# Selected Writings of Selma Fraiberg

# Selected Writings of Selma Fraiberg

EDITED BY LOUIS FRAIBERG

With a Foreword by Robert N. Emde, M.D.

Ohio State University Press: Columbus

*To the memory of Selma (1918–1981)*
*and to the future of our daughter, Lisa*

Copyright © 1987 by The Ohio State University.
All rights reserved.
Printed in the United States of America.

*Library of Congress Cataloging-in-Publication Data*
Fraiberg, Selma H.
    Selected writings of Selma Fraiberg.
    Bibliography: p.
    Includes index.
    1. Child psychology—Collected works.   2. Child
analysis—Collected works.   3. Infant psychology—
Collected works.   I. Fraiberg, Louis, 1915–
II. Title.
BF721.F66   1986        155.4        86-23454

ISBN 0-8142-0427-9 paper

9 8 7 6 5 4

# Contents

# Foreword

*Selma Fraiberg: Essayist, Clinician, and*
*Scientific Pathfinder*

The reader of these pages is in for a treat. When Selma Fraiberg published her much-acclaimed book *The Magic Years* in 1959, the world became more aware of what experience for the young child must be like. Insights from developmental psychology, psychoanalysis, and clinical work were set forth in beautiful and vivid prose. A fascinated world of adults responded by translating that classic work into eleven languages. In contrast, Fraiberg's essays, written mostly since *The Magic Years*, were published in a variety of outlets and have been less available to the general reader. This volume, assembled by Louis Fraiberg, corrects that problem for the reader while, at the same time, showing us that the whole is greater than the sum of the parts. Taken together, I am confident that the essays published in this volume will provide a treasure of insights for the clinician, educator, researcher, and, even more, for all of those who are interested in enriching family life through understanding development and what facilitates it.

The big themes of life—love, rejection, hate, good and evil—are replayed in these pages. In separate essays, Fraiberg, the humanist, writes not just for the clinician but for a wide audience of those participating in the drama of development. We encounter stories of adult problems and stories of repetitions of problems across generations. Such a portrayal heightens our sense of tragedy, to be sure, but it also enables us by virtue of our sensing heroic struggles that involve an emotion a bit beyond resignation. In spite of turmoil, the clinician-developmentalist remains optimistic. Infancy does that for us. Nowhere is such a drama portrayed better and with more literary grace than it is in these essays. The human condition is infused with hope, and the special adventure of childhood is revealed as giving us all a chance for new discoveries about ourselves. In reading these essays, we develop a piece of ourselves. It is hard to be in the same place afterward.

This foreword will comment on some aspects of Fraiberg's clinical approach and then suggest to the reader why Fraiberg, even today, deserves to be regarded as a "scientific pathfinder." The essays of this volume continue to point in new directions. Three "new looks" of developmental and clinical research are chosen to illustrate how we are still inspired and guided by such ideas.

## Clinical Work

Fraiberg's early clinical work, published after *The Magic Years*, provides a prototype for helping the handicapped infant and his/her family. Focusing on the congenitally blind, this work teaches us how delays and deviations of development can be used to understand developmental processes. Insights from the blind can be used in understanding the struggles of other handicapped children and their families; they can also deepen our views of normal development. Best of all, such insights can lead us to strategies for intervention, using the best opportunities available within the infant-parent relationship.

What has generally come to be known as "The Fraiberg Intervention Model" applies to infants and their caregivers who have a variety of psychological symptoms and troubles. The model refers to intensive worker-oriented and psychoanalytically informed treatment of mothers (and often fathers), usually with the infant present. It is focused around the infant's development, and home visits are often central. Treatment has an esteem-building focus with the mother and an optimistic-developmental focus with the infant, which, in turn, capitalizes on observed developmental accomplishments in the context of the mother's caregiving. Much of this model has its origins in the work presented in this volume. Recommended strategies use different levels of approach—crisis intervention, developmental guidance, environmental support, and infant-parent psychotherapy. In the latter approach, Fraiberg aims to free the baby and the parents from "ghosts" or intrapsychic transference objects from the parental past, sometimes with insights enabled both by trust in the professional worker and by a mother's appreciation of her infant's developmental advances. Further, with this form of treatment, a mother comes to feel understood in the midst of painful affects that accompany the emergence of memories of her own less-than-salutary childhood experiences. Her child's developmental experience can then be freed from distortions that arise from the past and that contain displaced affects. The aim of the Fraiberg model, in other words, is to liberate the infant from a focal parental neurosis.

Although the bulk of Fraiberg's published cases emphasize extremes of parental past maltreatment experiences involving psychological abuse and neglect, there is a spectrum of disorder that includes less dramatic parental problems from the past. These problems can also be brought into the light of day through working with infant *and* therapist so that the mother can become free to change and not repeat past maladaptive patterns. Fraiberg, as essayist and innovative clinician, puts forth this message through beautiful metaphorical prose in "Ghosts in the Nursery." The passages, in themselves haunting, are worth quoting here since they illustrate the essence of the model.

> In every nursery there are ghosts. They are the visitors from the unremembered past of the parents; the uninvited guests at the christening. . . . Even among families where the love bonds are stable and strong, the intruders from the parental past may break through the magic circle, . . . and a parent and his child may find themselves reenacting a moment or a scene from another time with another set of characters. Such events are unremarkable in the family theater, and neither the child nor his parents nor their bond is necessarily imperiled by a brief intrusion. . . . In still other families there may be more troublesome events in the nursery caused by intruders from the past. There are, it appears, a number of transient ghosts who take up residence in the nursery on a selective basis. They appear to do their mischief according to a historical or topical agenda, specializing in such areas as feeding, sleep, toilet training, or discipline, depending upon the vulnerabilities of the parental past. Under these circumstances, even when the bonds between parents and child are strong, the parents may feel helpless before the invasion and may seek professional guidance. . . . But how shall we explain another group of families who appear to be possessed by their ghosts? The intruders from the past have taken up residence in the nursery, claiming tradition and rights of ownership. They have been present at the christening for two or more generations. . . . The baby becomes a silent partner in a family tragedy . . . burdened by the

oppressive past of his parents from the moment he enters the world. The parent, it seems, is condemned to repeat the tragedy of his child-hood with his own baby in terrible and exacting detail.

But there is more:

> We have all known young parents who have suffered poverty, brutal-ity, death, desertion, and sometimes the full gamut of childhood hor-rors, who do not inflict their pain upon their children. History is not destiny, then, and whether parenthood becomes flooded with griefs and injuries, or whether parenthood becomes a time of renewal cannot be predicted from the narrative of the parental past.

In these pages, Fraiberg also identifies many instances of develop-mental triumph and protective factors that individuals find (often with the help of spouses and grandmothers) in order to overcome the cycle of tragic repetitions from their own past. She capitalizes on these instances by moments of intervention, whether educational or therapeutic, or through just acknowledging the human nature of the struggle and what seems to be working.

In the more extreme cases of parenting problems, therapy consists of helping the developmental relationship get back on track. Thera-peutic work with the mother is designed to provide support and guid-ance, using the infant's positive interactions and developmental prog-ress wherever possible. Often insights about what "belongs to the past" and not the present with the infant are used so that: (1) the mother's focal neurotic conflicts can be withdrawn from the child; (2) the loving bonds between the mother and the infant can emerge; (3) the mother now can appreciate the child's reciprocity, responsive-ness, and love; and (4) development can then "take off." In some cases, the Fraiberg model goes beyond these goals and tries for parental insight.

Fraiberg advocates a variety of techniques depending on one's op-portunity, including "psychotherapy in the kitchen." To begin with, there might be a focus on such interactive questions as: Why can't a mother hear her baby cry? Why does a mother avoid touching and holding her baby? Why does a mother persist with teasing games that have sadistic qualities of vengeance?

All of this requires patience on the part of the health care profes-sional who must build confidence and a therapeutic alliance. The expectation is that nearly all parents who have been traumatized and deprived can find it in themselves to bring the best to their children if helped by "professional allies" (Lebovici, 1985). In the Fraiberg model, therapy is ultimately aimed at helping the parent remember and reexperience an original childhood anxiety and time of suffering. Ghosts then depart, and, as Fraiberg has put it, "afflicted parents become the protectors of their children against the repetition of their own conflicted past."

## The Fraiberg Intervention Model Today: Use and Research

The Fraiberg intervention model provides an orientation for the burgeoning fields of infant mental health and infant psychiatry as can be seen in several active professional organizations (International Association of Infant Mental Health, World Association for Infant Psychiatry and Allied Disciplines, National Center for Clinical Infant Programs), a journal (Infant Mental Health Journal), a national newsletter (Zero to Three), and a variety of recent books and articles (for example, *Frontiers of Infant Psychiatry*, Volumes 1 and 2; *Clinical Infant Reports; The Handbook of Infant Development*, second edition; *Clinical Studies in Infant Mental Health*). Not only are the clinical approaches pioneered by Fraiberg in widespread use throughout the United States, but they are also regularly used in Europe. In Paris and Geneva, psychoanalytically oriented psychotherapy is being conducted with a parent while the infant is present. The goal is to work on focal conflicts that arise from the past and interfere with parenting. More and more clinicians are finding, as Fraiberg indicated, that there may be special access to developmental change in the adult when there is an infant and when joint attention can highlight the opportunities of a new relationship. There are many possibilities for all of us; there is room to explore and much to learn.

The model is being applied in many countries and contexts. But beyond noting its widespread application, I would like to highlight two aspects of Fraiberg's clinical work that represent "hot topics" for current clinical research.

The first of these is under rigorous debate in psychodynamic circles. It had been assumed that early childhood experience was riddled by imagination, fantasy intrusions, and creative fearful constructions, and that such childhood endogenous activities were largely responsible for generating later neurotic conflict. Following the likes of Freud's Oedipal complex, childhood memories were assumed to be distorted. But is it possible that maltreated children remember much of their early family experiences quite well (Bowlby, 1973; *Journal of Social Issues*, 1984; Miller, 1984)? In other words, when children have experienced trauma and deprivation or when they have experienced "tyranny" and "desertion," as Fraiberg has phrased it, do they remember? The work described in these pages suggests they do. When such children, as adults, talk in psychotherapy of early childhood abuse or of parental seduction, these accounts may not be fantasy distortions but clear memories. Such memories may remain unintegrated and subject to repetition, according to Fraiberg, because what is not available to the individual are the associated painful affects. The affects are warded off and reappear in "displaced" form when childhood memories are reexperienced in a special context, namely, within the intimacy of early parenting; in such a case, the infant becomes the object of what can be a devastating repetition. What is different from Freud's original account is that the parent's original childhood struggle is not primarily a result of fantasy intrusion; instead, what is pathogenic are warded-off affects connected with real memories. When these are expressed in the context of trust within a new therapeutic relationship and in the context of the infant's development, things can get better.

Another way of portraying this view is the following: What is "ghostlike" for such a parent is that the affect of the original experience (e.g., distress, helplessness, anxiety, or panic) is not remembered; rather, it leads to a shadowy form of pathological defense. Repression and isolation of childhood affect may occasion identification with "betrayers" and "aggressors"; this in turn may find expression in repeating the tragic dramas of parenting with infants of the next generation. Such matters represent current lively areas of concern not only for clinicians but also for basic researchers in the fields of early child memory, narrative construction, and studies of the "child as witness."

A second clinical research "hot topic" I would like to highlight is related to the first and involves pathological defenses in infancy. In one of Fraiberg's last essays (chapter 7), she enumerated what had, prior to that time, lacked systematic description, namely, pathological defensive patterns in the first three years of life. Such patterns had begun to impress themselves upon clinicians, particularly those working in the context of child maltreatment, but psychodynamic theorists, with a few exceptions (for example, Bowlby, 1973; Engel, 1962; Mahler, Pine, and Bergman, 1975; Spitz, 1961), had all but ignored them. What Fraiberg specifies in these pages gives the clinician-researcher an opportunity to identify early coping processes and problems in such a way as to offer more effective intervention techniques. All involve the infant's attempts to deal with painful affects connected with maladaptive caretaking. Because of their importance, it seems useful to indicate some of these defensive patterns in this foreword.

Pathological defenses are seen between three and eighteen months in infants who have experienced extreme environmental danger and deprivation. They include avoidance, freezing, fighting, transformation of affects, and turning of aggression against the self. According to Fraiberg, such defensive patterns are based on a biology of flight or fight and operate according to a goal of removing pain from consciousness. As a result, a symptom can "stand in the place of the original conflict."

Avoidance begins as early as three months. Examples are given of the infant selectively "editing" mother's face and voice. Avoidance behaviors in response to mother as a painful stimulus are presumably "activated" to ward off registration of painful affect, but such infants may also move into states of disorganization with, for example, uncontrollable screaming. This is often followed by an exhaustive "cut-off state" (cf. work on "conservation-withdrawal" by Engel, 1962).

The pattern of freezing is described in a five-month-old infant girl who sits glassy-eyed and immobile, staring off into space for twenty minutes. During an office visit, she does not look toward her mother or seek reassurance. Neither does she survey the room with interest or initiate social exchanges. Another example of freezing occurs in a sixteen-month-old, after which there is "collapse," followed by screaming and running to hide. The child then beats the mother with fists, a pattern that is labeled a "panic state" with "fighting." The depressive pattern of fighting begins, according to Fraiberg, in the second year of life and is characterized by tantrums in the midst of a "disintegrated state." The child is not only fighting against mother but fighting against the *danger of helplessness* and the *dissolution of self feelings* that accompany extreme danger.

Another defensive pattern involves transformations of affect. These also occur at the beginning of the second year. A vivid description is given of "laughter in a giddy way" and of "laughter in a ghoulish voice." Such laughter is triggered by anxiety, and, according to Fraiberg, it is a defensive pattern that "closely parallels" reaction formation even though it can occur as early as nine months. The reader will encounter an unforgettable example of hostile teasing by a mother of a nine-month-old. The mother takes the bottle out of her infant's mouth and puts it in her own. The infant then begins laughing with a kicking of legs, showing some kind of excitement. This frustrating sadomasochistic game is repeated six times in this fashion! Fraiberg speculates that in the face of a biological need there is a frustration and then a painful act. The painful affect then undergoes "transformation." Something akin to signal anxiety may play a role in this process.

Another defensive pattern is known as *reversal*. Here the process consists of a turning of aggression against the self. Fraiberg noted this pattern to begin at about thirteen months, although she comments that Spitz had seen this behavior in an orphanage child as early as eight months. The pattern itself consists of head-banging against the floor and the banging of body parts without evidence of pain.

These defensive patterns, activated in the context of pain caused by caregivers, are the result of extreme adaptations. They occur prior to language and prior to Piaget's representational intelligence, and yet these patterns share a striking coherence, often with a suggested specificity in relation to what it is that sets them off. Fraiberg's vivid descriptions deserve to be studied by all persons involved in infant intervention today. Not only do these observations raise questions that challenge our ideas about early cognitive, affective, and willful development, they also provide the seeds for our understanding of mediating processes involved in coping with stress. They challenge us with developmental psychopathology. It is an urgent task for today's researchers to use the "casebook" contained in these pages to address such questions as: What is the course of these defensive patterns over time? Under what conditions are infants or infant-caregiver dyads resilient with respect to the reestablishment of healthy developmental patterns? To what extent can a change in a parent's neurotic conflict or family circumstances result in enduring healthy changes in the child? The virtue of focusing on the child's defensive patterns is that child changes can be related to parental interaction changes, both in the short term and in the long term.

### Frontiers in Today's Research: Fraiberg as Pathfinder

In addition to the above-mentioned clinical topics, Fraiberg's pioneering work illuminates other areas of contemporary research. In some areas, research is just beginning; in others, it is well under way. I would like to comment on three "new looks" in today's research: (1) developmental continuities, (2) cross-generational transmission of maladaptive patterns, and (3) intervention and the capacity for change.

### *A New Look at Developmental Continuities*

The developmental research of the 1970s revealed few continuities from the behavior of infancy and early childhood to the behavior of school age and beyond (Emde, 1981; Kagan, Kearsley, and Zelazo, 1978). Contrary to expectations, prospective longitudinal studies provided little evidence for the continuity position—in other words, significant variations in early individual differences did not seem to be carried forward in any simple way. But today researchers are now appreciating some more profound features about developmental processes and continuities. There is a "new look," with angles of perspective revealing a more positive view of continuities. Fraiberg, in her writings, points the way.

We now appreciate that development is not well characterized as being linear. The behaviors and capacities of early infancy come and go. Development proceeds by periods of transformation, followed by periods of consolidation. Correspondingly, continuities in development "come and go," appearing in certain lifespan contexts and not in others. Some continuities may occur *only* during times of consolidation, others *only* during times of developmental transformation. Thus, one may see continuities in patterns of adaptation related to school entry at different ages, and one may also see continuities between adolescence and midlife, such as are being discovered in the Berkeley Longitudinal Study (Clausen, 1986; Eichorn, Clausen, Haan, Honzik, and Mussen, 1981). In a more complex way, one may also see continuities between adolescent experiences and later parental behavior, when the former adolescent's children become adolescents. Further, continuities appear in the organization of behavior rather than in specific behaviors. A clear example of this principle comes from "attachment" research. Infants who are found to be securely attached to the caregiver in the "strange situation" laboratory test at one year of age are found as toddlers (age two) to be more enthusiastic, persistent, cooperative, and more socially competent than insecurely attached children (Matas, Arend, and Sroufe, 1978). Such children are also more sociable and cooperative toward peers (Pastor, 1981). In other words, today's developmental research is beginning to indicate what Fraiberg, the clinician-researcher knew—namely, that continuities in development are apt to be *covert* rather than simple or overt.

New approaches in the search for continuities are appreciative of complexity. They take account of patterns of behavior in social affective as well as cognitive domains, as recommended by Fraiberg. Using an extreme group comparison, one research program has found strong developmental continuities from twenty-one months to five years of age among a group of children classified as either behaviorally inhibited or behaviorally uninhibited to the unfamiliar. Striking continuities have been found not only in social-affective and cognitive behaviors but also in autonomic arousal patterns (Reznick et al., 1986). Today's researchers are also finding that children's early temperamental and behavioral characteristics have some prediction for later behavioral problems (Daniels, Plomin, and Greenhalgh, 1984; Fischer, Rolf, Hasazi, and Cummings, 1984; Lewis, Feiring, McGuffog, and Jaskir, 1984; Matheny, Riese, and Wilson, 1985; Matheny, Wilson, and Nuss, 1984). What is only beginning, however, is testing the power of early interventions to overcome the effects of potentially troublesome early characteristics. Some research is indicating that there may be "sleeper effects" from early intervention, in which salutary developmental outcomes are seen in later development that have not emerged earlier. Indeed, much of the current perspective on continuities is being generated by intervention studies in which infants are seen to be at risk because of circumstances of family environment, perinatal difficulties, or physical handicap. Fraiberg's work with congenitally blind infants (see chapters 20-23) offers a dramatic example of the power of this kind of strategy, with interventions aimed at taking into account the individual infant's developmental competence (cognitive, social, and affective) while at the same time directing therapeutic work at the level of the caregiving relationship. Currently, such therapeutic approaches are being applied to Down's Syndrome and premature infants whose affective expressions and signals may be less clear and, therefore, may place them at risk for later difficulties.

Understanding the handicapped infant or the infant at risk for developing problematic social interactions is an important part of the new look at developmental continuities because researchers are now appreciating that infancy may be a crucial time when caregiving interactional patterns are being set. In other words, instead of early infant experience being thought of as a sensitive developmental period from the framework of the infant or the parent alone, it may be a sensitive period in terms of the *infant-parent relationship*. Thus, in a sample of prematurely born children, the quality of caregiving interaction when the infant was one month of age was shown to have a higher correlation with developmental outcome at two years than was initial perinatal risk status (Sigman and Parmelee, 1979). Such a point of view provides a context for understanding some recent dramatic findings of continuity between neonatal behavior and security of attachment as measured in the "strange situation" at one year. In one study, neonates who were less responsive, less motorically mature, and less regulated physiologically were more likely to be anxiously attached at one year (Waters, Vaughn, and Egeland, 1980) and in another study, there was a similar relationship to problems with newborn orienting (Grossmann, Grossmann, Spangler, Suess, and Unzner, 1985). In a third study, insecure attachment at one year was linked to newborn's irritability and distress as observed in a number of situations (Chen and Miyake, 1986). All of these findings imply the effects of infant temperamental characteristics on the development of one problematic infant-parent relationship characteristic at one year; namely, insecurity of attachment. It should be explained that much research remains to be done to clarify the role of infant and parent factors in understanding this form of developmental continuity. Similarly, much research is required to understand the significance of insecure attachment for later developmental psychopathology. But such continuities give us renewed hope for the kind of prevention the essays in this volume envision.

## A New Look at Cross-generational Transmission of Maladaptive Patterns

Fraiberg's work illustrates that there are two types of continuities— adaptive and maladaptive. Maladaptive continuities are marked by inflexibility in the face of environmental challenge; they puzzle us by their resistance to change in spite of what seems "logical." In Fraiberg's work, repetitive, stereotypic, constricted, irrational behavior, often accompanied by negative affect or withdrawal, was emphasized as a cardinal feature of the clinical problems of infancy. Evident in mothers' interactive behavior with their infants, this kind of behavior bespoke a continuity reaching back across a generation: to the mothers being mothered.

Recent developmental research on infant attachment has provided dramatic evidence for cross-generational transmission of maladaptive patterns. Three separate research programs now have shown significant relationships between a mother's own maladaptive environment with her parents and independently assessed insecure attachment patterns of her current infant (see reviews in Main, Kaplan, and Cassidy, 1985; Ricks, 1985). The clear inference from these studies is that, because of her internalized maladaptive patterns of caregiving from the past, such a mother is unable to be a "secure base" for her own infant's exploration and sense of social competence. The early childhood adverse relationship with her mother (or father) has interfered with her own developmental relationship as parent-to-infant. To use the Fraiberg ghosts metaphor, it is as if an earlier relationship has reached across the generations to haunt a later one.

Other recent research has illuminated cross-generational maladaptive patterns in a clinical group that commanded Fraiberg's attention, namely, infants with nutritional problems. It has been found that mothers of children with growth failure have often experienced highly stressful childhoods and inadequate parenting (Pollitt and Leibel, 1980). But more to the point, there is a search under way for mediating processes. Not surprisingly, these are being found in caregiver-infant interaction patterns. As an example, nonorganic failure-to-thrive feeding interactions are typically characterized by particular disturbances in mother-infant regulation with both intrusively controlling and unresponsive behavior patterns (Crittenden, 1985; Bithoney and Rathbun, 1983).

Today's researchers seem to have landed in territory rich in discovery. It can be said that interactional patterns involving caregiver and infant become, over time, relationship patterns that then become determinants of developmental continuity, both for health and disorder. Another promising research program in this area brings in physiology as well as behavior. Frodi et al. (1986) have shown continuities between a mother's autonomic arousal responses to a standard infant cry administered prior to birth and her later postnatal perception of her own infant as having or not having a difficult temperament. Striking continuities are seen in material attitudes, perceptions, and physiological responses. The link to the perception of her infant's difficult temperament may provide an important clue as to how deep-seated parental attitudes become transmitted. Because of such new research, one gains a strong conviction that we will soon learn a good deal about how enduring effects of the caregiver *and* infant become activated in the context of the early relationship experience involving both of them.

## A New Look at Intervention and the Capacity for Change

Fraiberg, like many developmentalists who are clinicians, was a sober optimist. Tragic, maladaptive continuities need not be repeated. Fraiberg convinces us that there is strength in development, in human nature, and in the opportunities for social relationships. She once characterized the psychotherapy of a mother with her infant as a little bit "like having God on your side"; the infant's rapid development acts as a strong force for progress and maternal self-esteem.

But aside from cheering us on in this difficult work of intervention, Fraiberg points us to the special importance of the caregiving relationship in infancy. Indeed, what is emerging from today's research is a new view about the nature of early development. Infancy may be a time of special importance, not because infant behavior gets set in some formative way but because *caregiving relationships get set.* When one observes patterns of behavior, one notes that interactional "sets" become relationship "sets." In other words, our previous idea that there are "critical" or "sensitive" phases for the individual infant's experience appears to have been misplaced. What goes forward in development is the relationship experience that becomes internalized by the child (see Sroufe and Fleeson, in press). Beyond infancy, the child learns to become connected to others in new ways, in addition to learning about being more autonomous; eventually, the child's early relationship set acts as a frame for becoming a parent.

Today's temperament research highlights another aspect of this view. Researchers are finding ways to characterize and identify temperamental misfits early in development so that intervention can prevent deviance in development and help relationships develop "on track." More research is needed, but there have been promising beginnings (for example, Frischer, 1985); and programmatic research attention is now being given to "interactional failures" (Papousek and Papousek, 1983). Perhaps we will soon be better able to identify, understand, and design interventions in instances of such "misfits" and "failures."

Infant intervention studies have been given a new rationale from research that indicates interactional patterns are being set in early infancy. Earlier findings of "resiliency" consequent upon infant placement in a new relationship context after early adversity now become more understandable. Previous thinking was too often in terms of developmental processes within the individual alone. Discussions of infant "resiliency" in that sense were misleading to our psychology. It now seems more appropriate to think of such concepts as phase-sensitivity, resiliency, and continuity in terms of relationship factors—not just in terms of the infant who cannot exist, let alone endure, alone. We should concentrate both our interventions and our research, as Fraiberg illustrates so poignantly in her writings, on caregiving relationships factors—not on infant factors or parent factors in isolation.

All of this, quite naturally, leads to a consideration of intervention and the general capacity for change. An obvious implication is that we should strive for earlier identification of problems in caregiving relationships. As Fraiberg has shown, intervention directed at the relationship level holds great promise for prevention of continued maladaptive patterns. A less obvious implication has to do with the fact that psychotherapy, at any age, is a relationship treatment. Perhaps we are at a time when psychotherapy research can elucidate what makes relationship matches and what makes mismatches, and on what facilitates adult development in a relationship context. The recent research of Luborsky et al. (1985) is particularly noteworthy in this regard. These investigators note that multiple studies of psychotherapy have found that the way the therapist and patient relate to one another early in treatment is an important predictor of therapeutic outcome. In a carefully controlled study of their own, they found that an early in-treatment measure of the patient-therapist relationship was a more meaningful predictor of outcome than were measures of either therapist characteristics or of patient characteristics alone.

We may be able to mobilize strong developmental functions in the process of forming relationships. Fraiberg illustrated the incentives to find new solutions when a mother and a baby are present. But there may be other opportunities in the life cycle for capitalizing on a developmental thrust. Presumably, these too involve new relationships. There is much to think about as we consider the effects of new relationships on old ones, and the possibilities of the present in the context of what has been brought forward from the past.

## And More . . .

These "looks" indicate a mere sampling of the kinds of new vistas that are possible for today's reader of Fraiberg. This volume also contains clinical contributions beyond infancy concerning the school-age child and the adolescent. It contains contributions to therapeutic endeavors with a variety of disorders and handicaps. It contains contributions to literary interpretation, philosophy, social work education, and public policy. Fraiberg, trained as a social worker as well as a psychoanalyst, demonstrates a keen sensitivity to social context and the broader aspects of environmental influence on the human condition and its vicissitudes. But mostly, Fraiberg represents for us what I would call a "strong developmentalist." In spite of adversity and detours along our developmental pathways, there is hope. For all of us—therapists, colleagues, clients, and patients—enlightenment and "new beginnings" are possible.

Read on.

*University of Colorado*          ROBERT N. EMDE, M.D
*Health Sciences Center*          *Professor of Psychiatry*

*Notes*

The helpful comments of Joy Osofsky, Ph.D., are gratefully acknowledged.

*References*

Bithoney, W. G. & Rathbun, J. M. (1983). Failure-to-Thrive. In *Developmental-Behavioral Pediatrics*, ed. M. D. Levine, W. B. Carey, & A. C. Crocker. New York: Saunders.
Bowlby, J. (1973). *Attachment and Loss, Vol. II: Separation Anxiety and Anger*. New York: Basic Books.
Chen, S. & Miyake, K. (1986). Japanese Studies of Infant Development. In *Child Development and Education in Japan*, ed. H. Stevenson, H. Azuma, & K. Hakuta. New York: Freedman.
Clausen, J. A. (1986, September). Early Adult Choices and the Life Course. Paper presented at the annual meeting of the American Sociological Association, New York.
Crittenden, P. M. (1985). Nonorganic Failure-to-Thrive: Deprivation or Distortion? Unpublished manuscript, University of Virginia.
Daniels, D.; Plomin, R.; & Greenhalgh, J. (1984). Correlates of Difficult Temperament in Infancy. *Child Dev.*, 55:1184–1194.
Eichorn, D. H.; Clausen, J. A.; Haan, N.; Honzik, M. P.; & Mussen, P. H.; eds. (1981). *Present and Past in Middle Life*. New York: Academic Press.
Emde, R. N. (1981). Changing Models of Infancy and the Nature of Early Development: Remodeling the Foundation. *J. Amer. Psychoanal. Assn.*, 29:179–219.
Engel, G. (1962). Anxiety and Depression-Withdrawal: The Primary Affects of Unpleasure. *Int. J. Psychoanal.*, 43:89–97.
Fischer, M.; Rolf, J. E.; Hasazi, J. E.; & Cummings, L. (1984). Follow-up of a Preschool Epidemiological Sample: Cross-Age Continuities and Predictions of Later Adjustment with Internalizing and Externalizing Dimensions of Behavior. *Child Dev.*, 55:137–150.
Frischer, L. J. (1985). Nonverbal Psychotherapy with Infants. *Inf. Ment. Health J.*, 6(2):76–88.
Frodi, A.; Bridges, L.; Shonk, S.; & Greene, L. (1986, April). Responsiveness to Infant Crying: Effects of Perceived Infant Termperament. *Infant Behavior and Development*, 9 (Special ICIS abstract issue).
Goodman, G. S., ed. (1984). The Child Witness. *Journal of Social Issues*, 40(2) (Special Issue).
Grossmann, K.; Grossmann, K. E.; Spangler, G.; Suess, G.; & Unzner L. (1985). Maternal Sensitivity and Newborn's Orientation Responses as Related to Quality of Attachment in Northern Germany. In Growing Points of Attachment Theory and Research, ed. I. Bretherton and E. Waters, *Monographs of the Society for Research in Child Development* 50 (1–2):233–256.
Kagan, J.; Kearsley, R.; and Zelazo, P. (1978). *Infancy: Its Place in Human Development*. Cambridge: Harvard University Press.

Lebovici, S. (1985). Review of *Clinical Studies in Infant Mental Health: The First Year of Life* by Selma Fraiberg in collaboration with Louis Fraiberg. *J. Amer. Psychoanal. Assn.*, 33:687–691.

Lewis, M.; Feiring, C.; McGuffog, C.; & Jaskir, J. (1984). Predicting Psychopathology in Six-Year-Olds from Early Social Relations. *Child Dev.* 55:123–136.

Luborsky, L.; McLellan, A. T.; Woody, G. E.; O'Brien, C. P.; & Auerbach, A. (1985). Therapist Success and Its Determinants. *Archives of General Psychiatry*, 42:602–611.

Mahler, M. S.; Pine F.; & Bergman. A. (1975). *The Psychological Birth of the Human Infant: Symbiosis and Individuation.* New York: Basic Books.

Main, M.; Kaplan, N.; & Cassidy, J. (1985). Security in Infancy, Childhood, and Adulthood: A Move to the Level of Representation. In Growing Points of Attachment Theory and Research, ed. I. Bretherton and E. Waters, *Monographs of the Society for Research in Child Development*, 50(1–2):66–104.

Matas, L.; Arend, R.; & Sroufe, L. A. (1978). Continuity of Adaptation in the Second Year: The Relationship between Quality of Attachment and Later Competence. *Child Dev.*, 49:547–556.

Matheny, A. P.; Riese, M. L.; & Wilson, R. S. (1985). Rudiments of Infant Temperament: Newborn to 9 Months. *Dev. Psychol.*, 21:486–494.

Matheny, A. P.; Wilson, R. S.; & Nuss, S. M. (1984). Toddler Temperament: Stability across Settings and over Ages. *Child Dev.*, 55:1200–1211.

Miller, A. (1984). *Thou Shalt Not Be Aware: Society's Betrayal of the Child* New York: Farrar, Strauss, Giroux.

Papousek, H. & Papousek, M. (1983). Interactional Failures: Their Origins and Significance in Infant Psychiatry. In *Frontiers of Infant Psychiatry*, ed. J. D. Call, E. Galenson, & R. L. Tyson. New York: Basic Books.

Pastor, D. L. (1981). The Quality of Mother-Infant Attachment and Its Relationship to Toddlers' Initial Sociability with Peers. *Dev. Psychol.*, 17(3):326–335.

Pollitt, E. & Leibel, R. (1980). Biological and Social Correlates of Failure-to-Thrive. In *Social and Biological Predictors of Nutritional Status, Physical Growth, and Behavioral Development*, ed. L. S. Green & F. Johnson. New York: Academic Press.

Reznick, J. S.; Kagan, J.; Snidman, N.; Gersten, M.; Baak, K.; & Rosenberg, A. (1986). Inhibited and Uninhibited Children: A Follow-up Study. *Child Dev.*, 57(3):660–680.

Ricks, M. H. (1985). The Social Transmission of Parental Behavior: Attachment across Generations. In Growing Points of Attachment Theory and Research, ed. I. Bretherton and E. Waters. *Monographs of the Society for Research in Child Development*, 50(1–2):211–227.

Sigman, M. & Parmelee, A. H. (1979). Longitudinal Evaluation of the Preterm Infant. In *Infants Born at Risk*, ed. T. M. Field, A. M. Sostek, S. Goldberg, & H. H. Shuman. New York: Spectrum.

Spitz, R. (1961). Some Early Prototypes of Ego Defenses. *J. Amer. Psychoanal. Assn.*, 9:626–651.

Sroufe, L. A. & Fleeson, J. (in press). Attachment and the Construction of

Relationships. In *The Nature and Development of Relationships*, ed. W. Hartup & Z. Rubin. Hillsdale, NJ: Erlbaum.

Waters, E.; Vaugh, B. E.; & Egeland, B. R. (1980). Individual Differences in Infant-Mother Attachment Relationships at Age One: Antecedents in Neonatal Behavior in an Urban, Economically Disadvantaged Sample. *Child Dev.*, 51:208–216.

# Preface

During our marriage of thirty-seven years Selma and I regularly discussed both her current clinical work and the process of its publication. I did not, of course, take part in the day-to-day activities of her staff (having full responsibilities of my own as a professor of English) but gradually evolved with her an informal relationship as editor for most of her writings before they were formally submitted for publication. In this, although my background in social work and psychoanalysis proved helpful, I served in a strictly advisory capacity. As everyone knew, particularly after the publication of *The Magic Years*, Selma was not only a talented clinician but a gifted writer as well. Her works were characteristically and unmistakably her own.

Selma was constantly absorbing new scientific experiences and seeking to find their relationship to her ongoing and established work. Having once placed an insight or a proposition in its context, she was not finished with it but kept it available for use in other connections. Thus there is in her writings an intricate series of signal associations, cross-references, and, in some cases, the embodiment of previously published material in new relationships. She was always ready to learn more from what she had already learned.

Her creativity was not limited to the computer model of retrieval from a memory bank but rather it involved the production of new ideas from a wealth of previous discoveries. Her work met the requirements of the ego-psychoanalytic description of the creative process: the gaining of ego control over id material and its sublimation and elaboration in the preconscious, permitting secondary elaboration largely under the influence of the conscious self.

But this "explanation" has a mechanical flavor and is therefore not ultimately satisfying. Selma was also creative in the larger, extra-scientific sense, the sense we associate with literature, not only as revelation but as joy and mystery. She took pleasure in confronting problems in her field, identifying them, and whenever it was possible, patiently and meticulously laying bare their reluctant secrets. When it was not possible, she calmly contemplated the seeming unknowability, expecting it to be more than likely that answers to at least some of the problems would be forthcoming, whether as a result of direct analysis or serendipitously from an apparently unrelated line of inquiry. She could be confident that her patience and persistence would be rewarded—as it so frequently was—because of her remarkable rapport with her infant friends. Once, when asked how she knew what babies were thinking, she replied, "They tell me."

With due regard for the scientific basis of her work, its accuracy, and the clarity with which it was presented, we may fairly say that a significant part of its value lies in its literary quality—a feature which is not ordinarily associated with clinical writing in the field of child development. Whatever Selma wrote—beyond bald "factual" reporting—exhibits her distinctive style.

Much of her writing is necessarily expository, particularly her discussions of technical and theoretical considerations. Here her clarity counts most: a direct statement of a subject without any more extraneous associations than necessary. Sometimes, as in the paper on object constancy, this becomes quite involved. But complicated or simple, her object is the effective transmission of information, and this her writing accomplishes with the precision and concision of an encyclopedia entry.

The chief merit of her prose, however, becomes evident in her narration. She always appreciated a good story, and I think this was in part because she came from a family in which a good story and the manner of its telling were much appreciated. This highly developed oral custom had its effect; those who did not have Selma's skill were at least eager listeners and applauded the teller by their appreciative responses. The older members of the family often repeated tales which were already familiar. As the years passed, some of these anecdotes constituted a kind of repertoire and their points were much savored. Outside the family there is usually not much substance to such tales, but they were listened to and appreciated because anyone could tell them and be applauded, especially if he embellished them suitably and was careful in preparing the punch line.

Technique was the issue here, and it influenced appreciation, just as Selma's writing ability influenced what she was able to communicate scientifically. As a number of these essays demonstrate, Selma was a talented practitioner who was not only successful in treating many difficult cases but also endowed with a superior ability to convey to the world the essence of her therapeutic experiences. This not only records her understanding of what happened but provides the means for others to follow in her footsteps.

In choosing which of Selma's papers to include in this collection, I had in mind these principal considerations: First, I wished to show the quality of her best work in the clinic and at the typewriter. Then I tried to demonstrate the variety of topics that interested her, the relationships between her scientific writings and her applications of their lessons to literary and social problems ranging from an analysis of Kafka's fictional depiction of dream states to the training of social workers. Within each major section of the book, the selections are arranged in chronological order. It is instructive to see her handling of certain ideas in papers written many years apart. Among other things, the book is suited to perform a teaching function, for, I believe, she would have wanted it that way.

Thanks for varying kinds and degrees of encouragement and assistance are due to Robert N. Emde, David G. Freedman, June and Paul Fullmer, Peter Givler, Jeree Pawl, Richard Rose, Vivian Shapiro, Albert Solnit, and particularly to my wife, Edna.

L.F.

# Acknowledgments

**Part 1.** *Chapter 1:* Selma Fraiberg, "The Origins of Human Bonds" is reprinted from *Commentary* (December 1967), 2–12; copyright 1986 by Louis Fraiberg. *Chapter 2:* "Libidinal Object Constancy and Mental Representation," *Psychoanalytic Study of the Child*, 24:9–47, ed. Ruth S. Eissler, Anna Freud, Heinz Hartmann, Marianne Kris, and Seymour Lustman, is reprinted by permission of International Universities Press, Inc.; copyright 1969 by International Universities Press, Inc. *Chapter 3:* "The Muse in the Kitchen: A Case Study of Clinical Research," *Smith College Studies in Social Work*, 40:101–134, is reprinted by permission of the Smith College School for Social Work. *Chapter 4:* (coauthored with Edna Adelson and Vivian Shapiro), "Ghosts in the Nursery: A Psychoanalytic Approach to the Problems of Impaired Infant-Mother Relationships," *Journal of the American Academy of Child Psychiatry*, 14:387–421, is reprinted by permission; copyright 1975 by the American Academy of Child Psychiatry. *Chapter 5:* (coauthored with Vivian Shapiro and Edna Adelson), "Infant-Parent Psychotherapy on Behalf of a Child in a Critical Nutritional State," *Psychoanalytic Study of the Child*, 31:461–491, is reprinted by permission of the Yale University Press; copyright 1976 by Ruth S. Eissler, Anna Freud, Marianne Kris, and Albert J. Solnit. *Chapter 6:* "The Adolescent Mother and Her Infant," from *Adolescent Psychiatry: Developmental and Clinical Studies*, ed. S. C. Feinstein, J. G. Looney, A. Z. Schwartzberg, and A. D. Sorosky, vol. 10, Annals of the American Society for Adolescent Psychiatry, is reprinted by permission of The University of Chicago Press; copyright 1982 by The University of Chicago. *Chapter 7:* "Pathological Defenses in Infancy," *Psychoanalytic Quarterly*, 51:612–635, is reprinted by permission of The Psychoanalytic Quarterly.

**Part 2.** *Chapter 8:* "Enlightenment and Confusion," *Psychoanalytic Study of the Child*, 6:325–335, ed. Ruth S. Eissler, Anna Freud,

Heinz Hartmann, and Ernest Kris, is reprinted by permission of International Universities Press, Inc.; copyright 1951 by International Universities Press, Inc. *Chapter 9:* "Clinical Notes on the Nature of Transference in Child Analysis," *Psychoanalytic Study of the Child,* 6:286-306, published and reprinted by permission as above; copyright 1951 by International Universities Press, Inc. *Chapter 10:* "Tales of the Discovery of the Secret Treasure," *Psychoanalytic Study of the Child,* 9:218-241, published and reprinted by permission as above; copyright 1954 by International Universities Press, Inc. *Chapter 11:* "Some Considerations in the Introduction to Therapy in Puberty," *Psychoanalytic Study of the Child,* 10:264-286, published and reprinted by permission as above; copyright 1955 by International Universities Press, Inc. *Chapter 12:* "A Therapeutic Approach to Reactive Ego Disturbances in Children in Placement," *American Journal of Orthopsychiatry,* 32:18-31, is reprinted, with permission, from the *American Journal of Orthopsychiatry;* copyright 1962 by the American Orthopsychiatric Association, Inc. *Chapter 13:* "Technical Aspects of the Analysis of a Child with a Severe Behavior Disorder," *Journal of the American Psychoanalytic Association,* 10:338-367, is reprinted by permission of International Universities Press, Inc.; copyright 1962 by the American Psychoanalytic Association. *Chapter 14:* "Further Considerations of the Role of Transference in Latency," *Psychoanalytic Study of the Child,* 21:213-236, ed. Ruth S. Eissler, Anna Freud, Heinz Hartmann, and Marianne Kris, is reprinted by permission of International Universities Press, Inc.; copyright 1966 by International Universities Press, Inc. *Chapter 15:* "The Clinical Dimensions of Baby Games," *Journal of the American Academy of Child Psychiatry,* 13:202-220, is reprinted by permission; copyright 1974 by the American Academy of Child Psychiatry.

**Part 3.** *Chapter 16:* "On Therapy," *Child Welfare,* 35:11-12, is reprinted by special permission of the Child Welfare League of America. *Chapter 17:* "Some Aspects of Casework with Children: (Part I) Understanding the Child Client; (Part II) Helping with Critical Situations," *Social Casework,* 33:374-381, 429-435, is reprinted by permission of the Family Service Association. *Chapter 18:* "Psychoanalysis and the Education of Caseworkers," *Smith College Studies in Social Work,* 31:196-221, is reprinted by permission of the Smith College School for Social Work. *Chapter 19:* "Legacies and Prophecies," the text of a speech delivered at graduation ceremonies at the Smith College School for Social Work, August 22, 1973, is reprinted by permission of the Smith College School for Social Work.

**Part 4.** *Chapter 20:* (coauthored with David A. Freedman), "Studies in the Ego Development of the Congenitally Blind Child," *Psychoanalytic Study of the Child*, 19:113–169, ed. Ruth S. Eissler, Anna Freud, Heinz Hartmann, and Marianne Kris, is reprinted by permission of International Universities Press, Inc.; copyright 1964 by International Universities Press, Inc. *Chapter 21:* "Smiling and Stranger Reaction in Blind Infants," from *The Exceptional Infant*, ed. J. Hellmuth, vol. 2, 110–127 (New York: Brunner/Mazel, 1971), is reprinted by permission of the publisher. *Chapter 22:* (coauthored with Edna Adelson), "Self-Representation in Language and Play: Observations of Blind Children," *Psychoanalytic Quarterly*, 42:539–561, is reprinted by permission of The Psychoanalytic Quarterly. *Chapter 23:* The Development of Human Attachments in Infants Blind from Birth," *Merrill-Palmer Quarterly*, 21:315–334, is reprinted by permission of the Wayne State University Press.

**Part 5.** *Chapter 24:* "The Mass Media: New Schoolhouse for Children" is reprinted from *Child Study*, 37:3–18. *Chapter 25:* "The American Reading Problem" is reprinted by permission from *Commentary* (June 1965); copyright 1986 by Louis Fraiberg. *Chapter 26:* "The Science of Thought Control" is reprinted from *Commentary* (May 1962), 420–429; copyright 1986 by Louis Fraiberg. *Chapter 27:* "Morals and Psychoanalysis: A Review of *Freud: The Mind of the Moralist*, by Philip Rieff, and *Psychoanalysis and Moral Values*, by Heinz Hartmann" is reprinted from *Partisan Review*, 28:109–117; copyright 1986 by Louis Fraiberg. *Chapter 28:* "Kafka and the Dream" is reprinted from *Partisan Review*, 23:47–69; copyright 1986 by Louis Fraiberg; selections from various works by Franz Kafka are copyright © by Shocken Books, Inc., and reprinted by permission of the publisher. *Chapter 29:* "Two Modern Incest Heroes" is reprinted from *Partisan Review*, 28:646–661; copyright 1986 by Louis Fraiberg; selections from *Invisible Man* by Ralph Ellison are copyright © by Random House, Inc., and reprinted by permission of the publisher; selections from *The Holy Sinner* by Thomas Mann, translated by Helen T. Lowe-Porter, are copyright © by Alfred A. Knopf, Inc., and reprinted by permission of the publisher.

The frontispiece, "Penelope," by Robert MacLean, is reprinted by permission of the Smith College School for Social Work.

**Part I**

Developmental and Theoretical
Contributions

# 1

# The Origins of Human Bonds

Konrad Lorenz (1967) has called it "the bond"—the enduring ties that unite members of a species in couples, in groups, and in complex social organizations. This personal bond is not the exclusive prerogative of man or of mammals. Stable and permanent partnerships for the propagation of young can also be found among some species of fish—and these partnerships endure beyond the period of spawning and the raising of young. Among greylag geese there are elderly couples which have raised their broods and remain demonstrative to each other and solicitous of each other's welfare in an exclusive and cozy domesticity that has outlived the biological purpose of union. Lorenz has described genuine grief reactions among widowed geese. Similar accounts exist of the fidelity of jackdaw couples, even after prolonged separation.

Yet, within the same species that produce permanent bonds among members, *fighting* among members is a common occurrence, regulated by formal rules of conduct and ritual forms of triumph and appeasement. It seems that the "problem" of aggression, which we like to believe was invented by the moral intelligence of man, is no less a "problem" to every species that possesses the bond. Conflicts between the claims of love and the claims of aggression did not originate with our own intelligent species. The devotion and fidelity of the greylag goose, for instance, is maintained through elaborate rituals designed to divert aggression from the partner. Even the device of the scapegoat appears in a simplified form among some species of fish and is ubiquitous among all species that exhibit bond behavior. To put it simply, aggression in these species is channeled away from the partner in order to preserve the bond.

The parallels between these phenomena and the data of human

development and human behavior are striking. In the course of development, the child modifies his aggressive urges through love of his human partners. If a child, for one or another reason, becomes deprived of human partners or of the conditions for attachment, the result may be a lack of inhibitions of aggressive impulses or of the capacity to regulate aggression. In the psychoanalytic view, conflicts between love and hate are central in the human personality. The need to preserve love from the destructive forces of aggression has produced in man great love, great works, and the highest moral attainments. The modification of aggression in the service of love has produced an infinite variety of redirected actions and mental mechanisms which serve to discharge the drive tendencies through substitute goals. And while the same conflicts between love and hate can also produce neurotic symptoms in the human personality, it is well to remember that there is a vast range in which man can find successful solutions to these conflicts without resorting to disease.

This essay is not intended as a review of Lorenz's book. Rather, I shall attempt to take up some problems in human psychology that Lorenz has illuminated from the biological side. Naturally, at a time when the most intelligent of animals seems bent on the extermination of his own species, a study of the natural history of aggression and its relationship to the love bonds should prove instructive. This is not to say that the solutions that have evolved among sea animals and birds or even the higher mammals are applicable to human society. When Lorenz urges us to regard the lessons from biology with modesty, he is not suggesting, of course, that we employ the rituals of waterfowl to regulate our daily aggressions or our foreign policy. He is telling us that there is an evolutionary tendency at work which has produced increasingly complex and effective means of regulating aggression, that the tendency is at work within human society in ways that we cannot easily recognize without following the biological narrative, and that there are as many portents for human solutions to the ancient problems of aggression as there are, at this point in our history, portents of disaster.

## II

At the center of Lorenz's book is a paradox. (1) Intraspecific aggression—fighting between members of the same species—is a characteristic of some species, but not of others. (2) The bond appears *only* in those species which also manifest intraspecific aggression. (3) There are species that have intraspecific aggression and no bond, but conversely there are no species that have the bond and do not also have intraspecific aggression. (4) Within those species which have evolved enduring attachments among members, there are biological mechanisms for inhibiting aggression under certain conditions and there are ritual forms of courtship and greeting ceremonials among members in which the characteristic motor patterns of aggression have undergone a transformation in the service of love.

It appears, then, that there are phylogenetic links between aggression and love. The coexistence of intraspecific aggression and the bond in certain species should inform us of the biological purpose and earliest interdependence of two instinctual drives which have evolved as polar and antagonistic. This is the territory that Lorenz explores.

Among the human psychologies, psychoanalysis maintains its original position with regard to the instinctual drives. In 1920, when the earlier libido theory was modified by Freud, aggression was given full status as an instinctual drive; a two-drive theory (sexual and aggressive) has remained central to psychoanalytic theory since that time. While recent advances in psychoanalytic theory have been in the area of ego psychology, psychoanalytic ego psychology has, on the whole, remained firmly rooted in biological foundations. Thus, it is the ego's role as a regulator of drives, the ego as the agency of adaptation, the ego as the mediator between drives and the demands of conscience, that define ego for psychoanalysis.

Now, it matters a great deal whether we include drives in our theory or not. If we believe that an aggressive drive is part of the biological inheritance of man, we add another dimension of meaning to conflict. It means that we grant motivational force to aggression as an instinctual drive that can, at times, be independent of objective circumstances. We thus have the means to explain what the behaviorists cannot well explain, the ubiquitous conflicts of love and hate, the admixture of aggression in the most sublime love, the "store" of aggression in human personality which can be triggered by a militant slogan or a boxing match or the buzzing of a mosquito. In this view the instinctual drive is given; it cannot be abolished—although it *can* be brought into the service of human aspirations by inhibiting those tendencies of the drive that can lead to destructive purpose.

We can learn, then, from the study of biology that the biological "purpose" of aggression is not murder. The killing of a member of one's own species is rarely encountered outside of human society. When it occurs among animals in the wild state, it is accidental. When it occurs in a zoo or an animal laboratory, it can be demonstrated that some component in the instinctual organization was deprived of a vital nutriment for functioning or of the stimulus for release, and that the intricate network which transmits signals within the instinct groups broke down. In one example given by Lorenz, hens that were surgically deafened for experimental purposes killed their newly hatched chicks by furious pecking. The hen, who does not "know" her young, normally responds to the call notes of the newly hatched chicks, which elicit appropriate maternal behavior. The deafened hens, unable to receive the signals of their young, reacted to the stimulus of the "strange object" and unleashed the aggression—heightened in this period by the necessities of brood defense—against the brood itself.

Lorenz defines aggression as "the fighting instinct in beast and man which is directed *against* members of the same species." Intraspecific aggression usually occurs in the service of survival. By warding off competitors within the species, aggression maintains living space and an equitable access to the food supply. Aggression is essential for defense of the brood; in any given species the primary tender of the brood, whether male or female, is endowed with the highest amount of aggressivity. With some rare exceptions, intraspecific fighting is limited to subduing the opponent or causing him to take flight. Lorenz describes ritual expressions of appeasement and submission in the loser of the fight as well as ritual forms of triumph (the "triumph ceremony") in the winner. Lorenz and other ethologists have collected thousands of examples from various species and have analyzed the components of each action in order to determine the specific patterns and variations. Each species, it appears, has its own forms of appeasement and triumph, and the ritual performance becomes a common language in which each gesture, each subtle nuance, has a sign function that is "understood" by every other member of the species. Among wolves and dogs, for example, the submissive gesture is the offering of the vulnerable, arched side of the neck to the aggressor. This is by no means an analogue to a "death wish" in the animal; it is the signal, "I give up," and it derives its function as a signal from the opposite behavior in fighting in which the animal protects the vulnerable region by averting his head. The triumph ritual among dogs is the lateral shaking of the head, the "shaking-to-death" gesture with mouth closed. At the end of this ceremony, the loser retreats and the victor marches off.

This ritualization of innate aggressive patterns is one of the most important links between instinct and the social forms that derive from instinct. The motor patterns for aggression are innate; when another instinctual need is manifested simultaneously, or external circumstances alter the aim of the drive, the innate motor pattern is still produced, but with some slight variation that endows it with another function and another meaning that is "understood" in the common language of the species.

What prevents a fight to the death within a given species? By what means can an animal check the intensity of his aggression before it destroys a member of his own species? There are inhibitions in animals, Lorenz tells us, that are themselves instinctual in their nature. There are inhibitions against killing an animal of one's own species or eating the flesh of a dead animal of the species. Nearly all species have inhibitions against attacking females or the young of the species. These inhibitions are so reliable that Lorenz regards a dog who attacks a female as aberrant and warns the reader against trusting such an animal with children. As we follow Lorenz we see that certain values which for humans are "moral imperatives" have antecedents in the instinctual inhibitions of animals.

Now if we grant that a certain quantity of energy is expended in an aggressive act, an inhibition of aggressive action can leave a quantity of undischarged energy in an animal that does not have a repertoire of behaviors or mental mechanisms for blocking discharge. In this dilemma the most common solution among animals is "redirection," to use the ethological term. That is, the animal switches his goal and discharges aggression on a substitute object. In one of many examples given by Lorenz, a female fish wearing the glorious colors of her "nuptial dress" entices a male. In the cichlid, the colors worn by the female are also the very colors that elicit aggression in the species. The excited male plows toward the female, clearly intent on ramming her. Within a few inches of the female he brakes, swerves, and directs his attack to a hapless bystander, a male member of the species. The foe vanquished, the victorious fish presents himself to his bride in a triumph ceremony, which serves as a prologue to the sexual act.

In this example, the inhibition is provided by the claims of another instinct, the sexual drive, and discharge of aggression is redirected toward another member of the species—an "indifferent object," as we would see it. This is a very simple example of conflict between two drives in a species less complex than our own. The claims of each drive must be satisfied, but the aggressive drive cannot satisfy itself upon the sexual object without obstructing the aim of the sexual drive. Redirection of the aggressive drive toward substitute goals provides the solution.

We can of course immediately recognize the behavior of "redirection" as a component of human behavior: in its simplest form it is analogous to "taking it out on" another person or an indifferent object, "displacing" the anger. Among humans the behavior of "redirection" has evolved into complex mental mechanisms in which drives are directed to substitute aims, as in sublimation, in defense mechanisms, and also at times in symptoms. In striking analogy with the drive conflicts of the unintelligent animals, it is the necessity among humans to divert aggression away from the object of love that creates one of the strong motives for the displacement, inhibition, and even repression of aggressive impulses. This means, of course, that the mental mechanisms available to humans not only permit redirection of the drives toward objectives that are far removed from "motor discharge of aggression," but that the drive energy is available in part for investing the substitute act with meaning far removed from "the fighting instinct." Where aggressive and sexual impulses enter into a work of art, for example, the original impulses undergo a qualitative change and the product in the work itself becomes a metaphor, a symbolic representation of the biological aims.

I do not wish to strain the analogies between "redirection" in animals and in humans. When complex mental acts intervene between a drive and its expression, as in human behavior, we are clearly dealing with another order of phenomenon. It is, for example, the human capacity for symbolic thought that makes it possible for the ego to block discharge of a drive or, more marvelous still, to exclude from consciousness (as in repression) the idea associated with the impulse. In non-human species, where there are no ideas and, properly speaking, no state that corresponds to "consciousness" in humans, there are no equivalents for repression.

Yet, we will find it arresting to see, in Lorenz's animal data, simple forms of symbolic action, a preliminary sketch for a design that becomes marvelously extended and elaborated in human thought. This is the process called "ritualization" in animals which we have already touched on in connection with the ceremonies of appeasement and triumph in animals. Lorenz presents us with an impressive body of data to show how courtship ceremonies among many species have evolved through the ritualization of aggression.

Any one of the processes that lead to redirection may become ritualized in the course of evolution. In the cichlid we saw earlier how aggression against the female is diverted and discharged against another member of the species in the courtship pattern. Among cranes there is a kind of tribal greeting and appeasement ceremony in which "redirected aggression" is simply pantomimed. The bird performs a *fake* attack on any substitute object, preferably a nearby crane who is not a friend, or even on a harmless goose, or on a piece of wood or stone which he seizes with his beak and throws three or four times into the air. In other words, the ritual redirection of aggression has evolved into a symbolic action.

Among greylag geese and other species, the redirected fighting and its climax are ritually observed in courtship, but they have also been generalized into a greeting ceremonial within the species as a whole. Greylag geese, male or female, greet each other ritually by performing the triumph ceremony. It is the binding ceremony of the group, and the performance of this rite with another member of the group renews and cements the bond, like the handshake or password of a secret society or a tribal ceremonial.

And here we reach the central part of Lorenz's thesis, the evolution of the personal bond. We recall that Lorenz and other ethologists have demonstrated that personal ties among members of a species—"the bond"—appear only among species in which aggression against members of the same species also occurs. Using the greylag goose as model, Lorenz shows how redirected forms of aggression become ritualized, then follow an evolutionary course to become the binding force among members of the group. Thus, among greylag geese, which show strong intraspecific aggression, stable and enduring friendships and lifelong fidelity exist between mates. These are bonds which are relatively independent of survival needs or procreation. Unlike partnerships found in some other species, these bonds are not seasonal or circumstantially determined. The mate, the friend, among greylags is individually recognized, and valued; he cannot be exchanged with any other partner. Loss of the friend or mate produces genuine mourning in the bereaved partner. And the ceremonial that binds these birds in pairs and in groups, the ritual greeting, the ritual wooing, the bond of love, is the triumph ceremony which originated in fighting and through redirection and ritualization evolved into a love ceremonial which has the effect of binding partners and groups. Aggression is made over in the service of love.

In the model of the greylag goose, Lorenz traces the pattern of the triumph ceremony in fine detail. The phylogenetic origins of the pattern are probably similar to those described in the cichlid: that is, a conflict between the subject's sexual aims and aggressive aims toward the same object finds a solution in the redirection of aggression toward another, "indifferent" object. The pattern evolved as a condition for mating and, through ritualization, became part of the courtship ceremonial. In the further evolution of the ritual fight, the triumph ceremony acquired a sign function for the affirmation of love; within the species it became a binding ritual. The ceremony, as Lorenz points out, has become independent of sexual drives and has become a bond which embraces the whole family and whole groups of individuals, in any season.

Lorenz adduces a large number of examples to show the evolution of greeting rituals from the motor patterns of aggression. Among certain birds, the "friendly" confrontation and exchange of signals is barely distinguishable from the threatening stance and gestures of the same species (thus, for example, the expressive movement which accompanies cackling among geese). But close observation and motivational analysis show a detail, such as a half-turn of the head or body, which alters the "meaning" of the motor pattern so that the sign value of the pattern is taken as friendly. The human smile, Lorenz suggests, probably originated in the same way: the baring of the teeth in the primal threatening gesture has been made over into the friendly smile, the uniquely human tribal greeting. No other animal has evolved the act of smiling from the threatening gesture of tooth baring.

Moreover, these greeting patterns, which are found among all species which have personal bonds, are not dependent upon learning. Given certain eliciting stimuli, the baby animal produces the greeting sign as part of his innate inventory of behaviors. If one bends over a newly hatched gosling, says Lorenz, and speaks to it "in an approximate goosy voice," the new-born baby goose utters the greeting sound of its species! Similarly, given certain "eliciting stimuli," the human baby in the first weeks of life produces our tribal greeting sign, the smile.

All of this means that in the process of redirection and the ritualization of aggression in the service of love, a new pattern emerges which acquires full status as an instinct and a high degree of autonomy from the aggressive and sexual instincts from which it derived. Not only are the patterns of love part of an autonomous instinct group, but they have a motive force equal to or greater than that of aggression under a wide range of conditions, and are capable of opposing and checking and redirecting aggression when the aims of aggression conflict with those of love.

While we can speak, then, of innate tendencies that produce characteristic forms of attachment in a particular species, it is very important to stress that these patterns of attachment will not emerge if certain eliciting stimuli are not provided by the environment. In the case of the newborn gosling, the cry of greeting is elicited by the call notes of the species, usually provided by the mother. Lorenz, by producing these sounds experimentally, elicited the greeting sounds from the newborn gosling and actually produced in hand-reared geese a permanent attachment to himself; he became the "mother." In experiments which Lorenz describes in *On Aggression* and elswhere, he was able to produce nearly all of the characteristics of early attachment behavior in young geese by providing the necessary signals during the critical phase of attachment.

In other experiments in which baby geese were reared in isolation from their species and otherwise deprived of the conditions for attachment, an aberrant bird was produced, a solitary creature that seemed unaware of its surroundings, unresponsive to stimuli—a creature, in fact, which avoided stimuli as if they were painful. It is worth mentioning in this context that Harry Harlow in certain experiments with monkeys accidentally produced an aberrant group of animals with some of the same characteristics of stimulus avoidance. In his now famous experiments in which baby monkeys were reared with dummy mothers (a cloth "mother," a wire "mother") the animals became attached to the dummy mothers in a striking parody of the species's attachment behavior, but the animals also produced a group of pathological symptoms that were never seen among mother-reared monkeys. They were strangely self-absorbed, made no social contact with other members of the species, would sit in their cages and stare fixedly into space, circle their cages in a repetitive, stereotyped manner, and clasp their heads in their hands or arms and rock for long periods. Some of them chewed and tore at their own flesh until it bled. When these animals reached sexual maturity they were unable to copulate. In the rare circumstance under which a female could be impregnated by a normal male from another colony, the female ignored her young after birth or tried to kill them.

To those of us who are working in the area of human infancy and early development, these studies of attachment behavior in animals and the correlate studies of animals deprived of attachment have had a sobering effect. For there are some striking parallels between them and our own studies of normal development and of certain aberrant patterns in early childhood which I will describe later as "the diseases of nonattachment." In all these studies of animal behavior and human infancy, we feel as if we are about to solve an ancient riddle posed by the polar drives of love and aggression.

## III

In the earliest years of psychoanalysis, Freud discovered that conflicts between the claims of love and the claims of aggression were central to all personality development. As early as 1905 he demonstrated through the study of a five-year-old boy, "Little Hans," how the animal phobias of early childhood represent a displacement of aggressive and libidinous impulses from the love objects, the parents, to a symbol of dangerous impulses, the animal. The phobia served the function of keeping the dangerous impulses in a state of repression and of preserving the tender feelings toward the parents in a state of relative harmony. This is not to say, of course, that conflicts between drives must lead to neurotic solutions. There are other solutions available in childhood, among them the redirection of hostile impulses in play and in the imagination. But in all these instances of normal development and even in the case of childhood neuroses, the motive for redirection of hostile impulses is love. *It is because the loved person is valued above all other things that the child gradually modifies his aggressive impulses and finds alternative modes of expression that are sanctioned by love.*

In all this we can see an extraordinary correspondence between the regulation of human drives and the phylogenetic origins of the love bond as constructed from the data of comparative ethology. Perhaps it might even strike us as a banal statement that human aggression should be modified by love. We are accustomed to take human bonds as a biological datum in human infancy. There would be no point in writing this essay if it were not for another story that is emerging from the study of a large body of data in psychoanalysis, psychiatry, and psychology on the diseases of nonattachment.

The group of disorders that I am here calling "the diseases of non-attachment" are, strictly speaking, diseases of the ego, structural weaknesses or malformations which occur during the formative period of ego development, the first eighteen months of life. These disorders are not classified as neuroses. A neurosis, properly speaking, can only exist where there is ego organization, where there is an agency that is capable of self-observation, self-criticism, and the regulation of internal needs and of the conditions for their expression. In a neurosis there may be disorders in love relationships, but there is no primary incapacity for human attachments. Similarly, we need to discriminate between the diseases of nonattachment and psychoses. In a psychosis there may be a breakdown or rupture of human bonds and disorders of thinking which are related to the loss of boundaries between "self" and "not self"—all of which may testify to structural weakness in ego organization—but this breakdown does not imply a primary incapacity for human attachments.

The distinguishing characteristic of the diseases of nonattachment is the incapacity of the person to form human bonds. In personal encounter with such an individual there is an almost perceptible feeling of intervening space, of remoteness, of "no connection." The life histories of people with such a disease reveal no single significant human relationship. The narrative of their lives reads like a vagrant journey with chance encounters and transient partnerships. Since no partner is valued, any one partner can be exchanged for any other; in the absence of love, there is no pain in loss. Indeed, the other striking characteristic of such people is their impoverished emotional range. There is no joy, no grief, no guilt, and no remorse. In the absence of human ties, a conscience cannot be formed; even the qualities of self-observation and self-criticism fail to develop. Many of these people strike us as singularly humorless, which may appear to be a trifling addition to this long catalogue of human deficits, but I think it is significant. For smiling and laughter, as Lorenz tells us, are among the tribal signs that unite the members of the human fraternity, and somewhere in the lonely past of these hollow men and women, the sign was not passed on.

Some of these men and women are to be found in institutions for the mentally ill, a good many of them are part of the floating populations of prisons. A very large number of them have settled inconspicuously in the disordered landscape of a slum, or a carnie show, or underworld enterprises where the absence of human connections can afford vocation and specialization. For the women among them, prostitution affords professional scope for the condition of emotional deadness. Many of them marry and produce children, or produce children and do not marry. And because tenderness or even obligatory parental postures were never a part of their experience, they are indifferent to their young, or sometimes "inhumanly cruel," as we say, except that cruelty to the young appears to be a rare occurrence outside of the human race.

A good many of these hollow men remain anonymous in our society. But there are are conditions under which they rise from anonymity and confront us with dead, unsmiling faces. The disease of emotional poverty creates its own appetite for powerful sensation. The deadness within becomes the source of an intolerable tension— quite simply, I think, the ultimate terror of not-being, the dissolution of self. The deadness within demands at times powerful psychic jolts in order to affirm existence. Some get their jolts from drugs. Others are driven to perform brutal acts. We can learn from Jean Genet of the sense of exalted existential awareness that climaxes such acts. Victims of such acts of brutality are chosen indiscriminately and anonymously. There is no motive, as such, because the man who has no human connections does not have specific objects for his hatred. When caught for his crimes, he often brings new horror to the case in his confession. There is no remorse, often no self-defense. The dead voice recounts the crime in precise detail. There was no grievance against the victim: ". . . he was a very nice gentleman. . . . I thought so right up to the minute I slit his throat," said one of the killers in Truman Capote's *In Cold Blood.*

Among those who are driven to brutal acts we can sometimes see how aggression and sexuality are fused in a terrible consummatory experience. It is as if the drives themselves are all that can be summoned from the void, and the violent discharge of these drives becomes an affirmation of being, like a scream from the tomb. Yet it would be a mistake to think that such criminals are endowed with stronger sexual urges than others. For the sober clinical truth is that these are men without potency and women without sexual desire, under any of the conditions that normally favor sexual response. These men and women who have never experienced human bonds have a diffuse and impoverished sexuality. When it takes the form of a violent sexual act it is not the sexual component that gives terrible urgency to the act, but the force of aggression; the two drives are fused in the act. When we consider the ways in which, in early childhood, the love bond normally serves the redirection of aggression from the love object, we obtain a clue: the absence of human bonds can promote a morbid alliance between sexual and aggressive drives and a mode of discharge in which a destructive form of aggression becomes the condition under which the sexual drive becomes manifest.

From these descriptions we can see that the diseases of nonattachment give rise to a broad range of disordered personalities. But if I have emphasized the potential for crime and violence in this group, I do not wish to distort the picture. A large number of these men and women distinguish themselves in no other way than in that they exhibit an attitude of indifference to life and an absence of human connections.

The hollow man can inform us considerably about the problem we are pursuing, the relations between the formation of human love bonds and the regulation of the aggressive drive. In those instances where we have been able to obtain histories of such patients, it appears that there were never any significant human ties, as far back as memory or earlier records could inform us. Often the early childhood histories told a dreary story of lost and broken connections. A child would be farmed out to relatives, or foster parents, or institutions: the blurred outlines of one family faded into those of another, as the child, already anonymous, shifted beds and families in monotonous succession. The change of address would be factually noted in an agency record. Or it might be a child who had been reared in his own family, a family of "no connections," unwanted, neglected, and sometimes brutally treated. In either case, by the time these children entered school, the teachers, attendance officers, or school social workers would be reporting for the record such problems as "impulsive, uncontrolled behavior," "easily frustrated," "can't get close to him," "doesn't seem to care about anything." Today we see many of these children in Head Start programs. These are the three- and four-year olds who seem unaware of other people or things, silent, unsmiling, poor ghosts of children who wander through a brightly painted nursery as if it were a cemetery. Count it a victory if, after six months of work with such a child, you can get him to smile in greeting or learn your name.

Once extensive study was begun on the problems of unattached children, some of the missing links in etiology appeared. We now know that if we fail in our work with these children, if we cannot bring them into a human relationship, their future is predictable. They become, of course, the permanently unattached men and women of the next generation. But beyond this we have made an extraordinary and sobering discovery. An unattached child, even at the age of three or four, cannot easily attach himself even when he is provided with the most favorable conditions for the formation of a human bond. The most expert clinical workers and foster parents can testify that to win such a child, to make him care, to become important to him, to be needed by him, and finally to be loved by him, is the work of months and years. Yet all of this, including the achievement of a binding love for a partner, normally takes place, without psychiatric consultation, in ordinary homes and with ordinary babies, during the first year of life.

This brings us to another part of the story, and to further links with the biological studies of Lorenz. Research into the problems of attachment and nonattachment has begun to move further and further back into early childhood, and finally to the period of infancy. Here too it is pathology that has led the way and informed us more fully of the normal course of attachment behavior in children.

## IV

Since World War II, a very large number of studies have appeared which deal with the absence or rupture of human ties in infancy. There is strong evidence to indicate that either of these two conditions can produce certain disturbances in the later functioning of the child and can impair to varying degrees the capacity of the child to bind himself to human partners later in childhood. A number of these studies were carried out in infant institutions. Others followed children who had spent their infancy and early years in a succession of foster homes. In each of the studies that I shall refer to here, the constitutional adequacy of the baby at birth was established by objective tests. When control groups were employed, as they were in some of the studies, there was careful matching of the original family background. These investigations have been conducted by some of the most distinguished men and women working in child psychoanalysis, child psychiatry, and pediatrics—among them Anna Freud, Dorothy Burlingham, René Spitz, John Bowlby, William Goldfarb, Sally Provence, and Rose Lipton.

The institutional studies have enabled us to follow the development of babies who were reared without any possibility of establishing a human partnership. Typically, even in the best institutions, a baby is cared for by a corps of nurses and aides, and three such corps, working in shifts, have responsibility for large groups of babies in a ward.[1] The foster-home studies, on the other hand, together with studies of "separation effects," have enabled us to investigate a group of babies and young children who had known mothering and human partnerships at one or another period of early development and who suffered loss of the mother and often repeated separations from a succession of substitute mothers. In one set of studies, then, the groups of babies had in common the experience of no human partnerships; in the other, the babies had suffered ruptures of human ties in early development.

Within these two large groups the data from all studies confirm each other in these essential facts: children who have been deprived of mothering, and who have formed no personal human bonds during the first two years of life, show permanent impairment of the capacity to make human attachments in later childhood, even when substitute families are provided for them. The degree of impairment is roughly equivalent to the degree of deprivation. Thus, if one constructs a rating scale, with the institution studied by Spitz at the lowest end of the scale and the institution studied by Provence and Lipton at the other end of the scale, measurable differences may be discerned between the two groups of babies in their respective capacity to respond to human stimulation. But even in the "better" institution of the Provence and Lipton study, there is gross retardation in all areas of development when compared with a control group, and permanent effects in the kind and quality of human attachments demonstrated by these children in foster homes in later childhood. In the Spitz studies, the degree of deprivation in a hygienic and totally impersonal environment was so extreme that the babies deteriorated to the mental level of imbeciles at the end of the second year and showed no response to the appearance of a human figure. The motion picture made of these mute, solemn children, lying stuporous in their cribs, is one of the little-known horror films of our time.

As the number of studies has increased in recent years and come to encompass more diverse populations and age groups, we have become able to see the "variables" at work here. (A "variable"—a monstrous term to use when one is speaking of human babies—signifies in this case the degree and kind of deprivation.) They can be tested in the following way. As we group the findings on all the follow-up studies it becomes clear that the *age* at which the child suffered deprivation of human ties is closely correlated to certain effects in later personality and the capacity to sustain human ties. For example, in some of the studies, children had suffered maternal deprivation or rupture of human connections at various stages in early childhood. As we sort out the data we see a convergence of signs showing that the period of greatest vulnerability with respect to later development is in the period under two years of life. When, for any reason, a child has spent the whole or a large part of his infancy in an environment that could not provide him with human partners or the conditions for sustained human attachments, the later development of this child demonstrates measurable effects in three areas: (1) Children thus deprived show varying degrees of impairment in the capacity to attach themselves to substitute parents or, in fact, to any persons. They seem to form their relationships on the basis of need and satisfaction of need (a characteristic of the infant's earliest relationship to the nurturing person). One "need-satisfying person" can substitute for another, quite independently of his personal qualities. (2) There is impairment of intellectual function during the first eighteen months of life which remains consistent in follow-up testing of these children. Specifically, it is conceptual thinking that remains depressed even when favorable environments are provided for such children in the second and third years of life. Language itself, which was grossly retarded in all the infant studies of these children, improves to some extent under more favorable environmental conditions but remains nevertheless an area of retardation. (3) Disorders of impulse control, particularly in the area of aggression, are reported in all follow-up studies of these children.

The significance of these findings goes far beyond the special case of infants reared in institutions or in a succession of foster homes. The institutional studies tell us how a baby develops in an environment that cannot provide a mother, or, in fact, any human partners. But there are many thousands of babies reared in pathological homes, who have, in effect, no mother and no significant human attachments during the first two years of life. A mother who is severely depressed, or a psychotic, or an addict, is also, for all practical purposes, a mother who is absent from her baby. A baby who is stored like a package with neighbors and relatives while his mother works may come to know as many indifferent caretakers as a baby in the lowest grade of institution and, at the age of one or two years, can resemble in all significant ways the emotionally deprived babies of such an institution.

## V

The information available to us from all of these studies indicates that the period of human infancy is the critical period for the establishment of human bonds. From the evidence, it appears that a child who fails to make the vital human connections in infancy will have varying degrees of difficulty in making them in later childhood. In all of this there is an extraordinary correspondence with the findings of ethologists regarding the critical period for attachment in animals.

If I now proceed to construct some parallels, I should also make some cautious discriminations between attachment behavior in human infancy and that in animals. The phenomenon of "imprinting," for example, which Lorenz describes, has no true equivalent in human infancy. When Lorenz hand-rears a gosling he elicits an attachment from the baby goose by producing the call notes of the mother goose. In effect he produces the code signal that releases an instinctual response. The unlocking of the instinctual code guarantees that the instinct will attach itself to *this* object, the producer of the signal. The registration of certain key characteristics of the object gives its own guarantees that this object and no other can elicit the specific instinctual response. From this point on, the baby gosling accepts Dr. Lorenz as its "mother"; the attachment of the baby animal to Lorenz is selective and permanent. The conditions favoring release of instinctual behavior are governed by a kind of biological timetable. In the case of attachment behavior, there is a critical period in the infancy of the animal that favors imprinting. Following this period the instinct wanes and the possibility of forming a new and permanent attachment ends.

It is not difficult to find analogies to this process in the attachment behavior of the human infant, but the process of forming human bonds is infinitely more complex. The development of attachment behavior in human infancy follows a biological pattern, but we have no true equivalents for "imprinting" because the function of memory in the first eighteen months of a human baby's life is far removed from the simple registrations of stimuli that take place in the baby animal. Yet even the marvelous and uniquely human achievements of cognitive development are dependent upon adequacy in instinctual gratification, for we can demonstrate through a large body of research that where need satisfaction is not adequate there will be impairment in memory and consequently in all the complex functions of human intelligence.

Similarly, there is no single moment in time in which the human infant—unlike the lower animals—makes his attachment to his mother. There is no single act or signal which elicits the permanent bond between infant and mother. Instead, we have an extended period in infancy for the development of attachment behavior and a sequential development that leads to the establishment of human bonds. By the time a baby is eight or nine months old he demonstrates his attachment by producing all of the characteristics that we identify as human love. He shows preference for his mother and wants repeated demonstrations of her love; he can only be comforted by his mother, he initiates games of affection with her, and he shows anxiety, distress, and even grief if a prolonged separation from her takes place.

I do not wish to give the impression that this process is so complex or hazardous that only extraordinary parents can produce a baby with strong human bonds. It is achieved regularly by ordinary parents with ordinary babies without benefit of psychiatric consultation. It requires no outstanding measures beyond satisfaction of a baby's biological needs in the early period of infancy through feeding, comfort in distress, and the provision of nutriments for sensory and motor experience—all of which are simply "givens" in a normal home. But above all it requires that there be human partners who become for the baby the embodiment of need satisfaction, comfort, and well-being. All of this, too, is normally given in ordinary families, without any reflection on the part of the parents that they are engaged in initiating a baby into the human fraternity.

Finally, where the attachment of a baby animal to its mother is guaranteed by interlocking messages and responses on an instinctual basis, we have no such instinctual code to guarantee the attachment of a human infant to his mother. This means, of course, that there are an infinite number of normal variations in patterns of mothering and great diversity in the mode of communication between baby and mother. Any of a vast number of variations in the pattern can be accommodated in the human baby's development and still ensure that a human bond will be achieved. The minimum guarantee for the evolution of the human bond is prolonged intimacy with a nurturing person, a condition that was once biologically insured through breast feeding. In the case of the bottle-fed baby, the insurance must be provided by the mother herself, who "builds in" the conditions for intimacy and continuity of the mothering experience. As bottle feeding has become common among all social groups in our society, continuity of the nurturing experience becomes more and more dependent upon the personality of the mother and environmental conditions that favor, or fail to favor, intimacy between the baby and his mother.

The bond which is ensured in a moment of time between a baby animal and its mother is, in the case of the human baby, the product of a complex sequential development, a process that evolves during the first eighteen months of life. The instinctual patterns are elicited through the human environment, but they do not take the form of instinctual release phenomena in terms of a code and its unlocking. What we see in the evolution of the human bond is a *language* between partners, a "dialogue," as Spitz puts it, in which messages from the infant are interpreted by his mother and messages from the mother are taken as signals by the baby. This early dialogue of "need" and "an answer to need" becomes a highly differentiated signal system in the early months of life; it is, properly speaking, the matrix of human language and of the human bond itself.

The dialogue begins with the cry that brings a human partner. Long before the human baby experiences the connection between his cry and the appearance of a human face, and long before he can use the cry as a signal, he must have had the experience in which the cry is "answered." Need and the expressive vocalization of need set up the dialogue between the baby and his human partners. Normally, too, there is a range of expressive signs in a baby's behavior which his mother interprets through her intimacy with him—the empty mouthing: "He's hungry"; fretful sounds: "He's cranky, he's ready for his nap"; a complaining sound: "He wants company"; arms extended: "He wants to be picked up." Sometimes the mother's interpretation may not be the correct one, but she has acted upon the baby's signal in some way, and this is the crucial point. The baby learns that his signals bring mother and bring need satisfaction in a specific or general way.

The institutional baby has no partner who is tuned in to his signals. As Provence and Lipton demonstrate in their institutional study, since there is no one to read the baby's signs there is finally no motive for producing signals. The expressive vocalizations drop out or appear undifferentiated in these babies. And long after they have been moved to homes with foster families, speech development remains impoverished.

The animal baby makes a selective response to his mother in the early hours of life, and distinguishes his mother from other members of the species. The human baby discovers the uniqueness of his mother in a succession of stages throughout the first year. How do we know this? Among other ways, through the study of the smiling response of the human infant. Our tribal greeting sign, the smile, undergoes a marvelous course of differentiation in the first year. Since the smile connotes "recognition," among other things, we may study differential smiling as one of the signs in the evolution of attachment behavior. In this way Peter Wolff of Harvard has found that the human baby in the third and fourth weeks of life will smile selectively in response to his mother's voice. Wolff can demonstrate experimentally that no other voice and no other sounds in the same frequency range will elicit the baby's smile. Wolff's finding should end the controversy over the "gas smile," and mothers who always disagreed with pediatricians on this score are thus vindicated in their wisdom.

At about eight weeks of age, the baby smiles in response to the human face. As René Spitz has demonstrated, the smile is elicited by the configuration of the upper half of the human face. A mask, representing eyes and forehead, will also elicit the baby's smile at this age. The baby of this age does not yet make a *visual* discrimination among his mother's face, other familiar faces, and strange faces. But between the age of six weeks and eight months the smile of the baby grows more and more selective, and at about eight months of age the baby demonstrates through his smile a clear discrimination of the mother's face from the faces of other familiar persons or the face of a stranger. Presented with a strange face at eight months, the baby will typically become solemn, quizzical, or unfriendly, and may even set up a howl. This means that a form of recognition memory for familiar faces has emerged in the infant. But in order that recognition memory appear, there must be thousands of repetitions in the presentation of certain faces, to produce the indelible tracing of *this* face with *these* characteristics, which can be later discriminated from all other faces with the general characteristic of the human face. This does not mean that a mother or other family members need to be constantly in the baby's perceptual field; it does not mean that, if someone else occasionally takes over the care of the baby, his memory capacity will be impaired. But it does mean that there must be one or more persons who remain central and stable in the early experience of the baby so that the conditions for early memory function be present. And it means, too, that such a central person must be associated with pleasure and need gratification because memory itself must be energized through the emotional import of experience. By the time a baby is eight months old, the mother is discriminated from all other persons, and the baby shows his need for her and his attachment to her by distress when she leaves him and by grief reactions when absence is prolonged beyond his tolerance. At this stage, when the mother has become the indispensable human partner, we can speak of love, and under all normal circumstances this love becomes a permanent bond, one that will embrace not only the mother but other human partners and, in a certain sense, the whole human fraternity.

The baby who is deprived of human partners can also be measured by his smile, or by the absence of a smile. If the human deprivation is extreme, no smile appears at any stage of infancy. In the institution studied by Provence and Lipton the babies smiled at the appearance of a human face, and while the smile was rarely joyful or rapturous, it was a smile. But whereas at a certain age babies normally discriminate among human faces by producing a *selective* smile, the institutional babies smiled indifferently at all comers. There was nothing in the last months of the first year or even in the second year to indicate that these babies discriminated among the various faces that presented themselves, nothing to indicate that one person was valued above other persons. There was no reaction to the disappearance or loss of any one person in this environment. In short, there was no attachment to any one person. And in this study, as in others, it was seen that even when families were found for these children in the second or third year of life there was a marked incapacity to bind themselves to any one person.

These were the same babies who showed a consistent type of mental retardation in follow-up studies. In the areas of abstract thinking and generalization these children and, in fact, institutional babies in all studies, demonstrated marked impairment in later childhood. In ways that we still do not entirely understand, this disability in thinking is related to impoverishment in the structures that underlie memory in the first year of life. The diffusion and lack of focus in the early sense-experience of these infants, and the absence of significant human figures which normally register as the first mental traces, produce an unstable substratum for later and more complex mental acts.

The third generalization to be drawn from all these studies has to do with "impulse control," and specifically the control of aggression. From all reports, including those on the model institution directed and studied by Anna Freud and Dorothy Burlingham and the "good" institution investigated by Provence and Lipton, it emerges that such children show marked impulsivity, intolerance of frustration, and rages and tantrums far beyond the age in childhood where one would normally expect such behavior. Over twenty years ago Anna Freud drew the lesson from her institutional study that the problems of aggression in these children were due to the absence of intimate and stable love ties. Under the most favorable circumstances, the group care provided by the institution usually cannot produce durable love bonds in an infant. Everything we have learned since this sobering study by Anna Freud has confirmed her findings twice over.

And this brings us back full circle to Lorenz's study of aggression and the bond. The progressive modification of the aggressive drive takes place under the aegis of the love drives. Where there are no human bonds there is no motive for redirection, for the regulation and control of aggressive urges. The parallel with animal studies is exact.

## VI

If we read our evidence correctly, the formation of the love bond takes place during human infancy. The later capacity of the ego to regulate the aggressive drive is very largely dependent upon the quality and the durability of these bonds. The absence of human bonds in infancy or the rupture of human bonds in early life can have permanent effects upon the later capacity for human attachments and for the regulation of aggression.

It would be a mistake, of course, to blame all human ills on failure in early nurture. There are other conditions in the course of human development which can affect the capacity to love and the regulation of drives. Yet, the implications of maternal deprivation studies are far-reaching and, if properly interpreted, carry their own prescription for the prevention of the diseases of nonattachment. As I see it, the full significance of the research on the diseases of nonattachment may be this: We have isolated a territory in which the diseases of nonattachment originate. These bondless men, women, and children constitute one of the largest aberrant populations in the world today, contributing far beyond their numbers to social disease and disorder. These are the people who are unable to fulfill the most ordinary human obligations in work, in friendship, in marriage, and in child-rearing. The condition of nonattachment leaves a void in the personality where conscience should be. Where there are no human attachments there can be no conscience. As a consequence, the hollow men and women contribute very largely to the criminal population. It is this group, too, that produces a particular kind of criminal, whose crimes, whether they be petty or atrocious, are always characterized by indifference. The potential for violence and destructive acts is far greater among these bondless men and women; the absence of human bonds leaves a free "unbound" aggression to pursue its erratic course.

The cure for such diseases is not simple. All of us in clinical work can testify to that. But, to a very large extent, the diseases of nonattachment can be eradicated at the source by ensuring stable human partnerships for every baby. If we take the evidence seriously, we must look upon a baby deprived of human partners as a baby in deadly peril. This is a baby who is being robbed of his humanity.

## Note

1. We should carefully distinguish this kind of group care from that provided babies and young children in a *kibbutz*. The *kibbutz* baby has a mother and is usually breast-fed by her. Studies show that the *kibbutz* baby is attached to his mother and that the mother remains central in his early development. The group care of the *kibbutz* does not deprive the baby of mothering, whereas such deprivation is the crucial point of the studies I cite in this essay.

## Reference

Lorenz, K. (1967). *On Agression.* New York: Harcourt, Brace & World.

# 2

# Libidinal Object Constancy and Mental Representation

This essay attempts to examine the concept of "object constancy" in psychoanalytic usage, as a term that embraces libidinal and cognitive aspects of human attachment in infancy. Our literature shows considerable range and variations in usage of the term "object constancy," which reflect its mixed origins in general psychology and psychoanalysis, and semantic changes in the word "constancy" as it came into the literature of psychoanalysis. In this essay, I shall take up these aspects of the problem: (1) historical roots of the term "object constancy" in psychoanalysis and general psychology; (2) variations in usage, definitions, and criteria for the attainment of libidinal object constancy as derived from the psychoanalytic literature; (3) mental representation and object constancy; (4) the problem of infantile hallucinatory experience as postulated in psychoanalysis and an attempt to infer from existing models of cognitive development the possible links between the negative hallucination and objective tests of the capacity to evoke the image of an object that is not present in reality; and (5) a proposal for a definition of mental representation which is consistent with the objective findings of genetic psychology and the inferences from the dream work derived from psychoanalytic study.

The term "object constancy" was first used in psychoanalytic literature by Heinz Hartmann (1952), who referred to it in this context:

Also there is a long way from the object that exists only as long as it is need satisfying to that form of satisfactory object relations that includes object constancy. . . . This constancy probably presupposes on the side of the ego a certain degree of neutralization of aggressive as well as libidinal energy . . . ; and on the other hand it might well be that it promotes neutralization. (P. 163)

In his 1953 essay on the metapsychology of schizophrenia, Hartmann links his use of the term "constancy" to Piaget's "object concept":

Here I want to say a few words about another aspect of the separation of self and object, which also is a step toward the *constancy* of the latter. First the infant does not distinguish between the objects and his activities vis-à-vis the objects. In the words of Piaget (1937), the object is still nothing but a prolongation of the child's activity. Later, in the course of those processes that lead to a distinction of object and self, the child also learns to make a distinction between his activity and the object toward which this activity is directed. The earlier stage may be correlated with magic action and probably represents a transitory step in ego (or, rather, pre-ego) development, interposed between simple discharge and true ego-directed and organized action. The later stage represents one aspect of "objectivation" which is an ego contribution to the development of object relations and an essential element in the institution of the reality principle. Piaget's finding agrees rather well with the findings of analysis, and it means, metapsychologically speaking, that from then on there is a difference between the cathexis of an object-directed ego function and the cathexis of an object representation. (P. 187f.; my italics)

In the 1956 essay on the reality principle, Hartmann says,

Both the development of ego functions and the *constitution of constant objects* represent a moving away from what Freud calls primary narcissism, and are closely interrelated. . . . In contact and communication with the object, the child learns to demarcate his "self" and to realize the first vestiges of objectivity. (P. 255; my italics)

From these references it appears that the introduction of the term "object constancy" was linked originally with Piaget's object concept, and while the dimension of "human object relations" was brought in from the psychoanalytic side, Hartmann was clearly seeking a formulation that would embrace both the cathexis of the human object and the constitution of its objectivity.

Yet, the term "constancy" is not Piaget's in designating the achievement of "objectivity." Piaget (1937) employs the term "permanence" for the achievement of an object concept (Stage VI in sensorimotor development, sixteen to eighteen months) and refers to "constancy" as an attribute of permanence; thus constancy is not identical with permanence. The term "constancy," however, appears in general psychological usage, and Hartmann, who was of course familiar with the term, employed it consistently in a number of his writings in contexts that clearly showed its reference to psychological usage. (In a letter to me, Hartmann, replying to my questions, attributes one source of this term to general psychology.)

In general psychology, "constancy" is employed with the specific meaning of an object that "preserves its essential character despite variations introduced into the situation surrounding it" (Werner, 1957, p. 108). "Constancy," then, refers to the stable, "objective," permanent attributes of things, which implies autonomy from the subject and his perception or his actions. Until this level of conceptual development is achieved by the infant, the psychoanalyst is in agreement with Werner that we can only speak of "things of action," phenomena which are experienced by the infant as a consequence of his actions or attitudes.

Hartmann's introduction of the term "object constancy" appeared in a paper presented at the symposium on "The Mutual Influences in the Development of Ego and Id," to which Anna Freud and Willie Hoffer also made far-reaching contributions. If we examine their papers along with Hartmann's essay, we can see the central tendencies in psychoanalytic thought that led to a later elaboration of the concept "object constancy" in psychoanalytic literature.

Hoffer (1952) differentiates two major phases in the first year of life, the first corresponding to the period of primary narcissism in which the relations with the mother are governed by body needs and their satisfaction and the mother is indistinguishable from the infant's own body. The transition to "the psychological object" (Hoffer's term) is seen by him as "a drawing away of cathexis" from the body to the mother as the consequence of her ministrations to need, a shift, then, from narcissistic libido to object libido.

Anna Freud (1952), working within the same framework as Hoffer—from the need-satisfying object to the psychological object—offered the hypothesis that the step from the first stage to the second stage is determined by a decrease in the drives themselves. She says:

While the infant is under the full impact of his needs—in terms of mental functioning; completely dominated by the pleasure principle—

he demands from the object one thing only, that is immediate satisfaction. An object which fails to fulfill this purpose at a given moment cannot be maintained as such and is exchanged for a more satisfying one. The needs have to lessen in strength, or have to be brought under ego control, before nonsatisfying (for instance, absent) objects can retain their cathexis. . . .

[She cites her own observations:] In the earliest months of life it seems possible to exchange the object, provided the form of need satisfaction given to the infant remains unaltered. Later (appr. after five months) the personal attachment to the object increases in importance; it becomes possible then to vary the satisfactions, provided the object remains the same. At that stage (appr. five to twenty-four months) separation from the object causes extreme distress, but the infant is so exclusively dominated by his needs that he cannot maintain his attachment to a nonsatisfying object for more than a given period (varying from several hours to several days). After this interval, which is most upsetting for the child, need satisfaction is accepted from and attachment (cathexis) is transferred to a substitute. As the ego matures and the pleasure principle yields to the reality principle, children gradually develop the ability to retain libidinal cathexis to absent love objects during separations of increasing lengths. (P. 44f.)

We should note that while the Amsterdam symposium gave birth to the concept of libidinal object constancy, the term "constancy" was not yet used by Anna Freud or Willie Hoffer to represent the establishment of the libidinal tie to the mother.

Anna Freud uses the term "object constancy" for the first time, I believe, in 1960 in her discussion of John Bowlby's paper "Grief and Mourning in Infancy and Early Childhood." The term appears in this context:

Any assessment of the eventual pathological consequences of a separation trauma is inseparable, in our belief, from the assessment of the level of libido development at the time of its occurrence. Results vary according to the fact whether at the moment of separation the tie to the mother was still of a narcissistic nature, dominated by the search for instinctual satisfactions; or whether in the relationship to the mother the personal and affectionate elements had begun to predominate, transforming the attachment into object love; or whether the child had attained *the level of so-called object constancy. In this last instance the image of a cathected person can be maintained internally* for longer periods of time, irrespective of the real object's presence or absence in the external world, and much internal effort will be needed before the libido is withdrawn. Such withdrawal happens gradually by means of the painful disengagement process known to us as mourning. (P. 61f.; my italics)

In this and a number of later essays, Anna Freud employs the term "object constancy" to represent the libidinal attachment to the mother, but she does not use the word "constancy" in its cognitive sense. She is explicit in her statement at the Panel Discussion (1968).

It is evidently a concept which has caused a good deal of confusion recently in analytic thinking, introduced by people who approached it not from the analytical but from the psychological side. They define object constancy as the child's capacity to keep an inner image of the object in the absence of the object in the external world. I have never used the concept in that sense and in our Clinic some people have followed my example.

What we mean by object constancy is the child's capacity to keep up object cathexis irrespective of frustration or satisfaction. At the time before object constancy the child withdraws cathexis from the unsatisfactory or unsatisfying object. Also in times when no need or libidinal wish is present in the child, the object is considered as non-existent, unnecessary. The turning towards the object takes place again when the wish or need arises. After object constancy has been established the person representing the objects keeps this place for the child whether he satisfies or frustrates. If you use the concept this way it is related closely to the overcoming of what we call the need-satisfying phase. The need-satisfying phase is pre-object constancy; when it has been passed and the next step has been taken, object constancy comes into being. The object keeps its place. That is at least how I use it; other people may use it differently. (P. 506)

Anna Freud's use of the term "constancy" connotes stability of the object cathexis in infancy and is in her view not related to "constancy" in general psychology. In Anna Freud's words, "the object keeps its place," has relative autonomy from the fluctuations of need states, in which case "constancy" means stability of the libidinal cathexis to mother and not stability of the object *qua* object in general psychological usage.

At the same Panel Discussion (1968), David Beres raised the question as to whether object cathexis on this level (libidinal object constancy) did not presuppose the existence of mental representation of the mother. I shall return to this very interesting discussion later, since it has bearing upon the relationship of "libidinal object constancy" and "object constancy" in general psychology.

## Variations in Usage, Definitions, and Criteria

As the term "object constancy" came into general usage among psychoanalysts, some writers retained its original meaning in general psychology; with others it acquired a meaning specific for psychoanalysis, that is, the establishment of the libidinal tie to the mother.

In context, among a number of psychoanalytic references, the term "constancy" is often used in its familiar, colloquial sense without reference to psychological constancy.

> . . . the establishment of lasting emotional relations with the mother, i.e., of object constancy . . . (Jacobson, 1964, p. 63)

> . . . institutions need not be pathogenic if object constancy is safeguarded in the ratio and schedules of nurses . . . (Alpert, 1965, p. 166)

> . . . a mothering person who could give the child an unwavering sense of object constancy . . . (Alpert, 1965, p. 275)

Here usage closely follows one of the dictionary definitions of "constancy": "Steadfastness of attachment to a person or cause; faithfulness, fidelity" (*Oxford English Dictionary*). In this context, "constancy" is a qualitative term connoting a durable, permanent attachment. Since constancy in its colloquial sense exactly describes the qualitative aspect of the infant's tie to the mother, the formation of the permanent love bond, it has gained some currency in psychoanalytic usage in this sense without any of its connotations in general psychology. It is, of course, perfectly valid for us to employ "constancy" in the sense of "steadfastness of attachment"—but the term has been preempted by general psychology. This is where the semantic differences arise.

To augment the semantic problem, some writers do introduce into the concept of libidinal object constancy (i.e., the "steadfastness of attachment") a "quality of being invariable" which has specific psychoanalytic connotations, yet is relative to psychological "constancy." The libidinal cathexis of mother, which remains stable regardless of fluctuations in need states or externally imposed frustrations, has the quality of being invariable; this presupposes a mother who retains her identity for the child regardless of variations in satisfaction or nonsatisfaction.

The factor of "invariability" is also introduced in the psychoanalytic concept of love object constancy by those writers who link the libidinal bond to mother with mental representation. The following sample is taken from John Frosch (1966):

> . . . consistency in the behavior of the primary love object is necessary; it facilitates the formation of an object representation which can remain constant in time and space and consistent with itself in spite of subsequent alterations and changes in the object relations of the developing individual (Spitz and Wolf, 1949, p. 100). When these features characterize object representation, we have object constancy. Its establishment facilitates the tolerance of temporary separation from the love object as well as the ability to tolerate ambivalence toward the love object. (P. 350)

Frosch specifically states that the psychoanalytic concept of object constancy "is not to be confused with the concept of the 'stable object' in academic psychology." This presents a puzzle to my mind, since Frosch's phrasing "an object representation which can remain constant in time and space" exactly defines "constancy" for Werner and Piaget. It is not inconsistent with psychoanalytic theory that the drive "object" can also be an "object" in the psychological sense, that is, "have objectivity" and autonomy from the subject's perception. This is apparently what Hartmann had in mind when he first introduced the term object constancy from general psychology and was seeking correlates in cognition for the libidinal investment of mother.

René Spitz makes his most explicit statement regarding the drive and conceptual attributes of "object constancy" in "Metapsychology and Infant Observation" (1966):

> These developments [referring to gratification and learning] combine with the growing memory, while apperception of mnemonic traces becomes more and more efficient. Both are instrumental in helping the baby to achieve a stable, consistent memory image of his mother. Hartmann (1952) refers to this as the establishment of object constancy.
> Up to this point, one and the same person, the mother, was alternatively a good or a bad object. She became a bad object when she refused to gratify the desire of the baby, for this refusal triggered his aggressive

drive; when shortly thereafter she gratified his wish, or rather his need, she became the good mother, toward whom libidinal drives were directed. (P. 137)

Spitz then links "object constancy" with "a stable, consistent memory image" (i.e., mental representation) of the mother. The achievement of mental representation is seen both in terms of drive organization (fusion of libidinal and aggressive drives) and cathexis of the memory image of the mother. The identity of mother is established through unification of "good" and "bad" memory traces.

Spitz places the establishment of object constancy at eight months, using the criterion of stranger anxiety (1957).

> The eight-months anxiety is a much simpler performance; the sequence is as follows. The child produces first a scanning behavior, namely the seeking for the lost love object, the mother. A decision is now made by the function of judgment "whether something which is present in the ego as an image, can also be re-discovered in perception" (Freud, 1925). The realization that it cannot be rediscovered in the given instance provokes a response of unpleasure. In terms of the eight-months anxiety, what we observe can be understood as follows: the stranger's face is compared to the memory traces of the mother's face and found wanting. This is not mother, she is still lost. Unpleasure is experienced and manifested. (P. 54)

In a letter, I asked Dr. Spitz whether I was correct in interpreting his statements on the significance of the eight-months anxiety as an indicator of the achievement of object constancy, and as a demonstration of the infant's capacity to evoke the image of the mother in her absence. He replied:

> You are quite correct in assuming my interpretation of the eight-months anxiety as an indicator of the child's capacity to evoke the image of the absent object. . . . However, this observation refers to a special stress situation. . . . I have . . . no sufficient systematic work on the subject to venture the statement that the mother's image can be evoked by the child at all times and under less stressful circumstances than at the stage of the eight-months anxiety, though I consider it highly probable.
>      . . . In other words, I consider the eight-months anxiety a proof of the establishment of object constancy in regard to the libidinal object.

Spitz, too, has sought links between the psychoanalytic theory of object constancy and the genetic psychology of Piaget. He has seen that where mental representation and objectivation are concerned, there is common ground between the psychoanalytic investigator of early mental processes and Piaget. In the appendix to *The First Year of Life* (1965), Spitz's collaborator, W. Godfrey Cobliner, attempts to work out parallels and stage-specific criteria uniting Spitz's findings in human object relations with those of Piaget in the development of the object concept. In a later section of this essay I shall return to this topic.

Humberto Nagera (1966) has used the term "object constancy" to connote the exclusive bond to the mother with emphasis on the developmental process which leads to the establishment of the stable attachment. He said:

> Obviously, the transition from the phase of need satisfaction to object constancy is a very slow and gradual process which starts in the third or fourth month, gains further impetus during the second half of the first year, and reaches its full development during the second year of life. In most cases it is already well established toward the end of the first half of the second year. (P. 415)

In placing the *attainment* of object constancy in the second half of the second year, Nagera provides clarification in usage which, I believe, successfully mediates the differences among a number of authors. Some of the differences which have appeared among psychoanalytic writers have arisen through usage in which "object constancy" connotes a developmental stage, and whether the term implies the emergence of that stage, or the attainment of a point on a scale with specific criteria, is often not clear or must be inferred from context.

Margaret Mahler follows Hartmann in usage of the term "object constancy." In her essay "On the Significance of the Normal Separation-Individuation Phase" (1965), Mahler uses "object constancy" in this context:

> *The fourth subphase* of separation-individuation is the period during which an increasing degree of object constancy (in Hartmann's sense) is attained (twenty-five to thirty-six months). At the beginning of this subphase, the child still remains in the original playroom setting, with the mother readily available in the mothers' sitting section. We have found that, as this phase proceeds, the child is able gradually to accept

once again separation from the mother (as he did in the "practicing" period); in fact, he seems to prefer staying in the familiar playroom without the mother, to going out of this room with her. We regard this as a sign of the *achievement of beginning object constancy.* (P. 167; my italics)

[Again, in 1966, she speaks of] the fourth subphase of separation-individuation in which a certain degree of *object constancy* will be attained: i.e., mental representations of the mother become intra-psychically available (Hartmann, 1952). The memory traces of the love object enable the child to remain away from the mother for some length of time and still function with emotional poise, provided he is in a fairly familiar environment. Presumably this is so because inner representations of the mother are available to him. (P. 156)

Mahler, then, specifically links the attainment of object constancy with the emergence of a stable mental representation which enables the child to tolerate separation from the mother.

Since the term "object constancy" has acquired diverse meanings in our literature, its stage-specific attributes are variously described and cannot be understood unless we can infer from context which usage the author follows. In this way, too, we can understand a puzzle in the range of age norms which appear in our literature for the attainment of object constancy. This range among eleven writers consulted extended from six months of age to twenty-five months. The apparent discrepancy seems to be the result of differences in definition. The writers who ascribe the beginnings of object constancy to the middle of the first year are using "constancy" only in the sense of attachment to the love object. The writers who give a range from eight months to eighteen months of age are adding some form of mental representation to the criteria for libidinal cathexis of the object; those who place object constancy at eighteen months appear to be following Piaget's criteria for mental representation and object concept. The one writer (Mahler) who placed object constancy at twenty-five months was using still more restrictive criteria on the libidinal-cognitive scale, in which mental representation of the mother had attained a high level of stability.

As we shall see further, it is *not* in the evidence for the libidinal attachment that the disparate views on libidinal object constancy appear, but in the evidence for "mental representation" of the mother and "objectivation" of the mother, the cognitive aspects of the exclusive, binding tie to mother.

The problem can be summarized in this way: If we can demonstrate that between six months and twelve months of age the infant's attachment to the mother becomes increasingly selective, exclusive, and relatively independent of need and the satisfaction of need, if we can demonstrate anxiety at separation from the mother during this period, what concomitant processes in cognition are at work in these increasingly selective responses? Do the highly differentiated responses require a particular form of mental representation of the mother? Does the reaction to loss indicate a capacity to evoke the image of the absent mother? Do the qualitative changes in the libidinal attachment to mother represent an achievement in "objectivation" of mother, that is, is mother seen as separate and autonomous from the infant self?

While all writers consulted take into account perceptual and cognitive aspects of the libidinal tie to the mother, there are wide differences among them in the attribution of (1) objectivation of the mother and (2) mental representation of the mother as conditions for the emergence of the stable, exclusive, permanent investment of the mother. I think these differences can be explained on this basis:

We are on firm analytic ground in a well-researched area when we speak of the investment of the mother and the primacy of the mother as love object in the period of six months to one year. Here, our data are derived from studies of normal infants and from the pathological sequelae in development, that is, absence of the bond to mother or temporary or permanent rupture of these bonds. Here, too, our data are largely confirmed by studies outside of the field of psychoanalysis.

We are on less certain ground—a circumstance that we share with other psychologies—in our investigation of the genetic aspects of memory and the stage-specific characteristics of "objectivation." Here, too, we have semantic disharmony in our use of the term "mental representation" and "object." In psychoanalysis we employ the term "mental representation" to cover a wide variety of mental phenomena, from simple registrations to evocative memory. We use the term "object" most familiarly as "object of drives" and also to represent a person, or thing, or universe of things which are perceived as external to the self and have autonomy from the self.

**Mental Representation and Object Constancy**

Nearly all writers consulted link the achievement of libidinal object constancy with some form of mental representation of the mother. Where differences occur among these writers, I think we can find the differences through usage:

1. The term "mental representation" is used to cover a broad spectrum of cognitive acts in psychoanalysis ranging from simple registrations and primitive hallucinatory phenomena to mental operations which involve a high degree of complexity in symbolic thought. Since our vocabulary does not designate gradients in this series, the kind of mental representation referred to in explanatory texts must be inferred from contexts.

2. There is not yet agreement among psychoanalytic writers regarding the level of complexity in mental representation of the mother which must be assumed as a correlate for libidinal attachment.

3. Some of the criteria for mental representation of the mother assume a higher level of complexity in symbolic memory than can be demonstrated through objective infant studies.

Some aspects of the problem of usage emerge in the following exchange at the Panel Discussion (1968) between David Beres and Anna Freud:

*Dr. David Beres:* The point I would like to make on the subject of object constancy is that I agree entirely with Miss Freud's and Dr. Lampl-de Groot's definitions of it. But I see no reason not to include, as part of the problem of object constancy, the psychological problem of mental representation. I would say that without the development of the child to the point where it has the capacity to form a mental representation of the object which remains in the psychic apparatus (and I am using a very crude metaphor here), in the absence of the object, object constancy in Miss Freud's sense would not be something of which the child would be capable. I think that there is no reason to eliminate the psychological aspect, I am not sure that Miss Freud meant to do so. . . .

*Miss Freud:* I certainly did not mean to neglect the psychological side altogether, namely, the establishment of an independent inner image. I only think that the two processes are different from each other. The capacity to retain an inner image comes before object constancy. To my mind it is characteristic and relevant for another advance in the child's life as shown in Spitz's book *The First Year of Life.* With this capacity the child takes the step from the object being an object for the id, to being an object for the ego. But that is not the same as object constancy. Object constancy means, on top of that, to retain attachment even when the person is unsatisfactory. (P. 507)

David Beres, then, is using "mental representation" as the capacity to evoke the image of the mother in the absence of the mother in perception. Here, mental representation means "evocative memory." On a scale of cognitive development, evocative memory requires a capacity for symbolic operations which many writers place at approximately eighteen months of age.

Anna Freud in her statement places "the capacity to retain an inner image" before object constancy. Since in her definition object constancy begins around the middle of the first year, she is undoubtedly speaking of a form of mental representation which is available to the infant at six to eight months of age, one of course which is far removed in complexity from the evocative memory of the second year. We do not have a descriptive term in psychoanalysis which differentiates this form of mental representation from evocative memory.

Some of the ambiguities in usage might be clarified if we distinguished between "recognition memory" and "evocative memory," following Piaget. Thus, a memory trace or a mental image of the mother does not in itself imply the capacity to evoke the image of mother independent of the presenting stimulus of her face or voice. *Recognition* can take place when the person or "thing" perceived has characteristics or signs which revive mnemonic traces laid down through previous experience. The test for *evocative memory* is the demonstrated capacity to evoke the image without the presenting stimulus. (Later, I would like to expand this definition to take into account the hallucinatory phenomena which we in psychoanalysis associate with the beginnings of mental life.)

The differences between recognition memory and evocative memory are acknowledged in everyday human experience. For example, if I should set myself the task of trying to remember the students in a class that I taught twenty years ago, I may be able to produce a picture of only three or four of twenty-five students. But if I should meet one of the students whose memory I cannot evoke, I may recognize his face immediately, and may even be able to remember which seat he occupied and a number of other details. This means that the presentation of that forgotten face revived the picture stored in memory; the face provided signs, the picture was "compared" by means of these signs, and recognition took place.

This matching of pictures by means of signs is "recognition" memory. We can only speak of "evocative memory" in the true sense, in the first example, when I can produce the picture without the presence of the student in reality. In infant development it is useful to discriminate between recognition memory, which can only be elicited by signs, and evocative memory, which has autonomy from objective signs.

It is "evocative memory" that Freud had in mind when he said, in the essay "Negation" (1925), "Thinking possesses the capacity to bring before the mind once more something that has once been perceived, by reproducing it as a presentation without the external object having still to be there" (p. 237).

David Beres (1968) carefully discriminates between "mental registrations" and "mental representation" and employs "mental representation" restrictively to connote "evocative memory."

At what point in development is the infant capable of evoking the image of the mother when she is not present in reality?

When the baby of six months begins to demonstrate his preference for his mother, through selective smiling and vocalization, when the baby demonstrates that his attachment to the mother has relative independence from need satisfaction, does this behavior toward the mother indicate a capacity to evoke the mother's image in her absence? Or can we explain these selective responses to the mother on the basis of recognition memory for a highly cathected object?

When the baby at seven to ten months displays anxiety in response to the stranger, is this a demonstration of evocative memory for the mother? Or can we explain this phenomenon on the basis of an advance in recognition memory? If the baby sobers or cries at the sight of the stranger's face, he certainly demonstrates the ability to make the perceptual discriminations between familiar faces and unfamiliar faces, cathected objects and noncathected objects, but the act of nonrecognition may only tell us that recognition memory has progressed to a certain level of complexity.

The anxiety which is manifest in this experience of nonrecognition can be interpreted without the attribution of evocative memory. While it has been suggested by Spitz that the anxiety is a reaction to "not finding" the mother in reality, even this hypothesis does not require the capacity to evoke the image of the "lost" mother. On the contrary, if a mother is "lost" when she is not perceived, this may be taken as evidence that the mental image of the mother is still unstable, is not independent of perception, and requires affirmation from visual experience.

If, as Spitz suggests, stranger anxiety is related to "not finding" the mother in reality, can we accommodate this interpretation within the framework of recognition memory? Recognition memory stabilizes itself through repetition. The appearance in the perceptual field of mother's face elicits the joy of recognition, the revival of highly cathected memory traces. In this transitional period for the baby, when mental operations begin to take into account the objective attributes of persons and things, we may suppose a kind of expectation in the baby that the people and things of his world should have resonance in memory. On the eight-month level of cognitive development, is it possible that the face that cannot be affirmed, "placed" through memory, is momentarily disruptive to the child's sense of the "real," that expectations are not confirmed? Is it perhaps a "spooky" experience, like the dream in which one enters the familiar kitchen of childhood, with mother at the stove, her back to the dreamer, and mother turns around . . . and suddenly one confronts the face of a stranger!

What I am suggesting is that an "expectation" that a familiar and beloved face should manifest itself in a familiar surround does not require the intervention of evocative memory. The child who is capable of evocative memory can sustain the image of the mother *not* present in perception which should theoretically diminish the disturbing effect of a strange face. Following this line of thought one might venture the hypothesis that the *waning* of stranger anxiety at twelve to thirteen months should have correlates in cognitive development, another step toward autonomy of the image from perceptual experience. (There is, I believe, some support for this hypothesis in Piaget's work.)

When the child demonstrates anxiety during brief separations from the mother, does this constitute evidence for evocative memory? Benjamin's studies show that the peak of separation anxiety appears around one year of age. Anxiety at loss of the mother certainly testifies to the strength of the libidinal tie to mother and of her valuation above all other persons. Does the anxiety constitute evidence that the child sustains a mental image of the mother in her absence? One could argue the other way, also—that separation anxiety is greater during the period eight to thirteen months because the libidinal bond has been forged, the mother is *recognized* as the all-important, indispensable person, but there is not yet a stable mental representation of the mother that can sustain the child during brief separations. All psychoanalytic writers consulted on this problem seem to agree that the stabilization of mental representations of the mother takes place gradually over a period of years. Our question is: When can we say the capacity to evoke the image of the absence object *begins?* What are the criteria? The criterion of separation anxiety remains arguable as long as we need the criterion "tolerance of separation" at the other end of the scale. That is, if we regard tolerance for brief separations at twenty to twenty-six months as an indicator of the stability of the mental representation, intolerance, bordering on severe anxiety states between the ages of eight to thirteen months, must testify to the instability of mental representations. Such an unstable representation, one that is still dependent upon "signs," cannot yet qualify as evocative memory in a strict definition of the term.

## Contributions of Piaget

Piaget's empirical studies of cognitive development in the sensorimotor period provide us with valuable criteria for the evolution of evocative memory during the first eighteen months of life. Piaget supports his findings with rich and detailed infant protocols which permit the psychoanalytic student of child development to follow the data and his inferences. These findings have made welcome additions to our literature, and, as we have seen, contributed in some measure to Hartmann's thinking on the subject of object constancy and to Spitz and Cobliner's studies of the cognitive aspects of libidinal development. Piaget has sometimes been criticized by psychoanalysts because he has not concerned himself with the affective components of cognition (although he does tangentially), and this, of course, is a central problem for the psychoanalyst in studying the mental development of infants. Further, his empirical work on the child's construction of an object world was based largely on the child's behavior toward inanimate objects, toys, and the problem of relevance to the human object comes into the psychoanalytic assessment. Finally, since Piaget's work on infant memory concerned itself with the percept and the withdrawal of the percept from the visual field, the whole large question of the hallucination in infant need states is left unanswered for the psychoanalyst who needs empirical data from infancy. This was not an area of interest to Piaget. In any case, the problem of setting up experimental conditions for the study of hallucinations in infancy is so formidable that we can only congratulate those who have left the field to us.

Yet, I think it can be demonstrated that Piaget's data have great importance for the psychoanalytic student of memory in infancy. We have from Piaget a set of stage-specific criteria for the development of memory based upon exteroceptive experience in infancy. Piaget's original work has since been validated by two independent studies, testing large infant populations (Décarie, 1965; Escalona, 1968). If the data for mental representation of exteroceptive experience are known, we can formulate certain hypotheses regarding the capacity of the infant to hallucinate during need states.

If we assume that the image of exteroceptive experience and the image of gratification in need states are united through a mutual feedback system, the infant's memory of an "object" that has been withdrawn from his visual field must have correlates in the infant's capacity to produce an image in need states. Since the picture must first be present as a visual percept, there is a given primacy in exteroceptive experience for the registration of the early mental traces. The most conservative inference that can be drawn is that no memory can be evoked through a need stimulus that is organized on a level of greater complexity than that present in the behavior toward the external stimulus. That is, if an infant cannot sustain the memory of an object hidden before his eyes under a screen, it is unlikely that the same infant can produce or sustain the memory of an object independent of a stimulus arising in a need state.

If this is true, the empirical data from Piaget's studies of the "object concept" and evocative memory can provide us with much needed baseline information for the study of the hallucinatory phenomena which we postulate in early mental life. To me, as for all psychoanalysts, the dream provides incontrovertible evidence that need gives rise to the image of its satisfaction. At what point in development is the infant capable of producing an image through need? At what point is he capable of producing a picture independent of need *and* the percept?

The dream can tell us that there was a time in mental development when sensory pictures emerged without unity and coherence and without taking into account time, causality, or the permanence of things not perceived. The dream has informed us of the phenomena of early mental life, but it cannot, of course, tell us how and when these disordered elements were bound together and how intelligence became free from the bond of the stimulus.

Does it matter? If reconstruction in the analysis of an adult or a child cannot tell us exactly when certain crucial events took place, it may not matter for the conduct of the analysis or for the patient's prognosis. It only matters that the memory can be revived. But for the psychoanalytic student of child development and for psychoanalytic theory itself, there must be something like a chronology and stage-specific criteria for the organization of memory in infancy or we are handicapped in the study of ego development. Such questions as: What is the relationship between libidinal object constancy and "the stable object" in general psychological terms? or: What do we mean by mental representation? are of central interest to us. In this way the objective findings of other psychologists can enrich our understanding of mental processes in infancy and can help us clarify a number of difficult problems in the area of libidinal object relations and the construction of an objective world.

For us, as well as other psychologists, the study of the genetic aspects of memory and its stage-specific characteristics must be inferred from behavior signs. The key to the dream was Freud's great gift to the psychology of thinking, and what is unknown and not yet fathomed in the genetic aspects of memory is really the fault of our subject, who is slow at picking up language before eighteen months. But if we have the key to the dream and data from a growing number of developmental studies in psychoanalysis, we can begin to chart the territory. Piaget's work gives us another key, a stratification of cognitive development during the first eighteen months of life with impeccable data for the study of memory when the percept is withdrawn.

In the final section of this paper, I shall attempt to bring together Piaget's thinking and our psychoanalytic views on the subject of evocative memory and suggest a formulation for evocative memory that is consistent with psychoanalytic data and the findings of Piaget.

At this point it might be useful to begin with a short summary of Piaget's experimental procedures and the findings which led him to deduce the presence of evocative memory in the infant eighteen months of age. The summary is my own;[1] since it was necessary to present this material in a highly condensed form in this essay, I worked out an abbreviated version which emphasizes for the psychoanalytic reader the progressive autonomy of memory from the presenting stimulus.

### Piaget's Case

Piaget deals most extensively with the problem of mental representation in his work *The Child's Construction of Reality* (1937). Evocative memory in Piaget's view is linked indissolubly with the development of the object concept, that is, the concept of an object as external to the self, having autonomy from the self and the subject's perception of it. There can be no "object concept" without "mental representation," no "mental representation" without an "object concept," both achievements involve mental operations on a symbolic level, both achievements must take into account the permanence of an object that is not present in perception. The experimental procedures which I shall summarize are well known—a sequence of screened-object tests presented to the infant during the first eighteen months of life. Piaget's sequence has been confirmed in the studies by Décarie and Escalona. Both authors have worked out object concept scales and age ranges. The larger samples employed by both investigators have resulted in slightly different age distributions from those obtained by Piaget. In referring to age ranges, I shall cite the ranges established in Décarie's testing.[2]

There are six clearly defined stages in the development of the object concept which correspond to six stages of mental operations which Piaget has adduced from his studies of infant intelligence. For purposes of our psychoanalytic examination of the problem I shall summarize Piaget's findings for Stages III through VI (roughly five months to eighteen months of age).

*Stage III—Five to eight months of age.* Until eight months of age, the baby will make no attempt to recover a favorite toy or a test toy that has been moved before his eyes and placed under a simple screen (e.g., a cloth or a pillow).

Inferences: *Object Concept.* The toy has no existence for the baby when it disappears from his perceptual field. The baby attributes no substantiality to an object not perceived; it has no objective stability. *Memory.* The baby cannot sustain the image of the object in memory when barriers to his perception are presented.

*Stage IV—Eight to thirteen months.* Between eight months and thirteen months of age the infant will search for an object hidden before his eyes under a single screen. He will remove the barrier and recover the object. If the examiner introduces two screens (and another level of complexity) and hides the object first under screen A and then under screen B, the baby, even though witness to the successive displacements, will search for the object only under screen A where he had first recovered it. When he does not recover the object, he gives up the search.

Inferences: *Object Concept.* The baby is now *beginning* to attribute some kind of objectivity to things screened from his perception, but he has no notion of objective permanence; the object can be found only in one place, the place where he first recovered it. *Memory.* The baby can sustain the mental image of the vanished object for the few seconds that elapse between his perception of it and the screening, which enables him to conduct his simple search. When another event intervenes (screen B), there is no evidence from the infant's behavior that after his failure to recover the object under screen A, memory of the object has been sustained.

*Stage V—Thirteen to eighteen months.* Between the ages of thirteen months and eighteen months the baby will search for an object under two or more screens, provided he has *seen* the object disappear under successive screens. If a single *invisible* displacement takes place (a sleight-of-hand maneuver in the examiner's hiding game), the baby will not be able to deduce the probable hiding place of the object and will give up his search.

Inferences: *Object Concept.* The baby has acquired the notion that an object can follow its own itinerary, so to speak, and is not bound to a single point in space (as in Stage IV), but this idea is *still linked to his own perception,* he must follow its displacements with his eyes. *Memory.* The baby can sustain the mental image of the vanished object through successive displacements but must still rely upon the object's continuous manifestations of itself to his eyes (each displacement is accompanied by discovery and verification). The failure of the object to manifest itself to him in the invisible displacement appears to have the effect of erasing the mental image; the baby does not continue his search and gives no sign that a cathected image persists.

*Stage VI—Eighteen months.* At approximately eighteen months of age, the baby begins to take into account invisible displacements. In the experimental procedures the object is subjected to at least one displacement which the baby cannot see. The baby conducts a search which for the first time makes use of deduction. He deduces the probable hiding place of the object from information and clues available to him and sustains his search until he finds the object.

Inferences: *Object Concept.* The baby demonstrates belief that the object exists independent of his perception of it; his sustained search in spite of the invisible displacement has the meaning: "It must be someplace." The object has "permanence" in Piaget's terms; it has autonomy from the infant self, from his actions, his perceptions. Its displacements in space follow independent laws. *Memory.* The baby can sustain the mental image of the absent object in spite of all experimental barriers to perception. In the absence of perceptual cues or *any sign,* he can *evoke the image of the absent object* and pursue it; his deduction regarding the probable hiding place involves mental operations in which the entire sequence of actions must be recalled, "played back" in the memory record, which constitutes a further extension of the capacity for evocative memory.

## Summary of Piaget's Position

1. For Piaget true mental representation is evocative memory. The capacity to evoke the image of the absent object is not demonstrated in his infant studies until eighteen months of age. Piaget reminds us that these findings correlate with other cognitive achievements at the middle of the second year. It is at this time that symbolic thought is manifest in speech through naming with correct referents. It is at this time, too, that the young child begins to demonstrate his capacity for "deferred imitation" in Piaget's terms, that is the ability to imitate in the absence of the model and without signs from the model, the period of the beginning of play, of imagining.

2. Until the middle of the second year when the child gives his first demonstrations of evocative memory (following the strict criteria described in the preceding section), the child is capable of increasingly fine perceptual discriminations and inferences which Piaget places in the category of "recognition memory." Thus, in the experimental demonstrations of the baby through Stage V, the child conducts his search only as long as "signs" are available to him, the sign given directly by perception before the object disappears, or the sign given by the screen itself as "a hiding place." No examples appear until Stage VI of the child's ability to evoke the image of the absent object independent of a sign.

### The Psychoanalytic Case

The applicability of Piaget's findings to psychoanalytic investigations in the mental representation of the libidinal object and the objectivation of the mother can raise questions among analysts. It can be argued, for example, that the libidinal object has primacy as a perceptual object and that tests involving inanimate objects do not fairly represent the cognitive aspects of the most highly invested human object relationships. It can be argued that tests involving barriers to visual perception in affectively neutral circumstances do not tap the heart of the problem for psychoanalysis, which is the hallucinatory image arising from need states as hypothesized in psychoanalytic theory. These are valid objections in my views, too, but these are problems for the psychoanalytic investigator, and the answers must come from our own research.

Such differences do not diminish the value of Piaget's findings for psychoanalysts. Piaget's meticulous work on the infant's construction of an object world and the mental operations that lead to evocative memory provide valuable baseline information for the psychoanalytic investigator. If we are correct in our assumptions in psychoanalysis that the human object has a nuclear primacy in cognition, then we can assume a relationship between the cognition of persons and things (which, in fact, we do), but this would affect only the temporal sequence by giving a kind of human priority to cognitive events. It does not change the structure of the cognitive act. Perception, recognition, evocative memory follow the same structural and maturational laws for human objects and inanimate objects; the differences that we discern in psychoanalysis are affective and are defined in energic terms; we can speak of degrees of cathexis but not of a different kind of mental representation. Similarly, we do not need a different set of criteria for objectivation of the human object and objectivation of the inanimate object. The human object may take temporal precedence, but the mental operations that lead to the construction of an object world are probably identical in each instance.

If we can accept these conditions, we can use Piaget's findings to construct certain hypotheses regarding mental representation of the mother (evocative memory) and objectivation of the mother. The hypotheses need to be tested through direct observation of infants by psychoanalytic investigators. Some of the work has been done in this area: some remains for further investigation.

*Some Hypotheses Regarding Evocative Memory for the Mother*

1. The capacity of the infant to evoke the image of the absent mother may precede the capacity to evoke the image of an absent "thing," but should appear in close temporal contiguity to "thing" representation. This gives us a baseline of eighteen months for "evocation of the thing" (Piaget) and the expectation that "evocation of the image of the absent mother" appears shortly before the eighteen-month period.

2. The capacity to "hallucinate" the mother, or another image of gratification, during need states is unresearched, and we have no stage-specific criteria. Since the hallucinated image at any point in the developmental scale can never represent a higher level of differentiation or complexity than the image produced through exteroceptive experience, the data available to us through objective tests of the infant's perceptual development should give us points of reference for inferring the characteristics of hallucinatory experience. Thus, (a) if need gives rise to the image of satisfaction, the picture produced through a rise in need tensions cannot be a better copy of the real object than one that registers through direct perception. And, (b) the capacity to evoke the image of an object withdrawn from perception must have correlates in the capacity to evoke the image of an object in need states.

3. The mental processes that lead to "objectivation" of the mother, the concept of mother as having autonomy from the self and a sub-

stantial existence when she is not perceived, can be presumed to follow the same sequential development as the construction of objective permanence of "things," although the time order may be altered on the basis of cathexis and valuation of the mother over "things." Since objectivation in this sense must be linked to the capacity for evocative memory, the location on a developmental timetable of evocative memory for the mother should establish the age of attainment of objectivation of mother.

### The Problem of Reconciling These Data from Two Psychologies

Both Thérèse Gouin-Décarie and W. Godfrey Cobliner (with Spitz) have attempted to reconcile the psychoanalytic criteria for mental representation (evocative memory) and objectivation of the mother with Piaget's criteria. Since 1960 I have been at work in the same area, seeking comparative data on blind and sighted infants.

Using psychoanalytic criteria for libidinal object relations and mental representation, and Piaget's criteria for the development of object permanence and mental representation, Décarie constructed two scales, an Objectal Scale for libidinal object relations and an Object Concept Scale, using Piaget's criteria. The psychoanalytic criteria were taken from authoritative sources in our literature and were employed with fastidious attention to nuances in psychoanalytic usage. Since nearly all of these criteria appear in one or another form on standard developmental tests for infants, it was possible to obtain age norms for each of these items and rank them on a scale. The Object Concept criteria were, of course, explicit in Piaget's work. Both scales were administered to a group of ninety infants. The sequence obtained through the administration of the Piaget scales was invariant, though the normative age groupings were corrected in this large sample. The sequence obtained through the administration of the Objectal Scale was variable in more than one half the subjects. Décarie herself offers a number of sound reasons for the heterogeneous protocols she obtained. They do not invalidate the psychoanalytic criteria as "indicators" of libidinal attachment, but they do suggest that the order of the appearance of signs has variability for at least some items. This will need to be investigated in future psychoanalytic research.

In Décarie's work, the most serious obstacle in seeking correlates between mental representation of the human object and mental representation of the "thing" was the absence of consensus among psychoanalytic writers in usage of the term "mental representation" and in identifying the characteristics of "evocative memory." Some of the behaviors which we in analysis interpret as manifestations of evocative memory were, in Décarie's view, uncertain signs; that is, while the behavior itself was manifestly a sign of libidinal cathexis of the human object, it did not require the intervention of evocative memory for its performance.

Analysis of the homogeneous protocols permitted the ranking of stage-specific characteristics in libidinal object relations and a comparison of these ranks with the Piaget scale ranks. Here the correspondence between stage-specific characteristics of libidinal object relations and the construction of the object concept showed closer correspondence. There remained, however, a gap in age intervals within the two scales. The gap appeared at the point on each scale where "evocative memory" is presumed to intervene. Décarie attempted to bridge the gap by advancing Piaget's criteria for evocative memory (from eighteen to fifteen months) and by placing evocative memory for the mother at one year of age, which left a three-month interval between the two scales which could be postulated as the difference represented between evocation of the human object and the inanimate object. Piaget, in an otherwise commendatory preface to Décarie's book, took exception to this revision of his criteria for evocative memory and affirmed his position on the eighteen-month criteria, citing corroboration from other studies.

W. Godfrey Cobliner, in his appendix to Spitz's *The First Year of Life*, also addresses himself to the problem of reconciling Piaget's data with psychoanalytic data, specifically Spitz's interpretation of the eight-months anxiety as an indicator of mental representation of the mother. The problem for Cobliner was to bring Spitz's eight-month criteria for evocative memory into harmony with Piaget's criteria. In order to do this, he had to give another value to Piaget's Stage V criteria and to place evocative memory for the inanimate object at approximately eleven months of age, where Piaget explicitly places it at Stage VI, eighteen months.

These efforts to conciliate the positions of Piaget and psychoanalysis on the appearance of evocative memory require us to stretch the evidence in ways that are uncongenial to both psychoanalysis and Piaget. If we accept Cobliner's criteria for mental representation of the mother at eight months (stranger anxiety), we have a ten-months gap between evocative memory for the human object and evocative memory for the toy, which is not demonstrated until eighteen months on Piaget's scale or the standardized scales of Décarie and Escalona. Even postulating a priority for the highly invested human object, we cannot account for this ten-months gap. If, in fact, there is a generalization in memory from the person to the thing, as Hartmann has proposed on a cathectic basis, such a generalization should take place without marked delay. It is difficult to imagine that once the capacity for evocative memory is achieved, it is isolated from all other experience. Generalization is the very nature of intelligence. (To illustrate, in the same eighth-month period that is under discussion, the attribution of qualities to the mother, the valuation of mother, has a counterpart in the child's new valuation and preferential treatment of toys and other "things." One could construct other parallels, stage by stage, but the case would be much strengthened by detailed day-by-day observations of infants by psychoanalysts who are interested in the problem.)

The problem of reconciling data really centers around criteria for evocative memory in psychoanalysis. As we have seen, such criteria as valuation of the mother, stranger anxiety, and separation anxiety, which come in during the second half of the first year, do not require more than a highly selective and differentiated "recognition memory" in the infant. I have been led in this direction not only by my interest in the theoretical problem but by the findings in my research on infants totally blind from birth.

*Some Data from Our Research on Blind Infants*

To study the development of libidinal object relations in blind infants we used criteria for each developmental stage for which there is agreement among psychoanalysts. In each of our observational sessions we made detailed narrative records of the baby's behavior in relation to the mother. As another aspect of our research, we studied the development of the object concept using highly cathected toys as well as test objects, following a modified Piaget scale.

The results for ten otherwise intact infants, totally blind from birth, can be summarized: Each of these babies met the criteria for human object relations that we accept for sighted children under one year of age. In the second half of the first year, the kind of exclusive love for the mother, the highly differentiated responses to mother, the discrimination of mother and stranger, negative reactions to the stranger, and the inability to accept substitutes for mother, were all demonstrated by these blind babies.

At the same time the results of our "object concept test," which is, of course, a test of mental representation, showed a stage-by-stage lag of three to six months in the ability to sustain the memory of an object after it had left the tactile or auditory sphere. The Stage VI demonstration, the ability to evoke the memory of the object independent of perceptual cues, was the most difficult task of all for our blind children.

We are then left with evidence that further complicates the relationship between libidinal object relations and the capacity for evocative memory. If we use the eight- to ten-months period as a point of reference, we have all the criteria for libidinal object relations including stranger reactions among the blind babies. But at eight to ten months, the sighted baby has attained Stage IV on Piaget's scale, which tests the capacity to sustain the memory of an object for a few seconds after it has disappeared from the perceptual field. Our babies are still in Stage III (no memory for an object that has left the immediate perceptual field). This means, of course, that a child who is retarded (by sighted child standards) in memory function need not be retarded in his libidinal object relations.

## The Problem of the Hallucinatory Image

At the center of all these problems of definition and criteria for evocative memory is the problem of the hallucinatory image which we, in psychoanalysis, regard as "the primary model of thought" (Rapaport, 1960). The dream provides us with compelling evidence that there are genetic links between drives and memory; need gives rise to the image of gratification. We can assume with Rapaport that the earliest forms of this imagery are diffuse and undifferentiated, and only gradually in the course of infant development do these images differentiate into discrete objects. It is further assumed in psychoanalytic thinking that memory gradually achieves some degree of autonomy from drive stimuli, and many psychoanalytic writers believe that the infant's capacity to retain the cathexis to the mother independent of fluctuations of need states is an indicator of the emerging autonomy of memory from drive stimuli. In the previous section I have raised some questions regarding the criteria which are employed for the demonstration of the infant's capacity to evoke the image of the mother independent of need and independent of her presence in reality.

Yet, the problem of the hallucinatory image and its relationship to evocative memory remains, and is most compelling for the psychoanalyst engaged in child development study. It is a vital link in the story of cognition, yet it can only be known by inference.

Our case is a difficult one because we cannot easily set up the experimental conditions for studying the infant's capacity to hallucinate. In the absence of language we must infer from behavioral signs, yet the signs can be ambiguous and cannot tell us the content of imagery if it is present. If the infant of eight months is hungry and begins mouthing or sucking movements, is this simply the activation of a sensorimotor schema to the stimulus of visceral sensations, is it an undifferentiated state of "expectedness" stimulated by visceral sensations, as Décarie suggests, or is there a picture of the mother or food stimulated by need?

## A Digression and a Possible Solution

To answer some of these questions for myself, I took a long detour which I shall now describe. The detour involves some animal observations. Here, I feel apologetic. I would have much preferred infant observations, but the elderly Beagle who is the subject of these investigations offered certain advantages for study. I can provide experimental evidence that his sensorimotor intelligence placed him not higher than Stage IV on a scale of mental representation. He was also capable of expressing a limited number of wants during need states. As a subject for the study of the negative hallucination he afforded one great advantage over the human infant. His range of mobility exceeded the possibilities of a human child at Stage IV, and, like most dogs, he translated his wants into specific motor actions which were sometimes very clear.

Late in the evening, usually around ten o'clock, Brandy would rouse himself from a doze, shake himself, and march over to my chair. He would stand before me, wag his tail in greeting, and bark in a peremptory fashion. I would then say, "What do you want, Brandy?" and stand up, waiting for a signal from him. He would then lead the way to the kitchen, and to one of two places in the kitchen. If he wanted a biscuit, he would stand before the packaged food cupboard and bark. I would then get the biscuits and feed him a snack. If he wanted something more substantial, like meat, he would stand before the refrigerator door and bark in the same commanding way.

Up to the time that the door to the cupboard was opened, or the refrigerator door opened, Brandy's behavior clearly indicated that he wanted "something" and his choice of two doors leading to (1) biscuits and (2) meat indicates that some kind of sensory image was evoked without the presentation of the stimulus in reality.

Is this evocative memory? I think not. Yet it satisfies the definition, "the evocation of absent realities"! Yes, but then something needs to be qualified in the definition. We are willing to credit Brandy with at least two sensory images without the presenting external stimulus, but both images are produced by an inner stimulus of need, and, I believe, *only by the stimulus of need.*

If we construct another test and qualify the definition we should ask: If there is no organic stimulus, can Brandy evoke the image of a biscuit or a piece of meat, even in the most diffuse form? I think this is highly unlikely on theoretical grounds. On this level of sensorimotor intelligence, "wanting" is united with an action schema; the registration of need, raised to a certain intensity, activates a motor pattern. We can be reasonably sure that if some form of motor expression is not manifest, no "image of satisfaction" is available to the dog. Brandy would probably not be able to keep to himself a lonely vision of delights in the refrigerator. If, then, the action schemas can provide signs of a sensory image of need satisfaction, they also tell us that *the image is entirely at the disposal of the stimulus.*

There is some correspondence, then, between the sensory image evoked through need states in Brandy and the hallucinatory image which we postulate in the development of human intelligence. But intelligence in human infancy becomes free of the bonds of the stimulus; there will be a point in the development of human intelligence when an image can be evoked with relative autonomy from need states *and* the presenting stimulus in exteroceptive experience. This leads us back to one of the recurrent questions in this investigation: Is there a correlation between the level of mental operations demonstrated for exteroceptive data (the object not present in reality) and the level of mental operations required for the hallucination of a drive object during need states?

What were the limits of Brandy's sensorimotor intelligence when presented with the problem of a desirable object that is withdrawn from his perceptual field?

Now I shall describe another set of observations on the same dog which derive from certain informal tests. Our daughter, Lisa, then nine, had been following some of my baby work with interest. She was intrigued with the baby's reactions to screened objects and began a series of tests with Brandy. When Lisa reported her first test results, she was visibly shocked and her confidence in our dog's intelligence was shaken for the first time. I then observed these tests, observed them many times, in fact, and this is what I saw:

Lisa showed Brandy a biscuit. Then slowly, so that he could follow the biscuit with his eyes, she concealed it in the rolled-up cuff of her jeans. Brandy recovered the biscuit. (This part of the procedure was part of a game with Brandy, and he could always recover the biscuit in the cuff of the jeans.) In the second part of the procedure, Lisa again placed the biscuit in her jean cuffs while Brandy followed the action with his eyes. Then Lisa removed the biscuit and did not give it to Brandy, but moved it slowly *in his visual range* to her *pocket*, and left it there. Brandy searched for the biscuit in the first hiding place, the jeans cuff! He then stared at the cuff of the jeans, waited for a decent interval, then whined piteously, begging Lisa with his eyes, and gave up the search.

In repeated experiments, the results were invariable. Brandy always searched for the biscuit in the first hiding place. This is all the more remarkable when we consider that Brandy was a scent hound and should have easily tracked the displacements of the biscuit on scent alone. He behaved in this test as if the data of vision had no connection with the data of smell and when the biscuit disappeared from vision behind the second screen, he could not account for its displacement and searched for it under the first screen. This was *the* place where a vanished biscuit must be found. Clearly, then, the biscuit had no "permanence" as an object in Piaget's terms, but was conceived as belonging to "a place."

I should say that when I reported these informal test results to my psychologist friends, they sneered. As one of them said bluntly, "Why use Brandy for these experiments? Everyone knows he's a dumb dog!" I will not debate the question of Brandy's intelligence. There may, in fact, be dogs who can do slightly better than Brandy on such a test, but no dog has yet presented evidence that he is capable of true evocative memory.[3]

### Correspondence between the Two Sets of Data

I think it can be shown that the "hallucinated" biscuit of need states and the biscuit that is screened from vision are organized on the same level of complexity and are mediated by "signs." *Both sets of mental operations are "stimulus bound."*

The level of sensorimotor intelligence demonstrated by Brandy on Lisa's biscuit test can be equated with Stage IV on the Piaget scale (eight to twelve months on a standardized scale for infants). Brandy can recover a biscuit behind one screen when he has seen it disappear before his eyes. That is, the mental image is still linked with the visual stimulus and its stability is conceived as "belonging to one place." Once the hiding place is moved, Brandy cannot "move" his picture to a second place and he pursues the biscuit at the place where he had first seen it disappear. The link between vision and the biscuit is the screen (the cuff of Lisa's jeans), where he had first seen the hiding of the object. Every time his gaze returns to the cuff of the jeans, he behaves as if the biscuit should materialize from the seams. When it does not, the screen loses its sign value, the cathexis of the mental image of "biscuit" wanes, and he gives up the hunt. Apparently he does not brood about the problem.

The child of eight months behaves in much the same way toward an object when more than one barrier to perception is introduced. And I can do the same thing myself when a series of distractions interpose themselves between a task set up in memory and the execution of that task! Given an hour or two of successive barriers to memory, I may forget where I left the grocery list when the phone began to ring. However, both I and a reasonably intelligent eighteen-month-old child can uncover a series of barriers to memory by mentally reconstructing the sequence, running the sequence over again in memory or running it backward. Unless my grocery list is caught up in intrapsychic conflict, I can employ evocative memory to reconstruct its displacements. I can recover a grocery list that has left my perceptual field two hours ago.

This grocery list (which now appears overdetermined in my argument!) can be turned another way for our purposes. No one will be surprised to learn that I can prepare a grocery list and produce a mental image of every item on that list without being hungry, and without any visceral signs or promptings. Somewhere around the middle of the second year of life, the child's vocabulary will tell us that he, too, can evoke the image of a small range of objects having relative autonomy from need states as well as exteroceptive experience. This dating through speech gives us the age eighteen months as a point of reference for the establishment of an image that has autonomy from exteroceptive experience.

Is it possible, however, that an image of the need-satisfying person or object can be evoked independent of the need stimulus or the presentation in reality at an earlier stage of development? There is really no way of proving or disproving this possibility, but if I can borrow our overworked Beagle once again for illustration, I think he can help us construct a useful hypothesis.

Brandy's performance on a sensorimotor scale places him at Stage IV for exteroceptive data. He has extended "recognition memory" to a point where he can sustain the image of an object as long as objective signs are available to him (i.e., seeing the object disappear, seeing the screen behind which it disappeared). Brandy's behavior during "need states" ("wanting" a biscuit or meat, signaling to me, walking to the kitchen) is also dependent upon a stimulus, this time we suppose an organic stimulus. In each set of observations we assume a kind of mental representation; in each set (inner and outer) we have evidence that the sensory image is at the disposal of a stimulus or sign. In both the image of need states and the image of exteroceptive experience there is no evidence that the image can be produced without a specific stimulus. If the stimulus biscuit is withdrawn from exteroceptive experience, Brandy can sustain some kind of diffuse image of the biscuit for a few seconds on the basis of a sign (the screen). Then the image dissolves, as we infer from his behavior. If somatic longings are stirred, Brandy can produce some kind of sensory image that leads him to seek one of two kinds of need-satisfying objects. He can apparently sustain such an image for the duration of the stimulus. If no organic stimulus is present to give rise to a sensory image, we have reason to believe that no image appears. (We infer this through the absence of motor expression.) *If all these observations have been fairly made, the hallucinatory experience of need is organized on the same level of sensorimotor intelligence as the image of the real object withdrawn from perception.* Both images are stimulus bound; i.e., the image of exteroceptive experience cannot be produced without a stimulus or sign and cannot be sustained for more than a few seconds after the real object has left the perceptual field; the hallucinatory image on this level of cognition cannot be produced without a need stimulus and it can be sustained only for the duration of that stimulus raised to a certain intensity. If memory for the real biscuit behind the screen is placed at Stage IV on the sensorimotor scale, then memory for the hallucinated biscuit of need states has excellent correspondence with Stage IV criteria; the level of mental operations for the hallucinated image is also Stage IV.

This is all that Brandy can tell us, however, since he never got any smarter, but the baby at Stage IV is moving toward complex mental operations which will obtain a high degree of autonomy from the stimulus in the next year. Yet, I think these animal observations can provide us with some useful hypotheses for the contruction of the intervening stages.

I would propose that images produced through need states and mental images produced through exteroceptive experience may be organized on a scale of coordinates. Given the data for exteroceptive experience in the screened toy experiments, the grades of progressive autonomy from the stimulus will be the same for the image of exteroception as for the image of need. Thus, the capacity to sustain the image of an object independent of perception which is measured on the objective scale of Piaget has short duration at Stage IV (eight to twelve months) but gains relative autonomy from the presenting stimulus at Stage VI (eighteen months). The capacity to sustain the image of need independent of the need stimulus may be presumed to have correlates stage by stage in which "distance from the stimulus" (drives, organic need) follows a progressive course toward autonomy, and the lengthening intervals may themselves have close correspondence with those on the exteroceptive scale, i.e., from stimulus, to sign (recognition), to evocation without a sign.

At the present time we have no experimental data to support this hypothesis on cognitive levels below the acquisition of speech. But this hypothesis is consistent with what we know of conceptual intelligence. Conceptual development is coherent; it synthesizes and organizes data from all perceptual experience ("inner and outer," as we would say in psychoanalysis); it generalizes and abstracts.

For these reasons it is difficult to imagine that the baby at eight months can employ mental operations on one level for exteroceptive data and another level, one of higher complexity, for the stimuli of need states. Where cathexis of the object, particularly the libidinal object, provides another variable, we may find a priority in the timetable, but we must suppose that the priority will appear close to the beginning of each new phase of mental operations; we cannot posit a gap of two stages, or ten months, on the cognitive scale.

If this argument has merit, the capacity to evoke the image of the mother with relative autonomy from need states and from the presenting stimulus of the mother will appear close to the time on the age scale that has been experimentally verified for evocative memory of the "thing." Piaget's empirical work gives us the age eighteen months for evocation of the inanimate object; we may postulate a period close to eighteen months for evocation of the image of the human object.

### An Expanded Definition of Mental Representation?

Finally, I would like to propose a reformulation to cover one form of mental representation (evocative memory) which may satisfy our requirements in psychoanalytic theory and which takes into account the sequences established by Piaget during the sensorimotor period of development (i.e., recognition memory to true evocative memory). If the objective criteria for evocative memory are based upon "autonomy of the image from stimulus or sign," there must be corresponding criteria for the image of need satisfaction, stated as "the image that has autonomy from the stimulus of need." In this formulation the hallucinatory image of need is not "evocative memory" as long as it is bound to a specific stimulus. And while the hallucination of need states is, in fact, a kind of "evocation of absent realities" and, we think, may be the vital link in the sequence of mental operations that lead to true evocative memory, it does not qualify as "evocative memory" in strict usage, as long as it is bound to a specific need stimulus or sign.

I would then suggest this formulation which brings the hallucination of need states into harmony with the scale of mental operations deduced from objective data: *Evocative memory is the production of a mental image that has relative autonomy from the stimuli of exteroceptive experience and the stimuli of drives and need states.*

## Summary

The concept of object constancy in psychoanalytic usage has been reviewed in its libidinal and cognitive aspects. There is agreement among psychoanalytic writers that the libidinal tie to the mother is formed during the first year of life and the term "object constancy" is employed by many psychoanalytic writers to designate the achievement of the libidinal bond. Where differences occur among psychoanalytic writers in defining the term "object constancy," these differences appear in the cognitive aspects of libidinal object relations. The mental representation of the mother is variously attributed to early and later phases of libidinal attachment, which suggests differences in definition of the term "mental representation." This essay suggests, following Piaget, that a distinction between "recognition memory" and "evocative memory" may clarify usage in psychoanalytic studies.

The problem of the hallucinatory experience of infancy was examined and an attempt was made to find correlates in the mental image of need states and the mental image of an object withdrawn from exteroceptive experience. A hypothesis was presented in which both sets of images are organized on a scale of coordinates with progressive autonomy from the stimulus or sign.

## Notes

An early draft of this paper was presented to Dr. Humberto Nagera's Psychoanalytic Concepts Seminar. I am deeply indebted to Dr. Nagera and to seminar colleagues for a close examination of the problems, for lively argument, and for expertise in a number of areas related to this topic. I wish to express my appreciation to Morton Chethik for assistance in surveying the literature, to Edna Adelson and Martin Mayman for reading and criticizing the revised version.
1. Excellent and detailed summaries are available in the writings of Peter H. Wolff (1960) and Thérèse Gouin-Décarie (1965).
2. Escalona's ranges were not available to me at the time of this writing.
3. See also David Beres (1968).

## References

Alpert, A. (1965). Introductory and Closing Remarks: Institute on Programs for Children without Families. *J. Amer. Acad. Child Psychiat.,* 4: 163–167; 272–278.

Benjamin, J. D. (1959). Prediction and Psychopathologic Theory. In *Dynamic Psychopathology in Childhood,* ed. L. Jessner & E. Pavenstedt, pp. 6–77. New York: Grune & Stratton.

———. (1961a). Some Developmental Observations Relating to Theory of Anxiety. *J. Amer. Psychoanal. Assn.,* 9:652–668.

———. (1961b). The Innate and the Experiential in Development. In *Lectures in Experimental Psychiatry,* ed. H. W. Brosin, pp. 19–42. Pittsburgh: Univ. of Pittsburgh Press.

———. (1963). Further Comments on Some Developmental Aspects of Anxiety. In *Counterpoint: Libidinal Object and Subject,* ed. H. S. Gaskill, pp. 121–153. New York: International Universities Press.

Beres, D. (1968). The Humanness of Human Beings: Psychoanalytic Considerations. *Psychoanal. Quart.,* 37:487–522.

Cobliner, W. G. (1965). Appendix: The Geneva School of Genetic Psychology and Psychoanalysis: Parallels and Counterparts. In R. A. Spitz, *The First Year of Life,* pp. 301–356. New York: International Universities Press.

Décarie, T. G. (1965). *Intelligence and Affectivity in Early Childhood.* New York: International Universities Press.

Escalona, S. K. (1968). *The Roots of Individuality.* Chicago: Aldine.

Freud, A. (1952). The Mutual Influences in the Development of Ego and Id. *Psychoanal. Study Child,* 7:42–50.

———. (1960). Discussion of Dr. John Bowlby's Paper. *Psychoanal. Study Child,* 15:53–62.

———. (1963). The Concept of Developmental Lines. *Psychoanal. Study Child,* 18:245–265.

———. (1965). *Normality and Pathology in Childhood.* New York: International Universities Press.

———. (1968). The Humanness of Human Beings: Psychoanalytic Considerations. *Psychoanal. Quart.,* 37:487–522.

Freud, S. (1925). Negation. *Standard Edition,* 19:235–239. London: Hogarth Press, 1961.

Frosch, J. (1966). A Note on Reality Constancy. In *Psychoanalysis—A General Psychology,* ed. R. M. Loewenstein, L. M. Newman, M. Schur, & A. J. Solnit, pp. 349–376. New York: International Universities Press.

Hartmann, H. (1952). The Mutual Influences in the Development of Ego and Id. *Essays on Ego Psychology,* pp. 155–182. New York: International Universities Press, 1964.

———. (1953). Contribution to the Metapsychology of Schizophrenia. *Essays on Ego Psychology,* pp. 182–206. New York: International Universities Press, 1964.

———. (1956). Notes on the Reality Principle. *Essays on Ego Psychology,* pp. 241–267. New York: International Universities Press, 1964.

———; Kris, E.; & Loewenstein, R. M. (1946). Comments on the Formation of Psychic Structure. *Psychoanal. Study Child,* 2:11–38.

Hoffer, W. (1950). Development of the Body Ego. *Psychoanal. Study Child,* 5:18–24.

———. (1952). The Mutual Influences in the Development of Ego and Id: Earliest Stages. *Psychoanal. Study Child,* 7:31–41.

———. (1955). *Psychoanalysis: Practical and Research Aspects.* Baltimore: Williams & Wilkins.

Jacobson, E. (1964). *The Self and the Object World.* New York: International Universities Press.

Mahler, M. S. (1963). Thoughts about Development and Individuation. *Psychoanal. Study Child,* 18:307–324.

———. (1965). On the Significance of the Normal Separation-Individuation Phase. In *Drives, Affects, Behavior,* vol. 2, ed. M. Schur, pp. 161–169. New York: International Universities Press.

——— & Furer, M. (1963). Certain Aspects of the Separation-Individuation Phase. *Psychoanal. Quart.,* 32:1–14.

——— & Gosliner, B. J. (1955). On Symbiotic Child Psychosis. *Psychoanal. Study Child,* 10:195–212.

——— & La Perriere, K. (1965). Mother-Child Interaction during Separation-Individuation. *Psychoanal. Quart.,* 34:483–498.

Nagera, H. (1966). Sleep and Its Disturbances Approached Developmentally. *Psychoanal. Study Child,* 21:393–447.

Panel Discussion. (1968). Held at the 25th Congress of the International Psychoanalytical Association, Copenhagen, July, 1967. *Int. J. Psychoanal.,* 49:506–512.

Piaget, J. (1937). *The Construction of Reality in the Child.* New York: Basic Books, 1954.

———. (1945). *Play, Dreams, and Imitation in Childhood.* New York: Norton, 1951.

Rapaport, D. (1960). *The Structure of Psychoanalytic Theory* [*Psychological Issues,* Monogr. 6.] New York: International Universities Press.

Spitz, R. A. (1957). *No and Yes: On the Genesis of Human Communication.* New York: International Universities Press.

———. (1959). *A Genetic Field Theory of Ego Formation.* New York: International Universities Press.

———. (1965). *The First Year of Life.* New York: International Universities Press.

———. (1966). Metapsychology and Infant Observation. In *Psychoanalysis— A General Psychology,* ed. R. M. Loewenstein, L. M. Newman, M. Schur, & A. J. Solnit, pp. 123–151. New York: International Universities Press.

——— & Wolf, K. M. (1946). Anaclitic Depression: An Inquiry into the Genesis of Psychiatric Conditions in Early Childhood. *Psychoanal. Study Child,* 2:313–342.

———. (1949). Autoerotism: Some Empirical Findings and Hypotheses on Three of Its Manifestations in the First Year of Life. *Psychoanal. Study Child,* 3/4:85–120.

Werner, H. (1957). *Comparative Psychology of Mental Development.* New York: International Universities Press.

Wolff, P. H. (1960). *The Developmental Psychologies of Jean Piaget and Psychoanalysis* [*Psychological Issues,* Monogr. 5.] New York: International Universities Press.

# 3

# The Muse in the Kitchen: A Case Study in Clinical Research

Our subject today is a consideration of problems of clinical research.

Those of us who are old enough to have followed the literature in this area for twenty-five years or more have witnessed a growing estrangement between clinical practice and clinical research. A marriage that should have brought mutually enriching rewards in human science and its applications seems to be drifting apart. The clinician has taken to minding the pots in the kitchen and the researcher is conducting an affair with a computer.

In the session we have planned for today I have agreed to bring in a case history of a clinical research project with some typical and some atypical marriage problems. I propose that we use this case history for discussion of the clinical problems that invited the research, the methods that were designed to get the answers, and finally the application of these findings to a program of prevention and rehabilitation.

The story begins, very simply, as a clinical problem in a social agency. In 1960 I was consultant to the Family Service Society of New Orleans when we were asked to take on a caseload of twenty-seven blind children between the ages of three and fourteen years. Viola Weiss, as chief supervisor of the FSS, asked me to give some time to the new work with blind children. Neither I nor any other member of the staff had ever worked with blind children. We were in no way prepared for the impact of these blind children on our eyes.

Of the twenty-seven blind children, at least seven presented a clinical picture that closely resembled autism in the sighted. There were stereotyped hand behaviors, rocking, swaying, mutism or echolalic speech. These were children who were content to sit for hours, sucking on a clothespin or a pot lid, rocking, detached, vacant, virtually unresponsive to the mother or to any other human being. The striking feature of these cases was uniformity. We had the uncanny feeling that we were seeing the same case over and over again. In reading our cases we had to provide ourselves with mnemonic cues to distinguish one case from the other. ("Martin is the one who likes to suck on clothespins; Martha is the one who chews rubber jar rings; Jane is the hand-banger; Chrissey bangs her bottom against the wall.")

Of the remaining twenty children, nearly all showed one or another form of stereotyped motility, but speech was organized and there were demonstrable ties to human objects.

When I first saw these autistic blind children I was convinced that they suffered brain damage. I think I would have rather believed anything than to consider that something in human experience could produce these automatons. We asked Dr. David Freedman, a neurologist and psychoanalyst, to consult with us. He reviewed the medical findings which included EEGs on several cases and personally examined certain children. In the end he confessed himself as baffled as we were. He found no evidence of neurological damage. This did not, in itself, rule out the possibility of brain damage of unknown causes, but in the absence of positive signs we were certainly free to consider other possibilities.

We reviewed the birth histories of each of the children and found no correlation between birth weight, length of time in oxygen (in the case of the premature baby), and the clinical picture of autism. Later, we were to find as Keeler (1958) did in his Toronto study, that the autistic patterns were not correlated with any specific disease or cause of blindness but were seen most commonly in children who were blind from birth, who were totally blind or had no pattern vision and who had received inadequate stimulation in infancy. From Keeler's studies and others we learned also that our population at the Family Service Society was more typical than we had guessed. Approximately one quarter of Keeler's metropolitan sample presented the clinical picture of autism. The incidence of autism in his group was, then, as high as our own.

The question of possible brain damage is still debated in the literature of the sighted and blind autistic child. It is still neither proved nor disproved by any scientific studies. However, we have learned since 1960 in our own work that if we can identify the autistic blind child in the early years, preferably under two years of age, we can bring this child to normal functioning. This means that whether or not there is a primary neurological defect, other factors in the environment or in the unique adaptive problems of a blind infant must play a decisive role.

## Clinical Observations

As clinicians, Dr. Freedman and I asked ourselves certain questions. First of all, we were impressed by the picture of developmental arrest in the autistic blind child, of personalities frozen on the level of mouth-centeredness and non-differentiation. There was no "I" or "you," but there was also no "me" or "other," no sense of a body self and "something out there."

All of this was of a piece with the most distinguishing characteristic of these children—the absence of human connections. The mother was barely distinguished from other persons; her comings and goings went unnoticed. There were no cries to summon her, no sounds of greeting when she appeared, no signs of distress when she left. We know, of course, that in the absence of a human partner the baby cannot acquire a sense of self and other, of "me" and "you." But should blindness be an impediment to the establishment of human object relations? How about our other blind children, the twenty children who had demonstrable human ties? How did these children make their human partnerships? The sighted child in the first year makes increasingly selective and highly differentiated responses to his mother. So far as we knew from psychoanalytic studies, the differential smile, the discrimination of mother and stranger, and indeed the whole sequence of differential human responses are predicated upon visual recognitory experiences. In the absence of vision how does the blind baby differentiate, recognize, become bound through love? There must be an adaptive substitution for vision. The mother of a blind baby must find some ways of helping the baby find the route. How? And if she does not?

We observed that in all of these autistic children, perception was largely centered in the mouth. The hand itself seemed to have no autonomy from the mouth. The cliché, "The hands are the eyes of the blind," had become a terrible irony in the case of these children. They had blind hands, too. The hands did not reach out for objects to attain them. The hands were not used to get information about objects. Most striking, the hands had remained in a kind of morbid alliance with the mouth. They could bring objects to the mouth to be sucked. And when the hands were not serving the mouth in some way they were typically held at shoulder height with stereotyped inutile movements of the fingers.

These children had virtually no independent mobility. Even walking with support was a late achievement, in some instances as late as five years of age; in one instance at the age of nine!

In the literature these children are classified as "the blind mentally retarded." If we are interested only in developmental measurement, this is certainly indisputable. But to the psychoanalytic investigator these blind mentally retarded children presented some inexplicable problems. If the systems for receiving nonvisual stimuli were intact (and this was demonstrable in the neurological examination) how could we explain this extraordinary picture of developmental arrest, this freezing of personality on the eight-to-twelve month level with virtually no gains, no small increments of learning thereafter?

## Inferences from the Clinical Picture

As clinicians we were accustomed to reading and interpreting behavior signs and there were a number of signs in the clinical pictures of these children that led our thinking along certain paths.

It is immediately apparent that the body schemas which normally lead to adaptive hand behavior had failed to integrate in these children. Normally, vision insures that at five months the thing seen can be grasped and attained. In the absence of vision other sense modalities must be coordinated with grasping. How is the adaptive substitution found in the case of the blind infant? And if it isn't found?

Next, our attention was drawn to the delay in locomotion. Were all motor achievements delayed in the case of these deviant blind children? No. A puzzle appeared in the developmental histories. Rolling over, sitting with support, sitting independently were not markedly delayed. But creeping, walking with support, and of course, walking independently were markedly delayed or never achieved. If the histories were reliable, there was neuromuscular adequacy demonstrated in the gross motor achievements during the first six months. Why the impasse in creeping and later locomotion?

As you can see our first questions were addressed to the unique adaptive problems of a child blind from birth. In the case of the autistic blind child the sensory deficit and unknown factors in early experience had produced a picture that suggested adaptive failure. But what about the twenty other children in our sample who had found the adaptive routes with varying degrees of success?

As a group, the remaining twenty children demonstrated human attachments with some variability in the quality of these ties or the capacity in later childhood to function independently. The range in adaptive hand abilities I cannot give you because in those days we did not yet know how to "read" hand behavior in blind children. But for most of these children, too, the achievement of independent mobility was very late by sighted child standards, between two and three years for independent walking. Typically, too, there was no mention of creeping in the developmental histories. But strangely enough in this "normal" group of blind children nearly all the children demonstrated one or another kind of stereotyped motility, rocking, swaying, hand-waving, eye-rubbing, or idiosyncratic movements. These behaviors were long known to workers with the blind, and have been called "blindisms." With the exception of eye-rubbing, all of these behaviors can be found in the sighted autistic child. These children were not autistic. What did this mean?

If we now looked at the entire group of twenty-seven children it appeared that certain characteristics such as the delay in locomotion and the stereotyped motility were found in both groups with qualitative and quantitative differences. The range for the achievement of independent mobility was not nearly so great for the "normal" group as for the autistic group. The stereotyped motility constituted a large part of the repertory of the autistic group and a small part of the repertory of the "normal" group. If we had known how to "read hands" in those days we might have learned through the study of the "normal" group what I have since learned through study of children in the general blind population. A large number of blind children who are not autistic and who have differentiated personalities may still have "blind hands," hands that do not serve as sensitive perceptual organs. But this brings us ahead of the story and we should really stay with what we knew at this point in our investigation.

At this point our observations and questions provided some kind of framework for our thinking. We were reasonably sure that what we saw in the range of personalities available to us in this sample of twenty-seven children was a range of adaptive behaviors to the problem of blindness during the first eighteen months of life. The picture of developmental arrest in the autistic blind child showed failure to find the adaptive routes on the six- to twelve-month level. We inferred this from the clinical picture of an undifferentiated self—not self, from the arrest in locomotor achievements and language, and from the absence of coordinated hand behavior to an external stimulus. *We reasoned that for every developmental failure in the blind autistic child there should be a correlate in the development of all blind babies in the form of a unique adaptive problem posed by blindness.* The difference between the autistic blind child and the child in the normal group might, then, appear in developmental studies in which one group found the adaptive solutions and the other group met a developmental impasse.

### A Need for Observation of a Blind Infant

Our own group of twenty-seven children could not help us in searching for clues. They had come to us with poor developmental histories from a variety of agencies that had no clinical interest in the problems with which we were concerned. The differences between the autistic blind children and the "normal" group in the first year of life could not be discerned from the records. In both groups the babies were described as "quiet" babies, content to lie in their cribs for the best part of the twenty-four hour day. In both groups the mothers were described as "depressed." In both groups there were the delays in gross motor achievements during the last quarter of the first year.

We then turned to the literature to find longitudinal studies of blind infants which could provide us with the detailed descriptive information on the blind baby's development. Then, to our surprise, we learned that no detailed longitudinal studies of blind babies existed. We found Norris's (1957) volume which described the developmental achievements of 200 blind children as measured by a modified Cattell scale. We found five useful case histories in this volume which gave some picture of the developmental achievements of a selected sample. But our problems were different from those of the Norris group when they undertook their study. We needed to know in fine detail how the blind baby finds the adaptive routes and how ego formation takes place in the absence of vision.

Until this point we had not intended to engage in research. We wanted to inform ourselves and be useful to caseworkers who were working with vast unknowns in their responsibilities for blind children. Yes—and something more, too. We were already excited by certain ideas that were beginning to emerge in our minds. The high incidence of autism in the blind might provide vital clues to autism in the sighted. Also, we knew that the blind baby could teach us about the role of vision in early ego formation.

If research begins at any one point I suppose our research began here. We waited for the first new baby to be referred to our Family Service Society program for blind children, and the baby turned out to be Toni, a five-month-old girl, blind from birth due to ophthalmia neonatorum. We ascertained that Toni was otherwise intact and healthy. The agency obtained the mother's interest and consent and we arranged to set up regular monthly observation sessions.

We had no research plan beyond observing and recording. We would use cinema film for documentation of certain behavior samples. We had no money or any hopes of getting any. Nobody liked our research proposal, such as it was, and at least two foundations questioned our qualifications for the study of blind infants. They were quite right, I think.

So, at the start, we were both unqualified and unfunded. It is possible, I suppose, to be either unqualified or unfunded and still conduct research. But to be *both* unqualified and unfunded is normally discouraging to an investigator. We agreed to support our venture out of pocket and to divide the bill for film and processing on the first of every month. We would, of course, give our own time. As for our lack of qualifications, this proved to be no deterrent.

On July 22, 1961, we borrowed a 16 millimeter movie camera from the man next door, packed ourselves and our equipment into an old VW, and like two innocents in a fairy tale, we set out for a journey to the land of the blind. The New Orleans map led us to a slum, to a tiny brown house on a dirt road, and there we met the first blind baby we had ever seen.

**Observations of Toni**

What can we learn from one case?

When David Freedman and I set out to visit Toni we brought with us a number of hypotheses. We had hypotheses regarding blindness as an impediment to the establishment of libidinal object relations. We had a hypothesis regarding the adaptive substitution of sound for vision. We had another hypothesis regarding the role of sound in prehension. And there were others which are fortunately obliterated by time. In the next eighteen months Toni threw out each of our hypotheses one by one, like so many boring toys over the rail of a crib.

Since Toni was selected with no other criteria than her blindness and her age, we were quite fortunate in our first baby. She was a healthy, robust little girl, the youngest of six children. She was the illegitimate child of a young Negro woman in her early thirties. Toni's mother was an experienced mother. In spite of her feelings of guilt and fears for the future of her blind child, she was a woman whose motherliness was called forth by need and this baby who needed her in special ways evoked deep tenderness in her.

Toni tossed out one of our hypotheses on the first visit. She was five months old, making pleasant noises in her crib as we talked with her mother. When her mother went over to her and called her name, Toni's face broke into a gorgeous smile and she made agreeable responsive noises. I called her name and waited. There was no smile. Dr. Freedman called her name. There was no smile. Mother called her name and once again evoked the joyful smile and cooing sounds. Her mother said, a little apologetically, "She won't smile for anyone. Not even her sisters and brothers. Only me. She's been smiling when I talk to her since three months."

Now since it is written in all our books, including my own, that it is the *visual* stimulus of the human face that elicits smiling in the baby at three months, Toni's smile had just shattered a major theory, which shows you what one case can do. Seven years later I can give you a long list of blind babies who smiled in response to mother's or father's voice at ages under three months. But it doesn't really matter. If only one blind baby smiles in response to mother's voice, there is something wrong with our theory.

In our notes of this session we recorded a number of observations showing the selective response of Toni to her mother, paralleling in all significant ways that of a sighted child at five months. Three months later, at eight months, Toni demonstrated another achievement in the scale of human object relations. Soon after she heard our voices, strange voices, she became sober, almost frozen in her posture. Later, when I held Toni briefly to test her reactions to a stranger, she began to cry, she squirmed in my arms, and strained away from my body. It was a classic demonstration of "stranger anxiety." Yet it is written in all our books, including my own, that stranger anxiety appears at eight months on the basis of the visual discrimination of mother's face and stranger's face.

We were good sports about it. We conceded that under favorable environmental conditions blindness need not be an impediment to the establishment of human object relations. Anyway, we still had a lot of other hypotheses tucked away.

One of these hypotheses had to do with the adaptive substitution of sound for vision. We all know that around five months of age the sighted child can reach and attain an object on sight. In the case of the blind child we expected that a coordination of sound and grasping would take place at approximately the same time. But at five months, at six months, and, astonishingly, even at nine months, Toni made no gesture of reach toward any of the sound objects we presented to her. We sneaked around with jangling keys, rattles, squeaky toys, always in a range where Toni could easily reach them. She looked alert and attentive. She made no gesture of reach. It did not matter whether we used her own familiar toys or Freedman's car keys; there was not a gesture of reach. Was the baby deaf? Certainly not. As soon as she heard the sound of the camera motor, for example, she would startle or wince. She could discriminate voices. She could imitate sounds at seven months. What was it then?

At ten months Toni demonstrated for the first time her ability to reach and attain an object on sound cue alone. Thereafter she became expert in grabbing sound objects within arm's range. As we drove back from Toni's house that day we were stunned by the implications of this observation. Toni had given her first demonstration of a direct reach for a sound object at ten months. The sighted baby coordinates vision and grasping at five months. But how did Toni solve the problem? We knew perfectly well that no developmental achievement appears overnight. A coordinated action of hand and external stimulus is the result of complex sensorimotor learning. There were antecedents which must have been present for months, unrecognized by us.

Now we were obsessed by the problem and its implications. Since memory could not serve us we went back over thousands of feet of film, frame by frame, to try to reconstruct the sequence. But the story was not there. And we knew why. Film and film processing is expensive. Since we were financing this research out of pocket we had to be thrifty in our use of film. We devoted only a small amount of footage to each of the areas we were sampling and we had thought that our sampling was adequate. In order to pick up our lapse we would have needed generous and unprejudiced samples. The story of Toni's coordinated reach on sound cue was lost to us and we already knew that this story would prove to be a vital clue in the study of the blind baby's development. (Three years later at the University of Michigan we got the answer. A generous department supported a highly unthrifty film study which made the work possible.)

To return now to Toni and to go back a bit in the story: At eight months Toni had excellent control of her trunk and was indisputably moving toward an upright posture. She could support her weight on hands and knees, she could elevate herself to a standing position and let herself down easily. There was no question, from our knowledge of babies, that Toni was getting ready to creep. As we were leaving Toni's house at the end of the eight-month visit, I said to the mother, "Well, I'll bet when we come back next month Toni will really be into everything!" These were foolish words and I came to regret them.

At nine months Toni was not creeping. Nor at ten months or twelve months. This is what we saw: Toni, with demonstrated postural readiness for creeping, was unable to propel herself forward. On the floor in prone position she executed a kind of radial crawl, navigating in a circle.

Why couldn't Toni propel herself forward? Clearly there needed to be an external stimulus for the initiating of the creeping pattern. What happens in the case of the sighted child? The sighted child at nine months, let us say, is supporting himself ably on hands and knees. He sees an out-of-range object. He reaches for the object. And what we see now is a reach and a collapse, a reach and a collapse, each time moving forward until the object is attained. Within a few days the motor pattern begins to smooth out and becomes a coordinated action of hands and legs in what we call "creeping."

Why didn't Toni creep? Clearly because no external stimulus was present to initiate the creeping pattern. Even eight years later, I can still remember the stunning impact of that discovery. Toni had brought a brand new insight into the understanding of motor development in sighted children. We—all of us—had never had occasion to question the assumption that locomotion in infancy follows maturational patterns that are laid down in a biological sequence. Toni demonstrated that motor maturation follows the biological pattern but in the absence of an external stimulus for reaching, the creeping pattern will not emerge. It was risky to generalize on the basis of only one case, but we reminded ourselves that in the retrospective histories of all blind children it is common to find that creeping was never achieved, and, in fact, there is a marked delay in the achievement of all locomotor skills from this point on, with independent walking a very late achievement in the second and third years.

Between eight and ten months we begin to see something in Toni that roused our own anxieties. At times during the observational session we would see Toni stretch out on the floor, face down on the rug, and for long periods of time lie quite still, smiling softly to herself. The passive pleasure in immobility was chilling to watch. Her mother, watching this with us, looked strained and anxious. "She does that all the time," she told us. She was an experienced mother, you remember, and she knew as well as we did that no healthy baby at nine months will lie on the floor for long periods of time, smiling softly to herself. And when did Toni assume this posture? At any time, we observed, when external sources of stimulation were not available to her, i.e., if no one was talking to her, playing with her, feeding her. In these moments of non-stimulation she would fall back on this form of self-stimulation in which the ventral surface of the body was in contact with the rug.

Did this mean that Toni's mother was neglecting her? We thought not. During the same period, pleasure in mother's voice, pleasure in being held by mother were clearly seen whenever mother resumed contact with her. But in a normal busy household, where five other children must make their claims upon a mother, there were, inevitably, periods when Toni was not being played with, talked to, held in mother's arms. It happens to sighted children too. What does a sighted child do at nine months when he is "by himself?" He occupies himself with toys, or, if he is creeping, he goes on excursions to visit the underside of the dining table or the top side of the living room couch, or the inside of the kitchen cupboard. And if he has no toy handy, and if he can't creep, he will occupy himself by looking, just plain looking around. Visual experience creates its own appetite for repetition; the hunger to see and the functional pleasure of vision are among the great entertainments of a baby after the first days of life. Vision keeps the baby "in touch" with his mother and with the world of things, giving continuity to experience. The sighted child at nine months does not have to be continually held by his mother or talked to by her in order to "be in touch" with her.

But when Toni could not touch her mother or hear her mother's voice, she was robbed of her mother and robbed of a large measure of the sensory experience that linked her to the world outside of her body. In this insubstantial, impermanent world, her own body and body sensations became at times the only certainty, the only continuous source of sensory experience in the discontinuous experience of darkness. And because proprioceptive experience provided the chief means for "keeping in touch" in the near void of blindness, and the only means for experiencing continuity of self feelings, Toni stretched out on the floor, face down upon the rug. In this posture, which afforded maximal contact between the body surface and the rug, she might obtain feelings of comfort, safety, pleasurable tactile sensations and a sense of body awareness. We are reminded too that the ventral surface of the baby's body is normally eroticized in the posture of being held against the mother's body and that pleasure, intimacy, comfort and safety are united for a lifetime in this posture—the embrace. What we saw in Toni, face down, nuzzling a rug was a form of stimulus hunger. Where vision would have insured abundant sources of stimuli and the visual alternatives to contact hunger for the mother, blindness caused this child in periods of external nonstimulation to fall back upon the poverty of body sensations. Like a starving organism that will finally ingest anything where there is not enough food, the stimulus hunger of this child led her to ingest the meager proprioceptive experience of body contact with a rug.

Later in my experience, I was to see variations of this posture in blind children. But when we first saw this in Toni we found it a chilling experience. We had not foreseen such a development in an otherwise healthy child. And remember, too, that during this period, at nine months, we were also sobered by the fact that Toni was unable to locomote in spite of the fact that she had maturational readiness for creeping. In other respects, too, Toni seemed to have reached a developmental impasse. Although she was still lively and responsive to her mother and her sisters and her brothers, there was almost no interest in toys, and at nine months she was not reaching for objects. Her mother, we observed, seemed anxious and discouraged. For the first time we saw a number of instances in which mother was manifestly out of rapport with her baby.

When we returned at ten months, the entire picture had changed. Toni's mother, entirely on her own, had purchased a walker, and within a short time Toni had become expert in getting around in it. She was still unable to creep but the walker provided mobility and Toni was cruising around the house with tremendous energy and making discoveries and rediscoveries at every port. Did she still lie down on the rug, we asked, concealing our own anxiety. Oh, no, the mother assured us. In fact, she absolutely refused to get into the prone position. Mother took Toni out of her walker and gave us a demonstration. The moment Toni was placed on the floor in the prone position, she yelled in protest and uprighted herself. This was now the posture of immobility and Toni had found mobility. The moment she was put back in her walker she stopped crying and took off like a hot rodder.

We never saw this passive prone posture again in Toni. Within three months, at thirteen months of age, Toni began walking with support, and now also creeping(!), Toni was "into everything" exploring the cupboards, the drawers, and getting into mischief. At thirteen months Toni had a small and useful vocabulary, she was using her hands for fine discriminations and she was now expert in reaching and attaining objects on sound cue. From this point on, Toni's development progressed without any major impediments. (Only one pathological behavior appeared in the second year, and I will describe it later.)

But now what about the stereotyped prone behavior which had so alarmed us at eight and nine months? It is clear from the sequence that once Toni acquired mobility she could not even be persuaded to get back into the prone position on the floor. Mobility provided functional motor pleasure, of course, but mobility also put her in touch with a world beyond her body and a world that she could act upon; mobility gave her for the first time a sense of autonomy.

Here, we thought we had found another clue to the ego deviations encountered among blind children. If we understand that the blind child lives in a near-void for much of his waking day, he can make few discoveries about the world around him until he becomes mobile. And if mobility itself is delayed until well into the second year, he will live for a perilously long time in this near-void in which the presence of the mother or other persons, or ministrations to his own body become the only experiences which give meaning to existence. In those periods where neither sound nor touch, feeding, bath or play occur there is nothing except his own body. Now we began to understand how some blind babies may never find the adaptive routes and remain frozen in the state of body centeredness, passivity, immobility, and ultimately non-differentiation.

I mentioned that one pathological trait was observed in Toni beginning in the second year. Let me briefly describe it. When Tony became anxious, when she was separated even briefly from her mother or when a strange person or a strange situation signaled danger to her, she would fall into a stuporous sleep. We observed this ourselves. It was as if a light were switched off. As far as we can reconstruct the onset of this symptom, it was first manifest in connection with a brief separation from her mother. She retained this symptom as late as the fourth year when we obtained reports on her. In all other respects she was a healthy, active little girl, able to ride a trike, play ball, join in children's games. Her speech was very good; eating and sleeping were entirely satisfactory. There was only this. We asked ourselves when we would find an otherwise healthy sighted child who defended against danger by falling into a pathological sleep. Never, of course. But then, one should ask, what defenses against danger does a blind child possess? I did not understand this until several years later.

This is a brief sketch of Toni and what Toni taught us. I should also tell you that during the same period that we were observing Toni, we took on the joint treatment of an autistic blind child and his mother. I was the child's therapist; Dr. Freedman analyzed the mother. I wish there was time to give you a report of this case as well (Fraiberg and Freedman, 1964). Perhaps it will suffice to say that Peter, the autistic nine-year-old child, taught us how blindness can lead to adaptive failure and Toni taught us how the route to successful adaptation is a perilous one for a blind baby. I worked with Peter for two years and saw him five times a week. There was considerable improvement but he never became a normal child. Today, when we get a Peter in the second year or even the third year, we know how to help him and we can bring about normal functioning. Much of what we now know we learned from Toni and from Peter.

Yet, it is worth mentioning that even with the small amount of knowledge we gained through the study of one healthy baby and one autistic blind boy we were able to help two blind babies in our Family Service Society caseload who were well on their way to autism by the time they were referred in the second year. Since we knew the danger signs and now had some pretty good hunches regarding the contributing causes, we worked out some simple guidance procedures which brought both babies to normal functioning within a matter of months.

In 1963 I moved from New Orleans and came to the University of Michigan. David Freedman also moved shortly afterwards to Baylor University. Since then, each of us, following his own special interests, has continued research in the area of sensory deficits.

In Ann Arbor, I received support and generous funds from my department to continue pilot work in the development of blind infants. Two years later we received a grant from the National Institutes of Child Health and Development to expand these studies. From this point on we were in a position to study the development of blind babies on a larger scale.

## The University of Michigan Study

A case history of the development of a research plan begins with the questions and proceeds logically to the methods and procedures which must be employed to obtain answers to these questions. I will try in the next few pages to give a sketch of our problems and the methods we employed. Then, in the last section of this presentation some sample problems encountered in this research are analyzed in terms of the questions, the methods, and the results.

We can already see that the problems we have isolated for study have reciprocal and interlocking relationships throughout the course of development. Human object relations, the differentiation of a self and an outerworld, prehension, gross motor development and language cannot be isolated as separate studies unless we first know the relationships which exist among these developmental schemas. In the case of the sighted baby we know a fair amount, which means that if we isolate areas for study we are working within a known framework. But if we are beginning the investigation of a previously uncharted territory, such as the psychological development of a blind infant, we cannot assume from the start that the relationships which exist among these sectors of development will be the same if vision is not available to the developing child. This means that we are practically obliged to conduct a systematic study of every sector of development in the blind infant in order to find the relationships which exist among them.

The methods and procedures for study which we worked out were the best methods, for us. They gave us, finally, the answers we were seeking. This means that they were valid methods for this study. But in this research as in any others, there is no such thing as "the correct" methodology. A quantitative study based upon a sample of 100 blind infants is not "better than" or "more scientific" than a qualitative study of ten blind infants. Controlled experimentation is not "more scientific" than a naturalistic study. All of these are scientific approaches to problems. The best scientific method is the one that produces the answers to the questions. If we want to know how the developmental capacities of totally blind babies compare to those of sighted babies we must examine a large sample of this population and employ statistical measures for working out comparative norms. But if we want to know how totally blind babies make their human attachments, differentiate a self and an object world, learn to speak, learn to use their hands as fine perceptual organs, learn to locomote, one blind baby can inform us considerably and ten blind babies with a range of environments and a range of assumed differences in endowment can help us identify the variables at work.

Since many of the problems we were studying had never been systematically examined before, we had to begin data collection within the large complex of behaviors that constitute infant development. Since there were no instruments standardized for our population (totally blind from birth) and the existing instruments for blind children with all degrees of visual loss are not reliable in themselves, we had to work out a system of observation in which the observer's selection and recording of data could produce a body of information that would permit comparisons within the group of blind babies and between the group of blind babies and sighted babies.

At this point I will try to give you a brief summary of the research design.

## Summary of Methods and Procedures

### The Sample

For our sample we chose babies who were totally blind from birth or who had light perception only; babies who had no other sensory or motor defects and no signs of central nervous system damage. Only by employing these restrictive criteria could we be sure that we were studying the visual deficit and its effects upon development. The total number of babies reported here is ten.

Blind babies who satisfied these criteria are rare even in a geographic range of 100 miles. In order to make home visits for observation we would need to travel in a radius of about 100 miles.

### Areas of Study

On the basis of our pilot studies we selected these areas of infant development for study: human object relations; behavior toward inanimate objects, toys; feeding; sleep; affectivity; language; gross motor development; prehension; self-stimulating behaviors; object concept.

### Observational Procedures

Each baby was assigned to a team of two observers. The primary responsibility for observation was placed in a senior professional staff member who was present at each visit. Our senior professional staff was composed of psychoanalysts and clinical psychologists. By placing the primary responsibility for observation in trained clinicians we insured as far as possible a high degree of sensitivity and clinical judgment in the work of data collection.

Why clinicians? Because, I feel, the clinical eye is trained to examine fine details and to regard every detail in the pattern as significant. The clinical worker, if he is well trained, has learned to regard himself as an instrument for observation and to protect his observations from prejudice. The clinician is also a pathologist, which means that a deviation in behavior from the expected and the typical will be recognized and invite inquiry. Above all, if he is a well-trained and well-seasoned clinician, he will allow the data to tell their own story; he will not impose a design upon the patterns observed. He will be open to the novel and the unexpected and he will welcome surprise.

The most serious drawback to using beginners or trainees in psychological investigation is one that I can remember with pain but with charity in myself. When I was a young worker I could only see what I was trained to see. When something emerged in my work that did not fit the pattern, my tendency was to screen it out, or to try to make it fit. In my research plan I knew that this must not happen. There was danger enough for all of us in drawing inferences from behavior of children whose perceptual field was radically different from our own. If we added to this the danger of "making things fit," our investigation would be doomed from the start.

*Methods*

The babies were visited in their homes at twice-monthly intervals. We chose a period in the baby's day, when he was normally awake and alert, when we might observe a feeding, a bath, a playtime with mother, a diapering or clothes change, and a period of self-occupation with or without toys.

One or the other of the observers recorded a descriptive narrative during the one-and-a-half hour observation period. In order to insure coverage of all items which must be gathered for comparative developmental study, the observers memorized our code schedule which included over 400 categories and sub-categories of behavior. This was not as difficult as it sounds. During any one observational session, the number of items relevant for a particular baby's developmental level might range from fifty to 100. An experienced observer could cover all of these items in the normal course of the session without disturbing the baby's routine or imposing a pattern upon the session. We never brought a schedule to an observational session. We did not need or want a checklist. What we wanted was descriptive detail.

At monthly or twice monthly intervals (depending on the age of the child) we recorded film samples of behavior in the areas of mother-child interaction in feeding or play, prehension, gross motor development, self-occupation. Because the photographing did impose a degree of artificiality on the observational session, we tried to keep this within the minimum required for useful documentation and study (approximately 450 feet of film per month).[1]

## Evaluation of Data

All of the data recorded in the descriptive narratives can be treated in two ways. They can be tabulated in shorthand form using the code schedule. This gives us a quick summary of the achievements of any baby at any age which can then be compared with the developmental characteristics of all other babies in our sample. At the same time every item tabulated has a reference by page and line to the original protocol, so that the descriptive and qualitative aspects of the behavior entered can be given separate treatment.

## The Educational Program

It is important to mention that for all babies in our study we have provided concurrent educational and guidance services to families. We know that the early development of blind babies is perilous. As our own research progressed we obtained important insights into the developmental problems of blind infants and we were able to translate this knowledge into highly effective prophylactic and remedial measures. In providing an educational service for our babies we have certainly altered our field in this investigation. But I am sure this audience will agree that no benefits to the research could justify withholding this knowledge from our families. It is only necessary that those who use our findings add to their information regarding our sample that these babies were probably advantaged by our educational intervention. It is necessary, too, that our records show explicitly how and when we intervened so that these parameters can be read into the assessment.

It is worth mentioning that even when our guidance work demonstrably affected the development of certain blind babies, it never obscured the study of the deficit and its effects upon development. In each case the visual deficit created a temporary roadblock in development which we were powerless to remove; in each case we saw the baby and his mother struggle to find the adaptive solution; in each case we gave assistance when necessary to find the adaptive routes. But what we needed to know we learned fully even though we influenced the outcome.

On the side of assets to the research I should mention two very important benefits brought to us through our educational work. First, the caseworker's guidance records gave us the kind of intimate knowledge of our babies and their families which we could never have obtained through the observational sessions alone. Second, our interventions at many critical points became a form of hypothesis testing, truly an experimental procedure.

## Sample Problems in Methodology

From the brief summary I have given you in the preceding section you can follow the general lines of our study. Since this is a case history of the development of a research program I think it would be very proper for my colleagues to ask the questions: Why these methods and not others? This is surely the clumsiest, most unwieldy system for data collection ever invented. Had you thought of less complex procedures? Or did you consider taking only one of these developmental areas and submitting it to exhaustive inquiry?

These are fair questions and very interesting ones. In this section, then, I propose to take some sample problems, discuss alternative methods, present arguments for the methods chosen and see how the methods were linked to the result.

SAMPLE PROBLEM 1: *What is the role of the mother in facilitating successful adaptation in the blind infant?*

If a blind child achieves a good level of adaptive functioning we will probably say that the mother of this child has done a very good job, and in colloquial terms speak of her as a "good" mother. If a blind child fails to make the grade we are inclined to regard his mother as a failure and to speak of her as a "poor" mother. If we want to elevate these notions to the status of science we could actually prove this. We could, for example, rate all our mothers on the Zweibach Maternal Warmth Scale, which I have just this moment invented, and rate all of our children on the basis of their developmental achievements. We would then find, predictably, that maternal warmth is highly correlated with the developmental achievements of blind children, in which case we would have spent a whopping chunk of taxpayers' money to deliver another cliché.

Now, of course, a provident nature has insured that almost any baby who is born with intact equipment will learn to walk and to talk, even if he has had the misfortune to get a mother who ranks low on the Zweibach Scale. This is just about what Hartmann (1958) means when he speaks of "the autonomous functions of the ego" and the guarantees for adaptiveness in "an average expectable environment." But if a baby is born with a deficit in his equipment the "average expectable environment" has some built-in hazards. The minus on the side of "state of adaptiveness" will require plusses on the side of a mother who will have to substitute for the deficit and take over the role of facilitating adaptation where the intact equipment would have virtually guaranteed it. This requires a mother with a high degree of adaptive capacity herself, and while mother love is certainly a great facilitator in responding to an infant's needs, the birth of a defective child can test love cruelly. Even if love passes the test, there is no guarantee that love alone will open up all the pathways of development that are imperilled by the defect. Toni's mother would be rated as "superior" on anyone's scale, "a very good mother," we would say. When Toni reached nine months and lay for long periods on the floor nuzzling a rug, or when she was condemned for months to the futile navigation of a circle, did the "good mother" become a "poor mother" because her baby's defective equipment led her to an impasse? No, clearly the problem is more complex. We will not learn about the role of the mother in facilitating a blind baby's adaptation if we use the Zweibach Scale or any other measure available to us. Since no one had studied the complexities of a mother's relationship to her blind infant, we needed to begin at the beginning.

## Method

We would need to observe and record in a detailed narrative everything that could be observed in the non-verbal communications between a mother and her blind infant, to learn how the baby's signals were read by the mother, how the baby learned to discriminate his mother from others, how the love bonds between mother and blind baby were forged, how the mother provided experiences for the baby that substituted for visual experience, how the mother helped her baby find the adaptive solutions when blindness created roadblocks in development.

We also want to know the differences and similarities between the progressive course of human attachments in a blind infant and the sighted infant. For the sighted baby we have criteria, indicators of the sequential development of human attachments. We arranged these criteria from several sources on a scale, relying heavily on the work of Thérèse Gouin-Décarie (1965) in testing a population of ninety children in Montreal. Since many of these criteria are also standard items on infant developmental tests we were able to obtain age norms for sighted children for certain key indicators. We avoided, very carefully, any temptation to substitute non-visual items for visual items in our own schedule and organized our data collection very simply on the basis of differential responses to mother, father, familiar figures and strangers.

All of our data in this category (and in every other category) were recorded, you remember, in narrative form. Clumsy, but essential for this investigation. Only by following a narrative form could we give value to the behavior reported in context and in temporal sequence. If we only cut across our data for significant events we might falsify these data. For example, if an eight-month-old baby howls as soon as a stranger picks him up, one might score this as "stranger anxiety." But suppose we read the protocol and find in the preceding paragraph that the baby had been playing a lap game with his mother and the stranger inadvertently interrupted the game. We cannot score this as "stranger anxiety."

The data from every protocol are sorted and indexed by student assistants who are rigorously trained in our coding procedures. If an item is scored "stranger anxiety" it must be unequivocal. When the same item is tabulated as I-8b in the code book there is also a page and line reference which will lead us back to the descriptive material in the text, so that the qualitative aspects of the behavior can be examined.

### Findings

The detailed descriptive recording in the area of human object relationships provided data for two different problems. Abstracted from the recording was: (a) a qualitative analysis of mother-infant communication (the "dialogue" in Spitz's terms) and (b) a sequence of differential responses to mother and other human objects which permitted comparisons with sighted baby achievements in any given quarter of the first eighteen months.

(a) *Mother-infant communication.* In the absence of that large repertoire of signals and signs which are normally provided by vision, nearly all of our parents experienced the feeling of being initially cut off from their blind babies. Since no educational help had been given any of our families before the time of referral to us, we can assume that the picture of mother-child interaction presented at the point of intake represented the mother's own unaided efforts to respond to her blind baby's needs and find her way into her blind baby's experience. In the sample that I am reporting, seven of ten babies were referred to us between the ages of three days and six months of life, and three babies were referred to us between six and nine months. (Ideally we would have wanted all babies referred to us as soon after birth as possible, but delays in diagnosis or referral gave us this distribution.) I cannot do more than summarize our findings in this rich and extraordinarily complex area. The following comments reflect the complexity of the problem.

"How will he know me?" was one of the first questions that these young mothers asked when they were still under the impact of the diagnosis of blindness. If the baby came to us as a newborn, we helped the mother to find a tactile-auditory language for communicating with her baby. When the baby came to us at four months or later, we were able to see at the point of referral how the mother found her way, or did not find her way, into her blind baby's experience.

Two of the older babies referred at eight months and nine months respectively, were well on their way to autism at the time we first met them. Jackie and Karen showed no differential responses to the mother or any human objects, were grossly retarded in all sectors of development, withdrew from stimuli and slept the better part of the twenty-four hour day. What kind of mothers were these? These were mothers who did not enjoy physical closeness with their babies. We saw this in their handling of their sighted children. Also they did not speak to their children except to make requests or give commands; having conversations with babies or young children was not their style. Were they "poor" mothers? That depends. Their sighted children were adequate, slow in speech development as you might expect with sighted children who are not encouraged to speak, and not inclined toward physical closeness, which you would expect, too. But the development of these sighted children was not imperilled by a mother who had a limited repertoire in the language of touch and speech. There was no danger of autism for these sighted siblings. Vision became a guarantor of development for these sighted children with a less than adequate mother; in the absence of vision, the blind baby with the same mother was cut off from all experience of knowing the mother. I should tell you that both of these blind babies were brought to normal functioning within a period of a few months through our education and guidance of the mother.

Now let's look at another baby, first seen by us at the age of four and a half months. Robbie, at the time of our first observations, was an extraordinary blind baby. He smiled in response to voices, he cooed and gurgled in response and for self-entertainment, and he was beginning to sit independently for a few seconds; his adaptive hand behavior would place him in the very superior range for blind infants. His mother had had no help in rearing her blind baby before the time we first met her.

Was this mother a very intuitive mother? A very superior mother? Robbie's mother would be rated by us as one of the least empathic mothers in our group and one who presented the most severe pathological signs. She was dull and extremely obese. She showed clinical signs of a severe depression which she warded off through eating and excessive talking. What made her an adequate mother for a blind baby during the first five months of life? She enjoyed physical contact with her baby. "I can't leave him alone!" she would say. We reflected to ourselves that she would probably have worn out a sighted baby through the amount of gross tactile stimulation she gave the blind baby, and her garrulousness, which we knew to be a defense against depression, made her known to her blind baby when she was not in physical contact with him! As long as she maintained her defenses against depression, she could meet her blind baby's needs. During one brief period at the end of the first year, when the depression broke through, she removed herself from physical contact with Robbie, and for that period he regressed alarmingly. We helped Robbie's mother to reestablish her defenses and Robbie once again moved back to the level of good functioning.

This is not to say that a mother's pathology will not have effects upon a baby's development. When Robbie ran into trouble with his mother in the second year, it was through conflict over feeding, which we can understand from the role of food in the mother's pathology. But Robbie never became an autistic child and Robbie's ego organization was not imperilled as long as the mother's pathology did not isolate her from her baby. All things considered, an intact ego and a feeding disturbance are to be preferred to autism.

From these brief case examples with their contrasts of babies and mothers we can see how unprofitable it would be to rate our mothers on a scale of arbitrary values. If we multiply these examples many times we can begin to get the picture of extraordinary complexity that emerged from our qualitative analysis of data in human object relationships.

Even the most intuitive parents of our group encountered impasses and crises in their rearing of the blind baby that were unparalleled in the experience of good parents with normal sighted babies. The blind baby was helpless before the most ordinary dangers of infancy. Brief separations were experienced as traumas, occasioning in four babies severe regressions that required our assistance. Each step in the achievement of locomotion, which normal babies pass through on a developmental express train, was encountered by the blind baby as another roadblock, another detour, and always another move outwards into the terrifying void. And since the baby never did things the way other babies do, every roadblock created fresh alarms in the parents, and periods during which a mother and her baby were demonstrably out of rapport.

In our educational work we became the interpreters to the parents of the blind baby's experience, helped the parents establish a dialogue in non-visual terms.

*(b) Comparisons with sighted infants.* Finally, how did our babies compare with sighted babies in the development of human object relations? Without any arbitrary substitution of non-visual items for visual items on a sighted-child scale, all but one of our babies showed increasingly selective and well-differentiated responses to his mother and other important persons and to strangers, leading to what we speak of in psychoanalysis as libidinal object constancy. I can summarize with a few key indicators: the smiling response, differential vocalization, stranger reactions, separation anxiety, display of affec-

tion and response to requests and prohibitions all appeared among our blind babies within the age range for sighted infants.

We must not generalize these findings to the blind infant population. Again we need to remember the selective criteria employed in choosing our sample and that the mothers of these babies received all the help we could give them in promoting the love bonds between the baby and themselves. But with all these cautions in interpreting our findings the result is a very significant one. This means, of course, that under the most favorable circumstances a blind baby need not be impeded in forming the vital human attachments. This probably means, too, that what we see in the sighted child as a sequence of differential responses expressed in visual terms must include every step of the way a large amount of non-visual experience, especially tactile and auditory experience, which is progressively organized under vision.

Having human object relations as a cornerstone in our investigation now permits us to draw inferences from our other data with a larger margin of safety. If, for example, the majority of our blind infants demonstrate adequacy in the area of human object relationships (even if we ourselves have influenced this) then any significant group deviation in other sectors of development can be treated more confidently as a possible effect of the visual deficit, or the restrictive experience of the blind infant, with relative independence of the variables in mothering.

SAMPLE PROBLEM 2: *How does the blind baby coordinate sound and grasping in the direct reach on sound cue?*

We already know that Toni did not demonstrate directional reach for an object on sound cue until ten months of age. We cannot generalize this finding from one case of the blind infant population, but one case can tell us that the substitution of sound for vision is not guaranteed in the same way that vision guarantees that the thing "out there" can be attained through reaching and grasping at five months.

If we are only interested in the study of prehension in the blind child there are a number of valid approaches to the problem. We can, for example, conduct a testing program for all blind infants in the state of Michigan, at quarterly intervals in the first year. We would then obtain statistical information on the characteristics of prehension in blind infants in each quarter of the first year and the age range for all blind infants in the attainment of an object on sound cue. This would be a very interesting and useful study in itself. But it would not give us the answers to our questions.

In our psychoanalytic study of ego formation in the blind infant, we want to know how the hand serves ego development. If there is an extraordinary problem in the adaptive substitution of sound for vision, this will have effects not only in the development of prehension, but in contiguous and/or reciprocal lines of development. For all babies, the hand becomes one of the executive organs of the emerging ego, the bridge between the body self and the external world. In the case of the blind baby, the hand must serve all these functions and must also serve as a primary perceptual organ. We need to know the adaptive process as well as the adaptive solution.

In designing this aspect of the research I was helped by a clinical hunch. The hunch was derived from observations of Peter, my nine-year-old autistic boy in New Orleans.

When I first knew Peter I was struck by the fact that when he dropped an object from his hands or lost an object, he did not search for it. He did not even make a gesture of reach. From these and hundreds of other observations it was very clear that when he lost contact with an object, it ceased to exist. We are reminded now that the sighted baby under eight months of age will not search for an object that has been hidden before his eyes. As Piaget (1954) has demonstrated, the belief that an object exists independent of perception is obtained around the middle of the second year and only gradually during the first eighteen months does the baby begin to take into account invisible objects and deduce their movements in space.

Watching Peter, I was struck by the fact that this must be an extraordinary problem for the blind infant. In the absence of vision, the baby must learn to track objects on sound alone. How does the blind baby learn that when he does not hear a person or hear a sound object, it still exists? How does he build a world of permanent objects? And if he fails in this learning, if he cannot acquire the concept of objects which exist independent of himself and his perception, there will be no differentiation between self and object world; he will be, clinically speaking, autistic, meaning that all experience and all phenomena are experienced as part of the body self.

My hunch was that Toni's inability to reach for and attain an object on sound cue until ten months of age might be related to a conceptual problem for a blind infant. In the absence of vision it was possible, I reasoned, that the sound of an object would not connote substantiality or "graspability." The ten-month achievement in an otherwise healthy and bright blind baby might be the clue. At eight months the sighted baby on the Piaget object concept scale begins to search for an object under a screen, meaning that he is just beginning to get the notion that the object can exist independent of his perception. It was possible, I reasoned, that the blind baby must reach this level of conceptual development before sound connotes graspability, that is, that an object exists independent of his manual tactile experience of it and manifests itself through a sound "out there." If this is a conceptual problem for a blind baby, it is very likely that no blind baby could achieve the concept before a sighted baby, which would place reach on sound cue in the last third of the first year.

*Method*

Our study of prehension, then, would include the testing of this hypothesis, but where nothing is known through direct observation of blind babies we must protect our investigation through designing experimental procedures that tested alternatives and variables without building in expectations. Also, since the factors we were seeking in this study were so complex and numerous, we needed to reduce the problems to manageable size.

There was a good solution, for which we are indebted to Piaget. Piaget's object concept scale, standardized in 1963 by Décarie (1965) on a population of ninety children, deals with the same complexities for the sighted child that we were examining in the blind child. In every step of the development of the object concept, the test involves problems in prehension, coordination of sensory-motor schemas, behavior toward inanimate objects, recognition and mental representation, the differentiation of a self and an outer world, in a progressive sequence. This becomes a highly economical test for our purposes.

How can we use this scale? Clearly it would be hazardous for us to take Piaget's scale and make arbitrary substitutions of sound items for visual items when we do not know how sound can substitute for vision and when, in fact, the adaptive substitution is just what we are looking for. But if we followed Piaget's principles we would ask the blind baby to teach *us* how he learned to coordinate sound with directional reach and grasping.

This is what we did:

At twice monthly intervals we presented problems of search to our blind babies. The procedures were very simple. In the first year, for example, we presented sound toys and soundless toys, the child's own toys and interesting toys of our own. We allowed the child to hold them and play with them, and gently removed them from his grasp and placed them within easy reach. We worked out procedures that would tell us clearly how the baby reacted when the toy was experimentally silenced or moved from one place to another, what sensory information he used to discriminate objects and identify them. We also followed the evolution of grasping, mutual fingering, transfer, the coordinate use of hands, unilateral reaching and thumb-finger opposition. We provided only enough structure in the testing to assure us that we could study the variables at work.

We recorded all of the testing on 16mm film. We then studied the film on a variable speed projector at approximately one-third speed or sometimes frame-by-frame. While viewing the film at one-third speed with the entire senior staff present, one of the investigators dictated a narrative record covering every gesture, every motion, in fine detail. If there was any disagreement on what was seen, we played the sequence over again until we had reached consensus. If there was no consensus, it was recorded as such. We then had a film record and a corresponding written document. The film protocol could now be used flexibly for coding and for sorting patterns.

This, too, is probably one of the clumsiest procedures ever invented. Yet it gave us all the answers we were looking for. I still do not know whether there were any short-cuts that we could have taken. Since nothing was known about adaptive hand behavior in blind infants we could not know what to look for. The situation is analogous to that of an archeological study of a site that is identified as potentially rich but has never been dug. Every fragment must be carefully examined, catalogued, and stored until the pieces can be arranged to tell a story.

*Findings*

When we sorted our data on each child, this is what we saw:

(a) The biogenetic patterns of prehension appeared in the grasping mode in a clear evolution throughout the first ten months. The hand unfolds, and at ten months the index finger explores and thumb-finger opposition appears, which corresponds to the norms of sighted children.

*(b)* Adaptive hand behavior, the route to acoustically directed reach and attainment, followed a very different course from that of the sighted child. The coordination of hearing and grasping appeared in our blind babies in the last quarter of the first year. *The modal age for ten babies in our sample was ten months!*

These data tell us that there is no adaptive substitution of sound for sight at five months. The blind baby must find the adaptive solution via another route. How does the blind baby find the adaptive route? To answer this question we analyzed literally hundreds of miles of film and classified the data in stages. I will not attempt to give the details in this short report. But this is an interesting story and I can give you a summary by choosing one baby as a model.

At five months Robbie enjoys holding a bell in his hands and ringing it. If we withdraw the bell from his hands and ring it within easy reach of his hands there is no gesture of reach, the hands remain motionless.

At eight months of age we bring Robbie's oldest and most treasured musical toy within easy reach of his hands. It is playing its familiar music. Robbie looks alert, attentive, shows recognition on his face. He makes no gesture of reach. We finally give him his musical dog and he hugs it and mouths it. After awhile we withdraw the dog from his hands. He is angry at the loss. He can still hear the music. It is within easy reach. He does not make even a gesture toward the toy. In hundreds of experiments during this period we can demonstrate that whether we use a familiar sound toy or an unfamiliar toy, whether mother presents the toy or the examiner presents the toy, whether sound is continuous or sound is discontinuous, there is no attempt to recover the toy.

At ten months of age if we sound the bell which Robbie is very fond of, there is still no gesture of reach. But now we see an interesting behavior of the hands. At the sound of the bell Robbie's hands go through the motion of grasping and ungrasping and once we see the hands executing the motion of ringing the bell. Still no reach, but now for the first time we can read the message in the hands that the sound of the bell connotes graspability and evokes a memory of bell ringing.

At eleven months and three days of age, Robbie hears the bell and for the first time makes a direct reach for the bell and attains it.

And now, from this model, we can reconstruct the problem for a blind baby. Sound alone does not connote substantiality for Robbie until eleven months. Until then the toy dog playing Brahm's Lullaby "out there" is not the same as the toy dog playing Brahm's Lullaby when held in the baby's hand. As a matter of fact, even the sighted baby at eight months will not search for a favorite squeaky toy if we cover it with a screen and cause it to squeak. But vision will unite the schemas of sound and touch so that the sighted child will soon take the sound to connote the object seen and grasped. The blind child has to make an inference that the familiar sound "out there" connotes the substantial object that he had held in his hands a few minutes ago. When, at ten months, Robbie's hands go through the motions of grasping and ungrasping and bell ringing we can see that he is getting the idea, and in a very short time we see him coordinate the schemas of prehension and sound in direct reach.

This means, of course, that the blind child has to reach a certain level of conceptual development before he can reach for and attain a sound object. The sighted child can achieve this on a much earlier level of conceptual development because vision will insure that the thing seen can be grasped at five months of age. This is not an advanced conceptual problem for the sighted baby; it is not even much of a memory problem. But for the blind baby, memory and an emerging concept of the qualities of things, independent of the self, are required for the solution of the problem.

We can now understand why many blind babies never find the adaptive solution and remain frozen on the level of body centeredness.

But now I should tell you, too, how the prehension study provided the vital clue to the problem of delayed locomotion in blind infants. Have you already guessed?

All of the babies in our sample were markedly delayed by sighted child norms in achieving locomotion through creeping, walking with support, and independent walking. As a group their achievements were very good for blind children; on a blind child scale their locomotor achievements would place them in the upper half of the blind infant population. This may reflect our educational interventions. But the developmental impasse which we observed in Toni appeared in each of our blind babies in the last quarter of the first year. There was maturational readiness for creeping which we can demonstrate through documentary films, showing a baby supporting himself ably on hands and knees, or pulling himself to a stand. These abilities testify for neuromuscular adequacy and "readiness" for locomotion. At ten months we see Robbie on film, supporting himself on hands and knees, acrobatically lifting one leg off the floor, maintaining beautiful balance. He has been "ready to creep" by all standards since nine months. For three months he maintains this posture, rocking back and forth on hands and knees. He is unable to propel himself forward. We had already guessed part of the story through observations of Toni. There was no external stimulus for reaching which would initiate the creeping pattern. But in those days we could not understand why a sound stimulus could not substitute for a visual stimulus. Now we knew.

Robbie demonstrated his first reach on sound cue at eleven months of age. Three days later while supporting himself on hands and knees he reached for an out-of-range sound object and began to creep.

This pattern or variations of it appeared in every child in our series. No baby learned to creep until he had first given us a demonstration of "reach on sound cue."

### Could We Have Used Some Shortcuts?

The methods I have described in these sample problems brought us the answers we were seeking. If you now add to these two areas of study the ten other major categories of this investigation, you can see that the work of data collection and analysis has been very demanding. Could we have simplified our procedures? Could we have found shortcuts? I still don't know whether there were other methods that might have produced the same answers.

All of our data are coded and sorted manually. Two years ago as I saw the mountain of data grow, I considered the possibility of working out a system for computer sorting and retrieval of items in their descriptive categories. I sketched the problem and the plan, and our data processing people thought it was workable. We never used it.

As we moved into the evaluation phase of our work each of us had the most compelling need to see the story unfold before his own eyes. Our descriptive data in certain categories are transcribed on large cards, one item per card, of course, and we will have to spend hundreds of hours, all of us, playing solitaire with thousands of cards. So far not one of us has complained about the work. I think I know why.

By the time I have read and sorted a thousand cards in Section I and re-read them and re-sort them for the study of twenty-five sub-categories, every card has been read hundreds of times. A large number of them have been practically memorized. Now, my mental storage and retrieval system is not nearly as efficient as the computer's system, but I have a usuable past which the computer does not have. When the computer registers information on card 456, it will know immediately that card 456 belongs to the same group as card 243. This is very clever of the computer, but it only knows it because I told it so. Now when I look at card 456 I also will know that it belongs in the same category as card 243, which does not yet give me much of an edge on the computer. But perhaps the fourth time I look at card 456, something leaps out of the printed text, and I say, "That odd behavior in Sally! That ear pulling! Where did I see that before? Oh, yes. Artie at eight months. Where is Artie's eight-month file?" I reach in and pluck a card. I re-read it. It's the same manifestation. Now we have two examples of a piece of incomprehensible behavior. My mind wanders for a moment. The picture of a twelve-year-old boy, a patient long ago, comes into my mind. How did Ozzie get into the picture? I wait a moment. The patient in my memory picture is agitatedly plucking at his clothing. It's that frightful hour eight years ago when I was afraid he was heading for the hospital. He is clutching his own skin through cloth, in panic, as he describes dissolution of self-feeling. Ah, that's the connection. Affirmation of self-feelings through repetitive touching of the body. Is that what the two babies are telling us? I will wait now for more evidence.

This kind of sorting in human intelligence takes place on a pre-conscious level. The computer has no history, no record of experience that can do this work. Even if we improve the model, the computer will never learn to do this. It is not just the lack of clinical experience that limits the computer. A system of mechanical retrieval can never make such associative leaps. The associative paths that can lead you and me from two babies to a twelve-year-old boy are not part of a logical system. There were probably affective pathways in my own mental processes that led me from the picture of two babies, pulling at their ear lobes, to a memory of a boy plucking at his clothes. In layman's language we might say the process began by "feeling" a similarity, even when I could not yet know what the connections were.

All this belongs to what we call "clinical imagination," which is simply another form of the scientific imagination. The insights of a physicist or a mathematician or a poet emerge in much the same way, through a collaborative process in which a preconscious ferment of ideas produces a hunch, or a connection, which is then examined and tested objectively by the instruments of logical intelligence. It is this imagination that is nurtured and developed in everyday clinical work. When we move from clinical practice to clinical research, this imagination becomes our most valuable instrument for the study of human problems.

The research which I have described today is the work of clinicians. If good and useful things have come out of this investigation, it is because of the extraordinary advantages that came to us through our clinical experience and training. Even our prehension study, which brought all of us into an area far removed from our clinical experience, became the unexpected beneficiary of this clinical experience. What we brought from the clinic were eyes trained for subtleties in movement patterns; we watch hands, body postures, faces with the same kind of attention that we use in listening. Since the blind baby's hands were going to tell us a story, we developed hand watching as a specialty in the research, where it was only a kind of sub-specialty in our usual clinical work. Then, in the way in which one thing leads to another in clinical research, the same clinical attention which was focused on hands was brought to bear upon other forms of motility, the trunk and head, for example. When we had analyzed these movement patterns in a group of normal blind infants, we found a scattered number of motility patterns that we will never see in normal sighted babies. Then we had the key to the so-called blindisms. We now know how they emerge, how they become stereotyped and how to undo them in the early years. But this story must wait for another time.

In the end, this study by clinicians of the development of blind infants gave us the answers to the questions that were raised at the beginning of the study, eight years ago in New Orleans. Since these were clinical problems we can test the validity of these findings in the clinic. If we have correctly identified the unique adaptive problems for the blind infant we should be able to translate our findings into methods of facilitating adaptive solutions for blind infants and young children.

The final stage of this research is application; which brings us back full circle. The clinician researcher is back in the kitchen—although, in a certain sense, he never left the kitchen. The research I have described is a kind of kitchen research, close to the source of supply, inventing with the materials on hand. It is plain in its design and functional. But then, science is not the practice of sacred arts. If we love science we can love it for its commonness, its everyday presence in the form of observing, questioning, examining—its everyday practice in our clinical work.

It was my husband who gave me the last line of this essay and the title. He paraphrased a line from Whitman. "Where is the muse? The muse is in the kitchen. . . ."

## Notes

This paper was presented at an institute sponsored by the New England Chapter of the Smith College School for Social Work Alumni Association, Boston, March 27, 1969.

1. For a more detailed description of the procedures for data collection, see Fraiberg (1968).

## References

Fraiberg, S. (1968). Parallel and Divergent Patterns in Blind and Sighted Infants. *Psychoanal. Study Child,* 23:264–300.

———— & Freedman, D. A. (1964). Studies in the Ego Development of the Congenitally Blind Child. *Psychoanal. Study Child,* 19:113–169.

Gouin-Décarie, T. (1965). *Intelligence and Affectivity in Early Childhood.* New York: International Universities Press.

Hartmann, H. (1958). *Ego Psychology and the Problem of Adaptation.* New York: International Universities Press.

Keeler, W. R. (1958). Autistic Patterns and Defective Communication in Blind Children with Retrolental Fibroplasia. In *Psychopathology of Communication,* ed. P. H. Hoch & J. Zubin. New York: Grune and Stratton.

Norris, M., et al. (1957). *Blindness in Children.* Chicago: Univ. Chicago Press.

Piaget, J. (1954). *The Construction of Reality in the Child.* New York: Basic Books.

# 4

## Ghosts in the Nursery: A Psychoanalytic Approach to the Problems of Impaired Infant-Mother Relationships

*With Edna Adelson and Vivian Shapiro*

In every nursery there are ghosts. They are the visitors from the un-remembered past of the parents; the uninvited guests at the christening. Under all favorable circumstances the unfriendly and unbidden spirits are banished from the nursery and return to their subterranean dwelling place. The baby makes his own imperative claim upon parental love and, in strict analogy with the fairy tales, the bonds of love protect the child and his parents against the intruders, the malevolent ghosts.

This is not to say that ghosts cannot invent mischief from their burial places. Even among families where the love bonds are stable and strong, the intruders from the parental past may break through the magic circle in an unguarded moment, and a parent and his child may find themselves reenacting a moment or a scene from another time with another set of characters. Such events are unremarkable in the family theater, and neither the child nor his parents nor their bond is necessarily imperiled by a brief intrusion. It is not usually necessary for the parents to call upon us for clinical services.

In still other families there may be more troublesome events in the nursery caused by intruders from the past. There are, it appears, a number of transient ghosts who take up residence in the nursery on a selective basis. They appear to do their mischief according to a histor-ical or topical agenda, specializing in such areas as feeding, sleep, toilet training, or discipline, depending upon the vulnerabilities of the

parental past. Under these circumstances, even when the bonds between parents and child are strong, the parents may feel helpless before the invasion and may seek professional guidance. In our own
work, we have found that these parents will form a strong alliance
with us to banish the intruders from the nursery. It is not difficult to
find the educational or therapeutic means for dealing with the transient invaders.

But how shall we explain another group of families who appear to
be possessed by their ghosts? The intruders from the past have taken
up residence in the nursery, claiming tradition and rights of ownership. They have been present at the christening for two or more generations. While no one has issued an invitation, the ghosts take up
residence and conduct the rehearsal of the family tragedy from a tat-
tered script.

In our Infant Mental Health Program we have seen many of these
families and their babies. The baby is already in peril by the time we
meet him, showing the early signs of emotional starvation, or grave
symptoms, or developmental impairment. In each of these cases, the
baby has become a silent partner in a family tragedy. The baby in
these families is burdened by the oppressive past of his parents from
the moment he enters the world. The parent, it seems, is condemned
to repeat the tragedy of his childhood with his own baby in terrible
and exacting detail.

These parents may not come to us for professional guidance.
Ghosts who have established their residence privileges for three or
more generations may not, in fact, be identified as representatives of
the parental past. There may be no readiness on the part of the parents
to form an alliance with us to protect the baby. More likely we, and
not the ghosts, will appear as the intruders.

Those of us who have a professional interest in ghosts in the
nursery do not yet understand the complexities and the paradoxes in
the ghost story. What is it that determines whether the conflicted
past of the parent will be repeated with his child? Is morbidity in the
parental history the prime determinant? This strikes us as too simple.
Certainly we all know families in which a parental history of tragedy,
cruelty, and sorrow have *not* been inflicted upon the children. The
ghosts do not flood the nursery or erode the love bonds.

Then, too, we must reflect that, if history predicted with fidelity,
the human family itself would have long ago been drowned in its own

oppressive past. The race improves. And this may be because the largest number of men and women who have known suffering find renewal and the healing of childhood pain in the experience of bringing a child into the world. In the simplest terms—we have heard it often from parents—the parent says, "I want something better for my child than I have had." And he brings something better to his child. In this way we have all known young parents who have suffered poverty, brutality, death, desertion, and sometimes the full gamut of childhood horrors, who do not inflict their pain upon their children. History is not destiny, then, and whether parenthood becomes flooded with griefs and injuries, or whether parenthood becomes a time of renewal cannot be predicted from the narrative of the parental past. There must be other factors in the psychological experience of that past which determine repetition in the present.

In therapeutic work with families on behalf of their babies, we are all the beneficiaries of Freud's discoveries before the dawn of this century. The ghosts, we know, represent the repetition of the past in the present. We are also the beneficiaries of the method which Freud developed for recovering the events of the past and undoing the morbid effects of the past in the present. The babies themselves, who are often afflicted by the diseases of the parental past, have been the last to be the beneficiaries of the great discoveries of psychoanalysis and developmental psychology. This patient, who cannot talk, has awaited articulate spokesmen.

During the past three decades, a number of psychoanalysts and developmental psychologists have been speaking for the babies. What the babies have been telling us is sobering news, indeed. This story you already know, and I shall not attempt to summarize the vast literature which has emerged from our studies of infancy.

In our own work at the Child Development Project, we have become well acquainted with the ghosts in the nursery. The brief intruders, which we have described, or the unwelcome ghosts who take up temporary residence, do not present extraordinary problems to the clinician. The parents themselves become our allies in banishing the ghosts. It is the third group, the ghosts who invade the nursery and take up residence, who present the gravest therapeutic problems for us.

How is it that the ghosts of the parental past can invade the nursery with such insistency and ownership, claiming their rights above the baby's own rights? This question is at the center of our work. The answers are emerging for us, and in the closing section of this essay we shall return to the question and offer a hypothesis derived from clinical experience.

In this paper, we shall describe our clinical study and treatment through two of the many imperiled babies who have come to us. As our work progressed, our families and their babies opened doors to us which illuminated the past and the present. Our psychoanalytic knowledge opened pathways into understanding the repetition of the past in the present. The methods of treatment which we developed brought together psychoanalysis, developmental psychology, and social work in ways that will be illustrated. The rewards for the babies, for the families, and for us have been very large.

In our collaborative work, Edna Adelson, staff psychologist, was the therapist for Mary and her family, Vivian Shapiro, staff social worker, was therapist for Greg and his family, and Selma Fraiberg served as case supervisor and psychoanalytic consultant.

## Mary

Mary, who came to us at five and a half months, was the first baby referred to our new Infant Mental Health Program. Her mother, Mrs. March,* had appeared at an adoption agency some weeks earlier. She wanted to surrender her baby for adoption. But adoption plans could not proceed because Mr. March would not give his consent. Mary's mother was described as "a rejecting mother."

Now, of course, nobody loves a rejecting mother, in our community or any other, and Mary and her family might at this point have disappeared into the anonymity of a metropolitan community, perhaps to surface once again when tragedy struck. But chance brought the family to one of the psychiatric clinics of our University. The psychiatric evaluation of Mrs. March revealed a severe depression, an attempted suicide through aspirin, a woman so tormented that she could barely go about the ordinary tasks of living. The "rejecting mother" was now seen as a depressed mother. Psychiatric treatment was recommended at a clinical staffing. And then one of the clinical team members said, "But what about the baby?" Our new Infant Mental Health Program

* This name, like all other patient names, is a pseudonym.—Ed.

had been announced and scheduled for opening the following day. There was a phone call to us and we agreed to provide immediate evaluation of the baby and to consider treatment.

*Early Observations*

From the time Mary was first seen by us, we had reason for grave concern. At five and a half months she bore all the stigmata of the child who has spent the better part of her life in a crib with little more than obligatory care. She was adequately nourished and physically cared for, but the back of her head was bald. She showed little interest in her surround, she was listless, too quiet. She seemed to have only a tenuous connection with her mother. She rarely smiled. She did not spontaneously approach her mother through eye contact or gestures of reach. There were few spontaneous vocalizations. In moments of discomfort or anxiety she did not turn to her mother. In our developmental testing she failed nearly all the personal-social items on the Bayley Scale. At one point in the testing, an unexpected sound (the Bayley test bell) shattered her threshold of tolerance, and she collapsed in terror.

The mother herself seemed locked in some private terror, remote, removed, yet giving us rare glimpses of a capacity for caring. For weeks we held onto one tiny vignette captured on videotape, in which the baby made an awkward reach for her mother, and the mother's hand spontaneously reached toward the baby. The hands never met each other, but the gesture symbolized for the therapists a reaching out toward each other, and we clung to this symbolic hope.

There is a moment at the beginning of every case when something is revealed that speaks for the essence of the conflict. This moment appeared in the second session of the work when Mrs. Adelson invited Mary and her mother to our office. By chance it was a moment captured on videotape, because we were taping the developmental testing session as we customarily do. Mary and her mother, Mrs. Adelson, and Mrs. Evelyn Atreya, as tester, were present.

Mary begins to cry. It is a hoarse, eerie cry in a baby. Mrs. Atreya discontinues the testing. On tape we see the baby in her mother's arms screaming hopelessly; she does not turn to her mother for comfort. The mother looks distant, self-absorbed. She makes an absent gesture to comfort the baby, then gives up. She looks away. The screaming continues for five dreadful minutes on tape. In the background we hear Mrs. Adelson's voice, gently encouraging the mother. "What do you do to comfort Mary when she cries like this?" Mrs. March murmurs something inaudible. Mrs. Adelson and Mrs. Atreya are struggling with their own feelings. They are restraining their own wishes to pick up the baby and hold her, to murmur comforting things to her. If they should yield to their own wish, they would do the one thing they feel must not be done. For Mrs. March would then see that another woman could comfort the baby, and she would be confirmed in her own conviction that she was a bad mother. It is a dreadful five minutes for the baby, the mother, and the two psychologists. Mrs. Adelson maintains composure, speaks sympathetically to Mrs. March. Finally, the visit comes to an end when Mrs. Adelson suggests that the baby is fatigued and probably would welcome her own home and her crib, and mother and baby are helped to close the visit with plans for a third visit very soon.

As we watched this tape later in a staff session, we said to each other incredulously, "It's as if this mother doesn't *hear* her baby's cries!" This led us to the key diagnostic question: *"Why doesn't this mother hear her baby's cries?"*

## The Mother's Story

Mrs. March was herself an abandoned child. Her mother suffered a postpartum psychosis shortly after the birth of Mrs. March and her twin brother. In an attempted suicide, she had shattered part of her face with a gun and was horribly mutilated for life. She had then spent nearly all of the rest of her life in a hospital and was barely known to her children. For five years Mrs. March was cared for by an aunt. When the aunt could no longer care for her, she was shifted to the house of the maternal grandmother, where she received grudging care from the burdened, impoverished old woman. Mrs. March's father was in and out of the family picture. We did not hear much about him until later in the treatment.

It was a story of bleak rural poverty, sinister family secrets, psychosis, crime, a tradition of promiscuity in the women, of filth and disorder in the home, and of police and protective agencies in the background making futile uplifting gestures. Mrs. March was the cast-out child of a cast-out family.

In late adolescence, Mrs. March met and married her husband, who came from poverty and family disorder not unlike her own. But he wanted something better for himself than his family had had. He became the first member of his family to fight his way out of the cycle of futility, to find steady work, to establish a decent home. When these two neglected and solitary young people found each other, there was mutual consent that they wanted something better than what they had known. But now, after several years of effort, the downward spiral had begun.

There was a very high likelihood that Mary was not her father's child. Mrs. March had had a brief affair with another man. Her guilt over the affair, her doubts about Mary's paternity, became an obsessive theme in her story. In a kind of litany of griefs that we were to hear over and over again, there was one theme: "People stared at Mary," she thought. "They stared at her and knew that her father was not her father. They knew that her mother had ruined her life."

Mr. March, who began to appear to us as the stronger parent, was not obsessed with Mary's paternity. He was convinced that he was Mary's father. And anyway, he loved Mary and he wanted her. His wife's obsession with paternity brought about shouting quarrels in the home. "Forget it!" said Mr. March. "Stop talking about it! And take care of Mary!"

In the families of both mother and father illegitimacy carried no stigma. In the case of Mrs. March's clan, the promiscuity of their women over at least three or four generations cast doubt over the paternity of many of the children. Why was Mrs. March obsessed? Why the sense of tormenting sin? This pervasive, consuming sense of sin we thought belonged to childhood, to buried sins, quite possibly crimes of the imagination. On several occasions in reading the clinical reports, we had the strong impression that Mary was the sinful child of an incestuous fantasy. But if we were right, we thought to ourselves, how could we possibly reach this in our once-a-week psychotherapy?

*Treatment: The Emergency Phase*

How shall we begin? We should remember that Mary and Mrs. March were our first patients. We did not have treatment models available to us. In fact, it was our task in this first Infant Mental

Health Program to develop methods in the course of the work. It made sense, of course, to begin with a familiar model in which our resident in psychiatry, Dr. Zinn, works with the mother in weekly or twice-weekly psychotherapy, and the psychologist, Mrs. Adelson, provides support and developmental guidance on behalf of the baby through home visits. But within the first sessions, we saw that Mrs. March was taking flight from Dr. Zinn and psychiatric treatment. The situation in which she was alone with a man brought forth a phobic dread, and she was reduced to nearly inarticulate hours or to speaking of trivial concerns. All efforts to reach Mrs. March, or to touch upon her anxieties or discomfort in this relationship, led to an impasse. One theme was uttered over and over again. She did not trust men. But also, we caught glimpses in her oblique communications of a terrible secret that she would never reveal to anyone. She broke appointments more frequently than she kept them. With much difficulty, Dr. Zinn sustained a relationship with her. It was nearly a year before we finally heard the secret and understood the phobic dread that led to this formidable resistance.

There are no generalizations to be drawn from this experience. We have been asked sometimes if women therapists are more advantaged in working with mothers who have suffered severe maternal deprivation themselves. Our answer, after nearly two years of work, is "not necessarily; sometimes not at all." We have examples in our work in which the male therapist was specially advantaged in working with mothers. We tend to assign cases without overconcern about the sex of the therapist. Mrs. March must be regarded as an exceptional case.

But now, we were faced with a therapeutic dilemma. Mrs. Adelson's work was to center in the infant-mother relationship through home visits. Mrs. March needed her own therapist, Dr. Zinn, but a morbid dread of men, aroused in the transference, prevented her from using the psychiatric help available to her. With much time and patient work in the psychiatric treatment we would hope to uncover the secret which reduced her to silence and flight in the transference to Dr. Zinn.

But the baby was in great peril. And the baby could not wait for the resolution of the mother's neurosis.

Mrs. Adelson, we soon saw, did not arouse the same morbid anxieties in Mrs. March, but her role as the baby-mother therapist, the home-based psychologist, did not lend itself easily to uncovering the conflictual elements in the mother's relationship to the child and the treatment of the mother's depression.

Since we had no alternatives, we decided we would use the home visits for our emergency treatment.

What emerged, then, was a form of "psychotherapy in the kitchen," so to speak, which will strike you as both familiar in its methods and unfamiliar in its setting. The method, a variant of psychoanalytic psychotherapy, made use of transference, the repetition of the past in the present, and interpretation. Equally important, the method included continuous developmental observations of the baby and a tactful, nondidactic education of the mother in the recognition of her baby's needs and her signals.

The setting was the family kitchen or the living room. The patient who couldn't talk was always present at the interviews if she wasn't napping. The patient who could talk went about her domestic tasks or diapered or fed the baby. The therapist's eyes and ears were attuned to both the nonverbal communications of the baby and the substance of the mother's verbal and nonverbal communications. Everything that transpired between mother and baby was in the purview of the therapist and in the center of the therapy. The dialogue between the mother and the therapist centered upon present concerns and moved back and forth between the past and the present, between this mother and child and another child and her family, in the mother's past. The method proved itself and led us, in later cases, to explore the possibilities of the single therapist in the home-based treatment.

We shall now try to summarize the treatment of Mary and her mother and examine the methods which were employed.

In the early hours of treatment, Mrs. March's own story emerged, haltingly, narrated in a distant, sad voice. It was the story we sketched earlier. As the mother told her story, Mary, our second patient, sat propped on the couch, or lay stretched out on a blanket, and the sad and distant face of the mother was mirrored in the sad and distant face of the baby. It was a room crowded with ghosts. The mother's story of abandonment and neglect was now being psychologically reenacted with her own baby.

The problem, in the emergency phase of the treatment, was to get the ghosts out of the baby's nursery. To do this we would need to help the mother to see the repetition of the past in the present, which we all know how to do in an office that is properly furnished with a desk and a chair or a couch, but we had not yet learned how to do this in a family living room or a kitchen. The therapeutic principles would need to be the same, we decided. But in this emergency phase of the treatment, on behalf of a baby we would have to find a path into the conflictual elements of the mother's neurosis which had direct bearing upon her capacity to mother. The baby would need to be at the center of treatment for the emergency period.

We began with the question to ourselves: "Why can't this mother hear her baby's cries?"

The answer to the clinical question is already suggested in the mother's story. This is a mother whose own cries have not been heard. There were, we thought, two crying children in the living room. The mother's distant voice, her remoteness and remove we saw as defenses against grief and intolerable pain. Her terrible story had been first given factually, without visible suffering, without tears. All that was visible was the sad, empty, hopeless look upon her face. She had closed the door on the weeping child within herself as surely as she had closed the door upon her crying baby.

This led us to our first clinical hypothesis: *"When this mother's own cries are heard, she will hear her child's cries."*

Mrs. Adelson's work, then, centered upon the development of a treatment relationship in which trust could be given by a young woman who had not known trust, and in which trust could lead to the revelation of the old feelings which closed her off from her child. As Mrs. March's story moved back and forth between her baby, "I can't love Mary," and her own childhood, which can be summarized, "Nobody wanted me," the therapist opened up pathways of feeling. Mrs. Adelson listened and put into words the feelings of Mrs. March as a child. "How hard this must have been. . . . This must have hurt deeply. . . . Of course, you needed your mother. There was no one to turn to. . . . Yes. Sometimes grown-ups don't understand what all this means to a child. You must have needed to cry. . . . There was no one to hear you."

The therapist was giving Mrs. March permission to feel and to remember feelings. It may have been the first time in Mrs. March's life that someone had given her this permission. And, gradually, as we should expect—but within only a few sessions—grief, tears, and unspeakable anguish for herself as a cast-off child began to emerge. It was finally a relief to be able to cry, a comfort to feel the understanding of her therapist. And now, with each session, Mrs. Adelson witnessed something unbelievable happening between mother and baby.

You remember that the baby was nearly always in the room in the midst of this living room-kitchen therapy of ours. If Mary demanded attention, the mother would rise in the midst of the interview to diaper her or get her a bottle. More often, the baby was ignored if she did not demand attention. But now, as Mrs. March began to take the permission to remember her feelings, to cry, and to feel the comfort and sympathy of Mrs. Adelson, we saw her make approaches to her baby in the midst of her own outpourings. She would pick up Mary and hold her, at first distant and self-absorbed, but holding her. And then, one day, still within the first month of treatment, Mrs. March, in the midst of an outpouring of grief, picked up Mary, held her very close, and crooned to her in a heart-broken voice. And then it happened again, and several times in the next sessions. An outpouring of old griefs and a gathering of the baby into her arms. The ghosts in the baby's nursery were beginning to leave.

These were more than transitory gestures toward rapprochement with the baby. From all evidence to Mrs. Adelson's observing eyes, the mother and the baby were beginning to find each other. And now that they were coming in touch with each other, Mrs. Adelson did everything within her capacity as therapist and developmental psychologist to promote the emerging attachment. When Mary rewarded her mother with a beautiful and special smile, Mrs. Adelson commented on it and observed that she, Mrs. Adelson, did not get such a smile, which was just the way it should be. That smile belonged to her mother. When a crying Mary began to seek her mother's comfort and found relief in her mother's arms, Mrs. Adelson spoke for Mary. "It feels so good when mother knows what you want." And Mrs. March herself smiled shyly, but with pride.

These sessions with mother and baby soon took on their own rhythm. Mr. March was often present for a short time before leaving for work. (Special sessions for him were also worked out on evenings and Saturdays.) The sessions typically began with Mary in the room and Mary as the topic of discussion. In a natural, informal, nondidactic way, Mrs. Adelson would comment with pleasure on Mary's development and weave into her comments useful information about the needs of babies at six months or seven months, and how Mary was learning about her world, and how her mother and father were leading her into these discoveries. Together, the parents and Mrs. Adelson would watch Mary experiment with a new toy or a new posture, and with close watching, one could see how she was finding solutions and moving steadily forward. The delights of baby watching, which Mrs. Adelson knew, were shared with Mr. and Mrs. March, and, to our great pleasure, both parents began to share these delights and to bring in their own observations of Mary and of her new accomplishments.

During the same session, after Mr. March had left for work, the talk would move at one point or another back to Mrs. March herself, to her present griefs and her childhood griefs. More and more frequently now, Mrs. Adelson could help Mrs. March see the connections between the past and the present and show Mrs. March how "without realizing it," she had brought her sufferings of the past into her relationship with her own baby.

Within four months Mary became a healthy, more responsive, often joyful baby. At our ten-month testing, objective assessment showed her to be age-appropriate in her focused attachment to her mother, in her preferential smiling and vocalization to mother and father, in her seeking of her mother for comfort and safety. She was at age level on the Bayley mental scale. She was still slow in motor performance, but within the normal range.

Mrs. March had become a responsive and a proud mother. Yet our cautious rating of the mother's own psychological state remained: "depressed." It was true that Mrs. March was progressing, and we saw many signs that the depression was no longer pervasive and constricting, but depression was still there, and, we thought, still ominous. Much work remained.

What we had achieved, then, in our first four months' work was not yet a cure of the mother's illness, but a form of control of the disease, in which the pathology which had spread to embrace the baby was now largely withdrawn from the child; the conflictual elements of the mother's neurosis were now identified by the mother as well as ourselves as "belonging to the past" and "not belonging to Mary." The bond between mother and baby had emerged. And the baby herself was insuring those bonds. For every gesture of love from her mother, she gave generous rewards of love. Mrs. March, we thought, may have felt cherished by someone for the first time in her life.

All this constitutes what we would call "the emergency phase of the treatment." Now, in retrospect, we can tell you that it took a full year beyond this point to bring some resolution to Mrs. March's very severe internal conflicts, and there were a number of problems in mother-child relationships which emerged during that year, but Mary was out of danger, and even the baby conflicts of the second year of life were not extraordinary or morbid. Once the bond had been formed, nearly everything else could find solutions.

## Other Conflictual Areas

We shall try to summarize the following months of treatment. Mary remained the focus of our work. Following the pattern already established, the therapeutic work moved freely between the baby and her developmental needs and problems and the mother's conflicted past.

One poignant example comes to mind. Mrs. March, in spite of new-found pleasure and pride in motherhood, could still make casual and unfeeling plans for baby-sitting. The meaning of separation and temporary loss to a one-year-old child did not register with Mrs. March. When she took part-time work at one point (and the family's poverty gave some justification for additional income), Mrs. March made hasty and ill-thought-out sitting arrangements for Mary and then was surprised, as was Mr. March, to find that Mary was sometimes "cranky" and "spoiled" and "mean."

Mrs. Adelson tried in all tactful ways to help the Marches think about the meaning to Mary of her love for mother and her temporary loss of mother during the day. She met a blank wall. Both parents had known shifting and casual relationships with parents and parent substitutes from their earliest years. The meaning of separation and loss was buried in memory. Their family style of coping with separation, desertion, or death was, "Forget about it. You get used to it." Mrs. March could not remember grief or pain at the loss of important persons.

Somehow, once again, we were going to have to find the affective links between loss and denial of loss, for the baby in the present, and loss in the mother's past.

The moment came one morning when Mrs. Adelson arrived to find family disorder: Mary crying at the approach of an old visitor, parents angry at a baby who was being "just plain stubborn." Thoughtful inquiries from Mrs. Adelson brought the new information that Mary had just lost one sitter and started with another. Mrs. Adelson wondered out loud what this might mean to Mary. Yesterday she had been left, unexpectedly, in a totally new place with a strange woman. She felt alone and frightened without her mother, and did not know what was going to happen. No one could explain things to her; she was only a baby, with no words to express her serious problem. Somehow, we would have to find a way to understand and to help her with her fears and worries.

Mr. March, on his way to work, stopped long enough to listen attentively. Mrs. March was listening, too, and before her husband left, she asked him to try to get home earlier today so that Mary would not be too long at the sitter's.

There followed a moving session in which the mother cried, and the baby cried, and something very important was put into words. In a circular and tentative way, Mrs. March began to talk about Aunt Jane, with whom she had lived during her first five years. There had not been a letter from Aunt Jane for some months. She thought Aunt Jane was angry at her. She switched to her mother-in-law, to thoughts of her coldness and rejection of Mrs. March. Complaints about the sitters, with the theme that one sitter was angry because Mary cried when her mother left. The theme was "rejection" and "loss," and Mrs. March was searching for it everywhere in the contemporary scene. She cried throughout, but somehow, even with Mrs. Adelson's gentle hints, she could not put this together.

Then, at one point, Mrs. March left the room, still in tears, and returned with a family photograph album. She identified the pictures for Mrs. Adelson. Mother, father, Aunt Jane, Aunt Jane's son who had been killed in the war. Sorrow for Aunt Jane. Nobody in the family would let her grieve for her son. "Forget about it," is what they said. She spoke about her father's death and her grandfather's death in the recent past.

Many losses, many shocks, just before Mary's birth, she was saying. And the family always said, "Forget about it." And then Mrs. Adelson, listening sympathetically, reminded her that there had been many other losses, many other shocks for Mrs. March long ago in her infancy and childhood. The loss of her mother, which she could not remember, and the loss of Aunt Jane when she was five years old. Mrs.

Adelson wondered how Mrs. March had felt then, when she was too young to understand what was happening. Looking at Mary, sitting on her mother's lap, Mrs. Adelson said, "I wonder if we could understand how Mary would feel right now if she suddenly found herself in a new house, not just for an hour or two with a sitter, but permanently, never to see her mother or father again. Mary wouldn't have any way to understand this; it would leave her very worried, very upset. I wonder what it was like for you when you were a little girl."

Mrs. March listened, deep in thought. A moment later she said, in an angry and assertive voice, "You can't just replace one person with another. . . . You can't stop loving them and thinking about them. You can't just replace somebody." She was speaking of herself now. Mrs. Adelson agreed, and then gently brought the insight back on behalf of Mary.

This was the beginning of new insights for Mrs. March. As she was helped to reexperience loss, grief, the feelings of rejection in childhood, she could no longer inflict this pain upon her own child. "I would never want my baby to feel that," she said with profound feeling. She was beginning to understand loss and grief. With Mrs. Adelson's help, she now began to work out a stable sitter plan for Mary, with full understanding of the meaning to her child. Mary's anxieties began to diminish, and she settled into her new regime.

Finally, too, we learned the dreaded secret which had invaded the transference to Dr. Zinn and caused her to take flight from psychiatric treatment. The morbid fear of being alone in the same room with the doctor, the obsessive sense of sin which had attached itself to Mary's doubtful paternity, had given us the strong clinical impression that Mary was "an incestuous baby," conceived long ago in childhood fantasy, made real through the illicit relationship with an out-of-wedlock lover. By this, we meant nothing more than "an incestuous fantasy," of course. We were not prepared for the story that finally emerged. With great shame and suffering, Mrs. March told Mrs. Adelson in the second year of treatment of her childhood secrets. Her own father had exhibited himself to her when she was a child and had approached her and her grandmother in the bed they shared. Her grandmother had accused her of seducing her elderly grandfather. This Mrs. March denied. And her first intercourse at the age of eleven took place with her cousin, who stood in the relationship of brother to her, since they shared the same house in the early years of life. Incest was not fantasy for Mrs. March. And now we understood the obsessive sense of sin which had attached itself to Mary and her uncertain paternity.

### Mary at Two Years of Age

During the second year of treatment, Mrs. Adelson continued as the therapist for Mrs. March. Dr. Zinn had completed his residency, and Mrs. March's transference to Mrs. Adelson favored continuity in the work with the mother. William Schafer, staff psychologist, became the guidance worker for Mary. (We no longer have separate therapists for parent and child, but in this first case we were still experimenting.)

It is of some considerable interest that in the initial meetings with Mr. Schafer, Mrs. March was again in mute terror as her morbid fear of "a man" was revived in transference. But this time Mrs. March had made large advances in her therapeutic work. The anxiety was handled in transference by Mr. Schafer, and brought back to Mrs. Adelson where it could be placed within the context of the incestuous material that had emerged in treatment. The anxiety diminished, and Mrs. March was able to make a strong alliance with Mr. Schafer. The developmental guidance of the second year brought further strength and stability to the mother-child relationship, and we saw Mary continuing her developmental progress through her second year, even as her mother was working through very painful material in her own therapy.

Are there residues in Mary's personality from the early months of neglect? At the time of this writing, Mary is two years old. She is an attractive child, adequate in all ways for her age, and presents no extraordinary problems in development. There may be residues which we cannot detect, or cannot yet detect. But at the present time they are not discernible to us. Are there depressive tendencies? None that we can discern. When frustrated, for example, she does not withdraw; she becomes very assertive, which we consider a favorable sign. What does remain is a shyness and inhibition of play, which seems related to temporary increases in mother's own social discomfort, as in new settings, or with strangers.

Mary's attachment to her mother and father appears to us as appropriate for her age. In spontaneous doll play, we see a strong positive identification with her mother and with acts of mothering. She is a solicitous mother to her dolls, feeding, dressing them with evident pleasure, murmuring comforting things to them. In her recent Bayley testing she threw the test procedures into disorder when she fell in love with the Bayley doll and could not be persuaded to do the next items on the test. She wanted to play with the doll; she spurned the block items which were next presented for tower building, and finally compromised on her own terms by using the blocks to make "a chair" for the doll.

It was in doll play at one year, ten months that Mr. Schafer heard her speak her first sentence. Her doll was accidentally trapped behind a door with a spring catch, and Mary could not recover it. "I want my baby. I want my baby!" she called out in an imperative voice. It was a very good sentence for a two-year-old. It was also a moving statement to all of us who knew Mary's story.

For us the story must end here. The family has moved on. Mr. March begins a new career with very good prospects in a new community that provides comfortable housing and a warm welcome. The external circumstances look promising. More important, the family has grown closer; abandonment is not a central concern. One of the most hopeful signs was Mrs. March's steady ability to handle the stress of the uncertainty that preceded the job choice. And, as termination approached, she could openly acknowledge her sadness. Looking ahead, she expressed her wish for Mary: "I hope that she'll grow up to be happier than me. I hope that she will have a better marriage and children who she'll love." For herself she asked that we remember her as "someone who had changed."

## Greg

Within the first weeks of our new program, we were asked to make an urgent call and an assessment of Greg, then three and a half months old. His sixteen-year-old mother, Annie, refused to care for him. She avoided physical contact with the baby; she often forgot to buy milk for him, and she fed him Kool-Aid and Tang. She turned over the baby's care to her nineteen-year-old husband, Earl.

Annie's family had been known to social agencies in our community for three generations. Delinquency, promiscuity, child abuse, neglect, poverty, school failure, psychosis had brought every member of the family to our community clinics and courts. Annie Beyer at sixteen now represented the third generation of mothers in her family who actually or psychologically abandoned their babies. Annie's mother had surrendered the care of her children to others—as did *her* mother. It was, in fact, Greg's grandmother, Annie's mother, who called our agency for help. She said, "I don't want to see what happened to me and my babies happen to Annie and her baby."

Vivian Shapiro of our staff called for an appointment and made a home visit immediately. Mother, father, and Greg were present. Mrs. Shapiro was greeted by a cold and silently hostile adolescent mother, a sad, bewildered boy who was the father, and a solemn baby who never once in that hour looked at his mother. Greg was developmentally adequate for his age, Mrs. Shapiro estimated, and her impressions were later sustained by our developmental testing. This spoke for some minimum adequacy in care, and we had good reason to believe that it was Earl, the father, who was providing most of Greg's care. At nearly every point in the one-hour session when Greg required care, Annie summoned her husband or picked up the baby and gave him to his father. He settled comfortably with his father and, for father, there were smiles.

During most of this session, and for many others that followed, Annie sat slumped in a chair. She was obese, unkempt, and her face registered no emotion. It was a mask which Mrs. Shapiro was to see many times, but when Annie brought herself to speak, there was barely controlled rage in her voice.

She did not want our help. There was nothing wrong with herself or her child. She accused her mother of a conspiracy against her and, in her mind, Mrs. Shapiro was part of the conspiracy. To win Annie's trust was to become the most arduous therapeutic task of those first weeks. To maintain the trust, after it was given, was equally difficult. It was a great advantage to Mrs. Shapiro, as it has been for all of us, to have come to this work with broad clinical experience with children and adolescents. An adolescent girl who defies her would-be helpers, who challenges, provokes, tests mercilessly, breaks appointments, disappears to another address, will not cause an experienced social worker to turn a hair. Mrs. Shapiro could wait to earn Annie's trust. But there was a baby in peril, and within only a few visits, we understood how great the peril was.

We began with the question to ourselves, "Why does Annie avoid touching and holding her baby?" To find the answers, we would need to know more about Annie than she was willing to give in those early hostile hours. And always there was Greg, whose own needs were imperative, and who could not wait for his teenage mother to make the therapeutic alliance which is slow-paced in adolescence. It was surely not ignorance of the needs of babies which distanced Annie from her child. Doctors and public health nurses had given wise counsel before we ever met the Beyer family. She could not use the good advice.

### An Illuminating Hour

In the sixth home visit, something of the therapist's caring for Annie as a lonely and frightened child came through. Annie began to speak of herself. It made her angry, she said warily, when her husband, when people, thought she wasn't doing enough for her baby. She knew she was. Anyway, she said, she had never liked holding a baby very much—ever since she was a little girl. When she was little, she had to take care of her younger sister. She would be given the baby and told to hold her. She much preferred leaving the baby on the couch.

And then, led on by tactful questions, she began to speak of her childhood. We heard about Annie, as a nine-year-old girl, responsible for the cleaning, cooking, and care of other siblings—after school hours. For any negligence in duties, there were beatings from her stepfather, Mr. Bragg.

Annie spoke of her childhood in a flat, dull voice, with only an edge of bitterness in it. She remembered everything, in chilling detail. What Annie told the therapist was not a fantasy, and was not distorted, since the story of Annie's family was factually recorded by protective agencies and clinics throughout our community. There was the mother who periodically deserted her family. There was the father who died when Annie was five years old. And there was Mr. Bragg, the stepfather, alcoholic, probably psychotic. For trivial misdemeanors he dragged Annie off to the woodshed and beat her with a lath.

When Mrs. Shapiro spoke to the feelings of Annie as a child, of anger, fear, helplessness, Annie warded off these sympathetic overtures. She laughed cynically. She was tough. Her sister Millie and she got so they would just laugh at the old man when it was over.

In this session, in the midst of Annie's factual account of childhood horrors, Greg began a fretful cry, needing attention. Annie went to the bedroom, and brought him back with her. For the first time in six visits, Mrs. Shapiro saw Annie hold Greg closely cuddled in her arms.

This was the moment Mrs. Shapiro had been waiting for. It was the sign, perhaps, that if Annie could speak of her childhood sufferings, she could move protectively toward her baby.

The baby clutched his mother's hair as she bent over him. Annie, still half in the past and half in the present, said musingly, "Once my stepfather cut my hair to here," and pointed to her ears. "It was a punishment because I was bad." When Mrs. Shapiro said, "That must have been terrible for you!" Annie, for the first time, acknowledged feelings. "It was terrible. I cried for three days about it."

At this point, Annie began to talk to the baby. She told him he was smelly and needed to be changed. While Annie was changing him, Greg seemed to be looking for something to play with. There was a toy beside him on the couch. It was, of all things, a toy plastic hammer. Annie picked up the toy hammer and tapped it, gently, against the baby's head. Then she said, "I'm gonna beat you. I'm gonna beat you!" Her voice was teasing, but Mrs. Shapiro sensed the ominous intention in these words. And while still registering, as therapist, the revealed moment, Mrs. Shapiro heard Annie say to her baby, "When you grow up, I might kill you."

It was the close of the session. Mrs. Shapiro said those things that would quiet the turbulence in Annie, supporting the positive strivings toward motherhood, allying herself with those parts of the ego of this girl-mother which sought protection against the dangerous impulses.

But this, we knew, as we talked together in an emergency session back at the office, would not be enough to protect the baby from his mother. If Annie had to rely upon her therapist as an auxiliary ego, she would need to have her therapist in constant attendance.

## An Emergency Clinical Conference

The question was, how could we help Annie and her baby? We now knew why Annie was afraid to be close to her baby. She was afraid of her own destructive feelings toward him. But we had read these signs from the breakthrough of unconscious impulses in the tease games with the baby. We could not interpret sadistic impulses which were not yet conscious to Annie herself. If we cooperated with the ego to maintain these sadistic impulses in repression, Annie would have to distance herself from her baby. And the baby was our patient, too. Our most vulnerable patient.

We were attentive to small positive signs in this session. *After* talking about her childhood terrors, even though the affect was flat in the telling, Annie did pick up her baby and hold him closely and cuddle him. And this was the first time we had seen closeness between mother and baby in six sessions. If Annie could remember and speak of her childhood suffering, could we open pathways which would free her baby from her own past and enable her to mother Greg? If Annie could be helped to examine her feelings toward the baby, if we could elicit the unspeakable thoughts, would Annie be able to reach out to her baby?

As an exercise in pure theory and method, we were probably on the right track in our thinking. The case considerations were derived from psychoanalytic experience. But this was not a psychoanalysis. As psychoanalytic consultant, Selma Fraiberg recalls that she suddenly found herself bereft of all the conditions and the protections against error which are built into the psychoanalytic situation.

First of all, the conditions of this therapy on behalf of a baby and his adolescent mother made it imperative to move quickly to protect the baby. Under all normal circumstances in therapy, we believe in cautious exploration; an assessment of the ego's capacity to deal with painful affects, an assessment of the defensive structure of the patient. As experienced therapists with adolescents, we also knew that to win the trust of this hostile girl might easily take months of work. And the baby was in immediate danger.

We were attentive to the defenses against painful affect which we saw in Annie. She remembered, factually, the experiences of childhood abuse. What she did not remember was her suffering. Would the liberation of affect in therapy increase the likelihood of her acting out toward the baby or would it decrease the risk? After thorough discussion of alternatives, we decided, with much trepidation, that the chances of acting out toward the baby would be greater if the anxiety and rage were not elicited in treatment. Selma Fraiberg recalls: "Speaking for myself, I clung to the belief that it is the parent who cannot remember his childhood feelings of pain and anxiety who will need to inflict his pain upon his child. And then I thought—but what if I am wrong?"

Then we would also be confronted with another therapeutic problem in this once-a-week psychotherapy. If we worked within the realm of buried affects, we could predict that the therapist who conjures up the ghosts will be endowed in transference with the fearsome attributes of the ghost. We would have to be prepared for the transference ghosts and meet them squarely every step of the way.

As we reviewed these conference notes one year later, we were satisfied that our treatment formulations had stood up well in the practical test. We now know, through the progress of our treatment, that the main lines of the work were well considered.

But now, we shall have to take you with us on a detour from the treatment, which turned out to be as important for the outcome as the psychotherapeutic plan.

Before any part of this treatment plan could be put into effect, Annie took flight from the therapist.

*Annie Locks the Door: A Flight from Treatment*

You remember that our emergency conference had followed the critical interview in which Annie began to speak of her childhood beatings in the sixth session. The seventh session was a home visit in which a number of Annie's relatives came to visit, and there was no opportunity to speak with Annie alone. In the eighth session, Mrs. Shapiro arranged to speak with both Annie and Earl about continuing visits and to invite them to raise questions with her about how we might best be able to help the Beyers. Earl was emphatic that he wanted Mrs. Shapiro to continue visiting them. He said that he felt that Mrs. Shapiro was helping them see things about Greg's development that they would never have been able to see themselves. Annie remained silent. When Mrs. Shapiro addressed herself to Annie's wishes, Annie said, with some hesitation, that she would like Mrs. Shapiro to continue to come. She would like to be able to talk about the baby and about herself.

In this hour, Annie herself picked up the narrative which had begun in the sixth session. She began, however, by speaking of her fears that Earl drove too fast, that he might have an accident. A child needed a father. Greg needed a father. This led her to speak of her own father,

her natural father, with some affection. After her father died when Annie was five years old, nobody ever really cared for her. There were several men in the household who lived with Annie's mother. There were six children, born to four different fathers. Millie was her mother's favorite. Annie said bitterly, "They didn't want me. I didn't want them. I didn't need anybody." She spoke again of Mr. Bragg and the beatings. At first, she used to cry, but he wouldn't stop. Then, later, she would laugh, because it didn't hurt anymore. He beat her with a lath. He would beat her until the lath broke.

After her father died, Annie's mother disappeared. She went to work in another city, leaving the children with an old woman. To punish the children, the old woman locked them out of the house. She remembered one night when Millie and she were locked out in the freezing cold and huddled together. Her mother never seemed to know what was going on. Even when she returned to her family, she went to work, and even when she wasn't working, she didn't seem to be around.

To all this, Mrs. Shapiro listened with great sympathy. She spoke of a child's need for protection. How frightening to a child to have no one to protect her. How much Annie missed her mother and a mother's protection. Perhaps she would be a different kind of mother to Greg. Would she feel she had to protect him? "Of course," Annie replied.

Very gently, Mrs. Shapiro spoke of the deep unhappiness and loneliness in Annie's childhood, and how difficult it was to be a young mother who had missed so much in her own childhood. Together, Mrs. Shapiro and Annie would talk about these things in their future visits.

It was, Mrs. Shapiro felt, a good visit. Clarification of the role of the therapist, an acknowledgment that Annie and Earl wanted help for themselves and for their baby. For Annie, the beginning of the permission to feel along with remembering. A permission that she was not yet ready to take. But this would come.

Following this visit, Annie refused to see Mrs. Shapiro. There were numerous broken appointments. Appointments were made, but Annie was not at home. Or Mrs. Shapiro would arrive at the door, with all signs of activity in the house, and Annie would refuse to answer the door. Annie, literally, locked the door against Mrs. Shapiro.

It is no consolation during a period like this to understand the nature of transference resistance while the patient barricades the door against the therapist. It is far worse to know that there are two patients behind the door, and that one of them is a baby.

As the memories of childhood terrors emerged in that last session, the original affects must have emerged—not in the treatment hour, but afterward—and the therapist became the representative of fears that could not be named. Annie did not remember or experience her anxiety during the brutal beatings by Mr. Bragg, but anxiety attached itself to the person of the therapist, and Annie took flight. Annie did not remember the terror of being locked out of the house by the woman who cared for her when her mother deserted the family, and to make sure that she would not remember, the ghosts and the ego conspired to lock Mrs. Shapiro out of the house. Annie did not remember the terror of abandonment by her mother, but she reenacted the experience in transference, creating the conditions under which the therapist might have to abandon her.

We were, ourselves, nearly helpless. But this is not to say that the psychoanalytic insight was without value. To understand all this gave us a measure of control in the countertransference. We were not going to abandon Annie and her baby. We understood the suffering behind the provocative, tough, and insolent adolescent posture, and could respond to the anxiety and not the defense.

The only thing we lacked was a patient who could benefit from the insight. And there was the baby who was more imperiled than his mother.

During the two-month period in which Mrs. Shapiro was locked out of the house, reports from grandparents, visiting nurse, and others increased our alarm. Annie showed phobic symptoms. She was afraid to be alone in the house. And she was pregnant again. Greg looked neglected. He was suffering from recurrent upper respiratory illness and was not receiving medical care. The paternal grandparents were alarmed for Greg and reported to Mrs. Shapiro that Annie was playing rough games with Greg, swinging him from his ankles.

Our own alarm for Greg brought us to a painful decision. In our hospital and in our community we were ethically and legally bound to report cases of neglect and suspected or actual abuse to Protective Services. In the case when treatment alternatives are rejected by the family (as in Annie's case), the report is mandatory. The law is wise, but in the exercise of our legal responsibility we would bring still another tragedy to the Beyer family.

This was a critical moment, not only for the family, but for Mrs. Shapiro and for our entire staff. There is no greater irony for the clinician than that in which he possesses the knowledge and the methods to prevent a tragedy and he cannot bring this help to those who need it. Clinically speaking, the solution to the problem resided in the transference resistance. Exploration of the negative transference with Annie would prevent further acting out. We all know how to deal with transference ghosts in an office with a patient who gives even grudging cooperation with our method. How do we deal with the negative transference when the patient has locked herself in a house with her baby and their ghosts and will not answer the door?

The considerations for Greg were paramount now. Mrs. Shapiro wanted to prepare Annie and Earl for the painful alternative which lay before us, a referral to Protective Services. But Annie refused to answer the door when Mrs. Shapiro called.

As a sad alternative, Mrs. Shapiro prepared a letter which was sent to Annie and Earl and to both sets of grandparents. It was a letter which spoke of our concern and deep caring for both of the young parents and for their baby. It cited the many attempts we had made to reach the family with our help and our continuing wish to help them. If they felt we could not help them, we would need to seek help for them elsewhere, and we would request the help of Protective Services. A reply was requested within the week.

We learned within a few days of the impact of this letter on Annie and Earl and the grandparents. Annie cried for the entire weekend. She was angry at Mrs. Shapiro. She was frightened. But on Monday she called Mrs. Shapiro. Her voice was exhausted, but she managed to say that everything in Mrs. Shapiro's letter was true. She would see Mrs. Shapiro.

*Extended Treatment*

This was the beginning of a new relationship between Annie and Earl and Mrs. Shapiro. Step by step, Mrs. Shapiro dealt with Annie's distrust, her anger toward Mrs. Shapiro and all "helping people," and clarified her own role as a helping person. Mrs. Shapiro was on the side of Annie and Earl and Greg and wanted to do everything possible to help them—to find the good things they wanted and deserved in life, and to give Greg all the things he needed to become a healthy and happy child.

For Annie, the relationship with Mrs. Shapiro became a new experience, unlike anything she had known. Mrs. Shapiro began, of course, by dealing openly with the anger which Annie had felt toward her and made it safe for Annie to put anger into words. In a family pattern where anger and murderous rage were fused, Annie had only been able to deal with anger through flight or identification with the aggressor. In the family theater, anger toward the mother and desertion by the mother were interlocking themes. But Annie learned that she could feel anger and acknowledge anger toward her therapist, and her therapist would not retaliate and would not abandon her.

It was safe to experience anger in transference to the therapist, and within this protected relationship the pathways of anger led back to childhood griefs and terrors. It was not an easy path for Annie. Yes, she acknowledged in a session soon after Mrs. Shapiro began visiting again, yes, she had felt bad about the therapist coming to see her. Yes, she resented her. "But what's the use of talking? I always kept things to myself. I want to forget. I don't want to think."

Mrs. Shapiro, with full sympathy for Annie's suffering and the need to forget, discussed with Annie how trying to forget did not get rid of the feelings or the memories. Annie would only be able to make peace with her feelings by talking about them to Mrs. Shapiro. Together, through talking, the therapist would be able to help Annie feel better.

In this same session, Annie did not reply in words. But at this point in the session she picked up Greg and held him very closely, rocking him in her arms. But the tension within her was transmitted to Greg; she was holding him too tightly and the baby began to protest. Yet we had seen Annie reach *spontaneously* for her baby, and this was a favorable sign. (Her awkwardness was to diminish over time, and we were later to witness a growing pleasure in physical intimacy with her baby.)

In successive sessions, Annie took the permission to speak of her feelings. The story of childhood privations, of brutality and neglect, began to emerge once again, as if the narrative begun two months ago could now be resumed. But this time Mrs. Shapiro knew what had caused Annie to take flight from treatment two months ago, and her own insight could be employed in a method which would prevent flight or acting out and would ultimately lead to resolution. It was not the telling of the tales which had caused Annie to take flight, but the unspoken affect which had been maintained in isolation from the memories. Annie, you remember, had described her stepfather's beatings with exact and chilling detail, but the affect was isolated. She laughed cynically throughout that early session. Somewhere between the factual reporting of beatings and neglect and the flight from Mrs. Shapiro, affect which had been maintained in partial repression had emerged and anger, fear, simple terror sought an object, a name for itself, and the name was Mrs. Shapiro.

This time, with the start of treatment, properly speaking, Mrs. Shapiro elicited affect along with the telling and made it safe to remember. When the story of childhood horrors emerged now, Mrs. Shapiro offered her own commentary. "How frightening to a child. You were only a child then. There was no one to protect you. Every child has a right to be taken care of and protected." And Annie said, with bitterness, "The mother is supposed to protect the children. My mother didn't do that." There was a refrain in these early hours which appears in the record again and again. "I was hurt. I was hurt. Everyone in my family is violent." And then another refrain. "I don't want to hurt anybody. I don't want to hurt anybody." Mrs. Shapiro, listening attentively, said, "I know you don't want to hurt anybody. I know how much you have suffered and how much it hurt. As we talk about your feelings, even though it is painful to remember, it will be possible to find ways to come to terms with some of these things and to be the kind of mother you want to be."

Annie, we saw, got both sides of the message. Mrs. Shapiro was on the side of the ego which defended against the unconscious wish to hurt and to repeat the hurts with her own child; at the same time, Mrs. Shapiro was saying, in effect, "It will be safe with me to speak of the frightening memories and thoughts, and when you speak of them, you will no longer need to be afraid of them; you will have another kind of control over them."

Mrs. Shapiro also anticipated with Annie the possibility of negative transference feelings that might arise during sessions where painful memories would be revived. Mrs. Shapiro said to Annie, "It may be that in talking about the past, you will feel angry toward me, without knowing why. Perhaps you could tell me when this happens and we can try to understand how your feelings in the present are connected to memories in the past."

For Annie, however, it was not easy to tell anyone she was angry. And she resisted putting into words her affect, so clearly evident in her face and body language. When Mrs. Shapiro asked Annie what she thought Mrs. Shapiro might do if Annie became angry with her, Annie said, "Sometimes I get close to people—then I get mad. When I get mad they leave." Mrs. Shapiro reassured Annie that she could accept Annie's angry feelings and she would not leave. With permission now to express anger, Annie's rage emerged in succeeding sessions, often in transference, and very slowly anger toward the objects of the past was reexperienced and put into proper perspective so that Annie could relate to her present family in a less conflicted way.

During all of these sessions, Mrs. Shapiro's watchful eye was upon Greg, always in the room. Would the rage spill over and engulf Greg? But once again, as in the case of Mary, we became witness to extraordinary changes in the young mother's relationship to Greg. In the midst of anger and tears, as Annie spoke of her own oppressive past, she would approach Greg, pick him up, enclose him in her arms, and murmur comforting things to him. We now know that Annie was no longer afraid of her destructive feelings toward the baby. The rage belonged to the past, to other figures. And the protective love toward Greg, which now began to emerge, spoke for a momentous shift in her identification with the baby. Where before she was identified with the aggressors of her childhood, she now was the protector of her baby, giving him what had not been given, or rarely given, in her own childhood. "Nobody," said Annie one day, "is ever going to hurt my child the way I have been hurt."

Mrs. Shapiro, in her work, moved back and forth between the story of Annie's past and the present. She helped Annie see how fear of the parental figures of her childhood had led her to identify with their fearsome qualities. As Annie moved toward a protective relationship with her own baby, Mrs. Shapiro fortified each of these changes with her own observations. Sometimes, speaking for Greg, Mrs. Shapiro would say, "Isn't it good to have a mommy who knows just what you need?" As Greg himself, now mobile, began to approach his mother more and more for affection, for comfort, for company, Mrs. Shapiro drew Annie's attention to each move. Greg, she pointed out, was learning to love and trust his mother, and all of this was due to Annie and her understanding of Greg. Annie was holding Greg now, cradling him protectively in her arms. We saw no more "playful" threats of beating and killing, which we had witnessed months ago. Annie was feeding the baby and using Mrs. Shapiro's tactful suggestions in providing the elements of good nutrition in the baby's diet.

In this family without traditions in child rearing, Mrs. Shapiro often had to be the tactful educator. In Annie's and Earl's families, even a seven-month-old baby was regarded as being capable of malice, revenge, and cunning. If a baby cried, he was "being spiteful." If he was persistent, he was "stubborn." If he refused to comply, he was "spoiled rotten." If he couldn't be comforted, he was "just trying to get someone's goat." Mrs. Shapiro always asked the question, "Why?" Why is he crying, why is he being stubborn, what could it be? Both parents, perhaps initially surprised by this alien approach to a baby, began to assimilate Mrs. Shapiro's education. More and more, as the weeks and months progressed, we saw the parents themselves seeking causes, alleviating distress by finding the antecedent conditions. And Greg began to flourish.

This is not to say that within a few months we had undone the cruel effects of Annie's own childhood. But we now had access to this past. When Annie's voice sometimes became shrill and she gave brusque treatment to Greg, Annie knew as well as Mrs. Shapiro that a ghost from Annie's childhood had invaded the nursery again. And together they could find meaning in the mood that had suddenly overpowered her.

As the baby progressed and Annie's conflicted past became sorted out, we began to see one figure emerge in Annie's childhood who stood for protection, tolerance, understanding. This was Annie's natural father, who had died when Annie was five. In Annie's memory he was kind and fair. He never beat her. He would never have allowed other people to be cruel to her, if only he had remained with the family. As she spoke of her own father, love and a remembrance of his loss overwhelmed her. Whether Annie's memory of her father was exact or not does not matter, of course. What does matter is that in the chaos and terror of her childhood there had been one person who gave her a sense of love and protection. In searching her past for something good, for some source of strength, this is what she found, and Mrs. Shapiro kept this good memory alive for Annie. We now understood another part of the puzzle. When we had first known the Beyer family, you remember, Annie had not only refused to care for her baby, but she regularly turned him over to her husband, the baby's father, for care. All of this had changed in the intervening months as Annie learned, through her therapist, how a mother, too, can be a protector to her child.

Greg himself began to show a strengthening of his bond to his mother within the early months of work. At ten months of age, just before Mrs. Shapiro left for vacation, his behavior toward his mother showed selective response and seeking of her, much smiling and seeking contact with her, approaches to mother for comfort and for company. But still some fear of mother, we saw, when her strident voice stopped him in the middle of some trivial misdemeanor.

During these months, we should now recall, Annie was pregnant. She rarely spoke of the coming baby to Mrs. Shapiro. It was as if the pregnancy was not real to her. There were no fantasies about the baby. She was fully preoccupied with her own self and with Greg, who was becoming the center for her.

In July, when Mrs. Shapiro was on vacation, Annie delivered a stillborn child. When Mrs. Shapiro returned, Annie was sad and burdened with guilt. The death of the baby, she thought, was a punishment to her. She had not wanted the baby, and she thought God did not want a baby to come into the world who would not be loved. Many hours were spent in putting together the experience of loss and self-reproach.

It was during this period too that Annie began to understand with help why she had not been ready for another baby. She was, indeed, drawing upon all of her impoverished emotional resources to give care and love to Greg and, in giving, she felt depleted. Many times we had the impression that she was sustaining herself through the warmth and caring of her therapist, borrowing strength, augmenting the poverty of her own experience in love through the relationship to her therapist. This was always a professional relationship, of course, but for a girl who had been emotionally starved and brutalized, this professional caring and understanding seemed to be experienced as the giving of love.

The unsatisfied hungers of childhood were persistent ghosts in this household. Often, when the therapist arrived, Annie and Earl were watching television. Their favorite TV shows were the children's programs and the animated cartoons. This was not for Greg's sake, we must assure you, since Greg himself had no interest in these shows. During the summer of the Watergate hearings, which were carried on nearly every channel, of course, Mrs. Shapiro saw Annie and Earl switch from channel to channel until they found a program they liked. It was The Jolly Green Giant.

When Mrs. Shapiro brought carefully selected toys for Greg (as we always do for our children when we know that the parents cannot provide them), Annie wore a conflicted look on her face. It was envy, Mrs. Shapiro realized, and longing. On one occasion, when Mrs. Shapiro brought some simple plastic toys for the baby, Annie said, in a voice full of feeling, "It's my birthday next week. I'll be seventeen." Mrs. Shapiro understood, of course. Annie wished the present were for her. The therapist, quickly responding, spoke of Annie's coming birthday, and her wish that it be a very special day. Annie said, "I never had a birthday. I never had a party. I'm planning to have one for Greg in August. My mother will probably forget my birthday." (Her mother did forget.) For Annie's birthday, Mrs. Shapiro brought a small, carefully chosen present for Annie.

On Greg's birthday, Mrs. Shapiro brought a toy bus for the baby. Annie opened the package. She was enraptured. She examined each of the little figures, opened the bus door, placed all the little people on the seats, and only when she had finished playing with it did she give it to Greg and share her excitement with him.

*The Last Ghost, the Most Obstinate One*

The last ghost to leave the nursery was also the first ghost to enter it. Its name, of course, was "identification with the aggressor." In its most formidable aspect this ghost no longer threatened the baby after the first months of therapeutic work; that is to say, there was no longer serious danger of abuse of Greg by his mother. We saw how the strengthening of the love bonds between Annie and her baby protected the child from physical abuse. We also saw how Annie's remembering of her own suffering became a form of protection to her baby. She would no longer inflict her pain upon her child.

At the end of the first year of treatment, then, Greg showed favorable signs of developmental progress and attachment to his mother.

But the ghost still lingered, and we saw it in many forms that still endangered Greg's development.

As Greg became active, independent, curious, and mischievous in his second year, Annie's repertoire of disciplinary tactics appeared ready-made from the ruins of her childhood. Maternal and protective and affectionate as she could be when Greg was quiet, obedient, and "good," there was a voice for disobedience or ordinary toddler mishaps which was strident, shrill, and of a magnitude to shatter the eardrums. Greg, at these moments, was frightened, and Mrs. Shapiro drew Annie's attention to the baby's reactions on many occasions. Then, very quickly it seemed to us, Greg acquired a defense against the anxiety produced in him by mother's anger. He would laugh, giddily, a little hysterically, we thought. This was of course exactly the defense which his mother had acquired in her childhood. Greg was sixteen months old when we witnessed the appearance of this defense.

Very clearly, an important component of Annie's defense—identification with the aggressor—had not yet been dealt with in the therapy. Annie had not yet fully experienced in therapy her childhood anxiety and terror before the dangerous, unpredictable, violent, and powerful figures of the past. From analytic experience we knew that the pathogenesis of the defense known as identification with the aggressor is anxiety and helplessness before the attackers. To reach this stratum of the defense structure through psychoanalysis is often a formidable task. How shall we reach it through our once-a-week psychotherapy-in-the-kitchen?

We examined the pathways available to us. Annie's voice, Mrs. Shapiro had observed, would shift in a single moment from a natural conversational voice which was her own to the strident, ear-shattering voice which seemed to be somebody else's. But Annie seemed not aware of this. The alien voice was also incorporated in her personality. Could we employ the on-the-spot manifestations of this pathological identification in a two-phase interpretive process? First, to make the voice ego-alien, identify it; then to interpret it as a defense against intolerable anxiety and lead Annie to reexperience her own childhood sense of terror and helplessness?

There was no difficulty finding the occasion in a home visit. The occasion, as it happened, appeared with startling clarity in a visit shortly after we examined the technical problems in our conference.

Greg, seventeen months old, was in his high chair, eating his breakfast. Mother kept up a stream of admonitions while he ate, "Don't do that. Don't drop the food off." Then suddenly responding to some trivial mishap in the high chair, Annie screamed, "Stop it!" Both Greg and Mrs. Shapiro jumped. Annie said to the therapist, "I scared you, didn't I?" Mrs. Shapiro, recovering from shock, decided this was the moment she was waiting for. She said, "Sometimes, Annie, the words and sounds that come out of your mouth don't even sound like you. I wonder who they do sound like?" Annie said immediately, "I know. They sound just like my mother. My mother used to scare me." "How did you feel?" Annie said, "How would you feel if you were in with a bull in a china shop? . . . Besides, I don't want to talk about that. I've suffered enough. That's behind me."

But Mrs. Shapiro persisted, gently, and made the crucial interpretation. She said, "I could imagine that as a little girl you might be so scared, that in order to make yourself less scared, you might start talking and sounding like your mother." Annie said again, "I don't want to talk about it right now." But she was deeply affected by Mrs. Shapiro's words.

The rest of the hour took a curious turn. Annie began to collapse before Mrs. Shapiro's eyes. Instead of a tough, defiant, aggressive girl, she became a helpless, anxious little girl for the entire hour. Since she could find no words to speak of the profound anxiety which had emerged in her, she began to speak of everything she could find in her contemporary life which made her feel afraid, helpless, alone.

In this way, and for many hours to come, Mrs. Shapiro led Annie back into the experiences of helplessness and terror in her childhood and moved back and forth, from the present to the past, in identifying for Annie the ways in which she brought her own experiences to her mothering of Greg, how identification with the feared people of her childhood was "remembered" when she became the frightening mother to Greg. It was a moment for therapeutic rejoicing when Annie was able to say, "I don't want my child to be afraid of me."

The work in this area brought about profound changes in Annie and in her relationship to Greg. Annie herself began to leave behind her tough, street-child manner, and the strident voice was muted. As the pathological identification with her own mother began to dissolve, we saw Annie seeking new models for mothering and for femininity, some of which were easily identified as attributes of Mrs. Shapiro.

And Greg began to respond to the changed climate of his home. As we should expect, the fear of mother and the nervous laugh as a defense against anxiety began to disappear. Since there were, in fact, strong bonds between mother and baby, there was much that Annie could now employ in an education of her son without fear.

Mrs. Shapiro enlisted mother as observer of Greg's attempts to communicate with her. Concrete suggestions and demonstrations were offered in a supportive noncritical way. This time, Annie was able to use the developmental guidance in a less defensive and more constructive way, working in alliance with the therapist on behalf of Greg. Within a month of first identifying Greg's need for help in language, he began to use language expressively and is now well within the normal range of the Bayley Scale.

Annie is pregnant again and is expecting her baby in the early fall. This baby, she tells us, is a wanted baby. Annie is anticipating the new baby with pleasure and with a new-found confidence in herself as a mother. She is carefully following medical counsel throughout the pregnancy. She and Earl have decided that two children will probably be just right for them. Annie does not think she has enough love or patience to spread over lots of children.

We don't know yet whether old ghosts will be present at this christening. There are positive indications, however, that the bonding process between Annie and this new baby has already begun. Annie is anticipating what the arrival of this new baby will mean to her, to Earl, and to Greg. As a young woman and not a fearful and defiant adolescent, Annie is telling Mrs. Shapiro now that babies are dependent, that they need a mother at home who will protect and comfort them, that Greg may be jealous, and that she will have to find ways to give Greg and Earl and the new baby the attention and the closeness they need. At the same time, Annie is able to express her own needs, to her therapist and to her husband. She is beginning to understand that she, too, can have the warmth and closeness she wants but has never had. Her relationship with Earl is also changing. Earl is planning to take two weeks off to be at home when the new baby arrives, to give help and support to Annie and the baby.

The bonds between Annie and her new baby are emerging. The

baby will be born at a time when Annie can establish a relationship unburdened by the ghosts of the past. If we can help ensure the bonds between Annie and her baby in the first days and weeks, we think the intruding ghosts will depart, as they do in most nurseries, when the child is protected by the magic circle of the family.

### Two Questions—And a Hypothesis

We began this essay with a question: "What is it, then, that determines whether the conflicted past of the parent will be repeated with his child?" Morbidity in the parental history will not in itself predict the repetition of the past in the present. The presence of pathological figures in the parental past will not, in itself, predict identification with those figures and the passing on of morbid experience to one's own children.

From the clinical studies of Mrs. March and Annie Beyer and from many other cases known to us, in which the ghosts of the parental past take possession of the nursery, we have seen a pattern which is strikingly uniform: these are the parents who, earlier, in the extremity of childhood terror, formed a pathological identification with the dangerous and assaultive enemies of the ego. Yet, if we name this condition in familiar terms, "identification with the aggressor," we have not added to the sum of our knowledge of this defense. Our literature in this area of defense is sparse. Beyond the early writings of Anna Freud, who named and illuminated this defense in the formative period of childhood, we do not yet know from large-scale clinical study the conditions which govern the choice of this defense against other alternatives, or the dynamics which perpetuate an identification with the enemy, so to speak.

We are on sound grounds clinically and theoretically if we posit that a form of repression is present in this defense which provides motive and energy for repetition. But what is it that is repressed? From a number of cases known to us in which "identification with the aggressor" was explored clinically as a central mechanism in pathological parenting, we can report that memory for the events of childhood abuse, tyranny, and desertion was available in explicit and chilling detail. *What was not remembered was the associated affective experience.*

Annie remembered her childhood beatings by her stepfather, and she remembered her mother's desertion. What she did not remember was the terror and helplessness in the experience of being abused and deserted. The original affects had undergone repression. When the therapeutic work revived these affects, and when Annie could reexperience them in the safety of her relationship to the therapist, she could no longer inflict this pain upon her child. Mrs. March could remember rejection, desertion, incestuous experience in childhood. What she could not remember was overwhelming anxiety, shame, and worthlessness which had accompanied each of these violations of a child. When anxiety, grief, shame, self-abasement were recovered and reexperienced in therapy, Mrs. March no longer needed to inflict her own pain and her childhood sins upon her child. With the reexperiencing of childhood suffering along with the memories, each of these young mothers was able to say, "I would never want that to happen to my child."

These words strike a familiar note. There are many parents who have themselves lived tormented childhoods who do not inflict their pain upon their children. These are the parents who say explicitly, or in effect, "I remember what it was like. . . . I remember how afraid I was when my father exploded. . . . I remember how I cried when they took me and my sister away to live in that home. . . . I would never let my child go through what I went through."

For these parents, the pain and suffering have not undergone total repression. In remembering, they are saved from the blind repetition of that morbid past. Through remembering they identify with an injured child (the childhood self), while the parent who does not remember may find himself in an unconscious alliance and identification with the fearsome figures of that past. In this way, the parental past is inflicted upon the child.

The key to our ghost story appears to lie in the fate of affects in childhood. Our hypothesis is that access to childhood pain becomes a powerful deterrent against repetition in parenting, while repression and isolation of painful affect provide the psychological requirements for identification with the betrayers and the aggressors. The unsolved mystery is why, under conditions of extremity, in early childhood, some children who later become parents keep pain alive; they do not make the fateful alliance with the aggressor which defends the child's ego against intolerable danger and obliterates the conscious experience of anxiety. We hope to explore these problems in further study.

The theory posited here, however incomplete, has practical implications for psychotherapy with parents and children in those families where the ghosts of the parental past have taken up residence in the nursery. In each case, when our therapy has brought the parent to remember and reexperience his childhood anxiety and suffering, the ghosts depart, and the afflicted parents become the protectors of their children against the repetition of their own conflicted past.

### Note

This paper is dedicated to the memory of Beata Rank, who asked the questions and sought the methods which illuminated the first years of life. The paper is an extended version of one given as the Beata Rank Memorial Lecture, Boston Psychoanalytical Society and Institute, May 23, 1974.

### Reference

Freud, A. (1936). *The Ego and the Mechanisms of Defense.* New York: International Universities Press, rev. ed., 1966.

# 5

# Infant-Parent Psychotherapy on Behalf of a Child in a Critical Nutritional State

*With Vivian Shapiro and Edna Adelson*

In this paper we describe the treatment of an infant boy who was referred to our Infant Mental Health Program at five months of age in a grave nutritional state. The baby was starving. His growth curve showed an ominous downward plunge which our pediatricians read as the profile of an infant who was moving toward the critical (and sometimes irreversible) state which is broadly covered by the term "failure to thrive." The term "failure to thrive" describes those infants who show growth failure in the absence of any organic cause. In strict usage it is employed for infants whose weight has fallen below the third percentile. It is almost universally associated with the impairment of the mother's capacity to nourish both in the concrete and in the psychological sense of the word.

The typical course of medical treatment for a failure-to-thrive infant is hospitalization with intensive one-to-one nursing care. With nurse-mothering and the introduction of a good nutritional regime, the baby begins to thrive. When his nutritional state is stabilized, he returns to his home. Typically, these gains are lost within a few weeks and the baby may return to the hospital again—and the cycle renews itself.

It is the mother who is the key. Whether or not the baby will thrive outside of the hospital depends upon the mother's capacity to follow the medically prescribed regime to insure adequacy in caloric intake for her baby and to provide the psychological nutriments for growth and development. But the dietary advice given by the hospital and the later guidance which focuses only on caloric intake and omits the developmental needs of infants are not successful (Whitten et al., 1969). All reports agree that families of failure-to-thrive infants are difficult to reach and to engage in continuing contracts. However, a more favorable outcome is reported by Leonard et al. (1966) and Barbero and Shaheen (1967) when mothers were able to collaborate with the physician, social worker, or public health nurse in a satisfying relationship established during the child's hospitalization and continued into the posthospitalization period. Barbero and Shaheen describe their experience in which parents are encouraged to become active members of the hospital care team. They speak with feeling for the parents who see the child's improvement during hospitalization as a threat to their competence. "It is around this point that the art of the physician is required to avoid such injury to the parent" (p. 644). In evaluating their experience, Barbero and Shaheen conclude: "Early case-finding and diagnosis are vital links in the process of intervention" (p. 644).

In our own experience at the Child Development Project we have benefited in several cases from "early case finding." We are indebted to the pediatricians, nurses, and social workers at the University of Michigan's Mott Children's Hospital who read the ominous signs in a child's nutritional state and a mother's incapacities to nurture.

Our Infant Mental Health Program brings the skills of a psychiatric team into the home. Clinical assessment of the child and his family and close collaborative work among the clinical specialists on our staff are carried out within the framework of home visits. The treatment program which evolves is provided by one primary therapist who may be a social worker, a clinical psychologist, an educational specialist, a pediatric nurse, or a psychiatric resident. The therapy is conducted in the family living room (or the kitchen). The baby as patient is usually present with one or both of his parents. The sessions are, of course, focused upon the baby and his development, the parental concerns, and inevitably the conflicts which are impeding the parent in his or her relationship with the baby. Our concerns for the parent as well as the baby have made us welcome visitors to many "hard-to-reach" families.

"Back at the office" there is a supporting team for every therapist and every family. The therapist—even the expert with years of clinical experience—discusses his case with a consultant in regularly scheduled sessions. We have found this plan vital to the conduct of our program. The work with infants in jeopardy and their parents is painful, often emotionally depleting to the therapist. To sustain energy, hope, and objectivity; to insure that the best professional resources of our clinic are brought to the treatment program for each child; to examine the treatment process in fine detail—we need each other and use each other's support and expertness.

Our work is guided by psychoanalytic principles and two of our senior staff members are child psychoanalysts who participate in the case review and planning in all intensive treatment cases. However, the treatment program for each family is properly speaking a collaboration of disciplines in which social work, clinical psychology, developmental psychology, special education, pediatrics, medicine, and nursing are united with psychoanalysis in every phase of the work.

In the case of Billy and his teenage parents which we describe in this report, Vivian Shapiro was the primary therapist, Edna Adelson and Selma Fraiberg were the consultants.

## Billy at Five Months

Billy Douglas* was referred to our project by the Child Health Center at the University of Michigan Medical Center when he was five months old. Billy vomited after each feeding. He had not gained weight in three months. He was a full-term healthy baby, whose birth weight of eight pounds put him in the seventieth percentile. At five months he weighed only fourteen pounds five ounces and was in the twenty-fifth percentile. He had become a tense, morose, somber baby who looked, in the doctor's words, "like a little old man." Dr. Robert Larson, then a pediatric resident at the Child Health Center, had worked intensively with Billy and his young mother for two months. Sensing the potential gravity of Billy's situation, he had begun to see Billy and his mother weekly at the outpatient clinic. He did extensive diagnostic studies and tried various medical interventions. He was puzzled, however, because there seemed to be no observable medical explanation for Billy's feeding difficulties. He also realized that the mother was becoming increasingly depressed.

Kathie Douglas was an anxious seventeen-year-old girl who had married Billy's twenty-one-year-old father, John, only two months before Billy's birth. She was often unable to carry through with sugges-

* This name, like all other patient surnames, is a pseudonym.—Ed.

tions regarding food and medication. Dr. Larson called in a public health nurse to see Billy and his mother weekly at home. Despite their best efforts, however, the doctor and the nurse observed that Kathie and Billy were not responding to their advice. At five months Billy's situation was critical. He was regressing and hospitalization was being considered. Further, Kathie seemed even more depressed, distant, and sometimes confused.

The medical team decided to make a referral to our Project. They requested both immediate clinical assessment and possible treatment for Billy and his mother. They were not certain there was a connection between the baby's health and the mother's deteriorating emotional status, but they felt that a better clinical understanding of Kathie and her baby might help explain why Billy was physically regressing and also indicate what psychological and medical interventions were needed.

**Clinical Evaluation**

Our first task, then, during this medical emergency, was to make a psychological assessment of Billy and his family. The therapist began twice-weekly visits to the home for direct observation of the baby, his parents, and their modes of interaction.

Under all ordinary circumstances we devote approximately five weekly one-hour sessions to the clinical evaluation period. In Billy's case, the nutritional and psychological perils were so great that we knew, after the first three visits (one and a half weeks), that intervention on a concrete educational basis must begin before the psychological complexities were fully understood. These earliest visits, however, gave us vital clues we could pursue in the emergency period.

*Initial Observations of Billy and His Parents*

When the therapist first arrived at the Douglas's small apartment, she met a timid, sad-faced seventeen-year-old-girl, who was Billy's mother, and a gaunt young man, the father, barely out of his teens, who was so uneasy that he did not acknowledge her presence until almost the end of this visit.

The therapist's first impression of Billy brought the doctor's words to mind. "Billy looked like a little old man." Billy was in his crib. He was up on his hands and knees, staring at the door, when she entered the room with his mother. His eyes met the therapist's with an intense stare and a fixed smile. His stare never wavered.

Billy was motorically very precocious and was able at five months to turn over quickly, to creep, to grasp and manipulate objects. On the whole, however, he was a very tense baby. All of his movements and efforts at communication had an urgency that was unusual in a baby of this age. When the therapist held him for a moment, she could feel the strain and tension in his body.

Billy seemed unusually aware of sounds. In particular, his mother commented that Billy responded quickly to any sounds related to feeding. She illustrated this by opening the refrigerator door while Mr. Douglas held the baby. Billy almost jumped out of his father's arms, his mouth opened, anticipating food, and his whole body strained toward the refrigerator. As his mother approached him with an eyedropper with vitamins, Billy, still in his father's arms, leaned back, opened his mouth, his hands became inert, and he looked like a starving baby bird awaiting food from his mother. Mother and father seemed uncomfortable with Billy. They treated him like a newly arrived stranger whom they had to approach cautiously and from a distance.

In early home visits the therapist saw that Billy spent his day either amusing himself on the floor or in bed. He was capable of spending a lot of time in solitary play with toys. There were few signs of human attachment. Even though he could creep, Billy rarely approached his mother. He rarely made eye contact with her. He rarely smiled unless his mother used gross tactile play. When he fussed his mother put him to bed with a pacifier and honey.

Billy's mother said sadly that Billy did not enjoy cuddling. She said that when she held him in her arms he seemed to turn away from her. In fact, neither mother nor father held Billy in a close ventral position. They held him so that he was constantly facing away from them.

Already, it was obvious to us that this baby and his parents were out of synchrony with each other. There was none of the normal spontaneity or joy in mutual gazing one would expect between parents and baby at his age. Billy was a somber, tense baby who seemed to be starving. His mother was also morose and somber and, as we shall see, both parents were hungry and starving in their own way.

We soon learned that this new family was in a state of great stress and deprivation. They were living in poverty, supported only by Mr. Douglas's small earnings and food stamps. In addition to the financial stress, Mr. and Mrs. Douglas had lost the support system of their extended families by their move to a strange city. They felt abandoned and overburdened. There simply were not enough financial or emotional resources in this new family unit to satisfy the needs of mother, baby, and father.

Billy's mother, at seventeen, seemed pathologically young and childlike. Her schoolgirl face, her T-shirt bearing a high-school insignia, gave her the appearance of a girl surprised by the events that had brought her to motherhood.

In response to the therapist's comment that this year must seem different from last year when she was still at school, Kathie spoke of her feelings of loss. She missed her hometown, her high-school friends. She missed going to school. So much was unfinished and now everything had come to an end. In her mind Kathie was not Mrs. Douglas; she was a misplaced teenager keeping house. All this emerged in a sad and distant voice. The therapist was struck by the depth of Kathie's depression, which was evident in her posture as well as in her words. Her range of affect was constricted. Her movements were slow. Her speech was halting, and she seemed distant and sometimes confused. She rarely made eye contact with the therapist.

The full weight of Kathie's depression soon became evident. She said that most of the time she was holding back feelings of rage that were so strong that "if I let go, I would kick the walls out of the house." She was having many somatic complaints, headaches, backaches, gynecological problems, and was also overweight. She sadly spoke of herself as feeling and looking like a fat old lady. She felt guilty about imposing on her husband for his time and attention.

John Douglas was also very young. At twenty-one, he was haggard, thin, frightened, and embarrassed by difficulties he could no longer cope with by himself. He was much more hesitant than Kathie to engage in any interaction with the therapist. He literally turned away from her during her first few meetings with him. When he did talk to her, it was through a teasing question to Billy. "Billy, do you want to go home with her?" We believe he was simultaneously expressing his ambivalence about Billy and questioning the therapist's attitude toward his own worth as a parent. The first time he directly looked at her and smiled was about a month after she started visiting when he told her that Billy seemed happier, that he liked to play more.

Billy's state and his feeding problem made intervention imperative, yet, after two sessions in the home, we had not yet observed a feeding which would provide tangible clues. Although the therapist had arranged to come at mealtimes, Kathie avoided feeding Billy in her presence. Kathie was, perhaps, not yet sure of her, not yet ready to reveal herself in the situation in which she was most inadequate. It was in the third session that Kathie volunteered to let the therapist see how Billy was fed.

*How Is Billy Fed?*

As part of our assessment a video play session was arranged at our office playroom. This session was primarily planned so as to permit the baby's own play as well as spontaneous mother-baby interaction.[1] What occurred gave us a sobering picture of the isolation and the estrangement of baby and mother. As if he were alone in the room, the baby engaged in solitary exploration of toys and furniture. He never once sought his mother with his eyes. He was mobile, but never crept toward his mother. His mother looked distant and self-absorbed.

Then Billy uttered sounds of complaint. His mother said that it was time for his bottle and volunteered to feed Billy. She said, "Watch what he does when I show him the bottle." She placed the bottle on the floor, several feet away from Billy, who was on hands and knees. Billy's face registered alertness and urgency—no smile, but urgency. And the five-month-old baby began to creep the long distance toward the bottle. He reached for it unsteadily, but could not quite grasp it. Finally he did grasp it, mouth open hungrily, but it was bottom up. He could not quite orient it. At last he got the nipple into his mouth. He sucked solemnly, greedily.

While the therapist watched this scene, masking her inner pain and horror, the schoolgirl mother explained that this was the way Billy took his bottle. "He likes it that way. He likes to have his bottle alone, on the floor."

After a while the therapist suggested that Mrs. Douglas sit with Billy in our rocking chair and feed him. The second observation gave us another piece of the puzzle. Kathie now held Billy loosely in her arms. Billy was still supporting his own bottle. The mother looking tired and apathetic, said that Billy usually finished his bottle in four minutes. "Sometimes, however, if the bottle is slow, it takes an hour." She talked as though it were his feeding, not something that she had anything to do with. She herself looked distant and empty. Our impression was that although Billy was in his mother's arms, he was still feeding himself. There was no mutual gaze, and little tactile contact. The mother was right: the baby turned away from her. She looked uneasy and sad and sometimes irritated.

Later in this visit Kathie started to rock herself in the rocking chair while holding Billy loosely in her arms. She looked like a little girl rocking herself, almost a parallel play situation, the hungry adolescent mother rocking and nurturing herself, allowing her baby to drink his bottle in her arms. Yet, as cold as the scene appeared to us, Kathie seemed to get some pleasure from this unusual closeness between herself and Billy. While watching this videotape later she commented that this was in fact a good feeding, a better feeding than usual.

### Why Can't Kathie Feed Her Baby?

As a treatment team we reexamined the videotape and the detailed notes of the home visits. We asked ourselves, "Where shall we begin? This is a schoolgirl mother who cannot feed her baby and who avoids physical contact with him." To encourage intimacy in feeding leads at best to mechanical compliance, as we saw on tape. There were few rewards for mother or baby.

Yet, we must promote this intimacy and proper feeding and we must, at the same time, seek the answers to the crucial diagnostic questions that will lead to help. What lies behind the avoidance of physical contact? Is it the destructive rage which Kathie had expressed in her first session? "I could kick the walls out of this house." Is it the mother's own unsatisfied hungers, body hungers as well as psychological hungers, which have led her unconsciously to withhold love and nourishment from her child? Was there something else on the mother's face and in her voice and manner as we watched the video story. An aversion to feeding? Disgust?

We would have to find out much more. But a teenage girl, even under more favorable circumstances, does not give her trust so readily to a helping person. We would need time to explore the dimensions of this conflict. But this teenage girl was a mother, her baby was our patient, too—and the baby was in great peril.

No case report can ever do justice to the feelings of the therapist who works with infants and their parents. There is an urge to rescue the baby who is in danger, to mother him oneself. There are deep reproaches, even anger toward the schoolgirl who is starving her baby, which must be expressed and which must be dealt with by the therapist lest it intrude in the work. In this situation we were helped by the fact that all of us are child therapists. We saw the mother herself as a child, an unfinished adolescent who still needed a mother herself. She was frightened, helpless, hungry, depleted. This did not imply that the therapist must become a mother or a mother substitute, but if we understood the child who was the mother and responded to her feelings of anguish and deprivation, we might earn her trust. Only on this basis was there hope for treatment.

In the home visits that followed the illuminating feeding session, Kathie began to respond to the therapist's deep concern for her as well as the baby. She began to speak of deep revulsion in the feeding of Billy. She was repelled by Billy's vomiting, she confessed, and had been since his birth. She was sickened by the sight, the messiness. The therapist saw for herself the horror and panic which came over Kathie when she anticipated—or only imagined—that the baby was going to spit up or vomit.

At the end of a bottle feeding (Billy was taking his bottle on the floor), Kathie hurriedly picked up Billy to burp him. We would expect, of course, that she would hold Billy upright against her shoulder. Instead, she rushed to the bathroom with the baby, faced him over her arm so that he was hanging over the bathroom sink—and Billy vomited his meal into the sink. In this way Kathie avoided her worst fears that the baby would throw up in her arms. And the strategy that she employed virtually guaranteed that the upside-down baby would throw up his dinner.

Until the therapist discussed her observations with Kathie, it had not occurred to the mother that she was precipitating the baby's vomiting. In her mind the only alternative was dreadful: to have the baby vomit in her arms.

Thereafter Kathie could tell us more. She had noticed that when Billy was three months old and had begun taking solids in his diet, the hue and texture of the vomit had changed. She was so repelled that

she reduced Billy's solids to a minimum as a way of avoiding the re-
volting mess. We now had another vital clue: the decline in Billy's
weight curve had started at three months.

What, in fact, constituted Billy's daily food intake? Kathie was not
sure. During the first visits the therapist often heard Billy's piteous
cries of hunger. When she said to both parents that Billy seemed very,
very hungry, they were astonished. The father said, "Do you think he
is still hungry? I think he is just like me. I could never be satisfied. I
could eat everything that was given to me right now." The mother said
resentfully that Billy never seemed satisfied; he was always begging
for food. "If we gave him everything he wanted, he'd eat us out of house
and home."

It soon became clear that neither of these young parents had any
real sense of how much food Billy needed. Actual hunger was part of
their daily experience and they had to limit severely their own appe-
tites in many ways. At some level both Kathie and John seemed to feel
that Billy would simply have to share in their hunger. Apparently,
they did not fully understand that his life was at risk.

### Assessment and Intervention Plan for the Emergency Period

Our initial assessment gave us many of the vital clues to Billy's
feeding problem. Billy was starving. But he was not "refusing" food, he
was being deprived of food. The vomiting, according to our observations, was induced by his mother's unique procedures for burping,
which were in turn related to her dread of being defiled by vomit.

The psychological picture was beginning to emerge: a teenage
mother who avoided contact with her baby; a baby who crept toward
his bottle on the floor and fed himself; a mother who had a deep inner
revulsion against messiness and possibly toward the baby himself; a
mother who was afraid of her own destructive rage; a mother who was
an adolescent with unsatisfied bodily and psychological hungers.

The baby was in nutritional peril and in great psychological peril,
for in none of our observations did he show signs of attachment to
either of his parents. At an age where preferential smiling and vocalization should emerge toward the baby's partners, we saw none. At an
age where the baby normally seeks eye contact with his partners, we
saw gaze avoidance. At an age when a mobile baby seeks his partners
through his own mobility, Billy sought no one. He did not enjoy

closeness in his mother's arms, and was stiff and resistant in the arms of any human partner. His mental abilities seemed well within the Bayley ranges, which testified for some adequacy in stimulation and experience.[2] But what could not be measured through any existing scale was the effect of emotional impoverishment and unsatisfied body hungers in this baby, now almost six months old.

At this point we faced a therapeutic dilemma. As clinicians we knew that the psychopathology of these young parents, and particularly the mother, would not be accessible to us within a few weeks, but the baby could not wait for the resolution of his mother's neurosis.

In this medical and psychological emergency we formulated our plans for the first phase of treatment. We would concentrate on the feeding problem, giving direct advice and guidance. We would do everything possible to promote the attachment of baby and mother. We would use our clinical insights to guide us during this emergency period, but we would not expect to gain full understanding of the parental psychopathology at this time.

The transference to the therapist would be fully utilized in this emergency period. This was an adolescent girl with her own developmental needs. The therapist's professional caring could be a form of nurturance for the mother. The adolescent need for identification models could be employed in a sensitive offering of this professional help.

## The Emergency Period of Treatment

The period that we speak of as "emergency treatment" lasted for two months. It was really synchronous in time with the assessment period. During this period Billy began to eat normally, the vomiting virtually ceased, and he began to gain weight in a stable and satisfactory manner.

### The Therapeutic Relationship

The therapeutic sessions with Billy and his mother took on a pattern that was set by Kathie. She had chosen a meeting time at home shortly before Billy napped. At the beginning of each visit, the focus was on Billy. Either the therapist and Kathie would observe Billy playing or Kathie would feed him or have some questions or—more often—complaints about Billy. Usually, midway through the visit, Kathie would put Billy to bed and the remainder of the time would be hers.

The therapist found out very quickly that if she responded to Kathie's own needs and feelings, either covertly or overtly expressed by her, Kathie would soon, and often in the same session did, attend to some of Billy's needs. For example, as the therapist acknowledged that she understood how hard it was for Kathie to try and hold a baby who turned away, Kathie was able to hold Billy with tears in her eyes instead of putting him down.

Many aspects of the positive transference became available to the therapist in helping Kathie on behalf of Billy. Kathie was initially very dependent and related to the therapist as a child to mother. (For example, when the therapist visited, she had to let herself in, hang up her coat, find a place to sit down while Kathie often continued to sit slumped in a chair in the living room.) The therapist responded to Kathie's need for a mother, while taking care, of course, to offer her another kind of "caring for Kathie" which was part of a therapeutic relationship.

The therapist sympathized with Kathie's sense of loss in leaving her own family and in leaving childhood as an unfinished adolescent. She responded to Kathie's feelings that no one cared for her and that she was physically deteriorating. She helped to arrange free medical service for Kathie at a health clinic which had been available but which she had not been able to seek out. She encouraged Kathie in her efforts to finish high school, and praised her for any accomplishments regarding her own efforts to continue her artwork.

We knew that Kathie felt inadequate, had been told she was by her mother, and in a sense by Billy himself as he repeatedly seemed to reject her food. The therapist was very careful not to compete with Kathie in any way for Billy's attention, nor did she actually intervene and do things for Billy, even though at times she could hardly restrain herself. It was important for Kathie to feel that the therapist, as a child consultant, identified with her as a mother facing problems in caring for her baby and that she had confidence that Kathie, with her help, could give Billy what he needed to be a healthy baby. Together they observed Billy, his preferences and his dislikes and took joy in any of his accomplishments. Billy's accomplishments were always related back to Kathie's efforts. The therapist especially shared her observations with Kathie of any special feeling that Billy expressed toward her, as his mother, such as a preferential smile or a reaching out to her. Kathie's feeling of failure was so strong that she was amazed when Billy preferred to go to her rather than to the therapist. She clung to any bit of evidence that Billy liked her. When she saw the scene of herself in the rocking chair with Billy, she said, "That looks so peaceful. Billy looks so contented."

## Guidance: Infant Nurture and Mother Nurture

Within this framework, and relying very largely upon the positive transference, the therapist introduced suggestions for feeding and burping Billy that were effective in a very short time. While these issues are treated topically in the pages that follow, they were actually concurrent and interwoven in every session.

The first concrete changes came in Kathie's willingness to try to hold Billy for a feeding. Kathie had said that Billy did not like to be held; she knew this because he turned away. The therapist commented that even though Billy turned away, his body seemed to be more relaxed and she thought this indicated that he did like his mother to hold him. It was obvious that Kathie's bland, sad face could not hold Billy's attention when she was trying to feed him in her arms. One time, as the therapist watched Kathie try to feed Billy in her arms, Billy repeatedly turned away. Seeking a tactful way to guide Kathie to a livelier exchange with her baby, the therapist asked her if she ever told Billy stories. She said, "No." The therapist asked if she could tell Billy a story while Kathie held him and she agreed. The therapist began her story, "Once upon a time there were three bears," using what Stern (1973) describes as "normal baby talk expression"—elongation of smile, rise and fall of voice, exaggerated nuances. All of these are typical exchange behaviors between baby and mother. All were missing from Kathie's conversation with Billy.

Billy and his mother *both* loved the story. Billy began to smile and make eye contact with the therapist and his mother, as together they watched him. Kathie so enjoyed this herself, as both child and mother, that she herself began to tell Billy stories and, of course, Billy quickly began to respond. However, this took so much effort on Kathie's part that she was often fatigued and once again lapsed into her silent behavior.

A major concern was the burping process. The therapist had made many suggestions to Kathie about burping Billy, and had tried to help Kathie understand how her method would precipitate vomiting. It was only when the therapist actually stood beside Kathie, however, and shared with her the tension she was feeling, as she put Billy gently over her sholder with the diaper underneath him, that she was gradually able to begin burping Billy in a normal fashion.

Kathie began to feed Billy the bottle in her arms on a regular basis, but did not yet give him solids. During a number of interviews it became clear that this was part of more complicated feelings about feeding Billy. At this point we identified two fears: Kathie's fear that "Billy would eat the family out of house and home" and that he would throw up endlessly.

While we recognized that these fears were deeply rooted in Kathie's personality, we knew that we could not uncover the origins of these fears in the emergency period. And Billy's needs were paramount. We would have to help Kathie in a concrete, educational way to provide caloric adequacy for Billy.

The therapist could use the positive transference in supporting Kathie step by step in a feeding program for Billy. It was futile, of course, to challenge Kathie's irrational belief that Billy would "eat the family out of house and home" or that he would "throw up endlessly." The therapist only sympathized with Kathie's fears and led her gently into a collaboration on Billy's behalf.

With pencil and paper and measuring cups the therapist and Kathie worked out quantities and sample feedings. We soon saw that Kathie could follow this regime. Long afterward we are still wondering how this was possible in view of the fact that quantities of food were still bound to profound conflicts in Kathie. Our best guess is that the objective, "on paper" feeding plan relieved Kathie of the responsibility for dealing with her own unconscious and dangerous impulses toward her baby. The therapist, "siding with the ego," was lending her own quiet authority to support Kathie's positive strivings to mother and her defenses against the destructive wishes.

In many discussions with the therapist, Kathie expressed her fear and revulsion of Billy's throwing up. The therapist acknowledged that she could understand how especially difficult it was for Kathie to hold and feed Billy. She told Kathie that together they would pay special attention to ensure that Billy would not throw up through overeating and that she wanted Kathie to observe carefully how much he ate and whether or not he threw up. With much relief that the therapist understood her difficulty, Kathie agreed to place Billy on a solid feeding schedule, which she and the therapist monitored carefully.

Billy began to gain weight steadily. Vomiting virtually disappeared. By seven months Billy had gained two and a half pounds and reached the fiftieth percentile in weight; Dr. Larson was satisfied that Billy was no longer in nutritional peril (see Fig. 1).

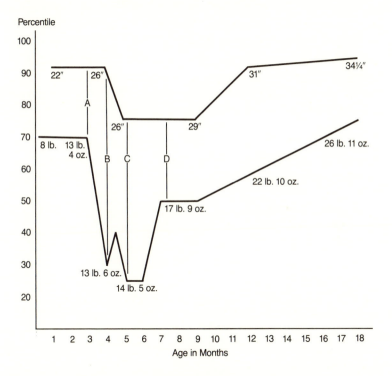

FIG. 1. Growth Curves Related to Intervention. Upper curve represents height in inches; lower curve, weight in pounds. Percentiles for infant boys are based on the anthropometric chart of the Children's Medical Center, Boston.

A. Mother depressed, baby vomitting (hospital notes)
B. Extensive medical outpatient intervention begins
C. Crisis referral to Infant Mental Health Program
D. Emergency ends; extended treatment begins

*The Family's Progress*

During the time this work was progressing, we were, of course, concerned with the well-being of the whole family, Mr. and Mrs. Douglas and Billy. An important part of the work was the help that was given Mr. Douglas. He came from a large, impoverished family and had suffered physical and emotional privations in his own childhood. As a young husband and father he was again struggling with poverty and hunger, and his depressed young wife drained his emotional resources. Each member of the family was hungry for physical and emotional sustenance. When John was home, he, too, shared his worries with the therapist, who responded with sympathetic understanding and with attention to his problems. She helped John and Kathie find ways to work out their present financial difficulties. She let them know that their hunger was her concern as well.

In summary, the work during the emergency period brought Billy to nutritional adequacy and his parents had formed a strong alliance with the therapist on behalf of their baby. Kathie, however, was still depressed, and we remained concerned about her and Billy.

## The Extended Treatment Phase

*Reassessment*

The period that we speak of as the extended treatment phase carried the work with Billy and his parents for a full year beyond the emergency period. While Billy had made progress, we still regarded him as a baby "at risk" in the psychological sense.

In the area of human object relations we saw much we considered ominous. Billy did not respond to his parents in ways that were appropriate for a child of his age. Billy still avoided eye contact with his mother, by turning away. He preferred play with toys rather than human partners. When he was hungry or in need, he still cried helplessly and piteously.

It seemed to us that Kathie was now able to follow much of the therapist's advice, but her responses were always mechanical. She was still unable to mother Billy in a harmonious and spontaneous manner; she still seemed estranged from her baby. She appeared to hold back food and only slowly responded to Billy's hunger cries. She was not empathic with Billy's attempts to communicate distress or hunger. The interaction between mother and baby was still erratic, and Billy could never really count on a pleasurable response from his mother. Very often Kathie teased Billy with food and seemed to be competing with him.

As part of our continuing assessment, when Billy was seven and a half months old, we videotaped another playroom visit which included a Bayley developmental assessment and a spontaneous feeding.[3] This tape spoke eloquently for the mother's ambivalence toward her baby and for pathological tendencies in both.

In one scene Kathie was holding Billy in her arms in a close and tender way while she was feeding him his bottle. Suddenly, Kathie pulled the bottle away, tossed back her head, dropped some milk in her own mouth, and then engaged Billy in a teasing game, in which she was competing with him for his bottle. It was painful to watch, but more painful was our witness to the baby's reactions: he was laughing. He had become a partner in this sadomasochistic game, a game that was repeated several times.

We have learned to give such "baby games" serious clinical attention. Some of our most important clinical insights have been derived from observing parents at play with their babies. The parent in conflict frequently reveals the essence of the conflict in play, in the "harmless games" (Fraiberg, 1974).

What we saw on tape, then, was a young mother competing with her own baby for his bottle. The moments of tender mothering were interrupted by an intruding thought, and feeding the baby became "teasing the baby," "taking food out of his mouth," "jealousy," "competition." As we watched this tape as a staff, we were struck by the thought that the mother behaved as if her baby were a sibling—and at that point the story began to come together for us.

## The Ghost in Billy's Nursery

By this time we had come to know a fair amount about Kathie and her own childhood. In the emergency phase of treatment, this was information which we could register and store, but could not put to use for Kathie's treatment. Kathie had regarded herself as the unwanted middle child of her family, the no-good child who could "never do anything right." While Kathie had spoken with some acidity about her mother and her older sister, she could barely control her rage when she spoke about Essie, her sister younger by five years. "Essie got everything," she said bitterly. Her memories of Essie, which may have been distorted, linked Essie to food in many ways. One of the bitterest memories, possibly a screen memory, was of a time when Kathie's parents took Essie out for an ice-cream cone and left Kathie home to do the dishes. Essie was the good child, the child that Kathie's mother favored.

We knew that Billy had been the "intruder" in Kathie's current life, the unwanted baby, the baby who "spoiled everything" for her, the baby who was taking food out of her mouth. There was a ghost in Billy's nursery, we thought, and the name of the ghost was Essie. Essie was the first intruder, the first baby in Kathie's life, who deprived her of the good things in life, of mother, and, in symbolic terms, of food.

If we were right, the therapeutic problem for us was to get the ghost out of the baby's nursery. We would need to help Kathie deal with the repetition of the conflicted past in the present, to disengage Billy from the figures of the past.

## The Infantile Conflicts and Repetitions in the Present

Our treatment during this period united guidance on behalf of Billy and a therapy which explicitly focused on Kathie's conflicts in mothering and their origins in her own childhood conflicts. The setting remained the same: home visits, scheduled twice weekly. Kathie was a willing and eager collaborator in her own treatment, to find out "why" she felt herself the victim of her own past.

Typically, the sessions would begin with Billy in the living room or the kitchen, and the therapist and Kathie would speak about his progress, or discuss any of Kathie's questions. The therapist continued, of course, to offer her observations and to help Kathie observe Billy, to interpret his needs and his signals, to praise his accomplishments and her own growth as a mother. Kathie's own needs for the therapist's time sometimes brought her into competition with Billy. Billy always had "his" time, during part of each session, and sometimes when Kathie felt most urgently in need of time with the therapist, she would say, "Shh, Billy, it's my turn now." Usually, the visits were timed so that

Billy's nap would divide the time and give Kathie some time for privacy.

In nearly every session childhood grievances appeared with more and more intensity. But vitriolic hatred toward Essie, the first intruder, dominated many of these hours.

The transference was employed both to open up the past and to offer Kathie the "unfinished adolescent," a new figure for identification and for undoing the powerful effects of her own mother, remembered as rejecting, critical, suspicious, and harsh, the "witch-mother" of early girlhood and adolescence.

The flow of memories converged again and again on the time following the birth of Essie, a period which marked a profound shift in Kathie's relationship to her own mother. Allowing for much distortion in adolescent memory, the figure of Essie, the baby who robbed Kathie of her mother, and the figure of the mother who "rejected" Kathie for the new baby were persistent ghosts. Along with these memories came overwhelming feelings of grief, depression, mourning for herself as a neglected, unwanted child. These were the feelings which had been revived with the birth of Billy. In Kathie's living room, with her own baby, the therapist often had the eerie feeling that she was witnessing another time, that Kathie was again the bereaved five-year-old robbed for the second time by a baby. Motherhood had brought regression, and Kathie was locked once again in the infantile conflict.

The relationship with the therapist opened up many pathways for "undoing." "My mother never listened to me," was Kathie's reproach, a recurrent theme in these hours, but the therapist listened and responded to Kathie's feelings of grief and rage. "My mother said I was bad. It was bad to hate my sister." The therapist acknowledged and accepted the feelings of jealousy and anger toward the sister "who got everything." "My mother never understood me." The therapist explicitly told Kathie that she wanted to understand her. "My mother said I couldn't do anything right." The therapist, siding with Kathie who wanted to "do things right," could give honest support to the many aspects of Kathie's growth as wife and mother in which she showed her good capacities. Since Kathie believed that her own mother did not find satisfaction in motherhood and did not provide a model for mothering that Kathie felt she could use, the therapist shared many moments with Kathie when she received great satisfaction with Billy. Moreover, she offered an alternative model for mothering, which Kathie could use if she wished.

When muted or sullen anger appeared in the transference, the therapist helped Kathie put her anger into words and to discover that the anger would not destroy the therapist, or the positive relationship to the therapist, and could, indeed, open pathways to the conflicted past and ways to find meaning in that anger.

We now select themes from the work of this period. In the process of treatment these themes were, of course, interwoven.

*Kathie, Essie, and Billy*

The story of Essie, the first intruder, emerged as a central theme in Kathie's sessions when Billy was eight months old. Kathie was still a reluctant mother to her baby, mechanically following the advice on feeding, now holding Billy for feedings and providing adequacy in caloric intake, but with little spontaneity or joy in her exchanges with the baby.

As memories of Essie emerged with rage toward that first baby "who spoiled everything," and as grief for herself as a small girl was revived, we began to see, for the first time, a spontaneous reaching out to Billy. The therapist described this in an excerpt from a visit with Kathie when Billy was eight months old:

> I had asked Kathie if she could tell me what it was like for her when her own baby sister was born. She said, "I've told you I hated my sister, how she always came between me and my mother. I don't remember much. When my sister was little, I remember being outside of the house much of the time. I do remember a couple of things. I didn't want to play with her. I hated to be told to play with her and I told my father that I hated her."
>
> At this time, Kathie had her hand raised and was shaking it in the air. (I think she was nonverbally imitating her father talking to her and speaking for her father.) She said, in a deep voice, "No child of mine can hate another sister, you play with her."
>
> After a while Kathie continued: "The first time I really got angry with my sister was when my parents took my sister out for ice cream and left me to do the dishes. I was so mad, I decided to run away. My mother found me and dragged me back to the house. She was angry at me for leaving." I asked if she had told her mother how she felt. Kathie said she

had told her mother that she had run away because she didn't want to be left at home when they went out. I asked if her mother had understood. Kathie said sadly, "She said she did, but," and she shook her head helplessly, "nothing changed."

At this moment a dramatic shift occurred: Kathie got up, went to Billy who was playing on the floor, swept him up in her arms, brought him back to her lap, hugged him, and started to play pat-a-cake with him, in a warm, thoughtful manner. She looked over at me, I was facing Billy's back, and she invited me to come and see Billy's face. Billy was ecstatic. This play was quite exciting for me to see. On previous visits I had suggested traditional baby games which Kathie could play with Billy. Kathie had never before picked up on this.

In this excerpt, then, we see that as Kathie reexperienced the rage toward Essie, she could turn toward her own baby and spontaneously show her affection for him. She played a game with him with full enjoyment, and we recall the words she had used in the early part of this session when she spoke of Essie, "I didn't want to play with her. I hated to be told to play with her." As the affective pathways led back to Essie, Kathie was able to disengage Billy from the first intruder and, as if some preconscious association had taken place around "play," she gave the "no" to Essie and the "yes" to Billy. Where Kathie's mother "didn't understand" and both parents sternly prohibited the expression of anger toward Essie, the therapist understood and accepted the words, "I hated her." The play with Billy was also, then, a gift to the therapist.

This was the first time that we saw this pattern. We were to see it many times in the sessions that followed. When Kathie expressed strong feelings of anger toward her sister or sadness in remembering the rejection by her own mother, she was able to reach out to Billy and to hold him close to her. The therapist could now become more active in interpreting to Kathie the displacement of feelings from Essie to Billy.

The ghost of Essie appeared in many disguises. For weeks the therapist was puzzled by a complaint from Kathie: Billy, Kathie said, drove her to distraction when he followed her around the house. From the therapist's point of view, Billy's following of mother and touching base with her were most welcome signs of the growing attachment between Billy and his mother. Kathie found it nearly intolerable and took a dim view of the therapist's ideas on the subject.

Then, in an interview, when Billy was eight and a half months old, Kathie quite unconsciously provided the vital clue. The therapist again described the session when Kathie was expressing a tirade against Essie:

> "The worst thing that I hated—I was about nine or ten—was when my sister followed me all around the house. She used to stare at me and whisper like me and repeat what I said. I used to tell my mother, but my mother said I was crazy and she could not understand what I was talking about. I couldn't stand it. I spent more and more time away from home. I wanted my mother to stop her, but my mother wouldn't." I asked her what it was that had bothered her so much. Kathie said that she didn't know, didn't care, she only hated it. She just didn't want to have anything to do with her sister at that time.
>
> After a few moments I asked her what it was like for her when Billy followed her around the house. Kathie said, "It's entirely different." Then she laughed. She understood. Kathie went to Billy and picked him up. She cuddled him, and put him on her lap so that he was lying on her knee, and tickled his back until Billy was laughing and giggling. He seemed delighted.

With this new insight, Kathie could now use more of the developmental and guidance information that the therapist offered. For example, regarding Billy's following her, the therapist explained that he wanted to keep her in sight at home because he was attached to her. At eight months mother's presence was reassuring. As Billy grew, he would be able to remember her presence even if she was in another room. He would not have to follow her all the time.

Kathie's relationship with Billy was beginning to have moments of tenderness, spontaneity, and joy. She was making obvious progress in becoming a mother to Billy. She was manifestly enjoying Billy, proud of his achievements, gratified by his steady weight gain, and eager for his response to her.

However, although the teasing games with Billy receded during this period, the therapist still caught glimpses of "teasing" which concerned us. On an educational level the therapist had dealt directly with the teasing games during feeding. She pointed out that these were games which might lead to problems which Kathie would not really want to see in Billy. She spoke of the meaning that food and love had for babies as well as adults. What did these games mean to Billy? Kathie consciously made an effort to give up the teasing games, an effort which was partially successful, yet the urge to tease Billy broke through in a game, and more explicitly in withholding food from Billy when he was manifestly hungry, Kathie responding only to his most urgent cries.

Billy meanwhile was responding to his mother's efforts by sometimes showing preferential responses to his mother in significant ways, but one aberrant tendency remained. At nine months of age he still avoided eye contact with his mother. Even in baby games with Kathie when she smiled and encouraged him, he turned his head away from her. In one sequence on tape we saw Kathie playing pat-a-cake with Billy on her lap, facing her, and the baby, though participating in the game, averted his head to avoid eye contact with his mother. Kathie, encouraged by the therapist, repeated the game until finally Billy rewarded his mother by smiling and cooing, but still turned away from her. The therapist interpreted the smiling and vocalizing as his way of telling mother he enjoyed the game. Perhaps soon he would also give her the reciprocal gaze she so wanted as affirmation of his affection toward her. Kathie, we saw with sadness for her plight, had to work very hard to woo her baby after the many months of avoidance and neglect.

Then, when Billy was eleven months old, the meaning of the teasing games and a facet of Kathie's uncontrollable urge to inflict pain broke through in a session. The therapist summarized the critical material:

> Kathie had recently returned from a visit to her own family, and was angrily recounting what had happened. Once again Kathie did the dishes while Essie disappeared from the kitchen, and once again Essie got all of mother's attention.
>
> Kathie said, "I hate my sister. She doesn't do anything. Just like now when my mother needs her. I have hated her ever since the time I was asked to take care of her and my little cousin together. I could have been with my friends, I really didn't want to do it, but I did. After a few days my sister said to me, 'Bug off, we all hate you, we don't want you here.' "
>
> In response to my question, "What did you do?" Kathie said, "I told my mother. She just shrugged it off." I asked, "How did you feel?" "I hated her." I said, "It really hurt, didn't it?" She replied, "Yes." Her face was red and she was very tense. I said, "It seems as though you are still angry." She said, "Yes."
>
> Kathie continued, "I told you how I would try to get her into trouble,

how I would make up stories, how I would tease her. I would tell my mother things that she would do. When she got me really mad I would shake her."

At this moment she turned to Billy who was playing on the floor, and took his arm and showed me how she would shake her sister, saying, "I would shake her like *this* and like *this*." Billy started to cry, obviously scared. I was scared for him. Kathie stopped abruptly. She was shocked and said, "Sorry Billy, I didn't mean to hurt you."

I said, "I can see how angry you feel at your sister and now I understand how you felt before." Kathie nodded. I asked her whether she sometimes got mad at Billy as she got mad at her sister, as though he were like her sister.

Kathie had an immediate response. She said, "No," in an emphatic voice and moved away from me. "I never get mad at Billy that way." Soon Kathie went over to Billy, started to play with him, got down on the floor, and for a long time held him and cuddled him.

Thus the teasing and sadistic rage toward Essie emerged from memory and could also be observed in a direct displacement toward Billy. After many interpretations, in this visit and others, of the repetition of feelings from the past in the present, Kathie's quick denial finally gave way to affirmation and insight.

The insight was very meaningful to Kathie and further freed Billy from being the target of her feelings of anger toward her sister. During the next visits we began to see a new depth in the relationship between Kathie and Billy. Teasing of Billy was significantly reduced and began to disappear. Kathie began spontaneously to reach out to Billy and, on her own, began to interact with him in such a way that both of them received great pleasure. Our observations also began to show some incidents of mutual gaze and approaches between Billy and Kathie.

### Kathie and Her Mother

The competitiveness with Billy was only one of the many themes that appeared throughout the work with Kathie. There was another important theme. We had often observed her seeming indifference to Billy's cries. Many times it seemed as if she and Billy were crying together. There was no mother present in the room. With great sadness and anger Kathie would say that her mother had not understood her. Once again the therapist acknowledged that Kathie too had many needs to be heard, to be loved, and to be understood and nurtured.

The therapist asked many times what it was that Kathie most wanted her mother and perhaps the therapist to understand. Gradually her true feelings emerged. She did not want to be a mother, she had never wanted to be a mother, and she was not ready to give up her role as a child. She had in fact not really separated from her own family.

With great sadness Kathie told the therapist of the very painful relationship she had had with her own mother. She felt that her mother was never satisfied with her, especially as a daughter. Kathie said that she had always been the family boy, loved by her father and ridiculed by her mother. As a little girl she had never played with dolls, but had always preferred to play with the neighborhood boys. As she approached puberty, she was accused by her mother of being too seductive. Nothing she did was right. With great hurt she described how her mother had said that she could never be as pretty as her older sister or as good as the younger sister. She began to go out with John, whom her mother had liked. During this time Kathie's mother had begun to enter menopause and was wishing explicitly for a grandchild. Kathie's older sister did not have any children. Kathie got pregnant and had Billy. Kathie, with hurt and anger, said that now her mother had a grandchild, but for her Billy's birth was not all that it was supposed to have been. The fantasy of renewed babyhood for Kathie never materialized. Now that Billy was born, he was the grandparents' pride, not Kathie. She was only seventeen and faced with an entirely new role, that of motherhood, which she did not want.

In work with Kathie, her ambivalence toward Billy now became overt. Even as she expressed her ambivalence, we began to see progress in her relationship with Billy. As Kathie spoke of these feelings, she began to be able to respond to Billy.

Nearly every session was related to Billy's needs in one way or another. Billy was approaching twelve months of age, a time when he did not yet have words for needs. As Kathie would weep for herself and berate the mother who never heard her cries and needs, Billy oftentimes needed her.

At first she was unable to interpret Billy's cries and the therapist would talk for him. For example, many times Billy was in his playpen and wanted to get out. Kathie was unable to respond. The therapist would talk for Billy and say, "Mom, I'm trying to tell you that I want out of the playpen, but I don't have any words yet." Kathie would respond. They had many discussions about the ways in which Billy tried to communicate with her without words. When Kathie did respond, the therapist always rewarded her efforts, speaking for Billy, who was not yet able to show her that he appreciated her efforts. The therapist might say, "Isn't it good to have a mommy who hears you and understands you? Even mommy has to be understood."

The first sign that Kathie was beginning to hear Billy and to be empathic with him was her ability to comfort him when he cried. She would pick him up in her arms, hold him closely, and pat his head. Eventually she anticipated his needs for both food and play. She took pride in his attempt to communicate and in her attempt to understand him, which the therapist encouraged and reinforced. She began to identify more strongly as Billy's mother. In fact, she started to let the therapist know that she knew Billy better, and the therapist, of course, stepped back from the role of active interpreter.

As we traced the content of these sessions "on being a mother" and the therapeutic work in this area, we could see the effects of reexperiencing, "undoing," and insight in Kathie's own ability to be a mother.

When Kathie's own cries were heard by the therapist, she began to respond to her baby's cries. When Kathie's needs were "understood" by her therapist, she began to interpret the signs of needs in her baby. When hostile feelings toward Billy could be put into words, they no longer exerted their influence in distancing Kathie from Billy; she was free to enjoy him. When the powerful ambivalence toward her own mother came into the therapeutic work, Kathie "completed" her own adolescence and became free of the "witch-mother" who impeded her own development as wife and mother.

### Termination of Treatment and Follow-Up

The major part of our therapeutic work was achieved by the time Billy reached his first birthday. Our work continued until Billy was eighteen months old, when the family moved to another community. John found new work, which brought financial security to the family.

Billy, at one year of age, already reflected both the changes in Kathie which were brought about in her treatment and the developmental guidance which Kathie could now use on his behalf with spontaneity and self-assuredness.

There were no residual feeding problems; Billy at twelve months and at the follow-up (twenty-five months) was a child who enjoyed food. He had no food idiosyncrasies or conflicts with his mother around feeding. There were no symptoms or disorders in the areas of orality or beginning autonomy. We watched carefully for signs of affective disturbances and saw none. We worried about possible residues from the sadomasochistic feeding games, which had so concerned us when Billy was eight months old, but we could identify no sequelae in the second year behavior picture. We did observe that John still occasionally teased Billy in words or games (Kathie did not) and that Billy at these times did not participate in these games, but turned away from his father, typically moving toward other games or toys. (We wish that we could have provided more help to John in this area, but we are satisfied that Billy did not offer himself as a partner in such games.)

In his second year, Billy was a cheerful, exuberant, busy little boy, curious, eager to learn, pleased with himself. Language development was excellent.

Most important of all, Billy's attachment to his mother was secure, mutually satisfying, and demonstrably joyous. In direct observations and in a number of vignettes on videotape we saw special smiles for mother, good eye contact, seeking of mother for comfort and protection, enjoyment of games and play with mother and father, and, equally important, a steady growth in self-confidence and independence. Billy had become an endearing child to both his parents and their pride and pleasure in him came through in nearly every visit. (He was also, objectively, an endearing child as others saw him.)

The therapeutic work with Kathie succeeded in freeing her and Billy from those aspects of a conflicted childhood which were being reenacted between her and her baby. To some measure, we believe, the work also resulted in the completion of Kathie's own adolescence. The resolution of infantile conflicts between Kathie and her mother freed her to become a mother and a wife in her own rights. For not only did Kathie become a mother who enjoyed her child, but we saw many positive changes in her relationship to her husband, and the marriage gained stability.

When Billy and his parents were seen in follow-up at twenty-five months, we were satisfied that he and his parents had sustained the gains of treatment. With only minimal support and guidance from the therapist during the period that followed their move from our community, both parents showed growth as young adults and had brought wisdom and good judgment to their rearing of Billy. They were justifiably proud of Billy and his achievements and spoke tenderly of his affectionate nature and his endearing ways of greeting his parents when he woke each morning.

Toilet training was proceeding smoothly. There was no sense of pressure in either Kathie or John. In Billy's play we discerned no anxieties in connection with the toilet or with cleanliness.

Recalling Kathie's earlier revulsion toward vomiting and messiness, we were interested to see that none of this had carried over to the toilet training of Billy. Since our work had not dealt with the deeper layers of this revulsion in Kathie, we wondered why the area of toilet training had not been contaminated. Then the therapist remembered that throughout the early critical period of the treatment, she had observed many diaperings of Billy, but at no time had Kathie shown revulsion toward the baby's feces or cleaning the anal region. It was, then, specifically an oral revulsion on Kathie's part in which food and vomit may have had anal determinants, but were curiously not manifest in connection with anal functions.

One vignette from our last records of Billy and his family is cherished by all of us. The therapist had made a visit to the new home of the Douglas's when Billy was twenty months old. Billy remembered her well and was very much a delighted child seeing an old friend. At one point he left the room and returned with a handful of Chinese noodles which he pressed in the therapist's hand. Kathie said, "He likes you. He always does this. He likes to share his favorite foods with people he likes."

*Notes*

1. We customarily videotape a play session and Bayley testing at this point in an assessment. This is done only with the consent of parents, of course, and we do everything possible to make the taping nonintrusive. We never invite intimate discussions at these times. We do not use video for treatment sessions, but we find that the taping of play sessions and testing is almost always of great interest to parents, and the playback of the tapes for the parents is valued by them and by us as an opportunity to observe the baby

and themselves. In Billy's case because of the urgency of the feeding problem, a formal Bayley testing was postponed until nutritional adequacy was achieved at 7½ months.

2. We did not observe Billy engage in age-related social personal behavior, such as frolic play and early vocalizations.

3. The Bayley showed that Billy was slightly above the median, in both mental and motor scores overall, but differentially lagged in beginning language items.

## References

Barbero, G. J. & Shaheen, E. (1967). Environmental Failure to Thrive. *J. Pediat.*, 71:639–644.

Bayley, N. (1969). *Bayley Scales of Infant Development.* New York: Psychological Corporation.

Fraiberg, S. (1974). The Clinical Dimension of Baby Games. *J. Amer. Acad. Child Psychiat.*, 13:202–220.

Leonard, M. F.; Phymes, J. P.; & Solnit, A. J. (1966). Failure to Thrive in Infants. *Amer. J. Dis. Child.*, 111:600–612.

Stern, D. N. (1973). Mother and Infant at Play. In *The Effect of the Infant on the Caregiver*, ed. M. Lewis & L. Rosenblum, pp. 187–213. New York: Wiley.

Whitten, C. F.; Pettit, M. G.; & Fischoff, J. (1969). Evidence That Growth Failure from Maternal Deprivation Is Secondary to Undereating. In *Annual Progress in Child Psychiatry and Child Development*, ed. S. Chess & A. Thomas, pp. 261–278. New York: Brunner/Mazel, 1970.

# 6

## The Adolescent Mother and Her Infant

In this chapter I will describe our work with adolescent mothers and their infants in an infant psychiatry program. I have gathered together some of our clinical observations of a group of young mothers struggling with formidable developmental conflicts of adolescence and their new and uncertain identity as mother to an infant. Later I will describe our treatment of one sixteen-year-old, severely depressed mother and her failure-to-thrive infant.

As the basis for this presentation I have chosen a group of ten babies and their eight adolescent mothers who constituted a subgroup in our intensive treatment case load in our University of Michigan program during the period from November 1972 to October 1978. The ten babies represented 20 percent of our intensive treatment case load of fifty. Since the only criteria for entering our intensive treatment program were our assessment of need for this form of treatment and the practical limitations of a small staff, it is important to note that teenage mothers constituted a substantial number of those we had identified as severely impaired in critical areas of functioning.

The ages of the mothers at the time of delivery ranged from sixteen to eighteen. Five were unmarried girls. Of the three mothers who were married, one was separated from her husband. The five fathers in the never-married group are unknown to us and, in fact, broke connections with the girls soon after pregnancy was confirmed. They appear in our records as nameless, faceless partners in casual encounters.

Seven of the ten babies were firstborn. All of the babies were full term with birth weights within the normal range. Congenital defects were later identified in three of the children. All of the mothers were living in poverty. The five unmarried mothers were supported by welfare services. In nearly all cases the young mother was living apart from her family of origin, and encounters with the extended family were caught up in conflict and turmoil. There was no psychological support for mother and baby nor were there traditions of child rearing to guide a young girl who was unready for motherhood.

The five unmarried mothers were attending school or were enrolled in job training. Their babies were being cared for in day-care centers or family day care. Mainly, the day-care arrangements, which we ourselves could assess through visiting, were poor and offered little more than custodial care. In three cases there was outright neglect of infants. As we came to know the babies and their families, we were sobered by the fact that the child, endangered by the considerable pathology in the mother and already showing signs of a severe attachment disorder, was further endangered by the circumstances in which he received indifferent or neglectful substitute-mother care. The baby who needed an optimal day-care program was receiving substitute care of the poorest quality.

The babies and their mothers had been referred to us by physicians, nurses, and social workers in Washtenaw County (population approximately three hundred thousand). The babies of teenage mothers were, as a group, among the most severely impaired children in our case load. A primary attachment disorder was present at the time of referral in each case. Four of the babies had been hospitalized for failure to thrive. The teenage mothers, as a group, showed grave impairment in psychological functioning and were virtually incapacitated in mothering a baby. Although they had been labeled by their community as "neglectful" and "rejecting," none of them had been evaluated by a psychiatric team before coming into our program. Ideally, we would like to see a psychosocial assessment of the teenage mother in every case at the point where the pregnancy is first identified by the health-care provider. After our own diagnostic study, six of the eight mothers were seen by us as severely depressed. Depression in each of these cases had been present for many months and even years before the baby was conceived. In fact, as I shall later discuss, depression and the unsatisfied psychological hungers which were entwined with depression had found their way into longing for a baby.

## Developmental Conflicts of Adolescent Motherhood

When I speak of the interlocking developmental conflicts of adolescence and motherhood that we saw in this group of young girls, I should preface these remarks with some caution. Clearly, the severely disordered teenage mothers in our case load do not represent the larger population of teenage mothers, in which we can find a fair amount of adequate or excellent mothering. The adolescent and mothering conflicts which we encountered are not typical but are exaggerated and heightened conflicts in which universal problems of adolescent maturation become distorted by disorder in the adolescent personality and the inability of the primary family of the girl to provide the vital pathways to resolution of conflict. The girls and their families, in our cases, were locked together in a morbid conflict.

The diagnostic study and treatment of this group of young mothers and their infants brought into focus the interlocking conflicts of adolescent development and mother-infant relationships. Each of these mothers had become pregnant at a point in psychological development when attachment and detachment from the primary family figures had produced conflicts of considerable magnitude. The unresolved conflicts of adolescence became the focus of new conflicts which embraced the child. The attachment and detachment problems of the mother were mirrored in the disorders of attachment that we saw in the baby.

The baby was caught up in the morbid past and uncertain present of his mother. But he was also, most poignantly, the symbol of hope and self-renewal in his mother. Each of the unmarried girls had examined the alternatives of abortion and adoption and had chosen to keep the baby. They wanted their babies and kept them against the wishes of their own parents. In each case, the baby, when we met him, was manifestly neglected and showed impoverishment in all areas of human attachment. The contradiction between the adolescent mother's daydreams for the baby and the actual state of the baby needed to be understood.

As we came to know these adolescent mothers, we saw how many of the typical conflicts of adolescence had become intensified and magnified for each of these girls before they became pregnant. Their own mothers were at the center of these conflicts. By the time we came to know them, these conflicts appeared to consume the life energies of each. In normal adolescence we may see the love-hate conflicts of the girl surface in daily life, but after the storm the beloved aspects of the mother can be reclaimed. What is preserved and eventually consolidated in the course of adolescence becomes available for positive identification and integration of personality in late adolescence. But among the young girls in our group, the mother as enemy and betrayer dominated the theater of conflict. There appeared to be no aspect of this mother that could serve maturation and identification. It also seemed to us that the mothers of these girls had become the unwitting collaborators in this tense family drama, transforming themselves into the enemy, so that the fantasy mother and the real mother sometimes merged.

Side by side with these consuming struggles with the mother was dependency in the girl and a longing for nurturance from the mother, which was explicitly brought to us in their stories and reenacted in transference with the therapist. Often, when the therapist was visiting the young mother and her baby in the home, there were two crying children in that living room.

The unresolved maternal conflicts of the girl became impediments to mothering and to the attachment of the girl to her baby. A girl who is fighting against her tie to her mother, who sees her mother as an enemy without redeeming features, has nothing good or solid to hold onto when she seeks a model for herself as a mother. And a girl who is still longing for a mother, who wants a mother to hold her close and nourish her, is not ready to become a mother herself.

Much of the important work that we accomplished in our treatment of these teenage mothers grew out of our exploration of the mother conflicts which were paralyzing the girl in her own psychological development. We examined the love-hate relationships to the mother, as they were described to us and as they were reenacted in transference to the therapist. We provided, through our treatment, a form of psychological nurturance for hungry girls. We offered a relationship in which independence could grow out of dependency. Affection and trust for the therapist could provide the conditions for new identifications with an adult figure and alternative models for mothering. The listening and understanding which the therapist gave the young mother could be transformed into listening to and understanding a baby. Again and again, in our records, the therapist is in a room with a crying mother and a neglected and crying baby. The therapist offers words of comfort to the mother and the mother turns to the crying baby as if she has heard him for the first time.

The adolescent girl's father, as he was described to us and revealed through the eyes of the girl, was also at the center of love-hate conflicts. We expect that in the normal adolescent process the girl's attachment to her father is gradually modified, that the oedipal wishes and fantasies are transformed, and that resolution paves the way to the discovery of new partners in love. Among the adolescent mothers in our group, the childhood daydream of father love had been preserved and was reenacted with male partners who appeared as transient lovers—if, indeed, the word "lovers" should be used.

Since the attachment to the father was still primary, there was no possibility of forming an enduring bond with another male partner. Typically, among our girls, sexual activity had begun at the age of thirteen or fourteen. The sexual partners were distantly remembered and seemed to have no more substantiality than figures in a fantasy. And, in fact, the sexual experiences resembled fantasies in which each partner was interchangeable with the other, like the masturbation fantasies of early adolescence. What was acted out in these transient sexual episodes was the fantasy of forbidden and dangerous love, a transparent oedipal fantasy. When pregnancy occurred, the unconscious childhood fantasy of having a baby with the father added another psychological dimension to a crisis, and the baby, when he arrived, became the embodiment of a shameful secret, a "child of sin," in the old-fashioned phrase.

The baby was also the child of a profound disappointment, the result of a promise that was not kept by whoever it is in our society who makes promises to the young. In the hyped-up sexual climate of our times, it is easy for the young to believe that puberty carries a passport into sexual bliss. But not one of the young girls in our group had experienced sexual pleasure of any kind in her many encounters. In fact, the serial encounters were motivated by the search for sexual joy. "It'll be different with the next fellow." But it never was. These girls were, in fact, unready for sexual fulfillment, like the majority of adolescents in their early and mid teens. But clearly, for the girl who is still pursuing a childhood fantasy love with her father, there is no place yet for a new partner and uninhibited sexual joy. The father love becomes the inhibitor.

The father love also becomes an impediment to motherhood. A girl who is still playing out an unconscious childhood fantasy of make-believe love and make-believe union with her father is likely to continue this fantasy as a make-believe mother with a make-believe baby. And this, in fact, is what we saw when we first met the mothers and babies in our group. Motherhood was somehow unreal; the baby was not quite real.

In our infant-focused psychotherapy, we listened to the tangled stories of fathers and lovers and helped the adolescent mother to find new solutions to old griefs and old longings. As we watched the mother and her baby together in session after session, we were attentive to those aspects of the baby and of mothering which were caught up in the old daydream. Where the baby was somehow unreal, and motherhood was unreal, we could make them real. This was not a fantasy baby to us; he was a person with all the unique qualities of his own personality. She was not a pretend mother to us; she was a real mother with real concerns for her baby and real problems. We played with this real baby and revealed his marvelous attributes to his mother. We talked to the real mother and most respectfully gave her the authority and prestige of mother. She was not a child to us, innocent and blundering, but a mother trying very hard to be a mother in the midst of terrible hardship.

The unresolved conflicts of childhood embraced every aspect of the childhood family. Repeatedly, in our work with adolescent mothers, we saw intense sibling conflicts reenacted with the baby. Jealousy toward the baby, competition with the baby, anger toward the baby, and the feeling of being robbed of something precious by the baby were recurring themes which we could trace back in treatment to a sibling who had been a rival in childhood. Normally in adolescence, the sibling conflicts of childhood undergo resolution along with other early and intensive love-hate relationships of the family. When the adolescent process has not been completed through maturation, the old jealousies and hostilities stand ready for transference to other objects. Tragically, in the case of teenage motherhood the new baby may come to represent the old rivals in the family of childhood.

In our work with the adolescent mother, we examined those ways in which the baby was caught up in old memories and the conflicts of the childhood family of the mother. We helped the mother to disentangle her baby from the figures of childhood and free the baby from the ghosts in the maternal past.

The inventory of unresolved adolescent conflicts in motherhood should include conflicts between self-love and love of others. Adolescence is normally a period in which self-love appears in heightened forms. The egocentricity and narcissism of the adolescent are, under all normal circumstances, only headaches that parents and teachers need to live with for a while. But when the adolescent becomes a parent, the self-love and self-centered goals come into conflict with the needs of a baby and the requirements of parenthood. A mother needs to put the child's needs before her own needs and is able to do this when psychological maturation has given her the possibility of subjugating self-interest and self-love in the interest of a child. The adolescent girl who has not completed this maturational step finds herself strained, or actually incapable, at times, of ministering to the ordinary needs of a helpless baby.

It is this colossal narcissism in the young that evokes anger in the parent generation. When the adolescent is also a mother, the self-centeredness of the mother united with neglect of her infant evokes anger in those who are called upon to help her. By the time we met our young mothers, they had been scolded by public health nurses, doctors, and social workers and grimly prepared themselves for a scolding from us. They seemed surprised, but certainly relieved, when no scolding awaited them.

Narcissism in parenthood, it strikes us, has two faces. There is the self-love that can endanger the child, and there is the self-love that can embrace the child. There is a large measure of healthy narcissism that goes into the parenting of many good and normal people. The baby is the most remarkable baby in the world. He's a genius, if we have to say it ourselves. Every achievement, even his first tooth, is somehow a credit to us, as parents. All this, the healthy narcissism, is available to the teenage parent, too. We began to see it happen in our work. As the baby began to thrive and reward his mother for her efforts, he became, for his young mother, a marvel, a precocious child, destined for a brilliant future.

From this brief summary, we can see how the intense unresolved conflicts of adolescence become psychological obstacles to the nurturance of a child and may, in fact, provide a theater in which the baby is caught up in the reevoked childhood griefs and disappointments of the mother. In our group, however, there was still another dimension of conflict which exerted its morbid influence upon the baby, and this was maternal depression.

Six of the eight adolescent mothers were suffering from severe and incapacitating depression. If these girls had not been mothers, they would have required intensive psychotherapy and, in two cases, might have required hospitalization for depression-related anorexia. While these young mothers had been labeled by their communities as rejecting, neglectful, or abusive toward their children, our clinical inquiry led us to understand that these were young girls who were barely able to function. In each case, the depression had antedated pregnancy and the birth of the child by many months and even years. Since each of these girls had considered the alternatives of abortion and adoption, the decision of these depressed young girls to keep their babies needed to be understood. What did the baby represent? In the course of our work we began to understand. In the hopelessness of depression the baby represented hope and renewal, the chance to live another life through the baby of fantasy. The hunger for love in the adolescent and the unsatisfied hungers seen in depression found the dream of a baby's love. And not only love, we saw, as we began to unravel the complex meanings of the baby. Periodically, in the course of treatment, the depressed young girl would speak of feelings of emptiness and a yearning for something to fill the emptiness. And, as we moved back into the historical events that had led to pregnancy and the decision to keep the baby, we began to understand. The yearnings for a baby seemed linked to an imperative need to fill the emptiness.

The baby, being a baby, could not fill the emptiness for needy and hungry girl-mothers. The baby, in fact, was a disappointment. Neither did the baby bring self-renewal or the fulfillment of old dreams. More likely, the bad dreams of childhood were reevoked by him. The baby had become the center of morbid conflicts by the time we met him.

## The Babies: Disorders of Attachment

It is time to talk about the babies. In each of these cases the baby had come to us because of severe disorders of attachment. Here, I am not generalizing to the larger population of infants of teenage mothers. We must remember that, as a psychiatric clinic, we were preselected by referring agencies for our expertise in the area of attachment disorders. The babies, as a group, were among the most severely impaired children in our case load. They were joyless, listless babies, who showed virtually none of the age-appropriate signs of attachment to the mothers, or who had a limited repertoire of attachment behaviors along with a constricted range of affect. Four of the ten babies were referred to us following diagnosis of failure to thrive.

As we follow the links between the adolescent conflicts of the mothers in our group and the disorders of attachment we identified in their babies, we can see how every component of the unresolved adolescent conflicts became an impediment to the attachment of mother to baby and baby to mother. Where resolution of childhood conflicts paves the way for parenthood and identification with one's own parents, nonresolution brings unreadiness, disappointment, and a turning away from the baby or the investment of the baby with the love-hate conflicts of the mother's own childhood. Where self-love is still dominant in adolescent psychology, there cannot be the selfless love of a parent. And when we add to this inventory of adolescent afflictions the severe depressions we encountered among the mothers in our group, it appears as if everything in the parental personality is negating the possibility of attachment.

Yet this is by no means a hopeless picture for therapy. Remarkably, when we consider the psychopathology we saw in mothers and babies, we found that we were able to engage each of these mothers in work on behalf of their babies and themselves, and the therapeutic gains were substantial in all but one case.

*Clinical Illustration*

The case of sixteen-year-old Karen and her baby, Nina, illustrates many of the interlocking disturbances of mother and baby.[1] It also illustrates our methods of diagnostic study and the formulation of treatment alternatives which grow out of the initial assessment.

No case can stand by itself in illustrating the clinical picture that we saw in our case load of teenage mothers and their babies. However, the case of Karen and Nina demonstrates many of the characteristics of our larger group. Nina, the seven-month-old baby, is referred to us following hospital diagnosis of "nonorganic failure to thrive due to maternal deprivation."

At birth, Nina had been a full-term healthy baby, birth weight six pounds one once (tenth percentile) and height twenty inches (seventy-fifth percentile). At the time of hospitalization for failure to thrive, Nina's weight had dropped to below the third percentile and height had fallen to below the twenty-fifth percentile. Medical study revealed no organic cause for failure to thrive, and the referring pediatrician and nurses concluded that growth failure was caused by severe maternal deprivation.

Her sixteen-year-old mother is unmarried and attending high school. The mother is described as neglected and unable to cooperate with physicians and nurses who have offered their help. When we meet the mother and baby, we see a young mother who is suffering with a severe depression and a depression-related anorexia which has antedated the birth of the baby by several years. Karen, the mother, weights approximately eight-five pounds. Food is repulsive to her, she tells us, and she eats barely enough for sustenance. She knows the doctors are concerned about Nina, but she is not sure why. Nina looks chubby to her, she says.

Karen and Nina are supported by welfare services. They are living in the home of the maternal grandparents in the midst of domestic chaos. There are violent quarrels between Karen's mother and father with periodic separations. Karen and Nina are given grudging shelter in this home. Nina is unwanted. Karen is taunted daily by her parents for bringing a baby into this home. No help is offered Karen. Karen would like to find another place to live, but she is afraid to live alone. She is a child herself, of course. The grandparents themselves are hostile to the treatment offered Karen and Nina. They will not permit us to visit the home. If Karen wants our help she will have to see us at our office. With all these constraints we will need to provide treatment for this endangered baby and her mother.

In the course of the initial evaluation period, we are asking ourselves many questions. The developmental testing of Nina will give us a fair assessment of the motor and cognitive development of Nina and the areas of deficit. But the test will not help us to discern the qualities of infant-mother relationship. In our observations, we want to look for the age-appropriate indicators of human attachment in the baby, the ability of the mother to respond to the range of signs and signals which a baby can send to the mother, and the ability of the mother to initiate and exchange social and affectionate signs with her baby.

In our initial observations we see a severely depressed young mother and her child who is suffering from growth failure and a severe attachment disorder. The depression of the mother is mirrored in the baby's face. The baby is silent, stares off into space, uninvested in her surroundings. She rarely turns to her mother for a social exchange or for comfort. In our broader observations, we see a limited number of attachment indicators. There is discrimination of her mother from others, there is preference for her mother. Nina has a limited repertoire of attachment behaviors, but they are muted and joyless. Similarly, Karen shows some signs of affection for her baby, but she sinks back into depression and solitude after each exertion.

As we look at the depressed and anorectic mother, we also look at our own therapeutic dilemma. Karen cannot read the signs of hunger and satiation in herself; how can she read the signs of hunger and satiation in her baby? In fact, in every observation during this assessment period of seven sessions, Karen seems unable to read hunger in Nina, or she misreads the signs.

Ideally, we would want our therapy to focus on the interlocking aspects of Karen's depression and her baby's attachment disorder. But soon after treatment begins, we find ourselves facing a formidable therapeutic problem. If the therapist begins to speak about feelings with Karen, to speak of sadness or anger, to touch ever so gently on the defenses against affect, Karen's depression deepens and her symptoms are exacerbated.

Clearly, we cannot yet deal with Karen's internal and objective conflicts without precipitating a grave conflict in personality and worsening the situation for Karen and Nina. We decide, then, that we will work with Karen and Nina, for the indefinite future, within the context of supportive treatment and developmental guidance. This treatment brings about very substantial changes for Karen and Nina.

Our treatment focused on both the nutritional and psychological aspects of Nina's and Karen's interlocking conflicts. But both aspects of this treatment were solidly embedded in the context of human attachments. On the nutritional side, we worked with Karen and the nursery in providing an optimal diet for Nina. Karen and the nursery staff were helped to see how a baby's pleasure in eating was intimately related to pleasure in the arms of a partner, most particularly the mother. Karen was encouraged to take over the lunch feedings in the nursery as often as possible. One or, at most, two aides at the nursery were assigned as Nina's special caregivers.

In our own sessions, with Karen and Nina and the therapist together in our playroom, the therapy focused on the relationship between Nina and Karen, emphasizing in every way possible how Karen was the most important person in the world to her baby, how no one, not even the therapist, could get the special smiles or comfort Nina in distress as well as her mother could. Karen, who had never in her life believed she was important or special to anyone, was deeply touched as she learned to recognize these signs of preference and love in her baby. And Nina, like all babies, gave generous rewards to her mother. Within four months of work, Nina made tremendous progress toward nutritional and psychological adequacy.

Karen, watching the therapist talk to Nina, was initially puzzled. After all, Nina could not understand English. Karen had no traditions in her family for talking to a baby, or, indeed, for conferring personality on a baby. As Karen watched her therapist, she saw that Nina began to make responsive sounds, and it was easy for the therapist to begin to speak about how babies learn to talk. Within a short time, mother-baby dialogues appeared in all of our sessions, and the quiet baby who never uttered a sound became positively garrulous.

Karen's conflicts with her own parents gave her no models for parenting. Her own mother did not like babies and considered a baby who cried as "just plain spoiled." Her own mother did not believe that a baby of Nina's age cared who took care of her. Mothers were not important. Karen's therapist listened to Karen and Nina with most respectful attention to each. To understand why Nina cried or what Nina was trying to tell us became central to every session. To understand Karen's sadness, inarticulate cries, and griefs was equally central to the sessions. Karen was profoundly touched by her therapist's concern for her, her listening, her sympathy, her praise, and her confidence in Karen. No one had ever cared for her in this way. Later she told the therapist how much this caring had meant to her. Karen, whose own griefs were listened to, then became a mother who could listen, in every sense of the word, to her child's cries and the everyday griefs of a small girl. She began to understand Nina's pain at separation from her each day at the door of the nursery. She had no alternatives in care for Nina, but she could now find words of sympathy and understanding for Nina which made the pain bearable. In short, what Karen received in emotional sustenance from her therapist, she could now give to her own baby.

At fourteen months of age Nina had reached weight adequacy. She also achieved adequacy in our affective-social evaluation and made substantial gains in cognitive motor development. Our health evaluation showed that Nina had gained weight steadily in these seven months. Her weight was now nineteen pounds, which placed her between the tenth and twenty-fifth percentiles. She was bright-eyed, animated, strong, active, and had good color and muscle tone. (She sustained these gains in later years.)

In the affective-social areas which had been seriously affected by the time we first met her at seven months, Nina was now age adequate. She had a good range of affective expression. She had strong and stable ties to her mother, with strong preference for and valuation of her mother (as we saw in social situations as well as need states). Her pleasure in being with her mother was manifest through warm and special smiles for her, animated "conversations" with her mother, and seeking her mother to share special moments and to touch base with her. She showed age-appropriate reactions to the daily separations from her mother at the nursery. She protested but then settled down (with resignation) to the less than ideal circumstances provided by this substitute care.

There were advances in cognitive motor development. At fourteen months she scored an MDI on the Bayley of 133. Her first testing at seven months had actually placed her within normal range (110), but now we could see that Nina's potential in mental development was higher than average. The gains reflected to some measure the tremendous progress in language development which was one result of our work.

During this period we saw Karen develop into a responsible and affectionate mother. It is important, however, to keep in mind that Karen was still a seriously depressed girl and was still anorectic. We had already discovered that our treatment of Karen had to be modified because of her inability to tolerate exploration of her profound conflicts (mainly internalized rage). She could not tolerate even the gentlest therapeutic probing of her feelings toward her mother and father, yet found comfort in the understanding and sympathy which the therapist expressed as she listened to the reports of fights between the maternal grandparents, their constant blame of Karen for bringing a baby into this home, and their depreciation of Karen as mother.

Thus our work with Karen was mainly supportive, and the supportive work was united with observations of Nina and developmental guidance. All of this brought significant developmental progress for Nina, as we have seen. And for Karen, too, there was brightening of mood, enhancement of self-image, and new confidence in herself as a mother. But the anorexia remained. Karen could now feed her baby, but she could not feed herself.

In describing the therapeutic approach to Karen, I should say that I am not generalizing about work with adolescents or work with adolescent parents. In nearly every other case we have worked with we were able to deal therapeutically with the inner conflicts of our adolescent parents and to do this fairly early in treatment. Only in Karen's case was such an approach contraindicated.

Actually, we had to wait two more years before Karen's love-hate conflicts toward her parents could be dealt with therapeutically (and, I believe, with great benefit to her). But what we learn from this work is that long before the clinical picture of a mother's disorder can change, there are large possibilities for change in the capacity to mother which can be brought about through supportive treatment and guidance.

Between Nina at age fourteen months and twenty-two months, we continued to work with mother and baby. For Nina, all gains in health and affective and cognitive development were sustained.

At twenty-two months, Nina was a healthy, enthusiastic, buoyant, outgoing child. In nursery school (a new school) she was regarded by her teachers as intelligent, creative, and socially mature for her age. She was well liked by her teachers and her peers. In doll play in our observation sessions we saw Nina as a tender and solicitous mother. She loved feeding and cooking for her dolls. We could not see residues of early oral conflicts.

Karen, herself, was a proud mother. Through guidance she had become a very sensitive and empathic reader of signs and needs in her child. She enjoyed Nina. She was proud of her spunkiness and assertiveness (vicarious pleasure for a young woman now eighteen years old, who could not yet assert herself with her own parents, except in defending Nina). Some measure of Karen's self-confidence was brought to improved schoolwork and a decision to enroll in a community college after high school graduation.

It was not until the final year of treatment, when Nina was three years old, that Karen's profound conflicts, which centered on the relationship to her own parents, could be dealt with. At last she felt strong enough as a person to allow herself to feel rage and disappointment toward her own parents and to speak of the heartbreaks, the childhood sense of worthlessness, and the fear of parental explosions. The depression lifted. The last vestiges of anorexia disappeared.

Karen's joy in her child had been sustained through our work. But now there was the beginning of pleasure for herself. Karen, at last, was ready to move out of her parental home. She made good plans for herself and Nina and entered a community college technical training program. With the liberation from parental love-hate bonds, Karen fell in love with a stable young man who became devoted to her and to Nina. Within a year after termination of treatment they were married.

## Discussion

A single case of an adolescent mother and her baby cannot, of course, illustrate all of the factors which I have identified as characteristics of the unresolved conflicts of adolescence which impinge on motherhood.

What we can see in the case of Karen and Nina are the effects of profound inner conflicts in adolescence on the capacity to mother a baby. Karen, when we met her, was a child herself, caught in a morbid love-hate conflict with her own parents. Her depression and anorexia spoke for intense internalized rage toward her own parents. The unsatisfied longings and hungers of adolescence had led her to early sexual experience with boys in casual encounters. She became pregnant. And she wanted to keep her baby. When we first met Karen and Nina we saw a starving mother and baby living in the home in which Karen's family gave grudging shelter and neither affection nor support to their child or their grandchild. If we give clinical attention only to Karen's own adolescent conflicts, the therapeutic task appears a formidable one: the anorexia is severe enough to warrant hospitalization. Depression has depleted Karen's resources. She is barely able to function in school. Failures in love have marked her life from childhood to adolescence, now marked again by the failures in seeking love from boys. There are unresolved oedipal problems in the pursuit of "forbidden love" through transient boys.

But this adolescent, with some ordinary and many extraordinary developmental problems, was a mother. And her baby was in great danger.

Anorexia has distorted Karen's ability to read her own signs of hunger and satiation. Anorexia has blotted out her recognition of hunger and satiation in her infant. Depression, which makes her psychologically absent in all social relationships, has made her psychologically absent to a baby who is in need of mother nurture.

The baby, herself, seems not quite real to Karen when we first meet her. She is uncertainly a mother. She still needs a mother herself. Her own longings for nurture collide at times with the baby's needs for nurture. And the fantasy baby, who would satisfy longings to be loved and the yearning for self-renewal which are universal in adolescence, is after all only a baby with imperative demands and no promise of bringing self-renewal. The baby of fantasy who would fill the emptiness only enlarges the sense of emptiness. At best, if Karen summons all of her meager resources, she can give mechanical care to Nina since Karen has no models for mothering. Her own mother's failure to mother leaves Karen bereft of knowledge and tradition.

We can sketch the treatment for Karen if Karen were not a mother. Many months of intensive work would be required. Hospitalization of Karen might be desirable. But Nina, the baby, is our patient, too. She cannot wait for her mother's depression to lift or for resolution of the complex problems that are bound together in anorexia.

Our work with Karen and Nina focused on the needs of both the baby and the mother. It was a delicate balance to sustain, for Karen, like many adolescent mothers we know, was desperately needy herself. Most sessions were held with both mother and baby in the room. When necessary, private sessions for Karen, herself, were arranged.

Psychotherapy is a form of undoing of the past. And so it was for Karen, too, even though our access to the emotionally laden memories of the past was limited by Karen's own defenses against powerful affects. Where rejection by parents had led to Karen's feelings of worthlessness, the relationshp to the therapist could give to Karen a sense of worth as an adolescent and as a mother. Where unsatisfied longings for mother love had led to morbid symptoms, therapy could provide a form of psychological nurturance which sustained the adolescent girl and had the effect of undoing some part of the injuries of the past. Where failures in understanding had marked the relationship with parents, understanding and profound sympathy from a therapist had the effect of healing the old wounds. Where the baby was somehow "a child of sin" with echoes from an unremembered past and censorship from the maternal parents, the baby was given, through our work, the rights of every baby to be cherished and to bear no shameful stigma.

Where the baby was a fantasy baby who belonged to an oedipal romance, we helped to make her a real baby, a real person, which had the effect of detaching the baby from childhood conflicts even though we were unable to deal with those fantasies directly. And long before we were able to deal with the inner conflicts of Karen in our treatment, Nina, herself, began to fulfill her mother's adolescent dream of renewal of self, a rebirth through giving birth to a child. Nina, through our work, became a loving, intelligent, social person who gave her mother huge rewards for motherhood. The mother who could not love herself or value herself when we first met her could know love and valuation from her child. Some measure of self-love could now grow in Karen—which means, of course, that for Karen, as well as all parents, a loving and rewarding child brought enhancement of self-love, the healthy narcissism that is the privilege of all parents.

Nina's progress in treatment was far in advance of her mother's during the first two years. Nina was brought to adequacy on all measures of personality development by the time she was fourteen months old. But in this work we had two patients, a mother and a baby. As long as Karen's depression remained, Nina was regarded by us as at risk and her mother's psychological state was regarded as precarious. When treatment was terminated at Nina's age three and a half, we were satisfied that Karen's internal conflicts had found resolutions and that Nina was progressing sturdily in her own development.

## Conclusions

Therapeutic work with adolescent mothers and their babies needs to accommodate objectives for the treatment of two patients, each of whom may be suffering from a developmental disorder. This therapy has the aim of bringing optimal development for an adolescent who is also an adolescent mother and for a baby whose development is endangered.

*Notes*

A version of this paper was presented as the William A. Schonfeld Distinguished Service Award Address at the annual meeting of the American Society for Adolescent Psychiatry, New Orleans, May 1981.

1. A full clinical report of this case and three other cases of adolescent mothers are included in Fraiberg (1980).

*Reference*

Fraiberg, S., ed. (1980). *Clinical Studies in Infant Mental Health: The First Year of Life*. New York: Basic Books.

# 7

# Pathological Defenses in Infancy

The fertility of René Spitz's mind and the inspiration of his work has changed the course of the professional life of many, including my own. More important, the world of infancy has been transformed through Spitz. Since 1945 it has not been possible to say that an infant does not experience love and loss and grief, or that tragic circumstances in infancy will not blemish a child who is "too young to feel or to remember."

In this presentation I will follow a line of inquiry that owes its inspiration to Spitz's work. His own studies of maternal deprivation originated in his observations of infants in institutions. The work that I will describe derives from the study and treatment of babies reared in their own homes. In the course of this work I have been able to examine a number of pathological defenses in infants who have experienced extreme deprivation. I will describe the behaviors and touch upon the theoretical and clinical implications of these findings.

In discussing "defense" in infancy, it is clear, of course, that I do not mean "defense mechanisms," which can be assumed to function only when an ego, properly speaking, has emerged. Here I find it useful to follow Wallerstein (1976), who distinguished between "defense mechanisms as a construct and defenses as actual phenomena" (p. 220). A behavior that serves defensive purposes can be observed. A defense mechanism, he points out, is a theoretical abstraction. We can, for example, observe exaggerated sympathy in a patient as a behavior, but we cannot observe the unconscious process in which a cruel impulse is turned into an opposite for which we postulate a mental mechanism that we call reaction formation. In this sense, we can observe behaviors that serve a defensive purpose at any point in development and, in the case of the infant, if the child is capable of registering danger or a threat to his functioning, he will react to the danger through a behavior that serves as defense.

In this sense, too, the term "defense" in infancy has validity of its own. We need not speak of "precursors of defense," the term which is commonly used in the literature for pre-ego modes of defense. Whether these defensive behaviors in infancy are linked to defense *mechanisms* in later development can only be examined through longitudinal study with *normal* children. In this presentation I will deal specifically with pathological defense in infancy as observed in a clinical population. Since our therapeutic work with babies and parents was largely successful in alleviating the conditions which brought about these defenses, and the defenses themselves dropped out of the clinical picture, we cannot know what the course of these defenses might have been if clinical intervention had not taken place.

Yet our observations of babies who came to us in extremity will generate useful hypotheses for the psychoanalyst. We come a little closer to the unanswered questions which Freud (1926), Anna Freud (1936), Hartmann (1950), and Spitz (1961) had posed in their writings, in which it was speculated that biological modes of defense might underlie the structure of certain defense mechanisms.

### The Questions

When we speak of "defense" in infancy, something within us resists the word and its connotations. The infant is helpless in the face of danger. His parents are his protectors, and so far as they serve as protectors we are unlikely to see a baby coping with external threats or physiological stress unaided. Under all normal circumstances the infant will not experience helplessness for more than brief periods, because distress is alleviated or modulated by the mother, usually before tension becomes intolerable. Even in the early weeks and months of life, the normally reared baby begins to turn expectantly to the mother for comfort and the alleviation of distress or pain.

But what happens to an infant in the first eighteen months of life when his human partners fail in their protective function and he is exposed to repeated and prolonged experiences of helplessness? How can he relieve his own pain? What means does he have to cope with extreme helplessness or to ward off "something out there" which is uncertainly associated with painful experience? And if pain is associated with the figure of the mother herself in daily and repeated circumstances, how can he ward off the person on whom he is absolutely dependent and who is associated with pain and disappointment? The questions seem to lead to nowhere: thinking the unthinkable.

These were certainly not the questions in my mind when I began a clinical research program in 1972 for the study and treatment of infants and parents who showed the early signs of impairment in relationships. But a very large number of babies who came to us showed affective disorders in the serious to severe range. Many of them were referred because of neglect or actual or suspected abuse. Their parents showed grave disorders in personality and were largely incapacitated in their ability to nurture a child. The research itself was designed to study and evaluate treatment methods in an infant mental health program and to assess the effects of intervention for the baby and his family. In the course of this work we came to understand the interlocking pathology between parents and infants; we saw the effects of maternal deprivation in family-reared babies; we were able to examine deviate patterns of object relations and their effects upon ego formation; and we began to identify certain aberrant behaviors in the babies which were considered to have a defensive function.

I will describe as well as I can the manifestations of these behaviors and their contexts. The description comes from detailed process notes. Some of these descriptions come directly from videotape records when, by chance and not by design, the camera recorded moments in which a baby with his mother or father, or with both, revealed total helplessness and a subsequent behavior which revealed his attempts to cope. The pictures are painful to watch, and the verbatim narrative transcripts of pictures or observed events are painful to read or hear. By way of reassurance I should begin by indicating that the largest number of these aberrant babies were brought to adequacy in our work with them and their parents.

In examining the occurrence of these behaviors, I selected items which I considered to represent defensive behavior and placed them in a chronological sequence according to the age of the child at the time of the observation. As the data grew voluminous, I chose to use eighteen months of age as the cutoff point for reporting. (Our program actually served children from newborn to thirty-six months of age.)

Since the first eighteen months embrace the sensorimotor period, the occurrence of defensive behavior in a preverbal period, prior to the constitution of the ego in psychoanalytic terms, will give us a context in which the earliest defense behaviors can be isolated for study as phenomena which are not yet related to the development of evocative memory (at approximately eighteen months) and not yet expressive of internal conflicts between drives and an emerging ego organization.

To examine the forms of pathological defense and their occurrence during the first eighteen months of life, I chose a group of babies who were judged by our staff to be the most severely impaired in object relations at the point of entrance to our program. There were twelve children in this subgroup, chosen out of a total of fifty. (I excluded one child of the original thirteen who was found in the course of treatment to have severe biological impairments which affected his capacity to respond to and relate to his mother and all other persons.) The twelve children who constitute the group selected for this study had no biological impediments known to us in the course of extended study and treatment.

Many of the children in this group were referred to us because of neglect or suspected or actual abuse. Twelve mothers were severely depressed women. One mother was schizophrenic. For all of the babies the mother was considered to be psychologically absent for a very large part of the infant's day. And for all of these children there was exposure to unpredictable eruptions from their mothers. Periodically, the mother's rage would break through the walls of depression, and we saw fear register on the baby's face. For the child of the schizophrenic mother there were experiences in which the mother was completely out of touch with her child, and moments when the child herself was caught up in the mother's delusional system.

Twelve of the thirteen children showed a characteristic behavior toward the mother: the baby avoided the mother through every system of contact he had available to him in a complete reversal of the social patterns that normally are exhibited at each developmental stage. In our exhaustive initial assessment period, which covered five to seven visits in the home, these are what we see as reversals: where the normal baby seeks eye contact and gaze exchange with his mother, these babies never or rarely looked at their mothers. Where the normal baby smiles in response to the mother's face and voice, these babies never or rarely smiled to the mother. They did not vocalize to the mother. At an age when a baby is motorically capable of reaching, they did not reach for her. If the baby was capable of creeping or walking he did not approach his mother. In circumstances that we could read as need or distress, these babies did not signal the mother for comfort. Wherever there should be "seeking," there was "avoidance." Avoidance, in fact, was the first defense which I can identify in this chronology, and it occurs as early as three months of age.

## Avoidance

The patterns of avoidance which I will describe were first noticed when we began our work with severely disturbed infants in 1971. We had never before seen babies who avoided their mothers with every system available to them. I had recently concluded a study of infants blind from birth (Adelson and Fraiberg, 1974), and along with my colleagues I longed to see babies again who gazed intently, who smiled in response to a partner's face. I had been following with much interest Stern's (1974) work in gaze interaction patterns between infants and mothers, and I was not prepared for what I saw in these babies. In 1971 Stern and I reviewed these new tapes together, and we were shocked to see a group of babies who negated every expectation for normal social interaction.

The avoidance patterns that I saw I considered to be a pathological defense. And I think that the detailed descriptions will support this view. However, it is of interest also that Mary Ainsworth and her colleagues have identified avoidance patterns in a subgroup of twelve-month-old children in an unselected and presumably normal population (Ainsworth et al., 1978). The differences between the avoidance patterns described by Ainsworth and those that I have seen appear to be these. Avoidance, in the Ainsworth study, was first identified in an experimental situation in which separation and reunion patterns in toddlers were being studied. The home observations of these babies and mothers showed avoidance of the mother in what I take to be a fluctuating pattern in response to circumstance. It was always associated with discord in the mother-infant relationship and with avoidant patterns in the mother herself. In our population we see avoidance manifest as early as three months of age and throughout the age span covered in our study (up to thirty-six months). The patterns of avoidance were total or near total, without fluctuations in the course of extended and intensive home observations. The mother's avoidance of her baby had reached a pathological extreme.

There are undoubtedly many links between the phenomena I will describe and those which Ainsworth has described which can best be examined through comparison of data. However, it is important to preface my own remarks by saying that avoidance as a form of defense can be identified in all infants, including normal ones; that a marked tendency to avoid as in Ainsworth's babies is, in my view, an early indicator of disturbance in the infant-mother relationship; and that the total or near total avoidance of the mother which I will describe represents a pathological extreme, a defense that has taken a morbid turn.

In what follows, I shall present the evidence for avoidance as a defense in infancy. I am mindful, of course, that without the evidence, our inclination is to find alternative and simpler explanations for the behavior I have described. One could argue that if deprivation is severe enough, it may be that these systems have not been activated by a nurturing person, as in the case of Spitz's (1945) babies in his "hospitalism" study. But if we look closely at the behavior I will describe (and videotape is nearly indispensable here), we will see that the avoidance of the mother is selective and discriminating. The baby avoids his mother, for example, and may not avoid his father or even a stranger. If the sign and signaling systems are available for exchange with someone in his environment and are not employed in social approaches to the mother, the avoidance patterns are selective.

To illustrate, I will describe the youngest child in this group, three-month-old Greg. Greg is the child of two teenage parents. His mother alternates between states of depression and outbursts of rage. Her voice when angry is shrill and penetrating. Whether depressed or angry, Annie, the mother, avoids her baby in every circumstance that is open to our observation. Annie, who had known brutality and abandonment in her own childhood, is afraid of the dangerous impulses which flood her at times. In the early sessions in the home we understood why Annie avoided her baby. She was afraid that she would kill him.

And Greg avoided his mother. At three months of age when a baby seeks his mother's eyes, smiles and vocalizes in response to her face and voice, Greg never looked at his mother, never smiled or vocalized to her. Even in distress he never turned to her. But when his father was present, there was gaze exchange, smiles, and vocalizations of pleasure. As clinicians, we could elicit eye contact and even small smiles.

We are inclined to argue with the evidence once again. Is *this* avoidance? If the mother herself avoids the baby and does not elicit these responses, is this avoidance? Not yet. However, the evidence from our observations supports avoidance, and the avoidance appears to be associated with fear and pain. When we examined this behavior in thirty minutes of continuous videotape, we saw sequences which are nearly indescribable. What follows describes Greg at three months and fairly describes the picture for other babies in this subgroup whether the age is three months, five months, seven months, or sixteen months.

What we see is this. The baby is scanning the room, his eyes resting briefly on the stranger, the cameraman, or an object in the room, and in the scanning he passes over his mother's face without a sign of registration or recognition. There is not a pause in scanning or a flicker on his face that speaks for registration. In situations where gaze exchange or a gesture is nearly unavoidable because of the line of vision or the proximity of baby and mother, we see the patterns again and again. It is as if perception has selectively edited the picture of the mother from the pictures in the visual survey.

The behavior is similar when the mother speaks. If she is for the moment outside the baby's visual field and she speaks to the baby or calls to him, there is no automatic turning in the direction of her voice, and there is no alerting or signs of attention. The editing process has taken place again.

When we consider that both visual fixation of the human face and alerting to the sound of the human voice are genetically programmed behaviors that normally subserve the earliest infant-mother relationship, how can we account for a modification in infant behavior in which vision and hearing selectively edit this mother's face and voice in a reversal of the form?

In the simplest possible terms, it appears that in the biological-social sequence in which sensorimotor systems are activated and organized around the experience with a mother as a nurturant, responsive, need-gratifying person, the percept of mother for these infants is a negative stimulus. It is also a defense which may, in itself, belong to the biological repertoire and is activated to ward off registration and, conceivably, a painful affect. When the visual and aural registration of this percept is closed off or the registration is muted, the associated affective experience remains dormant, that is, not called up by perception.

But avoidance, which defends against external "dangers," cannot defend against urgent somatic needs. What happens to these babies when need states or internal distress are experienced and are not satisfied by a mother or any figure in the infant's environment?

The same babies who avoid their mothers present another part of the story in states of distress. Hunger, solitude, state transitions, a sudden noise, or a stimulus that cannot even be identified can trigger states of helplessness and disorganization in these babies, together with screaming and flailing about—a frenzy that gathers momentum to a climax which ends in exhaustion. It is screaming in the wilderness, so to speak, since there is no comfort offered the baby and none that he seeks himself. In *this* extremity we have seen babies who never turn to their mother.

It seems reasonable to assume that the screaming babies I am describing are experiencing distress of such magnitude that pain reaches intolerable limits. Sometimes, in fact, the parents have reported to us that the baby's wailing and screaming abruptly stop after an interval which, in their view, suggests that the baby is "faking." He is not, of course. The behavior suggests that, at intolerable limits, there is a cutoff mechanism which functions to obliterate the experience of intolerable pain. Analogues with intolerable physiological pain suggest themselves.

The picture of the screaming babies represents helplessness in extremity. Kaufman (1977), in examining the biological response systems in monkey and human infants, says: "In very early life the reaction to danger is automatic and consists successively of two genetically pre-programmed biological response systems, namely, first 'flight-fight' and then 'conservation-withdrawal.' [Here Kaufman cites Engel's use of conservation-withdrawal.] Both are called forth by the condition in which the infant is helpless before a 'danger' which constitutes a threat to his functional status" (pp. 16–17). Kaufman regards these biological response systems as the precursors of psychobiological states of anxiety and depression.

What we are seeing in the babies I have described are certain behaviors that belong to the biological response systems and others that belong to a psychobiological system (well elucidated by Kaufman). In the extremity of biological helplessness, the screaming baby's agitated protest employs "flight-fight" responses followed by conservation-withdrawal. There are no defenses against imperative need states. But the same baby who flails in helplessness under extreme internal distress finds a defense which sustains him in the face of objective danger for most of his waking hours. One of these defenses is avoidance of his mother. Avoidance belongs to a psychobiological system. Avoidance has cognitive import (Schneirla, 1959). To "avoid" signifies that the baby has associated the figure of his mother with a threat to his functioning. There is an element of expectation, of anticipation of danger in avoidance, and since this anticipation is based upon experience and is no longer an instinctive reaction alone, we are observing a defense which appears to make use of signal anxiety. It is of considerable importance that this early defense also serves to ward off painful affects. If the baby selectively edits his mother's face and voice from experience, he will not encounter anxiety in intolerable repetitions throughout his waking day.

In the avoidance patterns exhibited toward the mother, I think it is reasonable to assume that the percept of mother has become associated with pain; that her face and her voice, if registered, would evoke painful affects. This level of recognition memory or associative memory is within the repertoire of the baby between the ages of three and seven months. What is remarkable is that a baby of this age can reverse the aims of the biological repertoire of signaling behaviors (gaze, smile, vocalizations, motor approaches) to avoid the mother and that perception itself can be caught up in conflict in the early months of life, so that registration appears to be closed off selectively. While we are unwilling, of course, to speak of a form of repression in infancy, the mechanism in which perception of a painful stimulus can be abolished from consciousness may be present in early development.

### Freezing

In the context of biological helplessness a form of defense that I have called "freezing" was observed. It has an easily recognizable counterpart in human and animal psychology in situations of exposure to the most extreme peril. The behavior is one of complete immobilization, a freezing of posture, of motility, of articulation. Among the babies we studied it was noticed as early as five months of age under circumstances that are objectively benign from the observer's vantage. It may occur when the baby finds himself in a strange situation such as the office playroom.

Mary, at five months, freezes during the first visit to the office. Her mother props her on the couch and Mary sits glassy-eyed and immobile for twenty minutes or more. Mary's mother is present, but she is not a protector, and the baby does not look toward her or seek reassurance from her through touch or voice. She does not respond to the tactful overtures of the therapist who wants to ease the anxiety. Normally, children at five months of age in a strange situation will seek closeness with the mother for an initial period, find reassurance through the mother, survey the strange room and strange persons with interest, then gradually, feeling protected, respond to and even initiate social exchanges with the stranger. But Mary, for an unbearably long period, remains frozen in place, staring off into space.

Halfway through this observation session, when a tester introduces toys to her, Mary makes a faint-hearted effort to touch a red ring, then hold a block, and suddenly she begins to cry. With the first outcry comes a motor collapse—rigidity gives way to disorganized motility, the cry becomes a scream, and the screaming escalates into a mournful howl that does not subside for five minutes, during which time the personality of the child appears to disintegrate before our eyes. There seems to be no awareness of her surround. She does not seek comfort from her mother; she never looks toward her although she is sitting on her lap. Her mother, during this interval of howling, makes a faint gesture to soothe the baby, gives up, and stares off into space. We do those things we can as therapists to bring some measure of relief in this situation.

This sequence represents the other face of freezing. Immobilization is a biological defense against the most extreme danger. However, its utility as a defense is probably exhausted in circumstances of chronic, unalleviated stress. The cost of maintaining immobility for a period of time will be physiological pain, and the tensions between the biological systems that ward off external danger and the systems that regulate internal stress cannot be resolved. Both systems break down, and the infant succumbs to a state of total disorganization.

Cindy, who was first seen by the intervention team at sixteen months, can sustain the posture of frozen mobility for an extraordinary length of time. Cindy is the one child in this subgroup who does *not* avoid her mother. She clings to her mother in mute terror. When we first visit her at a day care center, she is standing beside her cot, rigid, with a fixed stare and a face that registers no emotion. She maintains this rigid stance for forty minutes, oblivious to her surround and the occasional attempts of day care aids to distract her or lure her into activity.

Cindy's mother is a heroin addict. At home, Cindy is witness to brutal acts by men who are her mother's friends and lovers. Often Cindy wakens in a household where everyone is drugged and she tries desperately to arouse her mother. Sometimes her mother forgets to pick her up at the day care center. Cindy clings to her mother in mute terror, as we see in our early observations in the office.

Then, as we saw earlier with Mary, Cindy's defenses, freezing and withdrawal, collapse at certain times. Now we see the other side of defense in this sixteen-month-old child. Cindy is at home when she hears a noise from the basement. She is terrified. She screams, flails wildly, begins to strike her mother with her fists, and finally runs to a closet to hide. During the anxiety attack she cannot hear her mother's reassurances; she seems out of touch with reality. We, too, are witnesses to such panic states in Cindy. At times her personality, like Mary's, seems to disintegrate before our eyes.

Cindy's meager repertoire of defenses includes, at sixteen months, "fighting." With more advanced motor and drive development than five-month-old Mary, Cindy can strike out, at times, at the person who represents danger to her or at any available object which becomes a target. In the elementary scheme of defense, Cindy can take flight through freezing or withdrawal, or she can fight, at least briefly, in a futile exercise such as I have described. In the end, it is safer to hide in a closet.

### Fighting

This brings us to reflections on a group of children who are referred to our program in the second year of life because of severe behavior problems. They are also children who avoid their mothers, but no one refers to them as avoidant children. They are variously described to us as "little monsters," by their parents, or "holy terrors," or "stubborn," "mean," "spoiled," and they very often carry a label "hyperactive" which turns out not to be true.

For many years clinicians have looked upon these children as "un-disciplined," the product of laissez-faire child rearing practices or in-consistent discipline. Given the diagnosis, the treatment recom-mended was "discipline," "firmness," "let him know who is boss." I think it is possible that many of these children may, in fact, be the product of lax discipline, but the children that I will describe should be carefully discriminated from "spoiled" children. We cannot know this unless we are able to observe children in their homes.

A number of these toddlers presented an arresting clinical picture. They were, in every case, "little monsters" by day and terrified chil-dren at night who wakened in acute anxiety and could not fall back to sleep or be comforted.

A clinical observer could capture both the little monster picture and the terrified child picture in alternating sequences. Joshua, at thirteen months, gives his therapist a fair picture of both. He is obsti-nate, negative, and provocative with his mother, and he fights her with all his strength when she provokes him through her demands. Then when the fight fails before a stronger opponent, Joshua has a monumental tantrum. He throws himself to the floor; he screams, flails about. The screams become sobs, and tears stream down his face. He cannot be reached by his mother or his therapist. He is completely out of touch. On a few occasions the therapist recorded that it took nearly ten minutes to bring Joshua out of this state. Afterward he was exhausted, shaky, and wet with perspiration.

What we have seen is something that can fairly be called a disinte-grative state. But now how does this match with the picture of Joshua at night? His parents complain that he is up for hours at night. He wakens crying or in terror. Where is the anxiety in the day behavior? It is there, but it appears so fleetingly that only a trained clinical ob-server could see it. There is a moment before each of the fighting episodes with his mother in which fear registers on Joshua's face. Just for a moment. Then all trace of fear vanishes from his face, and he begins to fight. When the fight fails, the tantrum begins, and with it, the signs of a disintegrative state emerge.

We do not ordinarily think of "fighting" as a defense, certainly not as an ego defense. Fighting is accommodated in our defense theory mainly when it has become a complex and compounded ego defense, as in "identification with the aggressor." But in the period before there is an ego—and defense derives in large measures from a biological repertoire—we need to be attentive to the appearance of fighting as a form of defense. How this defense later makes its way into an ego defense cannot be answered from our research. However, I would propose that what we see in Joshua and other children of this age suggests that long before we can speak of identification, or "identification with the aggressor," fighting as a defense in earliest childhood appears in various manifestations, including the pathological forms that I have described. It seems to me that Joshua is not only fighting his mother because of terror; he is fighting against the danger of helplessness and dissolution of the self feelings which accompany extreme danger. The disintegrative states that I have described in Joshua and other children must constitute an extreme danger in themselves.

I should mention that for each of the children who showed this form of severe behavior disorder and disintegrative states we were able to bring about significant positive change. In each case we helped the parent recognize that it was anxiety that triggered the monster behavior and the tantrums, and when we could deal with the anxiety as anxiety, the pathological behavior disappeared. It goes without saying that these were children with the most severe disturbances in object relations—the children who avoided their mothers in every circumstance—and that our work had to move directly into strengthening the ties to parents at the same time that we dealt with the child's tremendous anxiety.

## Transformations of Affect

As we follow the chronological sequence in my records, we come upon a group of behaviors which first appear in the age range of nine months to sixteen months, in which affective transformations are displayed.

Billy had been referred to us at five months of age with the diagnosis of nonorganic failure to thrive. He was, at that time, one of the babies who consistently avoided his mother. He was a starving, solitary baby, the child of a depressed seventeen-year-old mother. Between five months and nine months our work with Billy and his family brought a number of positive gains. Billy gained weight steadily, and he was beginning to show some discriminating and preferential behavior toward his mother.

In the nine-month tape, Billy is being fed his bottle in his mother's arms. The beginning of this sequence seems unremarkable; Billy is sucking contentedly, his mother looks at him fondly; he shows less gaze avoidance than we had seen earlier. Then, abruptly, his mother turns the feeding into a tease game. She says, "Look here, Billy," and takes the bottle out of his mouth, holds it high, tosses her head back, and allows a few drops of milk to fall into her own mouth. And Billy, incredibly, begins to laugh and kick his feet with excitement. It is, in fact, the first time some of us had ever seen joy on this child's face. The mother returns the bottle to Billy, and he sucks contentedly again. Then, to our astonished eyes, after another interval, the mother again removes the bottle from Billy's mouth and renews the game. Again we see crowing and laughter and motor excitement in the baby as he joins his mother in the game. This game is repeated six times in the course of the feeding. It is intolerable to watch. We all wished the camera would stop.

Billy is a baby who has become a willing and enthusiastic partner in a sadomasochistic game with his mother. A hungry baby, one who has known starvation in his early months, has modified an imperative biological need for a goal that may be called "social" with some irony. Painful affects, which we must assume belong to unsatisfied hunger, are transformed into affects of pleasure. Why does this hungry baby not show anxiety or protest when the bottle is removed from his mouth? A baby who has once experienced starvation and chronic anxiety that his hunger would not be satisfied would, to our minds, be the least likely child to cooperate in a tease game in which his bottle is removed by his mother. Somewhere there must be anxiety, at least a moment of apprehension, but I do not see it on his face. Rather, I see a kind of excited expectancy. Is it conceivable that there is a fleeting moment of anxiety, with the expectation of loss of the bottle, and that the game ritual, which always ends in the return of the bottle, formalizes the expectation that loss will be followed by restitution? Anxiety would then be modified by anticipatory pleasure, the social aspects of the game would add their own increment of pleasure. In the case of Billy, it is easier to describe than to explain the transformation of affect. For the moment it may be enough to record that transformations of affect can be observed in a child as young as nine months of age, long before we can speak of an ego and long before we can speak of repression. There are other examples in the pages that follow.

We cannot leave the story of Billy and his mother without adding that we, as psychotherapists, were able to move quickly to undo the morbid pattern that we saw emerging. In the work with the mother, we understood that Kathy was repeating a sadomasochistic relationship with her baby that belonged to experiences surrounding the birth of a younger sister when Kathy was five years old. When we helped Kathy see the connections between Billy and that first baby who intruded into her life, the tease games disappeared.

Around the beginning of the second year, examples of affective transformations begin to proliferate in our records. At thirteen months Greg reacts to his mother's shrill and threatening voice by laughing in a giddy way. This is a child who, a few weeks ago, cried out of fright when he heard that voice. Also at thirteen months, Joshua, when threatened by his mother, would run around in a giddy fashion, laughing in a ghoulish voice. Once, when his mother threw a ball which hit his genitals, he winced, then laughed, and his therapist, searching for words in her record, said, "He laughed with an almost painful pleasure." Betty at sixteen months engaged in sly, provocative contests with her mother, in which aggressive intent is masked by smiling through clenched teeth. When she throws or kicks toys in anger, she laughs, and her laugh has a giddy, theatrical quality to it.

In each of these cases we must look hard for the anxiety that triggers laughter. It can sometimes be caught in a fleeting moment before the transformation takes place. But for each of these children, chronic and severe anxiety has been part of daily life from the early weeks. The theatrical laughter and the foolish grin on the face are most certainly defenses against intolerable anxiety, but how the transformation is accomplished is not so well explained. As I consider it, we do not understand hysterical laughter in later childhood and adult life very well either.

What we have seen, however, is that a form of defense that closely parallels "reaction formation," which we understand as an ego defense, can occur in infancy as early as nine months of life, as we saw in Billy, and can be observed with frequency in a clinic population of toddlers in the second year of life.

Grief, too, can be transformed through conflict in infancy, and we have at least one example of a symptom which closely resembles a tic. Cindy, sixteen months old, who spends long periods in an immobile stance, her face bleak and expressionless, has a stereotypic form of eye rubbing. Without visible emotion, her hand moves to her eye, rubs the eye in a pantomime of suppressing tears. But there are no tears, of course; there have not been tears of grief for a long time, as reckoned in Cindy's brief life. She is not permitted to cry. After being scolded by her mother and by day care aides for crying (for being a baby, they said), Cindy can no longer bring forth tears of grief. When her mother bids her good-bye each morning at the nursery, Cindy is silent and dry-eyed, then assumes her stance of frozen immobility before her cot. The stereotypic eye rubbing, we must assume, takes place when the affect of grief is about to register. It is suppressed or perhaps closed off before there is conscious registration, and the motor pattern of eye rubbing, of stopping the flow of tears, is executed as a trace of the experience of grief. But now there are no tears.

### Reversal

The turning of aggression against the self arrests our attention in the second year, beginning in our records of children about thirteen months of age. This is not to say that such manifestations may not appear earlier. Spitz (1965) described children in an orphanage as young as eight months of age who attacked themselves.

In our records we see Betty at sixteen months in a tantrum, banging her head against the floor. She seems oblivious to pain. Joshua at thirteen months is heedless, reckless, climbs to perilous heights and falls, runs giddily and collides with furniture, and when you want to run to him in anguish to console him, he looks, at the most, a little jarred, but he seems not to be in pain. Indeed, for Joshua and for Betty the threshold for pain is so high that only an accident of considerable magnitude provokes a cry or a response that we, as observers, could call fully commensurate with our sense of the quantity of pain. A normal child, after cracking his head against a floor or a piece of furniture, would shriek in pain and might not be consoled by his mother for many minutes. But Betty and Joshua can tolerate high levels of pain without wincing. And these two children never turn expectantly to their mothers for comfort.

To explain how a child of thirteen or sixteen months can turn aggression against himself is not at all easy. There is a straightforward explanation which we can examine, but as we pursue the problem it becomes more and more complex. The straightforward explanation is that the child's fear of a parent and of parental retaliation inhibits the expression of aggression toward the parent. Aggression is then turned back upon the self. But pain should then be the inhibitor of self-directed aggression. It should be, but the next puzzle appears in our observations that these children seem not to experience pain in their self-inflicted injuries, or not until pain crosses high thresholds. So we are back to our unanswered questions about pain and biological defenses against intolerable pain, the cutoff mechanisms that we seem to come upon at every turn in this study of aberrant children.

Is there any possibility of a biological fault in these children which affects the perception of pain? I think not. When our therapeutic work is successful in dealing with anxiety, when the parents become the protectors against danger, these children begin to look like normal children. Aggression is discharged along normal pathways, it is modified in the service of love of parents, it is no longer turned upon the self, and pain is experienced in a measure that is appropriate to circumstance. When a fall or bump takes place now that Joshua has found safety and affection with his mother through our work, he cries or screams, as we should expect, and runs to his mother for consolation.

I do not want to overstress the pain component in this picture at the expense of drive vicissitudes. I only want to include it because it needs to be explained. But if we now examine the larger picture of these pathological relationships of babies and parents, it appears that the aberrant development in object relations that is present in every case is closely related to the deviant course of the aggressive drive which is seen most clearly in these cases at the beginning of the second year. This is no surprise. The interrelationships between these two drives has been a tenet of psychoanalysis for many years. Aggression is normally modified in the course of infant development through the child's love for his mother. Here, too, the biological pattern is extended, since in all species that have strong social bonds, aggression is channeled away from the partner through rituals that preserve the bond (Lorenz, 1963). It is of some interest that aberrant forms of aggression, including self-injury and self-mutilation, are found in monkeys who have been experimentally deprived of mothering and of socialization (Harlow and Harlow, 1965).

In summary, I have identified a group of pathological defenses observed in infants between the ages of three and eighteen months which occur, I believe, only in babies who experience danger and deprivation to extreme degree. The early defenses, "avoidance," "freezing," and "fighting," are apparently summoned from a biological repertoire on the model of "flight or fight." The human infant, of course, does not have "fighting" capability until motor advances and concomitant drive progression emerge at the close of the first year. The forms of avoidance I have described in these deprived infants employ a cutoff mechanism in perception which selectively edits the mother's face and voice and apparently serves to ward off painful affects. I have suggested that this elementary form of defense against the perception of a painful stimulus may be related to forms of defense employed in later ego organization when repression and those compound defenses which make use of repression close off the perception of a painful stimulus at the threshold of consciousness. The transformations of affect which I have described in infants in the first half of the second year tell us that long before there is an ego, pain can be transformed into pleasure (as in the case of Billy), and pain can be obliterated from consciousness while a symptom, such as Cindy's eye rubbing, stands in place of the original conflict. The deviant course of aggression in these deprived and imperiled infants is seen at the beginning of the second year of life when aggression is discharged in wild outbursts in one moment and turned back upon the self in self-injury in another moment. And finally, our attention is drawn to the picture of the infant when these defenses fail before the formidable task of defending without defenders. I have described disintegrative states in which the child flails and screams and is demonstrably out of touch with his surround.

The question of how these pathological defenses in infancy evolve into later defenses and defense mechanisms cannot be answered from my work. Since we intervened in every case and our work has been largely successful, we cannot know what the progressive course of such defenses would be if no environmental changes were brought about. Whatever the fate of these defenses might be, we, as clinicians, will not let it happen, if we can help it.

In only two cases in this subgroup did we fail to bring about a satisfactory infant-mother relationship and modifications of the defense patterns. One child, Sandra, was recommended for foster home placement after six months of unsuccessful treatment in our program. Betty, the child of the schizophrenic mother, remained in her precarious relationship to the mother. When Betty was three, we arranged for outpatient treatment of her in another program, and we were pained to see that the fluctuating patterns of rage toward her mother and aggression turned against her own body had only acquired new dimensions in personality. At age two and one half Betty would tear at her toenails until they bled, then regard the bloody fragments with detached interest. There was no sign that she experienced pain. The smile that accompanied hostile intention at the age of sixteen months was now imbedded as a personality trait. The disorganization of personality at sixteen months took on more ominous forms at three years of age. Betty, in a play session which was recorded on videotape, represented a mother in whom the hallucinations of her own mother had found their way. As the voice of the persecuted and the voices of the persecutors spoke in this chilling dialogue with dolls, it was no longer possible for the observers to know when the voices spoke for the mother and when the voices spoke for the child.

The happier stories are those of the babies and parents who were able to profit from help during the critical months and years of infancy. The therapeutic work with parents and babies took place in the home. We employed a form of treatment that was informed through psychoanalytic principles and methods, and a form of developmental guidance on behalf of the baby that was closely united with the psychotherapeutic methods. In each case we considered that the work in the area of object relations was central. We identified the impediments to the mother-infant relationship (in all cases repetitions from the maternal past) and employed those methods that would disengage the child from old conflicts. We supported, encouraged, and promoted every aspect of the positive relationship between baby and mother as it emerged in the treatment. As the bonds between baby and mother developed, and as the mothers became protectors to their babies, the pathological defenses of these babies disappeared.

This leaves us with unanswered questions regarding the fate of pathological defense in infancy. We cannot know what the course of these defenses might have been if treatment had not taken place. But from our point of view as psychoanalysts we will call this the happiest of insoluble research questions.

*Note*

This paper was presented as the René A. Spitz Lecture to the Denver Psychoanalytic Society, April 11, 1981.

*References*

Adelson, E. & Fraiberg, S. (1974). Gross Motor Development in Infants Blind from Birth. *Child Devel.*, 45:114–126. Reprinted in *Exceptional Infants, Vol. 3: Assessment and Intervention*, ed. B. Z. Friedlander, G. M. Sterritt & G. E. Kirk, pp. 63–83. New York: Brunner/Mazel, 1975.

Ainsworth, M.; Blehar, M.; Waters, E.; & Wall, S. (1978). *Patterns of Attachment: A Psychological Study of the Strange Situation.* Hillsdale, N.J.: Lawrence Erlbaum Associates.

Freud, A. (1936). *The Ego and the Mechanisms of Defence.* New York: International Universities Press, 1946.

Freud, S. (1926). Inhibitions, Symptoms, and Anxiety. *Standard Edition*, 20.

Harlow, H. F. & Harlow, M. F. (1965). The Affectional Systems. In *Behavior of Nonhuman Primates, Vol. 2*, ed. A. M. Schrier, H. F. Harlow & F. Stollnitz, pp. 287–334. New York: Academic Press.

Hartmann, H. (1950). Psychoanalysis and Developmental Psychology. *Psychoanal. Study Child*, 5:7–17.

Kaufman, I. C. (1977). Applicability of Nonhuman Research to Psychoanalytic Theory. Presented at a meeting of the American Association for the Advancement of Science, Denver. Unpublished.

Lorenz, K. (1963). *On Aggression.* New York: Harcourt, Brace & World, 1966.

Schneirla, T. C. (1959). An Evolutionary and Developmental Theory of Biphasic Processes Underlying Approach and Withdrawal. In *Nebraska Symposium on Motivation*, ed. M. R. Jones, pp. 1–42. Lincoln: Univ. Nebraska Press.

Spitz, R. A. (1945). Hospitalism: An Inquiry Into the Genesis of Psychiatric Conditions in Early Childhood. *Psychoanal. Study Child*, 1:53–74.

——— . (1961). Some Early Prototypes of Ego Defenses. *J. Amer. Psychoanal. Assn.*, 9:626–651.

——— with Cobliner, W. G. (1965). *The First Year of Life: A Psychoanalytic Study of Normal and Deviant Development of Object Relations.* New York: International Universities Press.

Stern, D. N. (1974). Mother and Infant at Play: The Dyadic Interaction Involving Facial, Vocal, and Gaze Behaviors. In *The Effect of the Infant on Its Caregiver*, ed. M. Lewis & L. A. Rosenblum, pp. 187–213. New York: Wiley-Interscience.

Wallerstein, R. S. (1976). *Psychoanalysis as a Science: Its Present Status and Its Future Tasks. Psychol. Issues*, Monogr. 36. New York: International Universities Press.

# Part II

Clinical Findings

# 8

# Enlightenment and Confusion

In 1937 in his paper "Analysis Terminable and Interminable" Freud remarked incidentally about the effects of enlightenment on the sexual theories of children:

> I am far from maintaining that this [enlightenment] is a harmful or unnecessary thing to do, but it is clear that the prophylactic effect of this liberal measure has been vastly over-estimated. After such enlightenment the children know something that they did not know before but they make no use of the new knowledge imparted to them. We come to the conclusion that they are by no means ready to sacrifice those sexual theories which may be said to be a natural growth and which they have constructed in harmony with and in dependence on their undeveloped libidinal organization—theories about the part played by the stork, about the nature of sexual intercourse and about the ways in which children are born. For a long time after they have been enlightened on these subjects they behave like primitive races who have had Christianity thrust upon them and continue in secret to worship their old idols. (P. 336)

It is a common experience in analytic treatment of children to see how the child makes use of the enlightenment which his parents have painstakingly prepared for him. Almost all of our child patients come to us with a fund of knowledge at their disposal, a vocabulary of "eggs," "seed," "fertilization," and scientific terms for parts of the body. Frequently the modern parent responds to the child's first questions with a full and prepared account of the process from conception to birth. Often, too, the parent brings out a book which has been bought and saved against this day and the child is invited to listen to a story about how babies are made.

Yet we are impressed to find that such children who "know every-thing" will, in the course of their treatment, bring out bizarre and distorted ideas of procreation which are no less strange than those of our less sophisticated patients, but with the added complication that these theories of the "educated" child are often more obscure. The analogies of animals, birds, fish, and humans, which the parents and books have painstakingly drawn, may give rise to startling deductions on the child's part. The illustrations in the books of "egg," "seed," um-bilical cords, etc., have a way of surviving in the child's memory with surprising clarity, and of fusing with older and archaic images which the child has never surrendered.

From time to time in my work with children I have been interested to see the way in which children have employed the new ideas ac-quired in their sexual enlightenment to support or reinforce the older infantile theories, in spite of the great contradictions which existed between the old and the new. Some detail from the book or the paren-tal explanation is singled out, remembered, and imposed upon the infantile beliefs. The infantile theory is now supported in the child's mind by his belief that he "got it" from the book or "my mother told me so."

Often the child will defend himself against our exploring questions by flatly stating that he "knows all about it." Sometimes he will recite by rote the entire story from "the sperm meets the egg" to "the special passageway where the baby comes out." We can find nothing to con-tradict in his brilliant accurate exposition, yet we are left with the unmistakable impression that his statement of beliefs overlays a mass of confused and distorted images. As treatment progresses these come to light in striking ways. We find that "the sperm meets the egg" in novel and unexpected ways. The "special passageway" is not so "special" after all and is located in approximately the same place that the child imagined before he received his enlightenment!

The material which is presented in these pages is an inquiry into the fate of sexual education in certain cases of children. I have chosen five cases in which the failure of the enlightenment can be evaluated and studied in the light of the child's neurosis. In each case motives come to light which make it necessary for the child to hold on to his infantile theories. In four cases the child manufactured a new theory from his enlightenment which sustained his own beliefs at the same time that it claimed validity from a qualified source.

The first case, which I should like to cite, concerns a rare theory of conception which was derived, we find, from an illustration in a book on sex education designed for children.

Tony is six. He is in treatment because of his severe behavior problems. His sadistic attacks on other children have caused him to be ostracized in his neighborhood. His dreams and fantasies are filled with ideas of murder and of being murdered. In the tenth month of treatment he brings to the foreground his ideas of a sadistic relationship between men and women in which the man is damaged. Now he also begins a rapid-fire type of questioning of the therapist, questions on geography, history, science. The questions become more specific and lead, as might be expected, into the problem of origins. He answers my exploratory questions by saying, "I came from my mother. And my father had to help. He had to fertilize the seed." I ask him what he means by this. He becomes serious and says, "*That's* what I don't know. That's the big mystery question!" I encourage him to give me his ideas on this. "Well, he has a seed or sperm inside." And how does it get out? "I think from the belly buttom." Is he sure? "I think so. . . . Oh! I think the sperm is in the penis." (Now he is pleased with himself.) "And how does it get to the mother's seed?" Tony (gloomily): "There's only one way. I don't want to say it." Would he try to? "They . . . they cut it open (the penis). Just like they cut open the mother to get the baby out." "They do?" "Yes. 'Cause there's no other place for the sperm to come out." "Are you sure?" "Well, I'm pretty sure, but I'll look tonight." And now he hastily drops the subject.

Later I ask Tony why he is so sure that a daddy has to be cut open to get the sperm out. Tony: "Don't ask me all those mystery questions or I'll have bad dreams!" "Like what?" "Like . . . like murder dreams." I tell him that if we solve the mystery questions we will one day get rid of the bad dreams for good. Encouraged by my promise, Tony goes on. "They have to cut the Daddy's penis open," he explains, " 'cause the sperm is too big." "How big is it?" I ask. "This big!" he shows me. "*As big as a marble!* Then it meets the mother's seed and it gets to be a baby. . . . Then they cut her open." "Are you sure?" "Yes, my mother told me!" (I established that she had not.) He shows the greatest resistance to further discussion at this point. He firmly and noisily upholds his own theories.

We do not return to the subject for two interviews. Then an interesting interlude occurs. In a club, where he is the only Jewish boy among seven Christians, he engages in an exhibitionistic act. For some time he has been reluctant to go swimming with the boys and I suspected that this was because he was circumcized. He had formed a friendship with another boy in the group who, I learned later from his therapist, was also circumcized. Tony invited his friend, Jimmy, to engage in a stealing prank and then suggested that they both go to the club leader "and show her our pee-wees."

Following this episode we begin to solve "the mystery question." Tony returns to the subject of pee-wees and sperms. He has figured out that little boys do not have sperm because their pee-wees are too small and the sperm could not come out of such a little pee-wee. I ask him again how big the sperm is. Again he says, "About as big as a marble." I express my puzzlement. He is insistent. *"I saw it in a book. It was a picture!"* I ask now if he will draw this picture for me, which he did. Now we understand. It was a drawing of the sperm as seen through a high-powered microscopic lens! It was one of the illustrations in his book dealing with the sexual questions of children.

We are interested in the way in which Tony "saw" this illustration. I learned through further questioning that he had understood that this was the way the sperm looked under a microscope. He was an intelligent six-year-old who knew that a microscope enlarges. And the book which his mother read to him had clearly stated that sperm were invisible to the naked eye, "too small to see." He had misconstrued because he had a theory, antedating the book's theory, which could not yield to the new idea. I might fill in a few of the details here.

We know that he had a sadistic theory of coitus. He believed that the man was damaged, destroyed (as in the murder dreams he told me). But is there something even more specific? I asked him why they "cut open the father's penis" to get the sperm out. Before this I had encountered his preoccupation with circumcision in many different forms. The idea of an operation on the penis had such reality for him that I suspected a connection here. From the mother I learned that Tony had been present during his baby brother's circumcision. Tony was then three.

We see, then, how the ideas of "operation on the penis," "the mother and father do something together and the father gets hurt," and "how babies are made," are fused in Tony's mind. When the enlightenment is received he chooses a single detail which fits into his own system of ideas and distorts the new information so that it reinforces the old beliefs.

In the case of another patient, a four-year-old boy, a story of animal procreation in a book read to the child by his mother "in answer to his questions," produced a singular train of thought which I shall report here.

Allen is exceptionally intelligent for his four years. He is in treatment for a behavior disorder of unusual severity. During the first months of treatment I was impressed by his intense preoccupation with and fantasies about the activity of his parents in bed. One of his ideas was that his parents "chop off their heads and make a baby." He plays endless games with the little trucks and trailers in which they hitch at night "and make so much noise they wake me up." We do not handle this material directly at this time. Rather our work in the beginning months centers around his own anxieties and fears regarding his body, his belief that a little boy could be "broken," that something could be stolen from him, etc. From time to time in the beginning weeks he voices tentative questions about babies, then grows giggly and evasive when I invite his ideas on the subject.

At the beginning of the third month of treatment, Allen asks his mother a simple question about the origins of babies. Unfortunately I cannot recall the specific question but I had the impression that it was one to which he already knew the answer. His mother, who was pleased to feel that her son at last was confiding in her, brought out a book which she had used in the sex instruction of Allen's older sister and read it to him. According to the mother, Allen was very impressed. He listened attentively, asked few questions, but occasionally asked to have a passage or a chapter reread in a real effort to "master" the information. The book, I should say was much too advanced even for this precocious four-year-old. I was not familiar with it but when I read it later, I was interested to see that it dealt with coitus through analogy with animals, discussed the problem of menstruation, and in other ways presented material which could only be confusing to this four-year-old mind.

Allen did not tell me about the book and the enlightenment for some weeks afterward. But it was around this time that a renewal and a strengthening of many of the old problems occurred. The temper tantrums increased and his aggressive and destructive behavior at home reached new heights. The parents often were completely unable to influence him. At the same time the analytic material became diffuse. The games with the trucks and the little cars, the plays about the burglar who comes at night, had now come at an end. This usually inventive child often could think of "nothing to do" when he was with me. He would start several games in which favorite toys like the trucks were to be used and then a moment later would abandon them.

It is difficult to assign a single factor as the cause of these events. As always in children's work we cannot be certain of the influence of environmental factors in bringing about such a period of acting. Thus by her own admission his mother had felt more aggressive toward Allen at this time. A beloved nursery school teacher had left the school and Allen missed her very much. He may also have been reacting to material which had come up in the analysis in connection with his masturbation. But in addition to these possible contributing factors the later material points with some certainty to the role of the book and his enlightenment in this chain of events.

We obtain occasional clues during this period of treatment. Once he plays a game in which a baby doll is put into a tiny chest of drawers, which is "like an oven for firing something like clay," and "gets all burned up." There seems to be an idea here that a baby could be destroyed inside the mother. Then from time to time, I notice his intense jealousy of other children who come to see me. He tries to tear down their pictures, destroy their handwork. He admits that he does not want any other children to come to see me. He insists, giggling, that I have a baby inside me. His mother has a baby inside her, too. He seems to think, and I suggest that he may be thinking that all women have babies inside of them at all times. He says yes. When I assure him this is not so he looks puzzled but will not continue the discussion.

One day he discusses current events with me. He confides, "I'm glad that the war is 16 miles away! People are getting killed where the war is. . . . I'd like to go to Egypt 'cause all the bad kings and queens are dead now. I know all about Egypt 'cause I heard it on our Passover record. . . . *The bad king made the mothers kill their babies!*" There is some discussion of this. He agrees with me, although with some worry, that no mother would do such a thing.

Then one day, near the end of this long cycle he plays another game in which he hides the baby doll in a toy clothes hamper. We play this hiding game together. This leads into a discussion of where a real baby comes from. He answers promptly: "From the mother's tummy." He "can't remember" where the baby comes out. "I *know* this isn't right," he says. "I think it's the head but I know it isn't right. I knew but I forgot. I've got a book and it tells all about that. . . . *Did you know that some fathers eat up the eggs so no babies will come? It said so in my book!*"

And here we obtained our clue to Allen's preoccupation with the subjects of "babies getting all burned up inside the 'oven,'" the command to the Hebrew mothers to murder their babies, the fate of all the babies that might be inside his mother. I learned from his mother that the book mentioned the fact that although fish lay millions of eggs, few of these will ever become baby fish because the *father or other animals eat them up!*

We are interested in the fact that two months after Allen has had the book read to him, all the facts regarding procreation seem to have flown out of the window, including the very important fact of "how the baby gets out," which the book explained. He cannot remember the explanation, he can only think that the baby comes out of the head, though he says he knows that is not right. Thus it is the infantile theory which triumphs. All that remains of the book is the fate of the *fish eggs which are not fertilized!* The father eats the eggs.

Now we wonder why this is. From the earlier analytic material we recall his preoccupation with the activities of his parents in bed. He conceived of a sadistic act of procreation. "They chop off their heads and make a baby." At the same time, we recall his own fears of castration. The information which he obtained at this time when his mother read him the book was partially mastered intellectually, then almost entirely lost. All that remained was the memory of a sadistic act, the father's eating of the eggs. That he also attributed such murderous impulses to the mother is evident from our material. Since his fantasies at the time also dealt with the possibility of destructive or cannibalistic acts against his own person, we may assume that he transferred these ideas to his theories of procreation and to the fate of unborn babies. It should also be said that both Allen and his sister feared their mother's aggression, an oral aggression which sometimes took the form of shrillness and scoldings. (His sister, at the age of eight, had once said to me, "Of course nobody would eat up a child. . . . And anyway, . . . children wouldn't taste so good—would they?")

In books on sex education for children certain stereotyped phrases are employed for the process of conception. "The Daddy plants a seed in the mother . . ." is a phrase which many children have learned. One day six-year-old Peter comes to his interview with as guilty an expression as I have ever seen on the face of this small delinquent. He confesses with great apprehension that he has stolen something. I am interested because he has often stolen without a trace of guilt, but today he is very disturbed. At last he tells me. He had stolen a package of cucumber seeds! "I planted them under the telephone pole—the whole package of seeds." Then later, " . . . maybe me and my mother will have a baby next summer!"

Now we can be fairly sure that our knowing delinquent did not really believe that babies were made in this fashion. In the next interview Peter makes another confession. He admits that he knows a bad word. The word is "fuck." I ask if he knows what the word means. At this he becomes very angry. "I don't know what it means, but my mother she *don't* do it!" Thus Peter knew the facts very well! But his denial of "what mother and daddy do" finds support in the enlightenment which he had received. "A seed is planted. . . ." He then acts out his incestuous wishes by way of circumlocution provided by the bookish phrase.

In our analytic practice enlightenment is given the child strictly in accordance with the requirements of the analytic material and following a careful working through of his infantile theories. Yet, we are interested to see that our patient, from time to time, may revive one of his older theories of origins even after a careful working through of the material. I recall an eight-year-old girl who was nearing the end of the second year of her treatment when she gave me a theory of birth which had long been abandoned but was temporarily revived under the influence of her mother's pregnancy. In two years we had worked through her beliefs that babies came from the anus, from the urethra, from the belly button. All of these theories had existed side by side with the correct information which her parents had given her before she came to treatment. At the age of six, due to the enlightenment by the parents, she could give a complete account of procreation including "the father puts his penis into the mother." She had been enuretic and was severely constipated at the time she came to treatment. In the course of the treatment it was impressive to see how she had "learned the facts" while giving up none of her own infantile theories. The quantities of affect which had been isolated during this learning, emerged in the course of treatment, revealing how the learning had been accomplished while the symptoms were being formed on the basis of her primitive theories.

At the end of the second year of treatment she was symptom-free for a two-month period, and then her mother became pregnant. Shortly after Betty learned of this she developed a new symptom, a hysterical "burping." She clung to this symptom in a secret and satisfied way. She argued that this could have nothing to to with "feelings," that it came from something she ate, and that it was certainly nothing I could help her with. She would giggle as she said this in such a way that I was sure she consciously tried to keep something from me.

Then one morning she came in, looking tired and fretful. She burped constantly as she told me a nightmare which she had had the previous night. Betty, mother, grandmother, and Polly (a friend of Betty's), were in a land where bad animals were. There was a big animal with a beak and he was trying to steal something from them. Betty woke up screaming for mama. Her mother comforted her. Then Betty went to her story book. She read the story of the Gingerbread Boy and the story of the Wee Wee Old Woman. Then she went to sleep. When she woke up in the morning, she complained of a stomach ache and told her mother that she did not want to go to Selma's today.

I asked Betty to describe the bad animal with the beak. Her description fitted a stork very nicely though she could not remember its name until I suggested it. I took the story of the Gingerbread Boy as part of the dream and suggested that it might have something to do with the dream. She was far enough along in treatment so that I could suggest that this had something to do with "making a boy" or a baby. She giggled a little and burped continuously. Then I drew her attention to Polly in the dream. Polly had been the source of much discussion earlier in the treatment, for Betty and Polly used to play doctor games together. Now Betty admitted shyly that yesterday she and Polly had played "having a baby." (There had been no sex play for over a year prior to this period.) I asked how had they played "having a baby." Betty said she would explain:

"We put the baby in our clothes. Then the doctor cuts open the stomach." I asked her to show me on the doll. She made criss-cross cuts on the doll's stomach. In response to a question, she said, "Oh, I know that isn't the way and it comes out some place else." (She showed me the correct place on the doll.) "But we play it comes from the belly button. And Polly plays the husband and Margie plays the nurse. Then Polly and I go to sleep 'cause she's the husband."

I asked, "When children play having babies do the ladies feel sick?" "Oh, yes. They groan something terrible! This morning I woke up with a stomach ache, too!" I said, "Do they ever burp?" She exploded with giggles. "No! No! No! No! No!" she said. You're making that up!" she protested laughing. . . . And then she let out a profound belch and burst into laughter again.

Now the burping, I should say, was in identification with her mother who, during an earlier pregnancy which Betty remembered, had belched frequently. The detail of "cutting open the stomach" to get the baby out belongs, not only to the children's doctor game but to a game which Betty liked to play with her father when I first knew her. When Daddy came into Betty's room to kiss her good night she liked him to play with her which she called "operation." Daddy would make criss-cross motions with his finger on Betty's tummy which caused her to giggle because it tickled. When I learned of this game early in the treatment I had asked the father to give it up. There was little question that Betty enjoyed it and that in the doctor games with the children, the "cutting open" of the stomach was stimulating and exciting.

I think, then, we can understand why Betty reverted to an earlier theory of conception and birth when her mother became pregnant. The mother's pregnancy forces the child to the painful acknowledgement of the parent's intimate relationship which has produced the baby. At the same time she envies her mother who has been given a baby by the father. Her symptom of burping derives from an identification with her pregnant mother and an earlier theory of oral impregnation. In her doctor game the erotic element in the old game with her father is acted out in accordance with the wish to have a baby by her father. But also the infantile form of the game, and the manner of birth enacted, constitutes a denial of the facts of the sexual relationship between the child's parents. The mother's pregnancy is a painful proof to the child of the facts of coitus. She defends herself against these painful emotions by reverting to an earlier theory, one which is both pleasurable like the old game with Daddy, and which serves the useful purpose of denying the unpleasant truths.

I might conclude with one last case example which illustrates how enlightenment can come to grief even with an older child when it is imposed on infantile theories which have not been surrendered.

In the early days of my practice with children I was working with an eleven-year-old girl whose obstinacy, negativism and ill-tempered response to my therapeutic efforts left me with a twice-a-week feeling of futility and incompetence. I was gratified, therefore, after seven months of treatment to see some encouraging signs. Where for seven months she had loudly insisted that she wanted to be a boy, she now made some slight gestures in the other direction, which consisted of wearing skirts and combing her hair. She began to ask tentative questions about sexual matters, or rather to show interest in sexual matters in a disguised fashion. I took advantage of this new direction in treatment by enthusiastically presenting the facts of menstruation and conception while she listened with careful attention and some skepticism. In the course of these discussions (or lectures, perhaps) she asked a few questions regarding procreation. She did not believe that "you had to have a father to make a baby." She was unwilling to discuss this with me but seemed full of some secret knowledge and contempt for me which I did not understand. Then the discussions stopped. We had more negativism and more slacks and the hair was again uncombed.

One day Patty's mother called me before Patty's appointment to tell me that she had begun to menstruate that day. When Patty arrived she was silent and looked upset. She carried her school books into the office, sat down opposite me, picked up one of her library books, held it in front of her face and began reading to herself. The book was an effective barrier between her face and mine. On the cover of the book, I read its title: "The Mystery of the Missing Key."

Patty refused to talk during this interview. Then for about two weeks the interviews followed this same pattern. She brought one or another of the mystery books which she read constantly at school and at home, held it in front of her face and ignored me completely. Of course, I tried to handle the problem. I alluded to the mysteries and the avoidance of me and the relationship of the two factors. But she cleverly avoided getting into conversation with me.

Then one day she marched into the office with a look of triumph. She promptly told me that she had caught me in a lie. "You told me a baby had to have a mother and a father!" I admitted this. "There now I got you!" she sang out. *"Cause I read in the newspaper all about the lady who got a baby from artificial respiration!"*

I tried to straighten her out on this in vain. I knew that she was alluding to a newspaper account of a legal suit involving a case of artificial *insemination.* "No!" she insisted. "Respiration! I'll show you the paper. That's what it said. You can ask any of the kids at school."

I asked her to explain how one could "get a baby" from artificial respiration. She said, "Well *you* know what artificial respiration is when somebody drowns. Well, that's how it happened." I reminded her that we had already discussed that the seed of the male must come in contact with the egg of the female for conception to take place. She said knowingly, "You don't have to have the seed of a male." "Are you sure?" "Yes." "Give me an example." Patty said cautiously, "I heard of a girl who did something to herself and she got a baby." I asked what she could have done. "She did something like you do to have babies but she did it to herself." She went on. "But you have to *menestrate* first. And then if you do it after you *menestrate* why then you can have a baby!"

This naturally led into a discussion of masturbation and a story confided by Patty of sexual play with boys at the lake two summers ago. For our purposes here we need not go into this material.

The story of Patty seems to me of special interest in that it reveals how the infantile theories of procreation serve a purpose even at a later age in childhood. My enthusiastic and ill-timed enlightenment had entirely failed to reckon with this child's pubertal fantasies. Now it is easy to see that she had to deny the role of the male in procreation because of her anxieties about the sexual act. Her tom-boyishness was a defense against the heterosexual strivings which at that time were felt as dangerous.

Menstruation was perceived as a castration ("The Mystery of the Missing Key"). Her ideas of coitus were based upon her own masturbation (probably with fantasies of having a penis) but were also fused with the knowledge of a sexual act between two partners as we see in shadow behind the "artificial respiration" theory. Thus at the same time that she denies the facts of coitus and the role of the man, her "artificial respiration" theory testifies to some knowledge of a rhythmic act "performed upon" a woman lying prone.

In each of these cases cited we see many implications for those who enlighten the child, both for the parents and for the therapist. It seems that parents and beginning therapists share many of the same problems in enlightenment, the tendency to "tell all," to "read the book" to the child, to overlook the complex fantasies on which this new education is imposed. It is noticeable that in each case education did not "take" because the child's own theories served the neurosis in some way. In certain of our cases, as we have seen, isolated bits of the new education were appropriated by the child when these, too, served a neurotic purpose.

*Reference*

Freud, S. (1937). Analysis Terminable and Interminable. *Coll. Papers*, 5.

# 9

# Clinical Notes on the Nature of Transference in Child Analysis

In analytic work with children we are aware of factors in the conditions of therapy and the nature of the child as patient which differ markedly from the analytic situation with the adult. In the important field of transference these differences are such as to call for a reexamination of what we mean by transference in child analysis.

In this paper I shall review case material from the analyses of children in which transference phenomena are observable and permit inquiry into their motives and the manner of their appearance. In order that we can make a careful evaluation of such phenomena and judgments regarding differences and similarities in the transference with children and adults, it should be desirable to submit our data from child analysis to the test of the strict usage of the term "transference" in analytic terminology.

"By transference," says Anna Freud, "we mean all those impulses experienced by the patient in his relation with the analyst which are not newly created by the objective analytic situation but have their source in the early—indeed, the very earliest—object-relations and are now merely revived under the influence of the repetition-compulsion" (1946a, p. 18).

The role of transference in child analysis has met with different interpretations by Anna Freud and her co-workers and by Melanie Klein and her associates. It is the view of Anna Freud that a transference neurosis is not established in the case of the child patient. While recognizing in child analysis "manifold and variegated transferred reactions," she points out that in her own experience she has encountered no case of a child patient "where the original neurosis was given up during the treatment and replaced by a new neurotic formation in which the original objects had disappeared and the analyst taken their place in the patient's emotional life." "It is only a structure of this kind," she emphasizes, "which deserves the name of transference neurosis" (1946b, p. xii). Since the child still possesses the original objects and depends upon them primarily for his emotional gratification there would be no motive for the formation of a transference neurosis in Anna Freud's view.

Melanie Klein, on the other hand, holds the view that a full transference neurosis does occur with children "in a manner analogous to that in which it arises in adults," basing her belief on her experience in child analysis and on her own analytic theories. According to her theory, the major part of the oedipus complex has already undergone repression in the very young child, and the child is "far removed through repression and feelings of guilt from the original objects," and therefore fully capable of establishing a transference neurosis (1948, p. 165).

With these points in mind let us proceed to examine two cases which have been selected for study of transference phenomena in childhood.

## Transference of a Dog-Phobia

*Summary of Background and Pertinent Material*

Dottie, seven years old, had been referred for treatment of a serious behavior disorder. Her parents described her as a stubborn, defiant child who was insatiable in her demands, completely self-centered and indifferent to the feelings of those around her. She had wild temper tantrums and screaming fits which alternated with states of depression and lassitude. There was extreme rivalry with a younger sister of four whose charm, good nature and docility were in direct contrast to the older child's behavior. Both parents preferred the younger child, but the four-year-old Jeannie was the frank favorite of the mother. The mother's hostility toward Dottie was evident from the child's infancy. In fact, it was the father (then in analysis himself) who initiated plans for therapy for Dottie. The mother was indifferent and skeptical and would herself have preferred a boarding school.

The series of episodes which I shall report here, occurred in the third month of Dottie's analysis. To summarize briefly the development to that time:

The insatiable little girl had made the most exacting demands on the therapist before she could give her confidence. In games with Dottie I managed to cast myself in the role of a benevolent lady who would give a little girl anything she wanted. Her wishes were fantastic. She dreamed up vast quantities of candies, pastries and delicatessen. In game form these were presented to her and she consumed them all in a single gulp. Then she would cry that she was hungry and she wanted more and more.

Because of the inability of the mother to co-operate in Dottie's treatment during the early months, the therapist had to provide actual gratifications to a very large extent in order to establish the basis for a working relationship. The degree of earnest co-operation which the small girl was finally able to give in her treatment was quite exceptional. She seriously joined forces with the therapist to "get rid of the part of her that wanted to be bad." She made heroic efforts to control herself and thereby won a softened, much less hostile response from her parents.

Therapy was a lonely project for her. She came to interviews unaccompanied. (I lived only a few blocks from her school.) She went home alone, and the little seven-year-old took the bus back to her home about a mile away. Her mother was unwilling to call for the child and felt that she was quite able to get around herself. Thus Dottie had none of the feeling of parental participation which children should have in therapy. She came to interviews in all weather, regardless of the strong resistances which she felt at certain times. She was rarely late for her appointments. She carried on the business of therapy like an adult.

It is important to note that, just before the happenings which we report here, Dottie's mother had started her own analysis. It appeared for a while that the mother's rejection and hostility toward the child were temporarily brought under control although, of course, no fundamental changes had yet occurred in her attitude toward the child. The mother's own neurotic symptoms had become exaggerated, however. Her insomnia had grown worse and she excused herself more and more from family responsibility on the basis of "feeling tired and ill."

As is to be expected when a child begins to bring his impulses under control, certain neurotic symptoms began to appear more strongly in Dottie around the time that her improvement at home took place. A slight tic made its appearance around the corners of the mouth, testifying to the strength of those oral aggressive impulses which had been controlled at such cost. Also an old symptom, the grinding of her teeth in her sleep, became so pronounced that the father claimed to me that he could hear the child several rooms away. At the same time I received reports that Dottie had become noticeably afraid of dogs at home. Although her father asked her to tell me about her fear of dogs Dottie did not bring this to me.

The therapeutic work had already begun to focus on some of Dottie's fears but it was noticeable that she evaded such discussions. When the material pointed strongly toward the area of her anxiety and I would suggest the underlying fear to her, she would become blank, turn her face seriously to me and say, "What did you say? I didn't hear you." It was evident that she was truthful in this. If pressed a bit she would become further confused and vague. Now, also for the first time, Dottie began to ask why she should have to come here when she was "all better" now.

## Transference of the Dog-Phobia

During one interview of this period we encountered a "blankness" and unproductivity for the duration of the hour. Following this interview, which was remarkable only for its greater resistance, Dottie left the house.

Fifteen minutes later I heard a hammering on my door and screaming. It was Dottie. She ran wildly into the house and threw herself sobbing on the floor. Between sobs she told me that there was a dog sitting on the steps next door. No, he had not chased her. She had just seen him there and she was afraid to leave my house. She had been waiting on my doorstep all this time because she did not know what to do. This was a small dog which I knew Dottie had encountered at almost every visit to my house. She had never reacted to him before. I do not know now whether this was because he was previously "exempt" from the phobia or whether she would not or was not able to tell me. At least he had never before produced an anxiety attack in her.

She was comforted and reassured. Since I had another appointment I could not go into the episode in greater detail but offered to see her home if she would wait for me. After some moments she said that she would go home herself and had figured out a route by which the dog would not see her.

A few moments later—and before Dottie had reached home—I received a telephone call from Dottie's mother. Her mother gave no reason for the call but said that she wanted to tell me something about herself. She wanted me to know, she said, that no matter how much Dottie improved it would make no difference to her. She said that she found herself getting angry at Dottie "and then I can feel the cords of my neck tighten and I'm afraid of what I might do to her." It was a violent confessional outpouring, without precedent in my experience with this mother and completely unexpected. In reconstructing this strange conversation it appears that in the early weeks of her analysis the mother had reached growing awareness of the depths of her hatred for the child. In this call to the child's therapist we can also suspect that the mother was acting out something in the transference to her own analyst.

Now to return to Dottie. One would expect that the episode of the dog-phobia on my very doorstep would provide the opportunity I had been waiting for to begin the exploration of the phobia. On the contrary, Dottie's resistance was now even stronger than before. She was completely unable to speak of the incident with the dog, assured me that she really was not afraid of that dog, yet came to interviews and left interviews through back-alley routes. Any allusion to this fear or others brought about the now familiar blank look and the pleading, "What did you say? I didn't hear you." At the same time I was helpless and unable to handle this in any way because of her denial of all fear.

We have the impression now that Dottie's anxiety on the doorstep of the therapist's house was caused by something more than the mere presence of the dog on the neighboring doorstep. Why did the anxiety attack come on at this particular point and not earlier in her constant encounters with this dog? True, the therapist and her house had become dangerous virtue of the dog next door but had not the therapist been drawn into the phobia picture by something more than her proximity to the dog? Dottie's phobia had never been really severe in its other manifestations. It had never restricted her activities. The fact that she might encounter a dog on her way to school had never produced a resistance to going to school. The presence of dogs on her street did not prevent her from playing outdoors.

Several interviews passed. Then in one hour I happened to make a casual inquiry about the health of Dottie's mother, who was still ill and depressed. Dottie gave the conventional reply and then, in a fashion uncalled for by the nature of the question, began to build up a pathetic picture of an idyllic mother love, how her mummy had said this and that, how they did thus and so together. She seemed to feel compelled to defend her mother against deep-felt reproach. I said at this point that all of this was very nice and I was glad to hear it but I wondered if sometimes Dottie did not worry about her mother. Some minutes later Dottie said confusedly, "What did you say?" I repeated what I had said. Suddenly, on the verge of tears, she cried out, "I don't want to come here. I don't like to!" I used this remark to point out to her that almost every time we talked about her worries she had difficulty in hearing me, and that now when we talked of her mother she did want to come to see me. She nodded. I said that it was almost as if she were afraid of something here. Then I added jokingly, "What do you think I am, a dog who will bite you?" Reverting to play-acting I now proceeded to growl and bark timidly. She was momentarily startled, then laughed. In the next moment she was engaged in a game with me down on the floor, barking and yipping at me while I played the nursery game as a cowardly and harmless kind of pooch, crawling into corners and under the desk while she pursued me. She giggled throughout and screeched with joy as I simulated fear and whined as she approached me. She left the interview in high spirits.

In the next interview she arrived in an excellent mood. For the first time in several interviews she had taken the street route instead of the back-alley route from school to my house. She announced when she saw me that today when she saw the dog next door she just patted him on the head and she was not afraid. Her feeling toward me was once more relaxed and friendly, but it is interesting to note that we did not obtain any material at this time which led us further into the investigation of the dog-phobia.

The fear of the dog next door never reappeared in treatment although the dog-phobia was otherwise manifested according to the parents' reports to me. In the months that followed, analysis of the oedipal material brought about the dissolution of the phobia. In Dottie's later stories we learned of a wicked queen who was jealous of her beautiful daughter and had her taken out into the forest to be devoured by the wild animals.

## The Therapist as Witch

Before proceeding to an analysis of the transference of the dog-phobia, I should like to cite one other example from Dottie's case which throws additional light on the transference.

During the period of the analysis of the oedipal material, the full strength of the oedipal conflict was manifest when Dottie's mother went abroad for two months. Dottie became seductive toward her father, wanted to sleep in her mother's bed in the parents' room, and when thwarted by the father, had violent tantrums and wept uncontrollably. At the same time, of course, her anxiety increased and her stories and games in treatment contained the fear of violence from the mother in numerous forms. A basic formula appeared in many of these stories: A wicked queen jealous of her daughter, a scheme to get rid of the daughter (chop off her head, send her to the forest, etc.) and the beautiful daughter who learns of the plot and escapes. In one such version the little princess and her twin sister, who got her into trouble, fled from the castle at night. "They didn't even have a chance to take anything with them, only a refrigerator so as they wouldn't starve." There was a perilous flight across continents with the queen in pursuit. At one point the children sought refuge in a little house in the woods. It was a gingerbread house, Dottie said. An old, old woman lived there and lots of children came to see her and the witch turned them into candy. The story took another turn before I could explore this motif further. But I thought I caught a glimpse of myself in this old witch, in the words, "lots of children came to see her." I could not tell from the context just how I had emerged in this form, however.

Several interviews later the old witch cropped up again in another context. Now there had been evidence from Dottie's fantasies and stories, and reports from Dottie's father, that there had been sex play with a little boy of the neighborhood. Dottie told me a story one day. There were two children, a boy and a girl who were walking in the woods one day when they saw a sign saying: "Do not touch!" They touched it and they were enchanted and turned into statues. After a while a prince came along and disenchanted the children. And then in the rambling fashion of these children's stories we encounter the witch again in the next sequence. "The children come to a house in the woods and they see little statues of children turned to candy. So the children eat the candy and the witch is going to eat them up. Only she doesn't eat them up but they have to stay there for a year and then when the year is up they throw the witch in the oven and all the children come to life."

I was now quite sure I knew who the witch was. The witch wanted to eat the children up but she changed her mind. However, the children *have to stay there one year.* This detail made sense to me because a few days earlier Dottie had asked her father how long she would have to come to see me. (As our therapeutic work drew closer to her sexual activities and fantasies she had rapidly come to the conclusion that she had already stayed with me too long.) So she had asked her father with some show of petulance how long she would have to come to see me. Her father had told her rashly, "Oh, about a year."

Here we see the therapist again as a devouring woman, a witch who will eat up the children. But she changes her mind and commutes the sentence to one year. In this context the children have touched something forbidden (symbolizing the sexual activity) and the child expresses her fear that the witch (therapist) will do something dreadful to her when she learns about these sexual games.

*Analysis of the Motives for the Transference of the Dog-Phobia*

In reviewing the events which led up to the transference of the phobia we see the following sequence: The fear of dogs became intensified as the aggression against the mother was internalized during the first months of treatment. The dangerous animal is the mother. From the material we perceive that the dangerous animal embodies the child's aggressive and destructive wishes, yet represents from the side of reality the mother's aggression against the child and the objective danger which the child fears from the mother. It may be suggested, too, that the mother's illness plays a role in the intensification of the dog-phobia. For with the reality of the mother's illness the child is forced further to deny her hostile wishes against the mother.

We begin to see resistance to therapy at the point where the therapeutic work begins to deal with the anxiety. The child now defends herself against the analytic investigation in the same manner as she defends herself against the anxiety. The mechanisms of defense are isolation and projection.

It seems very important that at the point where the mother's own aggression and destructive wishes against the child break through the child is faced with her perception of a real danger coming from the mother. This serves to reinforce the symptom, for the ego of the child is now threatened from both sides, from within by the dangerous impulses, and from without by the dangerous mother.

At the same time another step is taken by the ego to ward off the "two-headed" dog. The therapist is perceived as dangerous, for if she removes the symptom the child will be exposed to intolerable anxiety. At the height of this conflict, then, the child suffers an acute attack of anxiety and her symptom is literally transferred to the doorstep of the therapist. She is afraid of the dog next door. At this point we may speak with some caution of a "transference neurosis" in that the neurosis is now transferred to the therapeutic situation.

We observe that the child does not recognize the "transference nature" of this development; she sees only a dangerous dog. We have great difficulty in isolating this phenomenon for analysis and meet only stronger resistances against coming for treatment. We are able at last to dissolve this transference through an interpretation and through the devices of play which we utilize with children. The therapeutic situation is now cleared for the further work required in the treatment of the neurosis.

We are interested in the question: Is this a transference neurosis? Considering the commonness of animal-phobias and the frequency of our encounters with such phobias in child analysis, I am impressed by the fact that this is the only time in my own experience that the symptom has been transferred to the therapeutic situation. As a rare occurrence, then, this "transference symptom" invites our interest.

Upon closer examination, however, we find that this is not, properly speaking, a transference symptom. For the phobia originated in the child's relationship to her mother and maintained itself on this ground at the same time that it appeared in transference to the therapist. The symptom was not detached from its original object and reformed around the person of the therapist. As we saw it, the symptom was only *extended into* the therapeutic situation in order to ward off the dangers which the child perceived there. We are not justified, then, in equating this manifestation with a transference symptom.

We could say that the transference of this symptom constituted a resistance against the therapeutic work, but this condition seems to have been made necessary by the *reality* in which this child lived at the time. In order to deal successfully with a phobia we must be able to unmask the object of danger and demonstrate to the patient how his fear is unrelated to external reality. However, when a mother reports to us that her own hatred of her child is so intense that she herself is afraid of what she might do to her child, we cannot say that the child's fear is not in some measure justified. And if our therapy has already deprived the child of her ability to fight back in her behavior at home, we must admit that we have put this child in real danger. We could show Dottie that the therapist was not dangerous to her, but at this particular point in her treatment and in her mother's analysis, we could not yet deal successfully with the reality factors at home.

Does the story of the witch cast further light on the transference of the dog-phobia? We recall how the witch in the house in the woods was first going to *eat* the children, then changed her mind, but made them *stay for one year*. Perhaps this story is a parody of the events. For first there was the fear of the therapist as represented in the dog-phobia (the fear of being bitten, eaten or destroyed). Then at a later point of resistance where the child's anxiety about her sexual activities is manifest, the danger perceived in the therapeutic work is not clearly defined; she will have to stay for one year.

## Transference of Anal Resistances in the Case of a Five-Year-Old Girl

*Summary of Background and Pertinent Material*

Margaret, five-and-a-half-years-old, was brought to me for treatment of her enuresis which had persisted from infancy. At the time of referral she was a docile, fastidious, very proper and well-behaved child, whose bed wetting appeared to be the only problem to the parents.

Margaret had been placed in a foster home at the age of three due to family circumstances and the mother's inability to cope with the child's soiling and smearing of feces. The father was at the time still in the armed services and hardly knew his little daughter. The soiling had ceased soon after placement but bed wetting had persisted. It was known that the foster mother had spanked the child for her bed wetting. After almost a year of placement the child was returned to her own home. At about the same time the father was released from service and the household was re-established. With the return of the child to her own home there was no recurrence of the soiling but frequent constipation became a problem. The mother administered enemas which the child herself sought and enjoyed. (This information was given by the parents and confirmed by the child herself.)

According to the history provided by the parents, Margaret had demonstrated her affection for the father and her jealousy of the mother in an open flirtation with the father when he returned from service and the family was reunited. In the course of a few months the flirtation had given way to an attitude, now characteristic, of renunciation and docile submission to unalterable circumstances.

At the time she came into treatment Margaret's character seemed already formed on the basis of rigid reactive defense mechanisms. Unfortunately the excessive tidiness and compliance were virtues highly admired by the mother, so that our initial task was difficult. From a clinical point of view the transformation of the tiny girl who soiled and smeared feces and defied her mother into the five-year-old who now appeared for treatment, was indeed an impressive one. No trace of the original impulses was visible. The pretty, healthy, social and talkative youngster impressed everyone she met with her charm and ease. There was no visible tenseness, not so much as a bitten fingernail to testify to the presence of those instinctual wishes which had been renounced with such completeness. There was only the bed wetting. During the two and half years of the analysis the investigation of this symptom revealed how every step of the way in ego development this single symptom accommodated the instinctual impulses which had been conquered by the ego.

The first months of treatment centered mainly upon the rigid defenses against dirt and messiness, for Margaret would permit herself none of the usual child's activities in the playroom because of her excessive tidiness.

Gradually she became freer with me, but at first this behavior was confined to the analytic hour, with no change in her behavior at home. After a while the degree of freedom achieved in interviews began to spill over at home. She allowed herself at first to become playfully aggressive toward her mother, then to show a little bit of defiance, and finally there were a few occasions on which she openly expressed anger with her—once defiantly wetting on the floor.

As a result of the partial freedom gained from the first months of analysis, she began to achieve occasional dry nights. She now entered a new phase of the treatment. Following the first stage of the analysis of the reactive defense mechanisms, there began to be signs of reactivation of the oedipal conflict at home. According to the parents, Dottie began a frank flirtation with her father, in every respect similar to her behavior of the previous year which had almost disappeared during the few months preceding treatment. Unfortunately the father found Margaret's flirtation amusing and for some time encouraged her fantasies by participating in little games with her. And now, too, Margaret began to make sly, giggling allusions to parental doings in bed and called her Daddy a "bad boy" with some amusement. I found it interesting, too, that this child who had been well educated—even overreducated—on sexual matters, now delighted in flaunting her own theories of birth. She insisted that babies came "from a man's rib" and defied anyone to disagree with the Bible. She revived her old and abandoned belief in Santa Claus and wept if either her parents or I cast some doubt on the matter or suggested that she was joking.

The more flirtatious she became at home with her father, the more fully she reverted to her earlier compliant, dutiful relationship with her mother. In interviews her former freedom and activity once more became restricted. She tediously arranged and rearranged my desk drawers or the doll house and begged me for compliments on her house-keeping. She compared herself to all my untidy and destructive patients and exclaimed in horror and disapproval at my lack of concern. When I reminded her that this was the way she had behaved at the very beginning with me and that we knew already why she had to do these things, she turned a deaf ear. More than that, she now denied all the earlier interpretations, intimated that I was a liar and that she would not talk to me at all. All this would be said with extreme politeness.

For several interviews after this Margaret engaged in this type of repetitive play and hardly spoke at all. When I attempted to help her see that this was her way of showing anger to me, she would insist gravely that she never got mad at anybody and that she could not talk because there was nothing to talk about.

So there we were; and we know that nothing hinders the treatment of children so much as this kind of resistance. For the child is under no obligation to communicate his thoughts to us in spite of inhibitory influences, and our technique must be based on the contents of these silences, of which we know very little at this point.

We see, therefore, that Margaret had transferred her defenses to the therapeutic situation. But why did they not yield as they had earlier to the attitude of the therapist and her interpretations of these defenses? What new factor had been introduced?

### The Stories of the "Teensy-Weensy Apples"

One day during this unproductive period I noticed that Margaret was making a little basket of plastilene. She modeled little balls which she put in the basket. When I inquired about this she explained, "They're teensy-weensy apples, because I want them to be teensy-weensy." Then as an afterthought she said, "And if you asked for one, I wouldn't give it to you. And if anyone asked for one I wouldn't give it to them, either. Ha. Ha. Ha. . . ." Her voice was serene and gave no evidence of the hostile nature of her statement.

Here we recognize immediately the significance of the little balls and their relationship to the general pattern of anal resistance, the stubbornness and refusal to talk. In order to analyze the content of this statement without arousing further resistance, I suggested that I would tell Margaret a story about a little girl and some apples.

My story went like this: "Once upon a time there was a teensy-weensy girl who lived all alone in a teensy-weensy house in the woods. One day there came a knock on the door. And there was an old, old woman. She said, 'Little girl, give me the biggest apple that you have!'" (This was a deliberate parody of the mother who still praised Margaret for her "fine b.m.'s.") " 'No!' said the little girl. 'You have to!' said the old woman. So the little girl was scared and went into her house and gave her the biggest apple she had. The next day the old woman came back and she wanted a still bigger apple. And the little girl gave it to her. The third day she came back again and the little girl fooled her and gave her the teensiest-weensiest apple she could find. And the witch was so mad! (To Margaret.) What do you think she did?"

Margaret (delighted): "She threw it in the garbage can!" I: "So the old witch went back to her house and she never went near that house again!"

Margaret: "No! 'Cause she comes back. 'Cause she's so mad and she tries to catch the little girl. Oh! Does the girl have a mother? Where is the mother?" I: "Let's pretend there's a fairy godmother, too."

Margaret: "Yes, so when the old witch tries to catch the little girl the fairy godmother puts her in jail."

I was interested to find that Margaret seized on this story and worked it over with fresh additions in several interviews that followed. Each time she would insist upon my telling the original story as I have reproduced it here and she would pick up the story at the point where the old witch was fooled by the little girl. For the most part Margaret's additions were tedious elaborations of her original theme in which the witch tried to catch the girl and was sent to jail. It seemed to me that there were countless repetitions of this tale and I was thoroughly tired of this creature I had conjured up, when one day Margaret brought forth a significant new addition.

After requesting the usual prologue from me, Margaret said: "Then the old witch goes away and gets a giant. And he's a *bad* giant. He's going to set the little girl's house on fire. And then the fairy godmother comes and puts him in jail. And the witch too. . . . And *then* a *bigger* witch comes, a big *fat* one and she wants the little girl to give *her* apples and she won't and the fairy godmother puts that one in jail, too. And then another big, fat witch comes. But she's a nice one. *She* won't do anything to the little girl. She'll just talk to her nice and help her with her troubles." (And, since Margaret already recognized this third old witch, she threw me a spurious smile and spoke her last words in a conciliatory tone of voice.)

On the basis of our knowledge of the child's history we have no trouble in translating this story. Beginning with Margaret's modeling of the "teensy-weensy apples" and her statement, "And if you asked for one I wouldn't give you one, etc.," we recognize that the little apples stand for feces and the refusal and obstinacy contained in these words and in her inability to talk, belong to the anal resistances.

The therapist's story was, of course, invented with this knowledge. But let us look at Margaret's additions and variations on this theme:

We recall that the basic story is always the little girl who will not give her apples to the old woman. And this part of the story is always rendered by me. Margaret adds this time:

*"The old witch goes away and gets a giant and he's a bad giant. He's going to set the little girl's house on fire. And then the fairy godmother comes and puts him in jail, etc."*

During Margaret's placement at three the mother (old witch) joined her husband at frequent intervals at his army post. The mother became pregnant at one point and miscarried. The child was later told of this. It will be remembered that at the end of placement the father had returned home. (The old witch goes away and gets a giant.) The giant who is bad and is going to set the little girl's house on fire, plays a part in many later fantasies and stories of Margaret. He is, of course, the father. We learn, later, of a characteristic oedipal dream of a "house on fire" which preceded the bed wetting in Margaret's case. On one occasion Margaret dramatically acted this out. Her father gave her a hug one day: Margaret wet her pants and cried out, "Daddy, daddy, you bad boy. You made me wet my pants!" We note that the fairy godmother puts the witch and the giant in jail in this and the second part of the story. Perhaps this makes sense if we interpret the punishment of the wicked pair as the punishment the little girl anticipates for her own naughtiness. "Going to jail," as we know, is a convention which children utilize in their fantasies as the appropriate punishment for the criminal, hence, for their own criminal and bad wishes.

*"And then a bigger witch comes, a Big Fat one, and she wants the little girl to give her apples and she won't."* The big fat witch is unmistakably the foster mother who was, indeed, fat, and who came in for much ridicule from Margaret on this point when she was mentioned in treatment. And the Big Fat one is thrown into jail, too, of course. "And then another big fat witch comes, but she's a nice one. She won't do anything to the little girl, just talk nice and help her with her problems." The third big fat witch is, of course, the therapist. Margaret's nice remarks about her are simply "apple polishing" for we see how she slips in a derogatory statement by making her a big fat witch. I should point out that in this respect I was identified with the foster mother because the child had been placed in a foster home for her soiling and now she was sent to me for her bed wetting, a symptom now used to express much of the stubbornness and defiance earlier expressed in soiling. I should also mention that I had already noticed

that Margaret identified me with the foster mother earlier in the treatment, and had dealt with her fear that I might punish or spank her, as the foster mother had, for wetting her bed.

Having identified the three witches and the giant, we must now try to discover why this material was brought out at this time. *Why did the anal resistances come to the foreground at this particular time?* Why was the therapist perceived as dangerous, too?

It will be recalled that the therapeutic work had been dealing in some measure with the defenses against aggression and had succeeded in bringing forth manifest aggression at home. Soon after Margaret became seductive toward her father she restored her earlier conciliatory and passive relationship to the mother. This tells us that she feared her aggressive feelings toward the mother. Yet we did not know why.

Perhaps the most important part of Margaret's "three witches" story is that of the first old witch. The first old witch, the mother, *went away* from the little girl and got a giant, after the little girl refused to give her apples. Margaret, we know, was placed in a foster home for her soiling while the mother later joined the father. We know that one of the earliest anxieties of the child arises from the danger of losing the mother. This fear exerts a major inhibitory influence on the early aggressions of the child. In Margaret's case the fear was realized through placement. The story of the witches tells us the fate of a little girl who becomes obstinate with witches.

We understand now why the child was unable to progress in her treatment. For to acknowledge the aggressive feelings toward her mother was to incur the danger of being sent away or losing the mother. Her earlier aggression toward the mother, which took the form of soiling and withholding of feces, had brought about her placement and loss of the mother.

But I had not considered this element at this point of treatment. I had failed to recognize the child's story as her fear of being sent away. Rather I had seen that she identified me with the old witches who wanted the little girl to give up her apples. With this insufficient diagnosis I pursued the fruitless course of demonstrating to Margaret that I did not feel that the little girl was "bad," etc., and that I would not be like the other old witches. I also spent weeks trying to help the child acknowledge her aggressive impulses.

Fortunately after some weeks, the material pointed so persistently in one direction that I was able to recognize Margaret's fear and deal with it. There was a sudden spurt of progress in the treatment when I finally made an interpretation to Margaret which dealt with her fear that if she became angry with mother she would be sent away. In the very next interview the child brought in her first anxiety dream in which she was pursued by a dog, marking the point in therapy where the anxiety at last broke through.

I wonder whether my technical error is not instructive for us in this study of transference phenomena in child analysis. For it appears that I recognized only one aspect of the transference. I had recognized the transference of the stubbornness and withholding from the mother to me, but I had, tentatively, attributed this to the child's acting out of her oedipal strivings at home. With an adult this might be a correct construction because of the interpretation we must put on "acting." But it is clear that this particular material must be differently construed.

### Analysis of the Motives for the Transference

We might at this point attempt to reconstruct the elements in the transference resistance.

In dealing with the reactive defense mechanisms in the early months of treatment, the therapist makes it possible for the child to bring out her aggression against the mother. Now begins a period of acting out in which the child becomes demonstrative and seductive with the father. We note that this "acting out" is by no means an "acting in the transference." The child does not revive her earlier libidinous tie to the father in order to resist the work of analysis. This is not "acting in order to remember," or in opposition and resistance to the analytic rule, since of course the child is under no obligation to observe the analytic rule in the first place. What we see is simply the result of our undermining of the defenses: a liberation of that portion of the libido which was the last, historically, to yield to reactive alteration.

With the acting out of this oedipal drama at home the child begins to fear the mother's anger and possible retaliation. She then effects a compromise. She permits herself flirtatious gestures toward the father and propitiates the mother through greater demonstrations of love and reactive defenses against her aggression. At the same time the child recognizes the therapist as a threat to this compromise solution since the therapist attempts to undermine the reactive defenses through interpretation. The child now reacts to the interpretations through a strengthening of the defenses.

The defenses which we now deal with in analysis derive their potency from three sources: (a) the strength of the hostile and aggressive wishes, (b) the fear of the consequences of these wishes "to be sent away," (c) the anxiety produced in the therapeutic situation as a consequence of the therapist's efforts to deal with the defenses. Of course the therapeutic error lay in the attempt to work with (a) without first dealing with (b).

The child adopts the same behavior with the therapist as with her mother in this dilemma, propitiating her through demonstrations of excessive tidiness and propriety and employing stubbornness and withholding as aggressive and retaliatory measures. But her story of the little girl and the witches tells us why. There is danger in this big, fat, nice, old witch who "just talks nice" to little girls. If the therapist should succeed in exposing her impulses she will be left to a dreaded fate, possibly of being sent away once more. The reactive defenses which the child has employed in dealing with her aggression toward the mother are thus transferred to the therapeutic situation for the purpose of warding off the dangers implicit in the therapy.

## General Conclusions

From our study of these two cases we see very clear evidence of the existence of transference phenomena. What interests us, however, is the limited field in which these transferences operate during the course of a child analysis. In neither case can we speak of a transference neurosis in the correct usage of this term, for we saw no evidence that the child gave up his neurosis in the course of therapy and centered it anew on the analyst and the analytic situation. When Dottie's dog-phobia is transferred to the therapist we see that it is merely *extended into* the analytic situation, it is not relinquished in the child's daily life. When Margaret transfers her reaction formations against aggression and dirt, we find the identical reactions in her behavior at home for the same period. In each case we found the motive for the transference in the child's perception of danger in the therapeutic situation.

Further study reveals other factors which make it difficult to establish an equation between transference phenomena in child and adult analysis. In considering, for example, the major types of transference phenomena which Anna Freud describes in her classification, we encounter some striking differences; moreover, we find certain manifestations which have no analogy in child analysis. As a frame for studying the transference manifestations in child and adult analysis I have grouped some of our findings in these children's cases around the three major types of transference phenomena described by Anna Freud (1946a, p. 18). These are: (1) transference of libidinal impulses, (2) transference of defenses, (3) acting in the transference.

With reference to the transference of libidinal impulses, we generally encounter in child analysis conditions very different from those in adult analysis. For although the child displays his affection for us, his dependence on us, and at times his anger or his jealousy of other patients, we only share these feelings with his own parents and, at that, we must say that we usually obtain such emotional reactions in a more diluted form than they appear in his family relations.

If we return for a moment to our two cases, we see that with both little girls we had occasion to observe a reactivation of the oedipus complex in the course of therapy. In each case this took the form of demonstrative and seductive behavior with the father and corresponding fear of the mother's retaliation. In Margaret's case this behavior had not been evident for almost a year prior to the beginning of analysis and we saw how the full strength of the original conflict was aroused again soon after we began to analyze the reactive defenses. In Dottie's case this behavior occurred a short while after the first effective work was done in relation to the dog-phobia, but the full strength of the oedipal strivings was not brought out until the mother took her trip abroad.

Yet in both cases when the therapeutic work brought about a temporary reactivation of the oedipus complex, the child did not direct the libidinal impulses toward the analyst, but directed them *once more to the original objects*. With the adult, when certain repressed features of the oedipus complex make their first appearance, they are centered first upon the person of the analyst and make their presence known in the analytic work either through direct transference of the libidinal wish, or the defenses against the wish. With the child the work of repression has not dealt completely with the oedipal strivings; the censorship is established but still corruptible. Even with the normal child well into latency, the temporary or permanent removal of the rival parent from the scene will easily serve to rearouse oedipal desires which have undergone only partial repression. The superego of the child is still largely dependent on the external presence of the parent or support from the environment.

So that in our work with the child the analysis of defenses may bring about a temporary reliving of oedipal desires and conflicts in relation to the original objects, which means that we have liberated certain impulses which the child with his still inadequate superego organization chooses to utilize in the most favorable manner for himself—through once again attempting to gratify these desires through the parents. This is in direct contrast to the adult patient, as we know. Where these same impulses are almost obliterated by repression, our work with the defenses may begin the liberation of the impulses, but these impulses cannot seek gratification through the original objects because of the strength of the superego. Instead, as we know, the impulses or their defenses are directed toward the analyst as a representative of the original object; they are transferred.

When we turn to the transference of defenses we find richer data for study in children's cases. We find that the child like the adult will defend himself against the analytic work at every point where he feels himself in danger. We saw how Dottie transferred her dog-phobia at a point when therapy presented the danger to the child that her symptoms might be exposed and that her own destructive impulses might break through. She now brought the phobia into analysis to serve its useful purpose in this new danger situation. The dangerous impulses which the child perceives may be exposed by the therapist; they are warded off by the same neurotic mechanisms which served the child outside of therapy and now serve to resist the analytic work. It seems important to add that Dottie was also facing at the time an objective danger situation, the mother's genuine hatred and destructive feelings toward the child. In the child's mind therapy could expose her to real danger.

With Margaret we saw how the reaction formations against aggression and soiling were transferred from the mother to the therapist at a crucial point in the analysis. When the child feared that her impulses might be liberated through therapy she utilized the same defenses against the therapeutic work as she employed against the impulses.

Again our work of analysis revealed how these strong resistances were set up by the child because these impulses might bring about an objective danger situation, the loss of the mother. Historical events had fixed this pattern. Earlier the child's soiling and withholding of feces had brought about her placement in a foster home.

Still another motive for the transference appears in Dottie's case. We observe that at a later point in treatment, as our work brought us close to her sexual activities with other children, the therapist made her appearance in the "Do not touch" story as a witch who wants to eat the children but changes her mind and just makes them stay for one year. The child fears that when her secret pleasures are discovered by the therapist she will be punished in some way. And something else, too. Around that witch's house were the many victims of the witch, the children who were transformed into candy. Dottie knew that in coming to see me she had submitted to an ultimate change or transformation of herself. Perhaps the "transformation" theme of this story has two meanings. One the fear of castration which presents itself frequently in the idea of transformation; the other an alteration of herself which implies the giving up of the pleasurable aspects of her behavior. I think this would be typical for children. The child guards his secrets from us not only because of the expectation of punishment but because he fears that in telling he will have to relinquish his pleasure.

Moreover, I think this material reveals even further differences between the child's motives for such transferences and the adult's. When the child transfers his defenses it would seem that he still appraises reality in terms of a child: he fears that his impulses may bring about an *objective* danger situation. He is still dependent upon his parents and we know that even in later childhood the superego has not achieved independence from the early objects. Thus when Dottie and Margaret resist the work of therapy we see how to their child minds therapy may bring about an objective danger for them. Fear of parental retaliation for his bad impulses is still a more powerful motivation than criticism from the superego. When a child fears castration as punishment for his libidinal wishes, such fears are very real to him. We have to strain the child's reality testing to the utmost to help him appraise his fears as unreal. The adult *knows* they are unreal and utilizes his mature perceptions of reality to co-operate in the analytic task of tracking down these alien and absurd fears. If the notion that his analyst will punish him for certain forbidden thoughts occurs to the adult patient, he will readily agree that such a fear has no place in objective reality. The child, however, sees such a danger from the analyst as real and often we have to *convince* him first of the unreality of such feelings before he will work with us to understand them and put them in their proper relationships.

A third type of transference phenomena is spoken of as "acting in the transference." In adult analysis we mean by this term the "acting out" of transferred impulses or defenses in the daily life outside analysis. It is understood that in such acting the patient has temporarily abandoned the analytic rule and "acts out" certain aspects of the transference neurosis in other relationships in preference to the analytic situation.

Here, we encounter real difficulties in establishing an equation between the behavior of the child in analysis and the adult. For although child analyses provide a store of examples in which the child acts out certain features of his neurosis in his daily life, some of which are under the influence of the analytic situations, such behavior cannot be called "acting in transference." This would presume that a transference neurosis was already in existence and that the child patient, in violation of the analytic rule, chose to give expression to his transferred impulses and defenses outside of the analytic situation. We have, so far, found no evidence for the existence of a transference neurosis in child analysis. In the two cases discussed here we have found ample material testifying to the existence of transferred reactions, but neither in these cases nor in others do we find that the child gives up the original neurosis and creates it anew in the analytic setting. Furthermore, the child is not committed to an analytic rule, or at least to anything which resembles the therapeutic conditions which we set up for the adult. So that when a child "acts out" at home or at school we cannot even say that he is doing this to resist therapy. We see connections between such acting and our analytic work and we utilize them for interpretation, but the conditions which bring about such acting appear to be different from those in adult analysis.

With Margaret we saw an "acting out" of the oedipal conflict during one phase of her treatment. The connection between this acting and our therapeutic work is obvious. For we had partially undone certain reaction formations against aggression which she had acquired for the purpose of warding off the dangerous feelings toward mother. When our therapeutic work centered on these defenses, we inevitably liberated impulses which the child promptly sought to gratify through reliving the abandoned oedipal wishes at home. This acting did not represent to the child a resistance to the analytic work. If anything she must have been pleased with the analytic work at this point. It was only later when Margaret herself became frightened at the strength of these impulses that she hastily began to rebuild certain of her defenses and transferred these defenses to the analytic situation.

In fact, "acting out" seems to be almost the first reaction of the child patient to the removal of neurotic inhibitions made necessary in the course of analytic work. It becomes our task to help the child bring these impulses under control and to establish defenses of a more satisfactory nature, but we are all familiar with periods in the child's analysis in which we expect to see acting out and even take the precaution of forewarning the parents.

One even has the impression that a child in analysis relives his neuroses on the familiar home ground. When we are able to obtain careful reports from home they provide us with a wealth of supplementary material. We discover old or abandoned behavior patterns or symptoms which are relived at home on a transitory basis. With Margaret, for example, there was a period during the analysis when this child, who had entered treatment with the most rigid reaction formations against dirt and aggression, again reverted to soiling and withholding. It was of the utmost importance to secure the co-operation of the mother in handling these episodes which were brief in duration but created the most acute anxiety in the child. The actual demonstration that this time she would not be punished for soiling, nor lose her mother, was much more effective than my assurances alone would have been. We do not replace the parents in the child's world and we must count heavily on the support of the parents for undoing neurotic mechanisms every bit of the way.

Melanie Klein puts a different interpretation on such a reliving of the neurosis in the environment by the child in analysis. She cites it as evidence of the existence of a transference neurosis in child analysis (1948, p. 165). I believe, however, that it is evidence of something quite the opposite. It demonstrates once again the primacy of the home and the original objects as the field of the childhood neurosis. Where the adult patient relives his neurosis in the transference, the child may undergo a parallel reliving of his neurosis, but in relation to the original objects and to the environment. Only secondarily and in diluted form do we perceive this reliving in the transference.

It may be worth while mentioning here the technical problems which we encounter in interpreting transference reactions to children in treatment. Although we utilize interpretations of transference in our therapeutic work and assist the child in understanding the unreal nature of his feelings toward the therapist, I cannot say from my own experience that I can credit the analysis of transference reactions with being the powerful agent of therapy in work with children that it is with adults. Sterba points out, in "The Dynamics of the Dissolution of Transference Resistance" (1940), that the analyst (with the adult, of course) allies himself with the ego of the patient, assisting the ego in accomplishing a separation of the reality-testing functions from the unconscious strivings which are re-enacted in the transference. The patient, with the assistance of the analyst, becomes an observer of his instinctual life. It follows that the patient must have sufficiently developed the function of reality testing to understand and to carry out this very difficult and indispensable analytic task. He must be able to recognize the transference nature, the unreal quality of the feelings and attitudes which attach themselves to the analyst.

Occasionally a child will delight us with his ability to accomplish this "splitting," to separate the observing functions and the instinctual life. Such a child, one with exceptional reality discrimination will seek out with us the cause and sources of his transferred feelings. But for the most part our child patients have great difficulty in recognizing many of their feelings toward us as unreal. If we are about to bring to light a secret pleasure or a criminal wish the child may behave toward us as if we were a gestapo agent, and as far as he is concerned his feelings are not unreal. With an impulsive child we may find ourselves in the dubious position of analyzing a transference reaction at the very moment—or immediately after—it has led him to destroy our furniture; not the most favorable time.

Our activity and participation in the child's play and his games creates its own difficulties both in establishing the transference nature of certain reactions and in interpreting them. In studying transference factors in one case, I found it difficult to appraise the child's behavior toward me because I had often played "house" with him and been given the role of mother.

There is one more question. At what age can we expect to find conditions which favor the development of a transference neurosis? It would seem that in puberty, when the instinctual strivings are revived but cannot be directed to the original objects because of the child's fear of the instincts, it would serve the purpose of the pubertal neurosis to transfer the libidinal impulses. In our work with children of this age, however, we have been impressed by the fact that the original neurosis is still centered to a large extent on the sphere of the home and the infantile objects; we cannot yet speak of a transference neurosis. It may be that we are not justified in looking for a transference neurosis at any point at all before maturity. We have little data on the subject of transference in adolescence, but here, too, it would seem that before the superego has become independent of the parents, and before new objects are sought to replace the parents in the child's love life, there can be no motive for the formation of a transference neurosis.

*References*

Freud, A. (1946a). *The Ego and the Mechanisms of Defense.* New York: International Universities Press.
———. (1946b). *The Psychoanalytical Treatment of Children.* London: Imago.
Klein, M. (1948). *Contributions to Psychoanalysis.* London: Hogarth Press.
Sterba, R. (1940). The Dynamics of the Dissolution of the Transference. *Psychoanal. Quart.*, 9.

# 10

# Tales of the Discovery of the Secret Treasure

Tales of the seeking or accidental discovery of treasure or wealth comprise one of the most persistent myths of all times. It is a striking fact that the essential characteristics of this myth have remained unchanged throughout the ages. The elements of the ancient folk tales of treasure are preserved in all the later versions of such stories down to modern times.

Typically the treasure story follows this pattern: A poor boy or man accidentally discovers a secret which leads him to buried treasure or to the acquisition of great wealth. Usually the treasure is the stolen loot of a bandit, a pirate or an evil sorcerer; it may be buried in the ground or in a mysterious cavern. The hero obtains secret knowledge of the treasure either through a conniving and evil person who wishes to use the innocent hero for a tool, or through the accidental "overhearing" or "overseeing" of an event which betrays the secret, or through the acquisition of a magic formula or device or a map or code. Usually, too, the hero must overcome an evil opponent who seeks the treasure. The treasure is successfully won by the hero who vanquishes his enemies, marries a beautiful princess, or brings wealth and prestige to his mother, elevating her from her humble and impoverished station.

The time of treasure hunting is childhood, and these stories of buried treasure are among the favorite tales of children. But they are not the exclusive property of children; they belong to all ages and all times. The evil magicians of the fairy tales gave way in time to one-legged pirates, and they, in turn, to eccentric millionaires and bank robbers. There have been mysterious caverns and desert islands, gothic castles and combination safes. But always there has been a fearless and honest fellow who accidentally discovered the secret, outwitted the sorcerer or the pirate, and entered the perilous enclosure to claim the heaped-up wealth.

The tales of the buried treasure are among the oldest mystery stories of the ages; a mystery which has engaged the imagination of men from ancient times to the present is of special interest to the student of psychoanalysis. What is the meaning of this never-ending search for the treasure? Who are these sorcerers, pirates, innocent boys, and simpletons in the unchanging cast of this drama?

My own interest in the tales of buried treasure derives mainly from two sources. My interest in the psychological meanings of the search for buried treasure came about through the contributions and fantasies of two small boys during the course of their treatment for neurotic disorders. The first patient, a seven-year-old boy, invented tales of piracy and buried treasure which provided me with most valuable insights into his neurosis and into the meaning of treasure seeking. My second treasure hunter, who was six, carried on a number of his excavations under my desk, providing a fortunate situation for the close-range study of the habits and mental activities of a treasure hunter.

My other source of interest is an old one. As a child I was a member of that large fraternity of treasure hunters which carries on its operations in vacant lots, basements, and ash cans. In the belief that a previous tenant had buried his fortune in the walls of our house, we pried up loose floor boards in the attic, tapped on paneled walls for a hollow sound, and searched for secret springs in desks and bureaus manufactured in Grand Rapids. In spite of a great deal of digging and prying and knocking, no tell-tale click answered from the furniture, no secret doors opened to our touch. We gave up hope after a while. I believe now that it may have been our failure to co-operate with all the requirements of the myths of treasure which delayed our discovery for almost ten years.

When we were children in our teens we moved into a new house. Some months after we began living there, a mysterious stranger came to our door. He said that he had once lived in this house and he had come to get something which he had left behind—in the secret room! Our mysterious stranger was not easily identifiable as an instrument of fate. He was neither lame nor bearded, had no tell-tale scars and had arrived on such a substantial vehicle as a bicycle. He was, in fact, an intelligent-looking lad of ten. He said he had left his model boat in the secret room, and we received his story with suspicion. We followed the mysterious stranger up three flights of stairs. We watched him as he stopped before a panel of recessed shelves, unfastened a concealed bolt, and swung open the entire panel. A small dark room was exposed to view. In the dim light we made out the outline of a model boat. We strained our eyes further. The room was empty. The mysterious stranger emitted shrill cries of joy, snatched up his boat and bolted. We stared into the empty room for a long time.

## II

In her remarks on Poe's "The Gold Bug," Marie Bonaparte refers to a conversation with Freud in which he speculated on the meaning of buried treasure. His words are paraphrased by Bonaparte:

> One hardly dares venture it, lest it seem too far-fetched, but there must be, in the unconscious, a connection between tales of seeking or finding treasure and some other fact or situation in the history of the race; something that belongs to a time when sacrifice was common and human sacrifice at that. The "buried treasure" in such cases, would then be the finding of an embryo or foetus in the abdomen of the victim.

Bonaparte, in her analysis of "The Gold Bug," traces the theme of the buried treasure to that period of Poe's life when he was occupied with the riddle of birth. In this analysis, gold-feces-fetus are symbolically equated as the buried treasure.

These findings can be borne out in each investigation of the buried-treasure motif which I have seen. However, when we extend the study to an examination of the various parts of the treasure myths, a picture emerges in which still other unconscious forces can be observed.

I should like to begin by citing fragments from the analytic material of the two small boys I mentioned earlier. In each of these two cases fantasies or games around the theme of treasure hunting appeared in the course of the treatment.

It was Jimmy who first brought my attention to the meaning of the discovery of treasure. Jimmy was seven, a solemn and brooding little fellow with excellent intelligence and imaginative gifts. He was in treatment for stuttering, bed wetting, and a general withdrawal and apathy. Jimmy's fondness for "making up stories" made it possible to carry on a good part of the therapeutic work through them.

A brief introduction to the case material may suffice for our purposes. The central figure of many of Jimmy's stories was a baby elephant named Sneezle. Sneezle, I learned, was dissatisfied with his trunk, and many of his secret wishes revolved around having two trunks instead of one or at least possessing a larger trunk than he had. Sneezle's trunk was frequently in danger. Sneezle wished that he could be as big as his father and he also feared punishment from his father.

From the parents I had already learned that Jimmy had always been very reluctant to ask questions about sexual matters and that, when information was given by the mother on one occasion, Jimmy vehemently denied the mother's explanation of sexual union. This occurred when Jimmy was four.

As Jimmy's treatment progressed he began to confide some of his dreams. One day he told me about a recurrent nightmare in which he is swallowed by a lion and can't get out. In the dream he would tell himself that he should not be afraid because "They'll cut open the lion's stomach and get me out soon." From this dream we began to explore some of Jimmy's ideas about "getting into a stomach" which led inevitably into a discussion of pregnancy and birth. Jimmy was eager to display his knowledge on at least one score. He told me that he knew *all* about that and that he knew about the "special passageway" for the baby to come out. He had no ideas how the baby "got in" and betrayed much confusion by describing the difference between men and women in this way: "The father has a penis and the mother has a littler penis." He spoke of "a mother's egg" and of "a father's seed." He did not know how they "met." *I tried to get him to tell me what he thought.* (This detail is mentioned because it plays an important part in his later fantasy.) The material which follows suggests strongly that I created some resistances in this interview.

Jimmy was reluctant to come in for his next appointment. But once in the playroom he said that he thought of a story and would tell it to me. *"This story is about an ole witch who makes Sneezle tell his father's secret. And the secret is about his father's buried treasure. She tries to get him to tell but he won't."* At this point I asked, "But why shouldn't anyone know the father's secret?" Jimmy was surprised at my ignorance. *"Cause if they knew the secret, why then they'd want to steal it!"*

We now see how the events of the previous interview are translated in this story. The old witch who tries to get Sneezle to tell his father's secret is, of course, the therapist. But how has the discussion about origins been transformed into "father's secret, the buried treasure?"

In the tales of the buried treasure there is always the discovery of a secret which leads to the treasure. In Jimmy's story we see clearly that the secret is a sexual one. From the analytic material we perceive an unconscious analogy between the act of coitus (putting something into the woman) and the burial of treasure. This suggests a twofold meaning for "treasure" here. The penis is "buried" in the woman and is equated with treasure, and the baby is the treasure which is buried in the woman. This last, of course, confirms Bonaparte's analysis of the treasure motif in "The Gold Bug."

*"If they knew the secret, then they'd want to steal it,"* Jimmy says. In tales of treasure the secret of the treasure is almost always stolen from a wicked person, usually a man. From Jimmy we understand, too, why he vehemently denied his mother's explanations of coitus. If he knew the secret, i.e., what father did with mother, then his own wishes to do such things with mother would become too dangerous for him. By denying what father did, he denied what he would like to do. If he "knew the secret," then he might steal it from father.

Some weeks later Jimmy reported an interesting dream with some consequences for us. "It was a real funny dream. A *real* funny one. I dreamed last night that there were two fire stations; a little one and a big one. And the big fire engine in the big fire house always got to the fire first and the little fire engine couldn't. It was too far away from the fire. Every time. Then one night the firemen in the big fire house were too busy playing checkers and they didn't hear the bell ring. So the little fire engine got to the fire and by the time the big one got there it was all put out. That was one time the little fire engine got there first. Wasn't that a good dream!"

Since we know that such dreams of putting out fires are often connected with sexual excitation and bed-wetting in children, I chose a moment later to inquire if Jimmy had wet his bed last night. "Oh, no!" he said. "Last night I slept in Mummy's room in my Daddy's bed, because my brother had a cold and I wasn't s'posed to sleep in the same room with him."

And now we understand how "this time the little fire engine got there first!" We will not go into all of the interesting ramifications of the dream but will mention only two points. First, Jimmy recalled that once before when he *had* wet his bed, he had gone into his parents' room and found them "sleeping together" in mother's bed. "I ran out fast," he said, " 'cause they were waking up." Second, a little while after relating the dream and some of his associations (the dream was based on a familiar nursery story called "The Little Fireman"), Jimmy said he had just thought of a new story and he would tell it to me. This was the story: *"Sneezle is captured by pirates who are after buried treasure. But someone learns of this and when the pirates open the treasure chest there's a bunch of lions inside who bite off their heads."*

The story of the pirates follows the dream and Jimmy's recollection of the circumstances of the parents sleeping together. "Sneezle is captured by pirates who are after buried treasure." Does this detail refer back to the episode just related in which Jimmy discovered the parents in bed together? He ran out then, he told me, because they were waking up. If the pirates represent the father, or possibly both parents, then the seeking of treasure in the story stands for the sexual activity, and the capture of Sneezle by the pirates might refer to Jimmy's fear of being discovered by the parents. "Someone learns of this," the story says, and "this" probably refers to the fact that the pirates are after buried treasure. The "someone" must be Jimmy who learns the father's secret by accidentally coming upon the parents. "And when the pirates open the treasure chest there's a bunch of lions inside who bite off their heads." The tricking of the pirates through the substitution of fierce animals for the expected treasure suggests that the treasure chest with the devouring lions represents the child's conception of the female genitalia in which the vagina is given the attributes of a fierce mouth which bites off the male organ in the act of coitus. The pirates are decapitated in Jimmy's story and the end of the story leaves us with the question, "Now who gets the treasure?" In the classical tales of treasure the hero gets rid of his enemy and acquires his treasure for himself. Our small treasure hunter leaves the fate of the treasure unanswered. Perhaps his unconscious motives came too close to light here, and he may have reasoned that, after all, a lion's appetite is capricious.

The theme of the mutilated pirate appears frequently in treasure stories. The most famous of these pirates is the peg-legged Long John Silver in *Treasure Island*. The terrible Captain Hook, the pirate in Barrie's *Peter and Wendy*, wears a wicked-looking hook in place of the hand which he lost to the crocodile. The classic stereotype of the pirate is that of a man of frightful ugliness with a patch over one sightless eye and a wooden stump beneath one thigh. Jimmy's story throws some light on the meaning of the mutilated pirates in treasure fiction. It suggests that castration is the price which may be paid for entering "the forbidden place."

From Jimmy's stories we acquire two valuable hints regarding the meaning of certain familiar motifs in the treasure tales. The immediate reference of the two stories to events in treatment and within the home permit us to interpret some of the symbols with certainty. The story of the witch who tries to get Sneezle to tell his father's secret of the buried treasure follows the interview in which I try to get Jimmy to tell me his theories regarding procreation. "Father's secret," we saw, was father's secret sexual activity. The buried treasure had the meaning of baby and penis. "If they knew the secret then they'd want to steal it" referred to knowledge regarding the sexual act and the small boy's wish to steal father's secret and replace him. In the tales of treasure there is commonly the discovery of the secret and the theft or cunning acquisition of the secret from a wicked person. In Jimmy's story of the pirates who have their heads bitten off by the lions when they open the chest, we obtain a valuable clue to the motif of the mutilated pirate in the classical tales of treasure.

Several months after this series of episodes in Jimmy's treatment, I encountered another treasure hunter who shed further light on the mystery of the buried treasure.

Danny, who was six, had come to me for treatment of a severe behavior disorder. He was capable of brutal and sadistic attacks upon other children, had violent outbursts of temper in which he would savagely destroy anything at hand. Along with these problems I discovered, after working with him for a while, a severe obsessional neurosis which involved numbers and calculations about death. Analysis revealed that the number compulsions involved a counting of the number of years before "someone" might die. The "someone" was his father, a middle-aged man who was considerably older than the mother.

The treasure games which I shall report shortly were preceded in Danny's treatment by a long prologue, a series of games which bear an important relationship to the treasure hunting which followed. In these earlier interviews Danny carried on an energetic search with a puppet named Mortimer who executed some of Danny's more daring ideas. They opened every desk and file drawer "because Mortimer is so curious." They examined minutely the compartments at the back of drawers which contained odds and ends of junk and desk paraphernalia. Danny was particularly interested in a file drawer which contained a large number of maps. I had told him once, in the feeble hope of making the map drawer "out of bounds," that these maps belonged to my husband. Of course this only stimulated his interest and Danny spent many hours with the maps spread out on the floor laboriously tracing out trips to places he liked to imagine he had been. But I did not entirely understand this absorption in maps at the time.

After some time, however, this seeking of hidden things and locating places on maps began to make sense. We had encountered in Danny a strong denial of sexual differences. Subsequently a curiosity about these differences began to weave in and out of his investigations with Mortimer into hidden places. One day Mortimer, the puppet, became bolder and, in the hands of Danny, attempted to lift the skirt of my dress. I could not permit this, of course, and said only that if Mortimer were so curious about ladies he could ask and I would tell him.

"Well, Mortimer," said Danny, "wanted to find out where ladies keep their penises."

Therapist: "Where does he think?"

Danny: "On their behinds."

Therapist: "Does Mortimer really think that ladies have penises?"

Danny: "Yes, they do!"

Therapist: "Did Mortimer ever see a lady with one?"

Danny: "Yes, he did!"

Therapist: "Where did he see a woman who had a penis?"

Danny looked baffled. Then he became noisy and blustery to cover up his confusion. "Well," he roared, "The girls in South America do!"

Now we understand Danny's games. And, since these games have a close relationship to the treasure games which I shall report next, we might briefly study them. The curiosity about things hidden appears to belong to a curiosity about the "hidden penis" of a woman. The absorption in maps and the examination of strange places could only be a displacement of interest from anatomy to topography. This is even nicely capsuled in his geographical allusion to the country where girls have penises: South America, which comes off the body of the northern continent in the shape of a penis-like appendage.

In the next few interviews Mortimer took a terrific beating from Danny for "being too curious." He was pounded on the floor and twice had his head separated from his puppet body, which made it necessary for me to do an emergency repair job. Then one day a new game appeared. The concern with "hidden objects" took a new turn.

Danny began a series of "excavations" under my desk. He explained that he was "digging for treasure." At his request I provided him with "treasure," and the odds and ends of junk which had fascinated him in the desk drawers now were handed down to him for his games. There were pennies, paper clips, erasers and other bits of office paraphernalia. Gradually the game began to take form. Now Danny assumed much of the conspiratorial manner of a robber, rather than that of a treasure hunter. His voice would drop to a low whisper as he would make a getaway from imaginary pursuers. The game continued along these lines for several interviews.

In the meantime I learned from Danny's parents that Danny was engaging in a number of petty thefts at school and in the neighborhood. He had acquired a number of toys and schoolboy trinkets which he was hoarding in his room.

One day the treasure game acquired a new twist. Danny was under the desk arranging his trinkets when he mumbled to me that the treasure belonged to "a mean king." "So," he murmured, "it was good to steal it because the king was so mean." "What did the king do?" I asked. "He was mean to all the people. And he was mean to the Queen. And the Queen was very sad." With this Danny seemed fascinated with new possibilities and began earnestly to play out another scene. "See!" he said with excitement. "The Queen is locked up. Then this guy comes along and he takes the Queen away so the King will never find her!" I could not resist asking at this point if the Queen might not miss the King. Danny was irritated. "No. See. The King is mean to her all the time. And she's *glad* 'cause she didn't like the King." Now Danny crawled out from under the desk and sat cross-legged on the floor. "Then the Queen sings a song. I'll sing you a song." With this Danny sang in his weird atonal voice a lament of the Queen. The "song" told how the King used to fight with her and hit her and how "she was glad she wouldn't have to live in his old castle no more."

Here we encounter another aspect of the treasure myth. Somehow, in Danny's game, stealing the treasure from the wicked king shades into stealing the Queen from the King. It appears then that the Queen is the treasure. To steal the treasure from the King is to steal the Queen.

For several interviews we heard nothing further about the treasure or the King and Queen. Instead Danny instituted a number of hiding games in which Mortimer the puppet hid in drawers, closets and file cases. I learned that Mortimer was hiding from a witch: "There is a witch and she could turn him into a tree or a stone or anything she wanted." More definitely, I learned later on, this witch could even turn boys into girls. In an "interview" with Mortimer the puppet I learned from his good friend Danny that "Mortimer was afraid that if witches and giants found out his secret, they would turn him into something." It seemed necessary at this point to learn something about Mortimer's secret. But I was not a match for a wily treasure hunter. I made a handsome deal with Mortimer and promised to get rid of his witches and giants worries for good if he would tell me his secret. Danny dragged Mortimer over for a talk. "Mortimer!" he ordered, "Tell that lady your secret." Mortimer was conveniently mute.

Then the hiding games began to develop into something new. Danny made secretive references to a game of his own, a game of hide-and-go-seek. The innocence of the game was out of proportion to the amount of secrecy employed by Danny. I asked him casually how he played this game. With this he obligingly got down on the floor and began to crawl under one of the little rugs. Now wrapped up like a mummy in the rug he announced unexpectedly, "Look! I'm digging for treasure. Give me the treasure. See I'm digging thirty feet down. There! Here's the treasure." Now I caught a glimpse of the meaning of his "hide and seek" game. For one was immediately struck by the fact that he was wrapped up in the rug as if in a blanket. His *treasure hunting* today must have something to do with activities in bed.

The new treasure game "under the rug" was now pursued with the same enthusiasm we had seen in the first treasure game. He asked me for jewels to put under the rug, and I provided him with more paper clips and an old string of pearls. Each time he would crawl under the rug, wrap it around him, then announce triumphantly, "Look what I found!" and produce the "treasure." The game was tirelessly repeated. Once I remarked, "You sure must like this game!" He said enthusiastically, "It's the best game I ever played!"

We can have no doubt about its meaning. The seeking of treasure while wrapped up in the rug is certainly a reference to another remarkable discovery "under cover." This digging for treasure alludes to masturbation. The discovery of "treasure" is the discovery of the penis and its pleasures. We might suggest a tie-up, too, between the two treasure games reported. For in the masturbatory activity hinted at in the second game we suspect oedipal fantasies of the type referred to in the first.

It is of some interest to us that at exactly this point in treatment Danny began to masturbate at home, particularly in his mother's presence. In interviews it became necessary to begin the analysis of anxieties around masturbation and this, I regret to say, ended our games of treasure and our opportunity to analyze further the theme of treasure seeking.

From Danny we have obtained additional clues to the meaning of treasure. The search for "hidden objects" which just preceded the treasure-hunting games, was an anatomical search, a search for the hidden phallus of the woman. The first treasure game involved the theft of the treasure from the mean king. The treasure, we saw, was the Queen. To steal the treasure, therefore, was to steal the mother from the father. The treasure in the second game involved the secret, undercover discoveries of the pleasures of the penis. There is the suggestion, too, that through the discovery of the secret of masturbation, the little boy has also discovered the King's secret with the Queen, which leads him to ideas of stealing the Queen for himself.


## III

The great myths and stories of treasure begin with the *accidental discovery of a secret* which discloses the means to great wealth and power. Usually the secret has to do with the hiding place of a treasure.

Aladdin, the ne'er-do-well son of a tailor, is enticed by a magician to enter a cave and obtain a lamp. The boy is given a ring by the magician to protect him against harm. In the cavern the boy discovers magnificent jewels growing on trees. He pockets the jewels and returns to the opening of the cave with the lamp. The magician refuses to help him out of the cave but demands the lamp. When Aladdin refuses, the angry magician closes the entrance. In his despair Aladdin accidentally rubs the ring which the magician has given him whereupon a spirit appears to transport Aladdin to the surface. One day Aladdin rubs the old lamp also by accident. The genie of the lamp appears to do Aladdin's bidding. With the discovery of the secret of the magic lamp, Aladdin now possesses the source of great wealth. He summons forth the genie whenever he wishes. In the tale we are told that Aladdin uses the lamp to keep himself and his mother supplied with everything they need.

Later Aladdin marries the Sultan's daughter, after first fulfilling the difficult conditions set forth by the Sultan. The old magician returns at last to get his revenge. Through a trick he obtains the magic lamp from Aladdin's wife, who does not know its magic power and is pleased to exchange it for one of the new ones which the wily magician is selling before her window. Now the magician has the palace and the princess transported to Africa. Aladdin, aided by the genie of the ring, retrieves the lamp through a ruse and kills the magician.

Certain details of the Aladdin story interest us here. First is the magician who sends the boy into the dark and mysterious cavern to bring back a lamp and then refuses to help him out. There is a quarrel over the lamp and the magician seals up Aladdin in the cave. We have the impression from these details that the magician who "puts Aladdin into" the cavern, is the father who originally "put him into" the mysterious recesses of the mother's body. Aladdin, now buried within, is deep in despair when he accidentally rubs the ring which the magician had given him. The accidental rubbing summons the spirit of the ring who transports Aladdin to the ground. In this way Aladdin is "born"!

Now the magical properties of the lamp are not discovered by Aladdin until after he leaves the cave. In examining the symbolism of the lamp it seems necessary to return again to the early part of the story. What is this object of great value which is hidden in the cavern and which can only be obtained from the magician by the boy? We have the impression that something has been left within, left behind in the cavern, which must be recovered by the boy and restored to the magician. We have advanced the theory that putting the boy into the cavern is a representation of "making the child," i.e., of procreation. In order to make the child, the father must first "put something in" which is of great value to himself, that is, the penis. In the infantile sexual theory the father loses his penis in the act of coitus. Does this line of thought lead us to any conclusions?

As a child I remember that I was puzzled by the fact that the magician made Aladdin go into the cavern to get the lamp. If the magician knew where the lamp was, I reasoned, why didn't he go himself? The fact is no less puzzling when we examine the detail analytically. It seems then that it is *necessary* that the boy Aladdin restore the lamp to the magician. Only he can do it, the story seems to say. Now if this detail belongs to the birth theories of childhood the magician's object of great value is the penis which is "left behind" in the woman and which is restored to the father in the form of the child. In this sense the son "restores" the father's penis, Aladdin restores the lamp.

But Aladdin's magician wants only his lamp. He would take it and leave Aladdin to perish in the cavern. Since Aladdin is no fool he refuses to give up the lamp and the magician, enraged, seals him up in the cavern. Aladdin now possesses the magician's priceless lamp. In the symbolic act we read that the boy possesses the father's penis.

Now here we have the echo of a great myth. Cronus, the son of Uranus, is imprisoned in the body of his mother, the earth, by the order of his jealous father. His mother induces him to repay the father and dethrone him. Cronus castrates the father and tosses the member into the sea. In this myth the son castrates the father while *in utero* (imprisoned in the mother) and becomes the ruler of the universe in his stead. In infantile sexual theories, too, there appear many stories in which the jealousy of son and father is placed back in time to intrauterine existence.

It is worth mentioning, too, that the theft of the lamp, a "fire-making instrument," attests to the kinship of the Aladdin story with universal myths of the Prometheus type in which the culture hero steals the original fire from one of the gods, typically through outwitting his opponent and employing clever strategems.

We understand that Aladdin did not know the value and the magical properties of the lamp until some time after he was delivered from the cavern. One day he accidentally rubbed the lamp and a genie appeared to do his bidding. Once again we have the accidental discovery of a secret which leads to great wealth. We are reminded now of Jimmy's discovery of his father's secret and of Danny's discovery of a priceless treasure under the covers. Aladdin's discovery of the magic lamp through "accidentally rubbing" is easily recognizable as the discovery of sexual pleasure through "rubbing" of the penis. The genie who appears to do his master's bidding is like the personification of the erect penis which does its master's "bidding."

We are told that Aladdin availed himself of the services of the genie to keep himself and his mother supplied with everything they needed. This detail is a familiar part of the child's fantasy. When he becomes rich and powerful he can supplant the father and give to mother all the things her heart desires. The fantasy of satisfying the mother's every wish must certainly derive from the child's envy of the father, his larger penis and his potency, and his realization that he, as a child, is "poor" in these respects; he can give nothing to his mother.

I should like to dwell on just another aspect of the Aladdin tale. The lamp which serves Aladdin is a source of never-ending wealth. As long as he keeps the lamp its genie will keep him in riches. The genital significance of the lamp, the equation of wealth and potency is evident here. But the lamp also seems to be a relative of those "bottomless purses" which we encounter in fairy tales. Such purses are never empty; they yield up gold whenever their owner opens them. Here we encounter an earlier theory of wealth. These remarkable purses produce gold in a manner analogous to the production of feces. There will always be more.

The Aladdin tale immediately calls to mind Andersen's "Tinder Box." The skeleton of the Andersen story is remarkably similar to Aladdin. A soldier is induced by a witch to climb into a hollow tree, "hollow to its roots." He is told that at the bottom he will find a great hall, with hundreds of lamps burning. He will see three doors each with a key which the soldier can turn to enter the room. In each room sits a chest. On each chest sits a dog. One dog has eyes as big as saucers. The second has eyes as big as windmill wheels. The third dog has eyes as big as the Round Towers of Copenhagen. In each chest the soldier will find money, the value of which is in direct proportion to the size of the dog's eyes. The soldier must place each dog upon the witch's apron in order to render the dog helpless. He may help himself to all the money he wishes. *The witch wants only the tinder box,* which will be found below.

When the soldier accomplishes his mission and subdues each dog in turn, he is pulled up to the surface by the witch. He demands to know why the witch wants the tinder box. The witch refuses to tell. The soldier threatens to cut off her head. When the obstinate witch refuses her secret, the soldier promptly strikes off her head.

The soldier now sets off for the next town. He is a wealthy man and spends his money lavishly. He encounters a beautiful princess, seeks her hand in marriage and meanwhile fritters away his wealth. He is quite without funds when one day he *accidentally discovers the secret of the tinder box.* He strikes sparks from the flint, his door bursts open, and there stands a dog from down under the tree. The dog serves his wants, bringing all manner of riches to him.

Now the soldier pursues his suit for the hand of the princess. There are innumerable obstacles set in his path by the King and the Queen. At the end he is captured and put in jail and is saved from hanging only through regaining his tinder box which is fetched for him by a little boy. The dogs arrive in time to save him and to punish the guards, the King and the Queen. The soldier is acclaimed King by the people and the princess is finally won in the bargain.

Certain details are similar to the Aladdin story. There is a witch for Aladdin's magician, a hollow tree for the cavern. An apron is provided by the witch to subdue the dogs and protect the soldier from harm. Aladdin's magician gives him a ring. The soldier refuses to give the witch her tinder box. Aladdin refuses to give the lamp to the magician. The secret of the tinder box is discovered some time after the ascent from the hole, just as the secret of the lamp is discovered by Aladdin after he emerges from the cavern. The dog appears to do the soldier's bidding just as the lamp genie serves Aladdin. The soldier wins his princess after fulfilling the difficult conditions of the Sultan.

A detailed analysis of the "Tinder Box" does not serve our study. However, it may be useful to examine certain features of the tale. The hollow tree into which the soldier is bidden to descend, is like Aladdin's cavern yet unlike it in its genital symbolism. We are reminded again of certain infantile fantasies concerning the female genitalia. The belief that the woman has a penis like the man gives way in time to understanding of the existence of the vagina. However, the first theory relinquished with such difficulty may sometimes be fused with the second, so that we encounter in some unconscious fantasies the belief that the woman has a "hollow penis." In the tale of the tinder box the witch induces the soldier to go down into the hollow tree and fetch for her a tinder box.

The witch's tinder box, like the magician's lamp, is "a hidden object of great value." In order to obtain the tinder box the soldier must strike off the head of the witch. In the symbolic act the witch is castrated and the soldier carries off the hidden object. We have little doubt about the nature of this hidden object. It must be the phallus, the hidden object, attributed to the woman. When we learn of the remarkable properties of this tinder box we are convinced. Through striking the tinder box one day he discovers the secret. The dog appears from under the tree and is ready to serve his master with all manner of riches. This is like Aladdin's genie. It is of interest, too, that the tinder box, like Aladdin's lamp, is essentially a "fire-making" instrument. The rubbing of the lamp and the striking of the box which brings forth their magic properties are unmistakable allusions to the arousal of sexual sensations in the penis.

Like Aladdin, the soldier who "discovers the secret" of the tinder box now overrides all obstacles and obtains the beautiful princess for his own. *Through the acquisition of a magical device, the hero achieves the means of obtaining the inaccessible woman.* The magical device, we have seen, is a penis which performs miracles.

Ali Baba discovers the secret of the buried treasure through another type of accident. He observes a band of thieves who stop near a large rock and unload their booty-filled saddle bags. He hears the leader say, "Open Sesame!" and a wide doorway appears in the rock. The men enter and the door closes. Afterward the men are heard to say, "Shut Sesame!" and the door closes. After the men depart Ali Baba addresses the rock with the same words. The cave opens and a store of silks, brocades and heaps of gold and silver are revealed. Ali Baba provides generously for himself and sets up his household in lavish style. Ali Baba's brother learns of his wealth and blackmails Ali Baba into telling the secret. Now the brother sets forth, finds the cave and loads his mules with treasure, only to discover at the last moment that he has forgotten the words to open the door. The bandits find him and promptly kill him. They hang his body at the entrance to the cave as a warning to the trespasser. Now the bandits go in search of Ali Baba. They enter his house through a ruse, posing as oil merchants, and ask to store their oil in the shed. A bandit hides in each of the oil jars. A servant comes upon them by chance and saves her master and his household by pouring boiling oil on the thieves.

We have added a third magical act for the discovery of treasure. To the accidental discovery of treasure through rubbing the lamp and striking the tinder box we have, in Ali Baba, the accidental seeing and overhearing of magic words. The magical devices of Aladdin and the soldier and the accidents of their discoveries were seen to be the discovery of sexual pleasure in the penis, an initiation into sexual pleasure. But what of Ali Baba's discovery?

He sees the thieves, he hears the magic words, and a door appears in the rock where no door was seen before. This suggests another type of initiation into a sexual mystery, one obtained through the accident of seeing and overhearing. The cave represents the body of the woman and the thieves who enter complete the symbolization of a sexual act. But we are intrigued by certain details of this description. The thieves with their booty-filled saddle bags bring to mind an image of exaggerated male genitalia as seen through the eyes of children. The magical opening of the rock, the appearance of a door where no door was seen, must be an allusion to the childhood mystery of the female genitalia, the puzzle of the opening where no opening is known to exist. The idea of a magical opening of the door belongs, too, to the child's conception of coitus.

Ali Baba introduces a new character in the treasure hunt. There is the jealous brother who steals the secret. But the simple-minded fellow forgets the magic words and is trapped within the cave. This method of disposing of a rival brother is a familiar one from ancient times to the present. Joseph was cast into a pit by his brethren. Many a modern child with the facts of life at his disposal has recommended to his parents that they put the new baby back into the mother. Trapped within the cave, the brother is discovered by the bandits, killed, and hanged at the entrance as a warning to other trespassers. The brother also fulfills the classic destiny of the son who would "enter the mother." In the act of "stealing the treasure," the brother is discovered by the bandits who promptly kill him. Ali Baba, of course, escapes such a fate.

The devices of magic in these fairy tales recede or disappear entirely in the modern tales of treasure. This is to be expected. But in their place come other *accidents of discovery* which lead to a buried treasure.

In the tales of pirate treasure, there is usually a map which falls into the hands of an upright young man who intelligently divines its meaning. The map is sometimes illegible, sometimes described in code, or in other ways makes requirements on the intelligence and ingenuity of the treasure hero. It is, of course, the map of the pirate who buried the treasure; many persons would give a great deal for it. But the treasure hero comes upon it through an accident of fate.

In the most famous of all modern treasure stories, *Treasure Island*, a small boy, Jim Hawkins, becomes the possessor of a map of buried treasure, through a series of curious events. Jim is the son of an ailing innkeeper, who owns an inn on the sea coast. Late one dark night an old sailor arrives at the inn with his sea chest. He is a furtive and suspicious fellow, asks many crafty questions of the boy, then demands lodging at the inn. This is Captain Billy Bones. Later the old man confides to Jim that he is pursued by enemies and engages the boy as a "look-out" to give warning when a one-legged man comes looking for Billy Bones. For weeks Captain Billy sits in the tavern and drinks quantities of rum, singing wild and mournful sea chanties.

The ailing innkeeper dies and Jim and his mother are left alone. Then come the mysterious men. First comes the crippled blind man, Pew, who frightens the boy into leading him to Billy Bones. Pew delivers "the black spot," the mark of death, to Billy. He leaves, and Billy fortifies himself with more rum and makes ready to escape, but it is too late. As the drunken old man attempts to rise he is stricken and dies of a heart attack.

There is no time to lose now, for the men are coming after Billy. Jim and his mother go to Billy's chest. The honest woman is determined that she will have what Billy owes her for his lodgings "but nothing more." Together they open the chest. The mother takes a few coins to pay for Billy's lodging. Jim takes a little pouch which he finds within the chest, a memento which seemingly has no value but has some appeal to a little boy. Mother and son escape before the pirates arrive. From a hiding place he sees the pirates enter and wreck the inn in their savage search for something which is missing from the chest. Later, in safety and among friends, the little pouch is opened and is found to contain a map. The Squire and the Doctor recognize it as a map of buried treasure. The treasure hunt begins.

Thus far we see that the little pouch in Billy Bones's chest is a descendant of Aladdin's lamp and the Soldier's tinder box. Like its magical forebears, it is *an object of seemingly little value, buried or hidden within, discovered and taken by the treasure hero, and found to be the key to infinite wealth at a later time.*

In Treasure Island, the Squire engages a ship and Jim and the Doctor join the expedition in search of the buried treasure. The Squire, a lover of good food, provides himself with an excellent cook, a former seaman, a one-legged fellow who hobbles about on a crutch. Only Jim suspects that Long John Silver is the one-legged man who pursued Billy Bones. But his fears are easily put aside by the others and by the ingratiating manner of Long John.

Halfway through the voyage Jim makes another important discovery. While looking for an apple in the huge barrel below deck he climbs into the barrel to reach the apples at the bottom. While thus momentarily hidden from sight he hears voices as Long John enters the room with several other sailors. From within the barrel Jim *overhears the plot* of Long John and his henchmen for capturing the ship and obtaining the map. In this way Jim and his crew are forewarned of the danger and are able to save their lives. The information does not prevent about a hundred pages of warfare between the two groups and at one point the capture of Jim by the pirates. In the end the treasure is found to be already in the hands of a marooned sailor who has spent his five years on Treasure Island in the discovery and excavation of it. He gladly shares his wealth with Jim and his friends in return for passage home. The story ends with an uneventful trip back to England with the pirates dead or marooned, except for Long John who returns a prisoner but escapes toward the end. Stevenson apparently developed an affection for Long John which prevented him from killing off the wily pirate in good style.

We are interested in some of the old and some of the new features of this more modern treasure tale. The discovery of the map concealed in the little pouch in the seaman's chest has already been mentioned in connection with the magical device of the fairy tales. But there are certain obvious differences in the relationship of the magic lamp or tinder box to discovery of treasure, and that of the map to discovery of treasure. All three are "concealed objects," and objects of seemingly little value. But the magic lamp and the tinder box have the distinction of being phallic symbols, which give up their secrets through an accidental manipulation. The map in this story has the properties of (1) belonging to the wicked man (pirate); (2) concealment in an enclosed place (first a chest, then a little pouch); (3) disclosing a secret which leads to wealth. But here the similarities with magical devices end. The map only *tells where the treasure is buried*. It contains knowledge which can be acquired through intelligent interpretation of its hieroglyphics. This is an intellectual discovery of a secret in contrast to the devices of the antecedent tales in which the secrets of the lamp and tinder box are acquired with the hands.

The map reveals the place where something is hidden. We recall now the interest in maps which we saw in Danny. We were able to follow, in the case study, a line of development from an absorption in maps and places on the maps to a strong curiosity regarding the anatomy of women. The map in the pirate treasure stories always answers the question: "Where did the pirate bury the treasure?" We have seen earlier in Jimmy's stories that "burying the treasure" has the double meaning of "burying the penis (treasure) in the mother" and "burying the child (treasure) in the mother." The question of where the treasure is buried must, then, have to do with an anatomical mystery, the mystery of the female vagina, which has confounded every curious child.

"Where is the *place* in the mother?" The discovery of the map in such stories, must correspond to the discovery of a necessary piece of information regarding origins. This discovery of "the place" where the treasure is hidden corresponds to Ali Baba's discovery of the mysterious door which opened into the cave. There are even a few reminiscent details of Ali Baba in *Treasure Island.* Jim watches from his hiding place as the thieves break into the inn and wreck the furniture as they search for something which is missing from Billy's sea chest. Later he overhears the pirate's plot to seize the ship and steal the map. The details of watching and overhearing in these two isolated episodes are points of high tension in the story. One wonders if this "watching" and "overhearing" which have to do with the search for the map and the treasure have a symbolic meaning in themselves. "The thieves who break into the house," "seeing an act of destruction" are familiar in dream language as the representation of a sexual act once seen through the eyes of the child. In the infantile conception such an act is seen as an attack upon the woman and a theft from the woman. The "overhearing of the plot to seize the ship" seems to belong also to such an observation. Here "to seize the ship" might represent the forceful taking possession of the woman, and the "overhearing" of the plot, an overhearing of the sexual act.

The figure of Long John Silver deserves some mention. He is the one-legged leader of the pirates, oily and ingratiating, and at the same time a man who has known violence and is capable of violence. Long John has sought this treasure before on Treasure Island, we are told in the story. We are not told how this pirate lost his leg, but there is a strong suggestion that this may have come about through one of the occupational hazards of his profession. We are reminded of the misfortune which befell Jimmy's pirates when they opened the treasure chest. A bunch of lions were concealed inside and bit off their heads.

In spite of a fast-moving plot and terrifying events which reach a climax when Jim is almost killed, the last part of *Treasure Island* is something of a disappointment. For after all, Jim Hawkins and his friends do not discover the treasure. Someone has been there before them. The old marooned sailor has employed his five years on the island in a leisurely excavation and storage of the treasure. Although he will share his treasure with the others in return for a voyage home, we admit to feelings of disappointment: "Someone has been there before; someone else got the treasure first."

It is another kind of "map" which leads to the discovery of treasure in Poe's "The Gold Bug." Properly speaking, the scrap of paper discovered by Legrand, in this story, was not a map of the place but a cipher which, when interpreted, established the description and the location of the treasure buried by Captain Kidd on the Atlantic Coast. Marie Bonaparte has analyzed the treasure theme in "The Gold Bug" minutely for purposes of her study of Poe. So far as our analysis here is concerned I should like to call attention only to one detail.

There is a quasi-magical feature in the discovery of the secret code. A scrap of dirty brownish paper is found and used to wrap a specimen beetle. Through the accidental exposure of this insignificant scrap to the heat of a candle, certain outlines appeared which aroused the suspicions of Legrand. When he holds the bit of vellum to the fire a number of characters take form which produce the cipher. It has been written in invisible, "magic" writing.

Again we have a "magical device" which leads to the discovery of treasure. But like Billy Bones's map, this requires an application of intelligence to the solution of the problem, to the "discovery." The cipher "tells the place" after Legrand ingeniously discovers the code. We have already suggested that the discovery of the map which "tells the place" refers to a necessary piece of intelligence in the unraveling of a sexual mystery in childhood. The idea of "invisible writing" in "The Gold Bug" may very well belong to the "invisible place," the "unknown place" of the sexual mystery. We are reminded of Ali Baba's mysterious, invisible door which opened in response to the magic words. In this sense the factor of invisibility, which belongs to the "unknown place" of the women, is placed in the context of the secret code, the map which tells "where." It is of some interest that the invisible code is revealed through exposure to fire. Here, again, the relationship of fire to sexuality is brought into play in a magical act, as in Aladdin and the "Tinder Box."

The analogy between "burial of the treasure" and the agricultural "burial of the seed" is so obvious that it hardly needs mention here. However, it may be worth while noting that in the child's conception of procreation he frequently construes human intercourse as a digging and burial of the seed in the woman. Such a detail as "digging a hole" may be literally carried over in a child's mind to explain coitus. I recall the theory of a two-and-a-half-year-old girl who developed a serious neurosis following an observation of coitus. The child maintained that "the man made the hole," that the penis was forcibly thrust into the woman's body like the hypodermic needle which had been thrust into her by the doctor when she was ill.

The agricultural theory was once carried to an extreme by an ambitious six-year-old I once treated. He confessed to me one day that he had stolen a package of cucumber seeds from the dime store and buried them package and all) underneath a telephone pole, "so maybe me and my mother can have a baby next summer." The unique site of this burial pointed to the anatomical misunderstanding which underlay many of his confused theories of origins. Is this why treasure is so often buried "under a certain tree" or so-and-so many paces to the left or right of the old oak tree? Are such prodigious phallic symbols a key to the errors of reckoning which foil the child in his first attempts to "find the place"?

There is another story which invites our study. I would like to propose that "The Rocking Horse Winner," by D. H. Lawrence, is a story which belongs to the family of treasure tales. It must be admitted that it does not immediately appear to be one. It has neither magicians, pirates, nor buried treasure. But let us review the main lines of the plot. The small boy who is the hero of "The Rocking Horse Winner" is the son of a vain and ambitious mother and a luckless, ineffectual father. The mother, a spoiled creature who grew up in a family of some means, complains bitterly and incessantly of her husband's failure to provide for his family. To Paul, the little boy, the house he lives in is a haunted house in which the very walls whisper, "There *must* be more money! There *must* be more money!"

Through the family's gardener, a kindly and sympathetic friend to the boy, Paul becomes interested in horses and in racing. Through the gardener, Paul places small bets at first, and he proves to have an uncanny talent for picking winners!

For Paul has discovered a secret. He must ride his rocking horse long and furiously and then the name of the winning horse will come to him. "When it gets there," he explains, "I *know!*" Within a very short time Paul's winnings are compounded into dizzying figures. The gardener and Paul's uncle, too, who is in the secret, have come to look upon the boy with awe.

His winnings, Paul decides, must all go to his mother to make her happy and to get for her all the things which she longs for. He arranges through his uncle for regular sums to be sent his mother under a plan which will not disclose their real source, so that his own part in the gift cannot be suspected by her.

But even with this new source of income and the luxuries which the mother now enjoys, there is still not enough money. The house still whispers, "There *must* be more money!" Paul's rocking horse is driven to new lengths. The furious rocking in the nursery becomes a sight too frightful to behold. The nurse pleads with Paul's parents to intervene, for the little children of the family are frightened by these rocking orgies. Even the cold and disinterested mother becomes concerned now.

The Derby approaches and Paul is frightened by a decline of his powers. He cannot call up the name of the Derby winner. Paul becomes ill. He is warned that he must not ride his rocking horse again, for the parents have divined some relationship between the illness and tension of the child and his mysterious riding of the rocking horse.

The night before the Derby Paul is put to bed and the parents go off to a party. When the parents return, the mother has a strange feeling that something is wrong. She goes up to the nursery, throws open the door with fear, and is terrified by the sight of Paul savagely rocking his horse, his eyes fixed and glazed with fever. He murmurs the name of a horse and collapses. From his sickbed the child tells the name of the Derby winner to the gardener. He is gravely ill now. As he lies dying he faintly hears the old gardener tell him that his horse has won.

A poor summary like this cannot do justice, of course, to the story by Lawrence. Recounted with these bare details its theme sounds almost maudlin. What is it then in this story which appeals so directly to the senses? How do the implausible details of this story evoke such genuine and deep-felt emotions?

The story is not meant to be plausible. This much is apparent. Its meaning and its appeal to the emotions lie entirely in its innocence and its character of a childhood daydream. It belongs to the category of little-boy fantasies which are universally familiar. It is Aladdin's story and Jim Hawkins' story, and possibly the story of all ancient and modern treasure hunters, the poor boys who accidentally discover a secret which leads to the acquisition of great wealth.

"Mother is unhappy," such fantasies begin, often enough with some truth. "Father is poor and there is never enough money." Or: "Father does not make her happy. . . . If I were rich I would give all my money to mother. I would give her everything she wanted. And she would love *me* best! But I am not rich. . . . Supposing. . . ." And now the daydream proper begins. "How can I get rich? . . . I am digging in the garden one day when I see a little tin box. . . . I am walking down the street one day when I see a purse. . . . I find a scrap of paper and I am just about to throw it away when I see something written on it. . . ." There are endless variations to such daydreams.

There is a second daydream which also makes its way into "Rocking Horse Winner." It is one of the earliest dreams of unrequited love and a great sacrifice. "Nobody loves me. They will be sorry when I'm dead. They will cry at my funeral and then they will realize how much they love me, but it will be too late." An imaginative child will visit his own funeral in this fashion and succeeds at such times in becoming his own chief mourner. These childhood fantasies of an unrequited love seem to belong to the early love of a child for an inaccessible object who cannot gratify the child's wishes. In clinical practice I have seen how this fantasy represents the child's grief in the surrender of his mother as object of his first love. The mother doesn't "love" the child. To die in these fantasies represents an act of revenge and an act of mourning for the lost love and for the self.

In "The Rocking Horse Winner" both of these common daydreams of childhood are combined. The little boy makes his mother rich through the discovery of a secret, and he dies at the end while the cold and undeserving mother is prostrate with grief. There is even a close relationship between these two themes in the story, and I should like to go into them further.

Where does the rocking horse fit into this childhood fantasy? How is it that Paul rides his horse and "when he gets there, he *knows*"? The weird and uncanny effect of these rocking scenes in the story must derive from a more profound experience in childhood than any induced by mere nursery rocking horses. This violent, rhythmic rocking and its climax corresponds to masturbatory activity. And now we return to a familiar theme in the tales of treasure. For when Paul "gets there" on his rocking horse, he "knows" the name of the winner. This is the discovery of a secret, the acquisition of secret knowledge which leads to riches, which we have already encountered in each of our treasure tales. The rocking activity on the horse is reminiscent of the rubbing of the lamp and the striking of the tinder box.

There is a further connection between the fate of Paul and his "rocking to win." For Paul grows ill from his incessant and frenzied rocking of his horse; we even have the impression, from the original story, that he has become "queer" and strange, "crazy," in a sense. We understand how this growing ill or "going crazy" belong to masturbatory threats to children and to the beliefs of children regarding their masturbation.

We must conclude that in all these stories, the recurrent theme of a magical act or discovery (masturbation), which serves as a means to the acquisition of great wealth, strongly suggests that these dreams of fortune belong to the masturbatory activity, we should say are masturbatory fantasies. In the purest form of these tales, the fairy tales, for example, the discovery of the treasure, or of great wealth, now enables the hero "to do anything he wants" and, like Aladdin and the Tinder Box soldier, to overcome all obstacles between him and an inaccessible woman (the princess). This element, too, seems to belong to the masturbatory fantasy in which the inaccessible mother (princess) is sought.

But how is it that in so many of these stories the acquisition of great wealth becomes the sine qua non for the fulfillment of the incestuous wish? I do not wish to ignore the real factor that to obtain a Sultan's daughter one must have wealth, but there must also be a deeper unconscious relationship between these two elements. Then I am reminded of an adult patient who was once seen by me at a social agency. The patient described a game which frequently absorbed him, a game with some compulsive features. He counted sidewalk squares on the route from a bus stop to his home. Each square was worth $10,000 in his game. If he avoided stepping on the cracks he awarded himself $10,000 and accrued earnings as he went along. If he stepped on a crack he forfeited all his "earnings" up to that point. His goal in these games was to make a *million dollars*. He had never achieved it.

Neither the patient nor I understood these games for some time. Then one day, while associating to a dream, the patient recalled a game which he used to play as an adolescent. The boys would ask each other, "Would you do it with your mother for a thousand dollars? For ten thousand? For fifty thousand?" My patient found himself incorruptible. But when he was asked, "Would you do it with your mother for a *million dollars?*" my patient did not admit to the others a gnawing doubt within himself. After all, he argued with himself, a million dollars was a lot of money. . . . The sidewalk game, then, had the meaning, "If I had a million dollars I could do it with my mother."

We have the impression, from the game and from the fantasies of children, that the incestuous barrier does not exist for those who have great wealth. The rich man can do anything he wishes. One wonders if the persistance of this belief derives from a historical truth. For the very rich until modern times were noblemen, and men of royal blood. The members of the royal families, especially in ancient times, were exempt from incest taboos. As descendants of the gods they had the prerogatives of the gods and this included the right to incestuous relations.

## IV

These tales of the buried treasure and the discovery of great wealth are among the oldest daydreams of the race. These are the longings of childhood which live on in the unconscious memory of the grown man. Their ageless appeal derives from the universal and perennial mystery which confounds the child in his first investigations of origins. In every life there is this momentous discovery of the secret through an accidental touching or an observation, a revelation of the "magic" of the genitals. And always there has been a magician with greater powers and a secret knowledge which is denied to a poor boy. There is the childhood mystery of "the place" where the treasure is hidden, the mysterious cavern which has no door, the hidden place deep under ground. And there is the unwavering belief of the child that if he should have the magician's magic lamp, the pirate's map, the key to the treasure, the knowledge of "the place," he could win for himself this treasure of treasures. In this ageless daydream of childhood, the poor boy who has nothing steals the magician's secret, the pirate's map, and outwits the powerful opponent who stands between him and the treasure.

# 11

# Some Considerations in the Introduction to Therapy in Puberty

The analytic method encounters special problems in work with the child in puberty. In a real sense we can say that the aims of puberty and the aims of analysis are hostile to each other. At a time when the ego must strengthen its defenses against the powerful resurgent drives, analysis must disturb the defensive structure in order to do its work. The precarious balance of the pubertal ego makes exceptional demands upon the analytic method. If the method succeeds in undermining the pathological defenses, it may, in some instances, precipitously release the dammed-up impulses to wreak new havoc upon the character of the child and upon the environment. If the method is perceived as a threat to the defensive structure, the ego may further strengthen the defenses, bring forth new defenses and elaborated symptoms, and marshall its resistances against the intruder, the analyst. The therapist, therefore, must walk a tight-rope in his work with the pubertal child.

As we pursue the problem further we see other contradictions of aim. Puberty is the age of secrecy. It closes the door upon the prying adult; it suspects the well-intentioned overtures of the parents, the invitations to confide. It hoards its secrets and, at times, sees the world of adults in grand conspiracy to spy upon them and ferret them out. The classical analytic technique requires the surrender of secrets. The spectre of the analyst as Spy who haunts the dreams of patients in analysis can be a tangible flesh and blood enemy to certain children in puberty. Where the enmity between parents and child is very strong, the analyst is certain to be suspect. Isn't he "hired by" the parents "to find out things"?

The pubertal child fears analysis for other and darker reasons. He is aware, as his parents are, that powerful forces are disrupting his psychic equilibrium. He experiences strange, overwhelming impulses, new sensations. He is frightened by the cyclic swings of affect which buffet him between the poles of depression and elation. He does not know this new self; his body seems to be inhabited by a stranger. But even his body has become a stranger to him! He observes its changes with mingled wonder and alarm, for with all its new excitements this oldest, most intimate and substantial fact of existence and personal identity has changed its landmarks. The stranger inside is the tenant of a house which does not seem to be his own. The sense of identity is assaulted from all sides. The pubertal child seems constantly preoccupied with the question, "Who am I?" and, as if to remind himself, he fills his schoolbooks, his notebooks and scraps of paper with his name and address in various fancy scripts and styles of lettering. And all of these things, the alienation of parts of the psychic structure, the altered body image, the disturbance of the reality sense, the masturbatory conflicts, give rise in puberty to terrible speculations regarding sanity. So he is afraid of analysis for these other reasons. "I'm not nuts!" he says. "I won't go to a nut doctor!"

The dilemma of the therapist lies not only in the technical problems which arise in the treatment of pubertal neuroses, but in the fact that puberty may bring forth the most severe symptoms, depressions, phobias, compulsive disorders, character disturbances and delinquencies in their most virulent form—symptoms which demand our immediate assistance and which cannot wait for a more propitious time in life for their treatment.

If we decide, in view of all these handicaps, that a pubertal child must have treatment, we are faced with our first and most difficult problem, that of overcoming the resistances to treatment which are commonly presented by the child of this age. While this is the problem which I have set out to study in this paper, it becomes immediately apparent that in order to do justice to this subject we would have to investigate every aspect of the condition of puberty. My intentions in this study are very limited in scope. They are to review some of my own cases of girls in early puberty in order to examine the early reactions to treatment and the technical problems posed by these reactions.

## II

Almost all writers recognize the adolescent's negative reactions to beginning treatment, and the powerful initial resistances, as factors which require special handling in the early hours of treatment. The possibility of an "introductory" phase in adolescent analysis is proposed by Spiegel (1951), who also suggests that some of Aichhorn's techniques for establishing contact with dissocial adolescents may find applicability here. Zachry (1945) gives special attention to the unfavorable position of the adolescent at the beginning of treatment. He might seek help himself except that to do so "is the result not of his own feelings in the matter but of the urging of his parents from whom he is seeking to free himself." Under such circumstances, Zachry stresses the importance of showing the patient that the therapist is not the authority from which he seeks independence, but someone who stands with the patient. This view is similar to Aichhorn's (1925), who, in speaking of the neurotic child with symptoms of delinquency, shows how the therapist must act toward the child "in such a way as to prevent a repetition with the worker of the situation with the parents which led to the conflict." In the case of the child who is in open conflict with society, Aichhorn found it necessary completely to take the child's part in order to win the child's confidence and bring him into a positive transference. In a case report of a twelve-year-old bed wetter, Anny Angel Katan (1935) describes the initial difficulties in the analysis due to the child's belief that the analyst was in league with the mother. Until the child's suspicions could be dispelled the analysis could make no progress. Deutsch (1944), speaking of the prepubertal girl, remarks on the special difficulties encountered by women therapists with this age group. The hostility toward motherly persons makes it necessary, Deutsch believes, for the therapist to adopt a role which is similar to that of a girl friend. Ella Sharpe (1950), supporting the view of Melanie Klein, believed it necessary to dissolve the initial resistances of the adolescent through early direct interpretation of symbolic actions.

Anny Katan (1951) examines a problem of resistance to the analytic process in the pubertal child in her work on the mechanism of "removal" and the pubertal defenses against incestuous strivings. The critical task of puberty is that of object removal, the displacement of the incestuous desires onto new objects. The term "removal" is employed by Anny Katan to differentiate this mechanism from displacement, and to give specificity to a process which has a single aim and direction (in contrast to displacement). The direction is forward moving and away from the incestuous objects, and the mechanism is exclusively concerned with the incestuous desires. The implications for analysis of the pubertal child are of the greatest importance. In an illustrative case, Anny Katan shows how a satisfactorily progressing analysis of a fourteen-year-old girl was abruptly terminated by the girl herself when she fell in love with a boy. There were no indications from the analytic material that this termination was a hostile act. The analyst saw this termination as a normal and necessary step. The girl's falling in love was seen as a successful object removal. Analysis would inevitably have disturbed this process in examining the repetitious nature of the new love and bringing forth once more the incest anxiety which impelled the removal. "In puberty," Anny Katan (1951) says, " . . . one is confronted with the entire force of the developmental thrust counteracting the analysis."

The negativism of puberty (which can become a formidable resistance to treatment at times) has been illuminated by Anna Freud (1952) in her "Studies in Passivity." The negativism which is investigated in these studies is a specific type, a primitive mode of defense. It is encountered in male homosexuals of the passive type, in certain borderline cases as an extreme defense against object relations, and as a characteristic of two developmental phases, the second year and puberty. Analysis reveals a common danger which is warded off by this defense. The danger is surrender, of complete submission to the love object—not alone a sexual danger, a danger of castration—but a danger of merging with the object, hence of losing the self and personal identity and of returning to an archaic oneness with the object. Here, love of the object would mean complete surrender to the object, loss of the self in the object, and the defense of negativism is employed against the object and against the danger of loss of personality. Such persons as these described by Anna Freud, are afraid "to be like" someone else, since "to be like" is "to be one with" the object (my paraphrasing).

In adolescence, Anna Freud shows how the two aspects of this process, negativism and emotional surrender, can exist side by side and are seen in the manifestations of passionate devotion to objects and, alternatively, extreme negativism to the same object. In a brief case illustration Anna Freud also shows how an extreme form of negativism in a child patient dissolved in adolescence to reveal the most passionate longing to surrender in a love relationship, as seen in her abandoned love for a man.

It is significant that our greatest progress in understanding puberty has come out of the developments in psychoanalytic ego psychology. In Anna Freud's study of negativism and emotional surrender, as in earlier studies of "defense motivated by fear of the strength of the instincts" in *The Ego and the Mechanisms of Defense* (1936), the study of puberty is incidental to a larger study of defense, but in each work puberty is illuminated by the study of defense at the same time that it serves the study of defense.

We understand that under conditions of severe stress, and puberty is one such condition, the ego behaves as if it were in danger of extinction and falls back upon primitive defenses which originated in the earliest struggle to preserve and maintain the boundaries of the emerging self from the danger of the backward step, of fusion with the object world. In any discussion of the therapy of puberty these defensive processes must be counted among the chief resistances.

For these reasons, and many others, there is disagreement among analysts regarding the treatability of adolescents. The relative weakness of the adolescent ego is regarded as a contraindication for treatment by Gitelson (1948). Zachry (1945), on the other hand, writes positively and optimistically about the possibilities of psychotherapy in adolescence. She regards the adolescent's introspective tendencies and his conscious recognition of conflict as specific advantages in treatment. Spiegel (1951), in his survey of the analytic literature on adolescence, notes the tendency among analytic writers to dwell upon the unfavorable aspects of analytic treatment in adolescence while comparatively little attention has been paid to the possibilities of "adapting psychoanalysis to the adolescent's particular situation."

### III

I have limited my own study here to cases of girls in prepuberty and early puberty. I should begin by explaining this selection.

It was my original intention to survey all my cases of adolescent girls within the age range, roughly, eleven to eighteen. I had expected, of course, to find important differences in the treatment of the very young adolescent and the older adolescent, but a preliminary review of the cases in this wide age range revealed such large differences that I could not justify the study of eleven to eighteen as a single group. I was struck by the fact that when we speak of "the special problems in the treatment of the adolescent," we are often not speaking of the wide range of adolescence but the phases of prepuberty and early puberty which precede the shift in object choice.

We know that the decisive point in adolescent development is the abandonment of the incestuous aim and the replacement of the infantile objects. While we recognize that this is a gradual process, the achievement of "object removal" distinguishes the later phase of development from the earlier and permits us to speak of two major phases of adolescence.[1] This achievement is reflected in ego changes, for the perilous balance between ego and drives which characterized the earlier phase has shifted and thrown the scales on the ego side. When this decisive step has been accomplished, however badly or contaminated by the incestuous motives, the ego has triumphed. A neurosis may persist with a change of personnel and scene, but the relative positions of ego and drives have changed and the implications for therapy have altered accordingly.

Now when I grouped my cases independent of age and only in reference to the phase of development as told by object choice, I achieved a much clearer picture. The "characteristic" problems of treatment which we speak of in connection with adolescence were actually characteristic of only the first phase, corresponding roughly to the age of biological puberty. Problems involving the early resistances to treatment and the establishment of a positive transference, technical considerations in interpretation, depth of analysis permitted, dangers of acting out, actually faded in importance when applied to the second phase, that which we sometimes speak of as "later adolescence." It almost seemed as if there were less differences between the analytic method employed for the "older adolescent" and the classical procedure for adults, than between the analytic methods employed for these two groups of adolescents with their separate developmental achievements. The "older adolescents" often strongly desired treatment for themselves; they understood its necessity, willingly accepted its conditions and showed readiness and aptness for the analytic process. Most important of all, this second stage of adolescence, marked by the successful removal of object choice, fulfilled the conditions for the development of a transference neurosis which altogether changed the character of the treatment from that employed with the pubertal child.

For these reasons I decided to limit my study to those girls who properly belonged to the earlier phase of development, the period which precedes object removal and which is still under the influence of "the biological onslaught of puberty," to use the phrase of Helene Deutsch (1944).

# IV

The problems of initiating therapy, of overcoming the initial resistances, are always in the foreground of discussions of treatment of the child in puberty. We find that if we are able to engage the child in a positive transference, many factors in the situation of puberty and the strong currents of puberty will come to the aid of therapy and work toward a favorable outcome.

## Initial Reactions to Treatment

From the beginning some children of this age show the strongest reactions to the idea of treatment even before the first meeting with the therapist. In only two of my cases did I have reason to believe that the parents themselves might have given a punitive tinge to the idea of treatment in preparation of the child for seeing me. Further, these negative reactions seemed to have little to do with the type of disturbance manifest in each case. We can understand that a delinquent girl or a youngster with conduct disorders can show strong resistance to the idea of treatment, but among other cases in the series studied were severe neuroses and symptoms of a type which critically handicapped the child and which we should expect might provide strong incentives to the child to come into treatment.

Some of these initial reactions seem worth while cataloguing:

Jeannie, who was eleven, was referred for treatment of a severe compulsion neurosis. There was a hand-washing compulsion, ideas of contamination through breathing, ritual prayers and hypochondriacal fears of cancer. Now, also, there was a reluctance to go to school.

She refused to come into my office to see me and pleaded with her mother not to seek help for her. In view of the severity of the disturbance I visited her first in her home in order, I hoped, to dissipate some of her exaggerated fantasies of me.

Upon seeing me the first time she burst into tears and cried out hysterically, "I'm not crazy! I'm not crazy!" then ran wildly out of the room.

With the greatest difficulty, in three visits to her home, I was able to reassure her and help her gain some degree of confidence in me.

Patty was eleven. She was a deeply unhappy child, without friends or special interests, and was failing in school in spite of better than average intelligence. She was biting and sarcastic to her parents, complained bitterly that she was a girl. She was untidy and flaunted her unkempt and unwashed appearance. Only girls, "sissies" washed and cared about how they looked.

Yet her loneliness and misery was evident to everyone. A sympathetic teacher found her sobbing behind a book one day, and took steps with Patty's parents to get her into treatment.

Patty's reaction to the idea of treatment was forthrightly hostile. "I don't need to go to see anybody. There's nothing wrong with me." And in her first visit to me she was hostile and uncommunicative, except that every now and then, she said, "I don't need to come here. There's nothing wrong with me."

Martha, aged twelve, referred for a serious conduct disorder and compulsive stealing, burst into tears at the entrance to my office on her first visit. "Mama, I'm not a psycho! Am I?"

Margery, aged twelve, was referred to me by her school. She was a stormy, defiant child who was so disruptive in the classroom and openly abusive of her teachers and parents that she could not be influenced by anyone in her environment. Yet, she spent hours in her room brooding and crying hopelessly. There was nothing wrong, she insisted, and she was not unhappy.

She protested with tears and tantrums when her parents proposed that she come to see me. Finally she capitulated and said craftily to her parents, "All right. I'll go to see her. But I won't talk to her. She won't get me to talk!"

At the time the child comes to us many fantasies about therapy and the therapist have already taken shape. Sometimes we are able to obtain these fantasies in early hours of treatment and make use of them in dissipating the child's fear of the treatment. But more often we may not get the content behind these initial reactions until a later stage in treatment.

At the beginning of her treatment, Judy, then twelve years old, would sit in complete silence with me. She suffered with a severe phobia which began as a school phobia and had extended itself to all areas outside of the home. Her apathy and withdrawal, her inability to communicate, had caused a psychiatrist to diagnose her as a schizophrenic the year before she came to see me, but this diagnosis was withdrawn after a period of observation.

Months after I had gained her confidence and our therapeutic work had progressed favorably, I asked her the question which I had asked at the beginning without getting an answer. "What did you think I was going to be like when you first came to see me? What did you think I would do?" She said, "I thought I was going crazy. I thought I had a brain tumor and that when you found out about it I would have to go to the hospital and have an operation."

I do not think that this fantasy was much influenced by the actual experience of a psychiatric interview, for it can be seen again and again, how such fantasies about treatment exist independent of experience in puberty.

Susan, fifteen, was a stutterer, a shy, lonely child who longed to be like other children. She was not unwilling to come to see me at first, but in the early interviews with me she found herself unable to talk and would sit wretchedly in a chair in evident agony. Once, in an early hour, she asked shyly if I didn't have to take notes, and in discussion of this I learned that she had expected me to behave like the movie psychiatrist who is equipped with a clip-board and fountain pen. But I learned nothing more about her fantasies about treatment at the time.

Then one day during a silence which was difficult for her, I asked her to tell me her thoughts. And then she blurted out, "I was thinking of a movie I saw." I asked her to tell me about it. "It was a mystery. There was a psychiatrist who was really a crook posing as a psychiatrist and he took notes to blackmail the patients."

The protests of these patients were, as we should expect, the first clues to the neurotic picture. But usually it was only later in treatment that the significance of these reactions became clear. It does not surprise us that in the case of Jeannie, the analysis of the hand-washing compulsion revealed her defenses against masturbatory activity, and that her hysterical protest, "I'm not crazy!" was the confession of her fear that her masturbation had made her crazy. Her fear of treatment was the fear that her secret would be discovered, a fear of the "examination." The reiterated protests of Patty, "There's nothing wrong with me!" testified to the deep fears that something *was* wrong with her, and I learned in the later treatment that she believed that she could become pregnant through her masturbation. Again the resistance against treatment was based on her fear that her secret would be discovered. Judy's fear that she was going crazy and that I would discover that she had a brain tumor for which she would have an operation, stemmed in similar fashion from the belief that she had damaged herself in sexual activity and from fantasies of impregnation through sexual activity with a sister. Susan's paralyzed silences in the beginning of her treatment had a direct relationship to her symptom, for her stuttering represented, among other things, the fear that she might blurt out forbidden words and thoughts. Her thoughts of the psychiatrist who blackmailed his patients with their own words stemmed partially from her own fear that she would betray (hence "be betrayed by") her own words. The behavior of Margery to the suggestion of treatment was seen to resemble that of a person accused of a criminal act who fears that if he speaks he will give evidence to the court, hence her absolute refusal to talk to the therapist. "I'll go but I won't talk to her. She won't get me to talk."

The occurrence of these reactions at the outset of treatment, even in many cases prior to the first meeting with the therapist, suggests that the therapeutic situation is ideally suited for the transference of certain elements of the pubertal neuroses. The fear of the pubertal girl that her secrets will be discovered finds rich possibilities for amplification in the girl's view of therapy and her view of the parents' motives in bringing her into treatment. The fear of "being found out" even reaches beyond the therapeutic hour. There is the fear that "others will find out" about their treatment. "What shall I tell the other kids when they want to know where I go so many afternoons? . . . If anyone of my friends found out I'd die." When asked: "Why?" she replied: "Because they'd think I'm nuts and had to go to a nut doctor." We find them making excuses to their friends regarding their absence from some after-school activities—most commonly, "I have to go to the dentist." We find that this fear of "others knowing" is a greater factor in puberty than at any other age. Our younger patients usually show such a casual disregard for "others knowing" that they may present embarrassing problems to their parents who do not wish the fact to be broadcast. Again in later adolescence there seems to be much less secrecy about treatment.

The factor of "being made to come" by the parents will also require skillful technical maneuvering on the part of the therapist. In the analysis of younger children the problem is quite different. Although the small child does not initiate the treatment and comes to his first hours chiefly because of his parents' wish, he is still dependent upon his parents and their influence will be sufficient usually to overcome any objections of his own at the beginning of treatment. But the child in puberty may actively resist the treatment *if only* because his parents wish it (Zachry, 1945). If we are not successful in divorcing our treatment from the pubertal tug-of-war with the parents, we may find that treatment can become a new battleground, ideally suited in some ways, for the continuation of the struggle.

In the case of the very strong hostility between patient and parents, resistance to treatment may satisfy revenge fantasies against the parents.

> Leslie, eleven, amused herself during unproductive hours of therapy with exhilarating fantasies, during which she calculated how much money her parents were throwing out on her treatment. (Her mother had once told her the fee when she asked.)

I have also suspected, at times, that "being made to come" satisfied certain masochistic tendencies which are so open and exposed in the early stages of puberty. It would have the significance of "being forced into intimacy with a woman," an idea which is both compelling and alarming to the pubertal girl during the period of her struggle to free herself from the incestuous tie to mother. I saw this most clearly in the case of a twelve-year-old girl who actually had entered treatment voluntarily; had requested treatment herself without any "pushing" from her mother.

> In spite of the fact that Eleanor had come to treatment through her own expressed wish, and on the basis of her deep unhappiness, her depressions and her withdrawal from normal interests of her age, the first signs of resistance appeared in this striking way: In the fourth hour of her treatment she announced that she had no problems, that she saw no reason for coming here, and only came here because her mother made her! I knew that no pressure had been put on Eleanor to come into

treatment or continue treatment. I reminded her that nobody had "made her come" here and that I would not wish this to be the reason she came for treatment. (My attitude, I felt, was a very neutral one. The implication was, of course, that no one would make her come here against her own wishes.)

She reacted with evident disappointment, but characteristically did not discuss this further with me. Later, in an outburst to her mother she said, "Selma was mean to me. She said if I didn't want to come in I didn't have to."

She arrived the next hour with intentions (she told her mother) to end her treatment. But as soon as she came in she relaxed, then said, "It's funny. I came today to tell you I didn't want to come any more but when I'm here I don't feel that way." When I encouraged her to discuss her feelings earlier of ending treatment she said, "I felt I *had* to come here and I didn't like it." I asked, "Did you feel that I was making you come here, too?" "Yes, that's what I thought. But I know you weren't really. That's what I can't figure out."

From the content of later hours I could understand the nature of this first resistance. For this hour ushered in a period of strong positive attachment to me, during which she tried to emulate me in many small ways, compared me, my house, my way of living with her mother, her house and her family's way of life to the latter's disadvantage, of course. She wanted to become a therapist one day and, as if to make a beginning, promptly had her hair restyled like mine.

It seemed to me, then, that the thought "I am being made to come here" alluded to the "compelling" nature of the emerging positive transference. It was this which the child felt must be resisted and was seen by her as a force emanating from the outside; I was "making her come"; mother was "making her come." We observe that my neutral attitude toward her continuation in treatment was interpreted by her as rejection I was "mean" to her.

Here, we see how without any external pressure on the young patient to enter treatment or continue the treatment, she behaves like so many of our other youngsters for whom the beginning of treatment is actually the outcome of the parental initiative.

*Technical Considerations at the Beginning of Treatment*

If an adult patient enters treatment with fantasies of a dangerous and powerful Spy-Psychiatrist who will wrest his innermost secrets from him, we will certainly hear about this spectre or see him in the patient's dreams, for the patient is bound to the analytic rule. The young child patient, if he has such fantasies, will bring them forth in Spy games, or robber games, or often in interminable guessing games in which he tests the therapist's ability to "read minds," for the small patient easily translates his fantasies into games and makes them accessible to us. But the pubertal patient can neither be bound to an analytic rule, nor will he act out his fantasies in play. We feel as if we are left without familiar access to the patient's inner life. I am reminded of a time when I spoke such thoughts out loud to Eleanor during an hour which was particularly difficult for her. She was evidently upset that hour and several times fell into paralyzed silence during which she could think of "nothing." Finally I said, "At your age it's so hard. The little ones who come here can play and they tell me their thoughts while they play. And grownups, you know, agree to a rule where they tell everything that comes into their minds. . . ." Eleanor stopped me right there with a horrified look on her face. "Do you mean," she said, "they tell *everything* that comes into their minds? *Everything!* Why that would be terrible! That wouldn't be . . . that wouldn't be *polite!*"

It seems to me this story nicely capsules the pubertal dilemma in treatment. We understand from Eleanor's reaction that she was struggling with such "impolite" thoughts about the therapist, but a therapy which should insist upon the telling of such thoughts stands for corruption to an ego which has concentrated its forces to resist corruption. This fear of "having to tell" can be dealt with even in puberty at later stages of treatment, but during the initial phase of treatment anything like an "analytic rule" would be countered with the greatest resistance by patients of this age.

How, then, can we deal with the initial resistances to treatment which have such critical importance for the future of the treatment? If the child brings transference fantasies to the treatment which are withheld from analysis, there is seemingly no means for the dissolution of the negative transference.

I have been impressed in work with some girls of this age with the fact that at the beginning of treatment, almost any interpretation, no matter how little, how superficial, constitutes a threat to the patient. Behind the transference fantasy of the sinister psychiatrist, the mad hypnotist, the "nut-doctor," is the image of the omnipotent parent, all-seeing, all-knowing. A display of the analyst's insights into the workings of the mind, however "correct" the interpretation may be, will only convince these youngsters that they are in the hands of the powerful superbeing of their fantasies. So we find, in the early stages of treatment, that we can best win the confidence of the pubertal girl by negating the transference image of the omnipotent psychologist if we cannot analyze it, and we can do this through being quite simply human, open, unmysterious, and not too clever. We may put aside, at first, our professional interest in dreams and fantasies for the more urgent worldly sorrows of youth—the traitorous girlfriend who spreads lies about our patient, the math teacher who likes to humiliate students, the blue taffeta dress or the lime velveteen for the school dance Saturday night. We are interested in whatever the patient brings to us, and we demonstrate from the beginning our sympathy, our special understanding of youth, and our ability to be helpful, very practically, on all manner of problems, small ones as well as big ones.

The transference fantasy of the omnipotent psychologist provided most valuable clues to me in the handling of the initial resistances to treatment in puberty. For when we consider this fantasy in another light, the danger of the therapist to the pubertal child is also the danger of *loss of autonomy*, of submission to a powerful being. In this connection, too, Anna Freud's "Negativism and Emotional Surrender" immediately comes to mind.

It is characteristic of the pubertal struggle that the ego, torn between two masters, should regard its loss of autonomy as the most terrible danger of all. In the transference fantasies of the omnipotent psychologist, the mad scientist, the mind reader, we see how the fear of being overpowered, of submitting, is a powerful determinant. Similarly the fear of "going crazy," while certainly connected with sexual ideas, is also a fear of loss of autonomy.

It appears then that if our therapy is to appeal to the pubertal child, the introduction to treatment must be managed in such a way that the threatened ego is given some measure of control in this new and strange situation, assurance that it will be an active, not a passive partner in this treatment. We will not only dispense with the analytic rule, we may find it advisable to reverse the analytic rule, as Aichorn did with his delinquents, "You don't need to tell me anything you don't wish to," to which one can safely add, "Though when you know me better you may *want* to tell me some things so that I can help you better." And since we understand the significance of the pubertal fear of the strength of the drives we will in no way reveal, at the beginning, our special interest in the instinctual sources of his conflict. We ally ourselves from the beginning with those forces within the ego which seek harmony and equilibrium, and we hold out to the ego the promise that our treatment will restore its autonomy.

The case illustrations which follow permit a more detailed analysis of some of these special problems of technique in the beginning of treatment in puberty.

The introduction to treatment begins, of course, before the introduction to the therapist. The manner in which the first consultation is presented by the parents to the child will greatly influence the initial reactions to the therapist, even, as I mentioned earlier, when the parents have not given a punitive tinge to the idea of "help."

I have found it very useful to give the child the initiative whenever possible, and this can actually be done in many instances. In noncritical situations where an immediate consultation with the child is not necessary, there is a great advantage in a "preparatory period" at home.

Nancy, fourteen, suffered with depressions which were of sufficient concern to her parents and me so that therapy seemed indicated, but the general picture of the child was not so alarming that immediate consultation was necessary.

When the suggestion of therapy was first made by her parents, Nancy reacted unfavorably. She was sure she could help herself, she protested, and she didn't need to go to an outsider. She couldn't talk about "personal things" with a stranger anyway. At my suggestion her parents did not press their offer but proposed that Nancy wait a while and think things over. For weeks Nancy tried valiantly to help herself, then the depressions returned. Her parents, following further advice from me, talked with her again, told her that even when parents loved their kids very much they could not help with such problems, and Nancy herself had tried so hard, yet could not help herself either. They asked Nancy if she would like to reconsider the possibility of "outside help" and this time Nancy asked questions about this "help" which were well answered by her parents. A few days later Nancy made her own decision to come to see me.

This was a good beginning for the therapy that followed. Had the parents been insistent at the beginning, we would certainly have encountered a negative youngster in the early hours of treatment, and much labor would have been expended on the achievement of a favorable attitude toward treatment which was better accomplished through waiting and permitting the child herself to come to terms with the first step in obtaining help.

I think there is an important indication in Nancy's initial protest and her wish to "help" herself. To seek help meant for Nancy (and for other youngsters, too) to admit a failure in control, a loss of autonomy, a dreaded admission in puberty. We know that the adult patient, too, finds it painful to acknowledge his own failure in dealing with his problems at the time that he comes to terms with his need for treatment, but the child in puberty is often terrified by his failure to find his own solutions to his problems. The pubertal fear "I am no longer master of myself" is realized in the admission, "I need someone to help me."

In more critical situations a "waiting period" during which the child can come to terms with the idea of treatment may not be desirable at all. In many such instances we are confronted with the need for an immediate consultation with a youngster who is strongly opposed to the parents' suggestion. Yet here, too, if we can bring the patient to the therapist with a more favorable attitude, if we can turn this disadvantageous situation into one which is advantageous from the point of view of the child, we stand a much better chance for a favorable outcome.

Diane, who was twelve, had displayed the most determined resistance to the idea of coming to see me. Her parents had consulted me following a rash of stealing episodes at home and in the community. Diane had long been a problem to her family. She was negativistic and obstinate, was passionately envious of boys, told "tall tales," and was having serious difficulties in school in spite of good average learning ability.

"I don't need to go. I'm not crazy!" she insisted when her parents introduced the idea of treatment. Although her parents had tried in every way to get across to her that I would be understanding and kind, she was suspicious of their motives and, of course, displayed the same obstinacy to this proposal as to most other proposals her parents made these days. She was reassured again and again that coming to a therapist did not mean one was crazy, but all this had no effect on Diane.

Of course I did not want Diane to feel she was being forced to come to me. I suggested to the parents that they tell Diane frankly that they had come to see me and that I felt I could not understand the situation without Diane's point of view, in fact that it would be most unfair to Diane if we had only her parents' view and not her own. I also suggested that the parents explain to Diane that it was quite possible that mother and daddy had not understood the problems of Diane, even though they had tried, and that Diane could tell the therapist everything she wanted to help her understand Diane's point of view. If she felt mother and daddy had made mistakes she could tell these things to the therapist, too. (With this last suggestion I was very careful, of course, to help the parents understand my reasons for saying this, and to assure them of my own uncritical attitude.)

This approach was successful. Diane came to see me willingly; she talked freely with me, and I was able to interpret treatment to her and to get her own consent to continue work with me.

The suggestions which were employed by the parents were based on the assumption that Diane would resist a visit to me if only because her parents had suggested it, and that she felt treatment itself was to be an "accusation" against her for her thefts and her other "crimes." The advantages, so far as Diane could tell, were all on the parents' side in this therapy business. When the parents surrendered part of their advantage to Diane (she could state *her* grievances, too), her own situation was changed from that of "being made to come," being passive, to the active role, choosing to come to state her own case.

> In the case of twelve-year-old Martha (stealing, conduct disorder) the initial reaction to her parents' suggestion was also hostile and defiant. She, too, was afraid she was "a psycho."
> Martha was very uncertain of her adoptive parents' love for her and feared that she might be sent away for being "bad." Here, I suggested to the parents that they tell Martha that because they loved her they could not bear to see her so unhappy and had consulted me to see how they could help her to become a happier girl.
> Martha was really very much touched by this explanation. She agreed to come to see me, although still worried that she might, after all, be "a psycho," and tearfully asking for reassurance as she came to my office.

In this case treatment which is first perceived by the child as a punishment, a banishment by the parents, is reinterpreted so that it can be seen as an act of love on the part of concerned parents.

In recent years, through giving more attention to the manner in which the child is introduced to treatment by his parents, I have been impressed to see how my work in initiating treatment has been lightened. As I review cases from the earlier period of my practice I observe how I tended to give "general" kinds of advice to parents in introducing the subject of therapy to the patient and did not concern myself sufficiently with details. I assumed, somehow, that the parents would manage to induce the patient to come to the first consultation and I would employ my own skills to bring about a positive transference. In the case of the negative adolescent, I burdened the early hours of treatment with the problems of undoing certain resistances which need never have arisen had I paid sufficient attention to the preparation at home. Granted that only the therapist should assume the task of *interpreting* treatment to the patient, only the parent can introduce the suggestion of treatment, and I am sure through my later experience as a therapist that even the most well-meaning parents can err in this without careful advice from the therapist. It is my practice now to counsel parents almost step-by-step in this process. The suggestions for introducing treatment are specific in terms of my knowledge of each child as far as it can be acquired through the parent consultation. If the adolescent patient does not react favorably to the parents' suggestions, the parents do not press or coax but are asked to discuss the child's reactions with me once more so that we can handle this in terms of the child's feelings. In this way we avoid the situation (some examples of which are provided earlier in this paper) in which a sullen and determinedly hostile youngster meets the therapist for the first time.

There still remains the very important work of the therapist in making treatment significant to the anxious and still uncommitted young patient. The question has been raised by Spiegel (1951) as to whether an "introductory phase" of analysis might have value in the treatment of adolescents in the same way that it has proved useful in the analysis of young children and delinquents. In her introduction to the last edition of *The Psychoanalytical Treatment of Children*, Anna Freud modified her earlier statements regarding the need for an introductory phase. Progress in psychoanalytic ego psychology and the study of defense mechanisms has made it possible for the child analyst to analyze the first resistances of the child patient and in this way to shorten the introductory phase or render it unnecessary. In general these remarks seem to apply as well as to the treatment of the adolescent patient.

Our understanding of the nature of the pubertal conflict provides us with the means for dealing with the early resistance. What the child in puberty fears is loss of control, surrender to the demands of the drives. What he fears in therapy is the further disturbance of his precarious equilibrium. What he longs for most of all is the restoration of harmony. If our treatment is to have meaning for him, if we can hold out to him a concrete goal, we need to help him see therapy as a means of re-establishing his equilibrium, of helping him become master of himself.

Nancy had recognized her need for help and had entered treatment willingly following the period, earlier described, in which she tried heroically to help herself. Now her depressions at home had alternated with violent outbursts against her mother, but early in her treatment, when she tried to tell me about these outbursts, all the circumstances fled from her mind and she could neither recall the events nor the strong emotions which had accompanied them.

She became afraid that coming to see me would make her worse. She begged me to arrange for her to go away to school. She considered giving up her treatment (then barely started). She was filled with self-loathing because she could not control herself. And she began eating enormous quantities of food which caused her now to castigate herself because she could not control her appetite. "Now that I come here I can't hate myself the way I used to and now I can't stop eating!" she wept. All interpretation was directed toward her fear of losing control and I assured her that therapy would help her achieve control. I showed her how her attempts to control through self-punishment had not worked, but that with help she would learn to control herself without being cruel to herself.

In one of these early, critical hours when she expressed her shame at letting me see her anger and her fear that she was getting worse I made a promise to her in the form of an interpretation. I told her that the more she was able to talk about her feelings here, the less she would lose control outside and that I could promise her that if she were able to do this she would actually gain more and more control over her feelings.

Nancy was really very much impressed with this statement. This made it possible for her to offer her co-operation in a very painful period in therapy, to begin at last to express feelings and to tell me for the first time about her obsessional symptoms.

This is, of course, a type of interpretation which we are accustomed to employ in order to penetrate a resistance which is produced by fear of the strength of the drives. I only wish to make special mention of the value of such interpretations in therapeutic work in puberty.

A variation of this interpretation served an important purpose in the very first hour of Diane's treatment.

> When Diane tried to speak of her thefts in this first hour, she turned pink with shame and could scarcely find the words to tell me. I remarked sympathetically on her feelings of shame. Diane: "I feel very badly about it. Most of all because I've hurt mother so. I *really* don't want to do it. I wish I could stop it. But I can't!" I told her I thought I understood, that she was telling me that she really didn't want to steal but at times she felt she had to and couldn't stop herself. Was that right? Diane: "That's right. Oh, and I really don't want to be bad. I want to be good so people will like me. And sometimes I can see money and it won't bother me. And sometimes—well it's just like eating." (Gesturing toward her round belly.) "I'll see it and I'll have to have it."
>
> Now I said, "It must be very frightening to have a wish to do something which you know is not good and yet not be able to control it." Diane was very much moved by this. "That's just it!" she said, and seemed close to tears. . . . "I'm so glad I'm coming here. You know all about that, don't you?"
>
> On this basis I interpreted treatment to Diane. I explained how it was as if another part of her makes her do these things against her better judgment. If Diane wanted me to, I would be able to help her so that she would gain control over that other part of her. A look of relief came over her face and then another thought seemed to cross it. "But some things which have good beginnings have bad endings," she said with worry. I asked if she were afraid that I might not be able to help her. She quickly denied this. Then I told her something of how I would help her and why it would take time. I explained that there were reasons behind her problem which neither of us understood now. But as we talked together we would be able to understand what made her do these things against her will and then she would be able to control them.
>
> On this basis Diane herself agreed to regular appointments with me. This proved to be a good beginning for therapy which was successfully concluded. Diane, throughout her treatment, accepted her own responsibility and her own need for help.

Here, then, we appeal to the child's anxiety in being at the mercy of uncontrollable urges. The promise of treatment is directed toward the part of the ego which strives for restoration of control over these urges.

When we encounter a well-established neurosis in puberty, we frequently find that the neurotic equilibrium will be preferred by the young patient to any possibility of relief which we can offer him. We can understand this very well for these symptoms which have been motivated by dread of the strength of the drives are regarded as indispensable by the patient. (They may, in fact, be indispensable, and we know how carefully we must judge the clinical picture in treating such patients analytically.) The ego which has achieved control in this way through pathological defense cannot easily be bribed through our therapeutic promise.

By the time Judy, then twelve, entered treatment her phobia embraced almost every area of functioning. It had started as a school phobia and she had not been in school for over a year. She rarely left her house, could not answer the door or the telephone. She had abandoned all friendships and even her relationships with her family were perfunctory and empty. The only thing in the world that she loved was her dog. The only traces of anxiety which remained were, of course, in connection with "going out" and "having dizzy spells" (which were chiefly connected with going out). Her fear in connection with the "dizzy spells" was that "people would see me and think something was wrong with me."

She came to her hours without fuss and without the slightest manifest resistance—but she was unable to talk! At best when she had reduced me to banal questions or leading remarks I would get from her a low "yes" or "no" or "maybe." Once I was rewarded with the longest speech she ever made to me. "But if I get rid of my dizziness, then I will have to go back to school." I promised her that I would never force her to go back to school and placed the emphasis in treatment on relieving her dreaded "dizziness." I think she believed me and trusted me, and yet she was unable in the hours that followed to talk to me.

It was a transference symptom which provided the first opportunity to make treatment meaningful to her. One day I observed a symptom which had never been reported to me by the parents. It was a leg-tic. The right leg moved jerkily up and down, pantomiming a motion of stamping the leg on the floor. I waited that hour to see if I could obtain any clues through behavior. None appeared. When the tic appeared again the following hour I called Judy's attention to it. She reacted with acute embarrassment. I said sympathetically, "Can you stop that if you want to?" She made a desperate effort, but the tic persisted. Then I told her that sometimes when we are unable to talk, our bodies do the "talking" for us. It was as if her leg were stamping the floor as someone might do when angry. Was she afraid to feel angry about something or toward someone. Perhaps me? Now to my surprise Judy burst into a tirade—not against me—but her sister Janie. It was an outburst that lasted several minutes. How she hated Janie. How Janie used to beat up Judy and threaten her. How Janie would get Judy into trouble, then blackmail her with threats of telling the parents. She went on and on in a voice full of impotent rage, cataloguing the grievances against her sister. (These were objectively correct statements.)

During the angry tirade the tic had ceased. I chose a moment after the outburst to draw Judy's attention to her leg. I showed her how, when she was able to talk about the feelings of anger and fear the leg had stopped its "jerking." She was surprised, even incredulous, and then broke into a smile of recognition.

Now in some respects I feel that this technique was disputable. It was successful (this marked the beginning of a true therapeutic attitude) but risky. With more experience in the treatment of puberty I would not be so sure of myself and would not so confidently undermine a defense before I ascertained the capacity of the ego to deal with smaller quantities of affect.

I can justify this technique, however, on the basis that it rendered inoperable the resistance of silence which completely blocked my efforts. It demonstrated to Judy that one can "talk" through a symptom. It also demonstrated that putting feelings into words could dissolve a symptom which she had demonstrably been unable to control. I, then, had the means to help her bring the disagreeable symptoms under control. It goes without saying that this technique worked only because this was an alien and embarrassing symptom. The phobias were not, of course. Above all this hour opened up the possibilities of exploring the negative transference which led us by way of the tyrannical sister whom she must placate to an infantile dog phobia, the prototype of the present neurosis. Her muteness in those early hours was the muteness of terror as well as repressed rage. One must not show any emotion to the dangerous animal or he will jump on you and bite you. Be nice to him. Make friends with him. And so she had! The only thing she loved when she first came to me was her dog. But I was a new dog, the strange dog.

Initially my therapeutic usefulness to Judy had to be based entirely on those symptoms which she herself found disagreeable. These were the conversion symptoms, the symptoms that "showed." Gradually as she lost her fear of me I acquired a role which became my greatest asset therapeutically. I became the watchdog, in effect, the one who protected her from dangers, from her father's rages (which I could "tame"), her sister's tyranny, and even (for a while) from going to school. Only when I had become the indispensable watchdog could I begin to approach the school phobia and encourage her to face the greatest danger of all.

In the following case we see how a short "preparatory" period was essential to reduce the anxiety of a child who was terrified at the prospect of treatment.

Earlier I mentioned Janet, the eleven-year-old with hand-washing compulsions and obsessional rituals. Her parents could not even induce her to come to the first interview with me and it was necessary to visit her at her home during the first hours. We recall how in the first hour she screamed hysterically upon seeing me, "I'm not crazy! I'm not crazy!" and fled from me in panic before I could speak to her.

Clearly there was nothing to do under these circumstances but to attempt to gain her confidence in me through whatever means seemed best. With her mother's help we induced her to come back and stay with me long enough so that I could offer some reassurance to her. While she sobbed, "I'm not crazy!" I managed to quiet her and to assure her that I knew very well that she was not crazy. I told her that she did not need to tell me anything about herself or her problems until she felt like it, in fact I would prefer that she tell me other things about herself, the kinds of things she liked to do, the subjects she liked in school, such things as that. She eagerly accepted this opportunity and asked if I would like to see her weaving and some of her metal work. She then brought me samples of her handwork which I wholeheartedly admired, and we talked enthusiastically about crafts methods.

In the next hour, still at her home, we continued to talk of her interests in crafts, school subjects, basketball, movies and books. She talked a great deal as if almost fearful that if she did not talk fast I might still change my tactics and begin to ask "psychiatric" questions. But more important, I could see how she wished to impress me with her normality and her good intelligence, to show me she was not "crazy."

In the third hour we continued our exhaustive survey of her interests.

In the fourth hour (now at my office) our patient announced that she was cured. "I'm feeling much better now. I think all my problems are solved." I told her I was surprised but glad to hear of this, and, if this were so I certainly could not take any credit for it, since we had not talked about her problems at all. I asked her with professional interest, how she had achieved this.

"Well, I'm all better now," she said bravely, but then couldn't go on because her voice shook so and she added, "Except my hands." And now she told me in an outpouring how she must wash her hands over and over because if she touches anything she might get sick, she might get cancer. She told me of her ritual prayers at night which keep her awake for hours and how she must sometimes hold her breath because if she breathes on someone, "they might get sick and die."

I am sure that in this case only such an introductory period could have brought the child into treatment. In such instances interpretations related to the child's fear of the therapist will only increase the anxiety and bring forth stronger denials and suspicion of the therapist. We understand that Janet needed to demonstrate to the therapist how well she was before she could admit she was ill. She had to show the other side of her "handwork," the good things she could do with her hands before she could speak of the bad things she did with her hands. And the introductory period probably succeeded in correcting the transference fantasy of the omnipotent therapist and an "examination" which would show that she was "crazy," that she had damaged herself.

## V

In many ways the introduction to treatment and the early hours of therapy appear to be crucial. In my own experience a case is more likely to be lost in the early stages of treatment, that is in the initiation to treatment, than any other time. If we can overcome these initial resistances and establish a therapeutic attitude we find many factors in the pubertal situation which go to work for us. I do not need to mention all those factors in puberty which do *not* work for us, the rigidity of defense, the fear of the homosexual transference, the acting out, etc. But the morbid aspects of the clinical picture in puberty are counterbalanced by the tremendous forward thrust of the drives. It is also, then, a time of hope and of promise and while the clinical picture in puberty can at times be alarming and can resemble in every aspect certain morbid disturbances of later life, the impetus toward growth, fulfillment, toward the future can work for puberty toward a favorable outcome. So it happens that a depression in puberty and a depression in the climacteric will present the same clinical features, but puberty is "not yet fulfilled" and the climacteric is "unfulfilled," and the therapeutic difficulties are by no means as great with the young patient as with the older one.

## Note

1. Our present nomenclature gives no descriptive categories for these two major phases of adolescence. Helene Deutsch's categories "early puberty" and "later puberty" take cognizance of the shift in object choice which sets off one phase from the other, but her scheme presents certain problems when, for example, she employs the term "adolescence" for the period which follows puberty and which is characterized by maturation and consolidation of trends set up in puberty. Current usage argues against standardization of the term "adolescence" in this special sense. More frequently now it is being used to designate the whole period of development commencing with the onset of puberty and ending with sexual maturation. There is evident need for a workable nomenclature which brings the phases of adolescence into the framework of the libido theory and for standardizing the terms "adolescence" and "puberty" which are used ambiguously and even interchangeably in our literature.

## References

Aichhorn, A. (1925). *Wayward Youth*. New York: Viking Press, 1948.

Deutsch, H. (1944). *The Psychology of Women*. New York: Grune & Stratton.

Freud, A. (1936). *The Ego and the Mechanisms of Defense*. New York: International Universities Press, 1946.

———. (1946). *The Psycho-Analytical Treatment of Children*. London: Imago.

———. (1952). Studies in Passivity. Address before the Western Reserve Medical School, October 25, 1952.

Gitelson, M. (1948). Character Synthesis: The Psychotherapeutic Problem in Adolescence. *Am. J. Orthopsychiat.*, 18.

Katan, A. A. (1935). From the Analysis of a Bed Wetter. *Psychoanal. Quart.*, 4.

———. (1951). The Role of "Displacement" in Agoraphobia. *Int. J. Psychoanal.*, 32.

Mahler, M. S. (1945). Child Analysis. In *Modern Trends in Child Psychiatry*, ed. N. D. C. Lewis and B. L. Pacella. New York: International Universities Press.

Sharpe, E. (1950). Contribution to Symposium on Child Analysis. In *Collected Papers on Psycho-Analysis*. London: Hogarth Press.

Spiegel, L. A. (1951). A Psychoanalytic Theory of Adolescence. *Psychoanal. Study Child*, 6.

Zachry, C. B. (1939). Contributions of Psychoanalysis to the Education of the Adolescent. *Psychoanal. Quart.,* 8.

————. (1945). A New Tool in Psychotherapy with Adolescents. In *Modern Trends in Child Psychiatry,* ed. N. D. C. Lewis and B. L. Pacella. New York: International Universities Press.

# 12

# A Therapeutic Approach to Reactive Ego Disturbances in Children in Placement

Among the gravest consequences of placement is the child's inability to form new object relationships following loss. A very large number of children in institutions and foster home care are permanently damaged and may never recover the capacity for making meaningful human ties. Frequently the casework treatment of such children is blocked by the characteristic defenses against affect which these children display and by their inability to make an attachment to the caseworker—the indispensable condition for treatment.

This paper describes and illustrates a casework approach that was developed in the course of working with a small group of latency-age boys in institutional placement. The treatment employed a specialized adaptation of an analytic technique that should be entirely within the competence of a caseworker and within the defined limits of casework treatment. It consisted mainly of working through the defenses against affects and of reviving the affects around the initial trauma of placement. Concurrent group treatment was employed for continuing diagnosis, to test the movement in object relationships, and to provide a milieu in which readiness for new ties might be gratified.

This work was part of a program jointly sponsored by the Tulane School of Social Work, the Children's Bureau of New Orleans, and the Protestant Children's Home. In this report I shall confine myself to the caswork treatment and illustrate with selected cases.[1] I wish to mention, however, that our experience in the use of concurrent group treatment demonstrated not only the value of the group as an adjunct to casework treatment but opened up the possibility in our minds that for selected cases, group treatment might operate independently to bring about favorable therapeutic results.

The setting in which this work was carried out is in many ways typical of institutions that provide care for the dependent and neglected child in our country. The Protestant Children's Home was built nearly one hundred years ago as an orphanage. There is a high iron fence surrounding the grounds and the children are still housed in dormitories according to age groups. The houseparents are mainly middle-aged men and women with limited education and, of course, they have no special educational preparation for work with children. Many of the children are severely disturbed and have been placed in the institution because of earlier failures in foster homes. There are no clinically trained staff members. At the time of our study casework services were provided for the children and their families by the Children's Bureau and other agencies in the community.

We chose the Junior Boys Division for our study. The ten boys in this group ranged in age from eight to eleven. The housemother, Mrs. Lindstrom, was a woman in her middle sixties, who somehow managed the difficult job of caring for a group of gravely disturbed children who would have taxed the best gifts of a clinically trained worker. She was strict in her discipline, and some of her demands for good behavior were undoubtedly excessive. But she also had sympathy and affection for her children, and as we worked together she learned to become more lenient and more tolerant in certain important areas.

## II

I will begin this report with a description of the treatment of George. George was eleven years old when we began treatment. He was the oldest of five children, all of whom had been placed by the parents two years earlier. At the time of placement the parents were considering divorce. The mother planned to return to work, and the children had become such an emotional and financial burden to her that she appeared dangerously close to a severe depression. The plan was for temporary placement, but as two years passed by it became clear that the mother might never bring herself to reunite her family. The father had disappeared after the divorce.

In preplacement interviews the mother described George as the chief problem among her children. He was described as very stubborn and aggressive and subject to stormy outburts of temper. In the early months of placement at the institution George presented the full battery of his behavior problems. Both the institution and the school reported belligerence and bullying of other children, much fighting, and provocative behavior. But gradually, the record shows, George gave up his fighting and his bullying and became a rather passive and tractable child. The complaints now were of another order. He had become whiny and fearful of bigger boys in the institution. He brought constant complaints of being beaten up by the bigger boys and of having his toys destroyed by them. About the second complaint the boys in his group seemed geniunely baffled and claimed that George himself had been seen destroying toys that his mother had sent him and would then accuse other children of having broken them.

Along with this shift from active to passive came two new developments. George had begun to gain weight rapidly, and at the end of the first year in placement he had gained thirty pounds. During the second year he continued to eat voraciously and to gain weight. He was about forty pounds overweight when I first met him. He had wet the bed occasionally prior to placement. By the time internalization of his conflicts had been completed, at the end of the first year, George had become a constant bedwetter. Often he wet two and three times a night.

When I first saw George he was an obese, sluggish youngster with a round pink face. He never smiled. His nails were bitten to the quick. His speech was mushy, indistinct—devoid of affect.

In the early interviews with George I was impressed by certain characteristics of his relationship with me. He was affable, superficially friendly, garrulous, and yet he was completely uninterested in the new caseworker. One had the impression that caseworkers were interchangeable, that one would do as well as another. He was sorry that he had to give up his previous worker. He had even expressed some regret to her when he learned of the transfer, but none of this feeling could be recovered when I invited him to talk about his feelings about the transfer. I began to understand that his relationship to me, to previous workers, and to members of the institutional staff derived from his feeling of helplessness. We were protectors against the danger of hunger, abandonment, and a variety of physical dangers. And because these relationships were important only for providing need satisfaction and protection, any one member of the staff could substitute for another. During the first months of treatment he almost never mentioned his housemother, Mrs. Lindstrom, unless I initiated discussion through questions. This, I learned, was not to be taken as a deficiency in the capacities of the housemother; it was a result of George's absence of interest in or involvement with the adults who cared for him. During the same period he never showed any interest in me or curiosity about me.

Like most children in placement George clung to a fantasy about his parents and the reasons for his placement. His mother, in the fantasy, wanted all of her children at home but she didn't have enough money to keep them. When she saved enough money she would bring the children back home. There was no criticism of his mother and there were no reproaches. On many occasions the mother neglected to visit the children when she had promised. George, if he discussed these occasions at all, reported them factually and without affect.

Our earliest work, then, began to deal with the defenses against affects. I used every good opportunity to give George permission to feel and to show him omissions of justifiable feelings of anger or disappointment and displacements of affect. Very early in treatment we began to understand why the defenses against aggression were so strong. On one occasion when George got into a fight with one of the boys in his school (and it was indeed nothing more than a mild fight in which they pushed each other around), George spent the better part of his hour alternating between restrained fury at his enemy and fear that he would be sent away to a correctional institution for delinquent boys.

There were two components in this exaggerated fear of consequences for aggression. One, of course, was the expectation that any aggression, no matter how mild, would result in his being sent away. The other clearly was that the exaggerated punishment was equal to the strength of the undischarged aggression; he was afraid of the destructive power of his rage. Through a number of examples of such exaggerated fear of punishment I began to help George see that he was really afraid of his own feelings, that the anger inside was so strong at times that he feared that if it came out he might really hurt someone. I helped him to understand that the more he talked about his feelings in the interview the less need he would have to fear these feelings.

Gradually we began to understand the various forms of displacement of anger. George's fear of attack by other boys, his constant complaints of being picked on, began to diminish when he understood how these fears were to a certain measure tied up with his fear of his own anger. Sometimes I could draw his attention to his savage nail-biting as he talked about anger, and he was impressed to see how feelings could be connected with such a symptom. We went further and began to establish some links between bed-wetting and the feelings of anger and fear that he kept inside him.

Yet he was only able to experience anger and resentment toward other children. He could in no way acknowledge feelings of anger toward the adults in the institution, toward teachers, or toward me. Once when I felt he was struggling with hostile feelings toward me I asked him what he thought would happen if he should feel angry toward me and tell me. And he said, without a moment's hesitation, "Why you would go away!" He said this with such conviction that I could tell him now that I thought that this fear was connected with a real happening in his life, that this must have been the way he felt when mother placed him in the home. I said that all children are afraid that if they are naughty or have angry thoughts mother or daddy might go away and leave them, and I said that when children are placed away from home they can't help but feel deep inside that maybe it was because of something they had done or because they had been naughty.

From this point on in the interview George seemed to be struggling with all kinds of feelings. Several times he was in tears or close to tears. I encouraged him to talk more about mother and father and his feelings about placement. When he began attacking his nails again I tried to get him to tell me what he was feeling. Was it possible, I asked, that even when a child loved his parents he might feel some anger toward them, too, for disappointing him? With this George turned away so that I might not see his tears, and in a voice full of fury he said, "Sometimes I think I'm gonna be in this place for four more years and that I'm never going to go back to my own home."

As more and more feeling welled up within him he began to talk for the first time about the beginning period of placement. He remembered when his mother first told the children they were going to a Home. He didn't know what it would be like and he even thought it would be fun to live in a place with many other kids and have swings and slides. "And then I remember the first night and everything was so strange and I woke up in the middle of the night and it was dark and I didn't know where I was and my bed was all wet. . . . And then the next day when I woke up I looked out of the window and I saw all the bars around the place and the gates were locked." (The "bars" were the high iron fences around the institution.) I said, "I think it must have made you feel as if you were in jail. It must have made you feel that being here was like a punishment." He nodded in silence.

In this session we established the first connections between George's fear of his aggressive impulses and his feeling that placement was a punishment for being bad. This hour initiated many new developments. George, who had been the scapegoat of his group and who exhausted the adults of the Home with his whining and constant complaints of persecution, now began to fight back. George was as astonished as his former tormentors were. There was tremendous relief in him when he found that he could fight back and hold his own even with the older and more powerful boys. For a while it was difficult to keep the fighting under control. I got him to exercise some judgment in the fighting and to get a good measure of his rage and hostility back into the therapeutic hours where it might do some good. At the same time I was in close communication with George's housemother and with the director of the institution. Their understanding of the meaning of this behavior enabled them to handle a number of difficult situations with a firm and nonpunitive approach. After a few weeks the aggressive behavior subsided to something close to normal for a boy of this age. Now we saw that George was no longer afraid of his own aggression or afraid of monstrous punishments for having aggressive feelings.

From this we could understand that one of the decisive factors in the transformation of aggression had been the experience of separation. To be aggressive was to invite abandonment, and when our work established the connection between these two factors and the separation experience George could experience anger once again. With even this much work there was some symptomatic relief. George's nails, which had been bitten to the quick, were now beginning to grow. The bed-wetting improved temporarily. Also there was now considerable improvement in schoolwork, with George boasting that he was getting a better report card than he had ever had in his life.

Yet the whole area of his ambivalence toward his parents remained barely touched at this point. Now, however, there was a new theme in George's communications. He worried about people dying. He worried about his father. He didn't know where he was. He could be dead for all anyone knew. He missed his Dad. Sometimes he worried that his mother might die. From his fantasies it was very clear to me that his fears were closely connected with destructive wishes toward his parents. I now understood, too, another reason why it was so difficult for George to express even mild hostility toward his parents. For the child who is separated from his own parents the hostile and destructive wishes are necessarily more dangerous than for the child who still has his parents. For all children the physical presence of the parents is a reassurance against the danger that the loved persons may be harmed or destroyed by the child's own bad wishes. In the absence of his parents George could not tolerate his own dangerous fantasies, for he could not have reassurance against the omnipotence of his thoughts.

"Is it really true," George wanted to know, "that you could put a curse on someone and make them die?" He didn't think so but he had seen a story on television once. In one session he brought forth a number of such stories having to do with fictional events in which evil wishes brought about the illness or death of "someone." When I began to relate these fears to his own fears that bad wishes might harm someone he quickly denied that he ever had such thoughts. Then, very tentatively, he began to explore this dangerous territory with me through offering stories about a fictional boy who did have such thoughts. In the course of this hour we talked about his fears that bad wishes could come true and I again linked these fears with the experience of placement and the feelings that angry thoughts could cause someone to go away. At the end of this session George, for the first time since I had met him, looked relaxed and happy.

In the play-group meeting the following week George did something unprecedented. He got angry toward his group leader for allowing someone to use his materials and he announced that he was quitting the group. But when he told me about this experience in his next session he assured me that he didn't really intend to quit the club. He liked his group leader a lot; he just got good and mad at her that day. Sally, he reported marveling, had not been mad at him; she was "real nice about it." He seemed tremendously uplifted by this experience. It was one of the first occasions offered us in which George could allow himself to show hostility toward an adult whom he liked and to do so without fear that he would lose the love of that person.

During the same week George's housemother reported a most interesting set of observations. For several days George had been playing baby, in a clowning act in the dormitory. The big one-hundred-and-fifty pound baby crawled from one end of the room to the other, under beds and under furniture, emerging to be petted like an infant by Mrs. Lindstrom, who went along with the game with some amusement. At the same time Mrs. Lindstrom reported that George had become very affectionate toward her, telling her how swell she was and how he loved her. He even made a written declaration of love in the form of a mock certificate of honor with her name on it.

These events marked another turning point in George's treatment. Now we began to see the beginnings of a strong positive attachment to Mrs. Lindstrom and qualitatively richer relationships with both the director of the institution and his play-group leader. And at just this point we were suddenly confronted with some new behavior that baffled all of us. With all the gains on the side of relationships with adults and with all the new satisfactions that he seemed to be receiving, George was now involved in conflict in another sphere. Both the group leader and the housemother reported that George was in constant battle with Jimmy, one of the scapegoats in his group. George had appointed himself chief tormentor of Jimmy and constantly provoked fights with him. From various pieces of material in treatment I was certain that George's hatred of Jimmy was based on an identification with him but I could not clearly establish the basis of this identification.

Then in one interview when George had spent most of his hour reciting a litany of hate against Jimmy I asked him what he thought was the trouble with Jimmy, what made Jimmy behave this way. "I'll tell you!" George said promptly. "He's full of hate. That's what his trouble is. Just full of hate. That's why he steals, too. Just full of hate." I replied, "Well, you may be right. But why do you think he is full of hate?" The answer was, "I don't know and I don't care." I said, "I think he is full of hate because he feels that nobody loves him." And then to my surprise George said, "Then I guess me and him is in the same boat, 'cause I ain't got nobody to love me either." He began to cry. "I'm just as bad off as he is. I ain't got no Daddy and my Mama, I don't think she's ever gonna take us home and I think the only way I'm gonna get out of this place is when I'm big enough to work."

Now I asked if this made George wonder if his mother loved him, too? He nodded, choked up. I asked if this made George "full of hate" at times, too, because he could not understand why his mother had done this? He hesitated, then said painfully, "Sometimes." Now for the first time George could express his bitterness toward his mother and his longing for her. In this interview he talked about how fat he had grown; he remembered that he had not been overweight before coming to the Home. I helped him see how miserable and lonely he must have been and how eating was a way of easing the hurt then and now.

From this point on in treatment George's ambivalence toward mother became accessible to us with the full strength of the powerful feelings involved. He no longer consoled himself with the fantasy that his mother was going to take the children back, and he made the heartbreaking observation that mother herself no longer talked about making a home for the children again.

On one occasion when two of the boys in his group were preparing to return home, several of the other boys circulated stories that they, too, were going home—stories that were really painful fictions. George was overwhelmed with jealousy and spent hours in bitter tirades against his mother. During this time he became involved in open conflict with his mother and there was one episode in which the strong feelings of George and his mother initiated a Sunday afternoon drama. The mother had taken the children home for a Sunday visit. George was apparently short-tempered and volatile for most of the day, quarreling with his mother and each of his siblings in turn. At one point when George and his brother Martin were bickering, the mother lost her temper and sent both children out of the house and locked the door. The two boys pounded on the door and screamed to come in but the mother would not open the door. George was in a fury as he told me this story.

When we sorted out all the complicated feelings in this episode I was able to show George two aspects of his reactions. On the one hand were the real and justifiable reactions to being locked out of the house. In another way, I suggested, the whole episode hurt him so deeply because it made him feel that mother didn't want him in her home, that she was "sending him away" and that being closed out of his house was just exactly the way he felt living away from home.

With this George's rage began to subside and he began to struggle with tears.

As we worked through the ambivalent feelings toward mother during these months George showed considerable growth in all areas of his life. That summer after the first eight months of treatment we all observed that George had actually become a happy child. His relationships to his housemother and the director of the home were warm and spontaneous and he could even afford now to express negative feelings toward them at times. At one period during the summer, when George's mother began to speak about the possibility of bringing her children back home. George's reactions were very interesting. He was genuinely happy at the prospect but, he told me soberly, he would miss Mrs. Lindstrom and the director very much. He said that if he went back to his mother he would ask the director if he could come back to the Home to visit "maybe three times a week." However, his mother changed her mind again, and even this George was able to manage, with understandably strong feelings but without regression.

In summarizing the casework achievements in the fall after ten months, we saw that George had demonstrated his capacity to make new love attachments and that his relationship to his own mother had grown freer. There was less overt conflict with mother now, and with increased satisfactions in other areas of his life he seemed able to accept the pain of separation and mother's own limitations. He was able to handle his relationships with other boys within the institution with confidence and without undue aggressiveness. But he could fight when he needed to. There was now real pleasure in school and in learning—an unexpected and welcome bonus for treatment. Arithmetic was still a rough spot, mainly because of academic deficiencies brought about by three years of daydreaming in class, but George was energetically applying himself to mastery of tables and other fundamentals neglected since the third grade and his teachers reported favorably on his progress. There was some modification of the symptom picture that came about very clearly through the therapeutic work on the defenses against affects. Nail-biting, for example, disappeared completely. The voracious eating was curbed. There were no further weight gains and even some slight weight reduction. (I made no effort to deal with eating as a symptom except to occasionally connect eating with longing and aggression.)

But the enuresis remained. Clearly the casework treatment that had centered on affects and their transformations would not bring about symptomatic relief in this area. I knew that the enuresis was intimately connected with fears concerning masturbation and sex play, and until this material could be worked through there was no possibility of cure. In the second year of treatment it was necessary to modify the therapeutic approach in order to deal successfully with the sexual conflicts associated with the enuresis. This part of the treatment does not concern us here, of course, since we are primarily concerned with the method employed in the first year for bringing about the restoration of object ties.

In summary, those conflict areas and transformations of affect that were clearly reactive to the separation from parents were accessible to the casework treatment approach I have described, and the morbid process proved to be reversible.

It was undoubtedly an advantage to the therapy that George was already in latency at the time that separation from his parents took place. And yet we were most interested to see that in another of our cases, ten-year-old Brian, who was placed in the institution at the age of four, we had a therapeutic achievement that surpassed our expectations. I shall only briefly mention this case for illustrative purposes. I hope that his caseworker Miss Ethel van Dyck will report on this case more fully.

Brian, when I first saw him, was one of the most severely depressed children I had ever seen. He was completely passive and withdrawn, a sad little gnome who sat on his bed looking into space, and who had no connections to any other human being. No one within the institution could say at this point that he had a relationship to Brian. I realized from reading his record that periods of severe depression had recurred throughout his stay at the institution dating from age four. There were other periods when he seemed less depressed, but characteristically he was withdrawn, and the picture of a grave, unsmiling, silent little boy remained little changed during the six years of placement. Brian's mother was described as mentally ill (diagnosis not available) and four of the six children were placed after mother demonstrated her inability to give even physical care to the children. Brian, the youngest, was mother's favorite. Throughout placement she has maintained contact with him through visits. The ties to father and his common-law wife were also maintained on an irregular basis.

My private estimate of the possiblities of reaching Brian through casework treatment was a pessimistic one. Brian had no conscious memory of a time before placement and the remaining ties to the parents were very thin. His capacity for object ties could not be judged. Ego functioning had broken down in vital areas. He had failed his last grade in school in spite of good intelligence.

Almost as soon as the caseworker began to touch upon "feelings" with Brian she found herself the object of transference reactions that were so dense and complex that at first we had great difficulty in understanding the events of treatment. At the beginning there was no evidence of a strong positive transference in the treatment sessions and yet the passive and lethargic little boy began to come alive and began to communicate with adults and other children at the Home. There was no question that the tie to the caseworker had meaning and value to him, yet many hours were spent in almost complete silence. Previous caseworkers had also reported such silent hours with Brian.

As the caseworker repeatedly encouraged expressions of feeling, and gave permission to feel, Brian became visibly afraid. And when feeling first emerged in these sessions it came through in the form of terrible inarticulate grief and rage. He would kick savagely at the chair while he sat mute and helpless. He would cry hopelessly and inarticulately. It was as if the grief and rage were so elemental that there were no words that could express them. As more and more affect emerged the caseworker found herself in the center of a strange, word-less drama, the object of passionate hate and longing yet walled off from understanding by the child's silence.

There were no words, we thought, because there were no conscious memories to which these feelings could attach themselves.

But as the pressure of these painful affects grew stronger we began to see elements of the past revived in the present. During a period when the caseworker saw many reactions in Brian that showed that he was jealous of other boys who came to see her, Brian characteristi-cally closed her out. Then on one occasion at the close of the inter-view Brian refused to leave and finally buried his head in his arms and burst into tears. He could not speak of his grief, but the next hour he entered in a hostile mood and for the first time put his rage into words. He didn't want to see the caseworker, he said. He wished she weren't his caseworker. He wanted to be left alone. Then, in a passionate out-burst he accused the caseworker of liking other boys who were her clients better than she liked him, and he burst into tears. When the caseworker attempted to talk with him he ran out of the room. In the next sessions he renewed his fury with the caseworker, and finally in one climactic hour he screamed, "I hate you! I hate you!" and then, sobbing, said, "Go see Roger. Go see Jimmy. Not me." At one point he jumped on a chair to reach a storage cupboard and pleaded with the caseworker to give him everything that he saw, crayons, glue, and color books. Finally he desperately demanded that she give him a model airplane that belonged to another child. When the caseworker explained that these things must remain in the office he began to cry and shouted, "You won't give me *anything!*" He ran out of the room sobbing.

Only after Brian could express grief and rage and longing in transference to the caseworker was he able to express his positive feelings for her and enter into a relationship that showed affection and trust. It is important to note that during this whole stormy period in transference, there was very little affect outside of treatment; all these strong feelings centered on the caseworker. In every other area—in the institution, in the play group, and in school—all of our reports showed Brian reaching out to people and finding pleasure in play and in schoolwork. He had become spontaneously affectionate toward his housemother; he had a strong attachment to his play-group leader, and as we followed his development in the play group we discovered skills and qualities of leadership that surprised all of us. Group treatment made a substantial contribution to the therapy by providing opportunities for growth and a favorable milieu for Brian's growing capacity for object relationships. It is also important to note that Brian, who had been failing in school the year before treatment, completed this academic year with an excellent report card.

In Brian's case, then, the affects associated with loss of the love object in the preoedipal phase were revived in transference, and the casework treatment permitted a reliving in the transference of grief and rage, with recovery of the capacity for object ties and excellent gains in ego functioning.

The therapeutic results in Brian's case surpassed our expectations. From an analytic point of view there is much in this case that I wish we understood better. The specific connections between events in transference and events in the past could not be established through a casework treatment; these could only be known through employing an analytic method. And we do not understand how a depression of such severity should have responded so favorably to a casework treatment. We cannot be certain, of course, that in a child with such severe depressive tendencies the tendency will not reassert itself. But this recovery through casework treatment is still a substantial gain, and the child in latency who can make attachments and who can feel again may be less vulnerable in adolescence and later life.

## III

In such cases as these, a child who has once experienced ties to the original object—however ambivalent these may have been—can recover the possibility of making new attachments through a therapy directed toward reviving affects and working through the experience of loss. As we should expect, the method will not have usefulness in those cases where a child's inability to attach himself derives from failure to establish meaningful human ties in the earliest stages of ego development. In one of our cases, for example, our earliest superficial observations led us to expect a favorable outcome in treatment. Pete seemed less damaged than any other child in our group. While his relationships were qualitatively poor there were no signs of serious withdrawal and no symptoms. But as we worked with Pete in casework and in the group we discovered that he had erred gravely in our original assessment. After eight months we found that none of us felt he really knew this child. Pete was charming, ingratiating, and somehow unconnected with any other person in his environment. We began to see that here there was real impoverishment in the ego, a deficiency and an incapacity in forming human ties that was not reactive to object loss but that derived from failures in human connections in the earliest phases of personality development.

In those cases where the child's inability to form new object ties is a reaction to loss with consequent transformations of affects we have, I believe, a generally favorable condition for recovery through therapy. One of the strongest therapeutic assets we have in working with such children in placement is the readiness to form a transference neurosis. As Anna Freud pointed out many years ago in her remarks on transference in child analysis, when a child is separated from his original love objects and moved to a new environment he may be expected to transfer to the new environment libidinal and aggressive impulses that originated in the relationships to the original objects. The condition of placement, of separation from the original objects, makes possible the development of a true transference neurosis.

If we observe closely during the early weeks and months of placement we can often find a variety of behaviors directed toward foster parents, cottage mothers, and caseworkers that are clearly repetitions of earlier experiences with the original objects. In a treatment home or institution with clinically trained personnel we can actually make use of these transference reactions in therapy and help the child achieve insight into his behavior. Or it may happen that reliving the past in the present with the corrective afforded by a benevolent institution and its personnel may, in itself, bring about the resolution of old conflicts. The transference neurosis and its handling should provide the key to the therapeutic effects of milieu therapy.

Now in the institution in which our work was carried out and most other institutions that provide custodial care for neglected and dependent children we have no clinical facilities and the houseparents ordinarily have little training to equip them to understand the complexities of child behavior following placement. The child's grief or withdrawal in the initial stages of placement is experienced by the cottage parents as a reproach or a criticism, as if they had failed to make the child happy. Mourning, then, is seen as something that must be gotten over quickly, and the cottage parent may exert himself in making the child happy and making him forget.

After an initial period of emotional neutrality toward the substitute parents we can usually expect some transference reactions to manifest themselves; old conflicts are revived in the new setting. Many children struggling with the crushing burden of their ambivalence toward the parents who deserted or surrendered them will transfer the hostile and negative feelings toward the new objects and preserve an unambivalent love for the absent parents. In the absence of clinical training, the cottage parent can hardly be blamed for reacting with injury and perhaps with anger to the child's repudiation of him and to the negative and provocative behavior that the child produces. The behavior from the cottage parents' point of view is bad behavior, "sassiness," impudence, and ingratitude—an indication to the cottage parents that this child needs to learn who is boss. There may be a period of conflict for a while and then we may learn that the child is much improved, that he is settling down in the institution and making a better adjustment. It sometimes happens, as in the case of George, that these achievements, which make the child far easier to live with, were made at the expense of symptoms, ego restrictions, and loss of the capacity to form new ties. The whole process is invisible to the cottage parents and no blame should be attached to their failure to understand this most complex sequence of behavior.

This brings us to examine the prophylactic measures that grow out of such studies of children in placement. The morbid process that eventually brings about a transformation of affects will only be visible to clinically trained eyes. This means that the caseworker of the child in placement must regard the first months following placement as the critical period, the time when the morbid process can be halted and reversed because the affects associated with separation are still available. Direct work with the child during this period and educational work with the cottage parents and other institutional personnel could make this a period of working through the reactions to placement. When grief and longing and reproaches to the parents are regarded as permissible feelings by the cottage parents and such feelings can be communicated to the caseworker by the child, the child may not have to resort to pathological defense. When hostility is transferred to the new objects and to the caseworker himself, cottage parents may be helped to understand the irrational feelings of the child, to see these feelings as displacements, and to deal with them without defensiveness and counteraggression.

The caseworker, himself, is often the object of the child's hostile feelings—realistically as the person who took the child away from his parents, in fantasy as the kidnapper of helpless children, and as a convenient transference object for hostile feelings toward the parents. If the caseworker makes use of the feelings that have attached themselves to his person and his role and if he makes use of transference reactions to cottage parents and institutional personnel, he can help the child to examine these feelings and to see them also as part of the ambivalence toward the original parents. It should then be possible to work through the ambivalent feelings toward the parents and to help the child find new solutions in his new environment. Only then is the child free to make new attachments in the institution.

## Notes

The writer wishes to express appreciation to these colleagues who collaborated in the program: Miss Ethel van Dyck of the New Orleans Children's Bureau carried major responsibility for the casework treatment in consultation with the writer. Miss Rita Comarda of Tulane University School of Social Work was supervisor of group treatment. Miss Sally Matlock, at that time a student in the Tulane School of Social Work, was leader of the treatment group. Miss Miriam Gaertner, director of the New Orleans Children's Bureau, Miss Adele Eisler, assistant director of the Children's Bureau, and Mrs. Carol Hamrick, director of the Protestant Children's Home, gave generously of their time and counsel throughout our study. The writer served as coordinator and consultant for the project and carried one child in casework treatment.

1. All cases reported here were seen in casework treatment on a once-a-week basis.

# 13

## Technical Aspects of the Analysis of a Child with a Severe Behavior Disorder

From the earliest days of child analysis, the treatment of the child with behavior problems has been regarded as a special problem. The child who acted out his inner conflicts and whose behavior obtained satisfactions for him was not, strictly speaking, analyzable. In order to make this child analyzable our earliest techniques were directed toward bringing about an internalization of the conflict, we "created a neurosis," in effect. The analyst actively intervened to bring about restriction of the behavior, to reduce the gratification obtained through direct discharge of impulses, and sometimes deliberately created anxiety in the child in order to give him an incentive to curtail his acting and to motivate him in analysis.

In the intervening years the mutually enriching progress of child analysis and ego psychology has brought about many changes in child analytic techniques. As Anna Freud has pointed out, many of the differences between the method of adult analysis and that of child analysis have begun to fade. Now, speaking generally of child analysis, we try as far as possible to relieve the analyst of educational functions and active interference in order not to obscure or distort the transference. As our knowledge of defense has expanded we are able to employ interpretation for certain analytic objectives where once we would have been obliged to intervene or prohibit.

There remains the special problem of the child with behavior problems, but he, too, has been the beneficiary of new insights and progress in child analysis. We have greatly enlarged our understanding of the defensive aspects of certain types of behavior and are in a position to use analytic means to bring about a restriction of acting that in earlier days required intervention. Analysis of behavior as defense against anxiety may bring about the desirable analytic cooperation in a child. When the child himself has learned to regard his behavior as a defense the analysis can examine the complex structure of the behavior, which almost invariably reveals a phobia of massive proportions at the core of the disorder. The readiness to transfer both id impulses and defense, which is characteristic of the child with behavior problems, can be employed to advantage in the analysis of transference resistances.

There remain, of course, those occasions when a child bent on destruction can close out the analyst's interpretations and oblige us to restrict or prohibit. I should not wish to minimize the practical problems of dealing with many severely disturbed children with behavior problems. However, the advantages are all on the side of the analytic measures for dealing with acting. When we must intervene out of practical necessity, we almost always pay a price and we learn nothing new about the significance of the behavior. If, on the other hand, we can handle the behavior analytically, we have the double advantage of restoring the child's control and of obtaining valuable insight and new progress in the analysis.

In the case example that follows I shall attempt to describe the resistances encountered in the analytic treatment of a severely disturbed boy and the technical problems that I encountered. The treatment extended over a three-and-a-half-year period and was brought to a very satisfactory conclusion.

## II

Roger began his analysis with me at the age of four. His parents had finally been reduced to complete helplessness in coping with his behavior problems. He was obstinate, negative, and relentlessly goading. He would seize upon any trivial point to challenge his parents and finally provoke them to anger and a spanking. At three he had once thrown his nursery school group into chaos by claiming that he was God and he could make everybody do what he said. His parents described destructive orgies in which he would run about the house in a giddy fashion, kicking doors, smashing objects, and giggling in a peculiarly joyless way. He showed no signs of remorse for any of his behavior.

His nursery school teachers and I felt that we could not assess his intelligence. He appeared to be at least normal, possibly bright normal. In the chaos of Roger's four-year-old personality none of us had been able to catch a glimpse of an extraordinary intelligence that revealed itself after better integration of the personality was achieved.

Roger's parents dated their conflicts with him to the second year. Roger's first year, according to the parents, had been uneventful. There were no problems in feeding; his health had been excellent. Speech and motor development appeared to have been accelerated. As the outlines of the history filled in during the three years of analysis I could reconstruct the second year along these lines: almost as soon as Roger became active he came into conflict with his mother. The contest between mother and toddler became the model for the later relationship; every wish of the mother had to be negated.

The parents at that time were very much preoccupied with their own conflicts in marriage and were contemplating divorce. Roger was the unplanned-for second baby. A sister, Judy, who figured prominently in Roger's analysis, was two years older than he. The unwanted baby made divorce more difficult now. At a time when the mother's hostility toward her husband was at its height, the little boy became the object of a good measure of her destructive feelings toward males. The children were witnesses to the verbal battles between the parents and at night they could easily overhear the parental quarrels in the bedroom next to the room they shared. Roger had witnessed his mother's destructive rages on many occasions. On one occasion she had literally smashed to bits a piece of furniture. We had good reason to believe that one of the motives in Roger's destructive behavior was an early identification with the dangerous and destructive mother. The mother herself began analysis a year before I began to work with Roger, and at the time the parents consulted me the family had acquired more stability and the mother had acquired far better control of herself.

A contest between mother and child over bowel training began in Roger's second year and continued until he was nearly four. Roger soiled himself and refused to use the toilet. According to the mother, when she finally "put her foot down" the soiling ceased.

The parents had found no effective means of discipline for Roger. He was spanked often in parental rage and helplessness, but there was no conviction on the part of either parent that spanking served any purpose in controlling his behavior.

Roger's father was harassed, resigned, and deeply wounded as a husband and a father. He, too, was drawn into conflict with his son. Roger's successful challenging of his father's authority further devalued him as a man, and he found himself impelled against his better judgment to take up the challenge and use physical force to subdue this relentless opponent, aged four.

In the early analytic observations of Roger I obtained a fair picture of his typical behavior problems. Almost from the beginning he transferred his provocative behavior to the analytic sessions. He gleefully smeared chocolate over my furniture, smashed the furniture of the doll house, tore up books and magazines, and ran up and down the halls of the apartment house banging on doors and annoying other tenants. When my words could not reach him I tried on two occasions to hold his hands to prevent him from destroying objects. This was a mistake. The first time he kicked me savagely and ran out of the room. The second time he giggled with excitement and tried to press himself against me. When I quietly withdrew he renewed his antics, now challenging me to punish him.

I knew that I could not influence him until I achieved a relationship with him, but here, too, Roger presented special problems. He could relate only through negating strenuously. When I invited him into my office at the beginning of the session he would refuse obstinately. If I quietly ignored him and entered my office alone, pretending to work at my desk, he would come barging in triumphantly five or ten minutes later, under the illusion that he was disturbing me. If he became destructive and I asked him to leave the room and come back when he could control himself, he would obstinately refuse to leave. Interpretations directed to his fear of me or his expectations of punishment fell upon deaf ears. He could negate interpretations, too.

In the early interviews he paraded around with a paper cigarette in his mouth, boasting that he was a daddy and that he was stronger than his daddy. He confided, with much giggling, that he would sometimes get up at night and get into his mother's bed. He played out his obsessive interest in parental activities at night in games with the dolls. The dolls wrestled together, they made noises, and regularly the play ended with a car wreck or an explosion.

There was little point in handling any of this material analytically. It is only useful to describe this material in order to show the naked and undisguised character of these communications. Much more significant is the fact that all this material emerged without any manifest anxiety or guilt.

There is no doubt that at this time Roger's behavior achieved certain satisfactions for him and that as long as these satisfactions existed there would be little motive for him to cooperate in his treatment. During the early weeks of treatment I was able to help Roger's parents understand one of the motives in his behavior, the relentless provocation of punishment. I enlisted their cooperation in giving up the spankings and we discussed other means of discipline. Much time was devoted to a re-education of the parents in this area, strengthening the positive ties to the child and enabling the parents to employ their relationship in a more effective discipline in which parental approval and disapproval might carry the necessary weight.

In the meantime I began to deal analytically with Roger, and used every good opportunity to help him see how his behavior was a defense against anxiety. When anxiety began to break through at home and in the analytic sessions I am sure that this first success was due as much to the parents and their change of discipline as to the analytic interpretations.

I mark the real beginning of Roger's analytic treatment as the day on which Roger announced, "I'm afraid at night. A man chases me." And when I asked about the dream and the man who chased him he said forlornly, "I don't want to tell you. It's somebody in my family."

And then in the sequence that followed I could see very clearly one of the patterns in Roger's behavior. He could not tell me what he feared from the man but immediately translated the thought into action. He became a burglar in his play, breaking into the doll house, then deliberately broke one of the andirons of the fireplace in the doll house. Suddenly he was off on one of his destructive orgies, breaking crayons, pencils, doll furniture, everything at hand. And there was no affect now; the anxiety that had briefly shown itself at the beginning of the hour had vanished. There was only the pixie Roger, gleefully destroying objects and closing me out. But now we could understand the pattern. In the moment that castration anxiety emerged in association to the dream, he acted out the dream, reversing the active and passive roles. In the dream he was passive and in great danger; in reenacting the dream he became active, he performed the symbolic destructive act. By identifying with the aggressor and by switching from passive to active, he did not need to experience anxiety. Now we can understand why Roger was capable of performing aggressive and destructive acts without any manifest anxiety. And now we were in a position to deal with the behavior as defense.

As soon as I was able to show Roger how his behavior was a defense against anxiety we had the means to bring about some control of the behavior and I was able to bring him into a therapeutic relationship. Often I could prevent a destructive orgy or his wild running around the room by the suggestion, "Now we know that something is making you afraid inside. Let's talk about it so I can help you." And when Roger began to understand that talking about his fears relieved him, the initial resistances to treatment began to dissolve. I was struck by the fact that the transference now had the same character as the transference obtained in phobic cases. He was strongly dependent upon me, he needed me as an ally against danger.

Meantime, too, the picture at home began to change. There was considerably less acting, and less need to provoke the parents, and the parents began to catch glimpses of the terror and helplessness of the child which gave them a new perspective on his behavior. With diminution of the acting, Roger became a more gratifying child to his family; his parents began to respond with some warmth and found qualities in him that were easy to overlook earlier. With greater satisfactions at home Roger had additional strong incentives to work on his problems with me.

Yet, I do not wish to give the impression that the communication of fears and the accessibility of his fantasies made Roger's analysis easier than any other. During the first two years of analysis we had a flood of material around the themes of castration, primal-scene observations, masturbation and sex play with his sister Judy. He could tell me, in so many words, that he feared that the faceless man in his recurrent terror dream would cut off his penis with a butcher knife. He could tell me that he thought mothers and daddies mutilated each other in intercourse. But the affect that accompanied these communications was thin and dilute, and I soon began to realize that isolation of affect played a very significant role in Roger's disturbance.

When we now turned our attention in analysis to the defenses against affects I encountered the most formidable resistance. It was difficult to explain to a little boy, now five years and a half, who was cooperating most earnestly in treatment, that it was really the feelings that were most important, and that it was the feelings inside that were causing all the trouble. Only gradually was Roger able to appreciate that when he put the ideas in one place and the feelings in another he got no real relief from talking. As anxiety began to emerge in small quantities Roger's suffering made me see why the defenses were so strong.

During a period in which we were dealing with sex play and his obsessive concern with the female genitalia he complained of dizziness in his hours. And for several hours he would begin each session with the ritual statement, "I am always the same Roger whether I come here or whether I'm home." During tense moments in the hour he would suddenly cry out, "I'm always the same Roger!" When I inquired about this he would say, "I *have* to say it. I *have* to say it!" It was clear that at such times he experienced feelings of depersonalization and that the formidable defenses against anxiety had been erected to protect the ego against loss of identity. During the same period he played a repetitious game with the doll house which he called "catastrophe." The game always began with innocuous doll play in which the doll family had dinner, looked at television, etc. Then the family would go to bed. Suddenly a "hurricane" or "tornado" would come up. Roger would throw all the doll furniture down the doll-house stairs or pile it in heaps on the floor of the doll house. Once he said there was a big explosion and he ran to call "The Red Cross" to come and rescue the people. "Oh, is this fun!" he would say, laughing in a singularly joyless way. And then suddenly in the midst of one of these games he turned pale, complained of dizziness and the "funny feeling" which I understood to be feelings of depersonalization.

The emergence of primal-scene memories was accompanied by an obsessive interest in his sister's and mother's genitalia; during this period his castration anxiety was so intense that it produced frequent episodes of depersonalization. Sometimes, during the same period, he would desperately clutch his penis which he understood, too, represented his fear that something could happen to his penis. As anxiety began to emerge more and more in our sessions each of his characteristic defenses was brought into play. Sometimes in the same hour he would revert to identification with the aggressor; and if this was pointed out to him, he would inhibit the acting but almost immediately isolate anxiety. At other times he would simply take flight. During several sessions he would stop in the midst of a dream analysis or play and cry out, "Oh, the feelings are coming, the feelings are coming," and run out of the room or run into a closet and close the door. He would return later, pale and tired. He understood fully now what tremendous anxiety there was within him and once, after much suffering, he said to me with marvelous wisdom, "I want to get it all out, but it will have to come out little by little, won't it?"

All the evidence pointed to the fact that the defenses against anxiety and guilt feelings were closely connected with masturbation fantasies. He was able to talk about masturbation and his fears of damage to the penis. He was also perfectly willing to communicate his fantasies to me, and I knew that certain of these were masturbation fantasies. But if I attempted to bring together the masturbation and the masturbation fantasies for analysis, I met the most determined resistance. In one of these fantasies, for example, he was a great inventor, greater, he said, than Edison. He had a secret invention, a rocket that could surpass anything invented to date. For a period of several weeks his mother reported that she could not get Roger up in the morning. He would lie in bed for an hour apparently masturbating. Roger's version of his reluctance to get up in the morning was that he was too busy thinking about his invention which, in a certain sense, was quite true. When it finally seemed necessary for me to bring together the fantasy and the masturbation for analysis he began to act up in his session, ran around the room in giddy fashion and sang, "cuckoo, cuckoo, cuckoo," over and over, hitting himself on the head. "You're making me cuckoo with all that talk," he yelled. On the following day he was somewhat subdued and regretted his antics of the day before. When I now tried to link up the antics with his anxiety about the invention fantasy he closed me out securely. "I've decided not to talk about my inventions any more," he said. And he explained prudently, "If someone knows about it, then they'd want to copy it, and I don't have a copyright yet."

Now I began to understand one of the functions of isolation as a defense in Roger's case. The masturbation and the attendant fantasies needed to be maintained in isolation from each other. If he acknowledged that they belonged together, he would suffer anxiety and guilt. At the same time isolation of the ideational content from the act served to maintain the affects in isolation. Now, too, it became clear that there was a close connection between the behavior disorder and the masturbation fantasies. There was some evidence that at certain times his masturbation fantasies became too exciting to him; at such times he would abandon masturbation and act out the fantasies. (Here the mechanism is identical with the one described by Anna Freud [1949].) During the period that the boy inventor, Roger, declined to bring his inventions in for analysis, he was both coy and seductive with his mother and mercilessly challenging of his father's authority, finally bringing his father's wrath down upon him one week end.

A good part of the three and a half years of Roger's analysis was devoted to analysis of the defenses against affects. In child language I succeeded in helping him see how he put feelings and ideas in separate compartments and how this was his biggest problem.

Perhaps it would be useful now to examine in a little more detail a segment of the analysis in which the analysis of the transference brought us a very good part of the way toward successful resolution of these conflicts.

## III

At this time Roger was six and a half years old.[1] This period of analysis coincides with the period I had earlier described in which Roger had shown the most determined resistances against the analysis of his masturbation fantasies.

This sequence begins with a daydream that Roger reported to me with dread and loathing. It precedes by one analytic hour a night terror and its accompanying daydream, in which the analysis reveals common themes. Roger confessed with great reluctance that there was something he just could not tell me. He didn't think he could ever tell me, he said, but maybe it wouldn't be necessary. If he could figure it out himself, it might solve the problem and he wouldn't need to tell me. When I explained to him that the big problems could not be solved unless we had all the parts, he made a heroic struggle and there followed this extraordinary sequence:

"I think I can tell you. I think it's coming. Wait a minute. I'll have to go into the closet to think." While I waited, baffled, he ran into the closet and presently I heard a queer, melancholy, atonal song, something like an infant's ah-ah-ah-ah "singing" when he rocks himself in bed. Then in the same sing-song Roger began to tell me. "If my mo-ther and my fa-ther had to go away for a lo-ong, lo-ong time. That's the first part. Now give me time so I can tell you the next part. . . ." There was a pause, then Roger burst out of the closet. "I can't say it. I just can't." I tried to help him to tell me. With help he managed to say, "Well, someone would come to live with me." "Who would that be?" "I can't say it." And finally, spelling, "a g-i-r-l." "Now the rest I can't tell you right out. I'll tell it to you backwards and you'll have to figure it out. I'll give you a clue. If I said, 'eight' that would mean 'sixteen or seventeen' so, I'll say a girl of eight." I: "Does that mean that someone, a girl of sixteen or seventeen, would come to live with you?" "Don't say it! Don't say it!" "But Roger, what makes you so scared and ashamed in all this?" "I don't know." "Is this a daydream?" "Yes." "What happens next?" "That's what I don't know either. Whenever I get to that part I get stuck and it's just blank. . . . My mother and father are dead, see [first time he had used this word instead of "going away"]. And then this g-i-r-l comes to live with me and she is you know how old." I tried to get at his feelings. If he has to spell, it must mean that there are some thoughts in connection with all this that make him ashamed. He agreed. He doesn't know what it is.

In the next hour Roger reported "a night dream" and "a daydream." When he woke up that morning after the "night dream" he had a day-dream while he was lying in bed. I should mention that he did not tell me the daydream until some time after reporting the night dream. I shall report them together here, only in order to organize the material better for study.

*The night dream:* There was a witch with Judy and it seemed they were fighting on one side against me and my boy friends on the other. Then in the next scene me and Judy and my mother and father were trying to dissolve a powder that would make a mask like a witch's.

*The daydream:* I'm in a boat with a girl, a girl about sixteen or seven-teen. The boat has wheels on it so it can go on land or water.

I had taught Roger to analyze his dreams through what we called "The What Pops into your Mind Game." When I now invited Roger to tell me what popped into his mind, he could only report an obsessive thought, "This is crazy; this is crazy." We had already encountered the obsessive thought on a number of occasions and understood that it served the purpose of blocking all other associations and had the significance of repudiating analysis and of disbelieving the evidence of analysis. When I asked for details of the dream he described the witch quite exactly, giving particular emphasis to the fact that the witch wore a Halloween mask. Now I proposed that the witch's mask might represent his wish to disguise, that the witch represented someone he knew whom he did not wish to know in the dream. Instantly he said, "I think the witch was you! And then it pops into my mind that you have a secret about me and Judy has a secret about me!"

In the next hour he remembered a forgotten detail of the dream. "It takes place on the porch. There's the witch and Judy and me. The witch has a needle or a pin or something and she dropped it on the floor. I was going to reach for it when Judy grabbed it and gave it to the witch." He goes on: "And that makes me think that you or Judy could play a trick on me. Judy used to play tricks on me. She used to say there was a burglar in the house and make me come into bed with her. But there was no burglar. . . ." Now I reminded him that it was through such a trick that Judy used to get him to play games in bed with her, the secret games that they used to think were like the things grownups did. Roger said, "That must be it!"

In associating to the dream detail in which Judy "grabbed at" the needle that the witch lost we found another connection with the sex games in which Judy would "grab at" Roger's penis, half playfully, half maliciously. The almost explicit meaning of Judy's behavior toward Roger's penis had been well understood by Roger. This was an old game and when Judy was younger she was outspoken in her wish to take Roger's penis and make it her own. Now Roger understood that in the dream and its attendant anxiety he feared that Judy could take his penis. The detail in which the witch lost her needle led us back to material in which Roger had earlier related his fantasies about the woman with a penis.

At one point I reminded Roger that the scary dream of the witch had occurred on the night of the day that he had told me about the daydream of the "sixteen- or seventeen-year-old girl" who came to live with him. I asked if there could be a connection. Now Roger remembered the daydream of the girl in the amphibian boat, a variation of the earlier daydream that took place on the morning after the dream. But he did not want to talk about it. "Do I have to?" he asked with dread in his voice. I asked him to try. He struggled with the narration again, and I saw that once again he needed to spell "girl" and avoided the age of the girl. He could not remember how the daydream ended "because my mother came to get me out of bed or something." (I was sure now that this was one of his morning masturbatory fantasies. There had been renewed difficulty at home in getting Roger out of bed, and his mother would come upon him openly masturbating.) Once, in the narration when he began his complicated game of disguising and reversing the numbers in the age of the girl, I asked, "Are you sure the girl was sixteen or seventeen?" Roger looked up sadly, as if he already knew the answer. "You guessed right the first time when I first told you the daydream." (From the number code I had first guessed Judy or me. He had denied it.) "What was the right guess?" "It was you." But it was not only I. In the complicated code he had worked out, sixteen was the double of eight, which was Judy's age, and the double of seventeen was thirty-four, my age at the time, which he knew. Roger, who knew the doubles of numbers very well (and had an almost obsessive preoccupation with doubling numbers) had nicely condensed Judy's age and my age. I now helped Roger make the connection between his guilty feelings and my identity in the daydream. I suggested, too, that this must have something to do with Judy and the secrets with her in the old days. I drew his attention to the way in which he had first told me the daydream of the girl sixteen or seventeen, in a number code and with spelling. A code and secret words and spelling had been part of the secret games with Judy, too, and had the function of warding off guilt feelings.

How had the sex games with Judy been draw into the transference? It seems to me that my analytic encouragement to talk about the forbidden games with Judy had made me, in the child's fantasy, the seducer, or the partner in "forbidden games" as Judy had been in reality. The games with Judy had been given up for nearly a year, and I have good reason to believe had survived in masturbatory fantasies of a sadomasochistic character. As the analysis at this point had begun to investigate the masturbatory fantasies, the analyst became the dangerous seducer and the fantasies were transferred to the person of the analyst and in turn made use of the analyst in elaboration of content. To Roger, I only explained at this point that the daydreams about me seemed to be a way of remembering the games with Judy and the fears and guilty feelings that went with them. I explained that if we understood the feelings that came out toward me in this way, we would have a way of solving the problems inside.

The transference fantasy and its accompanying guilt feelings made it possible for the first time to show Roger the full strength of his guilt feelings and to help him see how much guilt had attached itself to the old games with Judy. Yet as soon as we identified the guilt feelings, Roger succeeded in isolating them again. The serial daydream of the girl in the amphibian boat continued and now, from many clues, I began to understand how isolation of the guilt feelings served pleasure. I now understood better than before how Roger had engaged in sex play with Judy without apparent guilt. As long as he maintained the guilt feelings in isolation he could enjoy the games. In the masturbation fantasy he succeeded in isolating guilt and anxiety in order to enjoy the fantasy. Roger had already had a lot of experience in analysis in seeing how he "moved his guilty conscience into the wrong departments" and now it remained to show him how guilty feelings can be moved into other departments so that they will not get in the way of enjoying certain thoughts or games. Roger accepted this interpretation and then, characteristically, followed this session with a period of acting.

In the next session he was sulky and petulant, whined incessantly for a cookie, and I had none that day. He began throwing objects around the room in the monotonous driven fashion I had seen many times before. He would not discuss his behavior with me and several times walked out of the room. In the following hour he continued to sulk, and refused to talk about the wild behavior of the previous hour. When I asked what happened to make him move his guilty conscience into another department, he said, "Oh that's easy. I know the answer to that. I moved my guilty conscience so you won't find it." And then, suddenly intrigued by a thought, "Maybe it's like the witch again. Maybe I'm afraid you'll take it away from me." Then, "I figured out something else. You know who I think the witch was in my dream? My mother! That's who it was. And you and Judy and my father all wrapped up together. Maybe inside I'm afraid that you would play a trick on me. You know. Like someone would offer you a cookie if you did something, and then they wouldn't give it to you. . . . Oh! There's the cookie, yesterday. A trick. Something that witches do. And that must be why I thought of the Musicians of Bremen dream when I first told you the Witch Dream. A trick, see. And robbers."

Now I made a suggestion. I reminded him that it is said that witches have a magic, that they can change things. Roger came up with,

"Witches could change you into anything they wanted to. Oh! Oh! And *you're* trying to change me. Well you *are* in a way. Trying to make me better." I reminded him now of fears we had discussed earlier, fears of being changed into a girl. Roger said, "*That's* it. Maybe *inside* in the dream I thought the witch could change me and my boy friends into girls. We were fighting the witch and Judy in the dream. And wait a minute . . . that fits into the part of the dream where we're trying to dissolve a powder to make the witch's mask. . . . See magic again and changing something into something else. Oh! Oh! I see another connector. The daydreams. The part where I'm in a boat with the girl, the boat with wheels so it can go on the water or on land." What connections did he see here? Roger: "Why the changing over, of course. The boat can change over for land or water. . . . I wish I could remember the other dream, the one I had last night. But it was all chopped up in little pieces and I can't remember any part of it. . . . All chopped up! Oh! Oh! That's what witches are supposed to do too. They could chop you up into little pieces. Witches could kill you! That must be what I'm afraid of. And steal. Maybe inside I thought the witch could steal my penis and give it to Judy."

All of this expert analysis had been achieved without any display of affect. He had turned it into an intellectual exercise. Now Roger stopped and congratulated himself. "Don't you think I'm doing good today. I'm surprised myself at how good I can think when I don't try to. Now we're getting a lot of connectors." I said that this was good, but there was one very important connection that we didn't see here. Where were the feelings that would go with all of this? If a boy was so afraid of such terrible things, we would expect to see the feelings too. Roger took this in soberly. Then, surprisingly, he said that he thought he had better tell me another part of the daydream that he had not been able to tell me before (i.e., concerning the daydream of the girl in the amphibian boat). He started to tell me and a look of misery came over his face. He had to force himself to get the first words out. "In the daydream, I have a stick and it . . . it . . . has nails at the end of it." He couldn't finish the sentence. "I'll have to spell. To poke the g-i-r-l with." When I asked about this he was in agony again. "I don't want to say it. It's like what the needle in the dream was." And then, gathering courage, said, "like a penis, you know."

Now he stopped. He begged off from further work in this hour. Could we please talk about something else? I said, he could talk about anything else he wanted. The farthest thing from his problems he could think of. Roger said, "O.K." And then, "But you know what. I keep coming back to the same thing anyway. Then I think about Leila. Did I ever tell you about Leila? Well . . . well . . . It's about some games we played. You know the funny little penis girls have. Well . . . I have to spell L-O-O-K." I said, "look." Roger: "Don't *say* it! Don't say it!" I told him that the spelling would not help us. This was the way he was hiding his feelings, but the feelings were very important to us. Roger said, miserably, "All right. I won't spell." He exerted a great effort. "We looked at each other." I asked, "How do you feel right now?" Roger: "Sick in the head again." I told him I thought this was where his feelings were trying to come out. And he said, "That's my guilty conscience again."

At this point we began to experience increased resistance in analysis and a new period of acting. His behavior at home which had been much improved for some time now reverted to old patterns. He was tirelessly negative and provocative with his mother. Every one of the most ordinary demands that a parent might make was encountered with stubborn refusal. When I began to see some of this behavior in transference reactions I could show Roger that at such times he behaved as if he were in terrible danger. When grownups said something *had* to be done, he went to pieces. It was as if he were afraid that by doing what they wished they might get some kind of control over him and put him in danger, like a witch who could get power over someone.

Roger was immediately struck by this. "That's it. And the witch in the dream was my mother, too! But I know that my mother wouldn't hurt me so why do I do it?" I encouraged him to associate to this idea and he came up with "Witches can change you. . . . Maybe *inside* I wish I could have a little penis like a girl." He looked surprised himself when this statement came out. "I don't know why I said that. I just said it." When I inquired about the feelings in connection with such an idea a look of agony came over his face. And then he cried out, "Oh, the feeling is coming, the feeling is coming! Talk about something else. *Right* away." And then he began to talk quickly about trivial things, banishing the feelings in a few seconds.

The negativism toward mother continued, and Roger himself seemed baffled by his behavior at home. He said, "I know that my mother and my father aren't witches or ghosts, but I act like they were." He was reminded of the witch dream again.

In one hour he was suddenly struck by the fact that everything his mother asked him to do made him want to do the opposite. I remarked on his fear of women and girls. At this point he buried his head in a pillow. Then suddenly he brought a rabbit's foot out of his pocket. He asked if I knew the joke about the rabbit. "What does a rabbit hate to have most?" Answer: "A rabbit's foot." He began to fondle the rabbit's foot. He liked its feel, he said. This reminded him of Tumpis, his Teddy bear with whom he sleeps each night. (Tumpis had a prominent place in the analysis. He was properly a fetish.) I drew the analogy between the rabbit's foot and Tumpis, pointing out that both made him feel safe. I suggested that as long as he had Tumpis close to himself he might feel that he was not in danger of losing a part of himself, a penis perhaps. He started to say with surprise, "That's it! That's what Tumpis means." And then he cried out in pain, "My foot hurts! My foot hurts!" (This was an old hysterical symptom that had come up frequently in analysis.) He hugged his foot in misery. "I wish I could cut it off. So it wouldn't hurt. And if I didn't have it *then it couldn't hurt*. It would be nice not to have a foot. Cut off both of them."

I reminded him that we already had seen how the anxiety around the foot was displaced from the penis and could now make an essential point. We could connect this to his earlier statement about the wish to be a girl, that is, if one were a girl, one would not need to be afraid that something could happen to the penis because there wouldn't be any to lose. Roger said, "Yes." And then, in a suffering voice, he said, "Oh, I wanted to say 'No' so you wouldn't guess, but I made myself say 'Yes.' Wasn't that good of me?"

Later in this hour we returned to the conflict with mother and his own statement that everything mother wanted him to do made him want to do the opposite. I told him that it occurred to me that he was afraid if he did what mother wanted he would become like his mother; that is, he would be like a girl. He did not agree and it was not until I was able to handle this in the transference some months later that this insight was achieved.

Along with dread of castration, oedipal longings for mother were revived during this period. Roger had already discovered his mother behind the transference fantasies of the analyst as witch and the girl in the amphibian boat. Now as we reworked the daydream and the night dream with this new insight, he suffered agonies. He could not bring himself to give associations; his tongue just could not utter them. He would hide his face or alternatively become impudent and revive his provocative behavior. Once, he succeeded in telling me one of his shameful thoughts in connection with the girl in the amphibian boat, and he did it through spelling. "That I want *all* my mother's l-o-v-e." When I brought his attention to the spelling as a defense against guilt feelings, he could only nod, miserably. When we consider the depth and the intensity of Roger's guilt feelings as they came out in this period of analysis, it is impressive to remember the earliest period of analysis when Roger could bring out undisguised oedipal fantasies without a trace of guilt or anxiety. All this had been achieved through the most elaborate defenses against affect.

In the weeks that followed much of the material centered around dread of the female genitalia. Observations of his sister and his little girl friend came into the analysis again, now with strong anxiety. He could not rid himself of the conviction that girls and women do have a penis hidden somewhere, "Even though I know better." In the resistance I encountered an interesting specimen of disbelief which occasionally attached itself to my interpretations or the merits of analysis itself. Clearly, he had to hold on to his belief in the woman's penis in order to defend against his own castration fears. His sister was frequently cited to me as an authority on all kinds of subjects and eventually we were able to discover how she became an authority on anatomical differences between the sexes. She had told Roger that girls had something much better than boys hidden inside their vaginas. He was glad to believe her.

Tumpis, Roger's Teddy bear, finally became our most valuable tool in this phase of analysis. Tumpis was properly speaking a fetish and, as I mentioned earlier, Roger had already seen that Tumpis was a reassurance to him against the danger of loss. On a few previous occasions, Roger had brought Tumpis himself to see me in the hope that Tumpis could tell us something about his problems. As we might expect, Tumpis proved to be very resistant to analysis. Then on one occasion during this period when I had reason to believe I might get cooperation from Roger, I proposed that we try an experiment. I asked Roger (who still took Tumpis to bed with him) if he would be willing to put Tumpis in another room for a few nights in order to help us understand a problem. I told him that he could certainly take Tumpis back at the end of the experiment if he still needed him. The experiment was not immediately successful. There seemed to be some increase in anxiety, but no specific content that could demonstrate the role of Tumpis. At the end of the two-day period Roger did not ask to have Tumpis back, although he knew he could have him back if he needed him. And then one day he brought in what he called "a horrible dream."

> He was coasting on a sled down a steep hill with Tumpis sitting in front of him. They crash into a tree. Next thing he knows they have landed on a big toboggan and go coasting down on this one.

He did not want to discuss the dream. It was too horrible. I tried to help him out by reminding him of his analytic hour in which he had told me about the sex games with his girl friend, Leila. There had been considerable feeling, something close to panic as he told me about how Leila and he looked at each other and as he was reminded of "the little hole" of girls. He agreed. But then, instead of continuing associations, he fell back upon acting. He began roaming restlessly around the room, "I want *something!*" he kept saying. Would I give him something—a pad of paper, a pencil, a paper clip, *anything,* but he must have *something.* I interpreted the acting as a defense against anxiety which finally persuaded him to sit down and analyze the dream.

He associated the first accident to his fear of damage to his penis. Then his associations led to the disappearance of grasshoppers that he had been saving in a jar; then observations of Leila, as if something has "disappeared." Then he came forth brilliantly with the solution. "Maybe inside I thought a girl had one and lost it and then got a bigger one later on." (The sled is exchanged in the dream for the toboggan.) The "I want *something,*" which we may take as an association to the dream, had the same significance as the fetish, Tumpis, the illusory penis of the woman that protects him against his castration fears.

The analysis of the fetish and the surrender of the fetish (which was permanent) had the effect of liberating a large quantity of affect. For a time we had anxiety, guilt, and hostility erupting in unpredictable fashion in the analytic hours and often without content. In the resistance we had the affects, and the ideational content was now isolated.

He wandered restlessly around the room, complaining of funny feelings, of feeling afraid and not knowing what he was afraid of, or feeling crazy.

From clues I gathered that there was anxiety about masturbation and when I tentatively suggested this possibility he exploded with me. He denied that he masturbated "any more," then finally admitted that he did "sometimes." I suspected, of course, that his resistance had to do with masturbatory fantasies and encouraged him to tell me. There were more denials and then with much suffering he told me only this much, that it was the old daydream about me, the girl in the amphibian boat. He refused to give me details.

Now he reverted to the old provocative behavior in his sessions with me. He was negative, obstinate, and used any trifle as an excuse to try to engage me in arguments. Only later when I saw this behavior in a sequence I realized that this behavior had the significance for him of "fighting" with me; it was an attempt to engage me in a verbal wrestling match. This behavior culminated in a piece of acting at home that finally revealed the meaning of the whole period of resistance.

One evening he went on a rampage at home, goading his mother until her patience was exhausted and they both wound up yelling at each other. At one point during this evening both his parents were in their room and Roger locked them in. He refused to let them out for nearly an hour.

This time Roger really exceeded himself and when he arrived for his hour the next day he was tormented with guilt. As we analyzed this piece of acting he brought out his fantasy with much suffering. He said that he wanted to see what his parents would do. When I asked for his fantasies of what they might do he blurted out that he had forgotten everything I had ever told him about what parents do to make babies. He begged me to tell him again. I told him that this would not help, that it was much more important to find out what he thought and what the feelings were, since it was the feelings that prevented him from remembering. Now he became furious with me. He became very aggressive, yelled at me, knocked over a desk ornament, threw pillows around, and finally ran out of the room. With great difficulty I got him to return to the room and sit down with me to analyze the acting. Then I was able to show him how his acting was a way of telling me; that he was trying to fight with me and that this must be his idea, deep inside of him, of what the parents do. He must think it was something like fighting.

This was by no means a new insight for Roger. We had worked with his sadomasochistic fantasies of parental intercourse throughout the analysis. Primal-scene memories had emerged in a terror dream a year earlier in analysis. A dream which Roger called "The Musicians of Bremen" dream had occupied months of analysis and Roger recalled overhearing parental quarrels at night and the sounds of intercourse. But now we were able to tie up the primal-scene observations with his own castration fears, and Roger could see how his observations had confirmed for him his belief that the woman tried to castrate the man. This also provided one of the last important links in the "night dream-day-dream" sequence of the witch and the girl in the amphibian boat, his fear that his incestuous longings would lead to castration by the mother. But now, too, we could find an important motive in Roger's behavior problems. The fighting with his mother represented the acting out of an incestuous fantasy that incorporated a sadomasochistic conception of intercourse. Once again the behavior originated in a masturbation fantasy.

The analysis of this material had a dramatic effect. This ended the period of acting out, and it was also the last period of acting outside of the analysis that we experienced. Roger's behavior which had steadily improved through the three years of analysis that preceded these events now became so much better that his parents began to ask if he was not ready to terminate analysis. There was scarcely a trace of the old provocative behavior, and all the slow gains of analysis seemed to consolidate in the months that followed.

## IV

But in the analysis itself I now encountered new resistances. First of all he insisted he was all well and no longer needed analysis. He was irritable and whiny with me and often exploded in anger over the most trivial things. When I tried to show him that this anger toward me was, in itself, a reason for working further in analysis, he countered shrewdly by pointing out that he was much better every place but here in analysis and if he quit analysis, there would be no reason to be angry at me and no problems.

The content of this period was so chaotic that I had difficulty for a while in sorting out the many themes and their implications in transference. First of all I could detect in certain fantasies passive longings toward the father. These fantasies had emerged in various forms earlier in the analysis, most prominently in the form of a kidnaping fantasy. There was a bad man who would take little boys into the woods and play with their penises. (This had first appeared two years ago when his parents had warned him about playing in the woods near the house and, following a kidnaping scare in the community, had warned him against going off with strangers.) Our earlier analysis of the kidnaping fantasies had centered primarily in his wish to be loved by his father and his fantasy that his father would love him better as a girl.

A second theme in this disordered period was anality. There was a terror dream in which "a witch" and "a toilet" led him to recall his old fear of toilets and the association that the witch "wanted to steal me." Further analysis of the dream connected the fear of losing feces and fear of castration.

Meantime, too, it would be entirely correct to say that Roger at certain times in this analytic period behaved just like a two-year-old. He would litter my office with scraps of paper and gleefully empty the wastebasket on the floor. He recited a large collection of chants and songs about garbage cans, toilets, and feces. He was stubborn, negative, and completely unreachable at times. There were other times when he was charming and reasonable and sometimes announced himself at the door by saying, "Well, the old Roger is back today!" If on such occasions one reminded him of the other Roger who had torn up the place the day before, he assumed an attitude of amused and clinical detachment toward his alter ego. He was not interested in analyzing him.

For five months we had these visitations from "the other Roger" who, it strikes me, had marked resemblances to the Roger I had known at an earlier stage of analysis. At home and at school there were no complaints. He was progressing very well; he was a satisfaction to his parents and a joy to his teachers. His parents could see no reason for continuing the analysis and I am sure that if they had not had so much confidence in analysis, they would have withdrawn him or pressed me to terminate. Roger himself could point to his good behavior at home and at school, and argued strenuously against continuing this unprofitable business. In short, we had a behavior in analysis that might justifiably be called a transference neurosis. The analysis of this period proved to be very profitable and finally illuminated the origins of Roger's character disorder in striking fashion.

During these five months of acting in the analysis we were still able to make use of dreams and acting in a slow and laborious investigation and reconstruction of a period in early childhood before I knew him. The first important communication came through a dream.

> He was in a movie—lost in the dark—trying to find his way to the candy counter. Then he is eating a chocolate bar, "the round kind with nuts in it."

The insight must have dawned upon him almost as soon as he finished telling me the dream, because he suddenly became restless, began to wander around aimlessly, and positively refused to give associations. I suggested that there were feelings of shame in connection with it. He nodded, and now the familiar look of suffering came on his face. He could not say it, he told me. In the end I had to help him out and he was relieved when I asked him if the candy bar reminded him of a bowel movement. He looked as if he were about to gag and then said, "That's it, but I couldn't say it." I was able to show him how something was remembered in the dream, something that belonged to a time when he was very small. I commented particularly on the feeling of shame that attached itself to this experience and suggested that this experience and others like it might account for the very great shame that we have seen in Roger for so long, a shame that got itself attached to all sorts of things later on.

During one period of acting I became impressed that much of his provocative behavior and his stubbornness and messiness finally obliged me to become firm and to "put my foot down"; and when I did so, calling a halt to his behavior, he looked as if this was just exactly what he had wanted. When I mentally reviewed this behavior with his anal preoccupations I was very certain that this pattern exactly corresponded to the picture I had obtained in the early history. Roger had soiled until he was nearly four years old and his mother had been completely unsuccessful in trying to train him. When she finally "put her foot down," according to the record, he became trained within a very short time. But from the transference reactions and content of dreams I could also understand that Roger had not been simply defiant during this period. He had been afraid to use the toilet. He was afraid of the noise of the toilet and afraid of falling in. And in the witch dream reported earlier he had equated loss of feces with castration. I was able to help Roger see how his behavior during this period was a way of remembering important things that had happened to him when he was very little and began to reconstruct from behavior and dreams the critical second and third years.

Then I learned from Roger's mother that she had observed a return of anal masturbation which we had not seen for some time in analysis. Roger could not bring himself to tell me this and finally his mother and I decided that she should tell Roger that she knew about this and that she would like to discuss this with me unless Roger thought he could tell me himself. He preferred to have mother tell me and I was now free to bring this up with him. He was actually quite relieved to have me know. And now I learned that he had surrendered phallic masturbation "because I don't like it when my penis gets hard—it doesn't feel good." When I pointed out that this pleasure in the anus is a kind of pleasure that very small boys feel and I did not understand why he had gone back to this, he said very intelligently, "Well, I think it's because we've been talking about when I was a little boy and I've been remembering it, so I got to doing it again."

The anal masturbation was accompanied by fantasies of "what it would be like to be a girl." He equated the anus with "the hole that girls have." The old kidnaping fantasies were revived now and could be analyzed more fully. The idea of passive surrender to a man was exciting to him. His identification with his sister came out in fantasies and even in a brief period of acting out in which he persuaded his sister once again to let him look at her genitals. There was a terror dream during this period in which there were robbers in the house and a radio announcer said in a loud voice, "All the boys are going to have their a-s-s cut off!" (He spelled a-s-s.) He was scared and began to run away and then woke up. We were finally able to establish that he had renounced phallic masturbation out of anxiety once again, that he felt it was dangerous to be a boy and safer to be a girl, and yet when he fantasied being a girl this was a terrifying thought for him, too.

I now began to understand the origins of the active-passive conflicts that played such a prominent role in his behavior disorder. The danger of passive surrender to the mother was succeeded by the danger of passive surrender to the father. To "give in" was to invite castration. But there was also a more primitive defense in operation here, a good example, I think, of Anna Freud's (1952) "negativism and emotional surrender." In the transference during this period I was able to observe the negativistic patterns with a quality of urgency and necessity that I think was very close to that which had earlier been characteristic of his behavior at home. My summary of this period and of the analytic insights gained does not do justice to the labor of working through the resistances encountered every inch of the way.

For a time every help that I tried to offer him, every insight was first countered with the most obstinate negation. The nature of the resistance was partially obscured by material that suggested that he disbelieved analysis because it deprived him of the illusion that women had a penis. (For a time he returned to his earlier authority, his sister Judy, who offered him her own consoling theory that she had "something better inside.") But when we cleared this area once again the desperate negativism still remained and at last I was reminded that I had once seen this in a very specific way in relation to the mother. It was the fear that to be in accord with, to agree with, the mother, to comply with her wishes, would demand the surrender of his own identity, would compel him to become one with his mother. (I had heard Anna Freud's paper nearly a year earlier and it had illuminated Roger's case for me.)

When I now began to draw Roger's attention to his negativism in transference I suggested an anxiety behind the behavior. I suggested that he behaved as if he were afraid that if he agreed with me he would somehow not be Roger. I proposed that there might be some connection between his old fears of "not being Roger" and the negativism that we saw in transference. He, of course, negated the interpretation strenuously. Yet it became a useful measure, and on several occasions during this difficult period it was often enough just to say, good-humoredly, "You don't have to be afraid to agree with me. You'll still be Roger!" and he would laugh and relax.

This period culminated in the presentation of a most interesting gift to the analyst. Roger was very much absorbed in scientific projects at school and when he was not hating me or throwing trash around my office, he sometimes spent part of his hour describing his scientific experiments and his scientific ambitions. He was collecting specimens of bread mold during this period. I did not of course make any interpretations regarding the anal significance of his new hobby and as far as possible I had always tried not to interfere with sublimations that were being formed. I was privately amused and sympathetic with the dilemma of his mother who now had to put up with little dishes of bread mold all around the house in a way that was reminiscent of a period long ago when she had to put up with little deposits of feces around the house. In analysis I listened with attention to his scientific conversation. I was not myself interested in bread mold and I must have overdone my simulated interest. Following one climactic hour in which Roger had put on an infantile display and dumped the contents of the wastebasket on the floor and begged to be released from this horrible prison that was analysis, he came in for his next hour beaming with shy happiness. He had a package in his hands, clumsily wrapped and tied with ribbon. "I have a present for you," he said. I opened it and found a specimen of bread mold. "It's a very unusual strain," he said proudly.

A good part of the material of this period helped us to reconstruct Roger's earliest conflicts with his mother, and Roger was able to see that a part of his life that he could not remember in words was remembered through his dreams and his behavior during this period. The difficult work of this period finally brought about a very satisfactory resolution of the transference resistances, and Roger terminated his analysis at the end of approximately three and a half years.

I was able to follow Roger's progress for five years while I remained in the same city. He sustained all of his gains. He had become a gratifying child to his parents and presented no problems that they could not handle themselves during these years. His schoolwork was excellent and his precocity and joy in learning delighted his parents and his teachers.

### Summary

The analysis of this behavior disorder reveals in specific ways how the aggressive and destructive behavior was employed in the service of defense.

In tracing the motive for a destructive act we saw very early in the analysis how a fantasy in which the child was in extreme danger was translated into an action in which the content of the fantasy was reproduced and the ego spared itself anxiety through identification with the aggressor and through a shift from passive to active. (As in the first dream reported by Roger, the fear of castration by the faceless man was immediately translated into an action in which the child performed the symbolic destructive act upon objects in the room.) This defense served painful memories as well as fantasies. When primal-scene material emerged in the analysis, the memory of an act perceived as destructive, and as "fighting," was translated into aggressive acting in which destruction of objects and fighting was re-enacted and that which was passively experienced through observing and overhearing was transformed into action. Ultimately, the great danger against which the ego defended itself was loss of identity. The extreme negativism and obstinacy that characterized another aspect of Roger's behavior disorder was seen as a fear of surrender to the object, the fear of becoming one with the object (Freud, 1952).

The connections between the masturbatory fantasies and impulsive acting provided insights both into certain forms of erratic conduct and the role of isolation of affects in the behavior disorder. Anna Freud (1949) has brought our attention to a form of social maladjustment that can be traced back to the complete suppression of phallic masturbation and the consequent acting out of the masturbation fantasies:" . . . the masturbation-fantasy is deprived of all bodily outlet, the libidinal and aggressive energy attached to it is completely blocked and dammed up, and eventually is displaced with full force from the realm of the sex-life into the realm of ego-activities." In Roger's analysis it could be demonstrated that he periodically abandoned phallic masturbation under pressure of castration anxiety and in the erratic and apparently unprovoked periods of acting that followed we could trace a masturbatory fantasy.

But Roger also illuminated for me the process that led to abandonment of masturbation at certain times. On many occasions there was no evidence of a conscious struggle against the urge to masturbate. (The child who fights the urge to masturbate reveals the struggle in defense and resistance in analysis. The argument between the urge and the prohibition is seen in moral ambivalence, self-punishment, self-imposed taboos. He reveals the struggle in transference by identifying the analyst with the repudiated temptations and often behaves toward the analysis as if it were a bad habit that must be broken.) Through Roger I came to understand that at certain times when masturbation was apparently given up he lost "the good feelings" in his penis. His own description of this, in a period of the analysis that I have not included in this report, went as follows: "But my penis doesn't feel good when I touch it. It doesn't feel not nice, either. Not good and not bad. Nothing." In other words, anesthesia took place, probably on a hysterical basis, and masturbation could no longer evoke phallic sensations. Masturbation was then given up, not as the result of a struggle, but because of the loss of feeling and the inability to have sensations in the penis. The fantasies which had lost their connections with masturbation were now acted out, following the pattern described by Anna Freud.

One further connection is suggested in the acting out of the masturbation fantasy. In the earlier association of the fantasy with the act of masturbation, the fantasy was "made real" by the accompanying phallic excitations. (Another child once said to me, "The stories are more realer when I'm playing with myself.") I have wondered, then, if one of the elements in the acting out of the masturbatory fantasy is the attempt to make the story real through enactment, to recover the lost excitement, and to animate the fantasy gone dead with the penis. And since the fantasy had once served to excite the penis, is acting out also a magical device to bring back the lost feelings in the penis?

The most important part of the analytic work was that which dealt with the defenses against affects and it was here that analysis encountered its strongest resistance. The absence of anxiety and guilt which distorted the early picture of the behavior disorder was seen finally as the achievement of the most elaborate defenses against affect. By identifying with the aggressor and by switching from passive to active, the ego escaped both anxiety and self-reproach. The simultaneous acting out of libidinal and aggressive fantasies and the provocation of punishment spared the ego the necessity of experiencing guilt. The isolation of affect which proved to be the most formidable resistance of all, served many purposes in the mental economy. The barely disguised oedipal fantasies and castration fantasies were rendered less dangerous by depriving them of affect, making them "not real." Further, by maintaining guilt and anxiety in isolation, Roger was able to enjoy masturbation and its attendant fantasies. We saw that each time analysis re-established the connections between fantasies and affects the anxiety experienced by the child was nearly intolerable.

The analysis of the transference resistance in the last period of treatment shed further light on both the libidinal and ego aspects of the active-passive conflicts in which the behavior disorder had been rooted. Both the passive longings for the father and the defenses against these wishes were revived along with anal masturbation. The fight with mother over bowel training which had extended well into the fourth year was re-enacted in transference along with castration dread. The negativism which had been one of the primary defenses and one that had served resistance througout the analysis was seen as a defense against the danger of passive surrender to the mother, the "fear of loss of personality" as Anna Freud put it.

## Notes

This paper is an expanded version of one presented at the panel on Resistances in Child Analysis at the Midwinter Meeting of the American Psychoanalytic Association, December 1960.

1. In order to explain Roger's ability to spell and to do simple arithmetic in the sequence that follows, I should mention that Roger was in the second grade at this time, following advancement from nursery school to the first grade at the age of five.

## References

Freud, A. (1949). Certain Types and Stages of Social Maladjustment. In *Searchlights on Delinquency*, ed. K. R. Eissler. New York: International Universities Press.

———. (1952). A Connection between the States of Negativism and of Emotional Surrender. Abstract: *Int. J. Psychoanal.*, 33:265.

## 14

# Further Considerations of the Role of Transference in Latency

Some years ago one of the first of my child analysands returned to me at the age of sixteen and told me that she felt she needed help once again. Dorothy had been in analysis between the ages of seven and ten. She was, in fact, one of the children whose case material was used to illustrate my earlier paper on transference in child analysis (1951). The treatment of Dorothy in adolescence gave me an extraordinary opportunity to re-examine the role of transference in child analysis and to reconsider my earlier views.

Dorothy had been an aggressive, insatiable, and uncontrollable child when she entered analysis. Learning was impaired. She chose for her friends the neglected, quasi-delinquent children in her neighborhood, and, at the age of seven, seemed ready to form her own identity on the basis of "no good," "worthless," "cast off."

For the purposes of this essay there is no need to elaborate on the case history or on those details of the analysis which are summarized in the earlier paper. The analysis brought about radical changes in the child's personality, the oedipal conflicts were brought to a favorable resolution, anxieties over sex play and masturbation were extensively dealt with, and at the time of termination Dorothy showed all the signs of a favorable development in her femininity, her pleasure in learning, her relationships to parents and friends, and her self-valuation.

In this sketch I should call attention to one symptom that had been prominent in the early phases of the analysis. There was a dog phobia that had once been so pervasive that Dorothy could hardly bring herself to go outdoors at certain times, and during one period of the analysis the dog phobia had manifested itself in relation to me and to my house. (Later, I shall return to this detail.) It is also important to note that Dorothy had been enuretic until the age of four and that an ill-advised cystoscopy had been performed at four. Following the cystoscopy the enuresis ceased.

Between the ages of eleven and sixteen Dorothy sustained all of her gains, and early adolescence brought forth no extraordinary conflicts. I had followed her development through occasional visits with the parents, and Dorothy herself somehow kept in touch with me. Occasionally she sent a greeting card or called me to tell me about something nice that had happened to her. Twice, when she was thirteen, she asked to see me and on one of these visits told me that she sometimes still worried about the cystoscopy. She was afraid that it might happen again. Since Dorothy's overall functioning was unimpaired, I was not too concerned about this problem and felt that the old memories had been revived under the pressure of pubertal conflicts.

At sixteen Dorothy was an attractive, poised, very articulate girl, riding a tide of popularity at school and sustaining good grades along with an active social life. In general, she presented a picture of such wholesome good health that later, when we requested that she be excused from school for regular appointments with me, the school refused the request on the basis that there could not be anything wrong with this girl that would require her to be excused from school for psychiatric treatment. The hint was strong that either Dorothy was malingering or the therapist was making a mountain out of a molehill.

When Dorothy came to see me at sixteen, she stated directly that she needed further treatment. In a forthright and adult way she told me that in the past months she had come to recognize that she had a problem in relation to boys. She knew many "nice boys" with whom she went to parties and dances, but she felt very little sexual attraction for the nice boys. On the other hand, she formed an attachment to a boy who was coarse and really repulsive to her and yet she found kissing and sex play with him very exciting. She felt there were some problems that had not been worked out in her childhood analysis; in fact, she remembered deliberately concealing certain things from me. As I talked further with Dorothy, I reached complete agreement with her that further treatment was indicated at this time.

I saw Dorothy twice a week for a thirteen-month period. The story of the adolescent treatment may one day be reported in greater detail, for it illuminated the child analysis in an extraordinary way. From the material in the adolescent therapy I shall excerpt only a few details that throw light on the problem of transference in a child analysis.

In the early weeks of treatment Dorothy described her sexual relationship to Joe, the boy she described as repulsive and attractive to her. There was no genital sex play; the erotic high point of her relationship was achieved by having him lie upon her (both fully clothed) while she, imprisoned beneath him, moved her thighs and reached orgasm. Her shame as she described this act was overwhelming to her.

Dorothy's associations led back to the childhood cystoscopy at age four. She remembered being held down, screaming, while "that thing" was put into her. The memory was vivid and she could re-experience the terror as she told me. She had no difficulty in seeing the connection between her sex play with Joe and the cystoscopy. Then followed a period of resistance in the treatment, candid acknowledgment that she was withholding something from treatment, and even an admission that this was the same "something" that she had withheld in her childhood analysis. She was finally able to tell me that for years she had practiced a form of masturbation which involved thigh friction alone. The exciting fantasy for the masturbation was the memory of the cystoscopy. She was certain that she had never told me about masturbation in her childhood analysis. She was mistaken, but I shall return to this point later.

I was now able to show Dorothy how the sex play with Joe was the acting out of the masturbation fantasy. As we dealt with the masturbation fantasy in subsequent sessions, the relationship with Joe began to dissolve and within a few weeks Dorothy discovered that she no longer needed him. From this point on there was no longer a need for a degraded lover.

A new boyfriend now appeared. His name was Arthur. He was homely, tender, good-humored, and an amateur psychologist. The erotic high point of this relationship seemed to be an interminable psychologizing during the late hours, a sharing of adolescent woes, a continuous diagnosis of each other's weaknesses and failings, and clinical interpretations which sometimes led to quarrels. It was a long time before Dorothy was able to see some of the transference implications of this new friendship.

Soon this relationship, too, was caught up in conflict. One evening

Arthur had his arms around Dorothy and Dorothy found it exciting. Then Arthur began to nibble gently at the back of Dorothy's neck. At this point she had a feeling of panic. The thought occurred to her that Arthur was going to bite her. The sensations in her own genitalia stopped abruptly. The feeling of terror would not leave her and when she left Arthur that evening she was in tears.

In her session with me Dorothy immediately associated to this incident her old fear of dogs. She remembered, she told me, that her fear of dogs was one of the problems that had brought her into analysis in childhood. In the hours that followed we were able to trace the connections between genital sensations, the fear of attack by a dog, the masturbation fantasies, and the cystoscopy. For many weeks Dorothy remained completely anesthetic when Arthur held her or kissed her, and even later, when she recovered genital sensations, there were transitory occurrences of complete frigidity which required analytic work for months. The fear that she would not be able to control her excitement, that she would abandon herself and degrade herself, entered the treatment later. Unresolved residues of the oedipal ties to the father appeared as further obstructions to the experience of pleasure and were dealt with in treatment. And, finally, the very core of self-degradation, the early childhood experience of outright rejection by her mother, the feeling of lovelessness and worthlessness came into the adolescent treatment through the analysis of the transference.

This concise summary clearly implies that the childhood analysis had not effected a genuine resolution of the central conflicts in the neurosis. In the case of Dorothy I believe that resolution might have been achieved through a deeper analysis of the phobia in the transference.

When I reread my notes of the child analysis, I was struck by the fact that the method of that analysis was entirely alien to me only a few years later. Repeatedly I found instances in which my technical handling would now be very different. Even the criteria I had employed for termination of the analysis seemed questionable to me. It was in the area of transference that I found myself most critical of the early work. And it was in the handling of transference that I felt I had cut off access to precisely those conflicts that had re-emerged in the adolescent neurosis.

In reviewing the case notes of the child analysis, I found these differences in method and technique between the child analysis I·practiced in those days and that which I consider my present-day practice. To a large extent these differences also reflect the changes in the field of child analysis.

First, my attention was drawn to the ways in which I dealt with the earliest transference reactions in the childhood analysis. When the aggressive behavior first manifested itself in the analytic sessions, I employed techniques to arouse the child's anxiety in relation to her behavior. I showed great concern about the possible consequences of her uncontrolled behavior and brought about a situation in which the child made conscious efforts to control herself. The benefits in improved family relations were apparent very soon. The effort at self-control produced a mouth tic which appeared from time to time during the early months of analysis. In the child analysis of that period we regarded this as a favorable sign. This meant that we had converted the behavior disorder into a neurosis and had created a favorable situation for analysis.

Today, confronted with the same behavior manifestations in transference reactions I would view the aggressive behavior as defensive and begin to show the child how the aggressive behavior appeared whenever she was afraid of something. I would explore the anxiety in relation to me, trace it in its other connections, and help the child see her behavior as an identification with the aggressor. This would lead us into the analysis of the mother-child relationship and the same path would lead into the analysis of the cystoscopy. The analysis of the sadistic behavior as defense would bring me into direct contact with the phobic substructure of the behavior disorder and, by addressing myself to fear and helplessness, I would hope to bring about the kind of transference which we obtain with hysterical patients; i.e., the analyst becomes the ally against danger and the analysis has the purpose of freeing the child from anxiety. I would avoid, as far as possible, any measures that deliberately create anxiety in the child. The anxiety is there, it only needs to be uncovered through analysis of defense; and by following this analytic approach I would be in a favorable position to deal with transference reactions. I cannot easily show a child that her fear of me is unrealistic, and introduced by her neurosis, if I have, in fact, induced anxiety in her through the therapeutic approach I followed in Dorothy's case. Further, I would expect that through analyzing the relationship between anxiety and the aggressive behavior, the aggressive behavior would diminish without a heroic effort at self-control on the part of the child, an effort which in this case produced a new symptom. Experience tells us that the analytic approach which I would prefer in such an instance should bring about a more durable form of self-control than that obtained through turning the sadistic impulses back upon the self.

The dog phobia in the child analysis is of special interest. In my earlier essay on transference in child analysis, I described the way in which the dog phobia was manifest in the transference during one period of the analysis. As the analysis began to center upon Dorothy's relationship with her mother, and at a time when internalization of aggression had been achieved to a large extent, the dog phobia appeared in relation to me and to my house. Resistance was manifest in the analytic hours through a kind of frozen silence; then the child became afraid to come to her hours because of a little dog who lived on my street. During the same period the mother's own destructive feelings toward the child came to the foreground. Dorothy's mother was afraid that she might strangle her child. As I saw it, then, the phobia which represented in part the child's fear of her aggressive wishes and projection onto an external object had received massive reinforcement through the real danger of the mother's hostile feelings toward the child. When analysis centered upon the conflict between the child and her mother, danger was experienced as coming from the analyst and the dog phobia was transferred to the analyst. Thus far, I think, I would have no objections to the formulation I had worked out. In the earlier essay I also showed that there was no correspondence between the transference of the dog phobia and a transference neurosis because the conflict still centered in the relationship with the original objects, the still present objects for a child. In the illustration from Dorothy's case, we saw that the phobia was not withdrawn from the home ground as it were, but extended into the anaytic situation. From the evidence available to me at *that* time, I would not alter my views on this point either.

But my handling of the dog phobia in the transference struck me as quite alien to my present-day technique. In the child analysis I dealt with the transference of the dog phobia by showing the child verbally and through play devices that she behaved toward me as if I were a dangerous dog who might hurt her, and then in play and games with her I represented myself as a harmless old dog who would never hurt a little girl. On the basis of this reassurance to the child the dog phobia was withdrawn from the transference, the positive transference was restored, and the analysis went on to explore the conflicts of ambivalence in relation to the mother. With analysis of the oedipal conflicts the dog phobia disappeared. But it was the unlaid ghost of this dog that returned in adolescence.

Today, I reflected, I would have worked with the transference of the dog phobia in quite a different way. First, I would have educated the child patient to the meaning of transference reactions and through many demonstrations during the early period of the analysis would have shown the child how feelings and ideas can attach themselves to me and seem real yet belong someplace else. I would teach the child to trace these reactions and to find their origins. I would deal with the earliest negative transference reactions in a way that would make it possible for a child to express them and to see how we make use of them analytically. And through dealing with the dangerous affects in small quantities during this early period of analysis I would expect that the child will be less likely to feel overwhelmed by her feelings when certain conflicts appear full strength in the analysis. With this groundwork, if a dog phobia should make its appearance in the transference, I would have a patient who understood the meaning of transference, who would feel that the danger now emanating from the analytic situation was somehow alien and would work with me in unmasking the dog and her own resistance.

If I had analyzed the dog phobia as it was manifest in the transference, where might the dog phobia have led us? From the material in the adolescent therapy we know that there were links between the dog phobia and the cystoscopy in the fear of a genital attack. If I had analyzed the dog phobia in the transference, would the paths have led us back to the cystoscopy and the masturbation fantasies? Was the dog phobia another manifestation of a doctor transference, a "fear of the examination" that was analysis? Perhaps it is unprofitable to speculate, but it is very clear that by managing the transference instead of analyzing it I could not know exactly what was transferred.

As it happened both the cystoscopy and masturbation later appeared prominently in the childhood analysis and were analyzed on the basis of stories, daydreams, and play. But it struck me, as I reread the notes of that period, that the affective quality of these communications was thin, and diluted, I felt, in the context of play, storytelling, and "make-believe." The memory of the cystoscopy was a pale ghost of the memory that was reported to me in adolescence; there had been no reliving and re-experiencing of the event in the child analysis. Again, I do not attribute this to endogenous factors in the child analytic situation; the limitation lies in the method I employed. If transference analysis had been employed in the childhood treatment, the memory of the cystoscopy would have emerged in transference, made real and present to the child through the transference. Following closely the model in adult analytic technique, we would expect to revive this memory with a good measure of its original affective charge and the analysis of the event would have given meaning to dread of genital attack and castration anxiety.

In the child analytic notes the sadomasochistic fantasies appeared and links were established with the earlier cystoscopy, but I cannot find in my notes any connections that were established between the sadomasochistic fantasies and the masturbation itself! There were a group of masturbation fantasies, specifically oedipal in character, that occupied many months of analysis, but the sadomasochistic fantasies that Dorothy revealed in the adolescent treatment (the cystoscopy fantasies) were maintained in isolation from the masturbation itself. Only a young and inexperienced analyst could have overlooked this. We then have another explanation for the isolation of the memory from its attendant affects in the analysis. As long as the sadomasochistic fantasies could be maintained in isolation from the masturbatory context, the affects could be maintained in isolation.

Now, I think we can understand why Dorothy felt that she had concealed her childhood masturbation from me. Since she had never told me the cystoscopy fantasies as masturbation fantasies, she felt, in fact, that she had not told me. I also feel that so much of this analysis was carried on within the context of play and make-believe that even when masturbation was handled in the analysis it was somehow "not real" to the child.

This re-examination of a child analysis cannot stand by itself as an illustration of the role of transference in child analysis. At best we have only a kind of negative evidence that if the transference had been analyzed, the outcome might have been different. It might be more profitable to turn to another case illustration from latency in order to examine the role of transference.

## II

Nancy was eight when she began her analysis. Six months prior to referral seizures were observed and an EEG confirmed petit mal with grand mal components. A number of anticonvulsants were tried without success in controlling the seizures. With the onset of seizures there was marked deterioration in all areas of ego functioning and an impoverishment of affect that alarmed the parents. Analysis was begun with the hope of restoring ego functioning, but only after treatment was underway did we have hope that analysis might have some success in controlling the seizures. When analysis was terminated at the end of four years, Nancy was symptom free and there were significant characterological changes.

I shall not attempt a detailed history of the analysis. I have excerpted material from the third and fourth years of treatment in which analysis of the transference led to the uncovering of memories from the age of three. This was a critical year in the etiology of the neurosis, but it should be clear that the events that we later learned about cannot be construed as an etiology for the convulsive disorder itself.

During the first two years of analysis we dealt with the defenses against affect, masturbatory conflicts, a ball fetish, erotic looking games with an older brother, Fenton, and some aspects of the positive and negative oedipus complex. Nancy brought in dreams for analysis, learned to associate on the basis of a "What Pops into your Mind Game," and learned to candidly report reactions and feelings toward the analyst. At the beginning of the third year of analysis manifest seizures were rare, ego functioning was restored in all areas, and the affective picture was favorably altered. From a number of details in dreams and fantasies I was certain that there had once been a sexual observation of a couple, but the threads of this material seemed to lead nowhere.

In the middle of the third year of analysis a compulsive finger game appeared in analytic sessions and soon Nancy reported that she found herself playing the finger game at home and at school. In the finger game one hand was opened partially in a clawlike formation; the other hand with fingers partially closed entered the open hand in a rhythmic motion. Her associations led her into "what grownups do to get babies," then into "penis and mouth," and suddenly an interruption of associations and the experience of violent nausea in the hour. In later sessions the threads led back to sex games with her little friend Arthur which she herself blamed for bringing on her seizures, and the recovery of a memory from this period in which Arthur's mother, coming upon the children, had made a threat against Arthur's penis. Other threads seemed to lead back once again to a sexual observation of a couple (but I did not suggest this). The finger game ceased and there followed a period of strong resistance in the analysis.

One day Nancy arrived for her hour and immediately reported a thought that had been running through her head all during her trip from her house to my house. The thought was "Selma is a blackmailer, Selma is a blackmailer." I said, "Do you really think Selma is a black-mailer?" "Of course not!" she said, "I'm just telling you my thoughts!" She went on. Along with the thought was a fantasy that I would tell her parents that if they did not pay me more money I would discontinue treatment. There was no one else to go to, so her parents had to pay me more money.

Now I should mention that nothing in the objective picture could account for this fantasy. At no time in the analysis had the analytic fee been a problem for her parents or for me. Nancy herself was baffled and could provide no associations. I reminded her of criminal games in analysis the previous spring and the blackmailer who threatened to get the criminal if he did not pay off. "Yes," she said doubtfully, "but I'm not really afraid that you would tell anyone about anything I've told you, or that you would really blackmail anyone." I tried other leads. I reminded her of a maid who left Nancy's family because she thought she could get more money elsewhere. Yes, Nancy remembered. Then was I like a maid in this fantasy? "Yes." And the trail broke off again. Then, abruptly Nancy said, "Now I think of another blackmail. A black *male.* [This had turned up too in the blackmail fantasy the previous spring.] And that reminds me of a game Sally [her best friend] and I play. She's an all black horse and I'm an all white horse and we love each other." "What do you do?" "Oh, we just ran alongside of each other. Play together. See, that's where the black *male* comes in." We pursued this further. "Were there any other associations to a black *male?*" "No."

I asked her if another possibility of a black male was in connection with night. A white male would look like a black male at night. "No," Nancy said flatly. "You just lost the $64,000 question. I thought we were getting some place before, but that doesn't sound right to me. I keep thinking it was a *black* male." And we could not pursue this further that hour.

Soon afterwards, baffled by the detail of a black male and the child's own conviction, I found an opportunity to ask Nancy's mother some questions. I could not believe in the possibility that a protected middle-class child would have had an opportunity to see "a black male." Nancy's mother then told me that when Nancy was three and a half she and her husband had taken a two-week holiday in another city. The children were in the care of a Negro maid. When the parents returned they learned from the neighbors and from the children themselves that Cassie's boyfriend had visited her at night. Cassie was dismissed shortly afterwards. The parents had no evidence that the children had observed the couple in bed; Cassie's room was on another floor. The parents had never considered the possibility that Nancy could have observed a sexual act and had never told me about this incident.

I never told Nancy what I learned from her mother. The material that I now bring together emerged entirely through the analysis of the child's own dreams, fantasies, and transference behavior.

Soon after the appearance of the "blackmail-black male" material Nancy developed an upper respiratory infection and was in bed for a week. I did not understand until a year later that the upper respiratory infection belonged to the memory of the sexual observation. Only later, when still another sequence linked the observation and an illness and a separation from the parents, was I able to see this and use it analytically. (In the reconstruction, the three-year-old Nancy had wakened at night with cold symptoms and perhaps a sore throat. She had gone in search of Cassie. At the door of Cassie's room she heard voices. She opened the door and went in.)

When Nancy returned to analysis after her illness she reported that the fantasy "Selma is a blackmailer" had returned. Her associations were: "Selma is a robber. . . . You took my good feelings away." She was very careful to assure me, "These are just my thoughts you know. I don't really think this." She had lost all genital sensation that week and somehow felt I was to blame. There was a fantasy that I would cut off her hands at her wrists so that she could not touch herself. Then, still associating, she told me for the first time about "a picture" that kept coming into her mind during the time she was ill in bed, a "picture" that she had had before, when she was ill, and sometimes when she was not ill and was alone. The "picture," as she described it to me, had the quality of a hysterical hallucination in vividness and intensity. It was the picture of a chessboard with black and white squares and on the chessboard were "little creamy, skinny blocks" arranged on the board for a game. When she sketched it for me she showed a mass of little blocks placed in one corner of the board and two blocks isolated in the opposite corner. Along with the hallucination was a noise, "a noise," said Nancy, "that sounds like a big wh-i-ish."

In this hour and the next Nancy's associations again led in the direction of mutilation fears ("Someone will cut off my hand") and her associations to the chessboard blocks went on in this way: "They're people. It's as if the ones in the corner are mother and father with lots of children and a couple in the other corner without children." Then the phrase, "Evening Star" came into her mind. And then there flashed through her mind a picture. "A couple in the moonlight kissing. And there's the wh-i-ish sound again. . . . Another picture. A couple riding a horse in the moonlight." And then the associations stopped. There was a trancelike quality in Nancy as she gave these associations. Finally, I asked her if she could ever have seen a couple in the moonlight. She said, immediately, "Oh, yes!" I am not sure whether or not she had a brief seizure at this point. When I asked her about her last words, "Oh, yes!" she was surprised, and had not known she said this. She assured me she could not remember anything about seeing a couple and could not imagine what made her say that.

For over a month following this session, the analysis was at a standstill. Nancy had no problems to report, no conflicts, no fears. The seizures had practically disappeared from the picture, but something new had taken their place. Nancy told me that she was "forgetting" all kinds of things and she wanted to make it very clear that these episodes of forgetting were not at all like seizures. She carefully explained the difference. "In my forgetting spells I would blank out. Like the telephone gets disconnected. But this way I don't get disconnected. It's like I hear a person talking, but I can't remember what they said." Through careful questions I ascertained that Nancy was making clear that she never lost consciousness at such moments and that she was actually describing a hysterical absence.

This brought us close to the summer holidays. Nancy was obviously marking time in analysis until summer camp and when the time for departure came, she was relieved. It was an excellent summer, according to all reports. There were no symptoms, no conflicts that interfered with her pleasure at camp. It was as if banishing the analyst erased the memories.

Before proceeding to a new phase in the analysis of the primal scene material I shall briefly summarize the first appearance of primal scene material in the transference. We recall that much earlier in the analysis I had seen evidence of primal scene material in dreams and fantasies. None of this was available to analysis until it entered the transference. When the memory made its first breakthrough it appeared in the form of a transference symptom, the compulsive finger game, which manifested itself first in the analysis, then at home and school. In the finger games the memory of a sexual observation was still screened by later memories of sex play and masturbatory experiences. *However, when components of the memory of the original sexual observation became preconscious in the next phase of the analysis they no longer sought representation through compatible screen memories but found a new and independent route to preconscious representation in a transference fantasy: "Selma is a blackmailer."* Through the analysis of this fantasy we obtained almost immediately the associations that led back to "a maid" (the analyst in the fantasy, threatens to quit for more money) and "a black male" (from blackmail). In a rapid development in the next few weeks there appeared an upper respiratory infection, which, as I later learned, was a factor in the original observation, and the chessboard hallucination, a highly abstract representation of the act. I think we are justified in speaking here of transference neurosis.

The beginning analysis of the chessboard hallucination very shortly led to an impenetrable resistance. In the fall, when Nancy returned from camp, the resistance was still manifest. She had stopped working in analysis and the characteristics of the resistance eluded me as I tried to find a route back into the analysis. One evening, as I was reviewing my notes, I was struck by the fact that my interpretations seemed scattered and without focus and that many of them had a "pushing" quality that I did not like. I seemed to be trying to get her back to work by pressing and I was not sure why I was doing this. In the next hours I made no interpretations and resisted the temptation to get Nancy back to work and then, from various reactions, I had the impression that Nancy was inviting me to push her, to make her go back to work. Then a fantasy emerged. What would happen, Nancy wondered, if she should quit analysis? Her fantasy was that she would be forced to return. I would force her to return, she thought. Would I, though? Well, probably not, she considered. Well, then, her parents would force her to return, she decided. It was clear that this idea was somehow exciting to her and she saw it as real. When I pointed out to her that nobody had ever forced her to come to her analytic hours and that there was no reason to expect that anyone would, that I myself would not want this, Nancy still clung to the idea. When the fantasy persisted in the next hours I began to bring her attention to the detail of "forcing" as an analytic communication. I suggested that there was something in the idea of "being forced" to do something that could not be put into words, and was coming out in the form of a fantasy in which she would be forced to come to analysis. The meaning of the resistance was revealed very shortly afterwards.

One day Nancy arrived for her hour with a "back to work" manner that I could recognize. She began her hour. "Isn't it funny," she said, "how many of my daydreams are torture daydreams?" (It was indeed "funny," since she had never told me any torture daydreams during the three years I had known her.)

The torture daydreams I now learned were also incorporated in games which Nancy played with her friend Sally. In the games the two girls played horses together. One of the games we already know from Nancy's story of last spring. Nancy was a white horse and Sally was a black horse. Today, as Nancy began to give details of the current game with Sally, she made it clear that the game originated in her own daydreams and that she and Sally acted it out.

In Nancy's daydream there were two children who were captured by animals and enslaved by them. They were forced to do the work of dray horses. When they were too slow to work they were tortured. In one of the tortures a bit was placed in the mouth so that each effort at pulling would cause the bit to cut into the mouth. In another torture the girl was put in stocks, with head, arms, and legs through holes, while a man behind her threatened her with a whip (but did not actually beat her). The boy, however, was beaten on his arm by the whip. In still another torture the boy and girl were driven like horses while carrying heavy weights suspended from their backs.

In the following hour Nancy was nearly inarticulate with shame for having told me the torture daydreams. They belonged to masturbation, she needed them to get "a very strong feeling." Now each of the details of the sadistic fantasies came into the analysis. She associated to the bit in the mouth of the horse-humans her own hands in masturbation. "When I tighten up there with my hands." It was an exact displacement from vulva to mouth. The weights on the horses reminded her, she said, of "the balls . . . they hang down." The whipping did not yet yield any associations.

Gradually we established the links between the sadomasochistic masturbation fantasies and earlier sex games. Then the chessboard hallucination returned, and this time something new had been added. There were associated noises. "It sounds like people mumbling or jabbering and I can't make out what they're saying." Here the threads broke off once again and it was several weeks before Nancy provided another clue through a game with Sally. Again the game was confided with deep shame. The two girls pretended that they were two dogs, a male dog and a female dog. The male was wrongly thought to be savage and was chained up. Nancy, the female dog, tried to free him. She was to be punished by The People. In a climactic scene the Nancy dog is on her back (tied down) and the Sally dog is crouched over her legs with his paws under her while The People lower a heavy metal cast over Nancy's body. At first she can barely feel it. Then it hurts a little, then it hurts a lot and Nancy, in the game, can hardly breathe.

Nancy began to ramble. She confessed she did not want to associate to this material. "It makes me ashamed." Then she said, "There's a word that keeps coming into my mind and I keep forgetting it." And at this moment she had a seizure. The word was "intercourse" and when she remembered it shortly afterwards she said, "I feel like getting out of here, right now!" As we talked about her feelings she suddenly interrupted to ask urgently, "What would happen if something went wrong and instead of the seed coming out of the man, urine came out?" She looked ill again and I asked her about her feelings. "Like throwing up," she said.

As we worked over this material in this hour and the next I drew

Nancy's attention to the themes of torture and intercourse and fascinated looking and now I suggested for the first time that she might, in fact, once have seen a sexual act between a couple and that it might have seemed to her like a torture. She regarded me wide-eyed and then let out a little cry of disgust and horror. Yet she did not deny it. "Maybe when I was little." She was silent for some time. Then I heard her say, "Wa-wa-wa" in a musing voice, meanwhile blowing her bubble gum into a large, full bubble. Then she said, "Look at what I am doing with this!" She had blown it to the fullest extent, then inhaled and caused it to collapse. She stopped short in amazement and said, "I think that's what I saw! A penis, I mean. . . . Now I want to go home. I feel like getting out of here in a hurry!" I told her that if she had, indeed, once seen such a thing, she might have felt like getting out in a hurry.

There followed two hours during which Nancy found herself quite unable to talk and empty of feeling. When I asked what had happened to all the strong feelings she said, "All gone, I guess. Or maybe I should say they are in forgetting spells now." I then suggested that the inability to talk might be part of the memory, too. If I were right that she had once seen something between a couple, she might not have been able to talk about it afterward. She listened to this with some interest and then said, "You know what pops into my mind? That maybe someone told me I *mustn't* tell."

It was nearly two weeks later that Nancy brought a report of nausea and stomach pains and a new fear. In the darkness of her room at night she saw a picture. "A man with horns growing out of his head. A horrible monster. And I kept thinking about it [last night] and I couldn't fall asleep. . . . But today in class I thought of something. I think it's connected with what I must have seen when I was little, seeing intercourse, I mean. I don't know why, but when I made that connection I was *really sure* for the first time since we've been talking about it that I saw it. . . . He had a black face. Very ugly horns."

I have reported this segment of the analysis in some detail in order to permit close examination of the transference and a comparison with the adult model. The material shows that following the initial breakthrough of the primal scene memory in the transference fantasy "Selma is a blackmailer" a resistance appeared. The analysis of the resistance and the fantasy "to be forced" (in the analysis) led us into the sadomasochistic masturbation fantasies and the torture games with Sally. The analysis of the sadomasochistic games led back to the original observation of a couple, the recovery of partial memories in the transference, and the associated affective reactions—anxiety, guilt, nausea, an urge to take flight. There followed a period of resistance, conversion symptoms of nausea and stomach pains, anxiety at night, and the hallucination of the black man with horns. It was this that led to the patient's conviction that she had really seen intercourse.

In all the significant ways I think we can demonstrate a correspondence to the adult model of a transference neurosis. We note, too, that the technical handling of the transference followed closely the model of the adult analysis.

It may be useful to pursue the threads of the primal scene material in the next period of analysis. I should mention that the conviction that she had in fact witnessed a sexual scene remained with Nancy, but further analysis of the primal scene material encountered a new resistance. The defenses which now appeared led us into the analysis of bisexual fantasies, her masculine identification, and only many months later to the further analysis of the primal scene material.

Once again it was the analysis of the transference that led us back to the primal scene material. There was strong resistance, a fear of me that became explicit in a fantasy that analysis would take away her "boy part" (i.e., masculinity), and occasionally a feeling that analysis itself was a kind of torture. At the same time there was acting out in two directions. The torture games with Sally were back in the picture, and Nancy would give me only vague hints that the new games had something to do with a master and a slave and the command to the slave that she must exhibit herself to strange men. During the same period Nancy became provocative with her brother and, to a lesser extent, with other boys, teasing and goading until Fenton threatened to beat her up, then exciting herself through fantasies of being beaten.

In daydreams and one nocturnal dream of this period I could clearly see that I was represented as a sadist who exerted hypnotic effects upon a girl or a boy who was obliged to obey commands, and Nancy herself could acknowledge the transference implications. But it was much more difficult for Nancy to see the games with Sally or the provocation of Fenton as "acting."

During this period of acting I chose to deal mainly with the defensive aspects of the acting. I was able to show Nancy how she was afraid that her analysis would take away what she called her "boy part," how being a girl made her feel helpless at times, and how with me, with Fenton, and with Sally, she seemed to be telling a story over and over again of a helpless girl and a dangerous and terrible man who would command the girl to do all kinds of shameful and humiliating acts for his pleasure. The resistance dissolved and then, one day, Nancy arrived for her hour visibly distraught and told me a terror dream which she had the night before.

"My cat had kittens, but she had four kittens and two snakes. I watched them come out of her. The snakes escape and the whole family tries to get them out of the house. There are three little panels like doors in the house and if you could get the snakes through the little doors you could get them out of the house. . . . Then the snakes got into a fight. One was 'a rattler' and one was 'a gardener snake' [her words] and it was like they were wrestling together. Then the rattler stuck his head right into the mouth of the gardner snake and killed him."

It was this dream that led us into another dimension of the primal scene material. The anxiety centered in the snake fight; as Nancy described the killing of the "gardener snake," she cupped one hand and pushed a finger through the hole, a gesture that she had employed earlier in analysis during a period when she was trying to figure out with my help how the penis could enter the woman. As other details of the dream emerged in this and subsequent hours Nancy herself could make the connections between the terror dream and a sexual observation. "The whole thing must have looked like a fight to me and I thought someone was going to get hurt. The woman." Other details brought associations to mouth, teeth, biting, and the thought, "He had stolen the penis from the woman."

During the analysis of this material Nancy's parents took a two-week holiday. Typically, during parental holidays Nancy reacted with no conscious feelings of loss, but almost invariably she developed a cold, a sore throat, or an earache. Within a few days Nancy called, asking to cancel her appointment because she had a sore throat and sniffles. She had no temperature. I encouraged her to keep her appointment. When she arrived she looked quite miserable. She complained of a stuffy nose. Her eyes were tearing. "But I don't feel really sick. And the worst thing isn't the cold. I feel *hungry*, terribly hungry, just starving. But not *really* hungry. It isn't like I could eat something and feel better."

I was able to show Nancy how the hunger was connected with longing for her mother and how the tearing eyes and congested nose represented the suppressed tears. And then I could encourage the expression of grief and longing more directly. During the next three hours Nancy was overwhelmed by feelings of love for her mother and longing for her return. As the tears began to come freely in analytic hours the cold symptoms diminished—an exchange that greatly impressed Nancy. Then through a piece of acting and a new set of symptoms we were able to establish connections between this separation from the parents and an earlier, traumatic separation.

There was a fight with Fenton, not so different from a number of other fights with Fenton, and again there were the fears of Fenton and what he might do to her. But this time Nancy's own destructive rage toward Fenton broke through. "I'm afraid I could kill him! I hate him! There will never be enough years to get rid of my hate by talking about it."

Then, in a rapid development during the second week of the parents' absence, a group of facial tics made their appearance. These consisted of a widening of the eyes, a wrinkling of the nose, a distorted grimacing and stretching of the mouth. When I now saw this group of tics in a constellation, I realized that each of these tics had appeared fleetingly at one time or another during the past months, but until this week we had never seen anything like this. I drew Nancy's attention to this new group of symptoms and began to suggest a meaning in terms of body language. When Nancy could finally acknowledge the tics as symptoms, she also told me with some surprise that they appeared *only* in her analytic hours. I was later able to confirm this.

Nancy could provide no associations to the tics and I had to suggest the meaning to her, i.e., "To see something frightening," "disgust," "horror." I suggested to her that the tics represented memories in the same way that the cold symptoms and the hunger were ways of remembering an earlier time when mother and father were away. And if we added to this group of symptoms the fight with Fenton, and the dream of the snake fight that we had left incompletely analyzed, we now had a picture, I proposed, of that time that was not remembered, when Nancy had observed the couple. The tics and the cold symptoms disappeared shortly afterwards.

The analysis of the snake dream, the repetitious features of the illness during separation from the parents, the acting with Fenton, and the tics were employed for reconstruction in this child analysis in a manner that closely followed the adult model. As memories and their associated affects were revived and re-experienced by the child, I helped Nancy see how the memory had been broken up into several components and how the fragments could be reassembled to tell a story. In my own reconstruction I proposed that during the period of the parents' absence at three, Nancy had experienced the same sadness and longing for her parents that we had seen in the more recent separation. I suggested that the three-year-old Nancy might have developed a cold or a sore throat in the same way as she repeatedly did when her parents were absent during the time I had known her. She may have awakened at night in discomfort or pain and gone in search of Cassie. At the door of Cassie's room she heard voices which later appeared in the chessboard fantasy as mumbling or jabbering. She entered the room and saw the couple in intercourse. What she saw she interpreted as "fighting," "attack," and the castration of a woman by a man, as we saw in the analysis of the snake dream. She was frightened and "left in a hurry," as we saw in the transference during the analysis. She was either afraid to tell about what she had seen or had been told not to tell, something we inferred through transference behavior at one point in the analysis. During the first period following the observation and before the memory was completely repressed, a group of tics may have appeared; in these the experience which could not be told was represented in symptoms, possibly identical with those she had recently experienced in the analysis. (I should mention, however, that the parents were unable to confirm my hypothesis regarding the tics. They had never seen these tics and had no memory of ticlike symptoms at an earlier age.)

This phase of the analysis of the primal scene observation produced demonstrable effects in Nancy's personality. In the months that followed we began to see the emergence of a new integrity of the ego replacing the unstable bisexual integrity that had disposed the ego to neurosis. There was a new energy and self-confidence, satisfaction in femininity, and heightened pleasure in learning, friendship and new endeavors. No new symptoms appeared and the old symptoms which had dropped out or receded in the earlier phases of analysis now seemed definitely out of the picture.

**Discussion**

The excerpts from the case of Nancy were arbitrarily chosen in order to follow a single theme, a primal scene memory, as it emerged in the transference. The material demonstrates that a transference neurosis appeared in the analysis of this child in latency, that it manifested itself in ways analogous to those of the adult model, and that the analysis permitted technical handling which closely followed that of adult analysis. My own experience and that of other child analysts can provide a number of such examples in practice.

Both Sara Kut (1953) and Sylvia Brody (1961) have written about transference in prepuberty and puberty and have provided illustrations which show a close correspondence in certain features to the transference neurosis obtained in adult analysis. Both writers attribute the readiness to form a transference neurosis in prepuberty and puberty to the growing independence of the child from the original objects. Sylvia Brody asks the question "whether we have not discounted too readily the significance of transference neurosis in children, or relied too little on its appearance" (p. 252). Anna Freud (1945) wrote of "the open and controversial question as to whether the relationship of the child to the analyst is really wholly governed by a transference situation." She said, "Even if one part of the child's neurosis is transformed into a transference neurosis as it happens in adult analysis, another part of the child's neurotic behavior remains grouped around the parents who are the original objects of his pathogenic past" (p. 130).

The illustrations from Nancy's case show us that latency may also provide conditions favorable to the establishment of a transference neurosis, that the factor of independence from the original objects is not the only criterion. But "the open question" which Anna Freud raises must be raised in this case, too. For while the primal scene material appeared in the form of a transference neurosis and its correspondence to the adult model is demonstrable, the full report of this case would demonstrate that the whole of this child's analysis did not come under the influence of a transference neurosis.

During the first two years of Nancy's analysis transference manifestations were employed extensively in the analytic work and with great profit in reviving memories and affects of certain events that had preceded the outbreak of the neurosis. As these memories were revived they were tranferred, but they were also relived or re-experienced with the original objects, and this does not correspond to "acting in the transference" but to the mode of childhood, the translation of memories into actions and the availability of the original cast of characters for repetition and undoing.

Examples: When the analysis revived a memory of a traumatic episode of sex play between Nancy and her little friend, Mike, and Nancy experienced in her analytic hour the feelings of longing and humiliation, she did not re-experience this in the form of a love conflict or a feeling of rejection in the transference. She left the hour full of fury toward her faithless friend of four years ago and went in search of him. She found him dawdling in the front yard of his house, picked up a handful of mud and pelted him. She pursued him down the street flinging mud and insults at him.

Similarly, when Nancy in the second year of analysis re-experienced the love and longing for her mother that had undergone a transformation with the onset of the neurosis, it came about in this way: she produced fantasies in her analytic hours in which the queen was stolen from the king by a robber. However, when the affects themselves were revived during this period, they were not transferred to me, but re-experienced as love and yearning for the mother. In these examples we only confirm that which we already know about the child patient in analysis, namely, that the child who still possesses the original objects can relive on the home grounds certain conflicts which, in the adult patient, can be reproduced only in transference.

But now we are obliged to take into account that the primal scene material in Nancy's case was reproduced in the form of a transference neurosis and that the recovery of memories from the third year was achieved almost exclusively from the analysis of the transference neurosis. The analytic material provides its own answer. *For this memory was, properly speaking, "repressed."* It could be revived only in transference, in analogy with the conditions that facilitate the formation of a transference neurosis in adults. In the earlier period of analysis, when the analytic work centered mainly on the defenses against affects and the recovery of experiences that had led to the onset of the neurosis, the case material would show that these memories had undergone only partial repression. Once the affective links were restored each of the memories came through clearly and without distortion. To a very large extent these memories were re-experienced with the original cast of characters.

I believe that the question of "availability of the original objects" can also be qualified by a study of "kind and degree of repression." A brief example from Nancy's case illustrates the problem. I have already mentioned that the tender tie to the mother was revived in the analysis and experienced directly in relation to the mother, without transference manifestations as far as I could judge; but the erotic tie to mother emerged in the later analysis in the form of a transference fantasy. In one of Nancy's fantasies I was represented as a seducer of girls. When the fantasy was analyzed in the transference, memories of a very primitive kind emerged, a tactile memory of a hand, the rough texture of cloth, sensations of smoothness and roughness, and then a picture swam into consciousness of a mother bathing a little girl and washing her genitals. This memory, from a period under three years of age, could find its way into consciousness only by means of the transference. And unlike the earlier example of the tender feelings toward mother, the erotic tie to mother did not seek repetition with the mother herself, but found representation in a transference fantasy. Here, we have another demonstration of a memory that is, properly speaking, repressed and a libidinal aim that has undergone repression, both of which unite in a transference fantasy and in a manner entirely analogous to that of the adult transference neurosis. And while the original object, the mother, was still available, repression of the libidinal aim had prevented the repetition with the original object.

Where even a part of the child's neurosis is transformed into a transference neurosis the advantages for the child analysis will be as great as for the adult analysis. For it may be that only in this way can the analyst have access to the deepest layers of the neurosis. In the case of Dorothy, which I cited at the beginning of this paper, it was my failure to explore the dimensions of the transference that left untouched a pathogenic core that lay dormant and in a state of readiness to produce new symptoms in adolescence.

*Note*

This paper was presented at the Panel on Latency at the Fall Meeting of the American Psychoanalytic Association, December 4, 1964.

*References*

Brody, S. (1961). Some Aspects of Transference Resistance in Prepuberty. *Psychoanal. Study Child,* 16:251–274.

Fraiberg, S. (1951). Clinical Notes on the Nature of Transference in Child Analysis. *Psychoanal. Study Child,* 6:286–306.

Freud, A. (1945). Indications for Child Analysis. *Psychoanal. Study Child,* 1:127–149.

Kut, S. (1953). The Changing Pattern of Transference in the Analysis of an Eleven-year-old Girl. *Psychoanal. Study Child,* 8:355–378.

# 15

# The Clinical Dimension of Baby Games

Our longitudinal studies of infants blind from birth included interpersonal games as an area in which reciprocity between the baby and his partners could be examined in fine detail. Observations of games were recorded, along with all other data, in descriptive narratives by the observers in their twice-monthly home visits. Once-monthly film documentation also included "games" sequences. The games included a large number of the traditional nursery games and a number of games which appeared to have no tradition and were inventions of the parents themselves.

It was not until I completed the data sorting and constructed individual profiles for a study of human attachments that a "games story" emerged. I then saw that there was a remarkable correspondence between the characteristics of the *invented* games and the characteristics of parent-child interaction derived from all other observations in the area of human attachment. In many cases the conflictual elements in the parents' relationship to the blind infant, the defenses or the failure of defenses against negative and forbidden impulses, could be read as fairly through the games profile as through the human attachment profile derived from all other sources of study. This is not to say, of course, that the baby games provided as much information as the larger study, but rather that the baby games were equivalent, in some ways, to a projective test in revealing the main lines of harmony and conflict in parent-child relationships.

The children are blind, but our findings should not be interpreted as "blind baby and parent games," rather as "baby games" in which parents at play reveal to the clinician some aspects of their conflicted parenthood. We can read adaptive defenses at work as well as the tendencies that are generating further conflict in the parent-child relationship. In this way, I am suggesting, the observations of baby games can serve as a valuable diagnostic tool to all clinicians who are engaged in the study of parent-child interaction. (We have already learned in the past year, through our guidance program for sighted infants with emotional and cognitive disturbances, that the study of "baby games" may illuminate many aspects of parent-child interaction which are normally closed during the earliest period of assessment and diagnosis.)

In this paper, I have selected a group of case illustrations in which the "baby games" can be examined in relationship to conflictual elements in the parenting.

### General Characteristics of Sample: Notes on Observational Procedures

In introducing this material, we should first address ourselves to questions which arise from the nature of this sample and the observational methods. (1) What are the general characteristics of our sample? (2) Was there bias in our observational procedures which might distort the inferences from baby games?

1. Our observations are drawn from two groups of blind infants and young children known to our program between the years 1963 and 1973. Group I is the Restricted Research sample, the primary group in our longitudinal studies. N = 10. (Criteria: total blindness from birth or light perception only; no other handicaps; available for study within the first year of life.) Group II is the Consultation-Guidance sample. N = 71. (Criteria: blind infants and young children referred to us for developmental guidance; children who do not qualify for primary group; other handicaps accepted; all degrees of educational blindness; entrance into program at any point in the first three years.) It should be noted that our developmental guidance program was available to both Groups I and II (Fraiberg et al., 1969; Fraiberg, 1971b).

The range of socioeconomic status fairly represented the general population. The geographic limits which we accepted included urban and rural populations within a radius of fifty miles of Ann Arbor, Michigan.

The parents of our blind children had in common their grief, their anxieties for the child, their shattered daydreams, guilt and self-recriminations, and a helpless anger against a fate which had sent them a defective baby. With all this they were also faced with the extraordinary problems of raising a blind child whose adaptive incapacities require special forms of parenting, and whose development normally follows unfamiliar pathways.

All of this adds up to a very large number of hazards and potential hazards for the development of the blind infant and the formation of stable human bonds between the baby and his partners. For the parents themselves, the conflicted emotions produced by the birth of the defective child might lead the clinician to predict a conflicted partnership with the baby in every case.

Yet, in spite of the fact that we had a sample in which conflicted parenthood is the common condition, our experience shows that the majority of our parents did not inflict their pain upon the blind baby. Our study of the qualitative aspects of parent-child attachments gives eloquent testimony for the ascendency of protective love over anger and grief under circumstances which cruelly test that love.

The children themselves provided their own testimony for the qualities of parental love and nurture. With few exceptions, these imperiled babies achieved stable love bonds and demonstrated preference, valuation, and love of their parents in ways that can be fairly compared to the characteristics of human attachments in sighted children (Fraiberg, 1968, 1971a). Similarly, where the developing ego of the young child provides its own tests of adequacy in love and nurture, the majority of our children in Group I demonstrated adaptive capacities and developmental achievements which placed them in the upper half of a blind child population on all measures. While we credit our guidance program for some of these achievements, we must fairly credit the parents who were able to use our guidance.

2. There was no bias in our observational procedures which would have favored "baby games" over any other aspect of parent-child interaction. In our study of human attachments in blind infants, we recorded in descriptive detail all aspects of parent-child interaction in feeding and care-giving circumstances, in the tactile-vocal-auditory dialogue, in discrimination of parent and strangers, in separation and reunion behaviors. The game observations constituted one of twenty-five major categories in human attachments; we did not attribute special significance to games during our data-collection period. (My own bias was actually in favor of the significance of nurturing behavior, and in the games study I was really looking for something else. I had

included games in order to examine the purely social aspects of parent and blind infant reciprocity. I was looking for cooperation in games, the beginnings of baby initiative in games, etc.)

## What Can Baby Games Tell Us?

We should not be surprised to see that adults "at play" with a baby may use the freedom and the privilege of play to express love in many dimensions and many styles, to express anxiety, hostility, and even sadism in "the harmless game" or the "nonsense" of baby talk. If we grant ambivalence to all parents, and concede a larger measure of conflict to parents of a blind baby, we might also expect that the invented games of our parents would reflect these conflicts, rendered "harmless" in play.

This, in itself, adds little to our understanding of conflicted parenthood or the nature of play. But games and play have another function; they regulate, through ritual and through the conventional disguises of play, the discharge of forbidden impulses. In the case of parent and baby there is a biological contract, as old as the race, which normally guarantees that the love bonds will protect the baby against harmful or potentially harmful parental impulses, that aggressive impulses will not be discharged in physical acts against the body of the baby and must find pathways away from the body and the person of the baby. Normally, the game circumstance permits discharge in ways that are harmless to the baby, and the game conventions afford regulation and inhibition of hostile motives. If we are interested in the clinical significance of games, we will be as attentive to the defenses and regulation of discharge as to the conflictual material which is revealed in play.

In the following sections I shall present selections from a group of baby games from our narrative records, films, and videotapes of blind infants and their parents at play. I have chosen games illustrations from seven cases. For examination of the diagnostic problem, I propose that we arrange them in a contrast series. Two cases (Carol and Jamie) provide good examples of invented parental games in a category which I will call "Parental Conflict and Defense." (The game is, indeed, a harmless expression of parental conflict and the unconscious hostile motive is maintained in repression.) Five cases (Robbie, Ronnie, Jackie, Timmy, and Ernie) provide illustrations of a second category which we may call "Parental Conflict and Acting Out." (In these cases, hostile, sadistic, or erotic motives break through in the "harmless" game and the affective component emerges undisguised.) The five cases in the "Acting Out" group are exceptional ones.

For illustration, then, two cases in the "Defense" group adequately describe the normal function of games and play as seen in the majority of our cases. Here the game follows a familiar and unremarkable course. It maintains the function of rendering harmless unconscious motives. The five cases in the "Acting Out" group are both atypical and of particular clinical interest. The games "rules" are broken by the parents in conflict, and harmful impulses break through the defense barriers. In retrospective analysis these "Acting Out" games informed us of "danger" in many cases before other information was available to us. As a measure of pathological conflict in parenthood, the "Acting Out" games both described and predicted present and future disturbances of parent-child relationships with a fidelity which invites extended inquiry with other populations of at-risk infants.

It is important to note that the conditions of our intervention did not give us the privilege of the psychotherapist in making a clinical inquiry. While the observers and the guidance workers were trained clinicians, our parents had not come to us for psychotherapy, but for developmental guidance on behalf of their blind infant. Where pathological conflicts existed in the parents and when psychotherapy was indicated, or, sometimes, actively sought by one or both parents, we provided that help through mental health agencies in the family's own community. (In some cases it was needed, but not sought or not accepted.)

## Parental Conflict and Defense

In the two cases of Carol and Jamie, a "favorite game" is described. In each case, a parental conflict is revealed in the game which is consonant with clinical observations derived from all other sources of data. The game reveals an unconscious motive, and the game renders these motives harmless. There are many other examples in our records. The examples chosen will strike the reader as unremarkable, which they are. They belong to a repertoire of games which emerge in one form or another among all normal families. They have no morbid significance.

*Carol*

This game, a favorite between Carol and her mother, is a variant of a common nursery game. In citing it, we have no intention of reading "pathology" into this game between an adequate blind baby and a mother whose devotion is unquestioned. It is of interest because "the favorite game" has close correspondence with one area of the mother's greatest concern for her child: "She might fall. . . ."

0:9:5 (on videotape)
Carol is bounced on mother's knee while mother chants the rhyme, "Ride little Horsie/ trot downtown/ watch out Carol/ that you *don't fall down.*" The last phrase of the rhyme is slowed down when spoken, and on the word "down," mother extends her legs so that Carol (who had been seated on her mother's knee) falls backward onto her mother's legs. After a few seconds mother pulls Carol back up. Carol's enjoyment of the game was evident, and she vocalized "dada" and squealed excitedly with each bounce. At the end of the sequence, mother kissed Carol on the cheek.

Carol's mother is devoted to her blind baby and eager for all help that we can give her. But she is apprehensive when Carol pulls to stand, overprotective as Carol experiments in new postures. In spite of Carol's demonstrated readiness for advances in locomotion (creeping, and later, walking), the mother's anxieties sometimes impede Carol's experimentation. We understand that she had centered her unconscious anxieties about her blind baby in a fear that the baby might fall. This, in fact, is the only area in which mother's anxiety is an impediment to Carol's development.

In the "favorite game" mother's anxieties are given a voice and Carol becomes a game partner where falling down is safe, ritualized, rendered harmless in play. Is there an unconscious wish concealed in the fears that the baby will fall? This may be, yet the unconscious wish is maintained in repression and it is not directed against the child in the form of aggressive acts. The game is a paradigm here, for in no observations that we have in our records is a destructive wish openly expressed in words or acts. Mother's conflictual feelings about Carol may be responsible for a slight delay in taking first steps (this is achieved at eighteen months, in the low range for Group I babies), but the unconscious hostile impulse is not directed against the baby, and, in analogy with mother's defense, the baby is protected by love against the unconscious motives.

*Jamie*

> 1:1:9
> Jamie's father has taught him a game. When father says, "Tarzan! Tarzan!" Jamie starts thumping his chest, imitating the Tarzan call. This is regularly greeted by laughter in the family, and Jamie joins in with his own laughter.

Jamie's father's grief at the birth of his blind baby was overwhelming. It was many months before he could accept the fact that his son was blind. The wound to his own masculinity was very large, but he bore it with courage. The Tarzan game is an eloquent and touching statement of the father's shattered daydreams of a strong and powerful manchild, but the game is a harmless playing out of the old dream and the child's play-acting makes him a partner in the impossible daydream.

From all other observations of Jamie in his family, we know that the father has never inflicted his own pain on his child. He is a loving, tender man, adored by his blind child, and the love of his child has, to some measure, healed the wound.

Assuming that all parents have ambivalent feelings at one time or another toward the infant or young child, and considering especially the conflicted feelings of parents toward a blind child, it is impressive to see in our records the range of behavior manifest in our parent-child observations. The majority of parents protected the child from the acting out of their own aggression. While many of the examples that I shall now cite show the breakthrough of conflictual feelings and even direct hostility toward a damaged child, the largest number of the parents known to us did not inflict their pain upon the child.

## Parental Conflict and Acting Out

In a continuum from "Defense" to "Acting Out," the five cases described in this section represent a contrast group. They represent a small segment of the group of eighty-one cases, but in every case parental conflict engaged the baby as a partner in acting out. The baby games both described and predicted conflict between parents and child. Again, as with the "Defense" games, the "Acting Out" games were consonant with all other data in parent-child interaction which were available to us. As an early indicator of pathology in the parents and in parent-child relationships, these games should be regarded as clinically significant and merit study.

## Robbie

In a family in which domestic argument and aggression are commonplace, the invented games in Robbie's record become a paradigm for family relationships and show how the baby becomes a partner in conflict.

0:9:8
Mother has invented a "no" game with Robbie. Mother is very proud of Robbie's new achievements. He can pat-a-cake on request. He has also learned to shake his head "no" on request.
"Say 'no,' Robbie," says mother. Robbie shakes his head in response to her words. Mother (proudly), "He's so cute when he says 'no.' "

We may wonder why a mother would take pride in teaching her baby to say "no." In our records we can follow a curious correspondence between this game and characteristics in the mother's personality. "Negativism" is one of the distinguishing characteristics of her personality. In our work with Robbie's mother, she first negated nearly all the suggestions and help offered her by our staff. Our records tell a story of "first negating," "then affirming," in a pattern which we learned to use. Weeks after negating a suggestion, Robbie's mother would employ it, unselfconsciously, as an idea of her own. After making the suggestion her own (and typically without any memory of its source), she could use it; it became her own invention. Her pride in Robbie's "no" tells us how this trait in herself is narcissistically cathected. It is of some interest that among all of our blind children in the second and third year of life, Robbie ranks high above his peers in the traits of negativism and obstinacy.

1:0:19
Mother boasted about another "trick" which they have taught Robbie. She holds him close to her face and says, "Robbie, slap mommy." Robbie pats his mother's face. Mother claims that he "slaps" in anger, but we have no demonstration of this.

How did the game get started? Father tells this story: Robbie was patting father's face in an affectionate manner when mother said, "Slap daddy, Robbie." Father then took Robbie's hand and slapped mommy's face, saying, "Slap mama, Robbie." Now Robbie can "slap" on request.

Here, the game speaks eloquently for another aspect of the family; the child becomes an instrument for parental acting out of aggression against each other (a recurrent theme in our record). Again, an irony that we see later in Jackie's story: the aggression which is nurtured in infancy brings the two-year-old into conflict with his parents. Complaints in the second and third year have to do with Robbie's impulsiveness, his "stubbornness," and his "meanness."

The two games that I have cited, the only "invented games" that we have in our records of Robbie during this period, have perfect correspondence with a body of observations in parent-child relationships in Robbie's records during this period. The adversary relationship was well on its way. In feeding, in discipline, we saw variations of the theme. The games can be regarded as revelations through play of a central tendency evolving in the relationship of parent and child.

Yet, in order not to distort the picture, I should mention that Robbie demonstrated adequacy in other aspects of development. In language, concept development, and motor achievements, Robbie's development was not impaired as judged by our assessment at the three-year termination date.

Much help was given by us to the family during the first three years of Robbie's life, and the parents were able to use this help in many critical areas for promoting the child's development. We were, however, least effective in modifying the adversary relationship which existed in this family and which brought the baby into conflict with his parents. This must be regarded as a limitation of our guidance methods. Our guidance program was an educational program. Our parents did not come to us as patients. To modify the adversary relationships within this family we would have needed the permission and the privilege of psychotherapy to explore these relationships and bring about changes through insight.

### Ronnie

During the first year of Ronnie's life, the conflictual elements in his parents' feelings toward the blind baby were revealed in a sequence of games. In the early weeks we saw much tenderness on the part of both parents toward their baby. They could not fully share their grief with us, and since no parents in our program had come to us as psychiatric patients, we did not have the privilege that is given us in psychotherapy to explore the dimensions of their grief and conflicting emotions. Only when parents wished to share their feelings with us did we feel we were granted the privilege, and in the case of Ronnie's parents, we felt ourselves closed out.

During the first three months of our observations (Ronnie was first seen by us soon after birth), we have numerous examples in our records of joyful exchanges with mother in games, in feeding, and in bath play. "Give mommy a kiss," "give mommy a hug," were favorite games. Then a puzzle appears. It is a game which is curiously out of context in the record of affectionate play between mother and child.

The game is "hit mommy!" and a variation is "hit baby!"

0:3:9

Mother shows us a game that Ronnie "enjoys very much." With Ronnie lying on her lap, she holds his arms and brings his hands to her cheek in a striking motion and says, "Hit mama! Hit mama!" She repeats this chant for a minute or so with sustained movements. Ronnie smiles. Then mother takes Ronnie's hands and taps them lightly against his cheeks and says, "Hit baby! Hit baby!" Ronnie again laughs.

During this same period the love games continue: "Give mommy a kiss!" "Give mommy a hug!" and Ronnie showed much enjoyment in these games.

Between three months and six months the number of aggressive games begins to proliferate. At five months of age, we begin to see even more ominous signs. Ronnie is hitting himself in the mouth. It is the "hit baby" game now employed for self-stimulation.

0:5:3

He is very much absorbed in his private game and when mother attempts to join him in the game, he becomes fretful at the interference with his own activity. He immediately goes back to the game, striking himself repetitiously in the mouth with his fist.

One months later we have more examples of aggressive games with father.

0:6:10
Ronnie is playing with father. Father says, "Hit daddy! Hit daddy!" and takes Ronnie's hand in his, striking his own face with the baby's hand. Ronnie smiles briefly and then comes closer to father's face. Father says, "Bite daddy's nose! Bite daddy's nose!" Ronnie leans over and bites father's nose.

Between six months and twelve months we witness a gradual deterioration in the relationship between parents and baby. Offers of help from us are turned aside by the parents. We are permitted to visit regularly, to make observations, but the parents were seeking educational counseling elsewhere in the community. The advice they were receiving from another handicapped child program was very different from our own. Sternness, forcefulness, "early discipline" were now the principles which Ronnie's parents were following. (It was, we feared, a more congenial advice to Ronnie's parents.)

We then became helpless witnesses to increasing conflict between Ronnie and his parents. We had the impression that a critical change was taking place in the relationship of parents and baby, yet much information was withheld from us by the parents, who refused our guidance program. When the full year of records is reread, we see that the story could be read through the games.

While the "Hit mama, hit daddy, bite daddy's nose" games proliferated in the record, we also saw something new in the love games between mother and child. Our staff reviewed a play sequence between Ronnie and mother on film and in the records.

0:11:20
We are struck by the sensuality of mother's kisses, an open-mouthed, prolonged, lover's kiss, which the baby sustains with her.

During the same period, eight to twelve months, it is fair to mention that Ronnie's spontaneous gestures of affection, reaching up to kiss his mother, embracing his mother, extending his arms to mother to be picked up, would testify for libidinal investment of the mother. But we need the erotic kissing games to give us another dimension of the mother-child relationship.

The story of the baby games throughout the first year of Ronnie's life were telling an eloquent story. The aggressive "hit mama, hit daddy" games, along with many examples of tender and affectionate games, were already a sign that hostile feelings on the part of the parents were breaking through the protective boundaries of love. And the mother's sensual kissing, the lover's kiss, which we saw in the last months of the first year, were signs that erotic feelings had broken through the boundaries that normally protect the maternity of a woman and the libidinal development of her child.

It was very painful for our staff to review Ronnie's records. Since we had always placed clinical considerations above our research objectives, the parents' firm refusal of our guidance program placed us in the position of helpless witnesses to the unfolding of a tragedy. Ronnie, who was later seen at our hospital at the age of six, some years after the family had terminated its relationship to us, was a severely disturbed child, impaired in all aspects of interpersonal relationships, in language, mobility, and impulse control.

### Jackie

In Jackie's family, oral aggression is a dominant mode. The mother's periodic depressions (which antedated the birth of the blind baby) and her compulsive eating give their own testimony for oral-sadistic conflicts. "Love games" between mother and baby are playful biting games in which the baby at seven months solemnly accepts the playful nips, and at nine months responds with appreciative laughter. In our records there are no descriptions of tender kissing or embracing.

0:9:24
Mother says Jackie "loves" being bitten and "eaten" in his chest. She holds him against her and begins chewing his shoulder. Jackie responds with great smiles and laughter.

0:11:26
Jackie has a game with mother. Seated on her lap, back against her chest, he will lean forward, then backward, banging against her chest. Mother says he mainly plays this game with her. "He likes to beat me," she says fondly.

At an age when blind as well as sighted children can respond to simple requests, "Where is your nose?" or "Let's play pat-a-cake," we have only one example in Jackie's records.

0:9:8
When mama says, "Where is your tongue, Jackie?" he complies by sticking out his tongue. (Mother is vastly amused.)

Throughout our records, biting games and other aggressive games proliferate in this family, and Jackie becomes an active partner in them. The encouragement, and indeed the education of aggressive acts against the body of a partner, can begin early in life. The mother's enjoyment of the body-banging game, "he likes to beat me," speaks for her aggressive-erotic characteristics (very largely documented in our records), and the games with the baby tell us how such characteristics can be transmitted to a very small child. Ironically, when Jackie is in the second and third years of life, the aggression which was nurtured in infancy brings him into serious conflict with his parents.

*Timmy*

Timmy's mother is very tender and protective. His father is a man who values his own rough masculinity. The birth of a blind son has been a severe wound to his masculinity. He cannot confide his grief and pain to our educational consultant, who visits regularly. He plays rough games with his baby, which the baby endures helplessly. "Timmy likes to play rough," says his father. When our consultant points out Timmy's evident distress, the father brusquely disagrees. In this way, we become pained and helpless witnesses to a story of father-baby conflict which unfolds through "the harmless games."

0:1:26 (on videotape)
Father is playing with Timmy. At first impression, the game looks like an unextraordinary father-baby roughhousing. Then father's own actions begin to acquire an intensity, a physical energy that is more than playful aggression.

What is the father saying? The sound track is poor; he seems to be uttering gibberish. When we turn up the volume, we hear the words distinctly.

Father puts Timmy on his lap and begins to play with him. He taps Timmy's fisted hands, knocking them up and down. Father now plays with the baby's feet, something he calls "running" Timmy, holding him by the feet and moving his legs rapidly up and down. Father briskly pats Timmy's bottom as though spanking him and says, "You're bad . . . again." He then holds Timmy's arms and moves them in a mock boxing motion. He says, "Bet you like to be beat up, you like to fight. I could break you right in half. . . . "

[Later:] Father holds Timmy supine and elevated in his arms. He throws Timmy up a foot in the air and catches him several times. The consultant indicates her worry about Timmy falling. Father says humorously, "No. He won't fall. If he falls, that'll be the last time."

For Timmy's father (and his mother too), these are "harmless games" and "words in jest." To us, as clinical observers, these games were already revelations of conflict and danger. In reviewing this tape as a staff, we shared the alarm that our consultant had experienced as a witness in the home. It was the breakthrough of hostile affect that disturbed us.

These father-baby games, with only slight variations, are witnessed frequently in the months that follow. Our consultant repeatedly expresses her concern and tries to reach the father's conflicted feelings in areas that are accessible in the home visits, but the father is defensive. It appears to us that he is not even aware of the strength of his ambivalent feelings. "I'm gonna beat ya," "I'm gonna break you in half" becomes a ritualized speech in these games for many months, and the father, borrowing the protection and disguise of the game, can see this only as play.

Timmy's mother, who is always a witness, sometimes utters small protests when father's games become too rough, but more often she is the silent observer. Her own mothering capacities are very large. She is normally protective and tender. What prevents her from acting assertively to protect her baby in these rough games? She is, without any conscious intention, a co-conspirator, a silent partner.

Yet, the good aspects of mothering serve Timmy well for many months. He is a very responsive baby, deeply attached to his mother, and is progressing well in language and social development.

At thirteen months of age, the games between father and baby disintegrate. The father's destructive rage, which had emerged in muted form in play, words, and a too real pantomime of physical fighting, now breaks through in an act of abuse.

1:1:3
Father picks up Timmy and swings him roughly to one side. Timmy is frightened and begins to cry. . . . Father places him on the floor supine. . . . He is playing with a bell. When the bell drops, father returns

it. First he touches it gently to Timmy's stomach. Then, a sudden shift
of mood and intention. Father picks up the bell and strikes Timmy in
the genitals. Timmy screams. The father, strangely, is not contrite. The
mother makes no attempt to rescue Timmy.

At this point, our own alarm for Timmy and for his parents brings
us to move directly into the parental conflicts which are endangering
Timmy. In private sessions with the father, our consultant begins the
work which centers around the father's own pain and uncontrolled
anger which had emerged in the episode of abuse. There are no further
episodes of abuse. The "rough games" are moderated.

Timmy's father, at the time of this writing (Timmy's age: twenty
months), has found new satisfactions through his baby. Now there are
gentle and affectionate lap games in which Timmy and his father
carry on "conversations."

In Timmy's case, the baby games told their own story of conflicted
parenthood. The hostile and destructive wishes of the father were
barely disguised; the breaking through of affect in the games was ominous. When we witnessed the chilling episode in which the father
struck his baby's genitals, the full meaning of the games was disclosed. The cruel unconscious statement was, "This is where you hurt
me; this is where I will hurt you."

*Ernie*

Ernie is first seen in our program at 1:4:11. His mother is severely
depressed: the baby is neglected, retarded in all aspects of development. The baby is fearful—with cause—of the mother whose neglect
provides more safety than her attentions.

1:11:21
When mother feeds Ernie his bottle, she intentionally teases him,
stimulating his mouth with the nipple and withdrawing it. . . .
    Mother describes (with joy) a game in which she likes to "sneak up
on Ernie" because he can't see her. (Until the guidance worker discusses
the implications of "sneaking up" on a blind child, mother seemed unaware of its meaning.)
    Mother shows the guidance worker how she persuades Ernie to
creep. Ernie was in bridging position on the floor, rocking back and
forth. Mother: "I'm gonna get you. You'd better crawl away." (The guid-

ance worker notes to herself that Ernie's mother is the rare mother who teaches her child to creep by getting him to move *away* from her.)

There was no evidence of playful interaction between mother and her two boys (Ernie and his older brother) until the end of the hour.

She played a favorite game with them. "I'm gonna get you!" In the game she walked her fingers up their legs. Then she would say, "I got you" and tickled them.

The favorite game is "I'm gonna get you!" in many variations during this period. In itself, it is not yet ominous. There is even a kind of tradition in some families for such "scare-tease" games with babies. But we, in our guidance role, find it very disturbing to watch. The blind baby is frightened, and the mother not only does not see his anxiety, but appears to enjoy it. The guidance worker's tactfully expressed concern does not reach this mother.

Then, in the months that follow, the games begin to take an ominous course. The games and utterances become explicitly hostile and destructive. They are consonant with a large number of observations in the mother-child relationship which create alarm and dread in us.

2:1:2 (communication to guidance worker)
Mother begins to confide her fears to the guidance worker. She is afraid of losing control. She speaks of a man who killed several members of his own family. . . . Tells of a friend's father who had killed his wife with a hunting knife.

The other day, when Ernie was screaming, she had to drop him off at a friend's house. She was afraid she might hurt him.

The guidance worker discusses psychiatric treatment with the mother. (The family lives thirty miles from Ann Arbor.) The mother is reluctant to seek help. People would think she was crazy. All attempts to bring the mother to seek and use help meet opposition from her and her husband. There is a tense period described in the record, while we attempt to bring help to the family from psychiatric and protective agencies in their community and make frequent visits to the home to give support to the mother. No agency in their community wishes to be involved. "There have been no overt acts of child abuse."

During this period the baby games tell their own story, and our alarm grows with every visit.

2:3:26
At the end of the visit, mother picked up Ernie. She held him under his arms and bounced him in the air, saying, "You're too mean to be a baby," and, "I could beat you up!" (The observer notes that there was a tenseness in mother's voice that made her feel these words were not in jest.)

2:4:22
Mother sat Ernie on her lap. She began to play her favorite game. "I'm gonna get you," she said. And this time she closed her hand around the baby's neck, briefly, and then removed it.

The game, "I'm gonna get you," has become chillingly explicit.

She tried to tickle Ernie to make him laugh, but Ernie did not laugh and pushed her hand away. Mother said, "I could break you in two," and jerked at Ernie's crossed hands. Throughout, Ernie looked very apprehensive. . . . The observer notes, "Throughout this sequence mother's behavior was quite frightening to observe. Although she was saying things in a joking manner, there was something in her voice and her intense stare. . . ."

The mother initiates her own plans to place Ernie in an institution. While plans are proceeding for placement of Ernie, the mother's own destructive wishes toward the baby emerge with a terrible explicitness.

2:6:3
While dressing Ernie, mother handles him roughly, "I'm going to throw you against the wall," she says. "I could throw you out the window." When Ernie is dressed, she carries him over to the guidance worker, drops him on the floor and says, "Go see her."

"Throwing out" the baby, "giving him to someone else" is briefly acted out. This is no longer a game, and the utterance of destructive wishes which preceded this act during the dressing period tells us clearly that the placement represents protection of the baby against her own destructive wishes.

When the guidance worker speaks of psychiatric treatment once again in this session, the mother says, "I really belong in a mental institution."

2:6:8
The guidance worker calls "to see how things are." (She is keeping in close touch with the family during this ominous period.) The mother

is in despair. "I would like to shoot him," she says (meaning Ernie), "but I know I couldn't get away with it."

As plans move ahead for placement of Ernie, the mother's explicit destructive wishes begin to diminish. Between the 2:6:8 communication and the time of Ernie's placement at 2:10:23 the mother is more composed than at any other period in our records. There is some ambivalence about placing Ernie, but mother and father clearly have made their decision. The mother is relieved. "To send him away" is protection for the child whose mother is afraid she might kill him.

In this sequence from Ernie's records, the games provide a chilling paradigm for the sadistic conflicts of the mother. Before we can know the depths of this mother's destructive wishes, "the favorite game" is "I'm gonna get you." It is not the game alone that warns us, but the breakthrough of affect in a three-month sequence. The game is no longer a game. As mother's destructive wishes become more and more explicit in her communications to the guidance worker, the games themselves disappear from our records, in analogy with a recurrent dream which dissolves when the hidden motive breaks through disguise. (It should be noted that in our educational program our guidance worker in no way encouraged these revelations of motive.)

As we follow the sequence of baby games along with other observations in mother-infant interaction, we can see how the game at each stage of the record is consonant with other observed events and communications in the area of conflicted motherhood and mother-child interaction.

### Clinical Implications

The baby games in the examples chosen fairly describe conflictual elements in the parent-infant relationship which are supported in these cases through data derived from all other aspects of our study of the parent-child interaction. Our findings suggest that an extended study of "baby games" employing another sample may provide the clinician with a valuable diagnostic instrument for assessment of infant-parent relationships.

Our data also provide caveats for clinical inference. In Carol's mother's game, "Watch out, Carol, that you don't fall down," the unconscious wish "may she fall" does not endanger the child; maternal love, which is also manifest in the game, protects the child, in analogy with the defense, "Don't fall down." The hostile motive is *not* directed toward the child's body or her person in acts or words. On the other hand, Timmy's father, in his game of rough tossing of the baby into the air, expresses his hostile wish in his carelessness and in words, "No, he won't fall. If he falls, that'll be the last time." It is the breakthrough of the wish that is ominous, and it is Timmy's father who later brings his rage into acts of abuse. In Jamie's father's game, "Tarzan," father's wounded masculinity is given an eloquent voice, but the father's injury is not inflicted upon his baby; it is rendered harmless, as in the game. In contrast, we see Timmy's father, in rough and aggressive games in which the wish to hurt comes through in the too energetic play and the hostile words, "I'm gonna beat you . . . I'm gonna break you in half," and, finally, in the climactic striking of his baby's genitals. For Ernie's mother, it is not the tease game, "I'm gonna get you" which has morbid significance, but the breakthrough of sadistic affect in the game, which culminates one day in the words, "I'm gonna get you" and the chilling pantomime in which her hands close around the baby's neck. She is finally afraid, explicitly, that she will kill her child and places him in an institution.

This means, of course, that as we have become attentive to baby games in our new program for a heterogeneous population of at-risk infants, we are interested not only in the content or the dialogue of the game, but in the affect and the defenses against unconscious motives which appear in the game. The game (in analogy with play and jokes) normally serves to keep the unconscious motive and its original affective charge in a state of repression, allowing small charges of affect to emerge in conventional disguise. The game, in this sense, keeps the biological contract in which parental love protects the child against aggression. The aggressive and sadistic games which we have observed are ominous because they betray the wish, make it explicit, and give license for aggressive discharge. The ancient contract is broken; love does not protect against the aggressive wish; the child is in psychological and physical danger.

In our new work we are continuing to examine the clinical dimension of baby games in a population that includes a wide range of infants with developmental disorders and disturbances in their human attachments. Both the "baby games" and "baby talk" (adult monologues with the baby) are enlarging our clinical assessment and providing vital diagnostic information and guidelines for treatment.

## References

Fraiberg, S. (1968). Parallel and Divergent Patterns in Blind and Sighted Infants. *Psychoanal. Study Child,* 23:264–299.
———. (1971a). Intervention in Infancy. *J. Amer. Acad. Child Psychiat.,* 10:381–405.
———. (1971b). Smiling and Stranger Reaction in Blind Infants. In *Exceptional Infant,* ed. J. Hellmuth, vol. 2, pp. 110–127. New York: Brunner/Mazel.
———; Smith, M.; & Adelson, E. (1969). An Educational Program for Blind Infants. *J. Spec. Educ.,* 3:121–139.

**Part III**

Social Work Education

# 16

# On Therapy

Sometimes at social work meetings I have longed for an Alice, a blunt and impertinent child who might come uninvited to our Tea Party and ask the crucial questions. Over the years the fantasy of Alice has taken form in my mind, and I see her now as a second-year graduate student in a school of social work, earnest, intelligent, and unabashed. I really had no intentions of letting her into this paper; she doesn't belong here any more than she belongs in one of our closed meetings, but here she is, unbidden, and determined to be heard.

Enter Alice pursued by an urchin of six with a water pistol. The purple stain on her forehead must not alarm you; it is finger paint and serves to distinguish this tribe of social workers from all others.

"This Tea Party is not open to students!" says The Chairman, scowling at Alice and at the six-year-old who is taking deadly aim at him.

"That's why I came," says Alice pertly.

There is brief commotion while the six-year-old sprays his water pistol into The Chairman's face and bolts out the door at a gallop. In the disorder that follows only Alice retains her composure.

"Who is that child?" says The Chairman, mopping his face.

"That's my case, Dudley McPherson," says Alice. "He has enuresis."

"And what brings you here?"

"I have a question."

"State your question briefly and then kindly permit this Tea Party to continue its urgent business."

"My question is," says Alice, "what am I doing?"

The Tea Party is thrown into fresh disorder.

"How extraordinary! The child doesn't know what she is doing!"

"You haven't answered my question," says Alice.

"My dear young lady," says The Chairman, "let me ask you a question. What is your function in this agency?"

"I am a caseworker, a student caseworker, that is."

"Then it should be very obvious to you that what you are doing is casework!"

"It isn't obvious to me at all," says Alice. "Dudley has been squirting that water gun since September, and nothing has worked in this case at all."

"Has there been any movement in the case?" asks a lady in the audience with green finger paint on her forehead.

"Well . . . I have him listed as an active case on my monthly report," says Alice.

"Then there is still hope," says The Chairman heartily.

"What I've been thinking about is this," says Alice. "Isn't there something I might be doing that I'm not doing, something that . . . ?"

"My dear young lady," says The Chairman sharply, "are you suggesting, or are you about to suggest, that a caseworker can do *Therapy!*"

Shocked protests from the audience.

"I apologize for my language," says The Chairman, "but this girl is no longer a child and I must speak frankly to her."

"What does that mean, that word?" says Alice.

The Chairman looks embarrassed.

"Do you mean no one has ever told you?"

"Well, I know there are some things a nice caseworker doesn't do, but whenever I ask about it my supervisor says that I will find out when I am older. Sometimes I've been afraid that I might have done it without knowing it. I wish you'd tell me what it means!"

"Therapy," says The Chairman, averting his eyes, "Therapy is. . . . Damn it, young lady are you sure nobody ever told you about this?"

"Is it when two people love each other very much?" says Alice, wanting to be helpful.

"No!"

At this moment a Dormouse who has been sitting inconspicuously at the tea table, reaches into the samovar and pulls out *Webster's Collegiate Dictionary*. He is applauded wildly for his presence of mind.

"Therapy," he reads, "(1) therapeutics. (2) therapeutic nature or power. Therapeutics. (1) serving to cure or heal; curative."

In the pained silence that follows, Alice speaks.

"Why, what's wrong with that? Isn't that just what we want to do, serving to cure or heal?"

"You see!" says a lady in the audience, leaping to her feet. "You tell them about it and the first thing you know they want to do it."

There are cries for order and The Chairman recovers himself. He addresses himself to Alice's question.

"My dear Alice," he says, with commendable patience, "the desire to cure or heal is not abnormal. We now know that these desires arise in all caseworkers and there is no need to feel ashamed of them. It's like hunger or thirst. But when the desire to cure or heal leads a caseworker to commit Therapy, then she is going too far. If there are caseworkers who are doing Therapy, then they must know in their innermost selves that they shouldn't be doing it, and if caseworkers are not doing it then they must take care to see that whatever it is they are doing should not be done in such a way that it can be called Therapy."

"Suppose whatever it is they are doing results in curing and healing. Isn't that Therapy?" says Alice, addressing the Dormouse.

The Dormouse, who has been dozing during the liveliest parts of this discussion, is roused by his neighbor who shouts in his ear.

"What's that?" screams the Dormouse. "I never said it. I was only quoting Webster, and he's not an authority on casework practice. In casework we mean whatever we say we mean!"

His words are madly applauded.

"What happens to the caseworker who does Therapy?" says Alice, looking The Chairman straight in the eye.

"My dear Alice," says The Chairman, "I can only wonder again that your supervisor has not told you. You see, the caseworker who allows herself to go All the Way, who commits Therapy, will lose something very precious to her, something that can never be replaced. Something decent and fine in her will be lost forever. And when she graduates—*if* she graduates—this Thing will stand between her and her future happiness."

"You mean," says Alice, "she loses her technical virginity in the field?"

"I wouldn't put it so coarsely," says The Chairman, "and come to think of it young lady, if I were the dean of *your* school of social work, I'd want to have a talk with you—soon."

## 17

# Some Aspects of Casework with Children

**Part 1: Understanding the Child Client**

There is a certain type of client who creates special problems in the administration of social agencies and in the interviewing situation. This client seems totally unable to comprehend the function of a social agency. He frequently creates disorder and chaos in the waiting room. Often he talks loudly and shrilly, demanding numerous attentions, and has been known to look boldly over the shoulder of a typist as she transcribes confidential reports. In the initial interview with the caseworker, this client states more or less positively that he has no problem and he does not know why he has come to the agency. Further difficulties are encountered when it appears that he cannot sit in a chair for more than five minutes. He tends to concentrate on irrelevant matters like the operation of the Venetian blinds, the counting of squares on the asphalt tile floors, the manipulation of paper clips into abstract forms.

The client has neither marital problems nor employment problems. He is not in need of relief, although he will gladly take a hand-out. The sex of the client may be male or female. The age is roughly five to fifteen years. What shall we do with him?

The most disconcerting feature of the child client is his inability to behave like a client. He does not come to us because of his recognition of a need for services or counseling. Someone else—parent, teacher, physician, the court—has made him the reluctant consumer of our services. We are embarrassed by such a client. The body of our techniques is geared to the initial coming together of a willing and needful client and a willing and resourceful social worker. The client who has no recognition of a problem or who, having one, refuses to talk about it, is known as an "unco-operative client."

When we deal with the child client, our concepts of service and responsibility are turned about, for, willing or not, he becomes our client, our problem child. Frequently he, like the adult client, comes to us at a time of crisis in his life. Usually he has not come to us for direct treatment or psychotherapy; he may not even be in need of such treatment. Although a few children may be taken on for direct treatment by the agencies working in the field of family service, child welfare, school social work, juvenile court work, or group work, most child clients come to these agencies either for evaluation and social study or for practical planning and guidance around critical life problems. It is this group, the major category of cases referred to social agencies, with which this discussion is mainly concerned.

What do we mean by "help"? Ronnie is five. His father has deserted the family and the mother has arranged to place him in a foster home. The social worker, the lady who helps children, arrives on the scene. She will help him to find a nice home, she says, where people are very fond of little boys. But does this seem like "help" to a child? How helpful is the lady who takes a little boy away from his mother? We know how it seems to little children: "Mother has not sent me away. The lady has taken me away from mother."

Or it is another crisis. Peter is eight, and is threatened with expulsion from school after a long series of classroom incidents. He is "sent" to see the school social worker for diagnostic study. "This is a man who will help you," he is told. Everyone wants to help Peter. Papa wants to help him and that's why papa beats him with his belt when he is bad. The teachers want to help him, too, and that's why they have to tell him so many things for his own good and why they have to bawl him out even when they don't like to. And now look—here's another person who is going to "help" Peter. How will he help? Will he recommend that papa give Peter a good spanking? Will he bawl him out for his own good? Will he send him to another school? Or to the juvenile detention home?

I recall a little girl of six whom I saw some years ago and who received my offer of "help" with rather more open-mindedness than is usual with children. She was being seen for study and observation because of her fears regarding death. She seemed grateful to know of the existence of a strange animal like myself and, being a child of the Buck Rogers age, she was not really surprised that a creature known as a social worker had recently come upon this planet with a mysterious ray or a substance X for distressed children. But within a few visits I noticed a considerable loss in my prestige. My client became bored with my toys (hers were better anyway, she assured me) and skeptical of my methods. One day the client, squirming uncomfortably on a chair, twisted herself around until her head touched the floor. Then, balancing herself nicely, she stood on her head. At this moment, the client, legs in air but beautifully poised, was struck by a thought. She said to the worker, "You said you knew how to help children when they're afraid." "Yes," said the worker, leaning over to catch the first shy confessions. "Well, then," said the client sharply, "why don't you do it?"

If we ask ourselves why in the world this idea occurred to my client while she was standing on her head, we can only conclude that for her my proposed "help" was a kind of feat or trick, something I kept up my sleeve, in the same way that she kept her acrobatics on tap for display on special occasions. "Here, now I've shown you my tricks; you show me yours!"

Like the concept of "help," the concept of "worker-client relationship" requires a certain amount of re-working when we consider the child client. Sometimes, with uneasy acknowledgement of the differences in the relationship to adult and child clients, we feel that it is necessary to go under an assumed name for the benefit of the child. In this way a social worker may refer to himself not as a "caseworker" but as a "friend." Unfortunately this avowal of friendship may be received cynically by the child. To a scared youngster this offer of friendship is no more a guarantee of things to come than the famous overture of the Wolf to Little Red Riding Hood, or the invitation of the Spider to the Fly. Actually the word "caseworker" is a nice empty package for the child who meets one for the first time, and we are in a position to fill it and give it significance by what we do and by what we are to the child.

*Gaining the Child's Confidence*

With all these things in mind, we can see that there are very practical obstacles in the way of gaining a child's confidence and bringing him into a meaningful relationship with someone called a case-worker. If we grant that this relationship is the most important first objective with the child, we shall find ourselves behaving in unorthodox ways to achieve it.

We begin, of course, by putting aside formal interview procedure. We shall see the child, particularly the young child, in a room which is inviting to children but which can be equipped at modest cost. There will be paper and crayons and Plasticine, a few dolls or puppets from the dime store, some toy cars for the little boys, perhaps a small fire engine. A doll house and other such equipment can be used but are not necessary. The space under my desk has served at various times as a house, a garage, a fire station, a prison, a burial place for treasure, a secret hide-out for robbers, and a refuge for a sulking client. It is practical and economical. Dart games, guns, and other such weapons are found to be quite unnecessary, and besides they are hard on the caseworker. The aggressive urges in children rarely require these accessories. It is also noticeable that nowadays every little boy comes equipped with a built-in sound track for machine guns and bazookas; there is no need to strain the agency budget for lethal weapons that are only a poor imitation of a little boy imitating a lethal weapon. The cost of equipping such a playroom as this is probably under two dollars, including the space under the desk but not including a doll house. Any equipment beyond this is an indulgence for the caseworker. Here I speak from my own experience, for I suffer temptations in toy stores like everybody else and I have no difficulty in persuading myself that a certain doll is just what I need for a certain four-year-old who has been getting along just fine without it.

Perhaps this is as good a time as any to raise the question of the use of play as well as play materials in the social agency. Many of the fancy toys and play materials that fill our agency reception rooms and playrooms have dubious value in our work with children. I feel that this applies to child guidance centers as well as agencies that do not specialize in the treatment of children. Experienced child therapists find that such lavish displays of toys are a distraction to the child and do not serve the imagination nearly so well as the spontaneous, invented games of children which can be achieved through a minimum of props and toys. We must all admit, however, that they do serve a purpose for the worker. If we are uncertain about the nature of work with children—if we are troubled by the thought, "Now whatever shall I do with this child?"—the richness of our playroom equipment can allay our own anxiety.

In the past, too, I have seen how the special "therapy" toys—the amputation dolls, the ingenious little toilets, the weapons for bringing out aggression—have been defended on the basis that they "bring out material." This emphasis on "getting material" is well worth our attention. We shall dwell on the subject at other points in this discussion, but I should like to raise certain questions at this point. If the amputation doll brings forth from our little 5-year-old the expression of a castration anxiety, what do we know of him that is not true of every other little boy of his age? How does this enlarge our diagnostic picture? We cannot even consider this important *unless* the ego of this child has failed to deal satisfactorily with this anxiety; that is, if the ego has been compelled to develop pathological defense mechanisms or symptoms to ward off the anxiety. In other words, our criteria for diagnostic study are obtained not from observation of id-manifestations, but from observations of the ego and its efforts to deal with the instincts. For this we do not need the amputation dolls (which would in any event give a normal child the willies), and we do not need the little toilets. We need very little more than our educated eyes and ears.

But to return to this child whom we've just brought into the caseworker's office. Having put aside the formal across-the-desk interview, we now find ourselves on a completely uncharted course. We introduce ourselves to the child. We size him up—as he does us—and we wonder, "What *shall* we say to him?"

There are several gambits we can follow, all of which in my own experience lead into blind alleys. If we ask him whether he knows why he has come to see us, he will most certainly say "no." If we ask him to guess, he will probably say, "I don't know." If we ask him even in the friendliest way if he doesn't have lots of questions he'd like to ask us about why he is here and who we are, he will still, most probably, say "no." We can easily guess the trouble. Children hate being questioned. Furthermore, not one of these questions can be answered honestly until our youngster knows just what sort of person we are. If we give him time he will find out what he wants to know about us. And *his* interviewing technique, while devious and oblique, is remarkable in many ways. This junior interviewer can find out more about us in fifteen or twenty minutes than we can find out about him in the same amount of time. Let's see how he does it.

Jimmy is seven. He is referred for diagnostic study and planning by his school. He is reluctant to go to school; he is unable to learn to read although he has average intelligence. The caseworker, after introducing herself, invites him into her office and suggests he have a look around if he likes. He gingerly fingers the toys, picks up a crayon, looks as if he would like to scribble on a piece of paper, then changes his mind. He examines the drawings of other children which hang on the wall. "Who drew those lousy pictures?" he wants to know. This is a complex question. He doesn't really care "who" drew the lousy pictures since he doesn't know anyone who comes here. He wants to know the attitude of the caseworker toward such productions. He ridicules these other drawings as if anticipating ridicule from the caseworker for the drawing he might make which might be "lousy." The caseworker says: "Oh, we all draw here when we feel like it. We don't care if we draw good or bad. We don't have to be artists. We just draw for fun. This isn't school, you know."

He picks up a toy fire engine on which one of the parts is broken. "Jeez," he says with some effort at indignation, "who broke your fire engine?" Now this is really a very good question to test the reactions of adults under stress. Clearly this junior psychologist is not interested in "who" broke the fire engine, but in what happened to the guy who broke the fire engine. What does the caseworker do? Understanding this question (variations of this question are very common in first interviews with children), the caseworker says, "Oh, one of the kids broke it, accidentally, but I didn't get mad." Following this point neatly Jimmy says, "If he did it on purpose would you get mad?" "I wouldn't like it, but I don't get mad at children."

Jimmy brings out his next diagnostic point. "I like all my teachers in school except Miss Chase. She hits kids sometimes." The caseworker frowns with disapproval. Jimmy gives her five points on that one.

"You sure got a lot of drawers in that desk. What do you need all those drawers for?" The caseworker says, "Well, let's look and see." She opens all the drawers so that he can peek inside, finally opens one that is filled with odds and ends of junk, a supply especially maintained for youngsters. There are paper clips, stickers of various kinds, a broken automatic pencil, a pencil sharpener, a cigar box filled with the parts of a broken alarm clock, some marbles, a few sticks of gum, a box of chocolate niblets. He rummages happily, receives candy, a stick of gum, and the broken automatic pencil as a souvenir. He is sure he can fix it, he says.

Emboldened by this friendly opening of private drawers on the part of the caseworker, Jimmy now asks, "Do you have children? How old are you? Are you married?" The caseworker answers these questions simply but truthfully.

Now smeary with chocolate and at his ease in this surprising place, Jimmy ventures another question. "Do you have lots of kids who come here?" he asks. "Oh, yes." And then he says pointedly, "What do the other kids come here for?" The caseworker answers this by giving a few examples—a youngster who used to come here because he got mad too easily and got into lots of fights, a little girl who was afraid of things at night—"Oh, they come here for lots of reasons." Then the caseworker asks her question: "Now tell me," she says, "why do you think you come here, Jimmy?" Jimmy looks embarrassed, then mumbles, "Cause I don't like to go to school."

Admittedly this is a circuitous route to this most vital of questions in a first interview, but its advantages are obvious. The client has had plenty of time to interview the caseworker. We are impressed by his interviewing technique. In a relatively short space of time he has learned the following things about the caseworker. "She is not like a school teacher; this is not like school. You don't have to do things perfectly here." (This was obtained from the remarks about the drawings.) "She does not get mad at children." (Found out via the fire engine.) "She doesn't like kids to be spanked." (Derived from remarks about Miss Chase.) "It's all right to be curious here." (Information acquired through comments on drawers and invitation to look.) "You can ask her any question you want and she'll answer it." (Established through direct questions regarding worker's age, and so on.)

Now from the client's point of view this is highly pertinent information. If his difficulties lie with school and teachers and truant officers, the caseworker needs to be assessed in terms of enemy strength. Attitudes toward behavior, destructive urges, and the curiosity of little boys must all be inventoried ahead of time. Why tell this lady *anything* about the troubles in school if these revelations are to lead to a lecture, a bawling out, or threats? Since Jimmy has found that adults generally fall into the category of lecturers, scolders, and threateners, he reveals shrewdness and intelligence in first interviewing the caseworker around these vital points.

## Factors in Diagnosis

From the caseworker's point of view, too, we will not deny that a few important facts were gleaned from Jimmy's interview of her. His derogation of the other children's drawings is a possible clue to his own learning disability, a fear of not succeeding, a disparagement of his own products, a feeling that what he can achieve is so unworthy that it isn't worth trying. His fear of punishment from the adult is hinted at twice in his early remarks, and there is the possibility that the fear of adults may enter into his reluctance to go to school. On the positive side is the fact that when he feels safe with this adult he easily surrenders his wariness, and the caseworker knows that this reveals that his fear of authority figures is not all-pervading or frozen; it is manageable and yields to reality testing.

We may be disappointed in these meager findings. We do not know the symbolic significance of the interest in the broken fire engine or the curiosity about desk drawers. It might be argued that the worker could easily pursue these points. It seems to me that just here is where we so frequently get bogged down in child casework. For if the reaction to the broken fire engine has a deeper significance, we shall surely not learn of it in this first hour and the knowledge would do us very little good anyway. If this were a therapeutic situation, if we had behind us months of work, we might learn about its meaning—or we might find out that it was merely a natural interest in a broken fire engine. Actually the objectives of such a first interview with a child are simply those of establishing a relationship of confidence by whatever means are given us, and in observing those tendencies within the child which are brought into play in this new and strange situation for whatever value they hold in estimating the character of his disorder.

Every child reacts in unique fashion to this first meeting with a caseworker. If he feels endangered by this strange situation into which he is thrust, he will defend himself against this danger in ways that are characteristic for him and of the greatest importance for us, both in evaluating his behavior and in bringing him into a relationship with us.

Ellen, ten, is a constant daydreamer in school. Her teachers complain that she can't settle down to do her work. She is without friends, without any special interests. Ellen is in no sense a problem child in her foster home. She is a very "good" child and displays great affection toward the foster parents with whom she has lived for four years. Her teachers and foster parents are puzzled.

In the first interview with the caseworker Ellen is immediately chatty, quite frankly tells the caseworker she has difficulty in school and then, quite unexpectedly, draws an idealized picture of the caseworker under which she writes, "I love Miss Thomas" (the caseworker). Now we might count this as a triumph of relationship for Miss Thomas except that we know this is a most unusual reaction in a first interview with a child. Miss Thomas accepts the compliment pleasantly and without comment, then keeps her eyes open for some clues.

Later in the interview Ellen invents a drama with the puppets in which a little girl is very bad; she lies, talks back to her elders, and has secrets she will not tell her mother. The caseworker begins to understand Ellen's demonstration of love for her and an essential trait in Ellen's character. For it can be seen that Ellen has surrendered her aggressive tendencies, particularly those directed against adults, in favor of a compliant, dutiful attitude accompanied by exaggerated demonstrations of love toward the feared adult.

When we consider Ellen's background and a history of repeated placements because of behavior problems, we can understand how she made her adjustment to this foster home. Her fear that her aggression might cause her to lose these loved foster parents as she had lost others was a factor in the transformation of these tendencies into their opposite—exaggerated love such as she employed with the caseworker. This major defensive operation was not entirely successful, however, for we see in the inability to do school work and the preoccupation with daydreams, that so much energy is required to keep these bad impulses in check that there is little left at the disposal of the psychic apparatus for the activity of learning.

In the first interview she does not know what the caseworker will do about her learning difficulties. She only knows that she has displeased her beloved foster parents on this score. She knows that, in the past, adult displeasure has led to rejection and replacement, often through the offices of a nice lady like Miss Thomas. In this new situation of danger she defends herself in characteristic fashion—she propitiates the dragon through a declaration of love.

This type of diagnosis is immediately useful to the caseworker. It is true that Ellen hints at naughty secrets that a little girl withholds from her mother, but this is of no immediate value to the caseworker, who is obliged to make certain judgments regarding the depth and severity of this disorder in order to make suitable treatment plans for the child.

Ellen's caseworker is concerned with these larger patterns. She wants to know the extent to which these defensive operations of the ego have made inroads into the personality structure. She wants to know their strength and malleability in order to know where and how modification of these trends can be carried out. We can compare this task with that of the architect who is called in for advice on the remodeling of a structure. He must judge the existing structure in terms of the strength of its materials and its points of weakness but he need not tear down the walls and rip up the flooring in the course of his survey; he can judge by external signs.

This brings us to a next point regarding the important work of the caseworker in early diagnosis of childhood disorders. It goes without saying that the diagnostic study of a child which is undertaken in order to make suitable treatment or environmental plans requires the broadest and deepest kind of understanding and equipment on the part of the caseworker. We have borrowed largely from the field of psychoanalysis for our understanding of stages of libidinal development and for our knowledge of neurotic symptom-formation. The significant psychoanalytic developments in the field of ego-psychology, however, seem not to be widely understood by caseworkers. Yet the whole process of social study and diagnosis is dependent upon a knowledge of ego-psychology. Recently in an address to psychiatrists, Dr. Richard Sterba made certain remarks that I feel are specially pertinent for our field as well. He pointed out that in the past thirty years developments in the area of ego-psychology have made certain changes in the attitude of the psychiatrist in diagnostic interviews with patients. He said:

If we have to evaluate a patient today from a diagnostic therapeutic standpoint in an interview situation, we do not rely to such an extent on the symptomatology which he reports to us. Almost automatically

we observe the patient's general behavior, the peculiarities of his attitude toward us, his mannerisms, and the mode and inflection of his
speech. As we are aware of all these manifestations we use them for
evaluation of the neurotic trends which permeate the behavior, for
they indicate to the experienced therapist the extent and the manner
in which the neurosis afflicts the total personality and therefore the
character. . . . (Unpublished manuscript)

In the case of Ellen which we have briefly cited we are less interested in the fact that she daydreams—which is not in itself significant—
than in the fact that her fantasies inhibit a normal ego-function, learning. We are less interested in the fact that she has aggressive fantasies
and daydreams (which are allowable to any child) than the fact that
the ego of this child must deal with aggression in a specific way which
is unsatisfactory and which leads to breakdown of an ego-function;
the specific way, as we have already mentioned, is the transformation
of the aggressive impulses into their opposite.

Another case which illustrates the uses of ego-psychology in evaluating a disorder of childhood caused us some concern a year and a
half ago in a social agency.

The case of eleven-year-old Eddie was brought in for discussion at a
staff conference in the family agency. Three months earlier Eddie had
come to the attention of the agency in connection with its camp program. A school principal had asked that he be considered for placement at a clinical camp that is one of the valued resources of the
agency. The reason: Eddie acted peculiarly in school. He would often
burst out in classrooms and children's groups with bizarre and un-
called-for statements about death. The principal knew that a younger
sister had died of leukemia almost a year previously. As a matter of
fact a great deal of newspaper publicity had been given to the child in
the last months of her illness. The parents of Eddie had been deeply
depressed since the little girl's death and there was still an atmosphere of mourning in the house. The parents continued to talk about
the little girl to visitors, telling of her beauty and cleverness. There
was one other child in the family, a girl two years younger than Eddie.

Eddie spent four weeks at the clinical camp, following which we
obtained a report of the staff's observations. We saw that Eddie used
every opportunity to bring in the tragic story of his sister. He appeared
upset at the mention of death and once, after a church service that
reminded him of his sister's funeral, he spoke of his own death and

where he would like to be buried. On one occasion when the children were talking about murder stories, Eddie said quite seriously, "If you want to hear about a murder story I'll tell you about the death of my sister." This was evidently a slip, and a moment later he was remorseful. He then began to talk about his sister in heaven. When he looked up at the clouds, he said, he could sometimes see his sister sitting at the feet of Jesus. He described his sister as she looked in her coffin. The camp staff expressed something of the same concern for Eddie as had the principal of the school.

Admittedly this kind of preoccupation with death suggests pathology. We almost feel that we need very little more information to justify a recommendation for direct treatment. In our staff conference we investigated further the meaning of his symptoms. In a serious neurotic disorder with obsessional preoccupation with death we would find such manifestations as withdrawal, depression, inhibition, or turning inward of aggressive impulses, sometimes hypochondriacal complaints, or rituals and compulsive symptoms to ward off death or injury to the self. Yet as we examined the camp record further we saw that Eddie was capable of strong positive attachments to adults in the camp; he showed a lively interest in camp activities; he was able to engage in typical rough-housing with other campers. This was puzzling and certainly called for some modification of our views. We decided that the preoccupation with death had not invaded the total personality of this child. The ego was not restricted in its functioning. We combed the record for signs of pathological mechanisms in other areas of ego-functioning—and found none. We concluded that his preoccupation with death, because its sphere of operation was so limited and confined, was probably not obsessional in the clinical sense. "What is this, then?" we asked ourselves.

We began to think of other factors. We thought of the long mourning of the parents, the atmosphere of death in this household, and the withdrawal of the parents from their two living children. We thought of the way in which the dead became sanctified and how this little daughter who had been unexceptional as a live little girl had become saintly, good, beautiful, and clever since her death. We thought of what it meant to a modest, workaday family in a small community to achieve fame and much newspaper publicity because it had a little girl dying of leukemia.

In a real sense Eddie was placed in competition with his dead sister, but this competition was more devastating than anything he had known when the little sister was alive. He had nothing to offer that would compare with this spectacular illness and death. It might be, then, that his rather frequent and startling allusions to the dead sister and to the subject of death were his poor attempts to bring to himself some of the awesome respect that is given the dead and dying, to make himself important in the eyes of others through impressing himself upon them as the brother of a little girl who died of leukemia. Such speeches also may have served another purpose; by sanctifying the dead sister he allayed some of his guilt about her death. This is suggested in the slip about his sister's "murder." We did not, however, feel that it was necessary for us to dwell too much on the problem of Eddie's guilt feelings, since guilt after a death is not in itself pathological. We have already seen that his guilt feelings had not created serious neurotic mechanisms in Eddie.

Considering all these things, beginning with our appraisal of a basically intact ego in this child and the circumstantial factors that had played a specific role in his preoccupation with death, the staff recommended that no direct treatment be attempted with Eddie but that our casework efforts be directed toward the parents in an effort to help them achieve some recognition of his problems.

Eddie's parents, both serious and concerned people, came to grips with their own feelings about the death of a loved child and their responsibility to the living children. When they recognized and grew concerned about the effects of their mourning upon Eddie as well as upon their other child, they brought about important changes in the home and in their relationship to the boy. As the atmosphere of the home became more normal, as Eddie discovered himself to be once more a valued child with his ghostly competitor put at rest, we saw dramatic changes in him. He became a normally cheerful and busy little boy, showed unexpected talent for taking on responsibility, and gratified his parents tremendously by his change from a listless and fretful member of the family to an independent, even boisterous, youngster. He never became a star at school—the little dead sister had always been a better student—but we learned that Eddie was actually a little limited intellectually and the best he could do was "C" work. An understanding teacher and the parents accepted this limitation and helped Eddie achieve a feeling of importance for those other things that he did well, particularly in the area of mechanical skills.

The stories about death and leukemia stopped somewhere along the way. Now, a year and a half later, Eddie continues to function very well.

The case of Eddie illustrates a kind of casework which we speak of as "environmental." We see that an understanding of ego-psychology was indispensable to the casework staff in making an important decision regarding the type of treatment to be employed in a specific case. Had we considered the problem only from the point of view of the symptoms presented by Eddie we should have certainly felt that direct treatment of the child was indicated. But when the symptom is seen relatively and when the diagnostic eye of the caseworker is trained on the total configuration of ego functioning and environmental influences, the significance of the symptom changes immediately. Here, an environmental approach to the problem was diagnostically prescribed.

## Part 2: Helping with Critical Situations

Some of the problems involved in the initial meeting of caseworker and child and in the use of the diagnostic or study period in casework with children were discussed in the first section of this paper. At this point we turn to another important area of casework with children. Many typical casework tasks involve one or two interviews with a child client for the purpose of dealing with a critical situation in his life. Thus, the placement worker may find it necessary to see a child because of a specific difficulty in the foster home, for discussion of a new placement, or possibly for preparation of the child for a tonsillectomy. The school social worker may have to interview a child about a classroom difficulty. The institutional caseworker may be called on to see one of her charges because of a theft or a fire-setting incident. Sometimes the caseworker is already acquainted with the child (this is particularly true, of course, in placement or institutional work) and he does not have to deal with the problem of establishing a new relationship, but he does face the special problems that come with confronting a child with a painful reality or in dealing with the guarded feelings of a child who feels he is "on the spot." In such instances, we are still not dealing with problems of casework treatment or therapy with the child but rather with a casework approach to critical events in a child's life. We do not exaggerate, I am sure, if we consider that our handling of such interviews with a child may profoundly influence his management of the critical event, his attitude toward his own problems and their solution, and even the course of his future development.

Because such encounters between caseworker and child occur frequently in casework agencies, it may be interesting for us to examine an interview with a child which involves the handling of a crisis—in this case, stealing.

This material is taken from the record of a therapy group for boys of eleven and twelve years of age. The group leader was a trained caseworker who often found occasion to supplement her group handling of incidents with interviews with an individual child.

For several weeks there had been stealing in the group. A number of important items of equipment and many materials had disappeared. Finally, through many signs, the leader knew that Danny and Bill were chiefly involved in these thefts. When she was certain of the fact, she took both boys aside after a meeting, told them quietly that she wanted to talk with them privately about some of the missing items in the playroom, and asked them to see her in her office on a specified day.

Even in this brief talk the attitude of each boy toward his stealing was evident. Bill had a "Who? Me?" look written on his face and was well prepared with alibis; Danny looked shifty and uncomfortable although he made no admission of taking things. Formerly Danny had had a good relationship with the leader and it was not until the stealing began in the past few weeks that he had begun to avoid her. She already knew that Bill was the initiator and seducer in mischief and petty crime and that Danny was a willing partner who lacked boldness and cunning of his own but became daring and aggressive when he obtained a suitable partner. The boys were friends at school as well as in the group. Both had histories of stealing; Danny's seemed more sporadic while Bill's was a well-established pattern. Danny was living in the home of a maternal grandmother under supervision of a child-care agency which had earlier placed him in foster homes. His own parents were divorced and his mother had virtually abandoned him and his brother.

On the day of the scheduled interview Bill was ill. The worker had wanted to see the two boys together first and then have separate interviews with them. As it turned out, however, only Danny was able to come in for his interview. The following material is excerpted from the record.

Danny arrived early for his appointment. His face was streaked with dirt and his hair hung down into his eyes. He assumed a jaunty, unruffled manner. He said he couldn't find Bill. I said I had heard from Bill's mother that he was ill today. I commented it was too bad that Bill wasn't here but Danny and I could talk anyway. I suggested that maybe Danny understood why I had asked him to come in. He shifted uncomfortably. I said I knew that Danny and Bill had been taking things from the clubroom and so I thought it would be a good thing if we could get together and talk about this. He answered, "Yes," in a low voice.

I wondered what things Danny had taken. Danny hesitated. "Well, sandpaper," he said feebly. [Obviously the least valuable of the things he had taken.] "And some glue and some airplane stuff, and some other stuff that I can't remember," he went on. "Bill took some scissors and some knives and he took lots of big things." Then Danny was struck by his disloyalty to his friend. "I don't really know," he said. "I don't know exactly what."

I wondered whether Danny had taken things from other places and from other people too. He turned his head away. "Yes," he said. "But," he added, "not big things." I said little things could be important too. Like the things that Danny had taken from the club. It meant that other boys weren't able to use those things. Danny looked up at me gravely. "Guess so," he admitted in a low voice.

Then I said, "You know, Danny, I like you a lot. And this makes me kind of worried because I do like you. It makes me think that if you do these things, and if you get yourself into jams and you steal, that maybe there's something bothering you. When boys do things like that it sometimes means that they're worried about something." "Worry?" said Danny, as if he had never heard the word before. "Well, I worry about camp. I worry that maybe I can't go on account of my eyes. I had to go to the clinic about my eyes. And maybe they'll be so worse that I won't be able to go to camp this summer."

[Now the worker understood. The entire club was going to be sent to camp by the agency that sponsored the group therapy project. Danny obviously felt that, now that he had stolen, his chances for camp had ended.]

I said I didn't know about that. I didn't really believe that needing glasses would keep a fellow out of camp. But I felt that maybe Danny meant that he was worried that I would be mad at him and not let him go to camp. Danny immediately looked up. "That's what I was worrying about," he said. I said I was not going to punish Danny. There was no reason why he should not go to camp. I wanted him to go to camp very much. A look of profound relief came over his face. Then I said, "Was that the only thing you were worried about, Danny?"

"No," Danny said, "you see my grandma ain't gonna keep my brother and me no more." It cost him a lot to bring this out. Then he went on. "Teddy and me, we live with my grandma. My mother and dad are divorced. So now my grandma says she ain't gonna keep us no more and Miss Miller [caseworker at the placement agency], she's gonna take us to a home. Once me and Teddy lived in a home. The lady didn't like me. She was real strict. You couldn't make no noise and you always had to put your things away. You had to come straight home from school and you couldn't play agates on the way. And when you came home you couldn't even make yourself a jelly sandwich." This last was somehow the most unbearable. Danny began to cry quietly.

[The worker had not known about the new placement plans although she had known for some time that a new placement might be considered eventually.]

I said, "So it's pretty tough, isn't it, Danny? Now you don't know what'll happen. You don't know whether you'd like the new people or whether they'd like you?"

"I think all the time," Danny said, "I think that maybe it'll be a place where they won't like me. And then it won't be no better than at my grandma's. And maybe it'll be better if I just stay with my grandma. She don't like me. She don't like me because I stayed with my mother when I was a baby and my grandma always took care of Teddy. She don't like me because I like my mother. She says my mother is a bum. She likes Teddy best. When Teddy and me have a fight she always says that it's my fault. Teddy's stuff can lay around all the time and she don't say nothing. She always gets mad at me. When my stuff lays around she throws it out. I saved a dollar and half for a game and my grandma threw it in the garbage can. I guess she threw it in by mistake though. She says she wishes I was never born. She says I'm bad. She says I'm the trouble maker and I'm the cause of all her trouble. She says I'm good for nothing."

"Do you think you're bad, Danny?" I asked. "Guess so," Danny said briefly. "Why?" I asked. "Because I fight. And I always get into trouble. And—you know." "Yes," I said, "I think sometimes you do get into trouble and you do things you feel sorry for afterwards. But I don't think you're a bad boy, Danny." I do not recall that Danny responded to this in any way. But he continued to tell me more stories about the home.

"Yesterday my grandma hit me with the stick because I was fighting with Teddy. Sometimes she's nice to us, I guess. I guess she really likes us sometimes. But she don't like me. I wished I had a family and then I wouldn't have so much trouble. I wished I had something to play with. My grandma don't have no money to buy Teddy and me anything to play with. And any time I get anything she says it's junk and she throws it out."

I said, "Danny, is that why you steal things? Because you figure if people don't give you things, you'll take them?" Danny made no answer. I said that I felt, too, that boys should have things to play with. Miss Miller, I was sure, felt the same way. These were things that Danny could talk about with Miss Miller and I knew that she would try to get him some of the things he wanted.

Then I asked, "Danny, do you know what Miss Miller is there for?" and he answered promptly, "To help me." And that meant, I pointed out, that some of these things that Danny was so worried about and some of the things that Danny wanted, Miss Miller could help him with. He could talk to her about these things.

Danny continued to tell me more stories. At school, he said, he had a teacher who made him ashamed before the whole class because he had dirty hands. I said that I knew how that could feel; it was awful to feel ashamed before other people, other kids especially. It was better, I thought, for grownups and children to talk about these things privately as we do here. "Sure," Danny said, "that's what Miss Miller does too. We always talk private. Like if Teddy and me come down to the office we each see her private."

Again Danny brought up his fear of the foster home and the fact that "they" wouldn't like him. He concluded, "I never stayed with anyone who liked me." I asked, "Who do you feel does like you, Danny?" He replied, "My mother, I think. And my dad. Well, he used to but I don't know if he still does. And my aunt." He was silent after he recited this miserable little list. "And you know that I like you, don't you, Danny?" I asked. "Sure," Danny said, but then he added kindly, "but you ain't in my family."

Later on, as we talked, I asked Danny how he had felt last Thursday when I had talked with him and Bill about their stealing. "I was mad," he said, "I wasn't gonna come back. I thought to myself, 'She said I took tools. And I didn't take tools.' "

I pointed out that I had not said he took tools. "I know," he said, "that's just the way I was thinking. Then afterward, Bill and me, we played agates. Then Bill said he felt sick and he went home."

Suddenly there came over Danny a wave of feeling. "Bill, he made me spend a dollar and thirty cents I saved up. I wished I didn't listen to him. Then I could of had something. Bill he's always getting into trouble. Like at school. We ain't supposed to go into only one door. Bill he always wants to go into the other doors. He's always taking chances. And Bill he talks back to the teachers. He says, 'They can't do nothing.' "

Danny continued, "Once Johnny Peters said he didn't want to take no chances and Bill said he was a sissy. Just scared." I asked, "Just because he didn't want to take a silly chance and get into trouble?" "Yah!" was Danny's reply.

"I think taking chances like that is kind of dumb," I remarked. "Sure," Danny agreed. I said, "When Bill says that to you, what can you say?" "Tell him I'm not taking no chances," he said. I suggested, "Sure, I'd say, 'Not me. I'm not dumb.' "

Danny's next remark was, "Bill he gets into lots of trouble." "I know," I said, "I like Bill but I'm afraid he's going to get into a peck of trouble by doing these things. Bill sure needs someone to help him."

It was nearly time to end our interview. I said I was very glad that we had this chance to talk. Said Danny, "I got a lot of things off my chest."

Danny was at the door now. He turned to me and said shyly, "You know that boat you helped me with? It was the best boat I ever made." "It was a swell boat," I said, "and you made it too!" "Sure," Danny agreed, "but I knew how to make it good because you helped me."

In this interview with Danny certain typical problems in casework with children come to the foreground. With an adult client the caseworker usually grants the "right of self-determination"; with a child he must assume a different kind of responsibility. He must actively step in at times like this and interfere with "self-determination" of a certain kind. He must bring about a sense of responsibility for acts if his client is of an age and disposition that do not normally give rise to social feelings. Most unpleasant of all for the caseworker is the task of confronting a child with his juvenile crime.

In this interview we notice that the worker opened the discussion with a frank acknowledgment of the fact that she knew Danny had been taking things. She did not preface this with small talk and she did not try to make it easy for Danny. Earlier we spoke of the necessity for inviting a child's confidence in the caseworker and deliberately putting him at ease, and this bald opening of the caseworker seems to contradict everything we have discussed. But does it? First of all, this worker was known to her client as a group leader, and a good relationship had existed for months before the stealing began, at which time Danny became evidently less interested in her good opinion of him. The bald opening of the caseworker leads in this instance to a simple acknowledgment on the part of two people who know each other that something which concerns both of them and which is known to both of them must be discussed in the open. Since Danny knows precisely the reason for the interview, small talk is pointless. Also, the worker in this instance does not want to put her client at ease. She feels that it is best that he feel guilty for what he has done. She knows that he does not ordinarily feel much guilt about his delinquencies but here she is banking on her formerly good and warm relationship with Danny to cause him some discomfort and guilt. Clearly, without such an earlier relationship such an approach might bring hostility toward a nosy stranger, rather than guilt. She deliberately shows her concern for Danny. Because of his discomfort, Danny's attitude toward his delinquencies may change. Also, in order to handle the stealing episode at all with Danny, she must bring him to some acknowledgment of responsibility for his acts.

The worker has another objective in this interview. She wants to understand as far as possible the meaning of the stealing episodes so that she can handle these acts as symptoms. If the total picture seems serious, the worker may recommend to Danny's agency that treatment be sought for him. If, on the other hand, the stealing is largely a reaction to external circumstances and pressures, the worker may suggest to the agency, on the basis of her interest, that appropriate remedial measures be carried out. Therefore, soon after opening up the subject of stealing the worker directs Danny's attention to the fact that stealing is a symptom. She tells him that when boys do things of this sort it often means they are worried about something.

But what is Danny's response to this? He first denies any worry and then lamely expresses his fear that he will not be able to go to camp because of his eyesight. He fears that the worker will punish him for the stealing by not permitting him to go to camp. As soon as this is handled with Danny and he is assured that the worker actually wants him to go to camp, the interview takes a new turn. Now he can tell the worker about his big worry. His grandmother is not going to keep him any more. Miss Miller is going to take him and his brother to a home.

Actually Danny has no reason to expect that he will not be punished for his stealing, nor does any other child who comes to us following a delinquent episode. Danny can only expect that the worker will act like any other adult and he is already prepared with the full battery of defenses and alibis. His jaunty, unconcerned manner at the beginning of the interview is part of this defense. His admission to the theft of some trifles is the kind of compromise confession he feels it is necessary to make. Even though he knows this worker very well he still cannot measure how she will react under these conditions, what she does to boys when they steal. Only when he understands that she will not punish, when he experiences the relief of knowing he will go to camp, does he really perceive that her interest in his stealing is different from that of other adults. She wants to know *why* a boy steals, what worries make him steal. So he tells her.

As he talks we are impressed by the acuteness of this child's dilemma. He knows he is unloved and he is told he is bad. If there are no rewards for "being good" in Danny's life, if one is considered "bad" anyway, why shouldn't he be bad? And he is deprived, terribly deprived in every meaning of the word. He is without love, without meaningful relationships to any adult, without family, without possessions. As the worker suggests to him at one point, it is as if his defense for his stealing lies in the simple rationale, "If people don't give me things, then I will take them."

Our experience with children tells us that this type of stealing is perhaps the least complicated in the long category of stealing types. Such youngsters as Danny often give up their stealing when we are able to provide meaningful relationships for them, when the minuses are changed to pluses on the human relations ledger.

It may be worth while to mention that Danny's partner in crime, Bill, has far more complicated motives in his stealing. His defense against guilt feelings and against meaningful object relationships tells of a more entrenched delinquent attitude. Nor is Bill, strictly speaking, a deprived youngster. His stealing has to do with rivalry with a stepfather, with seductive attitudes on the part of his mother, altogether a more complex pattern. An interview with Bill would not be so simple as the one with Danny. A more developed delinquent type of youngster would protect his anxieties and inner feelings from the prying caseworker. The manner in which Danny surrenders his defensive attitude when the non-punitive and sympathetic attitude of the caseworker finally reaches him, tells us that this is not a very complicated delinquent.

We are interested in the way in which Danny understands this novel approach (for him) to his stealing. In his outpouring he mentions that a teacher once made him ashamed before his whole class because of his dirty hands. He seems to be saying thanks to the caseworker for not betraying him and humiliating him before the group. He must never have known before this experience where a boy's "badness" is handled in an interview, where stealing is seen as a symptom that "something is wrong inside." He confesses, too, that before this interview and at the time of the group meeting when the worker privately spoke to him and Bill, he had been angry at the accusation and had decided he would not come back to the club.

Finally comes the wave of feeling against Bill and the way in which he tempted Danny into delinquent acts. We recall that earlier Danny was loyal to Bill and was careful not to betray him. In the outpouring now against Bill, Danny tells us that in the course of the interview something has changed in his attitude not only toward Bill but toward his own delinquencies. It is as if Bill represents his "bad part" and in the outburst against Bill and his repudiation of Bill we see how he shows the wish, for this moment anyway, to repudiate his own "badness," his own inner temptations. The worker chooses to support this attitude in Danny and expresses concern for Bill and what will happen to him if such things continue.

Earlier we spoke of the difficulty that children have in understanding what we mean by "help." At the end of this interview with Danny we understand that he was giving shy thanks to the worker for her help. He spoke of the boat she had helped him make, we remember, the best he ever made. "But I knew how to make it good because you helped me." He seemed to understand "help" here. The question remains whether he would have understood it earlier. For the experience in the interview made "help" concrete and significant where earlier "help" would have been a word without positive content to this child who, like so many of our children, had never known what this kind of help could mean.

The outcome of this interview was a good one. There were no further stealing episodes in the group. Danny's relationship to the group leader was again a warm one and he sought many opportunities to be with her and to talk with her, though not necessarily about "private" things. The worker, of course, shared this interview with Danny's agency so that this material could be used in planning for Danny.

## Professional Responsibility

In every agency where caseworkers work with children, the worker carries the weight of the responsibility for making critical decisions for children and their families. Not only must we make judgments regarding the treatment of a wide variety of childhood disorders but we are often called upon to make decisions or recommendations regarding placement outside the home. We are, willingly or not, great manipulators of a child's life. This is an awesome kind of responsibility, and perhaps an attitude of awe toward such undertakings is a proper one for us. We need to feel inadequate before the magnitude of these tasks.

It is this responsibility that I want to talk about most of all. I feel that there are few professions in which are found such ideals, such dedication, and such seriousness of intent as in social work. Our errors, when we make them, are rarely from malice, or neglect, or self-interest. Surely we can be forgiven, I say to myself, if we err in our judgments sometimes. But then my thoughts travel back to the errors and the source of the errors and their consequences, and I feel bound to speak of them. For these errors, these mistakes in judgment, affect human lives profoundly, sometimes irrevocably. In the case of a child, a mistaken judgment can inalterably change the course of a life. Therefore, let us speak honestly to each other about one of the chief sources of error in our professional work with children. It is not lack of love and sympathy for children, or lack of proper concern for our charges. We abound in these virtues. I believe that the chief source of error in our work with children is the equipment we bring to our work. We need to know so much in order to help a child build a life, to help his parents build his life, and to rebuild a child's life when it has been destroyed. We need to know everything one can know today about the deepest sources of disease and health in the mental life of childhood. The most commonplace, everyday casework task requires the most thorough training in psychological development of the child, the richest possible experiences in work with normal and abnormal children under varied circumstances, with varied age ranges.

I do not know how this equipment and training for caseworkers will be obtained in the casework education of the future. But it seems to me that we must begin with an appreciation of the seriousness of the caseworker's responsibility for children. It is a fact that there are no elementary tasks in casework just as there are no elementary psyches among our clients; hence there is no place for an elementary education in human psychology for the caseworker. Already there are gratifying changes in the programs of schools of social work. We no longer believe (and new school catalogues testify to this) that the psychiatric social worker must have a broader education in psychology than the family caseworker, the child welfare worker, the medical caseworker. When we have achieved the broadest possible education for social workers (I speak here of the field of child casework) we shall do more than reduce the margin of error in our judgments; I think we shall begin to see the realization of an old dream in which social workers will be able to do preventive casework with children and their families on a scale not yet thought possible.

### Note

This paper was presented at the National Conference of Social Work, Chicago, May 1952.

# 18

## Psychoanalysis and the Education of Caseworkers

The education for social work, like all professional education, is an education for practice. The theoretical and technical content of this education has always borne a close relationship to the fields of practice. The social agency is the laboratory for the profession. It is through direct work with clients that we feel the pulse of social change and evolve new programs and modify old programs to meet new community needs. It is through direct work with clients that we test new ideas and the applicability of theories and research findings from allied fields to our own profession. When the usefulness of these findings has been demonstrated in practice, the curriculum of the professional school absorbs this new knowledge and makes it part of the professional education.

This means that a good curriculum reflects the best in current practice and thinking and derives its infusions of new knowledge from the work of thousands of practitioners. This means, too, that however restrictive it is to the academic imagination, we cannot be originators of new practices in the classroom and we cannot profess theories in the classroom until they have been tested in practice.

As an applied science, a user of other sciences, we find ourselves obliged to put our borrowings to a pragmatic test. Is it useful to our field, we ask. Does it explain things better; does it suggest new and better remedies for our problems? Now in asking these questions we are not inquiring about the validity of a theory—which can only be done within its own sphere of operation—we are only testing its application to our field, which puts us under another set of rules. Application implies use. This means, of course, that whether psychoanalysis or role theory or genetic psychology or cybernetics will find their way into social work practice and social work education will depend upon the usefulness of those theories for the performance of the social work job.

For nearly forty years psychoanalysis has been a major influence in the development of social work theory and practice and has supplied the basic psychology taught in schools of social work. It has become so much a part of the fabric of social work theory that we cannot easily identify many of the elements of our theory that are directly borrowed from psychoanalysis.

Now, in our current appraisals of social work theory and social work education the contributions of psychoanalysis as well as the contributions from all the behavioral sciences are being examined for their relative value to the professional content of social work. Such taking stock is an extremely valuable measure to a profession that is coming of age. It gives us the opportunity to separate the components in our social work theory and assign a value to them before we put them together again. It has a stimulating effect upon one's own thinking, I find. As one who believes very strongly that psychoanalysis is the indispensable component in social work theory and practice, I found it an excellent exercise and examination of my own beliefs to ask myself the question, "Why do I think so?"

Then I found myself very much stimulated by a question that is implicit in the curriculum study. If the goal of social work is described as "enhancement of social functioning" and "social functioning" is regarded as the unifying concept of social work, as defined in the Curriculum Study (I do not myself favor this definition), what is the place of psychoanalysis within such a formulation? What knowledge does psychoanalytic theory and practice bring to a profession that concerns itself with problems of social functioning?

To answer these questions for myself I began to think of cases. I reviewed all of the agency cases that had come to me for consultation during the past year and a few from previous years. In each case I attempted to identify the psychoanalytic knowledge that was employed in diagnosis and treatment. At the same time I submitted the data to a test: Will another theory explain these data better or provide better remedies for the problems presented? The test, I had to concede, was not entirely fair since I know psychoanalytic theory far better than I know any other theory of human behavior. But with these limitations I did succeed in clarifying some of my own thinking, and it seemed to me that this approach was one that we might follow today, with a selection of the cases I reviewed for myself. I would propose, then, that we review these cases together and see what they may tell us about psychoanalytic content in casework practice. And finally I would like to discuss the implications for social work education which can be derived from study of the cases.

## A Boy Gang Leader

Some time ago a nine-year-old boy was referred to a school social worker for evaluation. Larry was the leader of a little gang at school that molested other children outside of school and tyrannized younger children through physical attacks and threats. He was a child of good average intelligence and until this year had created no unusual difficulties for the school, although he had always exhibited some minor behavior problems. He was the child of conscientious middle-class parents who were frankly baffled by the complaints from school in recent months. He had always been difficult to manage at home and seemed to be in unceasing battle with his older sister, eleven. Often he seemed to be begging for punishment from his parents. But there were strong bonds of affection between the child and his parents and never before had the parents felt that his behavior was something they could not influence.

Both the parents and the school blamed these difficulties in part upon the changing neighborhood in which they lived and in which the school was located. There had been a large influx of Negro families into this neighborhood in a northern city and many of the Negro children who had lived in slums previously had brought with them the code of the street-child. A number of small delinquent gangs had sprung up among the Negro children of the neighborhood. I should mention that the middle-class Negro children were as threatened by the gangs and their culture as were the white middle-class children.

These are a few of the significant social factors as we knew them at the time of intake. If we now employ a diagnosis based upon the social factors we may say that Larry and the other middle-class children in this community are reacting to the impact of the street-child culture that has invaded their world. They are threatened by the aggression and tyranny of the newcomers. We can assume that certain middle-class values have been assaulted by the newcomers with their street code and we see this as a conflict between two groups who hold incompatible values and codes of behavior. From the standpoint of the middle-class child his role as defined by his group is threatened and violated by the alien group.

But now we are confronted with an interesting problem. If we grant that certain factors in the social situation have precipitated a conflict in Larry we are still left with the question, "Why did this externally induced conflict lead to the specific forms of behavior that we observed in Larry?" If he is afraid of attack by the tough boys, which is understandable, why doesn't his aggression manifest itself against the enemy, in fighting back? And if he forms a little gang we could understand it if the gang served as a mututal protection association against the danger of enemy attack—but this gang has as its purpose the tyrannizing of younger and helpless children.

Larry is modeling his behavior after the behavior of the delinquent boys. It might be proposed that Larry has taken the delinquent as a model because of the power status of the delinquent group within the school community. But with this factor in our tentative diagnosis we still have no explanation of the fact that Larry and his five gang members have reacted to the new status group by taking on the role of the delinquent, that other children in the school have reacted through an intensification of anxiety and sometimes reluctance to go to school, and still other children have managed to adapt themselves to the presence of the alien group without abandoning their own codes and without suffering paralyzing anxiety. Then, too, we are faced with the problem that this diagnosis does not carry with it its own prescription. To say that a child adopts the behavior of delinquent boys because they represent the power group in his community will not tell us what we ought to do about the situation.

Now let's try another diagnostic approach. We begin with the observation that Larry has taken over the behavior of the delinquent boys, that he models himself after them and now tyrannizes younger children in the same way that the delinquent boys have tyrannized him and his friends. We see this as an identification with the delinquent boys and we employ our psychoanalytic knowledge in a tentative formulation that this identification may be a form of defense. The details of this behavior suggest that Larry identifies with the aggressor and actively does to younger children those things that he has passively experienced at the hands of the tough boys. If we are dealing with a defense then we can employ our knowledge of defense in the appropriate treatment. But first we must study this behavior in detail in order to know what needs it serves.

The social worker in this case had a series of interviews with Larry in order to observe his behavior more closely. Larry was a lively, engaging youngster, absolutely on his best behavior during the first three interviews. He understood why he was coming to see the social worker and seemed quite unconcerned about it. He had little guilt about his gang activities and felt that everyone was making much too much fuss about the whole business. The caseworker was attentive to this omission of guilt feelings, knowing that she was dealing either with a defective superego or a defense against guilt feelings, and that the differentiation of these two conditions would be crucial in formulating treatment plans.

Then after a few interviews Larry began to give some surprising glimpses of the delinquent Larry. One day he whispered obscenities under his breath, giggling and casting furtive glances at the caseworker. He grew bolder in the next interview and sang a dirty song under his breath. In the same interview Larry, quite giddy and excited put on a bad-boy act in which he called himself "Ernie" and raced around the room shouting names at an unseen teacher in Negro accents. The caricature of Ernie was so well performed that the social worker had no difficulty in recognizing the real Ernie who was a celebrated problem child in the school. The caseworker watched with interest as Larry, clowning and excited, began to shadow-box with imaginary opponents, thumping the cushions of the chair and uttering obscenities under his breath. From the facial mimicry the caseworker understood Larry was now imitating someone else. "Who is this, Larry?" she asked. "JoJo," he said promptly, and now he imitated the random movements and disordered speech of another disturbed child in his classroom.

In watching this strange performance the caseworker discovered what she needed to know. The play-acting demonstrated very clearly the identification with the "bad" boys; now it remained to test this behavior as defense. The caseworker said, "All right, Larry, now I think you're getting a little too excited and I'd like to talk with you. Let's sit down." Still in his gremlin mood, Larry dived into a chair and boldly stuck out his tongue at the caseworker. He was preparing himself for a lecture. The caseworker said, "Larry, there are a lot of tough kids at school. I think it must be very scary for you and lots of other kids to be around tough guys and kids who lose control of themselves." Larry was momentarily surprised, then his play-acting came to a stop, and he said with great feeling, "You don't know the half of it!" "I'm sure I don't," said the caseworker, "so please tell me about it."

Then Larry told his story. He told of the small gangs that attacked kids on their way home from school. He described the extortionist tactics of these gangs and the ways in which many children at school were forced to pay for protection. (Much of this the caseworker knew.) Larry did not mention his own gang at this point. He went on to describe the chaos of his classroom with Ernie or JoJo running around the room in grinning defiance of the teacher. "We don't even learn anything any more," he said. And there was much more, he hinted, things he wouldn't tell anybody. When the teachers weren't around. . . . In the lavatories and the locker-rooms. . . .

Once the caseworker asked Larry if he could not have talked with his teachers about these things. "What good would *that* do," he said scornfully, "the teachers are scared of those kids themselves."

At this point the caseworker has learned a great deal. She knows that anxiety is the motive for this pathological identification with the aggressor, and here the diagnosis carries its own prescription. The caseworker knows now how she can help Larry.

In the weeks that followed the caseworker encouraged Larry to talk about the "bad" boys and his fears and carefully protected him from any implication that to be scared was to be a sissy. She helped him to see that his own gang activities were connected with his fears, that he was acting the tough-guy because he was afraid of the tough guys and that he was doing to the little kids just what he feared himself from the big, tough boys. And she helped him see that this was no solution to the problem. The caseworker, it was true, could not protect Larry against the danger of attack by the tough boys, but she soon discovered that Larry found much relief in talking about his fears to her and, feeling the psychological protection of this relationship, he began to find better solutions to the problems.

As Larry learned that he could trust the caseworker with any of the things he worried about he began to tell her about the lavatory and locker-room incidents that he had once thought he could not tell anyone. With great difficulty he described the sexual horseplay in the lavatories, the uninhibited exhibitionism of the tough-guys, playful threats against the genitals, dirty jokes, incestuous name-calling, the Dozens routine. The caseworker began to understand that the street-child code was a sexual as well as aggressive threat to the middle-class child and to Larry, particularly. Then, through tactful questions she learned that Larry had sometimes participated in these games and with this admission the one-time tough-guy Larry displayed the most agonizing guilt.

Now we understand that there was another motive for identification with the "bad" boys. Larry believed that he, himself, was a bad boy and by behaving like the "bad" boys he was making a confession. And now, too, we understand one of the motives in his provocative behavior and simultaneously we know why he did not show guilt feelings about his "bad" behavior. He regularly made his confession of guilt and invited punishment. When he received punishment from his teachers or his parents his guilt feelings were satisfied and he was free to renew the cycle of crime and punishment.

With casework help Larry gave up his gang activities and settled down to work in his classroom. Larry's parents were helped to gain a better understanding of his problems and to find more satisfactory ways of handling his behavior at home. With the caseworker's knowledge of the guilt-punishment mechanisms in Larry's personality she was able to give specific help to the parents in the area of discipline. Larry's behavior at home improved significantly.

We may say, then, that casework achieved its goal of more effective social functioning in the case of Larry. But in order to do this, the caseworker needed a precise and finally differentiated diagnosis. The factor of identification with bad boys could be established either by employing role theory or psychoanalytic theory during the first descriptive phase of diagnosis. But only psychoanalytic theory could establish the motive for the identification, and only through discerning the motive could casework treatment be effective. The motive, we found, was highly complex. This is not because Larry's case was more complex than others; it is because all human motives are complex. If we only know that Larry identifies with bad boys we have a description of the behavior, one that is perfectly valid as description but cannot tell us how we shall bring about change in the behavior. In order to modify behavior we must know its meaning exactly.

In Larry's case we saw that identification served as a defense against both an external and an internal danger. The external danger was represented in the threat of the delinquent boys; the internal danger was represented in the child's own aggressive and sexual impulses. We derived this from the data in the case, but it is also useful to remember that identification is one of the defense mechanisms that operates simultaneously against inner and outer dangers.

How useful are these case findings outside the case itself? Are these analytically derived data generally applicable? From my own experience with delinquent boys I would say that the factor of "identification with the aggressor" is one of the most important keys to an understanding of the "contagion" of delinquency. It is not, of course, a middle-class phenomenon. The delinquent street children who initiated the gang activities at school were also doing unto others what had been done unto them. Before they became the persecutors they had been the persecuted, the victims of older child gangsters. And the tyranny of the child culture is itself modeled after the tyrany passively experienced by many of these children in their own homes.

From the case of Larry we must also observe the external conditions which call forth the defense. The failure of adults, the teachers and parents, to protect Larry and others from the danger of attack and seduction, created anxiety in each child that summoned his characteristic mechanisms of defense. This suggests another application of the psychoanalytic case findings to prevention and treatment on a larger scale. When adults lose their protective role and function, the child is forced to fall back upon primitive defenses. If Larry's teachers had been equipped to handle the new problems that the delinquents brought to the school and had retained their role of adult protectors, the disorganizing effects of the street-child on the middle-class child might have been minimized and the spread of delinquency checked. Even such a simple measure as adult supervision of lavatories and locker-rooms may be highly effective in curbing anxiety if we understand how aggressive sex-games and incestuous name-calling can create both excitement and guilt in children who have not yet successfully repressed their oedipal strivings.

## A Failure in Foster Home Placement

Pete was abandoned by both his parents when he was seven and was taken into care by a child welfare agency. Nothing was known about

Pete's life before he entered his first foster home. Pete never spoke about his parents or his early life. The father was later traced, and it was found that he had died of acute alcoholism in an institution. Between the ages of seven and eleven Pete was in three foster homes. Each placement began with good hopes; the foster parents found him attractive, bright, charming, and most endearing. And each placement ended in disaster with the foster parents insisting that the child be removed, for they could no longer tolerate his strange and unpredictable behavior.

The pattern was identical in each of the foster homes. There was an initial honeymoon period during which Pete responded to the warmth and affection of the foster family. Then, at the point where strong positive ties seemed to emerge, this charming little boy began to reveal another aspect of his personality that shocked the foster family. He became aggressive toward the foster parents, relentlessly goading them into anger and punishment. He was insatiable in his demands. And he was capable of cruelties toward children and animals. In his last foster home he attempted to beat a foster brother with a baseball bat. He tormented and abused the puppy he had been given as a gift. He deliberately deprived the animal of food (he was in charge of its care and feeding) and could be seen with a strangely satisfied look on his face as the puppy begged for food and made pathetic mewling noises.

How shall we explain such behavior? The field of child placement will yield many, many examples of the child who goes through repeated placements in which certain patterns of behavior are reproduced in each home, in nearly unvarying form, regardless of the differences in foster parents, the variations in the family constellation, and the certain expectation on the part of the child that he will be sent away.

Here, a theory of role-interaction is inadequate to deal with the complex behavior. Pete's pleasure in hurting, for example, is not reactive; no one in his foster homes behaved sadistically toward him. Well then, one might say that he *perceived* his foster parents as sadistic and was reacting according to his perception of their role. But this would not be exact, here. I do not think Pete perceived his foster parents as cruel; such a distortion of perception will usually be revealed by a child in the form of accusations or persecutory feelings, none of which were expressed by Pete. All that one can safely derive from the facts is that he felt impelled to behave in certain ways and that this behavior generally was not initiated by external events.

To explain the repetition of certain forms of behavior without regard for objective circumstances we need the help of psychoanalytic theory. We need to understand the repetition compulsion and the phenomenon of transference. It is useful for us to know, then, in the case of children in placement, that when a child loses his original love objects or is separated from them, he will repeat in his new relationships to foster parents certain conflicts that originated in the relationships to his own parents. The child relives something from his past, sometimes only briefly but sometimes interminably. The child experiences this as a *compulsion* to behave in certain ways. If we, as social workers, take up with him one or another aspect of his apparently unmotivated behavior he will either rationalize it or will often tell us quite frankly, "I don't know why I do it." We are justified in calling this "transference" and we note that it is in many ways similar to the phenomenon of "transference neurosis."

Now, since foster parents are not clinicians, we can hardly blame them for finding these transference reactions quite intolerable. In a successful foster home placement, reality becomes the corrective for the transference fantasy, and the child after an initial disturbance will alter himself in accordance with reality expectations. But in many more placement situations the child's compulsion to repeat and to transfer will strain the foster parents to the breaking point and finally bring about the termination of the placement.

With these things in mind let us review the few details I have described in Pete's case. We observe that as soon as a positive attachment to the foster parents begins to emerge he reveals aggressive and sadistic behavior. This means that the sadistic behavior belongs to the condition of attachment, and from this we can now begin to infer something about Pete's unknown past. We now add to this the provocative behavior in which he attempts to get the foster parents to retaliate. And to this we need to add our observations of Pete's sadistic acts toward children and animals. This tells us that Pete is both active and passive in relation to sadism, and now we can deduce a portion of Pete's unknown case history. This child who finds pleasure in performing cruel acts has once been the passive partner in a relationship in which cruel acts were performed upon him. He has probably known brutal beatings (the incident of trying to hit the foster brother with a baseball bat) and he has probably known hunger and other forms of deprivation (the starving of his puppy). From the details we are fairly safe in assuming that the sadism that Pete had experienced had come from his own parents. (The provocative behavior is primarily directed toward the parent figures.)

But Pete himself has never spoken about his family or his life before placement, and the whole period of his first seven years is a blank in the history. And this is true. He does not speak of the past, but he repeats the past in his behavior. He transfers the past to the present, and if we understand the meaning of transference we can see that he is telling us part of his history. (It is very much worth mentioning that we were later able to unearth some facts about Pete's early life and that the brutality of the father was confirmed.)

But is all this really a help to the social worker? Do we have anything more than a refined diagnosis now? Here, we will see that the psychoanalytic diagnosis carries its own prescription. If we understand that the past is repeated in the present, the casework treatment which makes use of the present functioning of the client can help the child overcome the morbid influence of the past. The child can be helped to understand that his behavior is a way of talking, that he is telling us of painful and frightening things that have happened to him, but that he will find that if he *talks* about these things he will not need to *do* these things and that the memories will not hurt so much after a while.

Pete remembers his past (that is, these memories are not repressed), but whenever the painful memory emerges into consciousness, when he remembers being beaten or remembers hunger and fear and unsatisfied longing, the pain and helplessness that accompany the memory cannot be endured, and he must re-enact the memory and make himself active, doing to others what has been done to him.

The caseworker who wins Pete's confidence will find that if he can help him to express the painful feelings that accompany these memories Pete will be able at least partially to overcome the painful effects of his past experience and relinquish the acting-out of these memories. All of this we will grant is within the province of casework treatment. And all of this is necessary in order to achieve the social work goal of "enhancing social functioning."

In Pete's case we have borrowed the insights of psychoanalysis in order to understand the contradictions in one child's personality and the forms of behavior that have repeatedly led to failure in foster home placement. We can also see some general applications to casework treatment. An understanding of transference could illuminate many difficult problems in child placement. The understanding of the dynamics of this type of behavior disorder should assist us in working with a very large group of children who act out their inner conflicts.

## Casework Treatment of a Mother on Behalf of the Child

Now I am reminded of another case, one from a family agency, in which a mother sought advice in handling the problems of her eight-year-old daughter. The presenting problem was Margaret's reluctance to go to school, a problem which had existed since kindergarten days and now had reached serious proportions. Margaret complained of headaches and nausea each morning and begged her mother to allow her to stay home. Each morning a weeping, nearly hysterical little girl was dragged off to school. Once there she managed somehow, her mother said, and sat mute and docile in her seat, not taking in half of what was said in class. Her school grades were considerably below the expectations for a child of better than average intelligence.

When the parents were able to get Margaret to talk about her fears in connection with school, she could only say that she was afraid that the teacher might get angry at her. Since her teacher was not unduly severe with children, this explanation was not very helpful.

At home Margaret was described as a cheerful, well-behaved child who presented no unusual problems to her parents. If it were not for the difficulty in getting her off to school the parents would have no complaints. She occasionally wet the bed, her mother remembered. Margaret's strongest ties were to her mother, but her father had much affection for his children and was indisputably head of the family. There was an older brother, ten, whose school performance was very good, and Margaret often compared herself unfavorably with him.

Margaret's problem is one that the social worker sees very often in school and family agencies and in child guidance clinics. If the social worker's job is to bring about more effective functioning in the area of school and learning, the first question is "How shall this be done?" If Margaret's problem was clearly a reaction to a severe and punitive teacher, we might help the teacher acquire more understanding of Margaret and be more lenient in her expectations of the child. But here there is no evidence that the teacher enters into the conflict on a real basis, and we are left with a child's unreal fears. We may, if we like, tell Margaret that her fears are unreal. She will not believe us.

Let's try some theories here. Suppose we say that Margaret has failed in adapting herself to the role expectations of a school-child, that she sees herself as the baby of the family and prefers to remain dependent upon her mother. This may be true. If we now employ this diagnosis in treatment we should try to help Margaret become independent and to find that being a big girl has greater satisfactions. If this is only a dependency problem this method may work. But we will find that if we attempt to make Margaret independent of her mother her anxiety will increase and we will move further away from our goal of restoring social functioning. The dependency, we must reason, is only one facet of the problem.

What we need is a diagnosis that takes into account the factor of *dread* in Margaret's avoidance of school, dread of an imagined danger. The diagnosis needs to account for the fact that an eight-year-old child is a model of good behavior in her home and that she fantasies dangers when she is at school. The diagnosis must account for the outbreak of anxiety when Margaret is obliged to go to scool and for the conversion symptoms which appear at these times.

The diagnosis "school phobia" is correct here and immediately comes to our aid in treatment. If we understand the structure of a childhood phobia we will know that a conflict which originated in a child's relationships to his own parents is displaced onto objects outside of the home. The original ambivalence to parents vanishes, the dangerous aspect of the parent is split off and attributed to teachers and to the school itself. The child's own repudiated hostile impulses are projected outward and experienced as coming from the outside, and the child himself becomes free of conflict within the home as long as he can avoid the danger outside—the school. Again the diagnosis carries its own prescription. We must locate the sources of conflict in the child's relationships to his parents and help parents and child find new solutions to the conflict.

In Margaret's case the family agency chose to work with the parents, particularly the mother who seemed to be in the center of this invisible conflict. The caseworker began to help the mother to see Margaret's docility and obedience in another light. Gradually the mother was able to see how the child had acquired her obedience through completely surrendering naughty or aggressive impulses and that this had been achieved at great cost to the child. Margaret was afraid of anger, of her own anger and the anger of others, and this was one of the elements in the school phobia. When the mother understood this she began, with the caseworker's guidance, to become a more lenient mother, and to allow Margaret to express feelings of anger when this was appropriate and to ease the child's fear that anger would bring loss of love or monstrous retaliation.

As we might expect, when Margaret was given permission to feel anger toward the mother whom she loved, the conflict that had been displaced from home to school returned to home ground where now, with the help of the caseworker, better solutions could be found. Margaret's fear of school diminished rapidly. Within a few months the conflict was successfully withdrawn from the area of school, and school functioning improved markedly.

In the case of Margaret the casework treatment was aimed at "improvement of social functioning." The underlying phobia was not dissolved through this treatment. Margaret, for example, still had night fears. But this treatment was effective in bringing about the restoration of ego functions that had been restricted by the phobia. So we see that even such a simple objective as getting a child back into school and improving her scholastic performance depends upon a diagnosis that discriminates and organizes details. The psychoanalytic diagnosis not only describes but it explains, and when the caseworker understands the meaning of the behavior he can formulate the appropriate treatment.

### A Family Conflict

Mrs. B. has come to the family agency for counsel. Her problems are almost too many to enumerate. Her five-year-old son is a bully and generally regarded as a neighborhood menace. Neither she nor her husband seem to have any influence over him. Jon is passionately jealous of Lydia, the two-and-a-half-year-old daughter of the family. Lydia herself is a feeding problem and refuses to go to bed at night. There is considerable conflict between Mrs. B. and her husband, most of which centers around discipline of the children and the interference of Mrs. B.'s parents in their marriage. Mrs. B.'s parents have battled as long as their daughter can remember. Her father takes refuge from the abuse of his wife by spending several days a week at his daughter's house and takes over the cooking of evening meals at her home in shy apology for his too-frequent visits and in an attempt to make himself useful in a position where he obviously is not. Mrs. B.'s mother is erratic and opinionated, and rules her husband and her daughter by means of paralyzing guilt-producing tactics. Mrs. B.'s husband has grimly endured the involved relationships with in-laws for twelve years and now this long-suffering husband has made his own blunt protests. Something needs to be done.

Mrs. B. after several interviews with the caseworker in which she described the chaos of her home, finally began to see clearly that her problems as a wife and a mother were inextricably bound up in her problems with her parents. As long as she could remember she had been in the center of their own marital conflict and had been used by one or another of the parents as refuge and confidante and, as the only child, the sole reason for continuing the marriage. She was the peace-maker, or the trucemaker, and carried the intolerable burden through childhood of keeping her parents together.

Now, as a grown woman, she was still bound to them. She was weary of their quarrels. She was tired of her father's constant presence in her household and sympathized with her husband. But she could not discuss this with her father. Her mother's incessant demands and her interference in Mrs. B.'s family life exhausted Mrs. B., and impo-tent rage against mother and father made her a distracted and petu-lant wife and an erratic mother.

She could not even understand this tie to her parents, she confessed to the caseworker. Her mother and she had very little to say to each other. Her mother would call her frequently on the telephone and Mrs. B., who often yearned to end these conversations, could not ter-minate the calls because of her guilty feelings. Sometimes, she said, her mother would call and say nothing and each would hold on to the phone, in complete silence, unable to say "good-bye."

We have no difficulty in understanding why Mrs. B. is unable to function as wife and mother. As long as her infantile ties to her par-ents are not dissolved she cannot be a wife or parent in her own right. She repeats the infantile conflict with parents in her adult life, and with the best will in the world she cannot prevent herself from doing it. She is tied to her parents through guilt. The telephone calls from mother become a pregnant symbol; neither one can break the connection.

This constitutes our preliminary casework diagnosis. We might need a second thought to realize that everything that we have said derives from a psychoanalytic diagnosis. Psychoanalytic thinking is so closely woven into casework theory that we often cannot even identify it without a close look. We recognize in Mrs. B.'s relationships with her parents an unresolved oedipal conflict. The unconscious repetition of infantile patterns we have learned to identify through psychoanalysis. And the neurotic guilt feelings which bind this woman to her parents, and are an indispensable part of casework diagnosis, were first identified and described by Freud.

Now let us examine the casework treatment method employed in the case of Mrs. B. The caseworker began to show Mrs. B. the repetition of certain patterns in her behavior toward her parents. She did not interpret these patterns but she brought them to her client's attention. (This is an application of a psychoanalytic technique to casework.) Mrs. B. responded by examining for the first time in her life certain patterns of conduct which seemed so much a part of her personality that she had never even questioned their existence. (This, too, is a borrowing from psychoanalytic therapy. We create the conditions for self-observation and make the irrational behavior the object of inquiry.) Now the question "Why?" was raised in the casework interviews. "Because I feel so guilty if I don't do these things!" said the client.

Now the caseworker needs to make a judgment. To what degree can this pathological tie to parents be modified through casework treatment? There are compulsive patterns in Mrs. B.'s behavior. She seems too concerned with orderliness and cleanliness. Are we dealing with a compulsion neurosis? If we are, any attempts to alleviate Mrs. B.'s guilt feelings will only plunge her deeper into illness. In an unobtrusive way the caseworker collects data over a number of interviews and is finally satisfied that there are no systematized compulsions and that orderliness and cleanliness can be abandoned under a number of circumstances without creating anxiety in the client. (Here the caseworker makes use of the psychoanalytic theory of neurosis in order to safeguard her work with the client and to justify the use of casework treatment.)

From this point on the caseworker employs a method of treatment that in no way resembles psychoanalytic therapy and yet makes use of psychoanalytic knowledge in certain identifiable ways. The caseworker supports Mrs. B. in her wish to be free of this paralyzing tie to her parents. She gives her permission, as it were, to be free. And Mrs. B. through the support of the caseworker begins to take active steps in freeing herself. She becomes firm against their intrusion and their provocation of guilt in her. But with each step her own guilt feelings come to the surface and are brought to the casework interviews for clarification. As a consequence the relationship between Mrs. B. and her husband is strengthened and their conflicts diminished. There is considerable improvement in the behavior of the children and Mrs. B. demonstrates greater confidence and understanding in her handling of them. (There are, however, indications that Jon may later require treatment for himself.)

In casework terms the treatment method employed here might be called supportive although in certain areas treatment was directed toward modification of adaptive patterns. But our description of the method does not in itself describe the dynamics of this treatment. And in a scientific casework we want to be able to know exactly why a method works in a particular case or group of cases in order that we can duplicate the results under similar conditions. Here, again, psychoanalysis helps us to understand the dynamics of this treatment. The positive transference to the caseworker is employed for a kind of re-education of conscience. Through the relationship with the caseworker new standards of conduct and new attitudes are introduced to the ego, and the caseworker as a benevolent mother figure and authority has the effect of softening the harsh strictures of the tyrannical mother who was, of course, the original model for conscience. The unconscious sources of guilt feelings remain untouched by this treatment method, but this educational approach which utilizes conscious attitudes and feelings may be successful in freeing certain areas of functioning from their paralyzing effects.

## Psychoanalytic Perspectives on Adaptation

In each of the cases we have reviewed we began with a disturbance of social functioning, but the restoration of function could only be achieved after careful diagnosis of internal as well as external motives. Psychoanalytic insight provided a precise diagnosis, made the behavior meaningful, and prescribed the corrective measures. The psychoanalytic diagnosis made full use of the data pertaining to the social situations and the interaction of personalities.

Both psychoanalysis and social work are concerned with problems of adaptation. The study of adaptation has been at the center of psychoanalytic study during the past thirty years. Adaptation, in the psychoanalytic view, is a complex process which involves both external and internal regulation by the ego. While adaptation is largely the function of the ego, each of the mental institutions serves adaptation in special ways.

Psychoanalysis shares with other psychologies an interest in the ego's regulation of relationships to the environment and the effects of environment upon the ego's adaptive capacities. But psychoanalysis sees the ego as the regulator of internal as well as external processes, and adaptation in this view is given dimension and complexity. This means that adaptation is achieved not only by the ego's regulation of its relationship to the environment but by its regulation of the internal relationships between the mental institutions.

We can easily see the advantages of such a formulation. A disturbance between the ego and id, for example, can affect the relationship between the ego and the environment. (The classic example of such a disturbance and its effects upon adaptation may be seen in adolescence.) Similarly a disturbance between the ego and the environment may affect the equilibrium of the mental institutions. (We saw this in the example of Larry, when the conflict with the delinquent boys reactivated an inner conflict between ego and id.) And in the psychoanalytic view the ego's own functions that subserve adaptation may be disturbed if they are drawn into conflict. (An example would be Margaret's impaired learning.)

Such a view of adaptation is extraordinarily complex, but we find that because it is more complex than other theories it is more useful. It obliges us to consider adaptation as a process that engages every part of the personality. A failure or a disturbance in adaptation cannot be attributed to "a weak ego" or "environmental stress," but must be discerned through the most careful study of the internal and external processes that work for adaptation. In order, then, for the social worker to support the adaptive tendencies in personality or to modify adaptive patterns, he must know which parts of the personality are involved. The social worker does not need to be a psychoanalyst in order to make his assessment. Internal conflicts can be deduced through a study of the ego as we saw in the case reports we have reviewed, and their relative significance in a disturbance of functioning can be ascertained.

Such a comprehensive view of adaptation gives us a more stable diagnosis than one which measures behavior alone. I know a rebellious and hot-headed little boy who was placed in an institution at the age of nine. Within a year he was perfectly adapted to the requirements of the institution. He was well-behaved and polite and no longer gave anyone any trouble. He gained thirty pounds during that first year and began to wet his bed nightly. When I saw him at the age of eleven he was passive, obese and still a bedwetter. If we judge this adaptation by external signs this child was much improved in his behavior and was well-adapted to the requirements of the environment. But the psychoanalytic view of adaptation requires that a successful adaptation be assessed impartially by internal as well as external criteria. An adaptation that results in improved relationships with the environment at the cost of internalized conflict, symptoms, and a shift in the personality from active to passive aims is not a successful adaptation in the psychoanalytic view.

I know a child who was an exhibitionistic masturbator at the age of six. Her foster parents were deeply disturbed by this behavior and seriously questioned whether she could remain with them. The little girl loved her foster parents and feared the loss of her home. She gave up the masturbation, and her behavior within the home improved very greatly. From the standpoint of social functioning this was a successful adaptation. But the analytically trained social worker knows that when a serious symptom disappears it is a good idea to go in search of it. We went in search of it one day at a case conference nearly ten years after it vanished.

In the ten years that followed the disappearance of the symptom Julie suffered with a recurrent dermatitis which suggested that the skin had become eroticized in a displacement from the genitals. We followed her school history closely and saw that learning was severely restricted in certain areas, which told us that the catastrophic end to sexual curiosity had swept normal curiosity and learning with it. And now at sixteen when vocational training was indicated her teachers, the foster parents, and the social workers despaired at her potential. For not only was she restricted in her mental functioning, but she was the clumsiest and most inept child with her hands! She could do nothing with them, an observation that had first been made way back in the early school years. So we saw that the offending hands had been drawn into the conflict and its resolution. Here the social adaptation had been made at the cost of a dermatitis and a restriction of ego functions in vital areas. Should we call this a successful adaptation?

We social workers are always in the position of making crucial decisions in human lives. We make these decisions not always through advice giving but through a diagnosis and the treatment plan that grows out of it. A diagnosis that is based upon social functioning alone can be a perilous undertaking for a mental health worker. And a theory of social functioning and adaptation that does not take into account the inner mental processes that work for adaptation can lead us into the position of manipulators of social roles which calls for a divine wisdom that will not be achieved in two years of graduate study in a school of social work.

### Teaching and Learning Psychoanalytic Theory

What does a social worker need to know about psychoanalytic theory in order to make effective use of this knowledge in practice? If we only use the case examples I have cited, let us see what knowledge was necessary for diagnosis and treatment. A knowledge of ego and libidinal phases of development, of the structure of the ego and the mechanisms of defense; an understanding of transference phenomena and the repetition compulsion; knowledge of symptom formation and the structure of neurosis. All this is explicit. But then we find that implicit in this knowledge is the theory of drives, the concept of mental energy, primary and secondary mental processes—and before we have completed the list we will have covered nearly the entire structure of psychoanalytic theory!

I am not advocating, of course, a full curriculum in psychoanalytic theory in the two years of social work graduate training. We are satisfied if we can provide our students with the fundamentals of psychoanalytic theory, even as we are satisfied if we can provide them with the fundamentals of other aspects of social work theory. What, then, constitutes the fundamentals of psychoanalysis for students of social work?

In the present curricula of schools of social work the major concepts and theories of psychoanalysis are presented as part of a course called "Human Growth and Behavior," or "Growth and Development" which is designed to cover physical, mental and emotional growth throughout the life-span. The scope of this course is so vast that it is usually taught by a team of specialists in medicine, psychiatry, anthropology, and psychology with a social work faculty member serving as coordinator. The number of lectures specifically dealing with psychoanalytic theory may be a very small fraction of the total. In this respect psychoanalysis fares no worse than other disciplines represented at this smorgasbord. Out of this melange of ink-blots, chicken pox, chromosomes, cortisone, ego, libido and the Trobriand Islanders, the exhausted student may very well emerge with a disease that I once discovered in an examination paper in this course. It was called "prostrate trouble" and I was so touched that my student found this way of telling me what was wrong with my course that I could not even bring myself to correct his spelling.

There is general dissatisfaction with this course among both faculty and students in schools of social work, and at a time when nearly all schools are considering new ways of teaching this material I would like us to consider that part of the course content that deals with psychoanalytic theory. Because of the vast scope of this course the psychoanalytic content as well as the material from other disciplines is often so general as to be useless. In the short time available to discuss every aspect of human functioning the psychoanalytic content becomes "psychoanalytic information" instead of psychoanalytic theory.

What concerns us most of all is that our students emerge from their introduction to psychoanalysis with a terminology that seems to have very little meaning for them. The student knows the terms "ego," "id," "superego," "Oedipus complex" and "libido." He has learned the names of defense mechanisms with the same dutiful feeling that he once learned the Latin names for plants and with as little expectation that it will do him any good. He often misuses this terminology in ways that reveal his uncertain grasp of concepts.

If we analyze the typical errors of terminological usage of our students we sometimes get valuable clues to the learning difficulty. We find that many of our students treat the concepts of ego, id, and superego as if they were geographically defined regions in the psyche or even as if they were anatomical structures. The dynamic relationships between the mental institutions are then lost in the student's theory. "Psychic determinism," in the student's view, means that personality is "determined" in early childhood. "Anxiety" is a bad thing to have; a mature person shouldn't have it. Mature people don't have "repressions" either. Defense mechanisms are known to our students in the descriptive sense and are frequently understood in the layman's sense, not the scientific one. "Denial" for example is often understood as "to deny," following ordinary usage. "Reaction-formation" is used as a synonym for "reaction." "Undoing" is used to cover a wide variety of acts which have nothing to do with defense, in which an action "undid" or negated an earlier action.

On more than one occasion my students have shown me how my elementary exposition was responsible for their own untidy thinking. A few years ago when I was teaching a course in "Normal Development" I had introduced my students to the mechanisms of defense by identifying and illustrating the types of defense and showed them how anxiety created the motive for defense. I noticed that nearly all the students seemed quite unilluminated by this discussion, and as we were discussing reaction formations our discussion was particularly fuzzy. Finally one of my students asked, "What made the defense so strong in the example you gave? Why did it need to be so strong?" This was an excellent question. The problem of quantity could not be explained through the descriptive presentation I had given. And the mechanisms of defense could not be explained without quantity. I had not intended to go into energetic concepts during this introductory phase of the course, but I now saw how my elementary exposition was creating its own confusion.

At this point I began to discuss the concept of mental energy and illustrated how a defense "borrows" energy from the warded-off instinctual wish. The students were then able to see how the strength of a defense was a crude measure of the strength of the repudiated wish. From the questions that followed I knew that the students were beginning to grasp the principles of defense. We were also able to make a practical application of these principles to casework treatment. In order to support or to modify defenses in casework treatment we need to be able to judge the relative strength of a defense and to make inferences regarding the impulse warded off in defense.

On another occasion in a casework class we were discussing a case of learning disability in a child and got off into a theoretical discussion of sublimation. We saw that sublimation was a special form of displacement. I remarked parenthetically that in defining sublimation we no longer used the phrase "from a lower to a higher goal" because value judgments have no place in a scientific definition. At this point one of my students said, "I don't get it. Then what makes sublimation different from any other form of displacement? If I'm mad at my boss and I come home and kick the door or yell at my wife is *that* sublimation?" This was an excellent question. When I told my student that his question put him in excellent company among psychoanalytic theorists he looked terrified. But now consider the dilemma of the teacher. The elementary presentation got me into trouble again. Yet, to answer the question I needed to lead the students into rough theoretical territory. Hartmann's concept of "neutralization" which could lead us out of this tangle could just as easily bring our class into chaos. Hartmann, understandably, is not on Casework III reading lists.

I enlisted the help of the students. "All right," I said, "what do we need to explain the difference between sublimation and displacement?" Some students thought we would have to return to valuation of the act, after all. This was argued down by the purists in class. Then someone hit on the notion that the difference could not lie in the displaced goal, but, using the first student's example, in what happened to aggression. Aggression, she thought, would be changed, too, in the sublimated act. In what way? Well, she wasn't exactly sure, but she thought that it would lose some of its aggressiveness; it certainly wouldn't express itself in kicking a door! And there we had it; a homely but practical way of stating the concept of neutralization of energy. With a few more examples we were able to demonstrate that in sublimation there was a displacement of goal with a corresponding change in the mode of energy, that is a "desexualization" or a "deaggressivization" of the energy. When we now returned to our case the child's failure to acquire sublimations took on fresh meaning. With this much understanding of sublimation we could understand the child's failure, and the casework remedy suggested itself.

These are only two of many classroom examples that come to mind which illustrate the perils of over-simplification of theory. The fragments of theory which I had given my students had no meaning when they were plucked out of the context of the larger theory. My students' defense-mechanism jargon was not a measure of their intelligence or studiousness but a reflection of my own teaching. There is no possibility of understanding defense mechanisms or sublimation or any aspect of ego psychology without introducing the student to the theory of drives, the concept of mental energy, unconscious mental processes—in short to give unity to these ideas and to show the interrelatedness of mental processes.

Once last year my third semester students in casework had a lively discussion which centered around the use of psychoanalytic knowledge in casework practice. There was general agreement among the students that psychoanalytic ego psychology had demonstrable value to the caseworker, but what about dream theory, what about unconscious processes? Since social workers never deal with unconscious material, they said, was there any need to learn about these things?

I chided them a bit for being so thrifty in their attitude toward knowledge, but I took up the challenge. I reminded them that one cannot divide the mind into geographical territories. The very conception of an ego in psychoanalytic psychology implies the existence of drives and unconscious forces. Where there are no drives there are no mental processes. When the caseworker deals with the ego he must take into account unconscious mental processes even if he does not make them the object of his investigation as does the analyst. A social worker does not need to become expert in dream theory. But knowledge of unconscious mental processes is essential not only because it gives coherence to the study of psychoanalytic theory but because in practice we are obliged to take unconscious motives into account. When we observe a client's behavior, or his defenses, or repetitious patterns in his life we make inferences regarding unconscious motives. And these inferences serve our diagnosis and treatment even though the unconscious motive is not the object of our study.

So while a student may never interpret a dream in his professional life he may find it profitable and rewarding to become acquainted with the psychoanalytic writings on dreams because there is no better way of understanding unconscious mental processes. The dream, of course, is the model of unconscious mental functioning. If he understands the principles that govern unconscious mental functioning he will be able to understand defense, symptom formation, transference, and delusional states, and he will also understand the relationship of the ego to the id, which is a significant part of ego-psychology.

I have described some of the hazards in learning and teaching that may be attributed to our educational approach in the graduate school. A "psychoanalytic information" course can easily lead to fragmentary and inexact comprehension of psychoanalytic principles, which adds to the confusion of the learner and limits the possibility of applying these principles to social work practice. And, I should add, the best gifts of the teacher may be exhausted in the attempt to present coherent theory within the framework of a course that covers nothing less than the whole of human functioning.

If psychoanalytic knowledge is to be made useful to our students we will need to find ways in which the fundamentals of psychoanalytic theory can be taught as a coherent body of knowledge and ways in which we can promote transfer of learning from theory to practice.

I do not envision such a theoretical course or series of courses as a formal series of lectures. It would seem to me most satisfactory to teach this material on the basis of lecture-discussion in classes that should not exceed twenty-five or thirty students. The lecture, if used at all, should not deprive the student of the necessity to acquaint himself with basic writings in psychoanalysis. In our present teaching the psychoanalytic lecturer has served as a kind of reader's digest for the student, and it is not at all unusual for students to admit that they have never read a single work of Freud's. (When we persuade our students to read the neglected works of Freud on their course bibliographies they are always surprised to find that Freud is more lucid than his elucidators.) Perhaps much of the time that is now spent on lecture-digest of psychoanalytic concepts and theories might be more profitably spent in the libraries. The classroom time might be used for discussion of reading, and clarification of problems. Lectures or exposition by the teacher might be employed to bridge gaps in the student's reading or pull together materials that are not otherwise available to students or are too difficult to place on a student's bibliography.

Since this is a course for social workers it would seem very natural that this teaching should encompass not only the theory but the applications of psychoanalytic theory to social work practice. Illustrative case and group material from social agencies are excellently suited to demonstrate applications to diagnosis and treatment. While we also expect that the students are studying applications of theory in their methods courses, we should not wish to create rigid divisions in theory and practice. The students' learning will be enhanced throughout if, in each of the teaching areas, we demonstrate the interrelatedness of theory and practice. It is just as advantageous for the methods teacher and the field teacher to discuss problems of theory when this is appropriate.

If we value the contributions of psychoanalysis to social work we will need to make it the object of proper study in our professional schools. I do not think that anything less than serious study will yield returns to the student. And as our profession moves toward its objective of a scientific social work we are under a clear obligation to teach the component sciences of social work as science.

The student who understands psychoanalysis as science will know that it is not a speculative system but a body of knowledge that is derived from observation. He will learn to observe behavior with close attention to detail and be able to draw inferences from it. Having studied the complex processes that enter into ego functioning and social functioning he will not seek simple remedies and will understand that effective social treatment must take into account the complexities and dimensions of human personality. He will understand the general principles of mental functioning, but he will also know that each personality is uniquely constituted and reacts to its environment in ways that are its own. He should be able to discriminate through a scientific diagnosis between those conflicts that may be relieved through modification of the environment, those that can be helped through understanding and support of adaptive tendencies in personality, and those that require modification of the adaptive patterns themselves. And the student who understands all this will also know that professional intervention in a human life carries deep responsibilities and makes severe demands upon his scientific knowledge.

All in all, these benefits of a sound education in psychoanalytic psychology strike us as very familiar. They are, of course, identical with the objectives of a sound professional training in social work.

*Note*

This paper was presented at a meeting sponsored by the Psychiatric Social Work Section of the Eastern Massachusetts Chapter of the National Association of Social Workers, Boston, October 25, 1960.

# 19

## Legacies and Prophecies

The purpose of a commencement is to confer legacies, invoke ancestral spirits, and make prophecies. At the conclusion of these sacred rites we find that the legacy of the tribal elders is not as large as the young deserve, that it is encumbered by taxes in the literal and metaphorical sense, and that the inheritors, who deserve better, must put up with the improvidence and impaired vision of their ancestors. I promise to fulfill all of these ceremonial functions in the twenty-five minutes that have been given me.

Today I would like to speak about children and certain unpaid debts which we have contracted on behalf of children. The legacy and the debt are passed on to this graduating class, even as it was passed on to mine. But this generation of social workers has the means to discharge that debt and I would like to speak with some urgency on these matters. I think that if we do not pay off the debts to the children it may not matter very much what else we do in social work for the next twenty years.

The legacy in itself resides in social work. One part of the legacy is dazzling in its wealth and its promise. This is the scientific inheritance. Another part of the legacy is a powerful tradition in social work which has made each of us ministers to need and advocates for those who have no voice. A third part of the inheritance is encumbered. A chasm exists between the scientific treasure and the children in need. The children who should be the beneficiaries have received small sustenance, each year a little less, while we contemplate the treasure and invoke its glory in our classrooms.

In this century we have come into knowledge about childhood and the constitution of personality which can be fairly placed among the greatest scientific discoveries in history. The century began when

Freud discovered that the most severe and crippling emotional disorders of adult life have their genesis in early childhood. In the seventy and more years since Freud's early writings we have been led to discoveries about childhood and the nature of man which have left us reeling. During the past thirty years our studies have led us deeper and deeper into the unknown territories of childhood, into infancy and early childhood and the origins of personality. We now know that those qualities that we call "human"—the capacity for enduring love and the exercise of conscience—are not given in human biology; they are the achievement of the earliest human partnership between a child and his parents.

And we now know that a child who is deprived of human partners in the early years of life, or who has known shifting or unstable partnerships in the formative period of personality, may have permanent impairment in his capacity to love, to learn, to judge, and to abide by the laws of the human community. This child, in effect, has been deprived of his humanity.

How we learned this is no secret. It was a discovery that emerged from the wreckage of World War II. The lost children, the abandoned children, the children of Hitler's camps, the babies without mothers brought an impassioned inquiry on the part of scientists into the meaning of war to children. What emerged from this inquiry was that even the life-threatening dangers of war were not as destructive to the minds and emotions of children as separation from mothers and fathers. For many of these children the damage to personality was permanent.

At the war's end, the scientific inquiry moved ahead. It is not only in times of war that children are deprived of mothering and family nurture. There are circumstances today in which tens of thousands of children in our country are deprived of a mother or a mother substitute. Small children in institutions, children in foster homes, and children in their own homes with unstable partnerships form a vast population of sufferers.

As scientists from a number of disciplines examined the effects of maternal deprivation on the developing personality, a consensus of findings emerged. We learned that the developing ego of the young child is inextricably interwoven with the maintenance of the early love bonds and that deprivation of these bonds, or a rupture of bonds already formed, can have permanent effects upon the later capacities of the child to love and to learn. We also learned, from the clinical side of the inquiry, that the most severe and intractable emotional diseases of childhood are the diseases of nonattachment and the diseases of broken attachments. A commitment to love is normally given in the early years of life, the gift of ordinary parents, without benefit of psychiatric consultation. But a child who, at school age has not yet received this gift, may require the whole of our colossal apparatus in psychiatric clinics and remedial education to help him learn to love and to trust.

These are the extreme cases, yet the number of these children is growing year by year. There are also less virulent but ominous forms of the same disease that are afflicting tens of thousands of children in our country. The children of poverty know lost and broken human connections to a frightening degree. There is the father who is not there or has never been there. There is the mother who works at an ill-paid job whose babies and young children are delivered like small packages to substitute care-givers—on Monday to a neighbor down the street, on Tuesday to a grandma or an aunt, on Wednesday to an older sister, on Thursday to someone else. And finally over the months and years there is no one in this ghostly procession that is mother or stands in the place of mother. When Head Start began, its teachers were astonished to discover that there were children at the age of four or five who did not know their own names.

All of this tells us that during the thirty years in which our scientific world made revolutionary discoveries regarding the nature and origin of human bonds, and the origins of the diseases of nonattachment, the children themselves have not been the beneficiaries. We have identified a group of malignant diseases of personality, disturbances of the primary human attachments. These diseases are preventable at the source. In a rational world, an army of mental health workers and citizens would gather together to ensure the human bonds of children, to guarantee their human rights. Our problem as social workers is to bridge the chasm between what is known and what can be done.

The mending of children's lives is a very large part of the work of our profession. As a psychotherapist I know that there is no more rewarding work in our profession. It would be folly to say that all childhood disturbances of personality can be prevented. Even in Utopia I think that child therapists will have waiting lists. But a large number of the disorders of personality that I have seen could have been prevented; and these in nearly every case have been disturbances in the primary human relationships during the early months and years of life.

When we think of "preventive work" in child guidance we have traditionally considered child psychotherapy as a form of prevention. And so it is. If we are successful in treating the childhood form of the neurosis, we may prevent the crippling neuroses of later life. But prevention must be seen in social terms as well. For every child who has been cured of eneuresis, bogey men, and youthful pilfering there are thousands of children waiting, already endangered or damaged because our social institutions and our social policies have robbed them of some measure of their humanity. In the most terrible irony we, as social workers, have been witnesses and sometimes even unwilling collaborators in the tragedy.

Our own history as a mental health profession has many paradoxes and many lessons for us.

In the 1920s we were among the first to see the implications of Freud's theory of the infantile neurosis for the prevention of adult mental disturbances. In collaboration with psychiatry and psychology we set up child guidance clinics for the identification and treatment of the emotional disturbances of childhood.

The child guidance movement had barely entered its first decade when the great depression appeared. Poverty, hunger, the emasculation of jobless fathers, desertion of families by broken men, and the placement of children in foster homes were the problems that flooded social agencies and clinics. Social work was not, of course, responsible for the depression—at least nobody has blamed us for it yet—but we were responsible for the development and administration of programs of public assistance. It was during this period that we initiated a strange bureaucratic marriage that should not go unremarked.

The ancient division of soma and psyche prevailed in a division of the child. In our work, the soma of the child was given to the public assistance agencies to be fed and sheltered, and the psyche was given to the child guidance clinic. In the department of soma we collaborated with legislators to bring forth the first federal public assistance programs for dependent children. This was a remarkable achievement in itself for it guaranteed the subsistence needs of hundreds of thousands of children. But in order to feed the child we compromised, I believe, with intransigent legislators, and wrote into the enabling laws certain eligibility requirements which have had effects upon the psyche of the child for over thirty years. The model ADC child would have no father, an absent father, or a disabled father. In all cases, the family that qualified for ADC received higher relief allowances than a family might receive from local welfare sources. This meant, of course, that the family which had an absent father was rewarded by the system, and the system of rewards was so effective over three decades that it helped to institutionalize the family without a father among the poor.

The lesson can be summarized in briefest terms: at the same period in our professional history that brought forth new programs for child mental health, we launched and administered public assistance programs which eroded family structure. On one side of the street we had the department of soma, issuing mental health problems with its relief check. On the other side of the street we had the department of psyche rapidly expanding its waiting list. In the classic image of Penelope, we wove our cloth by day and unravelled by night.

The ghost of Penelope haunts the child guidance movement. History records that during the second, third, and fourth decades of our crusade for child mental health there were three wars. For half of those years tens of thousands of children in our country were reared in the family chaos bred by war, and the result was the steady erosion of family bonds which is the only certain and predictable outcome of war. If the era of child mental health has not brought forth freedom from fear in childhood we must reflect that child mental health is not sustained by science alone. Mental health is not a commodity that can be taken off the shelves during war time and put back on the shelves in times of peace.

The irony is underscored. These thirty years of intermittent war are the thirty years which gave us the research on the origins of love and the origins of human bonds.

As custodians of the scientific treasure we have somehow failed to share the wealth among the social institutions that serve children. Our juvenile courts, for example, are privileged to make decisions regarding custody and social treatment for tens of thousands of children. Their mental health principles were laid down in the Old Testament. In 1973 the child remains the property of his natural parents even though his natural parents may be strangers to him. This means that a child who has formed his permanent attachments to foster parents, to grandparents, or other relatives may be returned to his natural parents upon their petition if no evidence of parental unfitness is presented to the court. In adoption cases the rights of natural parents have prevailed even after surrender, as in the well-known case of Baby Lenore and a very large number of other cases known to me.

Many thousands of babies and young children spend the early years of their lives in a succession of foster homes and institutions while decisions regarding surrender and custody drag through the courts. The court is empowered to act in the best interest of the child. Since the best interest of the child is incontestably served through sustaining stable human partnerships for the child, the power to act decisively to protect the child and his future surely resides within the law.

These unwanted children who have never known stability or continuity in human partnerships fill the waiting lists of our child guidance clinics and psychiatric hospitals. In truth they are not wanted there either, for no one has yet invented a treatment that fills the vacancy in a personality that occurs when no human partners entered.

The archaic principle of ownership prevails strangely in another group of custody cases. There are children of psychotic and criminal parents whose lives as well as their psyches are endangered if they remain in their homes. But today, even as it was fifty years ago, the court is loath to take protective custody of children who are the property of deranged parents. These children, too, are brought to the doors of the child guidance clinic. But we have not yet found a cure for children whose nightmares are real.

And, finally, in 1973, since no one has yet banished Penelope from the social policies that affect children, we have come full circle on poverty too. In 1940 we rewarded the families that had an absent father. Since 1970 we have inaugurated relief policies which make employment mandatory for welfare mothers. Since our government has also closed the door on a bill for the development of day-care facilities, we are now creating an expanded population of little wanderers who are already arriving at the doors of mental health agencies.

We have become partners in a surrealist charade in which society assaults the developing ego of the child and charges the child guidance clinic to repair it.

The legacy to this generation of social workers is a mixed one. But it is entirely within the capabilities of this generation to banish the spectre of Penelope and bring forth a rational policy for child mental health. To do this we need to abolish the ancient division of soma and psyche which has bedeviled our social policies.

In our profession the public assistance worker, the child welfare worker, the court social worker, the family caseworker must regard themselves fully as guardians of child mental health, in no way second to the child guidance worker who repairs it. We must examine the social policies which affect children, examine our agencies and services, and ask hard questions of ourselves. We must become advocates for the children who have no voice. We must speak for them to our legislators and our judges. We must develop new programs of mental health for infants and young children to insure the stability of human bonds.

To do this we need a generation of social workers to serve as the scientist-intermediaries between developmental psychology and children in need. The scientific legacy is already yours; beyond this we need a moral commitment to children who are the true inheritors of the legacy. This generation of graduate students is uniquely endowed with both the scientific training and the highest order of social commitment. My prophecy—I promised you a prophecy—is that the Penelope principle that has bedeviled our work and our social policies will receive its sternest challenge in the next forty years.

I am sorry that the ghost of Penelope has risen so insistently on this occasion. I had never intended to invite her to our graduation party. How did she get here? Who is Penelope? I know her well. I am Penelope. And you invited me.

Thank you. And good luck!

## Note

This paper is the text of a speech delivered at graduation ceremonies at the Smith College School for Social Work, August 22, 1973.

# Part IV

## Blindness in Childhood

# 20

# Studies in the Ego Development of the Congenitally Blind Child

*With David A. Freedman, M.D.*

Our interest in the process of ego formation in the congenitally blind infant originated in our first encounters with certain ego deviations found among blind children. We and other investigators were impressed by the high incidence of ego deviations encountered among children totally blind from birth and the clinical picture presented by such children which closely resembled autism in the sighted child. Since many children blind from birth may achieve a level of ego integration comparable to that of the sighted child we had to conclude that the absence of vision was not in itself the primary predisposing factor to deviant development. The deviant blind children showed a uniform development arrest and a freezing of personality on the level of mouth primacy and nondifferentiation. These and certain details in the retrospective histories suggested that the process of ego formation had been impeded during the critical period nine to eighteen months. The role of blindness as an impediment and the unique adaptational problems of the blind infant were yet to be understood.

In a review of twenty-eight blind children who constituted the first year's admissions to a guidance program inaugurated by the Family Service Society of New Orleans in 1959 we found seven cases in the age range three to thirteen who presented an extraordinary picture of developmental arrest. The clinical picture resembled that of infantile autism, but close examination revealed significant differences as well. Later we will describe these children.

Between 1959 and 1962 the authors engaged in the collaborative treatment of a deviant blind child and his mother. The case of Peter, which is presented in Part I of this essay, is typical of the deviant children we encountered in the agency population. The opportunity for close study of the deviant behavior and development of this child brought our attention to certain critical phases in ego formation during which the absence of vision impedes or may imperil integrative processes. The adaptive failures seen in Peter and other children in the blind group brought forth a large number of unanswered questions regarding the adaptive solutions found by normal blind infants and young children. We must assume from the evidence presented by large numbers of healthy and educable blind children that other sensory modalities can substitute for vision in the process of ego formation. There remain the questions: how are these substitutions made, and how does ego formation take place in the absence of vision? All theorizing concerning the process of ego formation is predicated upon the utilization of vision. It occurred to us that developmental studies of infants should help delineate the role of vision in ego formation and the vulnerable points in this early development which may lead to adaptive failures and ego deviations.

In July of 1961 we began our observations of an infant, then twenty-two weeks old, who had been totally blind from birth with the diagnosis ophthalmia neonatorum. She was followed through monthly observations and a motion-picture film record until twenty-eight months of age. A report and discussion of our findings in the study of the infant, Toni, is presented in Part II of this paper. The blind infant achieved at two years of age a level of maturation that was well within the norms for a blind child. At the time our observations terminated we saw no evidence of ego deviations. But as we followed the development of this child we began to understand how her blindness created a roadblock in her development at certain critical points in ego formation. As we watched this healthy blind child find circuitous routes to get onto the main developmental paths, we understood how, under less than favorable environmental circumstances and with less adaptive capacity than that shown by Toni, the complex solutions may never be found at all.

For these reasons the adaptive solutions found by a blind infant are best viewed against the background of adaptive failure in the cases of the deviant blind children.

The following description of the deviant blind child is based upon the group of cases in our Family Service Society case load together with those reported in the literature by Keeler (1958), Parmalee (1955), and Parmalee, Cutsforth, and Jackson (1958). The striking feature of these cases drawn from three sources is "uniformity." The investigator finds himself with the uncanny feeling that he is reading the same case over and over. In studying our Family Service Society records we had to provide ourselves with artificial memory cues to distinguish one case from another. ("Martin is the one who likes to suck on clothespins; Martha is the one who chews rubber jar rings; Jane is the head banger, and Chrissey bangs her bottom against the wall.")

The child may be two years old, five years, nine, or even thirteen years old and the picture is almost unvarying. Typically the deviant child spends hours in bed or in a chair or lying on the floor, absently mouthing an object. There is no interest in toys or any objects that are not in themselves need satisfying or stimulating to the mouth. Contact with human objects is often initiated by biting and even more often by a primitive clutching and clawing with the hands. For all these children the mouth remains the primary organ of perception. New objects are brought to the mouth and are rarely explored manually.

The behavior of the hand is striking. While many of the children can use the hand for self-feeding and can even use spoons and forks, the hand appears to have no autonomy of its own. It can serve the mouth, it can bring objects to the mouth, but it is not employed for examination or manipulation of objects. Discrimination of objects remains centered in the mouth; however, as already seen, objects are important not for their own characteristics but for their qualities in stimulating the mouth.

What we see in this superficial picture of the deviant blind children is a personality that has remained mouth-centered to an extent that is almost never encountered among sighted children except, perhaps, for certain children who have suffered extreme deprivation in infancy (Provence and Lipton, 1962; Spitz, 1945). And we should note that although mouth-centeredness and failure to achieve hand autonomy are two factors uniformly present in the deviant blind children, these are not characteristics commonly found among sighted autistic children. If we consider, further, that the hand of the blind child must serve as a primary organ for perception, the adaptive failure of the hand in these deviant blind children must be regarded as an important factor in the total picture of adaptive failure.

However, these children do display behavior such as body rocking, head banging, arm and hand waving, and bizarre posturing which is strikingly similar to that observed in the sighted autistic child. Language is rarely employed for communication or expression of need and consists mainly of echolalia and the repetitive use of apparently meaningless words and phrases. Discrimination of "I" and "you" has not appeared and self-reference is made in the third person.

In some cases the mother is not discriminated from other persons in the environment. In other cases an attachment to the mother is demonstrable, and reactions to separation from the mother are discernible through biting or clawing or a frenzied display of the whole repertory of autistic behavior. Still other children who seem to be oblivious to mother's presence and efforts to stimulate them will react violently to any threat of separation.

The early developmental histories of these deviant blind children are not significantly different from those of blind children who have achieved a good level of ego integration. They are described as quiet babies who were content to lie in their cribs for hours, and this is a common description of the infant who is blind from birth. The reports on both groups uniformly stress the mother's guilt and depression at learning of the child's blindness. But, as Keeler has reported, the histories of the deviant blind children often show the failure of the mother to offer stimulation and to make emotional contact with the sensorially deprived infant.

The gross motor development of the deviant children is within the norms for blind infants during the first nine months. Learning to hold up the head, to turn over, to sit independently were usually achieved without marked delay according to the histories. But many of these babies either do not creep, or learn to creep at a very late date, and walking is markedly delayed in nearly every case. Several of the children did not achieve independent walking until the age of four or five. It should be noted that among blind children, walking is normally achieved much later than it is among sighted children. In the Norris (1957) study between 50 and 75 percent of the 295 blind children achieved independent walking between the ages of two and three, with a range from fifteen months to five years. We have some evidence from our records that those infants who have even a small amount of form perception follow patterns of motor development that are very close to those of sighted children and achieve independent locomotion without significant delays.

One of the striking features of this group of deviant blind children is the picture of developmental arrest. The picture of the thirteen-year-old deviant blind child is not different in any significant way from that of the two- or three-year-old in the deviant group. In one case we were able to compare our picture of a ten-year-old blind boy in the deviant group with home movies of him that dated back to the age of three. Except for some progress in independent locomotion there was almost no difference in the developmental achievements at three and at ten.

The deviant blind children present a picture that begins to lag at the end of the first year and falls off progressively during the second year. In the third year we have the impression that development has come to a standstill. If independent locomotion is achieved at four or five, it seems to have little effect upon the over-all developmental picture.

This clinical picture remained unevaluated until recent years. Speculations regarding possible brain damage have been offered, but the available evidence does not give stronger support for a neurological etiology in these cases than for autism in the sighted. Until the past decade the large number of retrolental fibroplasia cases in the blind child population had further obscured the picture and, in the eyes of many clinicians, weighted the possibilities in favor of a neurological etiology. It was not until the publication of studies by Norris et al. (1957) and Keeler (1958) that a comparison of the children with retrolental fibroplasia and children blind from other causes was made, and the new evidence required a clinical reassessment of the blind child with gross ego deviations.

The Norris report which involved 295 blind preschool children is one of the most extensive studies to date. The sample included 209 children (71 percent) with the diagnosis retrolental fibroplasia; the remaining 86 cases (29 percent) included children blind from other causes. Testing was conducted at intervals throughout the first six and a half years of the child's life. Tests included the Cattell, adapted for use with the blind child in this study, and the Interim Hayes-Binet Intelligence Scale for the Blind. It was found that the performance of the children in the retrolental fibroplasia group was well within the range for blind children in general with a distribution pattern that did not distinguish this group from the group of children blind from other causes. Actually, if a correction were made for prematurity, the ratings in the retrolental fibroplasia group would have been better than those in the second group. In summarizing their findings Norris et al. say: "Within the limitations of the methods and subjects employed by this study there is no evidence that retrolental fibroplasia is associated with a specific or a generalized brain defect. When a child with retolental fibroplasia is retarded in his functioning and there are no specific neurological findings, the retardation must be presumed to be directly related to complex social and environmental factors."

It was necessary, then, to make a new assessment of the retrolental fibroplasia group. Evidently, this group which, until a decade ago, constituted more than 70 percent of the total blind child population, had distorted the over-all clinical picture by including among their numbers a large group of deviant children whose arrested development and bizarre motility gave apparent support to a neurological etiology. In this comparative study by the Norris group the distortions that were brought about through the impact of numbers were corrected and the clinician was obliged to look for other factors in the development of blind infants which might explain the adaptive failure of a significant number of these children.

Keeler's work in Toronto brought fresh insights to the problem of etiology in the deviant blind group. His investigation began with five preschool blind children who presented a clinical picture that struck him as remarkably similar to that of "infantile autism." The description of these children, as given by Keeler, is incorporated in the profile of the deviant child we have presented earlier in this essay. The cause of blindness in all five of Keeler's cases was retrolental fibroplasia. Keeler then selected a sample of thirty-five additional cases of children with retrolental fibroplasia (total registered in Ontario was 102 cases). He found that the histories and behavior patterns of all thirty-five cases were in many ways similar to those he had seen in the five intensive cases referred to his hospital, but none of the second group of children showed ego deviations to the degree seen in the intensive group, and the ten children in the sample who were in school were up to grade in spite of their disturbances of personality. In order to analyze more closely the factors at work in the ego disturbances found among the retrolental fibroplasia cases Keeler decided to study two other categories of blind children; one group blinded at birth and another group blinded postnatally, in infancy or early childhood. The first group consisted of eighteen children who were congenitally blinded by such conditions as cataracts, familial macular degeneration, buphthalmos, endophthalmitis, etc. It is important to note that in all these cases the amount of vision was much greater than that present in the children with retrolental fibroplasia, but none of them had more than 20/200 vision in the better eye. In this group the developmental patterns more closely approximated those of sighted children; there were not the developmental delays in motor achievements, feeding, toilet training, etc. Among these children Keeler did not find autistic patterns and abnormalities in motility to the same degree that he saw them in the retrolental fibroplasia group. In the second group, which consisted of seventeen children blinded postnatally, abnormalities in development and behavior were least conspicuous. The majority of the children in this group became blinded during the first and second years of life and in many cases motor maturation, acquisition of language, feeding and toilet habits, etc., had been established before blindness occurred.

Keeler's analysis of the developmental histories and behavior patterns of the blind children in each of these three groups focuses clinical attention on these points: the gross abnormalities encountered in certain blind children appear to be associated with total or nearly total blindness from birth and a history of inadequate emotional stimulation in the early months of life. If the incidence of abnormal ego development is conspicuously high in the retrolental fibroplasia group, we are obliged to include in this assessment the fact that it is the largest single category of blindness in which total or nearly total blindness from birth occurs. Each of Keeler's five children who showed gross abnormalities and developmental arrest also had a history of inadequate emotional stimulation in infancy. The number of children in Keeler's retrolental fibroplasia group who were in fact functioning adequately appears to confirm the findings in the Norris study and also shows clearly that blindness from birth is not in itself the predisposing factor to deviant development. Both studies bring attention, finally, to the factor of emotional stimulation and incentives for development in an infant blind from birth.

Our cases at the Family Service Society gave additional support to the findings of both Norris and Keeler as reported here. We may add, however, that the severe ego deviations which Keeler reported only in his retrolental fibroplasia cases appeared in our agency cases outside of this group as well. In the two years following our initial survey we found two such examples among new cases, one a girl of three, the second a girl twenty-two months old. In both cases the diagnosis "optic atrophy" had been made. The clinical picture in these two cases differed in no significant way from that of deviant children in the retrolental fibroplasia group. In each case, too, there was a well-documented history of inadequate emotional stimulation and neglect in infancy. In both cases, of course, we have the factors "totally blind from birth" and "inadequate stimulation in infancy" as Keeler has hypothesized for the etiology of autism in the blind child. In Keeler's own control group (the congenitally blind) the amount of vision present in all cases was greater than that of the cases in the retrolental fibroplasia group.

Our Family Service Society cases provide us with one additional footnote: Among the retrolental fibroplasia cases we were unable to find any correlations between the clinical picture of developmental arrest and such factors as birth weight, degree of prematurity, or length of time in oxygen.

None of these studies, of course, rule out the possibility of brain damage in the deviant blind children. While the question remains to be answered, it should be noted that we and others have found that if the pathological signs are detected in the early months or years, remedial measures can be employed which may bring about dramatic reversal of these tendencies and a favorable ego development. In the case of children under three years of age guidance of the mother may be sufficient. In the brilliant case report of Omwake and Solnit (1961) an educational and psychotherapeutic approach brought about normal ego functioning in a child who, at three years of age, resembled in every way the clinical picture of developmental arrest we have described here.

### I. A Nine-Year-Old Blind Boy with Arrested Ego Development

The case of Peter which follows is typical of the group of deviant blind children we have described.

Peter was eight years ten months when his treatment was begun. Some months after the work with Peter was under way, his mother began her own analysis which then made possible a more detailed study of the complexities of the mother-child relationship and illuminated portions of the child's history that had earlier been obscure.

Peter is the youngest child of his family. His mother was thirty-five and his father forty at the time of his birth. The pregnancy had been unplanned and was unwelcome. Peter is a surviving member of a set of identical twins who were born prematurely. His birth weight was two pounds and two ounces. Immediately after delivery he was placed in an incubator with an oxygen-rich atmosphere. At approximately six months of age the parents became concerned about his lack of responsiveness and his apparent indifference to his surroundings. At this time the child was examined and a diagnosis of retrolental fibroplasia was made.

Both parents are intelligent and well educated. They have demonstrated their capacities for parenthood in the rearing of two older daughters, now in adolescence, who present no unusual problems, have performed well in school, and are attractive and responsive youngsters.

The mother became depressed immediately after learning that Peter was blind. She remembered the early years of Peter's life as a kind of bad dream. We have the impression from our observations of the mother both in analysis and in relation to her child and his treatment that much of her handling then, as now, was mechanical, driven by guilt, and that at times when her suffering became too great for her she simply withdrew. There is evidence that Peter was in the care of servants a good deal of the time and that there was a succession of maids, so numerous that their names could hardly be recalled by the mother when later we needed to verify one or another of the allusions which Peter made to them in his treatment.

We have very little information, therefore, regarding the early development of Peter. We are told that his motor development was a little slow during his first year, but his mother could not give us dates or approximate dates for any of the achievements. We know, however, that he never crept, that walking with support was achieved sometime between two and two and a half, and that even at the age of three, when he entered a nursery school for the blind, he did not walk independently and moved from place to place by hanging on to objects.

When Peter was eight his parents grasped at a new hope for their apparently uneducable child and arranged for him to be sent to an eastern community where a new residential program for disturbed blind children was being set up. Since there were initial difficulties in establishing the new facility, Peter lived in a foster home for several months and was finally transferred to the institution, where he remained for approximately five months. The institution closed its program unexpectedly at the end of this period and Peter was returned to his home. We have been unable to obtain any reports from the clinical staff of this institution and the little we know we can only piece together from the child's communications to his therapist and from the mother's observations when she visited.

As Peter grew to know his therapist and progressed in his ability to communicate he gave us vignettes of this year. He re-enacted nighttime scenes in which he made the noises of crying and imitated the voice of one or another of the nurses in this institution: "Sh-h! What's the matter?" "Stop that!" "Stop that crying. You're not a baby!" "You'll wake up all the boys!" And on other occasions he would mimic an angry adult voice, "Sit there!" "Just sit there until I come back!" (referring to the toilet) and "You made a mess!" The degree to which he had regressed during this period also came out in unexpected ways. A disgusted voice is imitated, "What! Eating your stool!" and when he was first seen approximately a month after he returned from the institution, he was emaciated and in such poor nutritional state that it seemed certain that this child had been refusing food for some time, for there was no question that in this institution the children were adequately fed. Occasionally one caught a hint from Peter's verbal memories that his nutrition had become of great concern to the staff at the institution for he would repeat in alien voices, "Eat your custard now! Now, come on—just a little bit, just a little bit more!" Variations on this theme were common in his "reports."

## Initial Observations

When I first visited Peter at his home I saw him on the front lawn with his nurse, entwining himself around her body.[1] He was tall for his age, extremely thin, pale, with an absent self-absorbed look upon his face. His arms and legs seemed to flop like a rag doll's. He walked uncertainly with support and several times his nurse picked him up in her arms and carried him from place to place.

Later we moved to the garden. Peter paid no attention to me or to my voice and sat or lay on the picnic table absently mouthing a rubber toy. Occasionally he made an irrelevant statement. Once he sang, in perfect pitch, "Pussy cat, pussy cat, where have you been?" His mother told me that he spent hours at his record player.

After a while he came close to me and fingered me. Then, without any change of facial expression and without any show of feeling, he began to dig his fingernails into the skin of my arm, very hard, and causing me to wince with pain. From this point on it was nearly impossible to divert Peter from digging his nails into me or alternately pinching me with great intensity. It is impossible to describe this experience. I cannot call it sadistic. It was as if he did not know this was painful to me and I really felt that on the primitive undifferentiated level on which Peter operated he was not able to identify with the feelings of another person. This digging into me had the quality of trying to get into me, to burrow himself into me, and the pinching had the quality of just holding onto me for dear life.

I observed that when Peter lost an object he was mouthing, he showed no reaction to loss and did not search for it. Repeated observations in this session and in others confirmed this point. Very clearly this child had no concept of an object that existed independent of his perception of it.

While his mother was with us I observed that his reaction to her was in no discernible way different from his reaction to me, to the nurse, or to the dog. At no time, then and for many weeks after I began to work with him, did he ask a direct question, express a need through gesture or language, or answer a question put to him. His mother told me that until very recently he did not call her "Mama" but referred to her as "Too-hoo." She explained that this word derived from her own greeting to him when she entered the house.

Peter always referred to himself in the third person. The word "I," his mother told me, had entered his vocabulary before he had gone to the institution last year, but when I was able to observe him directly I felt that "I" was not employed for self-reference and was mechanically interpolated into speech as if he had been given lessons in "I" and "you."

There were no toys to which Peter had any attachment. When he showed transitory interest in objects he brought them to his mouth, sucked on them, chewed them. He did not explore them with his hands, he did not manipulate them. Prehension was poor and the fingers were rigidly extended. The only well-coordinated movements observed were those employed in bringing an object to the mouth.

Peter's mother reported that he could feed himself adequately and I was able to confirm this through direct observation. He still preferred soft foods, had great difficulty in masticating, and usually spit out the masticated food rather than swallow it.

In speech samples which I obtained in later sessions there were typically much echolalia and toneless repetition of stereotyped phrases.

When my early efforts to work with Peter and his mother began to bring favorable results, I suggested with all necessary caution to the parents that we might attempt a treatment program, that we should have reservations regarding its outcome, but that I thought I could promise some improvement in functioning. The parents were able to accept a treatment program on this basis. Both parents said honestly that they did not expect that Peter would ever be able to go to school, that they did not even know whether he was educable to any extent, but if only he could come alive, be responsive, be a happier child, be a member of the family, they would consider the treatment well worth while.

I shall briefly describe the treatment approach. Peter was visited at his home five times a week. From the beginning I discovered that there were great advantages in having his mother present during my visits with Peter. Not only did it constantly afford me a picture of mother and child together, but the mother could gain insight into Peter's behavior. As Peter began to communicate more and more to me, the mother could share the knowledge and the insight and make use of them in her handling of him.

Peter was in no sense "analyzable," of course. What I attempted to do was to apply analytic insights in a kind of education and therapy for a particular child.

The report that follows is a summary of observations over a two-and-a-half-year period.

### The Mother-Child Relationship

The earliest educational work with the mother was, of course, focused on promoting ties between her and the child who barely discriminated her from other human beings in his environment. Mrs. M. was encouraged to take over a major part of the child's care and she was helped to understand how need satisfaction and constancy were the indispensable first steps in establishing human ties. Gradually in the early months of treatment Peter's attachment to his mother became evident. He showed joy when she appeared and reactions to separation. He began to use the word "Mama" consistently for the first time. Out of the need-satisfying relationship gradually evolved the expression of need in language and there was a rapid expansion of speech.

Concurrent with the work in building the mother-child ties was the education of the mother to the unique needs of a blind child in acquiring knowledge of his world. Ironically, much of this education was not new to the mother, who had read widely in the literature of education of the blind; but until the treatment of Peter was begun and her own analysis was under way, she had been unable to apply this knowledge. Where the blind child is almost entirely dependent upon mobility for discovering a world of objects, Peter had been very largely restricted in his home. As opportunities for free movement and exploration of his environment were opened up to him, and as the range of his experience expanded, his exploration and manipulation of objects became more and more absorbing, the discovery of objects led to naming of objects, and there followed a rapid expansion of his vocabulary.

The mother's own reaction to the child's evolving ties to her was ambivalent. On the one hand, she was gratified by the signs of progress, on the other hand, the demands of the child who had wakened to a human relationship were at times nearly intolerable to her. She confessed to irritation and anger and a longing to have someone else take over. It was as if this treatment which required her to be a mother to the child had evoked an ambivalence that was very close to her experiences in the early months of Peter's life. She had not yet begun her own analysis and in my educational role I could not easily explore the dimensions of this conflict. But one thing became clear as we talked together in the early months. This mother, who had impressed everyone with her devotion to the blind child, had in fact avoided contact with him and had turned over most of his care to servants.

Many months later, when Peter's feeding had become the topic for discussion, I inquired about details and learned that Peter usually ate alone or in the company of a servant. When I encouraged Mrs. M. to join Peter for at least one meal a day and report the results to me, she burst into tears and said, "You don't know what you're asking of me!" He was repulsive at mealtimes, she said. He threw food, spit out food, smeared it. "I feel that if I am paying someone to work here I shouldn't have to put up with that myself!" But behind the complaints about the child's repulsive eating habits was a profound revulsion which was illuminated later in the mother's analysis. This analytic material and her own communications to me revealed that she had avoided the feeding of Peter in infancy and that the revulsion against the infant had expressed itself, among other ways, in an inability to feed him. The pattern of turning over the feeding of the child to servants was a very early one. From the analytic material there was good reason to believe that the mother's inability to respond to her infant had antedated the discovery of his blindness (at six months). Her ambivalence toward the infant was associated with a crisis that preceded the child's birth and which, for various reasons, must be excluded from this report. But it is equally important to note that even before the diagnosis of blindness was made, this baby, like all infants totally blind from birth, had appeared to the mother as curiously unresponsive. He was quiet and content to lie in his crib for hours. "He never seemed to need me!" the mother told us, and because this was a woman whose capacities for relationship were largely called forth by expressed needs of a partner, this baby who did not seem to need her could elicit no response.

With some working through of this material in her analysis, Mrs. M. was able to come to grips with her need to abdicate at the time of Peter's meals. She found, to her surprise, that when she joined him at mealtimes, the repulsive food habits declined in a very short period, and the child's own ties to mother were strengthened by the association of mother with eating pleasures.

Another motive in the mother's avoidance of contact with her child appeared early in treatment. In the period that preceded the mother's own analysis, I saw how typically she employed reaction formations against anger and rage, both in relation to her child and to me. With encouragement she was able to express more and more of her feelings toward Peter and then, on one occasion, was able to admit with considerable anxiety that she was afraid that if she "let go" she might kill Peter. She was able to see how, when her anger became dangerous to her, she avoided contact with Peter. When her guilt about and fear of her destructive feelings became evident to her, she accepted my recommendation of analytic treatment for herself.

The mother's analysis made it possible to conduct my educational work with greater freedom and flexibility. Mrs. M. continued to work closely with me and to be present during Peter's sessions, but it was no longer necessary for me to deal with aspects of her own conflict that impeded the child's treatment. With analytic help the mother demonstrated unusual capacities to support the child's treatment.

## The Mouth and the Hand

I hope my description adequately conveyed the picture of mouth activity as I saw it in Peter at the beginning of treatment. The mouth, it appeared, had remained the center of his primitive personality organization. All objects were brought to the mouth; the mouth was almost never empty. Perception largely centered in the mouth. There was almost no handling or exploration with the hands. We know that this is not typical for normal blind children, and yet it is important to note that for all blind persons the mouth functions as a discriminating sensory organ throughout life (Villay [1930] describes how, even as an adult, he relied upon his mouth, and particularly his tongue, to make the finest perceptual distinctions.) In Peter the mouth had also remained the center of erotic and aggressive impulses, and when I first knew him it did not even appear that these were differentiated. When he made contact he mouthed, and often the moment after, he bit, and this biting had the quality not of intentional aggression but of incorporation.

Very early in Peter's treatment I began to understand the behavior of the hand in the clutching and clawing, that I described earlier. Peter could at first make contact with me only by clawing me, burrowing his fingers into the skins of my arm and neck. When at such times I moved away from him and maintained contact with him merely through my voice, he would immediately revert to apathy or to autistic mannerisms (rocking, swaying, etc.). But on one such occasion as I withdrew in pain, he stopped his clawing of me, withdrew his fingernails from my arm, then bit me on the head. When I recovered, I was again struck by the fact that there was no sadism in this act—again it had the quality of taking me in so that I could not go away. Then, recalling the sequence of the frustrated digging into me with his fingernails and biting that immediately followed, I understood the fuller meaning of the hand behavior. The hand behaved like a mouth, the fingernails like teeth, and the pinching activity like biting also. The oral-incorporative aspects of mouthing and biting had been transferred to the hand.

When I understood the oral-incorporative significance of this clutching and clawing, I was able to make a useful interpretation to Peter. The next time he seized me and clawed me in this way, I did not immediately extricate myself, but said, "You don't have to be afraid. I won't go away." And with this he released his "death grip" on me. In the same session when he began to claw his mother I repeated the interpretation, "You don't have to be afraid. Mother will not go away," and he released his mother. From this time on we were able to bring about control of the clutching and clawing with these words. His mother was deeply impressed. It was "like magic," she said; but most important of all, she had achieved insight into a piece of behavior that she had always interpreted as aggressive and now began to understand as a kind of inarticulate terror. (Later, when this same hand behavior acquired the significance of intentional aggression, other ways of handling it had to be employed.)

In this connection it is worth mentioning that this biting, clawing, pinching behavior is commonly observed among preschool blind children, and it is retained by the blind children with severe ego deviations. It is as if grasping has not freed itself of the oral mode and the hand has not achieved autonomy from the mouth.

For Peter the progress from mouth to hand was slow and laborious. The mouth retained its primacy as a perceptual organ for most of the first two years of my work with him. Even after he progressed in grasping he was slow to acquire pleasure in manual exploration of objects. For the most part it appeared that an object was desirable or not desirable to the degree that it stimulated the oral cavity in some preferred fashion. When I tried to encourage tactile discrimination by bringing him various textiles and textures for him to handle, he brought them to his mouth and discarded them when the texture or taste was not pleasing to the mouth. When Mrs. M. and I covered bean bags with a variety of materials, velvet, satin, corduroy, he did not discriminate among them on the basis of their qualities. When we introduced him to a "tonette," hoping that mouth satisfaction, audition, and manual proprioceptive experience might make this an attractive object to him, he produced one note and tossed it away. He did the same thing on subsequent attempts.

However, there were small and encouraging achievements along the way. There were periods during which he evidently enjoyed fitting together pots and lids, or jars and covers. He began to enjoy filling and dumping a milk bottle with clothespins and successfully inhibited the impulse to bring the clothespin to his mouth.

A big step was achieved at the beginning of the third year of treatment. He became interested in sea shells and brought a number of them home from the beach. He played with them for long periods, tracing their whorls with his fingers and gradually discriminating among them. In a box of several dozen there were a few that he preferred and he quickly sorted them with his finger tips until he found these. He used his mouth minimally for discrimination. His mother and I encouraged this newly found interest and collected shells for him.

Then, almost as soon as Mrs. M. and I became aware of this new progress in use of the hands, we noticed something else. The clawing and pinching had disappeared altogether! Prior to this period there had been much intentionally aggressive scratching and pinching—a later sequel to the undifferentiated clawing we had seen earlier. The hand, which had largely functioned as an auxiliary mouth, now appeared to be freeing itself of the oral mode, a corresponding neutralization of drive qualities.

There is nothing in my observations that tells us exactly how this was achieved and why it occurred at this particular time! In the meantime, there was a new behavior toward inanimate objects in general. Objects that had once served only self-stimulation now began to acquire independent values. An old wooden bowl that Peter used to suck on and earlier had used to bang his head with, now, for the first time, became a vessel and he spent long periods filling it with shells or other small objects.

During this period I had the feeling that something new was taking place in Peter's personality. And then, at the end of a six-week period, the new behavior was lost, the shells and the bowl were again brought to the mouth to be sucked, the pinching and scatching returned, and the promise of these new developments faded. (This regression will be discussed later along with other data from the same period.)

A number of provocative questions derive from these observations of a personality that has remained mouth-centered, as in the case of Peter and other deviant children. Following a suggestion given to us by Dr. Joseph Michaels at an early stage in this study, we began to consider the implications for ego development when an organ that has retained a high degree of instinctual cathexis also serves as a primary organ of perception. The prolonged mouth-centered perception of the blind infant and young child may impede the development of "conflict-free" perception. In the development of the sighted infant the primary autonomy of vision becomes one of the guarantees of conflict-free perception. In the normal development of blind infants and young children, the hand takes over as the leading organ of perception and achieves autonomy from the mouth.

We are accustomed to speak of the hands as the "eyes" of the blind. Until we studied the infant Toni, we did not understand that the achievement of hand autonomy in a blind infant is a feat of extraordinary virtuosity. *In this healthy, normally developing infant, we saw that perception remained mouth-centered until well into the second year, and the hand did not achieve primacy as a perceptual organ until the last half of the second year.* Where vision mediates the evolution of hand autonomy in the sighted child, the absence of vision obstructed this crucial progress in the healthy blind infant, and hand autonomy was achieved finally through an elaborate detour. From the history of Peter and other deviant blind children we began to understand that in less than favorable environmental circumstances the progress from mouth to hand may not be achieved at all and the personality may remain arrested on the level of mouth-centeredness and nondifferentiation.

### Object Concept

We have already described Peter's inability to search for lost objects or even to attempt to recover them after he lost contact through mouth or hand. At the same time, he could orient himself to a certain degree in his own room, could find his bed, could make his way from his bed to his record player. When I observed him in the family kitchen at a mealtime it was clear that he was not well oriented there, and his behavior in the downstairs rooms suggested that he had explored them very little. His own room, it is important to know, isolated him to a very large extent from even the ordinary household noises. This was a large house and his room was so situated that very little sound carried from the first floor to the second floor, and a circular staircase broke up sound so successfully that on occasions when I had to call his mother or nurse for assistance, my own voice could not be heard.

Peter had in many ways shown that he had no concept of the existence of an object after he lost contact with it; in the same way he showed that he had no concept of the existence of human objects independent of his perception of them. He did not call for his mother, he did not search for his mother. He showed his concern over the disappearance of persons through repeated questions, "Where is Aunt Cora? Where is Roger? Where is Jonathan?" It did not even matter that some of these people had had only the most casual relationship with him. He would ask one question most urgently, "Laura, Laura! Where is Laura!" Laura was a cousin of his mother's who had died during the time when Peter was in the institution. He of course did not know what "dead" meant, but his mother had told him that Laura could not come back.

The "where is . . . " questions need clarification. "Where is Aunt Cora?" for example, did not mean that Aunt Cora must be "someplace," i.e., that she had an existence for Peter when he was not in contact with her. This could be tested by means of Peter's behavior toward inanimate objects during the same period. When Peter dropped his bowl or his block there was no attempt at recovery or even a gesture of recovery. He would say in a flat voice, "Where is my bowl?" and his mother or I would retrieve it. If we did not pick it up for him, he would shift his attention. "Where is . . . " then was a magic formula to bring back the object. The "where is . . . " construction was also the magic formula in peek-a-boo games and hiding games that Mrs. M. and I played with Peter, an incantation that "caused" someone to return. Following Piaget (1937), we should probably take the failure to search for human or inanimate objects after loss of contact as a fair sign that he had not acquired a concept of the independence of objects from his perception. At a later stage in treatment, which will be described, Peter demonstrated active search and with this achievement his behavior toward people and things altered in significant ways.

For many weeks at the beginning of my work with Peter I played hide-and-seek games with him and taught him to find me through tracing my voice. These games gave him enormous pleasure and we played them repetitiously hour after hour after hour. After a while he began to formalize the games, sending me away with a push, saying, "Good-by!" then finding me and spontaneously hugging me in a greeting. I had also encouraged his mother to play these games with him, but during the early months of treatment she had very little luck in engaging him in such games. I soon understood why. Once when I asked her to join in a game during one of our sessions, Peter himself refused to go on. I saw through his behavior that it was too dangerous for him to play "going away and returning" with mother herself. As a neutral object I could serve the game purpose very well; his mother could not.

On one occasion I employed an innovation in these games in order to test his ability to follow cues in locating objects. I began the game with the ritual, "Good-by, Peter!" and then walked to a corner of the room clicking my heels on the wood floor to give him an opportunity to trace my movements. Then I waited in my corner, but did not give him the signal of my voice as I usually did. He started in search of me, was obviously not oriented, walked right past me, went through the door of the bathroom that communicates between his room and his parents' room, passed on into his parents' room, and then there was silence. He did not return. After a little while his mother and I went in search of him. We found him lying on his mother's bed, his shoulders heaving convulsively and a look of mute terror on his face. He could not cry in those days, he could only go through a kind of motor parody of grief. I tried to put his feelings into words and I tried to explain to him what had happened and that I had not been lost at all. But he refused to have anything to do with me for the rest of that hour and he would not play the hide-and-seek games with me for a very long time.

For many months Mrs. M. and I found every means available to us to teach Peter the substantiality and permanence of objects through games and other devices. We taught him to find the cookie jar in the kitchen and get his own cookies. We taught him to find the cracker cupboard. He discovered the joys of the pots and pans cupboards, and then, of course, there came a rapid expansion of searches into everything. From the initial discovery of objects that could always be found in the same place he moved on to the discovery that the same object could be found in a different place and was still the object he had known before. And yet it was nearly a year of work before Peter demonstrated real gains in this area. Then he was searching actively for objects and if he did not find them in the expected place, he would search for them in another place. When he wanted his mother he went in search of her.

There was an interesting corollary in speech development at the same time. We recall that in the beginning Peter did not call for his mother and, as a matter of fact, he did not even cry to summon her. Since his mother did not have a substantial existence for him, speech did not possess one of its vital functions—to summon the lost object, to bring back the lost object. But later when Peter clearly demonstrated his ability to search for objects and recover them and when the concept became stabilized, the change was reflected in speech. He began calling his mother, summoning her to his side, or even calling her while she was in the same room in order to locate her. At this time his incessant calling of mother nearly exhausted her. Mrs. M. also provided us with an interesting observation. On the one hand, she understood very well that this was a wonderful achievement for Peter; on the other hand, she found herself disturbed. For now, she told Dr. Freedman and me, when he was able to express his needs for her in words, she felt herself bound to him in a new way and one that was not altogether satisfying. "When he couldn't express his need for me before I didn't feel quite so guilty about going out and leaving him, and now that he puts it into words, I feel torn each time I go away." While the ambivalence of the mother needs no comment here, we were struck by the fact that for the first time something like a genuine human relationship was developing between the child and his mother.

These observations regarding the emergence of an object concept raise a number of questions. As Piaget (1937) demonstrated, during the period nine to eighteen months the sighted child makes a series of experiments which lead him to discover that an object exists independent of his perception of it. The sighted infant demonstrates an evolving concept of the object through his behavior toward a screened object, a failure to search for the object under nine months of age, followed by recovery of the object in successively complex situations in which the displacements of the object are traced by means of visual reconstructions. Somewhere between fifteen and eighteen months the sighted infant demonstrates through his search for screened objects that he has a concept of the object that has achieved independence of his perception of it; when he conducts his searches he demonstrates that he knows the object is "some place." This is, of course, one of the crucial developments in the process of differentiation of self and outer world.

When we consider the role of vision in constructing an object's displacements in space, the parallel achievement in the case of a blind infant must be regarded as an adaptive feat. In the first stage of building the object concept the blind infant must trace the object's displacements by means of perceptual cues that are highly inadequate substitutes for vision. Audition, for example, can substitute in tracing only certain classes of objects—those that have sound-making properties. Tactile experience cannot tell the infant where the object is located when he has lost contact with it. The blind infant, then, has a fragmentary and discontinuous experience with objects during the period of tracing, and probably can evolve a concept of the independence of objects from his own perceptions only after his own locomotion provides him with spatial references and repetitive experiences with object finding.

In all this it is undoubtedly the human object that provides maximum experience for the blind infant's building of an object concept. Where no one sense modality can substitute for vision as a distance receptor and an organizer of perceptual wholes, the mother and other highly invested human objects carry the main burden of "teaching" the blind infant about the permanence of objects and through their own persons offer the possibilities of synthesizing and uniting these impressions. Where cathexis of the human object and nonvisual sensory data have established a stable object representation for the blind infant, the goings and comings of the mother, the tracing of the mother through auditory cues, and later the search for the mother by means of the child's own mobility will all lead the blind child to the concept of a mother who exists even when he has lost contact with her. In the early stages of the evolution of this concept it is unlikely that inanimate objects can serve the blind child's learning in the same way, although the sighted child's learning during the same period is achieved through countless experiments in which both human and inanimate objects are employed. The totally blind infant has a restricted range of interest in inanimate objects, as we saw in the blind infant, Toni, and infants known to us in the Family Service Society project. Within this range (which may in the first year include the bottle, a pacifier, a rattle, or bells) only the noise-making objects are useful in tracing the movements of an object.

It is, then, probably the mother who becomes the center of this learning for the totally blind child and while a parallel development can be constructed for the sighted infant, the functional advantages of vision over other sense modalities and the infinitely larger experience with objects provide the sighted child with rich and diverse data for constructing a world of objects; the mother is not the exclusive teacher. Since the blind child's learning must emanate from the experience with mother, insufficiencies in mothering or deficiencies in the mother-infant ties can cut off all possibilities for learning in this sphere.

The arrested ego development of Peter and other deviant blind children shows, almost uniformly, the failure to acquire an object concept. While this is only one of a number of interrelated problems having to do with differentiation and individuation, the adaptive failure in this area suggests that the absence of vision creates a developmental hazard. The mother's resources must be heavily exploited to compensate for the impoverished fund of information available to a blind infant, and when the mother can provide such compensation a normal sequence in ego formation takes place. In those cases where developmental arrest occurs we also find a tragic failure on the part of the mother to get her blind baby's signals and to serve as the unifier of perceptual experiences. In this way the double handicap of blindness and insufficiencies in the experience with mother may cut off for many blind children the developmental path that leads to the achievement of an object concept.

*Mobility*

The importance of mobility and particularly the achievements of independent locomotion have been stressed by Norris et al. (1957), Burlingham (1961), and other writers and students of the blind child's development. Until the blind infant is free to explore his world, he has very limited possibilities for learning about his world. Peter, we are told, never crept at all. (Many blind babies do not.) In this respect his mother blamed her own ignorance, since she did not put him on the floor and did not give him opportunities for creeping. This is certainly a valid point; but as we observed in the blind infant Toni, in the absence of a visual stimulus there is not a strong incentive for the child to creep. And, as mentioned earlier, the blind child achieves independent walking much later than the sighted child.

Peter was still supporting himself by touching walls and other objects when I first met him. He had had very limited opportunities for exploration of his own house. It was a house furnished with antiques, a house of china lamps and crystal and silver ornaments, and clearly, from the furnishing of the downstairs rooms, it was not expected that a still clumsy blind child would enter them. His mother, who had so much anxiety about this retardation and who tried to employ her own experience as a teacher in educating Peter to handle toys and to manipulate toys, had not understood that a crucial experience had been omitted in learning. He needed mobility and the opportunity to explore.

When Peter's mother fully understood this, she was able to bring about many changes in his life. She and I encouraged independent walking, simple climbing, swimming, playing ball. Within a very short time he was walking independently and motor skills improved rapidly. During this period we saw a great improvement in Peter's over-all physical appearance. He gained weight, he acquired muscle in his pipe-stem arms and legs, and his skin lost its pallor. He was encouraged to explore the house and although his mother had thought that he never had shown interest in exploring, once these opportunities were opened up to him he was very soon "into everything"—cupboards, drawers, all the rooms of the house.

As we would expect, Peter's language began to make tremendous leaps. As he discovered objects, handled them, discriminated and named them, his vocabulary enlarged very quickly. He was actively encouraged, at the same time, to express his needs and wishes in words, and his mother learned to be not so quick in anticipating his gestures and tactfully to postpone gratifications until he expressed his wants in words. While these were good achievements, it is important to note that a good deal of his speech was echolalic and did not, properly speaking, serve communication. Also, for a very long time, his speech had no affective quality.

*Aggression and Motility*

As I have mentioned earlier, the biting, pinching, and scratching, which I had observed at the very beginning of treatment, reappeared later in connection with intentional aggression. It was impressive to realize that until the second year of treatment Peter had not used his hands for hitting, or his feet for kicking, in directed aggression. Aggression was expressed either through the mouth or by means of the hand following the oral model. At the same time Peter was reluctant to masticate and only through encouragement by me and his mother did he learn to use his teeth for biting food.[2]

I observed fairly early in treatment that Peter did a lot of throwing of objects, particularly of his blocks, but this throwing was aimless and without energy and reminded me of the way a child throws food or toys in the last quarter of the first year. It seemed as if Peter could do only two things with objects, either put them in his mouth or throw them away. At that time, because I was still groping in my educational and therapeutic approaches, I would, after a certain point, interfere with this aimless throwing of objects. For example, when we were "making cookies" with play-dough and Peter began to throw the play-dough, I would repeatedly remind him that play-dough was for making things, for playing games with me and Mommy, and that when he wanted to throw things he could throw balls. If he was in rapport with me on these occasions, he would accept the prohibition but almost immediately, I saw, he would revert to passivity and lethargy and begin his swaying, or rocking, or nonsense chants.

I began to understand that this throwing was necessary to him. I then changed my tactics and permitted, even encouraged, the throwing without knowing where this would lead. During these throwing sessions he was undoubtedly in better contact with me and his mother and there were evident signs of release in his personality. Yet my conscience as a child analyst troubled me very much during this period as I watched play-dough, blocks, and plastic toys go flying through the air in an apparently meaningless barrage. Never before in my therapeutic career had I given permission for such aimless throwing or ever had the feeling that it was justified for therapeutic purposes. While all of this was going on I would sometimes remind myself that normal infants go through such a phase in the last quarter of the first year, but I had never observed this closely or reflected upon its significance in development.

As I watched Peter in many such sessions I saw that gradually the throwing itself became energized and lost its aimless quality. He was throwing hard, and showed evident satisfaction when the object made contact with the floor or the walls. He began to make noises and to accompany his throwing with little cries and sounds that had an aggressive quality. As the throwing acquired aggressive quality, his mother and I, in self-defense and as part of Peter's education, began to provide him with good substitutes for the blocks and other toys for throwing. His mother made about a half dozen bean bags which had enough weight and made a sufficiently satisfactory noise on contact so that they gave satisfaction to Peter. Gradually we now began to limit the throwing to bean bags and balls, and Peter was able to accept the substitution in a way that earlier he could not.

As I recorded my observations and reviewed notes I saw very clearly another connection that seemed to be very significant. As Peter became more active in throwing, and as throwing became more energetic and more aggressive in quality, the biting, pinching, and scratching diminished markedly.

Circumstances provided me with several good tests of the relationship between the different modes of aggression. On one occasion, for example, I arrived to find Mrs. M. bitten and scratched and she reported that she had had a very bad weekend with Peter. In order to get a picture of the weekend, I asked to what extent Peter had also been throwing. Mrs. M. became embarrassed by my question and said a little defensively that she had decided to put a stop to it this weekend. She knew I had recommended that he be given permission to throw, but it all seemed so pointless and so chaotic. (Naturally, I could sympathize with her in all this.) I then suggested that there was probably a connection between his attacks on her and the deprivation of throwing and asked her if she could bear with us for a while. She agreed. When throwing was permitted again the attacks on the mother ceased.

Somewhat later, however, Peter himself gave up the throwing, without any external prohibition as far as we could judge. He reverted once again to biting and scratching, and at the same time his mother reported a severe eating restriction. He was "eating next to nothing except milk and soft foods." There had been progress in masticating for a while and this was lost entirely. The content of our sessions gave me a few clues. He talked incessantly about Laura and other absent persons. "Where is Laura? Where is Bryan? Where is Aunt Cora?" At the same time he repeated the admonishing voices of adults, "You don't want to bite Aunt Cora! Stop that! Stop that!" And then, "Where's Aunt Cora? Where's Aunt Cora?" Or, "Don't scratch Laura. Don't scratch Laura! Where is Laura? Where is Laura?" During this time I saw how he tried to inhibit his biting and scratching and observed a mouth tic exactly representing the urge to bite and the inhibition of biting. Along with the tic Peter would begin swaying, rocking, or bouncing, or uttering gibberish.

The repetitive content of this period strongly suggested that he thought that he could cause people to go away in analogy with eating. Once he even put it quite exactly, "Laura is dead. Laura is all gone." (All gone, of course, was a phrase he would use when he had eaten all of this food.) I decided to put my understanding of the eating inhibition in the form of an interpretation. I told Peter that when he bites his celery or apple he makes it go away inside of him and it is all gone. "But Mommy is not food. Daddy is not food. I am not food. Laura is not food. You cannot eat a mommy or daddy or me. You can't make me all gone." He listened intently to me. After this session his mother reported that he had a hearty lunch, accepted an apple which he had not done for a very long time, and enjoyed his dinner that evening. The eating inhibition returned several times in the weeks that followed. Each time I made a similar interpretation. Each time the eating inhibition disappeared. Along with this he once again returned to throwing and showed much less biting, scratching, and pinching.

Later he demonstrated a similar fear that his own aggression could destroy objects. He had broken a couple of his favorite phonograph records. In the old days we used to replace these. Now he had made enough progress to begin to learn that breaking is an end to things and that they cannot be magically brought back. He was saddened with this knowledge, of course, but then we noticed that he became very anxious when he accidentally broke things; at such times he would revert to apathy and solitude. We would hear his melancholy chant, "The record is all gone! Mommy's vase is all gone!" Then on one occasion when I found him depressed because his mother had not returned at the time she had promised, he used the same melancholy refrain, "Mommy's gone away. Mommy's all gone." It was very clear that once again he needed help in understanding that while his aggression could destroy phonograph records and certain other inanimate objects, his aggression would not make "Mommy all gone" or other people "all gone." I had to repeat this interpretation to him many times until he appeared to grasp it.

We think we can now understand, or begin to understand, the relationship between the aimless throwing of the early period and the differentiation of the aggression described here. In the sequence from oral-centered and undifferentiated aggression in the early behavior to directed and energetic throwing in the later behavior the aimless throwing forms a bridge. This must represent part of the process of separating the skeletal muscles from the mouth. We would need to make close observations on normal infant development in the last quarter of the first year to carry our thinking further; but if our interpretation of Peter's behavior has any validity, the transfer from the mouth to the skeletal muscles constitutes an essential progress in the differentiation of aggression, and the aimless throwing by infants must signify that the skeletal muscles are beginning to take over. We must remember, however, that in the sighted child progress in locomotion normally is made during the same period—a period in which so many events occur that this transitional state in normal development might ordinarily be obscured. In the blind infant there commonly is a maturational readiness for crawling and a failure, in the absence of vision, to achieve locomotion. The fate of aggression during this crucial period merits careful study. This may be another vulnerable period in the development of the blind child, and the particular fate of aggression may be another of the predisposing factors to deviant ego development.

Is the delay in motor development, specifically in locomotion, a key to the fate of aggression in the deviant children? At the point where the skeletal muscles should take over and serve discharge as well as integration of new patterns, a failure in motor function takes place. The achievement in the deviant child may be delayed for another two years or longer. During this period, if we follow the history of Peter and other deviant blind children, libidinal and aggressive impulses remain undifferentiated and centered in the mouth; perception remains centered in the mouth. By the time locomotion is achieved, a state of oral-centered adaptation may also have been achieved and locomotion can no longer lock in with progressive tendencies in ego development that were in a state of readiness during an earlier stage.

*Body Image*

When I first met Peter he was unable to identify parts of his own body when asked such questions as "Where is your nose?" "Where is your ear?" He had so little awareness of internal sensations that he gave neither sign nor signal when he was about to urinate and defecate, and of course could not be trained to use the toilet. He showed little interest in his penis. As we should expect, there was no awareness of sexual differences. As our work progressed it was evident that some crude image of his own body began to emerge. He was able, at the end of the first year of treatment, to identify parts of his own body and to find the corresponding parts (nose, ear, fingers, etc.) on his mother and me. He was able to ask to go to the toilet for urination and defecation.

The discovery of sexual differences took place in an extraordinary way around the eighteenth month of treatment. He had walked into the bathroom as his mother was emerging from the bath. According to the mother's report, he began to explore her body with his hands. The mother chose to use this occasion to enlighten Peter on sexual differences. She allowed him to explore her breasts and the genital area and told him that she had breasts but she did not have a penis. The mother said that Peter showed no reaction at the time.

Peter's mother was much pained when I raised questions about these means of enlightening her child in sexual differences. How else, she wanted to know, could a blind child learn about body differences? There were no good answers to this question, but I recommended verbal explanation along lines that we were following in Peter's treatment sessions.

Following the anatomy lesson in the bathroom, I began to see Peter's reactions very clearly in my sessions with him. I saw him make reaching gestures for his mother's breasts, giggling with excitement when he made contact. On two occasions he reached boldly into her blouse and his mother explained to me with some embarrassment that he had recently discovered that she wore "falsies" in her bras and had even succeeded in removing them in one swift gesture. He called them "little hats" and searched them out in her drawers, bearing them off as trophies.

During the same period Peter began to suffer from constipation. He would withhold for days in evident discomfort. When he sat on the toilet he was visibly frightened, but could not put his fears into words. At the same time his mother reported that he had been wandering around the house for several days searching for "something," but he could not say what he was looking for, and in fact did not seem to know. In a session during this period I saw Peter jumping wildly on his bed and saw his hand move furtively to his penis. His mother then told me privately that the night before Peter had been snuggling close to her at bedtime and had suddenly taken her hand and put it on his penis. She had withdrawn her hand and said, "But you may put your own hand there." Today, as I watched Peter, he was evidently preoccupied with his penis and more than once I saw his hand move to his penis and move away. When I made a neutral comment to Peter on his wish to touch his penis—as a way of opening up the topic for discussion—he suddenly switched to "The hat! I want the little hat!" His mother asked whether it would help if she brought in one of the "falsies" and I agreed. When Peter was given "the little hat" he became completely preoccupied with it, brought it to his mouth, and explored it manually.

Clearly, the anatomy lesson had added to Peter's confusion. He behaved toward "the little hats" as if they were breasts and could be removed. And there was the strong suggestion in his switch from penis to little hats that he believed that a penis could be removed in similar fashion. Since his exploration of his mother's body in the bathroom had already confirmed for him that she did not have a penis, he could only conclude that a penis, was portable and removable. And when we add to this his most prominent symptom at this time, the retention of his stool, it seemed most probable that fear of loss of a body part was operating in all these spheres.

In this session Peter and I talked a little about "the little hats." I told him that the little hats were something that Mommy wore inside her clothes. The little hats were not breasts. Mommy had breasts and all ladies had breasts. They belonged to a mommy and stayed right on her. He listened to me without comment. At the end of the session his hand moved to his penis once again and then he said enigmatically,

"The ski is all gone." I asked him what a "ski" was and he did not answer. But in Peter's magic language I knew that he sometimes substituted one word for another when he needed to disguise a painful thought or memory.

For several weeks Peter's concerns with penis, no penis, loss, and breaking became repetitive themes. He began a chant in his hours with me. "Where's your penis, where's your penis, where's your penis?" I used the opportunity to clarify his mother's earlier statements in the bathroom and told him that boys and girls and men and women were made differently. Peter was a boy, made just like Daddy. Margaret (older sister) was a girl, just like Mommy. After a while a new chant made an appearance, "I am a she. I am a he. I am a he. I am a she."

Stool retention continued off and on during this period, but there was no opportunity to make a meaningful connection between the fear of loss of his stool and fears regarding his own penis. Then in one session I arrived to find Peter disturbed and almost immediately ambivalent toward me. He first reached out for my hand and stroked it softly, then began to bite it. Suddenly, most urgently he asked, "Where is Laura? Where is Laura?" (the dead cousin). And scarcely waiting for an answer he began a recital of the names of absent or long-forgotten people. Then again in an urgent voice, he began to inquire about lost and broken phonograph records. "Where is Hokey Pokey? Where is Genie?" "Where are they, Peter?" "Broken. All gone. Broken" (sadly). I said, "Records can be broken. But people can't be broken." As I said this Peter's hand went swiftly to his penis. I said, "Peter can't be broken. A penis can't be broken." He seemed not to take this in.

But now for many sessions the theme of "broken" appeared as a refrain. In the session following the one reported above, Peter began by uttering the single word "tooth" and showed me the place where he had lost a tooth several weeks ago. We talked about the tooth, and how another would grow. I spent a great deal of time in this session telling him how a nose could not go away, a finger could not go away, etc. They belonged to Peter. "Laura?" he said plaintively. "Where is Laura?" (Laura, of course, belonged to the category of objects which go away and cannot be restored.) Once more we talked about Laura. At the end of the hour he said, again with some urgency, "Where is the penis?" and made a tentative reaching gesture toward me. Again I told him that I knew he had found that Mommy and ladies do not have a penis and that it was very hard for him to figure out. Again I gave the explanations, and again I said explicitly that nobody could make a penis "all gone." Peter's penis would always stay with him.

For many weeks the anxiety about "broken" and "all gone" was dealt with in ways very similar to those I have described. I was present on one occasion during a period of stool retention when Peter asked to go to the toilet and I could see the anxiety on his face. I used the occasion to make a connection between his fear of losing the feces and his fear of losing his penis and again gave reassurances. His mother reported that soon after I left that day he asked to go to the toilet again and had a bowel movement. There were to be a number of occasions thereafter when I was able to handle the stool-retention problem through such interpretations. However, I should mention that this problem was very complex; a number of other motives were uncovered before the problem finally cleared up.

The inadequacies of Peter's speech were serious handicaps to an investigation of his blind-child's version of castration anxiety. It was impossible, of course, to get details of his fantasies or to get him to elaborate his cryptic comments. I employed an approach which is of course very different from child analysis. I had to use "educational" techniques to deal with his body concerns, to promote, if possible, the integration of each piece of knowledge into a stable body image.

There were other observations of anxiety in connection with the penis. Though the meaning of these observations remains obscure, I believe they should be reported. On several occasions both his mother and I saw that Peter was manifestly anxious when he had an erection. Erections typically occurred while he was straining for a bowel movement or when he was about to void. The moment the erection appeared he became frozen and immobilized. At these times he would never touch his penis, nor did he do so when erections appeared spontaneously on other occasions. It seemed to me that he then avoided touching his penis.

He refused to hold his penis under any circumstances when he was voiding. For long periods during the two and a half years that I knew Peter he avoided handling his penis. In the early days of treatment I discerned prohibitions in an alien voice, "Uh! Uh! Uh!" which Peter chanted in a warning voice when he chanced to touch his penis. When this and similar material was handled with Peter he would take a more relaxed attitude toward touching his penis, but before long the avoidance was manifest again. After many months of observations I was unable to come up with a better explanation than that offered by his manifest anxiety in connection with erections. Was the experience of erection and detumescence an equivalent of loss or "castration," the "disappearance" of the penis? Was the loss of sensation that accompanies detumescence a disturbance to this deviant child whom strong sensations were an affirmation of self? I do not know. Occasionally when I talked with Peter about how sometimes his penis got big and sometimes quite small I had the impression from his response that I was on the right track, but I never received any positive confirmation from him or further material that permitted investigation. Perhaps the only justification for including this in the record is the possibility that such a detail may be useful to another investigator.

## Grief, Pain

When I now describe and bring together data relating to the affective disturbance in Peter it is with some uncertainty and incompleteness of observations.

When I first became acquainted with Peter, he was incapable of expressing grief. If he reacted at all to loss or the danger of loss, it was through the convulsive heaving of shoulders and distortion of face which I described earlier in the hide-and-seek game. We do not think that such behavior is typical of the deviant blind children.

The measures by which Peter warded off grief, however, were similar to those that he employed in warding off any strong undesirable or unpleasurable stimulus, external or internal as judged by the observer. His reaction to pain may be considered a model. (And here, incidentally, we do have parallels with other deviant blind children and autistic children in general.) Initially Peter showed no reaction to pain. When he injured himself, even badly, he did not cry out, did not complain, but typically reverted to autistic mannerisms. Once when he burned himself severely his mother, who was with him in the kitchen, had no way of telling the moment at which the burn occurred and discovered it only later on. Once when he had the flu we inferred that he had severe stomach pains and internal distress because he waved his hands in a gesture of warding off an external bothersome stimulus. More typical, however, was his attempt to ward off the perception of the painful stimulus—a device he adopted with regard to pain and a variety of other stimuli originating within or without.

I have already reported that he would ward off an aggressive impulse by means of repetitive speech or nonsense words. He employed identical mechanisms in the warding off of grief. His mother and I would sometimes see him with shoulders heaving and the tic-like grimacing of the mouth. We would encourage him to cry, tell him it was all right to cry, that all boys cried sometimes. And sometimes we would see the muscles of his face reacting to our words, giving us the impression that he was on the verge of tears, but suddenly he would come forth with a repetitious phrase like, "I want a triangle cracker, I want a triangle cracker, I want a triangle cracker" and would repeat this sometimes for as long as fifteen minutes.

We cannot attribute to this primitive personality anything like repression. In my notes I employed the provisional term "blocking" of affect, but finally discarded this, too, as being not descriptive. Even blocking has the connotation of a countercathexis, and nothing in my observations of Peter suggested that his ego at that time was capable of forming countercathexes. What I saw could best be described as simple shifts of attention cathexis, a withdrawal of cathexis from a painful perception and an indiscriminate shift to another perception. The repetition of such a phrase as "I want a triangle cracker" showed that the original impulse was still active while the goal had shifted. When the impulse had exhausted itself the repetitious phrase would cease. I could bring about a complete repetition of the whole sequence if, after Peter became quiet, I should say, "I still think that you want to cry." What I have described here, then, is a very primitive mechanism for warding off a disturbing stimulus. Such shifts in cathexis are not, properly speaking, "displacements," for in displacement the original impulse would break through since only the goal is changed. What we see in Peter is something close to what we mean in laymen's language by the term "distractions." It is what the patient does in the dentist chair when he counts the squares on the ceiling to take his mind off the drilling.

Very early in treatment my efforts to help Peter to express his grief were rewarded by several episodes in which grief broke through. This was during a period in which Peter expressed his fear that he was bad and would be sent away (to the institution). Then, following a real but brief separation from his parents when they took a holiday over a week end, these favorable signs disappeared and it was actually many months before he could again express grief with genuine emotion. When grief emerged once again it took the form of a series of emotional storms all in connection with his fear that his mother would go away and be "all gone." One of these episodes appeared during one of my sessions with him, the others took place with his parents at times of leave-taking.

In this essay I shall not go into the details of but only comment on a significant change which occurred in Peter when he once more acquired the ability to express grief. For the first time he began to react to physical pain. There were several episodes in which he cried after an injury. He even acquired the word "hurts" and was able to say on several occasions when he was constipated and could not expel his stool, "It hurts! It hurts!"

## Differentiation, Separateness

While in the two and a half years of treatment a slow progress toward separateness and a sense of identity could be observed, the boundaries between "me" and "other" remained unstable and were easily blurred or temporarily lost. As late as the third year of treatment Peter could occasionally lapse into states of confusion between his body and his mother's body. For example, when Peter and his mother were swimming in a pool, she said, "Peter, come here and pour some water on my feet." Peter came over and carefully poured water over his own feet.

The use of "I," which appeared to have stability at the end of the first year of treatment, became a kind of barometer for the whole period I knew Peter. "I" could disappear from his vocabulary for days or even weeks and self-reference in the third person would come back. After a while "I" would emerge once again, stay with us for weeks and mysteriously disappear once again. At such times I studied my notes for cues regarding the conditions under which "I" became lost or reemerged. At first I thought I saw patterns related to separation. Following the parents' short holidays there was nearly always some regression accompanied by loss of "I." But after I had accumulated more observations I saw that the loss of "I" occurred just as frequently when no separation had taken place. At the end of the second year of treatment I could trace another pattern that I had missed throughout. "I" disappeared just as frequently immediately following a period of relatively good integration and functioning, often accompanied by healthy strides in the direction of independence!

I saw this most clearly toward the end of the second year of treatment. We had made good progress in reducing the anxieties in connection with separation from mother. Bowel and bladder control were good and Peter was now dry at night for the first time in his life. Peter was often in good contact with me and could now even put into words some of the things he was afraid of. "What are you afraid of, Peter?" "I'm afraid of Mommy" (i.e., "I'm afraid *about* Mommy"). "What woke you up last night, Peter?" "I had a dream." "Tell me a story about the dream." "The garage was all gone." (On the dream day the garage *had* been torn down in order to enlarge the garden.)

Peter now had a new awareness of states of waking and sleeping. At the same time he showed reluctance to go to sleep. Often Peter was wakeful until 12:00 or 1:00 in the morning, bringing frequent requests for food or soft drinks or playing with his phonograph. In part the reluctance to go to sleep may have been the warding off of a disturbing dream. Moreover, since being awake now brought pleasure and satisfactions to Peter, the wish to prolong contact with his family must have been another motive. But there was also something else. Peter had a favorite shell which he now took to bed with him; when he awakened at night and could not find it, he was greatly disturbed until it was restored to him. The shell, like the transitional objects of children in their second year, appeared to symbolize the absent mother and also affirmed his own identity, a substantial something that could be clutched in the hand when the insubstantial self feelings dissolved in sleep. From this and a number of small details I inferred that one of the motives in the reluctance to go to sleep was the fear of loss of identity. I suggested that at such times his mother tell him stories about how Peter goes to sleep, but he doesn't lose Peter. He's always there. And when he wakes up he is still Peter and he will find Mommy and Daddy and everyone waiting for him. These little stories seemed to help him go to sleep.

With all these small signs of an emerging sense of identity the use of "I" appeared to have more stability for a time. Then new anxieties appeared. Suddenly in the midst of play in the garden, with mother and me present, he would stop, go indoors, and climb the stairs to his room. When we followed him we could see his tremendous relief at entering his own room. Typically he would then go to his bed, cover himself up, ask for his favorite shell, and lie there in complete self-absorption. In a very rapid development, he now became reluctant to leave his room and would have been content to stay there all day if we had not encouraged him to come down for meals or go for walks. This behavior was not connected with fear of loss of mother, because at these times his mother was usually present and he knew it. It seemed rather to be associated with an urgent need to establish the connections with a base, the room which affirmed his own unstable core of identity. And during this period "I" was lost again, his contact with mother and with me was poor, there was regression in eating and toilet habits. After a period of weeks the anxieties diminished and he climbed back to a level of integration that was fairly close to the one preceding the regression.

It was during this period that I began to see the pattern that I had missed. There was no apparent external reason for the regression. It struck me that each time Peter had achieved a new level of integration around "I" and separateness, there were fresh anxieties and regressions which I was helpless to prevent. It was as if the achievement of separateness, of aloneness, was in itself a state of danger that promoted regression to the tension-free state of nondifferentiation.

## Termination

Peter's treatment was terminated after two and a half years, when Peter was eleven. While his over-all functioning was greatly improved, the limits of therapeutic possibility seemed to have been reached. Now, too, an early puberty added its own complications to the picture of this unstable personality organization. Growth of pubic hair and changes in the size of the genitals had been noticeable already at the age of ten. As puberty advanced we saw increased excitement and indiscriminate discharge through gross body activities, e.g., jumping on his bed with wild hilarity and a sustained erection until he reached exhaustion. This behavior was not, strictly speaking, new but now appeared more frequently and with a marked increase in excitement. We could foresee the difficulties ahead for Peter and the entire family, and the family had already made extraordinary sacrifices in accommodating itself to Peter's unique demands. I began to prepare the parents for the possibility of institutional care for Peter and to help them accept the fact that we had gone as far as we could in treatment in the home.

## Summary

The clinical picture of Peter and that of other blind children with arrested ego development shows certain resemblances to the picture of autism in sighted children, but there are significant differences as well. We are struck by the fact that these deviant blind children show a picture of uniform developmental arrest. The mouth has remained the center of this primitive personality; perception is largely mouth-centered and those qualities that we call "aggressive" and "erotic" remain mouth-centered and appear to be undifferentiated. Tactile perception is minimal; in fact, the hand appears to have no autonomy from the mouth. These characteristics of the blind deviant child have no parallel among sighted autistic children.

The unique characteristics of the blind deviant group and the uniformities encountered in the clinical picture must be linked to the common defect in the group—blindness from birth. We must assume that during critical phases of ego formation the blind infant is faced with unique problems of adaptation which have led, in these cases, to adaptive failure.

Each of these deviant blind children had a mother who felt estranged from her blind baby, who could not establish a "dialogue" (in Spitz's terms [1963]), and who became in this way one of the tragic determinants in the child's adaptive incapacity. But we must give equal attention in studies such as these to the adaptive problems presented by blindness itself. When we consider our present knowledge of the role of vision in ego formation, the substitutions and circuitous routes required of the blind infant must be regarded as adaptive feats.

The observations of Peter and other deviant blind children open up two lines of inquiry: (1) blindness as a communications barrier between mother and infant with extraordinary demands upon the mother's own adaptive capacity; (2) blindness as an impediment during critical phases of ego formation with extraordinary demands upon an infant's adaptive capacity. (The two problems are, of course, interdependent.)

1. Many of the mothers of the deviant blind children, like Peter's mother, were adequate or more than adequate mothers in rearing their other children. While we may suppose that in each of these mothers the blind baby struck old wounds in personality, we need to be attentive to blindness as a barrier in the establishment of the mother-child dialogue. Before the diagnosis of blindness was made (usually around five or six months among the retrolental fibroplasia cases) the mother was already aware that this baby did not respond in expected ways. He was strangely uninterested in his surroundings; the unseeing eyes made the face seem blank and remote. When the mother sought contact with him through her eyes the child's eyes did not meet hers, which feels curiously like a rebuff if you do not know that the baby is blind. The appearance of the mother's face did not cause the baby to smile. All those ways in which the eyes unite human partners were denied to this mother and baby. It seems reasonable to suppose that when these early signals between mother and child failed, the dialogue between mother and child became halting and uncertain. A mother might still carry on a tactile and auditory dialogue with the baby whose eyes never met hers, and some mothers succeeded in this even before the diagnosis of blindness was made. (In those cases where the diagnosis of blindness was made soon after birth, as in the case of the infant, Toni, the mother could more easily exploit the nonvisual repertory that was open to her.) But many of the mothers of the deviant blind children seemed unable to find some bridge of communication, and the estrangement of mother and child began in the early months. When the diagnosis of blindness was made, depression and a sense of hopelessness completed the estrangement for some mothers.

While it is true that the mothering of the deviant blind babies was deficient, the successful mothering of a totally blind infant requires extraordinary qualities indeed. And while the developing ego of the sighted infant is insured when the mother is unexceptional or even less than adequate, the blind infant's ego development is imperiled when his mother does not have adaptive capacities which are exceptional.

Omwake and Solnit (1961), in discussing the case of Ann, point out that "The absence of a visual representation of the mother may seriously impair the capacity to form a useful memory of the mother if the mother is unable to provide other modes of libidinally cathected perceptual experiences, especially touching, to compensate for the absence of the visual experiences."

While the histories of Peter and other deviant blind children show marked deficiencies in the earliest ties with mother, other deviant blind children achieve a demonstrable human tie by the seventh or eighth month which is then followed by a developmental impasse during the crucial nine- to eighteen-month period. Typically the child regresses, reverts to passive postures, exhibits autistic behavior, and remains frozen on the level of mouth-centeredness and nondifferentiation. Clearly there are a number of points in the process of ego formation where blindness creates hazards.

2. The specific ways in which blindness may impede the process of ego formation can be inferred from the characteristics of the blind children with arrested development.

*Perception remained mouth-centered.* The hand appeared to have no autonomy from the mouth, and tactile discrimination was minimal. The mouth, as a strongly endowed instinctual zone, is ill adapted for the achievement of conflict-free perception. The adaptive substitution of the hand as a primary organ of perception is an indispensable step in the development of the blind child. However, our study of the development of Toni, a healthy blind infant, shows that hand autonomy evolves very slowly during the first two years and that the hand did not achieve primacy over the mouth as a perceptual organ until twenty months of age. Clearly, since vision mediates adaptive hand behavior in the sighted infant, the adaptive use of the hand as a primary organ of perception requires the blind infant to make an elaborate detour, even under the most favorable circumstances. Under less favorable circumstances, as in the case of Peter and other deviant blind children, there may be no incentives for this complex adaptive task. Perception remained mouth-centered and the adaptive failure had a morbid significance for the future of these children. When the mouth remains the primary organ of perception the distinctions between "inner" and "outer," "self" and "not self" will not emerge. Perceptual experience is restricted to a narrow range of objects—those that stimulate the mouth in some preferred way. The qualities of objects cannot be known. The failure to achieve hand autonomy was one of the crucial factors responsible for maintaining these personalities on the level of nondifferentiation.

*Those qualities that we call "erotic" or "aggressive" remained mouth-centered and were in fact not differentiated.* The biting and oral-incorporative behavior of the mouth in relation to human and nonhuman "objects" had, as its corollary, a hand behavior in which scratching, clawing, and pinching were employed in a frenzied seizing and holding of human objects. In the case of Peter we saw that this behavior was not intentionally aggressive; the hand had not freed itself of the oral mode and oral-incorporative characteristics of the mouth had been transferred to the hand.

*There was a striking failure to employ the skeletal muscles for the discharge of aggression.* Dorothy Burlingham (1961) reported that nondeviant blind children show an inhibition in the expression of aggression, but we cannot suggest parallels here because of the great difference in ego organization between the children studied by her and our deviant blind children. That which is clearly "inhibition" in Burlingham's group actually appears to be a developmental failure in our group. In the case of Peter, for example, we saw inhibitions in expression of aggression only after he had made considerable progress and after aggression had become linked to specific intentions.

Peter affords an extraordinary insight into the process of differentiation of aggression which may have implications for general studies of early ego development. The work with Peter demonstrated that as opportunities for motor discharge were provided (throwing, large muscle activity), the biting-pinching-scratching behavior receded and patterns that were recognizably "aggressive" emerged from the undifferentiated behavior of the mouth and hand which had previously not been intentionally aggressive.

*A significant delay in the achievement of independent locomotion was reported in nearly all of our deviant blind cases.* Many of these children did not crawl at all and most of them did not achieve independent walking until the age of three, four, or later. We have mentioned that for all blind children independent walking is a late achievement by the standards of the sighted child. In our study of the blind infant Toni we found that the delay in creeping was closely linked with the absence of an external stimulus usually provided by vision. Nonvisual stimuli did not provide the same incentives for reaching and, by extension, crawling. The healthy blind infant with good adaptive capacity and very good mothering found the route to these later motor achievements by means of a detour which we describe.

Our deviant blind children were immobile during the first three or four years of life. There may be a close connection between the failure to discharge aggression through the skeletal musculature and the inactivation of the apparatus during a crucial period in development. When independent locomotion was finally achieved a critical period in ego formation and drive differentiation was lost, and it may no longer have been possible for the components of this process to lock in and produce new patterns.

The delayed locomotion may be another factor in maintaining the personality on the level of nondifferentiation. Until the blind child achieves independence in locomotion he cannot fully experience separateness. Nor can he, in the absence of vision, construct a world of objects until he has made physical contact by means of his independent locomotion.

*The failure to acquire an object concept* was demonstrable in the case of Peter and other deviant blind children. The concept of an object that exists independent of the field of perception is achieved among sighted children by means of a visual construction of its displacements in space. In our earlier discussion we described the unique adaptive problems presented to the blind child in making such a construction on the basis of nonvisual information. This is another of the adaptive feats which fell beyond the capacity of the deviant blind child and another of the factors that maintained the personality on the level of nondifferentiation.

## II. Developmental Patterns in a Blind Infant

With the picture of the deviant children in the background of our thinking we approached our developmental study of blind children with the following propositions. There are certain characteristics found uniformly in the deviant blind children that are not found uniformly among sighted children with severe ego deviations. The uniform characteristics in these blind children must be linked to the defect that the children have in common—blindness from birth. If blindness has led to adaptive failures in this group, there should be correlates in the development of all blind children in the form of specific adaptational problems. With this view we began the first of our developmental studies.

Toni R. was the youngest of six children, the illegitimate child of a Negro mother. The father of the older children had deserted the family some time after the birth of the next older sibling. When the mother learned of Toni's blindness soon after birth, she became depressed. She told us that she had no hopes for the child's future until the family agency social worker gave her assurance that Toni had excellent chances of becoming a normal and healthy child and offered the help of the agency in understanding the special problems of rearing a blind child. The family agency has continued its educational work with the mother throughout the period we have known the family.

Toni was observed at monthly intervals from twenty-two weeks through twenty-eight months of age. A film record was maintained throughout the study which we refer to in this report.

*Smiling Response*

In our first visit at twenty-two weeks we found Toni in her crib in the tiny family living room, very much in the center of family noise and family activities and keenly attentive to the variety of sounds around her. In the midst of the pleasant confusion we observed that when Toni discriminated her mother's voice she broke into an enthusiastic smile accompanied by joyful kicking. We were impressed to find that our observation at five months as well as the social worker's report from three months showed a *selective smiling response* to the sound of mother's voice. Mrs. R. told us that Toni smiled only for her and for no one else in the family. Our film shows her in games with the mother in which the mother chants nonsense to the baby and the baby's whole face radiates anticipation and joy. The uninformed observer could not easily guess that the child is totally blind.

*Stranger Anxiety*

As we followed Toni's development we were impressed by the fact that her blindness per se was not an impediment to the establishment of the vital human connections. At eight and nine months we saw in the film that she clearly discriminated between her mother and a stranger (one of the investigators) on the basis of auditory and tactile cues. She showed a strong anxiety reaction at eight months and violently clutched at the stranger's arm; at nine months she cried as soon as the stranger made contact with her, and we saw her fingering the stranger's face with mounting anxiety and turning her head as if in search for the mother.

It is apparent, then, that if cathexis of the object is achieved, a mental representation of mother can be formed on the basis of a variety of nonvisual sensory data. The retrospective histories of some of the deviant blind children indicate that a smile did not emerge in infancy and that discrimination between the mother and a stranger was not demonstrable in infancy or later in development. Other data in these records show that the mother failed to respond to and stimulate her blind infant and help him utilize perceptual capacities that could lead to an image of mother. Omwake and Solnit (1961) gave emphasis to the same point in their discussion of Ann.

It should be mentioned, however, that there are other cases among the deviant blind children in which the establishment of preobject and object ties followed an apparently normal sequence during the first year, and then reached an impasse, for causes unknown, resulting in developmental arrest or even regression and a freezing of personality at these points. It seemed likely to us that there were a number of vulnerable phases in the process of ego formation for the blind child.

*An Impasse in Motor Development*

Toni's motor development during the first eight months was good and even precocious judged by standards for sighted children. At seventeen weeks the social worker observed that Toni could turn herself over and at twenty-two weeks she could sit briefly without support and could stand for one minute with slight support. At seven months when we arrived for our visit we found Toni sitting confidently without support at the open front door. During the same visit one of the investigators observed Toni supporting herself briefly on hands and knees. An observer, judging by experience with sighted children, would say that Toni was on the verge of crawling.

And then for the last third of the first year, this picture of an unimpeded maturational progress began to change and we saw patterns in development that are not familiar to the observer of sighted children.

There was maturational readiness for creeping as evidenced by Toni's ability at seven months to support herself on hands and knees and at eight months to lower herself unassisted from a sitting position in a chair to a standing position on the floor. Yet, until she was fourteen months old she was unable to creep in directed linear fashion. At that time creeping actually coincided with the beginning of walking. At eight months we first observed a form of locomotion that persisted for months. (Actually it had appeared earlier but had not been observed by us.) We have described it as a kind of "pinwheel locomotion" resembling, in some feature, the pivoting that typically initiates the sequence that leads to creeping, yet it was distinctly inappropriate in this child whose postural behavior placed her within the forty-week norms for sighted children. The "pinwheel locomotion," a rotating which brought her around full circle, remained Toni's only form of locomotion on the floor until she was fourteen months. We learned that this behavior could be set in motion by either pleasurable or unpleasurable excitement. In our films we have an unforgettable picture of the blind child in futile navigation of a circle. It is as if the machinery has been set in motion, but the child has no place to go. The apparatus appears to function in a vacuum.

We have since uncovered other examples of this pinwheel locomotion among blind infants, but until we have made further direct observations we cannot generalize. We do know from the extensive study of Norris et al. (1957) that locomotion is markedly delayed for all blind children. Many observers of blind infants attribute the delay in locomotion to "lack of opportunity" provided by the environment, the undue anxiety of the mother, and the frequent failure to permit the child to get on the floor. But our observations of Toni showed no such lack of opportunity. The pinwheel locomotion points clearly, we think, to the importance of the absence of an external stimulus, usually provided by vision.

The attraction of the visual stimulus leads the sighted child to directed linear creeping. At the time when there is maturational readiness for creeping he is already expert in reaching for an object in space, and the attraction of the object stimulates a sequence of motions that can be described as a reach and a collapse, a reach and a collapse, each time accompanied by some progression. This gradually evolves into a smoothed-out rhythm in which the reaching gesture of the hands coordinates with the legs and the whole body takes over the function of reaching, leading to continuous directed movement.

The sighted child reaches for objects and secures them as early as twenty-four weeks. Toni could grasp an object on contact at thirty weeks but made no attempt to reach for an object in space until ten months of age. When we experimentally jangled keys or bells within the range of her grasp, she did not reach for these. She made no attempt to recover an object which had fallen from her mouth or her grasp; the object had no existence in space for the blind child at this stage. (As a conceptual problem it corresponds to the sighted child's behavior toward a screened object at the same age; here blindness itself constitutes the screen.) We understood then that until Toni could reach for an object in space, there could be no incentive to linear creeping. But here, too, Toni's blindness created a tragic dilemma, for until she could achieve some degree of mobility, the concept of an object in space would be difficult to achieve.

During the same period (the eight- and nine-month observations) we had the general impression of an impasse in development. Toni now appeared dull and lethargic. She still showed no interest in toys or any objects except her bottle and her pacifier. And there was one new behavior that gave us concern. *In the absence of any other stimulation Toni was content to lie passively on the floor, for long periods, face down, smiling softly to herself.*

Mrs. R., we observed, was now often out of rapport with the child. She was anxious, irritable, and inclined to push Toni toward performance. Toni's pinwheel locomotion was baffling to her. The passive prone position was disturbing to see, and the baby wasn't doing anything "new," she complained. To the mother, who had reared five healthy children, the blind baby now appeared "different" and even dull. All the old fears that Toni might never be normal seemed to rise to the surface again.

Yet there were, in fact, evidences of progressive maturation during these two months, although they were not meaningful to the mother. Toni had learned to lower herself from a chair to the floor. We observed that when she dropped her pacifier she now made tentative reaching gestures for it, although she did not search for it. We watched a feeding in which Toni grabbed the spoon from her mother and inserted it in her own mouth. And, in spite of evidence of the disturbance in the mother-child relationship, we also observed that when the mother actively stimulated her in games, Toni responded with the joyfulness and excitement that we had seen in earlier months. But none of these things were reassuring to the mother. The baby didn't "look" normal to her.

In assessing this period we had to take into account those impediments to maturation that were directly or indirectly related to blindness, and those impediments that were now presented by a disturbance in the mother-child relationship. Clearly they were mutually reinforcing in an intricate pattern. Blindness was an impediment to the achievement of locomotion. Until mobility could be achieved, the blind infant could not make discoveries that would lead her to explore, to discover objects, or to manipulate them. Until objects acquired a value independent of need satisfaction or self-stimulation, Toni could not move beyond the bottle and pacifier. All of this added up to a picture of arrested development to the mother, who reacted with anxiety and withdrawal.

From the standpoint of Toni, who was almost exclusively dependent on stimulation provided by her mother and other human objects for the maintenance of interest in the outside world, inevitable periods of nonstimulation seemed to leave her in an exteroceptive vacuum. At such times she assumed the prone position and fell back on proprioceptive experience, which to us seemed to be erotically stimulating.

During this period Mrs. R. was given guidance and support by her social worker. We ourselves felt it necessary to depart from a neutral position and give reassurance. In addition, we felt that our study was itself a factor in increasing the mother's anxiety about the child's achievement. Toni, in her mother's eyes, had become a movie star and the pressure for performance was increased by our visits and filming. The educational work of the social worker was chiefly in the area of promoting the positive ties between mother and child and of diminishing the mother's anxiety.

At ten months the picture changed again. Toni was not yet able to creep in a linear fashion, but she now strongly resisted being placed in the prone position. Concurrently she achieved mobility of another kind through a walker which her mother had purchased for her. We saw her "scooting" about the room with great energy and enthusiasm. When her mother called to her she could steer her walker in the direction of the mother's voice. This was accomplished through reaching her body in the direction of mother's voice, and the reach of course propelled her. The reaching of the body toward a desired object had a correlate in another behavior. We saw in the same session that Toni could now reach for an object in space. In two experimental situations, one involving a bunch of keys and one a candy cane, she recovered the object by reaching out into space even after she had lost physical contact with it.

It is of interest that the presence or absence of auditory cues seemed irrelevant in this situation. We have no observations indicating that she was able to reach for and recover a noise-making object earlier than a nonnoise-making object.

During the same ten-month observation we saw that Toni and her mother had recovered their old rapport. The mother reported with pride that Toni was "getting into everything," scooting about the house in her walker, exploring rooms, kitchen cupboards. The passive prone position was no longer in evidence.

We observed Toni's behavior toward inanimate objects. Among a series of toys presented to her, cloth dolls, stuffed animals, and a plastic hourglass-shaped rattle, she examined each with her tongue and lips and minimally with her fingers and clearly discriminated among them, choosing and discarding on what seemed to be a basis of "least desirable" and "most desirable."

We asked the mother, "What does Toni do when she gets mad?" (We had no direct observations.) The mother gave some examples. If Toni was in her walker, she began to scoot around the house with great energy. If she was frustrated by a member of the family, she might pinch, and her pinching, we gathered in response to questions, was specifically directed toward the person who was frustrating her. She did not bite in anger but did bite playfully and in demonstration of love.

Toni now imitated sounds. We heard her say "dada" in response to mother's "dada" and cluck in response to mother's cluck.

From these observations we could see a new progress which was probably facilitated by a number of factors. The change in mother's feelings toward Toni was seen clearly in response to the new achievements of the child and may also have been a vital factor in promoting progressive currents in the personality.

The child's new-found mobility probably played an important role in the changes that we saw. A decisive shift from passive to active was achieved, and the thrust toward activity became so powerful that the child made vigorous protests against the posture of passivity which, for her, was being put on the floor. Mobility brought her into a new relationship with the world of objects; she now actively explored and discriminated a widening range of objects. Toni's behavior toward objects that were removed from her field of perception told us that she had an emerging concept of the independent existence of objects. In the case of this blind child, mobility perhaps aided the evolution of the concept; and it would also be correct to say that the emerging concept afforded incentives to locomotion. Now, too, motor activity appeared to facilitate discharge of aggression (when she was mad she "scooted around the room"), and there may be a connection between this achievement and the newly reported goal-directed aggression against the frustrating person.

As we review this critical period in Toni's development we can identify some of the hazards in development that confront the blind child. This child with better-than-average endowment and adaptive capacity, living in a home that provided favorable opportunities for development, reached a point in development when absence of vision was an impediment to progress and the adaptive solutions could be found only through an elaborate detour.

We have mentioned earlier that the retrospective histories of the deviant blind children almost uniformly showed a delay in achieving locomotion that was even beyond the norms for blind children in general. We know that the normal, sighted child is given a tremendous impetus toward the achievement of separateness and individuation by the experience of independent locomotion. The blind child is to a far greater extent dependent upon locomotion to make the crucial distinctions between self and outer world and to construct a world of objects—and here, ironically, the absence of vision becomes an impediment to the establishment of locomotion. In a less than favorable environment, the blind child may not have strong incentives to find the complex adaptive solutions, and the failure to achieve locomotion within a critical period of time may be one of the factors that brings about a developmental arrest in the deviant children.

## The Mouth and the Hand

In his essay "The Primal Cavity" Spitz (1955) investigated the role of the oral cavity as interoceptor and exteroceptor; here all perception begins. The oral cavity, he said, fulfills the functions of a bridge from internal reception to external perception. Integrating the contributions of Hoffer, Lewin, Isakower, Linn, and Halverson with his own observations, Spitz examined the early alliance of hand and mouth. The participation of the hand in nursing (clutching, stroking, clawing, and scratching the breast) is in the nature of overflow at birth; the sensorium of the hand is not yet cathected. This activity of the hands becomes more and more organized in subsequent months, probably, Spitz suggests, as a function of the progressive cathexis of the hand's sensorium. The fusion in early infancy of oral, tactile, and visual perceptions into an undifferentiated unity is hypothesized by Spitz (later given experimental support through the work of M. Bender [1952] and L. Linn [1953]). Hoffer (1949) in his study "Mouth, Hand, and Ego-Integration" describes how in the second and third quarters of the first year the hands achieve a progressive independence from the oral zone and are more under the influence of the eyes, "playing the part of an intermediary between eyes and mouth. They have developed from instruments serving as a means for discharging tension into tools which control the outer world. They have at this stage become a most active extension of the growing ego." Gesell and Amatruda (1947), speaking of the blind infant and tactual experience, say, "The senses were made to function in synesthesia, two or more modalities blending. Even the primary tactual sense does not normally function in pure form. Tactual perceptions are visual-tactual perceptions for the normal mind. If this close reciprocal interacting relationship between vision and touch is not recognized it is impossible to appreciate the gravity of the handicap under which the blind or near-blind infant labors."

In our observations of Toni we were impressed to see that the mouth remained the primary organ of perception well into the middle of the second year. The hand was employed minimally for discrimination during the first year and did not achieve autonomy from the mouth until the second half of the second year. Since the hand, for the blind child, must achieve primacy as a perceptual organ, the progress from mouth to hand becomes an important area for study in the blind infant. We recall that one of the characteristics of the deviant blind children was mouth-centered perception and a failure to achieve hand autonomy.[3]

At nine months of age Toni had no interest in objects other than the bottle, a spoon, and a pacifier. There was transitory interest in rattles and bells. Each of the items in the first group has retained its oral cathexis, while for the sighted child of this age (and even much earlier) a large number of objects that are independent of need satisfaction will attract and excite the child and invite his handling and exploration. If a novel object was presented to Toni at this age—and even much later in the second year, she brought it to her mouth. So will the sighted child, of course, during the first year. But there are these differences. The object, to be meaningful to Toni, had to stimulate the mouth in certain preferred ways. If it did not, it was immediately discarded. The sighted child of this age, in the act of exploring an object, will employ his mouth to acquire certain data about the object which are added to the group of data already acquired through the eyes, the hands, and other sense modalities. The qualities of the object itself are discovered in this way, and the attraction of the object has relative independence from mouth satisfaction.

During the period when Toni showed no interest in inanimate objects (and distressed her mother by appearing so dull) we saw, on the other hand, that her discrimination of human objects had achieved a high level. She discriminated her mother from a stranger; she recognized each of her siblings and responded selectively to them. Among sighted children we know that the interest in inanimate objects advances from the cathexis of human objects (Hartmann, 1952), and absence of interest in inanimate objects in a sighted child of Toni's age would indicate grave deficiencies in object ties. Evidently, for Toni, the path from human objects to inanimate objects was slow and circuitous compared to that of the sighted child, yet essentially the same path was followed.

To illustrate, we turn to a group of observations which tell us something about the way in which Toni recognized objects during the second half of the first year.

In our early film sequences we observed that Toni recognized the bottle only at the moment when her mouth or fingers made contact with the nipple, that is, the cathected portion of the bottle. At seven months Toni lost her bottle while lying on the floor. In random movements of arms and hands she came in contact with the glass bottle itself without showing signs of recognition. In a sequence at nine months when the bottle was presented to her inverted, she showed no signs of recognition although she took the bottom of the bottle in her mouth and sucked on it as she did with all objects at this time. When the bottle was righted for her and she made contact with the nipple, there was immediate recognition on her face. At eleven and a half months when the bottle was again presented to her inverted, she handled it familiarly, extended her fingers down the sides of the bottle until she reached the nipple, and slowly, quite unselfconsciously reversed its position and brought the nipple to her mouth. From this behavior we inferred that she now had a concept of the whole bottle. Where vision would have conferred wholeness to the percept of bottle many months earlier, the blind baby had to achieve this through a laborious additive process.

In the behavior with the inverted bottle, we can also see that the perception of wholeness was achieved through the hand alone. The hand began to function as a discriminating sensory organ. This was a new behavior with regard to inanimate objects although it was not a new behavior with regard to human objects. As already indicated, at eight months when Toni was held experimentally by one of the investigators, she reacted with immediate anxiety to the stranger and followed this with anxious, exploratory fingering of the stranger's face; she was relying upon her hand for fine discrimination and for reality testing. At nine months we saw her hand exploring the faces of her brother and sisters as they played with her. The progression from human objects to inanimate objects in the behavior of the hand was first observed by us in connection with the bottle. It was not observed in connection with objects that were not libidinally cathected or were unfamiliar to her until many months later.

At seventeen months when Toni had already demonstrated very good tactile perception, we made observation: Toni was playing a game with her bottle on the porch of her home. She repeatedly threw the bottle away and recovered it. Once, she lost the bottle and conducted a search for it. We then saw her crawling along the floor licking the floor with her tongue! In the emergency she fell back upon the mouth as the organ of perception.

For all blind persons the mouth retains its function as a leading discriminating perceptual organ throughout life. Villay (1930) describes how, even as an adult, he relied upon his mouth, and particularly his tongue, to make the finest perceptual distinctions. Our observations of Toni show the extent to which the mouth was required to serve as a substitute for vision from the third through the eighteenth month of life. The use of a highly cathected instinctual zone for perception has important implications for the study of ego formation. This line of inquiry, which was suggested to us by Dr. Joseph Michaels at an early stage of our work, is one that we consider central to this and subsequent studies.

The mouth, of course, dictates its own terms of perception. As we saw in Toni, in order for an object to be desirable, it must be need satisfying or associated with oral stimulation. When the mouth remains the primary organ of perception, it restricts the range of experience with objects and obstructs a crucial development that leads to the discovery of the nature of objects.

We have no analogy in the development of sighted children. The primary autonomy of vision guarantees the conflict-free development of perception. The prolonged mouth-centered perception of the blind infant promotes an alliance between drives and perception that can be a serious impediment to learning. The hand will later serve the development of a "conflict-free" perception, but the hand itself in the blind maintains its partnership with the mouth for an extended period that is not paralleled in the development of sighted children.

We are accustomed to speak of the hands of the blind as their "eyes." When we consider how the achievement of hand autonomy for sighted infants is facilitated by vision, the same achievement in the blind infant appears as a feat of extraordinary virtuosity. It may not be achieved at all—as we see in the deviant blind child. While we are not prepared to say how the adaptive failure of the hand should be weighted in the whole complex of factors that have led to developmental arrest in these cases, it is striking that this failure is consistently found in our own observations as well as all reported cases of deviant blind children.

As we followed Toni's development we saw that the hand very gradually took over perceptual functions that were centered in the mouth. The early partnership of mouth and hand facilitated a transfer of perceptual qualities and even oral-perceptive modes to the hand itself (Spitz, 1955) until, as we saw, near the end of Toni's second year the hand achieved autonomy from the mouth and was capable of increasingly complex discriminations.

As we traced the progress of the hand through the film record we saw that at seven months Toni recognized the nipple of her bottle when her fingers came in contact with it. At eight months when she was held by one of the investigators, she cried in distress and anxiously fingered the stranger's face, verifying that this was a stranger. At nine months we saw her playing with her brother, alternately mouthing him and fingering his face. At ten months she demonstrated tactual recognition of her bottle when it was presented to her inverted and, in a sequence where various stuffed animals and dolls were presented to her, she used the mouth and her hands alternately for discriminating among them. Novel objects were still brought first to the mouth as late as twenty-one months. The progress in tactual recognition evolved from human objects and the cathected inanimate objects such as the bottle and gradually spread to include a wide range of objects that were not, in themselves, libidinally cathected. And this last achievement, which corresponds to the autonomy of the hand from mouth, was seen only in the last months of the second year.

We contrast this with the picture of the persistently mouth-centered deviant blind child. The invariable picture of these children showed them lying on a bed or sitting on the floor absently mouthing or sucking or tonguing or chewing a clothespin, a rubber toy, or a mental ashtray. In the case of the deviant child, perception could not free itself from the erotogenic overload of the mouth and remained in a kind of morbid alliance with the drives. There was no interest in objects other than those that were connected with need satisfaction or self-stimulation (as we saw in Toni, too, during the first year).

We do not know why the deviant children failed to develop hand autonomy. As already indicated, however, we feel that this failure is crucial and is one of the factors that maintains the personality on the level of nondifferentiation. What we can see through the study of Toni is that the adaptive use of the hand as a primary organ of perception is an extraordinary feat which even under favorable circumstances evolved very slowly in this one blind child. We are accustomed to take this adaptive achievement for granted in the case of the blind child. The study of deviant blind children teaches us that the route to hand autonomy for the sightless child is so complex that it may never be found at all.

We hope that further developmental studies on blind children, including deviant blind infants, will illuminate this and other developmental failures.

## Notes

1. In the case narrative, "I" refers to the child's therapist, S.F. The mother's analyst was D.F.

2. We should note also that repeatedly in our records and those of Keeler (1958), Parmelee et al. (1958), and others the deviant blind children were reported to be unable to masticate. Among our children in the nine- to fourteen-year range at the Family Service Society, many were still on soft baby foods.

3. Shortly after this paper was submitted for publication, Anne-Marie Sandler's paper "Aspects of Passivity and Ego Development in the Blind Infant" appeared (1963). Mrs. Sandler's views and ours are strikingly similar in certain areas, particularly in her considerations regarding the role of the hand and the mouth in the early development of the blind child.

## References

Bender, M. B. (1952). *Disorders in Perception.* Springfield: Thomas.

Blank, H. R. (1957). Psychoanalysis and Blindness. *Psychoanal. Quart.,* 26:1–24.

———. (1958). Dreams of the Blind. *Psychoanal. Quart.,* 27:158–174.

Burlingham, D. (1961). Some Notes on the Development of the Blind. *Psychoanal. Study Child,* 16:121–145.

Gesell, A. & Amatruda, C. (1947). *Developmental Diagnosis,* 2nd ed. New York: Hoeber.

Hartmann, H. (1952). The Mutual Influences in the Development of Ego and Id. *Psychoanal. Study Child,* 7:9–30.

Hoffer, W. (1949). Mouth, Hand, and Ego-Integration. *Psychoanal. Study Child,* 3/4:49–56.

Keeler, W. R. (1958). Autistic Patterns and Defective Communication in Blind Children with Retrolental Fibroplasia. In *Psychopathology of Communication,* ed. P. H. Hoch & J. Zubin. New York: Grune & Stratton.

Klein, G. S. (1962). Blindness and Isolation. *Psychoanal. Study Child,* 17:82–93.

Linn, L. (1953). Psychological Implications of the "Activating System." *Amer. J. Psychiat.,* 110:61–65.

Norris, M.; Spaulding, P.; & Brodie, F. (1957). *Blindness in Children.* Chicago: Univ. of Chicago Press.

Omwake, E. G. & Solnit, A. J. (1961). "It Isn't Fair": The Treatment of a Blind Child. *Psychoanal. Study Child*, 16:352–404.

Parmalee, A. H., Jr. (1955). Developmental Evaluation of the Blind Premature Infant. *A.M.A. Amer. J. Dis. Child.*, 90:135–140.

———; Cutsforth, M. D.; & Jackson, C. L. (1958). The Mental Development of Children with Blindness Due to Retrolental Fibroplasia. *A.M.A. Amer. J. Dis. Child.*, 96:641–648.

Piaget, J. (1937). *The Construction of Reality in the Child.* New York: Basic Books, 1954.

Provence, S. & Lipton, R. C. (1962). *Infants in Institutions.* New York: International Universities Press.

Sandler, A.-M. (1963). Aspects of Passivity and Ego Development in the Blind Infant. *Psychoanal. Study Child*, 18:343–361.

Segal, A. & Stone, F. H. (1961). The Six-Year-Old Who Began to See: Emotional Sequelae of Operation for Congenital Bilateral Cataracts. *Psychoanal. Study Child*, 16:481–509.

Spitz, R. A. (1945). Hospitalism: An Inquiry into the Genesis of Psychiatric Conditions in Early Childhood. *Psychoanal. Study Child*, 1:53–74.

———. (1955). The Primal Cavity. *Psychoanal. Study Child*, 10:215–240.

———. (1959). *A Genetic Field Theory of Ego Formation.* New York: International Universities Press.

———. (1963). Life and the Dialogue. In *Counterpoint*, ed. H. S. Gaskill. New York: International Universities Press.

Villay, P. (1930). *World of the Blind.* New York: Macmillan.

# 21

## Smiling and Stranger Reaction in Blind Infants

We have strong evidence in the study of human infancy that the healthy, sighted baby establishes his human bonds during the first eighteen months of life. From the maternal deprivation studies we know that the absence of human partners or a rupture in the early love ties during this period may produce permanent impairment in the capacity to form enduring bonds in later life.

When we consider the central role of vision in the process of human attachment—in the differential responses to the human face, the development of recognition memory and the acquisition of a stable mental representation of the mother—we can see that the study of human object relations in the blind infant can afford an extraordinary opportunity to examine the non-visual components and the extent to which these can lead to adaptive substitutions in human attachment.

Since 1963 we have been engaged in a series of longitudinal studies of blind infants at Children's Psychiatric Hospital, University of Michigan Medical Center. Our study covers these areas of development: human object relations, behavior toward inanimate objects, language, gross motor development, prehension, object concept, affectivity, body and self image, self-stimulating behaviors, sleep patterns, eating patterns.

In this essay, we have selected items from our study of human object relations which are generally accepted as indicators on a scale of human attachment: (a) differential smiling and (b) stranger reactions.

*The sample.* The data which are summarized in this report are derived from a study of ten babies, seven boys and three girls. So far as possible we have brought babies into the study soon after birth, but the actual age at the point of first observation has ranged from twenty-three days to seven months for eight children and two children were first seen at nine months and eleven months respectively. Within the range of medical certainty we have selected babies who are totally blind from birth or who have light perception only and no other defects.

Our sample, then, is highly selective and our findings cannot be generalized for the total blind infant population. (A typical blind population includes children with a range of useful vision who are still legally classified as "blind" and children who have other sensory and motor handicaps and neurological damage.) Our babies, then, are advantaged in a blind child population by the intactness of other systems and are disadvantaged as a group by having no pattern vision. (These restrictive criteria have given us a small population even though we called upon the referral network of a major medical center.)

It is important to note that we have provided a concurrent educational and guidance service for all babies in the research program. We know that the early development of blind babies is perilous. In the general blind child population we see a very high incidence of deviant and non-differentiated personalities and arrested ego development (even when we exclude cases of brain damage and multiple handicaps which are also common to this population). As our own research progressed we were able to link certain developmental road-blocks with a clinical picture seen in the older blind child (Fraiberg and Freedman, 1964; Fraiberg, 1968). As these findings became available to us they were readily translatable into a program of prevention and education. We felt that no benefits to the research could justify withholding this knowledge and began to provide a home-based educational program which has been highly effective in promoting the development of our blind babies (Fraiberg, Smith, and Adelson, 1969).

We can say then that the observations in this report are derived from a group of healthy, otherwise intact infants; their families represent a good range of socioeconomic conditions; their mothers are at least adequate and, in four cases, would be rated as superior. The development of these babies has probably been favored by our intervention.

*Observers.* Each baby is assigned to a team of two observers. The primary responsibility for observation is placed in the senior staff member who is present at each visit.

*Methods.* The baby is visited in his home at twice monthly intervals for an hour and a half session. (We travel within a radius of one hundred miles to cover our home visits.) We try to time our visits to coincide with a morning or afternoon waking period and to fit our observations into the normal routine of that period. Nearly all of the data required for our study can be obtained through observing a feeding, a bath, a playtime with mother, a diapering or clothes changing and a period of self-occupation with or without toys. A small amount of time in each session may be employed for testing procedures by the examiner in the areas of prehension and object concept.

The observers record a continuous narrative with descriptive detail. Once a month we record a fifteen minute 16 millimeter film sample covering mother-child interaction, prehension, and gross motor development which will be employed for close analysis by the staff using a variable speed projector.

Since the areas we are studying have not been previously researched, our data collection procedures had to insure coverage of hundreds of items for comparative study, yet needed to be open, flexible and rich in detail for qualitative study.

Our study of human attachment was, of course, one of the central areas of this study. Since nothing was known regarding the characteristics of human attachments in the blind infant we had to design a study which permitted the blind baby to teach us what kinds of sense information he used when he made selective responses to his mother, his father and other familiar persons, how he differentiated mother and stranger, how he reacted to separation from his mother, how he demonstrated affection, joy, need, grief, anger, and the range of human emotion that will normally tell us about the quality of human bonds during the first eighteen months.

Our observations, then, covered differential responses (smiling, vocalizing, motor responses) to the human voice, to touch, to holding, to lap games, with familiar and unfamiliar persons, with mother present and, when appropriate for testing, with mother absent. The data covering the first eighteen months of life were classified, yielding twenty-five categories which could be employed for analysis of differential responses.

From these data we have selected two areas which afford interesting comparisons between the blind child and the sighted child in the sequence that leads to the establishment of human bonds: smiling and stranger reactions. In the following sections we will present brief summaries of the literature pertaining to normal development in each of these areas and brief summaries of our findings in the study of the blind infant.

## Smiling

### The Sighted Child

Wolff (1963) reports a response smile to the human voice in the third week of life, and a selective response to the mother's voice in the fourth week. Emde and Koenig (1969) describe *irregular* smiling at three weeks to two months as a "response to unpatterned kinesthetic, tactile, auditory and visual stimulation" leading to a *regular* smiling response at two to two and a half months. There appears to be general agreement among investigators that by the second month the response smile to the configuration of the human face appears and that it is the most successful stimulus for regularly evoking the smile (Spitz and Wolf, 1946; Gewirtz, 1965).

Between four and six months Benjamin (1963) reports that the experimenter's smile will elicit a smile from the baby, and that discrimination of faces will appear during the same period. Emde and Koenig speak of the further differentiation of the smile during the period two and a half to six months with more frequent and intense smiling to mother than to unfamiliar persons. During the period six to eleven months there is a marked decline in the smiling response to strangers reported by Spitz and Wolf (1946), Ambrose (1961), Polak, Emde, and Spitz (1964). Emde and Koenig speak of this period as an "all or none" smiling; that is, smiling occurs to mother and familiar persons. There is some disagreement among investigators regarding this last point (Gewirtz, 1965; Morgan and Ricciuti, 1969). Since the experimental conditions in these two sets of studies were not identical, the "not smiling to the stranger" or the "smiling to the stranger" may be related to variations in the introductory stage of the stranger-reaction testing.

The differentiation of the smile, then, gives information regarding the baby's increasing selectivity and valuation of human partners during the first year and may be taken, as Spitz and Wolf (1946) long ago proposed, as a key indicator of stages in the growth of human attachment during the period of ego formation. The negative demonstration is seen in the institutional baby, where the absence, or infrequency, or non-differentiation of the smile can be regarded as a sign of impoverishment in human relations. The indiscriminate smile for all comers, seen by Provence and Lipton (1962) in year-old babies in an institution, was regarded by these investigators as a sign of failure or absence of human connections, speaking for no valuation of one person over another.

## The Blind Infant

D. G. Freedman (1964) reported on the characteristics of smiling in response to touch and voice in four congenitally blind infants tested under six months of age. He described the smiles of these infants as "fleeting"; that is, they quickly formed and disappeared, as in normal infants during the first month. In two cases observed by Freedman through six months of age, the fleeting smiles gradually changed to normal prolonged smiling. In this study Freedman did not test differential smiling, and his observations did not extend beyond the six-month level. S. Fraiberg and David A. Freedman[1] (1964) reported a longitudinal study of one blind infant followed from five months to thirty-six months of age, in which selective smiling to the voice and touch of mother and familiar persons was described in some detail. Studies by Thompson (1941), which included smiling in twenty-six children, employed a mixed population of children with congenital and acquired blindness, and his findings are not applicable to the problem we are investigating in the present study.

Four of our ten babies were seen by us under three months of age. These babies were able to demonstrate a clear response smile to the sound of the mother's voice in the early weeks of life. Our findings show close correspondence with those of Peter Wolff's (1963) study, in which he demonstrates that the sighted baby shows a selective smile to the sound of his mother's voice as early as four weeks of age.

Example: Ronny, at 0:0:28 days, just wakening from his nap, drowsy, briefly alert with eyes open, then slipping back into sleep. Mother calls his name. A smile appears, eyes open briefly. Father calls his name. A smile appears. Mother and Father take turns calling his name. After calling his name several times, either of the parents can elicit a smile. The observer now calls his name several times. There is no smile.

Mother calls. The smile returns. Observer tries repeatedly to elicit his smile without success. Parents in several repetitions can nearly always elicit the smile.

At this age, as Emde and Koenig (1969) point out, the familiar voice as well as a number of other stimuli can irregularly elicit a smile in the sighted child. And, while it is impressive to see how the blind Ronny can respond selectively to the sound of one or another of his parent's voices, we should note that this is not an automatic or a regular response. Even with the familiar voices, several repetitions are required to elicit the smile. At this point, however, where voice is the stimulus for the smile, there is good equivalence between the blind baby's smiling response and that of the sighted baby.

But at two to two and a half months, where the visual stimulus of the human face evokes an automatic smile with a high degree of regularity, there is no equivalence in the blind baby's experience. The blind baby's smiling becomes more frequent from the second month on, and the pattern of selective smiling for the familiar voice or sound becomes increasingly demonstrated in favor of the mother, but even the mother's voice *will not regularly* elicit the smile. There is no stimulus in the third month or later that has true equivalence for the human face gestalt in the experience of the sighted child.

At a meeting in May 1969 with René Spitz, Robert Emde, and David Metcalf, we presented some of our data and were satisfied that this constituted the essential difference between the smile of the blind baby at two to three months and that of the sighted baby. Robert Emde proposed that what we saw in the blind child's smile was an adaptive modification of the characteristics of smiling observed in sighted children between the ages of three weeks and two months in which the human voice was one of a pool of stimuli which elicited *irregular* smiling. Out of this pool, only the visual stimuli will be differentiated for automatic response in the third month to the stimulus of the human face gestalt. In the case of the blind baby, the human voice afforded the means for selective smiling but lacked the sign value of the visual stimuli which release the automatic smile.

Between three and six months (now reporting on seven babies), the smile remains selective for the parents' voices and we have only isolated instances in our record in which the smile was elicited by the observer's voice. Yet, in this period, too, it is never an automatic smile to the sound of the parent's voice.

Now, in our records of this period, we begin to see that the most reliable stimulus for evoking a smile or laughter in the baby is gross tactile or kinesthetic stimulation. As observers, we were puzzled and concerned by the amount of bouncing, jiggling, tickling, and nuzzling that all of our parents, without exception, engaged in with the baby. In several cases, we had to judge the amount of such stimulation as excessive by any standards. We had rarely seen, among parents of sighted babies in such a range of homes, so much dependence upon gross body stimulation. Then we began to understand; these games provided the almost certain stimulus for the smile, while the parents' voices, alone, provided at best, an irregular stimulus. The parents' own *need* for the response smile, which is normally guaranteed with the sighted baby of this age, led them to these alternative routes in which the smile would be evoked with a high degree of reliability.

During the same period, lap games, particularly "patty-cake," provided patterened motor stimulation which almost always elicited a smile from the baby. Such games had the advantage, of course, of giving the baby some means of regulating stimuli through anticipating pattern and rhythm and became favorite games for all of our children in the second half of the first year.

Smiling and pleasure in the game were clearly linked to the mother. When we tested differential responses through our observers by repeating a favorite game, we were unable to elicit a smile or responsive vocalizations, except in rare instances.

Ronny, at 0:4:6, is playing patty-cake with mother. (In our region this game is played with five sequences, usually involving five motor patterns. Pat a cake, pat a cake, Baker's man. Bake me a cake as fast as you can. / Roll it / and pat it / and mark it with a T; / put it in the oven for baby and me.) As soon as mother begins the first sequence with hand clapping, Ronny smiles. As the shift in rhythm is about to appear in the second sequence, there is anticipatory excitement on his face. As the new pattern appears, a big smile. At the conclusion of the game, laughter and vocalizations, then distress, which mother reads as "more." Mother resumes the game. At one point in repetition of the game with mother, mother interrupts the game to address a comment to the observers. There is a loud outcry from Ronny and mother must resume.

Later, the observer plays patty-cake with Ronny, using the same chant and motor patterns. There is no smile and no active participation. When the observer experimentally interrupts the game at a point where a shift in rhythm and motor pattern would occur (a high point in the game with mother), there is no discernible reaction. Ronny maintains his hands limply in the posture of the point of interruption.

During the period six to twelve months (now reporting on ten babies) our records of smiling show no patterns of further differentiation, and parallels with the smiling of sighted infants break down at several points. For each child known to us in the first and second quarters, our records show an increase in the number of observations of smiling during this period. The pattern of preferential smiling for parents and familiar persons remains unchanged. The stimuli themselves, voice, tactile, kinesthetic, nearly always united with the familiar person, remain unchanged, except that the range of smile-eliciting experience now enlarges to include a variety of games, which had not been in the child's repertoire in the earlier period. (A notable favorite among games, a sure stimulus for joyful smiling and laughter, is a version of "peek-a-boo" in which a cloth is pulled over the blind baby's face with the ritual, "Where is . . . Johnny?")

When we consider the course of the differentiated smile in the case of the sighted infant, an attempt to find further parallels with our blind infants would be spurious. Smiling in the sighted infant is differentiated through vision. The automatic smile to the sign gestalt of the human face becomes a differentiated smile as recognition memory discriminates facial characteristics; it becomes a preferential smile for the face of intimate persons, and some observers (Benjamin, 1963; Spitz and Wolf, 1946; Emde and Koenig, 1969) report that in the second half of the first year the smile is reserved for mother and familiar persons and not elicited by unfamiliar persons.

Now, of course, since the blind infant's smile to voice is selective from earliest infancy on, the differentiating criteria which we employ for sighted infants later in the first year have no meaning in the study of the blind infant. Since, in our observations, unfamiliar persons rarely elicited the smile, "not smiling" to the stranger in the second half of the first year had no value as a criterion for stranger reaction. (Other criteria were employed for stranger reactions, as we shall see in the next section.)

Actually, as we studied the characteristics of the blind baby's positive attachment to mother in the second half of the first year, we found that responsive vocalizations offered more differentiating criteria for valuation of the mother than the smile itself. The recorded "dialogues" between mother and child with "question and answer" cadence, play on sound, imitation of sound, could not be elicited by an observer experimentally reproducing cues with the baby. We have isolated examples in our record in which, for example, a blind baby says "Hi!" in response to the observer's "Hi!" but no examples of the extended "dialogue" with an observer in cases where we had clear demonstrations in relation to the mother or father.

When we exclude vision as a factor in the socialization of the smile, other differences in smiling emerge. Since the sign value of the smile in greeting can only be a visual sign (the exchange of smiles) the blind baby does not automatically smile in greeting; the blind baby does not *initiate* or invite contact with a smile. Our babies do not smile as frequently as sighted babies do (the consensus of our own staff and a very large number of independent observers who have reviewed film with us over the years). And even when we have all the criteria for a mutually satisfying mother-child relationship, the smile of the blind infant strikes us as a muted smile. The joyful, even ecstatic, smile that we see in a healthy sighted baby is a comparatively rare occurrence among blind babies. This suggests that the smile on the face of "the other" is a potent reinforcer—even in infancy—of one's own smile. The contagion of smiling is clearly dependent upon visual experience.

And what about the contagion of laughter? Since laughter is vocal, we should expect not only imitation, but the possibility of contagion. All of our babies laughed, of course. Typically, laughter was associated with peaks of excitement in games.

Under what circumstances did laughter of "the other" evoke laughter in the baby? We have only isolated examples in our records of laughter in response to laughter! We have a report from Ronny's mother that Ronny "laughs when his father laughs," at the age of ten months. But we never observed this. Was he imitating the sound of laughter (mechanically) or was this, properly speaking, laughter evoked by the laughter of "the other"? We have an observation of Teddy at eight months in which he laughed in response to laughter. We have an example of contagious laughter in Paul at the age of two years. We have this example in Robbie's records.

Robbie: age 2:6:0. His mother reported during our visit that Robbie had been taught to say his prayers. "God bless Mama, God bless Daddy." Recently, Robbie invented his own litany: "God bless Mama, God bless Daddy, God bless television!" This, of course, broke up the research team and we all roared with laughter. Robbie, hearing our laughter, began to laugh. To get more mileage out of his joke, he repeated the litany, and we laughed again. One of us said, still laughing, "Robbie, you are a clown." "I'm a clown," he said, squealing with laughter. We kept up this nonsense for a few moments, in which one wave of laughter from us initiated another wave of laughter from Robbie. . . .

After we left the session and drove home, we realized that this was the first time we had ever encountered "contagious laughter" in Robbie.

These exceptional examples lead to some reflections. Is the contagion of laughter related to the contagion of the smile? In the absence of the visual signs that lead to the contagious smile, is the evolution of contagious laughter altered or impeded?

## Stranger Reactions

### The Sighted Child

On the scale of increasing differentiation and valuation of the mother and other human partners, a complementary series of reactions toward the unfamiliar person begins to emerge before the middle of the first year. Benjamin (1963) describes "fear of the strange" during the period four-to-five months, which he discriminates from "stranger anxiety proper" at approximately seven months of age. At this age, fear of the stranger is closely connected with, or identical with, "fear of the strange" and has little to do with the human attributes of the stranger. It may be related to the sudden movement of the unfamiliar person, or a loud voice, reactions which can also be elicited by unfamiliar toys at the same age. There will also be reactions to physical handling by the unfamiliar person where shifts in the postural mode of holding or differences in feeding techniques will elicit fear reactions.

The phenomenon of "stranger anxiety" or "negative reaction to the stranger" which appears between six and ten months of age has been variously described in the literature. Some of the differences among writers regarding "onset" and "peaks" may be related to differences in criteria and experimental procedures. Spitz, who has written extensively on the subject, uses the term "stranger anxiety" to cover a broad spectrum of behaviors which he referred to most recently under the more general term "negative reaction to the stranger" (1969). As described to us by Spitz, his procedures for eliciting stranger anxiety involve a direct approach by the experimenter to the child, preferably without mother in the room, in which the experimenter brings his face close to the child and speaks. The reactions of the child may range from "sobering," "averting the head" to "distressed crying." Any of these reactions are scored as negative reactions to the stranger. Morgan and Ricciuti (1969) employed distance and a gradual approach in the introduction of the stranger and scored "sobering" as neutral rather than negative. In their sample, the intensity peak for negative reactions to the stranger appeared at twelve months while Tennes and Lampl's (1964) sample (using procedures and criteria that involved a direct approach to the child) demonstrated a peak at nine months.

On a scale of human attachment, the negative reaction to the stranger is regarded as a significant criterion for the assessment of the positive bonds to the mother and other human partners (Spitz, 1957; Benjamin, 1963; Provence and Lipton, 1962). It speaks for another level in valuation of the mother in which the positive affect is bound to a partner, in which persons are no longer "interchangeable."

It is significant, again, that in the institutional studies of Provence and Lipton the non-attached babies showed no negative behavior toward the stranger in the last quarter of the first year and, as previously noted, smiled and vocalized indiscriminately for all comers. Ainsworth (1967), in her Uganda study, rated her sample on an attachment scale and found a significant correlation between the rating of attachment and the manifestation of stranger anxiety in the last quarter of the first year, while the babies rated as "non-attached" did not, as a group, manifest negative reactions toward the stranger.

### The Blind Baby

During each twice monthly visit, we recorded in descriptive detail differential responses to mother and the observers. Reactions to the observer's voice and to being held in the observer's arms were recorded at each visit. In several cases, too, where a game and vocal dialogue were important elements of mother-child interaction, we experimentally reproduced the conditions of the game, substituting an observer, and recorded the baby's participation and response. Our longitudinal findings were then classified on the basis of (1) discrimination of mother and unfamiliar persons, (2) negative reactions to the stranger in which we attempted to discriminate between *(a)* fear of the strange and *(b)* fear of the unfamiliar person.

### Discrimination of Mother and Strangers

During the first year, the blind baby in our sample shows increasingly selective and well-differentiated responses to his mother, his father, to other intimate persons, and to strangers. In addition to voice cues, the blind baby begins to inform himself through his fingers around five months of age and explores the face of familiar persons with his hands. Not only does he smile more frequently for mother and father, but his responsive vocalizations are far richer and more fluent with his parents or siblings than with the stranger, even after a warm-up period. Similarly, when we as observers attempted to play games with the baby, attempting to approximate in every way discernible to us the motor pattern employed in the game with parents, or the song or chant that accompanied the game, there were discernible differences, as described earlier, in the baby's response, his participation, and the registration of interest or pleasure on his face, compared to the game with one of the parents.

### Negative Reactions to the Stranger

In the analysis of our data we have tried to differentiate (following Benjamin) between "fear of the strange" and "fear of the stranger." Thus, we have a large number of observations during the first year which show that the blind baby will react to "something different" in the situation, or in a voice characteristic, or in being held, or in touching an object that has novel tactile properties. The parallels with sighted babies are close here. During this period, as Benjamin has said, "a stranger is best defined as someone who does things differently." We have reserved the term "stranger anxiety" for manifest fear reactions to unfamiliar persons, following criteria which exclude the element "fear of the strange" and which offer fair evidence that the unfamiliar *person* is the object of distress.

There are obvious difficulties in setting up criteria. "Fear of the strange" flows into "fear of the stranger" in the case of the blind child as well as the sighted child. For example: Nine of our ten babies reacted to being held in the observer's arms in ways that contrasted with the easy molding to the mother's body. These babies quieted, stiffened, strained away, and showed discomfort or distress in the stranger's arms. When the baby was then returned to the arms of his mother, he settled and relaxed. (This behavior is, of course, very close to that described by Benjamin [1963] and Ainsworth [1967] in sighted babies of the same age. The baby reacts to subtle postural differences in the stranger's arms.) We have classified these reactions as "fear of the strange"; that is, something new has been introduced into a familiar situation.

Between seven and eighteen months, we find that something new begins to emerge in the behavior—manifest fear, struggling, crying—which, for the majority of the babies in our sample, occurs when the observer holds the baby. As we will see later, these fear reactions appear even though the observer, a twice-monthly visitor, is not, strictly speaking, a stranger. At the same time that these reactions are manifest in relation to the observer, we have parallel reports from the mothers, showing that fear of strangers has emerged with other visitors to the house as well.

In examining differential reactions to unfamiliar persons, we recorded, beginning with the first observational session, (a) reactions to the voice of the observer in the first encounter of the session, (b) reactions to being held in the observer's arms.

*Reactions to voice alone.* Among those children who were observed under six months of age, we have already mentioned that smiling was rarely evoked by the stranger's voice and appeared as a selective response to the voice of the mother and other intimate persons from the earliest weeks on. During the first six months, the baby was attentive to the sound of the stranger's voice. We have no reports of negative reactions to the stranger's voice.

Between six and thirteen months, we obtained reactions in all ten babies which we have called "quieting" in response to the stranger's voice, that is, a cessation of action or vocalizing (without signs of distress) which may last for several minutes, or longer. Mothers have told us that this is a typical reaction to strange voices. Indeed, we were to learn, the quality of vocalizations was affected by the presence of unfamiliar persons, something mothers had told us, but we were unable to verify until recently.

> When Teddy was seven months old, the observer became concerned by the sharp drop in vocalizations in a child who had been one of our most vocal and "conversational" babies. His dialogue had been almost exclusively with mother but now, during the past two visits, the observer was impressed to see how little vocal exchange was present even in relation to the mother. The observer found a way to make tactful inquiry regarding Teddy's language, and the mother, perhaps amused, assured the observer that Teddy was as talkative as ever—he just shut up when strangers were around. To prove her point, Teddy's mother tape recorded some samples of Teddy's "conversations" during the day. There was no question in listening to the tapes that mother was right. Teddy was reacting to strangers by a constriction of vocalizations and exchange with his mother.

The meaning of "quieting" for all of our babies during this period is open to several possible interpretations. We should state at the outset that we have not scored "quieting" as a negative reaction or as stranger anxiety. However, it regularly precedes the period in which a manifest stranger anxiety occurs. "Quieting" is also one of the characteristics of the reactions to strangers among sighted children in the period before the onset of fear of the stranger. For the sighted child, too, there is a reduction in vocalizations and vocal exchanges when strangers are present, as Ronald Tikofsky tells us (1970). Is "quieting" in the blind child an equivalent of "staring" in the sighted child, which Ainsworth and others describe in the period that precedes fear of the stranger? Is it a form of focused listening, as the blind child sorts out the information coming to him from familiar and unfamiliar voices, as Edna Adelson of our staff suggested? (Dorothy Burlingham [1964] also describes the intent listening of older blind children as a characteristic orienting device.) Is the immobilization at the sound of unfamiliar voices a defensive posture on the part of the blind child who has a limited repertoire of mechanisms for regulating or "turning off" novel, unexpected, or excessive stimuli? (Another possibility proposed by Mrs. Adelson.) At the present, we cannot provide answers to these questions, but as we move into other areas of data evaluation, the characteristics of "quieting" as defense will be studied in an extended range and we may obtain further clues.

*Reactions to being held.* In addition to "voice alone," we tested the reaction of the baby to being held in the observer's arms at each of the twice-monthly visits. Typically, the observer spoke to the baby while holding him. (This was not by design, but intuitively we felt that to hold the blind baby without speaking to him would introduce another factor of strangeness and produce a shock reaction that could not be discriminated from stranger reaction—without vision, the baby cannot anticipate the stranger's approach signs, the open arms, for example, that signify "I would like to pick you up." Without the voice the blind child cannot have information regarding the person who is holding him.) So, while "holding without speaking" would have been a procedure that would differentiate between the reactions to voice and the reactions to being held, it would not have provided fair analogies to the situation with the sighted child and would probably have been an unwarranted disturbance for the baby.

The cumulative record for each child on "reactions to being held" was analyzed for each of our ten babies. Our problem, then, was to discriminate between those reactions that could be classified as "fear of the strange" and those that were, properly speaking, "fear of the stranger." Thus, if "stiffening" and "straining away" are characteristic reactions in our sample from the early months on (fear of the strange), we will need other criteria to define "stranger anxiety" as such at a later stage.

A number of criteria employed for stranger reactions in sighted child studies are not applicable to the blind child at all. "Sobering," for example, is inapplicable because there is actually not enough contrast in the facial expressions of blind children to produce a valid judgment of "sobering." The blind child typically wears a "sober" (solemn, serious) look. And since his smiles, too, are rare for the stranger, *not* smiling to the stranger, or regarding him solemnly, have no value in assessment. "Frowning" is not an expressive sign for all of our blind babies, and we have some evidence that when it appears at all it occurs among those babies who have light perception. But, as an infrequent or atypical sign in our sample we cannot use "frowning" as a criterion of negative response.

We are left, then, with a limited number of signs in our blind children that can fairly be called "fear responses" or "negative reactions" to the stranger. Vocal displeasure—whimpering, crying, screaming—remains the same for the blind baby as the sighted baby. Motor resistance and avoidance to the approach of the unfamiliar person, followed by active seeking of the mother, will also provide fair equivalence to the behavior of the sighted child.

As we analyzed the protocols of each child for differential responses to strangers, eight of the ten children between the ages of seven and sixteen months showed fear and avoidance reactions to the observer even under the circumstances in which the observer had been a twice-monthly visitor in the home. Since holding the baby or approaching the baby for games and testing had been part of the regular observational procedure, the appearance of the first fear reactions could be placed against a background in which no fear reactions had been observed in previous visits. There was close correspondence, too, between our first observations and the parents' reports of fear of strangers.

The following examples represent, in each case, the first appearance of fear of the stranger in eight cases which provided unambiguous evidence.

Toni: age 0:7:2. Soon after the observer (a woman) picks her up, she freezes, then bursts into tears. She frantically fingers the face of the observer, registers increasing distress on her face, strains away from the observer's body, turns her head and trunk as if seeking to locate her mother by voice. She claws at the examiner's arms. She begins to scream loudly. When she is returned to her mother, she buries her head in the mother's neck and is gradually comforted.

Teddy: age 0:8:18. During an observation session at the project office, S. F. was used to test stranger reactions. Teddy had not previously met her. Teddy was lying supine on a rug, playing a game in which he brought his clapsed hands to his mouth. He was vocalizing "gaga" and "ah" and seemed very comfortable with three observers and his parents nearby. When S. F. spoke to him he seemed attentive to her voice; there was no smile or responsive vocalizations as we observed with the parents. S. F., while talking with Teddy, now picked him up, speaking throughout. Teddy now became very still and quiet. Then he began to finger her mouth. He stiffened more and more and then began a quiet whimper which got louder and louder. He mouthed her scarf. S. F. continued to talk to him and his whimper became louder. He began to cry. S. F. handed him to his mother. He snuggled in her arms and was soon comforted.

Jamie: age 0:9:12. E. L. is visiting with the team today. Jamie has never met him before. E. L. picks up the baby and begins to talk to him. As soon as he is picked up, Jamie begins to cry. He is handed to his mother who diverts him with a game and succeeds in comforting him.

Paul: age 1:1:5. Later in the morning, when he was standing on the floor, I offered him my hand while talking to him. Once again, he listened but made no move on his own to approach closer. Both with S. F. (second observer) and myself, he turned away from us as soon as he heard his father's voice, and reached toward his father.

Cathy: age 1:1:16. The observer speaks to Cathy. She is attentive. Now the observer picks her up. Cathy stiffens, feels the observer's face with her right hand, clutches her shirt with the other hand, whimpers, is transferred to her mother's arms.

Joan: age 1:3:17. As the observer began to engage Joan in play, he noticed fear and withdrawal for the first time in his regular visits. When he spoke to Joan and touched her, she drew her hand away. Later, too, when he attempted to place her on his lap, Joan withdrew from contact and tried to get away from him. When he offered her objects in a testing situation during this session, she was unwilling to touch and explore any of the items.

Ronny: age 1:3:29. . . . While mother went to get coffee, Ronny was still in his teeterbabe. He was fretful and upset. I (observer) asked him if he wanted to get out and he instantly raised his arms (as he does when mother asks him this question). However, as soon as I had him in my arms, he stiffened and arched away and didn't want to have any contact with me at all and began to cry noticeably. . . . I was talking to him. "Mama's coming right back." He still very definitely and angrily kept pushing away from me, and mother then takes him from me. . . .

Jackie: age 1:6:21. Jackie is sitting on his mother's lap, not at the moment engaged with mother or the observers. The observer picks him up and brings him to stand, holding his hands. There is not an immediate negative reaction. On film we see an initial smile on his face. But this is followed by constraint and motor signs of discomfort (observer's own notes). Now, on film he turns in the direction of mother, on the couch, correctly orienting himself, and holds out his arms to mother. Mother offers her hand, and as soon as Jackie makes contact with the hand he begins to crawl upon his mother's lap. Once on mother's lap he makes chance contact with the observer's hand, fingers it, then turns back toward mother, very actively climbing on mother, and settles in a supine position on her lap. He then engages mother in a favorite game.

This leaves two cases out of ten children who have not given evidence of stranger anxiety during the first eighteen months. It may be worth reporting briefly on each of them to give a picture of the sample:

> Karen provided no clear examples of fear of the stanger at any point in the second year. Since she had always resisted being held, and did not enjoy being held in her own mother's arms, the examples of protest in the stranger's arms had no meaning in assessing differential responses. On the other hand, her positive attachment to the mother could be seen in following the mother when she became mobile and in frequent excursions to mother to "touch base."

> Robbie provided one example of "quieting" to the observers' voices at 1:0:0 and no other examples of negative reactions to strangers at any time in the second year. During the second year he allowed our own observers and other unfamiliar persons to hold him and to play with him. We have examples in our hospital waiting room and other unfamiliar places in which his indiscriminate friendliness to strangers is recorded. He is also the one child in our group whose attachment to his mother was regarded by us as unstable, without signs of active seeking of the mother for pleasure or comfort.

If we can accept, then, those differences in testing stranger reactions which were required when we needed to translate procedures for testing sighted infants into procedures for blind infants, there is fair equivalence in the characteristics of stranger anxiety in our blind baby sample and those reported for sighted children.

However, if our criteria are fair, there is a marked difference in age of onset of fear of the stranger in our blind group. For five of the eight children the first observations of fear of the stranger appeared between the ages of thirteen and fifteen months. The one child (Toni) who showed the most extreme fear of strangers, at seven months, two days, sustained a fear of strangers that I would now regard as pathological in its intensity. As late as four years of age, when Toni was last seen, this otherwise healthy and bright child, reacted to strangers through the most complete withdrawal. We have always felt that the early and intense stranger anxiety must have been related to other events, very possibly a brief separation from the mother.

The full significance of these differences between the age of onset of stranger anxiety in our blind sample and age of onset in sighted children awaits further study. The links with separation anxiety will be described in a separate report (Fraiberg, 1971). The relevance of locomotor achievements, prehension and object concept (in Piaget's terms) will be examined as our data analysis moves ahead.

## Notes

I wish to express my gratitude to colleagues in the Child Development Project who have participated in the primary research. I am specially indebted to Edna Adelson, Lyle Warner, Evelyn Bruckner, and Marguerite Smith of our staff for examining problems of criteria with me and for reading and criticizing the first drafts of this paper.

1. Not to be confused with D. G. Freedman, whose work is cited above.

## References

Ainsworth, M. D. (1963). The Development of Infant-Mother Interaction among the Ganda. In *Determinants of Infant Behavior*, ed. B. M. Foss, vol. 2, pp. 67–104. London: Methuen.

———. (1967). *Infancy in Uganda: Infant Care and the Growth of Love*. Baltimore: Johns Hopkins Univ. Press.

Ambrose, J. A. (1961). The Development of the Smiling Response in Early Infancy. In *Determinants of Infant Behavior*, ed. B. M. Foss, vol. 1, pp. 179–196. London: Methuen.

Benjamin, J. D. (1963). Further Comments on Some Developmental Aspects of Anxiety. *Counterpoint*, pp. 121–153. New York: International Universities Press.

Bowlby, J. (1958). The Nature of the Child's Tie to His Mother. *Int. J. Psychoanal.*, 39:350–373.

———. (1960). Separation Anxiety. *Int. J. Psychoanal.*, 41:89–113.

———. (1969). Attachment. In *Attachment and Loss*, vol. 1. New York: Basic Books.

Burlingham, D. (1964). Hearing and Its Role in the Development of the Blind. *Psychoanal. Study Child*, 19:95–112.

Emde, R. N. & Koenig, K. L. (1969). Neonatal Smiling, Frowning, and Rapid Eye Movements States: II Sleep-Cycle Study. *J. Amer. Acad. Child Psychiat.*, 4.

Escalona, S. (1953). Emotional Development in the First Year of Life. In *Problems of Infancy and Childhood*, ed. M. Senn, pp. 11–92. New York: Josiah Macy Foundation.

Fraiberg, S. (1968). Parallel and Divergent Patterns in Blind and Sighted Infants. *Psychoanal. Study Child*, 23:264–300.

———. (1969). Libidinal Object Constancy and Mental Representation. *Psychoanal. Study Child*, 24:9–47.

———. (1971). Separation Crisis in Two Blind Children. *Psychoanal. Study Child*, 26:355–371.

———— & Freedman, D. A. (1964). Studies in the Ego Development of the Congenitally Blind Child. *Psychoanal. Study Child,* 19:113–169.

————; Siegel, B.; & Gibson, R. (1966). The Role of Sound in the Search Behavior of Blind Infants. *Psychoanal. Study Child,* 21:327–357.

————; Smith, M.; & Adelson, E. (1969). An Educational Program for Blind Infants. *J. Spec. Educ.* 3:121–139.

Freedman, D. G. (1964). Smiling in Blind Infants and the Issue of Innate vs. Acquired. *J. Child Psychol. and Psychiat.,* 5:171–184.

————. (1965). Hereditary Control of Early Social Behavior. In *Determinants of Infant Behavior,* ed. B. M. Foss, vol. 3, pp. 149–161. London: Methuen.

Gewirtz, J. L. (1965). The Course of Infant Smiling in Four Child-rearing Environments in Israel. In *Determinants of Infant Behavior,* ed. B. M. Foss, vol. 3, pp. 205–248. London: Methuen.

Gouin-Décarie, T. (1953). *Intelligence and Affectivity in Early Childhood.* New York: International Universities Press.

Morgan, G. A. & Ricciuti, H. N. (1969). Infant's Responses to Strangers during the First Year. In *Determinants of Infant Behavior,* ed. B. M. Foss, vol. 4. London: Methuen.

Polak, P. R.; Emde, R. N.; & Spitz, R. A. (1964). The Smiling Response to the Human Face: I. Methodology, Quantification, and Natural History. *J. Nerv. Ment. Dis.,* 139:103–109.

Provence, S. & Lipton, R. (1962). *Infants in Institutions.* New York: International Universities Press.

Schaffer, H. R. & Emerson, P. E. (1963). Some Issues for Research in the Study of Attachment Behavior. In *Determinants of Infant Behavior,* ed. B. M. Foss, vol. 2, pp. 179–199. London: Methuen.

————. (1964). The Development of Social Attachments in Infancy. *Monogr. Soc. Res. Child Develop.,* 28, No. 1, Serial No. 94.

Spitz, R. A. (1950a). Anxiety in Infancy: A Study of Its Manifestations in the First Year of Life. *Int. J. Psychoanal.,* 31:138–143.

————. (1950b). *A Genetic Field Theory of Ego Formation: Its Implications for Pathology.* New York: International Universities Press.

————. (1957). *No and Yes: On the Beginnings of Human Communication.* New York: International Universities Press.

————. (1965). *The First Year of Life.* New York: International Universities Press.

————. (1969). Personal communication.

———— & Wolf, K. A. (1946). The Smiling Response: A Contribution to the Ontogenesis of Social Relations. *Genet. Psychol. Monogr.,* 34:57–125.

Tennes, K. H. & Lampl, E. E. (1964). Stranger and Separation Anxiety. *J. Nerv. Ment. Dis.,* 139:247–254.

Thompson, J. (1941). Development of Facial Expression of Emotion in Blind and Seeing Children. *Arch. Psychol.,* 264.

Tikofsky, R. (1970). Personal communication.

Wolff, P. H. (1963). The Early Development of Smiling. In *Determinants of Infant Behavior,* ed. B. M. Foss, vol. 2. London: Methuen.

# 22

# Self-Representation in Language and Play: Observations of Blind Children

*With Edna Adelson*

Among children blind from birth there is typically a delay in the acquisition of "I" as a stable pronoun. The meaning of this characteristic has been necessarily obscured because of the heterogeneous population usually designated as "blind," one that includes children with damage to other systems as well as children with minimal vision and those blinded postnatally.

In our longitudinal studies of the early ego development of blind children, we have followed ten children, blind from birth. The children in this sample are, to the best of our knowledge, free of any other sensory or motor handicap and are neurologically intact. Infants admitted to the research program were totally blind or had only light perception. A concurrent guidance program was provided for all infants in this group.

Our group is advantaged, then, within a blind population by the intactness of other systems and by a guidance program that has facilitated development. They are disadvantaged in comparison with the general population of blind children by their total or near total blindness and blindness from birth. Both the selection process and the guidance program enabled us to examine the developmental characteristics of blind infants and young children under the most favorable circumstances.[1]

All of the children in this group were followed by means of biweekly home visits from the first year through age two-and-a-half. Four of the older children were available for continued study through age five. In this advantaged group of blind children we saw delays in the achievement of "I" as a stable pronoun, and a concomitant delay in the representation of the self in imaginative play. As we analyzed the descriptive protocols and reviewed the videotape samples, we began to achieve some insight into the interlocking components of self-representation in language and play, and were able to follow the extraordinary problems for the blind child in constructing an image of self and a concept of an objective self.

In this essay we examine the relationship between the blind child's acquisition of "I" as a correct grammatical form and the correlates of "I" in representation of the self in play. We have selected one of the four older children, Kathie, as the subject of detailed study.

## II

The four blind children who were available for continued study to the age of five years included three who were in the upper half of our group on most measures and one who placed in the lower half of the group.

Jackie who consistently ranked in the lower half of the group, had not achieved "I" when last seen at age five years. At two-and-a-half years his language achievements placed him in the lowest rank in our group of ten. The failure to achieve "I" was also a measure of his impaired ego development. He presented the picture of a disordered personality with frequent regression to echolalic speech. This brief description of Jackie, who had no "I" at age five, is included because he fairly represents the large number of uneducable blind children who do not achieve "I" or "me" even at school age or later. In Jackie's case, and others known to us, there was no evidence of neurological impairment, and one can fairly consider an alternative explanation for this form of deviant ego development: that blindness imposes extraordinary impediments in the development of a self-image and the construction of a coherent sense of self.

The remaining three children in the older group all achieved "I." Kathie, Paul, and Karen ranked in the upper half of our group on nearly all measures. Their language achievements at two to two-and-a-half years (judged by vocabulary, two-word combinations, and the use of words to make needs known) fell within the sighted age range.

A syncretic "I" ('Iwanna') appeared in their language records in the age range two to two-and-a-half, which again does not distinguish them from sighted children.

From this developmental picture in the language area we would have predicted an unremarkable course, leading within a few months to a stable concept of "I" and versatility in the use of "I". We were not prepared for our findings. The ages for the achievement of the non-syncretic "I" for these three children were as follows: Karen, two years, eleven months; Paul, three years, five months; Kathie four years, ten months.

The differentiation of a *syncretic* "I" from a *nonsyncretic* "I" follows Zazzo's (1948) usage. The syncretic "I" typically appears in the two-year-old's vocabulary imbedded in verb forms of need or want. In the course of weeks or months, "I" is gradually disengaged from this early set and is used inventively in new combinations. The two levels of "I" represent two levels of self-representation. The achievement of the nonsyncretic "I " requires a high level of inference on the part of the child in which he demonstrates his capacity to represent himself as an "I" in a universe of "I's." ("I am an 'I' to me; you are an 'I' to you; he is an 'I' to him," etc.)

We credited the children with the achievement of a non-syncretic "I" when these criteria were met: (a) "I" used inventively in new combinations (disengaged from set phrases); (b) "I" employed with versatility in discourse (management of "I" and "you" with rare or no confusion or reversals). It is of some interest that although these criteria were met by the three children at the ages given above, both Paul and Kathie had occasional lapses in "I"-"you" usage for many months afterward.

While the achievement of stable "I" usage impresses us as markedly delayed in these blind children, comparisons with sighted children cannot be fairly made through the use of any existing measures. There are no normative data for the achievement of the nonsyncretic "I" in sighted children. Gesell (1947), who offers the only developmental scale which includes personal pronoun usage, does not discriminate between the syncretic and the nonsyncretic "I". He scores pronoun usage on two levels: At twenty-four months he credits the child with the pronouns " 'I,' 'me,' and 'you,' not necessarily correctly" (p. 422); at thirty months the child receives credit when he "refers to self by pronoun rather than name. [The child] may confuse 'I' and 'me' " (p.

423). Gesell accepted parent reports for his language items, and his scoring, as cited, does not discriminate for our purposes the cognitive values of "I."[2]

In the absence of comparative measures in standard developmental tests for sighted children, we cannot pursue some of the problems of apparent difference between the range for achievement of a stable "I" in three otherwise healthy and adequate blind children and that of sighted children. Yet, the differences, on any level of comparison we can borrow, impose themselves upon us. If three blind children demonstrate language competence at the age of two to two-and-a-half years which can be objectively rated as normal for sighted children, if the syncretic "I" appears as a grammatical form in the range for sighted children, how can we explain a developmental course which detours in the middle of the third year and comes back on the sighted child's route in the fourth or fifth years? Were the apparently very late achievers of "I" (Kathie and Paul) cognitively impaired? Was Karen, the earliest achiever of "I", the smartest in the group? Here again, all expectations and reasonable predictions come undone as strangely as the blind child's pronoun usage. At age two-and-a-half years Kathie and Paul were among three of the highest ranking children in the group of ten in language achievements and in over-all developmental achievements. Kathie's good intelligence will speak for itself in the history we present later. Paul, at five years, had a command of language and a capacity for abstract thinking which impresses us as superior even by sighted child standards. Karen, the first achiever of "I" was a very adequate blind child, whose good language and cognitive capacities at five years did not equal those of Kathie and Paul. We are not able to explain this puzzle.

While we watched the protracted struggle with pronoun usage, another piece of the puzzle was emerging from the patterns of play which we had observed and recorded. At the age when sighted children begin to *imitate* domestic life in doll play (approximately two years) we find no such examples for the blind children in our group. If we tried to elicit such play, "Let's give the dolly her bottle," "Let's put her to bed," we got no response, not even mechanical compliance. In some instances there were other infants in the house being mothered, or other children in the family playing with dolls. Models were available but were not used.

Again, at age two-and-a-half years, when sighted children begin to *represent* themselves and their world in play, endowing the doll with a personality and an imaginary life, our blind children could not represent themselves or other personalities in play and could not invent in play. Between the ages of three and four-and-a-half years, we began to see imaginative play emerge in the records of Karen, Paul, and Kathie. In each case the emergence of representational play had correspondence with the emergence of self-reference pronouns "me" and "I." The data invited closer scrutiny. They suggested that the acquisition of personal pronouns was closely united with the capacity for symbolic representation of the self, and that vision normally plays a central facilitating role in each of these achievements.

After we worked our way through this thicket, we discovered that Zazzo had arrived there by another route in his study of a sighted child. His observations on Jean-Fabien, which will be summarized in the last section of this paper, were most welcome and provide another framework in which to place our detailed observations of Kathie as she pursued an elusive "I" between the ages of two and five years.

### III

In order to examine in detail the blind child's extraordinary problems of self-representation in language and play, we have chosen one of these children, Kathie, for illustration.

Kathie has been followed by us since nine months of age, and is now six years old. She is totally blind. She was born three months prematurely. The diagnosis, retrolental fibroplasia, was made at five months of age. She is a healthy, very bright child with no other sensory defects, and is neurologically intact.

Kathie is the youngest of five siblings. Her parents have shown extraordinary ability to intuit a blind child's experience and every help that parents and our staff specialists could give has been available to promote the fullest use of her good capacities. Now at six years of age, she has excellent command of language; she is inventive in imaginative play; she is well-behaved but also mischievous and fun-loving. She is in the first grade in a class for sighted children and is able to hold her own. She has considerable appetite for new experience and enjoys cooperative play. She is independent in dressing and feeding, and is fully responsible for her own safety in outdoor play.

The story of Kathie's language and representational intelligence followed a different route from that of the sighted child. In the absence of pictorial memory, there were delays in the evolving forms of mental representation, the concepts of time and causality, of self-representation and the construction of a world of permanent objects. Yet, a simple vocabulary count and identification of word and thing, or an analysis of phrase and sentence patterns would not have distinguished her speech at the age of two years from that of sighted children. It was between the ages of two and four that the study of Kathie's speech and play gave us a slow-motion picture of the relationship of language to other cognitive processes and thus provided the means for identifying those elements in self-object representation which are dependent upon a coherent and intact sensorimotor organization.

*Observations at Two Years of Age*

When Kathie was two years, one month old, she became the subject of linguistic study conducted by Eric Lenneberg* with our staff. Speech samples were obtained in home visits and Dr. Lenneberg and a member of our staff, Nancy Stein, worked out a dictionary based on the question: What does Kathie *mean* when she *says* . . . ? Following a three-month study, Dr. Lenneberg felt that Kathie's language competence compared favorably with that of the sighted child of the same age. Her vocabulary at that time was well within the range for sighted children. She correctly identified members of her family and a number of people outside the family. She identified by touch or sound, and named all the objects in her home with which she had contact. She quickly learned the name of novel objects. She had four- or five-word phrases in which present tense verb forms were imbedded, but not yet used inventively in new combinations.

She could express her wishes in phrases; for example, "Wanna hear a record." "Wanna go walkie." "Wanna go lie down." "Wanna hear music." "Want to feel, . . . What's that?" (when confronted with a novel object).

She had a range of useful words for the expression of affective experience. "Feels good!" "Tastes good." And the dictionary records that she used the words "damn" and "shit" when she was angry.

*Eric H. Lenneberg, author of *Biological Foundations of Language*, was consultant to the Child Development Project in 1969.—Ed.

She employed parental admonitions to inhibit forbidden actions. "Don't put your finger in your eye," she said to herself, imitating her mother's voice when she pressed her eye, and sometimes succeeded in inhibiting the act. "Hot!" she said, to warn herself when near the stove.

There were examples of generalization in our records. At Christmas time, when we brought her a toy-sized Christmas tree, she explored its plastic bristles thoughtfully and said, "Feels like a brush!" She could identify a chair and name it, and generalize from chair to chair.

We heard pronoun reversal and pronoun confusion in nearly all the speech samples we have during this period. When she touched the hair of one of her observers, she said, "my hair," using the wrong pronoun. "Want me carry you?" she said to her mother when she meant that she wanted her mother to carry her. The pronoun "I" was rarely used and, typically, appeared as a syncretic form "Ahwonna" or as an "I"-"you" reversal. However, at two years of age the pronoun reversals and the unstable use of "I" do not distinguish Kathie from sighted children.

In Dr. Lenneberg's unpublished notes he records one item that puzzled him. "All attempts to make her listen to short stories (while sitting on laps and being quiet) have failed." In a summary statement he draws attention to the disinterest in stories as being one factor that points to "a somewhat different language beginning from that found in sighted children." As it turned out, in retrospect, this puzzle was already one of the clues to certain incapacities in symbolic representation which were later to be of considerable interest in our study of blind children.[3]


*Observations at Three Years of Age*

Between two-and-a-half and three years of age Kathie's language and her capacity to represent showed marked deviations from that of the sighted child. In both our detailed home observations and in the reports of the mother, it was very clear that Kathie could not represent herself through a doll or toy. She could not re-create or invent a situation in play. She could not attend to a story or answer questions regarding a story or tell a story herself. She could not spontaneously report an experience. And still between the ages of three and four, she continued to confuse and reverse pronouns, and the concept of "I" had not emerged as a stable grammatical form.

To illustrate the problem, we now propose to present some of our own observations of Kathie at the age of three.

When Kathie was three years, twenty-three days, we arranged for her to visit us in our nursery. The nursery visits had been a special treat for Kathie in preceding months. Since we already knew from home observations that Kathie could not invent in play or represent herself in play, we sketched an observational plan and procedures which would tell us more precisely where the incapacities lay and what her limits might be.

We worked out a group of experimental play situations which would permit us to compare a blind child's capacity to represent herself in play with that of a sighted child. We were satisfied that the "pretend" games we had in mind could be played with any sighted child between the ages of eighteen months and two years, giving much leeway for three-year-old Kathie. In order not to strain Kathie's tolerance, we moved freely between structured play periods and unstructured "free play intervals." In the one-hour observational period which was recorded verbatim and documented on 16 millimeter film, the structured portions of the observation totaled twenty minutes. This gave us a balance between the two modes of observation which favored the spontaneous productions and permitted us to fairly assess Kathie's play capacities and language. Kathie's mother was present throughout.

As we present material from this play session at three years of age, it is important to keep in mind that we already knew Kathie's play incapacities from naturalistic observations in her home, and that the purpose of the structured play observations was to get more precise information regarding the level of symbolic representation available to this bright, three-year-old blind child. When one of the authors (S. F.) pursued certain elements in play, although it was clear that Kathie could not follow her, it was because we needed the negative demonstration as much as the positive demonstration, both for this period of observation and for our projected retesting at four years.

S. F. was not a familiar person to Kathie and gave her a good deal of time to greet old friends at the project, to get accustomed to a new voice, and to begin some verbal exchanges. When Kathie seemed at ease and came close to S. F. at the work table, S. F. hinted that there was something on it. Kathie came over, sniffed, and said, pleasantly surprised, "Play dough." S. F. waited to see what Kathie would do. She squeezed it, handled it, put it down. When it was evident that she would not invent with the play dough, S. F. suggested they make a cookie and guided her hands with the cookie cutter. Kathie was interested but did not extend the possibilities. Later, to test her notions of "pretend," S. F. asked, "Can I have a bite of the cookie, Kathie?" Kathie, clearly confused but amiable, said, "You have a bite!" and put it in *her own* mouth. Kathie said, reflectively, "This cookie different."

Because of the confusion in "me" and "you" elicited in this sequence, we used a later occasion to test facial analogies. S. F. asked, "Where is my mouth, Kathie?" There was no response to "my mouth" but Kathie's hand moved to *her own* mouth. S. F.: "Where is my nose?" She made no effort. Neither the other author (E. A.) nor Kathie's mother had been able to get Kathie to correctly name parts on their faces if they used the pronoun "my," for example, in the question, "Where is my nose?" However, if Kathie's mother asked, "Where is Mommy's nose?" she could respond correctly.

Knowing how much Kathie loved her own bath at home, we had sketched out a sequence for doll play. There was a basin of water, a doll, a towel. S. F. brought over one of our dolls and suggested giving the doll a bath. (We knew, however, that Kathie had no interest in her dolls at home.) S. F. introduced the doll to Kathie, who gave it a few cursory touches but was clearly not interested. S. F. tried to elicit interest. "Where is the dolly's mouth?"—no answer. "Where is the dolly's nose?"—no answer. Clearly Kathie could not endow the doll with human characteristics. (We were also unable to get a response when we played this game with other blind children of Kathie's age.)

Kathie made it clear she did not want to give the doll a bath but we were not prepared for what took place within a few moments. As soon as Kathie touched the water, she herself stepped into the tiny tub, giving S. F. only a second to remove her new red shoes. She curled up in the tiny tub, legs folded up, and joyfully screeched. Then followed a series of little chants and songs, her own bathtub songs at home. After several minutes S. F. decided to re-introduce the doll. She suggested washing the doll's hair (guiding Kathie's hands to the doll's hair). S. F. even went through a performance in which, representing the doll, she squealed protests and said, "No, no, I don't want a shampoo." Kathie did not enter into the game but now did something else.

As Kathie squatted in the tub, pushing herself up and down in the water, she began to carry on a dialogue in two voices: "Swimming in the water." "Mama look at that!" "Whee, whee." "Can you feel it?" "Okay, you stay in the water." "Okay, you sit down in the water." Very clearly, one voice in this speech belonged to Kathie and one voice to her mother, bathing Kathie.

Before drawing inferences from this last anecdote, let us give a second set of observations which are very similar. Later in the session, Kathie was walking around the room when she discovered the sink in the nursery. We did not tell her what it was. She climbed in and examined the sides and faucets with her fingers. One of us said, "What is it?" and, after a moment, she said, firmly, "It's a sink!" Kathie curled up inside it. She was unmistakably pretending that the sink was a bed and said, in a mother's intonation, "Night-night, have good sleep, night-night. Go sleep in the sink." She closed her eyes, then opened them mischievously, and went through the whole routine again, with some variation. "Right here. You be a good girl!" Once S. F. tried to extend the game by saying, "Good morning Kathie!" Kathie, not to be distracted, said, "See you in the morning, good night. Then go in pool." (Echo phrases—apparently her schedule for summer.)

Obviously, then, Kathie could "pretend" when she herself was the subject. Could she pretend now with a doll? It was doubtful, but S. F. brought her the doll for an experimental demonstration. She said, "The dolly wants to go to sleep. Let's put the dolly to bed." She gave the doll to Kathie. Kathie promptly dropped the doll over the side of the sink and pursued her own game.

In these two examples (and others which we had in this and other sessions), it is very clear that Kathie had a form of "pretend" in which she could take herself as object and play subject and object in a game. But she could not yet move beyond to further objectivation (actually *projection*) which would permit the doll to represent Kathie, while Kathie herself represented her mother to the doll. Note, too, how important it was for her to get *into* the basin, to put herself *into* the sink for "pretend." Where a sighted child would be able to imagine herself in the basin or the sink, and then also *imagine* her doll as herself in the basin or sink, Kathie was still obliged to go through the motions—to transpose through action that which the sighted child would transpose through vision. We must remember, of course, that sighted children in nursery schools also enjoy fitting themselves into the doll bed or the doll carriage, but by this age they move flexibly between such egocentric play to representational play, sometimes placing the doll, sometimes themselves, in the bed or carriage.

Along with Kathie's failures in self-representation, we could see throughout this session, even in this condensed form, that "I" and "you" were not yet used correctly. This corresponds to our observations in which subject and object pronouns are confused in comprehension, as in following the directions for the game "Where's my nose?—Where's your nose?" Kathie's pronouns did not yet define subject and object, which may indicate the level of her conceptual development; she could not yet *see* herself as an object to others. She was indisputably "Kathie" to herself and to others, and her mother was "Mommy," but she could not assimilate the semantic ambiguity in which she is a "you" to others and they are a "you" to her. The same ambiguity was apparent in her comprehension of "me" and "my" usage in the game, "Where's my nose?" Yet Kathie could correctly identify facial parts by pointing if the questioner used the form "Where is Mommy's nose?" "Where is Mrs. Adelson's nose?" "Where is Kathie's nose?"

From the protocols of this session and home visits during this period we do not yet have an example of "me" usage in self-reference. Typically, when Kathie wanted something she would say, "Give it to her!" in the echo form.

The first example of "me" in self-reference (not echo or reversal) occurred at three years, six months, and the context happens to catch exactly a transition point. Kathie's mother called her in the midst of play. Kathie was clearly annoyed at the interruption. She roared at her mother, "You leave her alone!" and then, shortly afterward, "Leave *me* alone!"

The question should be raised: Would Kathie's performance in the nursery have been more fairly tested if the play sequences had been undertaken by one of her old friends on the staff or by her mother? To test this possibility, four months later we invited Kathie and her parents to another play session and recorded the visit on videotape. This time E. A., a familiar person, took over some of the play sequences and we also involved the mother in the game of "Where's my nose? Where's your nose?" Even under these most favorable circumstances the limits of Kathie's performances remained the same.

These experiences suggest to us that the observations on subject and object in play and the problem of expressing subject and object in language have a unified core in the capacity for a certain level of mental representation. The capacity to represent oneself in play is a measure of the level of conceptual development in which the self can be taken as an object and other objects can be used for symbolic representation of the self (Piaget, 1952). Kathie's play incapacities at three years were exactly mirrored in speech, in her pronoun reversals, and in her difficulties in achieving "I" as a stable concept and a stable grammatical form. Yet, this child at the age of three years had a rich vocabulary, if we make allowances for the restricted experience of a blind child, and her syntax did not jar the ear except for sentences in which pronoun usage governs order and coherence. She was not retarded nor in danger of autistic development.

## Observations at Four and Five Years of Age

Between the ages of four and five years, Kathie began to represent herself in doll play and, in a parallel development, we also began to see new complexities in syntax, a stabilization of pronoun usage, and, finally, the emergence of "I" as a concept and a grammatical form.

At four years, six months, our observations of Kathie's doll play paralleled in all significant ways the doll play of sighted children at two to three years of age. Kathie was a solicitous mother to Drowsy and Pierre, her two dolls. She fed Drowsy from a toy nursing bottle, filling it herself and capping it with the nipple. She murmured endearments to Drowsy: "Want to give me a kiss?" "Bye bye, Drowsy." "Did you bump your head?" (rubbing it to make it feel better). "She's crying. She wants her bottle." She also spanked her dolls in anger and scolded them for misdemeanors. She toilet trained both dolls by placing them on her old potty chair.

Around the same time, Kathie acquired an imaginary companion she called Zeen. Kathie carried on conversations with Zeen in two voices. When addressed by a friendly adult, Zeen was willing to extend the conversation. At lunch, when the observers were having coffee, E. A. asked what Zeen would like. Kathie, in an animated voice, said, "Here he comes. He's driving up the driveway driving a car. He has got to go home to make a cup of tea." It was Zeen who spilled the macaroni all over the kitchen floor, Kathie told her mother righteously when she herself was caught in the act.

After tracking Zeen for several months in our study, E. A. one day asked the direct question: "Where is Zeen's house?" Kathie said, "You gotta walk outside," and then, "Wanna go for a walk?" E. A. accepted the invitation and Kathie took her for a walk to Zeen's house. Kathie told her that she would show her Zeen's sand box and Zeen's house which had a door that you could open and close. It was a long walk to Zeen's house and it was a cold day. E. A. complained of the sniffles and her need for a kleenex. Kathie said, "Here's a kleenex," and produced an imaginary tissue which she used to wipe E. A.'s nose. They walked for a long time and had many interesting encounters on the way. Finally, it dawned on E. A. that since Zeen was an imaginary person with an imaginary house, they were probably never going to get there. And they never did.

Around the same period, we received the first report of a dream. Kathie wakened one night very much upset and told her mother: "I stuck my foot in it and it turned on." In the morning, Kathie reported her dream again but changed the detail to, "She bumped her foot." Her mother could give us no clues regarding this dream. While this may not have been Kathie's first dream, it was the first dream reported to her mother.

Verbatim speech records from visits at this time showed an increase in the number of sentences which included a grammatically correct use of "I" but there were still instances in which pronoun reversals appeared.

At four years, eight months, Kathie's mother reported that she began to ask, "Today is what day?" And then, in a very rapid progress, it was reported to us that she began to learn the days of the week and the time concepts of "tomorrow" and "yesterday." As we were sorting data for this period, we made a discovery. The first record of use of the past tense appeared at the same time. Kathie had taken a walk to the outer limits of her home property. She reported when she came back, "I found Robinsons' house!"

One month later at four years, nine months, we have the first report in our records of Kathie's ability to reconstruct from memory an event of the previous day. Kathie was playing with her mother's cigarette lighter. The next day Kathie's mother could not find the lighter and asked where it was. Kathie thought for a moment and said, "It's on the floor by the rocking chair." It was.

As late as Kathie's fifth birthday there were still occasional lapses in her use of "I." On the day of her birthday there was a routine visit to the doctor's office. Her mother reported that Kathie told the doctor that it was her birthday. He asked her how old she was. Kathie replied: "She's four. No, *I'm* five years old."

Here are a few samples of Kathie's conversations at the age of five years as reported by her mother:

> Kathie bumped into a little girl in the doctor's office.
> Kathie: "Who is this?"
> The little girl said, "Karen."
> Kathie: "Where does your daddy work?"
> Little girl: "At Marshall's."
> Kathie: "Does he work on a farm?" (Kathie's father did.)

> Kathie overheard a mother spanking her baby during a visit to Kathie's home.
> Kathie said: "*Don't* spank the baby."
> The mother, embarrassed, said she wasn't hurting the baby.
> Kathie: "Oh, did you do it gently and softly?"

> Kathie, at five years, one month of age, overheard the bus driver of her school bus say, "Darn!"
> Kathie: "Are you swearing?"
> "No," said the bus driver, embarrassed.
> Kathie, persisting: "Do you swear?"

At five years, three months, we have the following observations which tie together concepts in language and in play.

Evelyn B. Atreya was videotaping a session at Kathie's house to document play and language.[4] At one point Kathie was feeding Drowsy, the doll, with the toy nursing bottle. She stopped for a moment and addressed the photographer: "Joy, what are you doing?" Joy said that she was taking pictures. Kathie said, "Oh, are you going to take my picture while I feed the baby?"

At another point, Kathie said that Drowsy was taking a nap. She whispered, "Don't wake him up!" Kathie began to make snoring noises as if pretending that Drowsy was asleep. "That's Drowsy," she explained.

Later, everyone reviewed the tape in the kitchen. As Kathie heard the voices on the tape she asked: "Evelyn, who is talking?" E. B. A. told her that it was Kathie talking to her mother. Kathie seemed to listen intently to the voices on the tape and to respond to them. She began to identify her own words on tape, and when she heard herself snoring for Drowsy on tape, she laughed out loud.

In these fragments from five years, three months of age, we see versatility in syntax, good pronoun usage, stable forms of "me" and "I," and an objective concept of self which permits her to identify her own voice on tape and to laugh at her own clowning on tape.

In summary, Kathie's capacity for self-representation in play and the acquisition of the concept "I" finally did emerge in a coherent cognitive structure. Yet both were late acquisitions compared with sighted children who attain this level of development between two-and-a-half and three years of age.

## IV

The relationship between self-representation and personal pronoun usage has not been rigorously examined in the literature on the sighted child. Zazzo (1948), whose longitudinal study of one child is unique in the literature of developmental aspects of pronoun usage, produced promising hypotheses which he had hoped would lead to controlled experimental research. His work has not yet been extended. While our own work was designed without knowledge of Zazzo's study and his hypotheses, there is close correspondence between his findings and ours on self-representation and the pronoun "I."

In his study, *Image du corps et conscience de soi,* Zazzo follows the grammatical transformations of self-reference pronouns in relation to the child's behavior toward his mirror image. The child was his son, Jean-Fabien, and the mirror observations were recorded between the ages of three months and two years, nine months. (Photographs and home movies were also employed for picture identification, but our summary will confine itself to mirror image.)

At two years, three months, Jean-Fabien made his first (and untutored) identification of the baby in the mirror. After a moment's hesitation, he said, "Dadin," the name he used for himself. (From Jean-Fabien's behavior during this period, it appears to us that the response "Dadin" is an identification of his image, but the "Dadin" in the mirror is uncertainly himself—perhaps in the nature of "another Dadin.")

At two years, four months, Jean-Fabien used a syncretic form of "*je*" ("*ch' sais pas*"). At two years, five months, Zazzo reports he had the pronouns *"elle," "i"* (*"je"* [syncretic]), *"ca."* At two years, six months, he began to use *"moi-tu."*

At two years, eight months, Jean-Fabien responded to his mirror image for the first time with the phrase, *"C'est moi."* At a later point in the essay, Zazzo adds that the phrase *"C'est moi"* was accompanied by a gesture in which Jean-Fabien pointed to his own chest. In all later variations in responding to his mirror image, the child used the phrase, *"Moi, Jean-Fabien."*

At two years, eight months, the pronoun *"je"* is disengaged from syncretic forms and the author cites examples of discourse in which *"je"* is used inventively and in free combination. During the same period, Zazzo reports in his later text, the momentary confusion before the mirror which preceded each self-identification had disappeared.

Zazzo's findings corroborate our own in essential aspects. The grammatical transformations of self-reference pronouns follow a progression that is linked with stages in the evolution of the self-image; the nonsyncretic "I" closes the sequence and signifies the child's capacity to represent himself as an object in a universe of objects. For the sighted child, and more so for the blind child, the achievement of the concept "I" is a cognitive feat. The consistent, correct, and versatile employment of the pronoun "I" tells us that the child has attained a level of conceptual development in which he not only endows himself with "I," but recognizes that every "you" for the child is an "I" for the other, and that he is a "you" to all other "I's." This is a leap out of his own skin, so to speak, and one that is normally facilitated and organized by vision. Even when there are no mirrors and no pictures to consult, self-image evolves through increasingly complex forms of mental representation in which the body self is given objective form, a "double" as Zazzo suggests, an image of the self.

For the blind child, the constitution of a self-image and its representation through "I" can appear in a protracted development. We have used self-representation in play as the only means available to us to examine parallel representation of the self in pronoun usage. If we can grant some equivalence to Kathie's self-representation in play and imagination with Jean-Fabien's response to his mirror representation, we can compare the characteristics of self-representation and pronoun usage in the two children.

Kathie, at two years, two months, and Jean-Fabien at two years, four months, both employ a *syncretic* "I" and, more commonly, their own first names for self-reference. Jean-Fabien can name himself in the mirror. Kathie has no form of self-representation in her play.

At two years, eight months, Jean-Fabien has "*moi*" and "*tu*" in his vocabulary. In the mirror, he identifies himself with the words, "*C'est moi.*" Kathie's "me" and "you" appear in echo responses which inevitably lead to reversals. She cannot represent herself in play.

At two years, ten months, Jean-Fabien's "*je*" has completed the course of disengagement from syncretic usage and is used freely and inventively in discourse. The momentary confusion which had preceded mirror identification of himself has now disappeared, which indicates that he now feels at one with his mirror image. It is assimilated to "I." Kathie's "I" is still employed in syncretic forms. "Me" and "you" are still embedded in set phrases as echo responses and appear as reversals. She cannot yet represent herself in play.

At three years, six months, Kathie employs "me" for the first time in our records.

At four years, six months, Kathie becomes a solicitous mother to her dolls and invents an imaginary companion.

At four years, ten months, Kathie's "I" is now demonstrably a stable form which is used inventively in discourse, but there are still occasional lapses.

From this concise summary, we can see that the two children whose "I" first emerged in syncretic form at two years, two months, and two years, four months, followed divergent paths in the acquisition of the nonsyncretic "I." The sighted child traveled a route which brought him to a stable concept of "I" at two years, ten months. The blind child's route brought her to the same point at the age of four years, ten months. Jean-Fabien's travels took him six months; Kathie's took her two years and eight months.

The parallel developments in self-representation and pronoun usage from these two independent studies speak strongly in favor of Zazzo's view, which is also our own: that the acquisition of personal pronouns goes beyond practice with grammatical tools. It goes beyond the influence of the language environment which we can demonstrate through the incapacities of Kathie in self-reference pronouns, while living in a home with six highly verbal family members. The hypothesis in these two independent studies links self-reference pronouns to self-image.

The blind child's delay in the acquisition of "I" as a concept and a stable form appears to be related to the extraordinary problems in constructing a self-image in the absence of vision. The blind child must find a path to self-representation without the single sensory organ that is uniquely adapted for synthesis of all perceptions and the data of self.

In infancy, most of the data of self are integrated into a body schema by submitting to visual tests. We need only reflect on the hands as a model. Through countless experiments before six months of age, the infant makes the discovery that the hand that crosses his visual field, the hand that he brings to his mouth, the hand that grasps an object is part of himself, an instrument that he controls. The games he plays with his hands before his eyes are experiments in self-discovery. It is vision that gives unity to the disparate forms and aspects of hands and brings about an elementary sense of "me-ness" for hands. Body image is constructed by means of the discovery of parts, and a progressive organization of these parts into coherent pictures. In constructing a body image, vision offers a unique advantage that no other sensory mode can duplicate: the picture replicates exactly, and the picture by its nature can unite in one percept, or a memory flash, all the attributes and parts into a whole. Once the picture is there, it does not need to be reconstituted from its parts.

The blind child has no sensory mode available to him which will immediately replicate his own body or body parts. The blind child is obliged to constitute a body image from the component of nonvisual experiences available to him, not one of which will give him, through objective reference, the sum of the parts. His tactile, auditory, vocal, kinesthetic, and locomotor experiences will give him a sense of the substantiality and autonomy of his own body, but these sensory modes bind him to egocentric body and self-experience and cannot lead him easily to the concept of self in which the self can be taken as an object—the indispensable condition for the nonsyncretic "I." Self-image, which Zazzo suggests is a double, a replicate, a kind of mirror image of one's own person, is literally a picture of oneself, however distorted that picture may be. "I" is the externalization of that picture into a community of pictures each of which is an "I."

For the blind child there is no single sense that can take over the function of vision in replicating body image. When Kathie, at five years, three months, identifies her own words and her voice on tape,[5] she has demonstrated a form of self-recognition which still offers imperfect comparisions with Jean-Fabien's identification of himself in the mirror at two years, eight months. The voice on tape is an aspect of self, one of the components of self-image that can now be identified in objective form. But the voice does not replicate body image; the mirror image replicates exactly and instantly.

For the blind child, the level of inference required for the construction of the nonsyncretic "I" goes beyond that of the sighted child. The blind child must infer from his own consciousness of himself as an entity a commonality with the consciousness of others who are "I's"; he must construct a world of human objects each of whom is an "I" to himself by granting forms of substantiality and "I-ness" to those human objects whom he has identified as having attributes similar to himself. He must do this without the one sensory mode that would describe, through the visual picture, the commonalities and the generalizations that lead to the concept "I." Yet, when he does achieve "I" as a stable form and when he represents himself in play by means of a doll or an imaginary companion, he has indisputably externalized a form of self and reconstituted the self as an object. Our scientific imagination is strained to reconstruct the process

The blind child's route to "I" and self-representation is a perilous one. Many blind children do not make it. In the blind child population a very large number of children at school age or later do not have "I" or any other self-reference pronouns in their vocabularies. From the study of Kathie and other healthy and adequate blind children, we can understand without difficulty why the pronoun "I" and forms of self-representation in play are delayed in comparison with sighted children. The more difficult problem is to understand how the blind child achieves this prodigious feat.

## Summary

The blind child's delay in the acquisition of "I" is examined as a problem in self-representation. In a detailed longitudinal study of Kathie, the authors describe the extraordinary problems for a blind child in representation of the self in play and language. Kathie's achievement of a stable "I" at the age of four years, ten months, corresponds exactly with her capacity to represent herself in doll play and to invent an imaginary companion. Zazzo's protocols are employed for a comparison of a sighted child and a blind child in acquisition of

"I." Our data invite extended inquiry with a sighted child population. Detailed study of the developmental sequence of the representation of the self in language and play should add to our understanding of the evolution of the concept of self and the capacity to take the self as an object.

The ego is "I," yet we find ourselves, strangely, without empirical studies of the acquisition of "I" in early childhood. The blind children with their typical delays in self-representation have given us a map which should be valuable in identifying the strata of self through observations of the capacity to represent the self in language and play. We are pursuing these problems in empirical studies with sighted children and will report on these studies later.*

*To the best of my knowledge such studies were not completed or published.—Ed.

## Notes

1. For an early report of the findings, see Fraiberg (1968). The intervention program is described in Fraiberg, Smith, and Adelson (1969), and Fraiberg (1971a).
2. The primary source of data for our research group was naturalistic observation in the home, recorded as objective narrative description and documented on film or videotape. Parent reports were a secondary source and will be indicated when used.
3. Dr. Lenneberg had no opportunity to follow Kathie's language development beyond the age of two years, three months. When we now report further developments in Kathie's language history, we will find much that interests us from a developmental point of view but we also miss much that Dr. Lenneberg would have brought to us from linguistics.
4. Kathie's development after age four years, ten months was followed by Evelyn B. Atreya of our staff.
5. Even as Jean-Fabien had had the mirror available to him for many months before he identified himself, Kathie had had experience with tape recorders in her home for some time before this occurrence. This need not have been her first identification of herself on tape, but it was our first observation of it.

## References

Fraiberg, S. (1968). Parallel and Divergent Patterns in Blind and Sighted Infants. *Psychoanal. Study Child,* 23:264–300.
———. (1971a). Intervention in Infancy. *J. Amer. Acad. Child Psychiat.,* 10:381–405.

———. (1971b). Smiling and Stranger Reaction in Blind Infants. In *Exceptional Infant*, ed. J. Hellmuth, pp. 110–127. New York: Brunner/Mazel.

———; Siegel, B.; Gibson, R. (1966). The Role of Sound in the Search Behavior of a Blind Infant. *Psychoanal. Study Child,* 21:327–357.

———; Smith, M.; Adelson, E. (1969). An Educational Program for Blind Infants. *J. Spec. Educ.,* 3:121–139.

Gesell, A. & Amatruda, C. S. (1947). *Developmental Diagnosis.* New York: Paul B. Hoeber.

Lenneberg, E. H. (1967). *Biological Foundations of Language.* New York: Wiley.

Piaget, J. (1945). *Play, Dreams, and Imitation in Childhood.* New York: Norton, 1962.

———. (1952). *The Origins of Intelligence in Children.* New York: International Universities Press.

Ulrich, S. (1972). *Elizabeth.* (Introduction by S. Fraiberg; Commentary by E. Adelson.) Ann Arbor: Univ. of Michigan Press.

Zazzo, R. (1948). Image du corps et conscience de soi: Matériaux pour l'étude expérimentale de la conscience. *Enfance: Psychologies, pédagogie, neuropsychiatrie, sociologie,* 1, pp. 29–43.

# 23

# The Development of Human Attachments in Infants Blind from Birth

In this paper I will describe characteristics of attachment behavior which are derived from the study of ten infants blind from birth. The data, covering the first two years of life, will include: (a) smiling, (b) discriminating tactile behaviors, (c) stranger avoidance and distress, and (d) separation and reunion behaviors.

For the sighted child, the developmental course that leads to stable human partnerships in the course of the first eighteen months is charted by us through affective signs and by a sequence of increasingly discriminating behaviors toward the partner which speak for preference and valuation. Without exception, these are signs that are mediated through vision. Differential smiling, discrimination of mother and stranger, separation and reunion behaviors, unite the affective experience of the mother with sensory pictures, and the picture itself is the synthesizer of all sense experience.

But in a world without pictures, how does the infant learn to discriminate his mother from other persons, how does he express preference for, and valuation of, his mother? How does the visual deficit affect reciprocity between the baby and his partners and the reading of signs which must underlie every human partnership?

In this paper I will describe the sequential development of discriminating and preferential behaviors of blind infants towards their human partners and compare these characteristics with those of sighted children during the first two years of life.

## Method

*Subjects*

Ten infants, five boys and five girls, constitute the group on which this report is based.[1] Children who were accepted for the primary research group satisfied these criteria: (1) blind from birth, (2) total blindness or minimal light perception, (3) no other handicaps, neurologically intact (Table 1).

It is important to note that we have provided a concurrent educational and guidance service for all babies in the research program (Fraiberg, 1971a; Fraiberg, Smith, and Adelson, 1969). We know that the early development of blind babies is perilous. In the general blind child population we see a very high incidence of deviant and nondifferentiated personalities and arrested ego development (even when we exclude cases of brain damage and multiple handicaps which are also common to this population). As our own research progressed we were able to link certain developmental road-blocks with a clinical picture seen in the older blind child (Fraiberg and Freedman, 1964; Fraiberg, 1968). As these findings became available to us they were

---

**Table 1**

Characteristics of Blind Infant Group (Child Development Project)

*Criteria:*
Total blindness from birth or only minimal light perception
No other known handicaps or neurological damage
Less than one-year-old
Within fifty miles of our office

*Description:*

| | |
|---|---|
| Sex | 5 boys, 5 girls |
| Age at referral | 1 to 11 months (1 to 8 months with correction for prematurity in 3 cases) |
| Age last seen | 2 to 6 years |
| Ordinal position in family | Only (5), first of 2 (1), first of 3 (1), second of 2 (1), fifth of 5 (1), sixth of 6 (1) |
| Diagnosis | Hypoplasia of optic nerve (3), retrolental fibroplasia (3) (3 months premature birth), infantile glaucoma (2), ophthalmia neonatorum (1), resorption of vitreous humor (1) |
| Light perception | 2 boys, 2 girls |
| Social class by father's occupation* | Managerial (1), college student (2), skilled (2), semi-skilled (3), unskilled (2) |

*\*Edwards' Occupational Index.*

readily translatable into a program of guidance and education (Fraiberg, Smith, and Adelson 1969; Fraiberg, 1971a).

Finally, then, this study is based upon a unique sample and we cannot generalize our findings to the larger blind population. In a typical blind child population we will have children with a range of useful vision who are still legally classified as "blind," and we will have a high incidence of multiple handicaps and neurological damage. The babies in our sample are advantaged in a blind child population by the intactness of other systems and are disadvantaged as a group by having no pattern vision.

In summary, we can say that the observations reported in this paper are derived from a group of healthy, otherwise intact blind infants; their families represent a good range of socioeconomic conditions, and the development of these babies has probably been facilitated through our intervention.

## Observational Procedures

The five major areas of the study were: human attachment, prehension, gross motor development, language, and object permanence.

Each baby was visited in his home twice a month for sessions ranging from one to one and a half hours. Visits were timed to coincide with a morning or afternoon waking period, and observations were fitted into the normal routine of that period. Nearly all of the data required for our study could be obtained through observing a feeding, a bath, a play time with mother, a diapering or clothes change, and a period of self-occupation with or without toys. A small amount of time in each session was employed for testing procedures in the areas of prehension and object concept.

The observers recorded a continuous narrative with descriptive detail. Once monthly we recorded a fifteen minute 16 millimeter film or video sample covering mother-child interaction, prehension, and gross motor development which was employed for analysis at one-third speed.

Since the areas we were studying had not been previously researched, our data collection procedures had to insure coverage of hundreds of items for comparative study, yet needed to be open, flexible, and rich in detail for qualitative study.

*Evaluation of Data*

In examining the course of human attachments in blind babies we recorded and analyzed hundreds of items for each child in a chronological sequence which gave us differential responses to mother, to familiar and unfamiliar persons, behaviors showing pleasurable response to and preference for mother, the ability to be comforted by mother, reactions to temporary separation from mother, tracking and seeking mother (when the baby was mobile). Profiles for each child were constructed, a selection of indicators was made, and a composite profile was developed for the ten babies.

When our data were sorted and evaluated we saw that there were differential responses in certain areas which could be examined in relation to sighted child criteria and sighted child norms. There were also a number of indicators of human attachment which appeared in our blind children which represented the blind baby's exploitation of tactile-auditory modes. These may also be tactile-auditory components of human attachment that are normally obscured when vision is available to the baby.

The summary that follows is highly selective and may not do justice to the complexities of the problem for the blind baby and his mother in achieving their bonds. Table 2 summarizes for the reader the ranges and medians for milestones in human attachment in our group. These milestones will be explained in the text. Four papers by the author deal with aspects of human attachment in blind infants (Fraiberg, 1968, 1971b, 1971c, 1974). A volume summarizing and analyzing our data (and including protocols) is in preparation.

**Table 2**
Human Attachment Milestones (Child Development Project blind group)

| Item | Range | Median Age |
|---|---|---|
| Smiles to familiar voice* | 1.0–3.0 | 2.0 |
| Manual-tactile discrimination familiar-unfamiliar faces | 5.0–8.0 | 5.0 |
| Stranger avoidance | 7.0–15.0 | 12.5 |
| Person permanence Stage 4 | 10.0–16.0 | 13.0 |
| Separation protest | 11.0–16.0 | 12.0 |

NOTE: Ages rounded to nearest half month; 3 cases corrected for 3 months prematurity.
* Parent report credited for this item only. All children had achieved this item at time of entrance to study. All other items credited by our direct observation.

**Smiling**

The course of smiling in the blind infant is of exceptional interest and provides an entry through "known territory" to the "unknown territory" of the blind infant's development. Our findings during the first year of life are described in "Smiling and Stranger Reaction in the Blind Infant" (Fraiberg, 1971c).

In the sighted child, the differentiation of the smile and the increasing selectivity of the smile for the valued partner gives us a sequence of milestones or indicators of human attachment. (Spitz and Wolf, 1946; Ambrose, 1961; Polak, Emde, and Spitz, 1964; Gewirtz, 1965; Emde and Koenig, 1969). From the automatic smile at two months to the selective smile which is well established at six months the prime elicitor of smiling is the visual configuration of the human face. Indeed, the facial gestalt is biologically overdetermined as a stimulus for attention and smiling in the infant.

For the blind infant, the familiar *voice* is the prime elicitor of the smile. As early as the fourth week we have examples of selective (but irregular) smiling to mother's and father's voice. When we, the observers, tried to elicit the smile through our voices, in repeated experiments, we failed. The smile to voice is also reported by Wolff (1963) for sighted children of the same age. Emde and Koenig (1969) report, however, that voice is one of a number of unpatterned auditory, tactile, and visual stimuli which elicit the smile as an *irregular* response in the period three weeks to two months.

At two and a half months, however, the smile of the sighted child becomes regular, and is relatively automatic to the gestalt of the human face. The blind child smiles more frequently to the voice of mother and other familiar persons, but there is no stimulus except gross tactile stimulation (tickling) which *regularly* elicits the smile.

In the period two and a half months to six months the sighted child's smile becomes preferential for mother, with greater frequency for mother than unfamiliar persons. This preferential smile speaks for an affective-cognitive advance in which the baby can discriminate the familiar face from the unfamiliar face. The blind child, whose smile has been "preferential" from the second month on, continues to smile selectively to mother's voice; the smile to voice is still irregular.

In the period six to eleven months the sighted child reserves his smile, almost exclusively, for mother and familiar persons (Emde and

Koenig, 1969). The blind child's smile is not further differentiated from the earlier stage; it is still an irregular smile to the mother's or familiar persons' voices.

Using sighted child criteria for smiling as an indicator of attachment behavior, the course of smiling in the blind infant would tell us nothing of the development of human attachments. A preferential smile to voice, which does not undergo a course of further differentiation in the first year, leaves us without vital indicators of progression in human attachment. Yet, even though the blind baby's smile does not inform us of complex discriminations, or tell us how he gives unity to the disparate aspects of mother, how he "knows" mother, how he comes to value her, we can demonstrate that there are components of sensorimotor experience which are exploited by the blind baby and his mother and which lead him to a stage in human attachments which becomes recognizable to us immediately as an indicator of a level of human attachments.

Between seven and fifteen months of age, the blind baby, like the sighted baby, repudiates strangers, resists their arms and their ministrations, cries in protest, and is comforted only by mother's voice and embrace. The blind baby has kept his appointment, and meets the sighted baby at a certian time and a certain place on a developmental pathway, but he got there by another route.

## The Tactile Language: Discrimination and Preference

The hands of the blind baby tell a story which begins in the first months. As the story unfolds in the course of the first year we see the progressive adaptation of the hand as an organ for maintaining contact with human partners and, later, for fine discriminations. When we consider that in normal development it is vision that facilitates all adaptive hand behavior, the blind child's exploitation of the hand as a perceptual organ is an extraordinary adaptive feat. In our studies we have compelling evidence that this adaptation, which is unique, of course, for blind children, is given impetus and motive through the primary human attachments and tactile intimacy between the baby and his human partners.

Yet, the beginning of the story of the blind baby's hands does not distinguish for our eyes the blind child and the sighted child.

In the early weeks of life, we see a form of contact-seeking in the blind baby which closely parallels that of the sighted baby. In the mother's arms, both the blind baby and the sighted baby in the second month will engage in a brief pursuit of the mother's hand which has been withdrawn from contact, or in other ways attempt to restore a contact that has been momentarily lost. (Our own protocols for three children and Piaget's protocols for Laurent at 0:1:19 show close correspondence; see Piaget [1952]).

But for the sighted child, manual tactile experience becomes one of several modes which are available "to maintain contact." By the third month, visual regard and tracking are capable of taking over the functions of "making contact" and "sustaining contact" when the child is at tactile and auditory remove from his mother.

The blind child in the third month and for many months to follow can only maintain contact with his mother when she manifests herself to him through tactile experience and through her voice. When his mother does not manifest herself to him through touch or voice, the blind baby is "not in contact" with his mother.

Yet the condition of physical proximity to the mother can be exploited fully by the blind child, and what we see is a pantomime of hands which begins in the first month as "chance encounter," then moves toward "tactile seeking" and grows progressively more discriminating and intentional by five months of age. For many months before the ear-hand schemas are coordinated, the blind child's hands send and receive messages in an archaic language: "Are you there? . . . I am here."

Between five and eight months something new emerges in manual tactile experience. The blind baby's hands begin to explore the face of the mother, father, and other familiar persons.

Robbie 0:5:18 (on film)
Now sitting on father's lap, father nuzzling his face and jiggling him on his lap, Robbie's hands are stretched outright. A sequence of Robbie fingering his father's nose and face with great interest follows. Robbie is pinching his father's cheek. Father is talking to him and he strokes father's chin and mouth with his fingers. Now examining with his fingers father's glasses, he grabs hold at one point of the glasses and nearly pulls them off father's nose.

Far less frequently in our records are examples in which the blind baby explores the observer's face. Our protocols and films give numerous examples from all children in the sample of a sustained, fascinated exploration of facial features of mother, father, siblings, other familiar persons, which gives the sense to the viewer of pleasure in tracing a familiar map and knowing what is to be found. The few examples of manual exploration of the observer's face are qualitatively different; they are brief scannings which appear to give some minimal information. In this behavior the blind child clearly differentiates between the familiar person and the stranger. As an early form of recognition behavior it may be compared fairly with the recognition behaviors which we discern in the sighted child of the same age, in preferential smiling, for example.

The appearance of manual-tactile exploration of faces follows a distribution pattern which is of some interest for comparison. Crediting the first example in the child's protocols of "exploration of the face," we have five children in the range five to six months, two at seven months, and one at eight months. ($N=8$ for this age period.)

There appears to be some correspondence, then, with forms of discriminatory and recognitory behaviors which appear in the sighted child around the middle of the first year. My hypothesis is that the correspondence between visual recognition behavior in the sighted baby and manual-tactile recognition behaviors in the blind baby is a function of brain maturation as well as libidinization of the partner. Both factors must be present, of course, to lead to recognition behavior.

## Negative Reactions to the Stranger

On a scale of human attachment, negative reaction to the stranger is regarded as a criterion for the assessment of the positive bonds to the mother and other human partners (Spitz, 1957; Benjamin, 1963; Provence and Lipton, 1962; Ainsworth, 1967; Yarrow, 1967). It speaks for another level of valuation of the mother, in which the positive affect is bound to a partner, in which persons are no longer "interchangeable," and for a new level of cognitive discrimination.

Among sighted children it is the visual discrimination of the stranger's face which elicits avoidance behavior or fear in the child between the ages of seven and fifteen months (ranges from Morgan and Ricciuti [1969]). The experimental situations which have been designed to study the developmental characteristics of stranger reaction require, of course, the presentation of the stranger's face and the reactions of the baby to the visual stimulus of the face.

When I now summarize our findings on the stranger reactions of the blind babies in our sample, I do not wish to strain the comparisons between blind and sighted children. The conditions which elicited negative reactions to the stranger for blind children are not identical with those observed and studied in sighted children; there is no true equivalence between a non-visual percept of the stranger and a visual percept.

All that can be said with confidence is that in longitudinal study of ten babies blind from birth negative reactions to the stranger were manifest in naturalistic observation and elicited in experimental approaches by the stranger. *The first manifestations of stranger avoidance and fear emerged in the period seven to fifteen months for nine of the ten children.* This corresponds to the period of onset in sighted children.

For both sighted and blind children discrimination of familiar persons and strangers is manifest some weeks or months before the onset of stranger avoidance or stranger anxiety. We have already seen in our discussion of smiling and the "tactile language" that the blind baby shows differential responses to familiar persons and strangers in the period under six months of age. I should also add—and this is an important bridge to the material that follows—that the blind baby, like the sighted baby, in the period under six months reacted with squirming and discomfort to subtle postural differences when held in the stranger's arms. Ainsworth (1967) describes similar reactions in sighted children during the same period. But this is not yet fear of the stranger; rather, as Benjamin (1963) suggests, it is the experience of something different, something strange.

As the data emerge from the descriptive protocols and films there is nothing in our records for any child under seven months that can yet be classified as "a negative reaction" to the stranger. Reactions to the observer's voice and to being held in the observer's arms were recorded at each visit.

Then, between seven and fifteen months, we find that something new begins to emerge in the blind baby's behavior toward the stranger—struggling, straining away, crying—which, for the majority of the babies in our sample, occurs when the observer holds the baby. These fear and avoidance behaviors appear even though the observer, a twice-monthly visitor, is not, strictly speaking, a stranger. At the same time that these reactions are manifest in relation to the observer, we have parallel reports from the mothers, showing that fear of strangers has emerged for other visitors to the house as well.

To the stranger's voice only (no touching or holding) we have only one observation of fear reaction during this period. A typical reaction to "voice only" is something we have called "quieting" in response to the stranger's voice (i.e., cessation of activity or vocalizing—without signs of distress—which may last for several minutes, or longer). I should state at the outset that we have not scored "quieting" as negative reaction. However, among our blind children it regularly precedes the period in which manifest stranger avoidance or fear occurs. Among sighted children Ainsworth (1967) and others describe "quieting" or "staring" in the period that precedes fear of the stranger.

In addition to "voice only" we tested the reaction of the baby to being held in the observer's arms at each of the twice monthly visits. The observer employed a modulated approach to the baby, speaking to him both before picking him up and during the period of being held. The cumulative record for each child was then analyzed and examples of the first manifestations of negative reactions to the stranger were sorted and credited, first by me, then jointly in senior staffing where we debated criteria. The credited "first examples" were made through staff consensus.

The following examples represent in each case the first instance in our records of the appearance of negative reactions to the stranger in nine cases which provided unambiguous evidence.

Toni, 0:7:2
Soon after the observer (a woman) picks her up, she freezes, then bursts into tears. She scans the face of the observer with her fingers, registers increasing distress on her face, strains away from the observer's body, turns her head and trunk as if seeking to locate her mother by voice. She claws at the examiner's arms. She begins to scream loudly. When she is returned to her mother, she settles, still crying, scans her mother's face with her fingers and is gradually comforted.

Carol, 0:8:22
The observer picks up Carol and holds her. Twice Carol strains away from the observer's shoulder. When the observer takes Carol's hand in hers to bring it to the observer's face, Carol's hand closes in a fist.

Jamie, 0:9:12
Eric Lenneberg is visiting with the team today. Jamie has never met him before. EL picks up the baby and begins to talk to him. As soon as he is picked up, Jamie begins to cry. He is handed to his mother, who diverts him with a game and succeeds in comforting him.

Kathie, 0:10:16
The observer speaks to Kathie. She is attentive. Now the observer picks her up. Kathie stiffens, feels the observer's face with her right hand, clutches her shirt with the other hand, whimpers, and is transferred to her mother's arms.

Karen, 0:12:19
Mother reached out and took EA's (observer's) coat; she walked to the dining room with the coat and EA said "Hi, Karen" very quietly. Karen turned in the direction of the dining room and, crying and whining quietly, crawled after her mother.

Paul, 1:1:5
Later in the morning, when he was standing on the floor, I offered him my hand while talking to him. Once again, he listened but made no move on his own to approach closer. Both with SF (second observer) and myself, he turned away from us as soon as he heard his father's voice, and reached toward his father.

Ronny, 1:3:1
Avoids contact with the observer today for the first time. Withdraws from her touch (while in earlier sessions he reached out to her). While he made no overt objection to my picking him up, he would not sit on my lap nor make any attempt to mould in the sitting position, but stiffened and arched back, so that his head hung over my feet.

Joan, 1:3:17
As the observer began to engage Joan in play, he noticed fear and withdrawal for the first time in his regular visits. When he spoke to Joan and touched her, she drew her hand away. Later, too, when he attempted to place her on his lap, Joan withdrew from contact and tried to get away from him. When he offered her objects in a testing situation during this session, she was unwilling to touch and explore any of the items.

Jackie, 1:3:21
Jackie is sitting on his mother's lap, not at the moment engaged with mother or the observers. The observer picks him up and brings him to stand, holding his hands. There is not an immediate negative reaction. On film we see an initial smile on his face. But this is followed by constraint and motor signs of discomfort (observer's own notes). Now,

on film he turns in the direction of mother, on the couch, correctly orienting himself, and holds out his arms to mother. Mother offers her hand and as soon as Jackie makes contact with the hand he begins to crawl up on his mother's lap. Once on mother's lap he makes chance contact with the observer's hand, fingers it, then turns back toward mother, very actively climbing on mother, and settles in a supine position on her lap. He then engages mother in a favorite game.

This leaves one subject out of ten who has not given evidence of stranger avoidance during the first eighteen months. It may be worth reporting on this child to complete the picture.

Robbie provided one example of "quieting" to the observers' voices at 1:0:0 and no examples of negative reactions to strangers at any time in the second year. During the second year he allowed our own observers and other unfamiliar persons to hold him and to play with him. We have examples in our hospital waiting room and other unfamiliar places in which his indiscriminate friendliness to strangers is recorded. He is also the one child in our group whose attachment to his mother was regarded by us as unstable, without signs of active seeking of the mother for pleasure or comfort.

If we can accept, then, those differences in testing stranger reactions which were required when we needed to translate procedures for testing sighted infants into procedures for blind infants there is fair equivalence in the characteristics of stranger anxiety in our blind baby sample and those reported for sighted children.

## Separation and Reunion

For sighted children, there is now a fair consensus among investigators that separation protest or distress emerges in the third quarter of the first year. Stayton, Ainsworth, and Main (1971), in a report of their longitudinal studies, place the median age of onset of separation distress in a "mother leave room" situation at twenty-two weeks or five and a half months. Other studies (Schaffer and Emerson, 1964; Tennes and Lampl, 1964; Spitz, 1965) give us a range of six to eight months in average age of onset. However, criteria and observational procedures differed among these studies.

Allowing for these differences, the age of onset of separation protest or anxiety appears to have some correspondence with the emergence of a concept of permanence for the mother (approximately Stage 4). This means, of course, that both an affective investment in the mother and a cognitive advance enter into the experience of separation distress. *There must be at least an elementary concept of mother as an object before her absence is perceived as loss.*

In briefest summary, we see that between the ages of six months and eight months there is a confluence of events in the development of the sighted child in which affective, motor, and cognitive advances unite in the service of human attachments. Valuation of and preference for mother, established under six months of age, is now given poignancy by the cognitive awareness of loss and the baby protests even the momentary disappearance of his mother. An advance in motor development permits him to follow his mother and maintain contact with her. An advance in conceptual development confers upon the mother some measure of permanence as an object, but it is still an uncertain belief which binds her to place and requires frequent confirmation or verification through vision. During the next twelve months the sighted baby's experiments and a tremendous advance in representational intelligence will permit him to account for his mother's displacements in space and finally to constitute his mother as an object (Stage 6).

*For the blind children in our group, the first manifestations of separation protest and distress appear in the age range 10:22 to 1:9:24; median age 11:20.* There is, then, nearly a six-month difference between the age of onset of separation distress in our blind children and that reported for sighted children ranges six to eight months (see Table 2). This delay (by sighted child standards) corresponds exactly with the blind child's delay in the achievement of a Stage 4 level of object permanence (Table 2). For the blind child as well as the sighted child, there can be no concept of "loss" or "absence" until the mother is constituted as an object at least on a Stage 4 level.

In the following pages I propose to examine the onset of separation protest in relation to (a) the blind child's awareness of "absence and presence," (b) his concept of mother as an object, (c) tracking on sound, and (d) locomotion as experience in learning the displaceability of objects.

For comparison with sighted children we will find it useful to discriminate between the forms of separation protest and the conditions which elicit them, following Ainsworth (1972).

Ainsworth differentiates between anxiety following prolonged separations ("definitive separations") and "separation protest" in minor everyday situations. In her 1972 essay and elsewhere, she agrees with other authors that separation protest is a criterion of considerable value in the assessment of human attachments, but in her view it should not be employed as the only criterion of attachment. When separation protest is present along with other behaviors ("following" when mother leaves the room, active contact behaviors, affectionate behaviors, approach through locomotion and the use of mother as a secure base to explore, flight to mother as a haven of safety, and clinging), Ainsworth feels that the judgment of "attachment" can be fairly made.

Our data on the emergence of separation anxiety or protest in a "mother leaves room" situation are derived entirely from naturalistic circumstance. We recorded descriptively all occurrences in which mother left the room for a few moments and described the baby's reactions. Until the close of the first year we have no examples in which the blind baby registered in any discernible way an awareness of mother "not present," except in circumstances where hunger or an interrupted game with mother were antecedent conditions. To fairly approximate the "neutral conditions" which provided the base for sighted child observations of "separation protest" I chose only those examples in our records in which the baby's state would not introduce other variables (e.g., the baby is alert, shows no signs of hunger or discomfort, is pleasantly occupied with a toy, may be sitting on the floor listening attentively to conversation in the room, and mother leaves the room for a few moments).

We might begin now with a general frame of reference for the examination of a blind child's experience of separation: How does the blind child experience what we know as "mother not present"?

## Blindness and the Experience of "Presence" and "Absence"

In the case of the blind infant even the concept of "momentary separation" must be modified and expanded to include a range of experience that may be called "not in contact" and "maintaining contact." It is more difficult in the case of the blind baby to isolate those conditions which mean mother is "absent" in everyday experience. In the case of the sighted child, mother is absent when she is not seen.

Vision also permits the sighted child to give meaning to the "goings" and "comings" of his mother, since he can track her with his eyes to the point at which she leaves his visual field (goes to another room, closes a door, etc.).

For the blind child, mother can be present in the room and if she is not in physical proximity and refrains from talking or moving, she has left the child's perceptual field. Silencing of mother's voice is not an equivalent in the blind child's experience to disappearance of the mother for the sighted child. Vision, by its nature, is continuous; visual tracking confers temporal order to events, and a break or closure of the visual record is read as the sign of "gone." Sound is discontinuous, and for large periods in a blind child's day, things and people do not manifest themselves to him through sound (or touch). Since there is no predictability in events that are experienced through intermittent sound, the breaking or closure of a sound sequence need not denote "separation" or "loss" or "absence."

For these reasons we chose not to define "separation" for the blind baby at the start of our study, but to examine the experiences of "not in contact" and "maintaining contact" with the mother's voice or her person, with the expectation that at certain unknown points in development during the sensorimotor period, the experience of "loss" would be registered in identifiable ways and the means of perception of loss would be revealed to us.

In the early weeks of life the sighted child maintains contact with the people and the things of his world by fixating near objects and by tracking movement through vision. As recognition memory becomes available to the baby (and he demonstrates this at under three months in the response smile to the configuration of the human face), the sighted infant scans his environment and can "rediscover" both human and inanimate objects that are momentarily "absent." Repetition of the game of scanning and recovery probably affords a kind of elementary belief in permanence, that things "lost" can be "found" and are somehow at the disposal of vision (Piaget, Stages 1 through 3). Visual tracking of moving objects, both human and inanimate, affords the sighted child the first practical demonstrations that a person or object (sensory picture) located at point *A* can appear again or be "rediscovered" at *B* and at *C, D, E,* etc. And long before the child achieves even an elementary notion of causality visual tracking prepares him for the discoveries at the end of the first year that an object is not bound to place, that it can be subject to multiple displacements (Stage 5) and, finally, between thirteen and eighteen months, to the discovery that the displacement of objects can occur independently of his perception of their movements, which then enables him to take account of invisible displacements and to employ an elementary form of deduction regarding an object's probable route (Stage 6). At this stage the sighted child conducts a sustained search for a lost object, which testifies to the emergence of a belief in permanence: the person or the object "must be some place."

The human partner leads the way to these discoveries, as psychoanalysts and as Piaget have shown. The person-object sequences which lead to object permanence have been experimentally worked out by Saint-Pierre (1962) and Bell (1970), and in these reports we see that *person permanence normally precedes toy permanence;* that when the search for the not-present mother takes account of her invisible displacements, discoveries leading to belief in the permanence of inanimate objects follow closely in temporal sequence.

For the blind child during most of the first year there is no equivalent for the sighted child's visual scanning or tracking to locate and maintain contact with the mother if she is momentarily out of the child's perceptual field. And where vision guarantees the perception of movement and the "displaceability" of human and inanimate objects, the blind infant cannot confer movement to objects, or "comings" or "goings" until his own mobility in the second year gives him the experimental conditions for tracking and recovering persons and toys in multiple displacements.

As we reported in other papers (Fraiberg, Siegel, and Gibson, 1966; Fraiberg, 1968), acoustical tracking and localization of sound is not achieved by any child in our sample until the last quarter of the first year. But when the blind child reaches directionally for or creeps toward a person or toy on sound cue only, he demonstrates an emerging concept of permanence, probably on the level of Stage 4. The sound "out there" now denotes a person or a toy, and his reach or his locomotor approach signifies that he confers substantiality, a sound-touch unity to the person or object.

This is, I believe, a virtuoso achievement for the blind child. From all of our evidence, substantiality is affirmed tactually by the blind child for most of the first year. To endow the sound "out there" with meaning he can employ only one distance sense, hearing, one that was "intended" in the biological program to evolve in synchrony with vision.

This means, of course, that during the first year the awareness of "mother not present" and the experience of "mother not present" for the blind child can emerge only under two types of circumstances: (1) in need states, if the cry or signals of distress do not summon the mother, if there is a delay in answering the signal or satisfying the need, the blind baby may have an acute sense of "loss" or "not present"; (2) if the mother is constituted as an object, at least on the level of Stage 4 and 5 (i.e., if her voice and footsteps connote substantiality to the blind child), "presence" and "absence" become open to objective confirmation. Mother is "present" when she manifests herself through voice and "absent" when she does not manifest herself through voice or sounds of movement. Under all favorable conditions in which the mother has become the central person, the affectively significant person, awareness of "absence" can also evoke protest, distress and anxiety in ways that are entirely analogous to the experience of separation in sighted children.

For both the blind child and the sighted child, then, the manifestations of separation protest and anxiety are linked to the emergence of object permanence, in which the human partner is endowed with objective attributes. If we can employ my provisional crediting of Stage 4 to the level of concept development achieved by our blind children at the close of the first year, the emergence of separation protest and anxiety during the same period has close correspondence with sighted child data which link the emergence of separation anxiety with Stage 4.

Next, we should examine the possible relations between the onset of separation protest and the onset of locomotion in our blind group. In Adelson and Fraiberg (1974), we report the typical delays in creeping and free walking in our blind group.

In our group, creeping was achieved in the range of ten and a half to sixteen and a half months for nine of ten children; free walking in the range of twelve to twenty months. We also described the relationship between the onset of self-initiated mobility with the coordination of ear and hand. (No child could creep before he first demonstrated reach for and attainment of the sound object.) This links locomotion in the blind child to the achievement of a Stage 4 level of object permanence.

With the onset of locomotion, the blind baby can begin to conduct a large number of experiments which will inform him of the displaceability of human and inanimate objects and he will now be able to use his newly acquired ability to track movement by sound with his newly acquired locomotor skills, in a discovery and rediscovery of his mother hundreds of times every day. It is even possible that the discovery, in a sense, of his own "displaceability" through locomotion gives some substance to the concept of "movement" which the blind child cannot perceive in any ways that are analogous to the experience of the sighted, which for us is a sequence of pictures. In all these ways, then, mobility plays a central role in the blind child's construction of an object world and specifically, in the problem under examination, in constituting the mother as object.

*Illustration: the course of separation and reunion behavior between eleven months and twenty-five months.* To illustrate the course of separation and reunion behavior I have chosen a set of protocols from Edna Adelson's record of Karen. Karen falls within the upper half of our group on nearly all dimensions studied. She was blind from birth due to retrolental fibroplasia and was three months premature. She was first seen by us at eight months. (Age is corrected for prematurity in these examples.) Karen was totally blind during her first eighteen months. Light perception (but no form perception) was observed beginning at eighteen months.

Until 0:11:13 we have no observations in our records which show that Karen registered the momentary absences of her mother from the room. Since there was a baby sister (Debby) who required mother's attention, there were numerous examples in which mother left to respond to Debby. Typically Karen did not interrupt her activities, did not protest, did not appear to be listening for cues of presence or absence. At eleven months we began to see the first signs of separation protest now reported by mother and confirmed in our observations. (Karen, it should be noted, began to creep at ten and a half months.)

Karen, 0:11:13 (Mother's report)
Mother remarked that she can't leave Karen with anyone anymore, which has not been the case until very recently. Karen cries and is unhappy even with her grandmother, whom she has known since birth. Added to Karen's behavior today is her need to always be in contact with mother.

Karen, 0:11:13 (Observer's report)
Karen let herself down to the floor and started to creep to the box
which was about two feet away from her. She was somewhat hesitant or
cautious, but she was curious. At this moment, mother got up to go to
Debby to give her the pacifier because she was fussing. Karen immediately started to whimper, reversed direction, and went back to cling
to mother's chair and when mother sat down again, reached to touch
mother's arm. Mother reached out and touched Karen's hair.

In the 0:11:13 observation we see that both awareness of mother's
absence and distress at absence have emerged together. But Karen's
new-found mobility does not yet lead her to tracking mother on
sound cues and her concept of mother as object is illustrated in her
behavior following loss of mother. *She seeks mother's chair which is
now vacant, of course, and clings to the chair.* Mother "belongs to" the
chair, as it were, and is conceived as having one position in space, the
place where Karen had last had contact with her. This is a Stage 4
behavior.

At 0:12:4 we see the beginnings of search for mother after mother
leaves the room.

Karen, 0:12:4
Mrs. Cook offers her visitors coffee. When she leaves the room Karen
begins to whine. Karen crawls out of the living room into the dining
room, apparently in search of her mother. Mrs. Cook returns to the
room and asks Karen, "Where are you going?" Karen turns around at her
mother's voice and crawls to her mother's chair. She smiles and stops
crying when she finds her mother's knee. She proceeds to touch her
mother's legs again.

Karen's apparent search for her mother (who is actually in the kitchen) leads her to the dining room, which is on the route. If we assume
that Karen's mother has, for Karen, left the child's perceptual field, the
search to another room must represent an advance in object concept.
She does not return to an empty chair, as she did in the eleven-month
sequence, she searches for the mother in another place, which means
that she can conceive of her mother as a "displaceable" object. Analogies with Stage 5 behavior suggest themselves.

Two weeks later, Karen is tracking her mother from room to room,
and a summary of observations in this session shows that crying has
diminished when mother momentarily leaves the room. One example
will illustrate:

Karen, 0:12:19
Mother picks up Debby and carries her into the bedroom talking very quietly to her. Karen, who is busy with a necklace, picks up the distant voice of her mother and, without crying, crawls over all the toys and follows her mother into the bedroom.

In the 0:12:19 example Karen can track her mother on sound and use her own mobility to locate mother and reunite with her. The discovery that a temporarily "lost" mother can be "found" appears to be a potent antidote to separation anxiety, at least within the safety of the home which is now well-mapped by Karen.

Two observations at fourteen and fifteen months show sustained tolerance for momentary separations.

Karen, 1:1:23
Mrs. Cook leaves the room to get Debby. There is no reaction from Karen when her mother leaves the room.

Karen, 1:2:7
Karen came and went, sometimes seeking mother, sometimes on her own, sometimes out of sight, since I did not feel I could follow her around.

Then, at 1:2:28 we have an observation that shows us that separation anxiety will still be evoked under certain circumstances. In this example, we should note, we had inadvertently created two barriers to search for mother. We were filming at that visit, and our tripod obstructed Karen's path. To make space for filming in this small living room we had moved one of the living room chairs so that the chair was not only out of place, but partially obstructed the kitchen doorway.

Karen, 1:2:28
Mother leaves the living room to see why Debby is fussing in the bedroom. Karen crawls after her, gets tangled up with the tripod, but manages to make her way through anyway without tipping it over. Here is a problem for Karen. She is not quite sure where mother is and goes to the kitchen for her first try. We have moved one of the living room chairs, so that it is in the dining room, almost in the kitchen doorway, not at all where it should ordinarily be. Karen has to move around it in order to get to the kitchen. She makes the detour, goes into the kitchen, then hears her mother in the bedroom with Debby and heads for the bedroom. Karen is crying by the time she gets to her mother.

In this example, we had inadvertently created the conditions under which there were two barriers to memory and locomotion. Assuming that some form of mental representation of mother is available to Karen as she conducts her searches during this period, the tripod and the chair may constitute distractions or obstacles to memory by introducing competing problems for attention. Assuming that Karen can, for short intervals, sustain a mental representation of mother in spite of barriers to perception and memory, the tripod and chair are obstacles to locomotion and, therefore, to her recovery of mother. Karen, who has been able to accurately track mother from room to room during the past three months, becomes slightly disoriented. Like Ariadne in the labyrinth, she must find her path by a thread, but Karen's thread has become tangled in barriers. Under these conditions mother becomes "lost" again, in her own house, and Karen, by the time she picks up the voice thread again, is crying.

Between fifteen and twenty-six months Karen (who began free walking at fifteen months) has a variety of ways in which she "keeps in touch" with mother, and anxiety at momentary separations is no longer recorded.

At sixteen months she is still experimenting with her new freedom in walking and stays in close touch with her mother.

At nearly two years of age, Karen has begun to make more and more use of language to locate her mother. The word "mama" can be used as a probe, to take soundings of her mother's whereabouts.

Karen, 1:11:25
Mother was busy in the kitchen. An interesting interaction between Karen and her mother followed. Karen would be ordered into the living room, she would go to the dining room, pause, then return to the kitchen where she would maintain contact with her mother by saying, "Mama." Her mother would answer, "What?" and Karen would say, "Mama" again. This was repeated to the distraction of Mrs. Cook, who would order her out to the living room again. During Karen's sojourns in the dining room, she seemed to be waiting a decent interval before she could sneak back into the kitchen.

By the close of the second year examples of anxiety at momentary separations are rare for Karen. We do not see distress again, except during periods of prolonged daily separation during a period when mother is working part-time.

The illustrations from Karen's record of momentary separations fairly describe the process for our group of blind children: (a) awareness of loss of contact with mother, (b) distress, (c) tracking and locating mother on voice or sounds of movement, (d) following, (e) accounting for mother as a displaceable object, (f) diminution of distress, and (g) use of language as a probe (a "radar device" as Lyle Warner of our staff called it) to locate and to keep in touch with mother.

## Notes

Senior staff of the Child Development Project who participated in the research and intervention program were Edna Adelson, Evelyn Atreya, Morton Chethik, Winnifred Connelly, Ralph Gibson, Barry Siegel, Marguerite A. Smith, Lyle Warner, Marion Ross, and the author.

1. We have no census information on the incidence of blind births in our state, or in the counties that we covered in our referral network. Our state is by no means alone in its failure to obtain compulsory or obligatory registration of cases by physicians. When blindness is identified at birth the circumstances favor registration by the attending physician or nurses. But in the largest number of cases blindness is identified some weeks or months after birth and central reporting may not follow. At the time of this writing both state and national agencies are at work in developing efficient methods of registration, but there is no way in which we can place our ten-year cumulative sample within a larger population designated as "blind from birth" or within a subgroup of unknown number—"blind from birth, no other handicaps."

## References

Adelson, E. & Fraiberg, S. (1974). Gross Motor Development in Infants Blind from Birth. *Child Dev.*, 45:114–126.

Ainsworth, M. D. (1967). *Infancy in Uganda: Infant Care and the Growth of Love.* Baltimore: Johns Hopkins Univ. Press.

———. (1972). The Development of Infant-Mother Attachment. In *Review of Child Development Research*, ed. B. M. Caldwell & H. N. Ricciutti, vol. 3, pp. 1–94. Chicago: Univ. of Chicago Press.

Ambrose, J. A. (1961). The Development of the Smiling Response in Early Infancy. In *Determinants of Infant Behavior*, ed. B. M. Foss, vol. 1, pp. 179–201. London: Methuen.

Bell, S. M. (1970). The Development of the Concept of the Object and Its Relationship to Infant-Mother Attachment. *Child Dev.*, 41:291–312.

Benjamin, J. D. (1963). Further Comments on Some Developmental Aspects of Anxiety. *Counterpoint.* New York: International Universities Press.

*Blindness in Childhood*

Emde, R. N. & Koenig, K. L. (1969). Neonatal Smiling, Frowning, and Rapid Eye Movement States: II Sleep-Cycle Study. *J. Amer. Acad. Child Psychiat.*, 4:637–656.

Escalona, S. K. & Corman, H. H. Albert Einstein Scales of Sensorimotor Development. Unpublished.

Fraiberg, S. (1968). Parallel and Divergent Patterns in Blind and Sighted Infants. *Psychoanal. Study Child*, 23:264–300.

——. (1969). Libidinal Object Constancy and Mental Representation. *Psychoanal. Study Child*, 24:9–47.

——. (1971a). Intervention in Infancy. *J. Amer. Acad. Child Psychiat.*, 10:381–405.

——. (1971b). Separation Crisis in Two Blind Infants. *Psychoanal. Study Child*, 26:355–371.

——. (1971c). Smiling and Stranger Reaction in Blind Infants. In *Exceptional Infant*, ed. J. Hellmuth, vol. 2, pp. 110–127. New York: Brunner/Mazel.

——. (1974). Blind Infants and Their Mothers: An Examination of the Sign System. In *The Effect of the Infant on Its Caregiver*, ed. M. Lewis & L. Rosenblum, pp. 215–232. New York: John Wiley.

——, with L. Fraiberg. (1977). *Insights from the Blind: Comparative Studies of Blind and Sighted Infants*. New York: Basic Books.

—— & Freedman, D. (1964). Studies in the Ego Development of the Congenitally Blind Child. *Psychoanal. Study Child*, 19:113–169.

——; Siegel, B.; & Gibson, R. (1966). The Role of Sound in the Search Behavior of Blind Infants. *Psychoanal. Study Child*, 21:327–357.

——; Smith, M.; & Adelson, E. (1969). An Educational Program for Blind Infants. *J. Spec. Educ.*, 3:121–139.

Freedman, D. A.; Fox-Kolenda, B. J.; Margileth, D. A.; & Miller, D. H. (1969). The Development of the Use of Sound as a Guide to Affective and Cognitive Behavior: A Two-Phase Process. *Child Dev.*, 40:1099–1105.

Gewirtz, J. L. (1965). The Course of Infant Smiling in Four Child-rearing Environments in Israel. In *Determinants of Infant Behavior*, ed. B. M. Foss, vol. 3, pp. 205–248. London: Methuen.

Griffiths, R. (1954). *The Abilities of Babies: A Study in Mental Measurement*. London: Univ. of London Press.

Morgan, G. A. & Ricciuti, H. N. (1969). Infants' Responses to Strangers During the First Year. In *Determinants of Infant Behavior*, ed. B. M. Foss, vol. 6, pp. 253–272. London: Methuen.

Piaget, J. (1952). *The Origins of Intelligence in Children*. New York: International Universities Press.

——. (1954). *The Construction of Reality in the Child*. New York: Basic Books.

Polak, P. R.; Emde, R. N.; & Spitz, R. A. (1964). The Smiling Response to the Human Face: I. Methodology, Quantification, and Natural History; II. Neural Discrimination and the Onset of Depth Perception. *J. Nerv. Ment. Dis.*, 139:103–109; 407–415.

Provence, S. & Lipton, R. (1962). *Infants in Institutions*. New York: International Universities Press.

Saint-Pierre, J. (1962). Étude des différences entre la recherche active de la personne humaine et celle de l'objet inanime. Master's thesis, University of Montreal.

Schaffer, H. R. & Emerson, P. E. (1964). The Development of Social Attachments in Infancy. *Monographs of the Society for Research in Child Development,* vol. 29, no. 3a.

Spitz, R. A. (1950). *A Genetic Field Theory of Ego Formation.* New York: International Universities Press.

———. (1957). *No and Yes: On the Beginnings of Human Communication.* New York: International Universities Press.

———. (1965). *The First Year of Life.* New York: International Universities Press.

——— & Wolf, K. A. (1946). The Smiling Response: A Contribution to the Ontogenesis of Social Relations. *Genet. Psychol. Monogr.,* 34:57–125.

Stayton, D. J.; Ainsworth, M. D.; & Main, M. B. (1971). The Development of Separation Behavior in the First Year of Life: Protest, Following, and Greeting. Paper presented in part at the biennial meeting of the Society for Research in Child Development, Minneapolis, April 1971.

Tennes, K. H. & Lampl, E. E. (1964). Stranger and Separation Anxiety. *J. Nerv. Ment. Dis.,* 139:247–254.

Wolff, P. H. (1963). Observations on the Early Development of Smiling. In *Determinants of Infant Behavior,* ed. B. M. Foss, vol. 2, pp. 113–138. London: Methuen.

Yarrow, L. J. (1967). The Development of Focussed Relationships During Infancy. In *Exceptional Infant,* ed. J. Hellmuth, vol. 1, pp. 427–442. New York: Brunner/Mazel.

———. (1972). Attachment and Dependency: A Development Perspective. In *Attachment and Dependency,* ed. J. L. Gewirtz, pp. 81–137. Washington, D.C.: Winston.

# Part V

Applications

# 24

## The Mass Media: New Schoolhouse
## for Children

Many, many years ago when I was a child—in the time of the dino-
saurs and Abraham Lincoln, and the Pilgrim Fathers—a home was a
shelter against the dangers outside. I had heard, as a child, that there
was savagery in the world, that men committed murder, that homes
were burglarized, that a child had been kidnapped and ravished, and
that in far-off lands there were revolutions and wars. But all these
things happened in another world. Murderers, kidnappers, and bur-
glars lived on another planet—not so far away as dragons, witches and
monsters, but almost as far—and in any case they had not much more
reality for me than the creatures of the fairy tales. I saw a few movies
when I was a child, carefully selected so as not to bruise a child's
sensitive nature. I was a ripe age for a child before I saw a murder or
horror film, and in those days the industry that has since perfected the
drama of violence was still in its infancy, just cutting its fangs on such
things as Fu Manchu and Dracula.

There were threats of war in my childhood in the twenties, just as
there are now. And once, during such a scare, we children read the
headlines and were terrified. We were not afraid that we would be
killed; children in the twenties were still operating under the old rules
of warfare. We were afraid, of course, that our father might be killed.
We could hardly bring ourselves to tell our parents what we feared.
And then, when bed-time came and we couldn't sleep and we were
exhausted by our unspent emotion, we blurted out our fears to our
parents. And what do you think they said to us? It lifted our spirits and
sent us off to dreamless sleep. They said, "Don't worry. There's noth-

ing to be afraid of. There will never be another war." Did they mean it? Did they believe it? Of course they did.

The world in which I lived was undeniably a different world from that of my mother's and my grandmother's, and yet my upbringing was not so different from theirs. In my family and many thousands of others, the laws governing childish lying, stubbornness, greediness, talking back to elders, and quarreling with siblings were transmitted cleanly down the line of three generations with serene confidence on the part of the child rearers and without serious challenge from the young—who were under the impression that laws governing family manners were written into the American Constitution. All this seems incredible to me now, for I cannot imagine how a child today could be governed so completely by his family code and insulated to such a degree from external and hostile forces.

## The Crack in the Family Fortress

At this point I will not go into the question of how much shelter a child needs for healthy growth. I only wish to point out that it was *possible* thirty years ago for parents to protect their children from influences which they felt to be alien to their educational purposes and that there were few competing agencies for the control and influence of a child's imagination and conduct.

For today's child, a home is no longer a shelter against the dangers outside. The child is a fascinated spectator of the whole of our world. From the earliest years he can control a switch that causes the window blind to fly up and reveal the most ordinary and extraordinary aspects of this world in a continuous parade before his eyes.

It is a parade of exhorting statesmen, gloomy commentators, and ladies praising floor-wax; of cowboys and nasal sheriffs and district attorneys and Neanderthal gunmen; of the story-hour lady with fruity voice and the monster decanted from a madman's laboratory; of Mozart selling 1960 station wagons and station wagons selling Mozart; of hopped-up comedians fading out in a riot of canned laughter.

The child will hear his President, his congressmen, and atomic physicists speak man-to-man with him about the perils of the world. He may watch the brotherhood of nations to see how older and wiser minds are at work on the problems that imperil him. He may finally escape from the wisdom of his elders to the diversion of ghouls or interplanetary monsters.

The average nine-year-old today has experienced the best and the worst of our world, and we can only hope that he is in favor of letting it go on. It is true that he is far better informed on world affairs and scientific developments than the children of my generation. And it's also true that he has a lot more to worry about. We can hope that this precocious knowledge will bring him political wisdom when he receives our legacy in twelve years.

He is precocious about lots of other things, too. He has a wider knowledge of the habits and customs of the underworld than the average sociologist in my time. His knowledge of sordid domestic intimacies and intrigues is nearly equal to that of a child reared in a slum. He has witnessed domestic brawling on his television screen; he is wise about love and unfaithfulness and divorce and psychiatrists and mental hospitals and alcoholism and dope. He can witness three or four murders on the television screen before his 8:30 bedtime and double the number when the sitter is there on parents' night out. On Saturday afternoons, when he is in the mood for a change of pace, the local movie house will provide a carefully selected children's program featuring exotic forms of torture, vampires, and monsters from outer space.

## The Ubiquitous New Educators

We are obliged to reckon with the mass media as a potent educational force in our society, and I use "educational" in the neutral sense, not necessarily as elevating but as capable of influencing ideas and emotions. The scale of this education is so vast that the primary institutions of education in our society, the home and the school, must struggle to compete. Our scientific measurement of the influence of mass media is fragmentary and inconclusive. We can only guess at the magnitude of this influence through consumer studies in those areas where media are employed to educate a consumer's appetite or to create a new market. Here the crude test of buying and consumption may be applied to measure the educational means, and, at least in this measurable area, we have amassed a mountain of data which testify to the efficacy and potency of education through mass media.

If the subject of the influence of mass media on today's children has brought all of us together today, it is because we recognize the power of these new educational forces that go their own way unhampered by tradition or the social obligations of families and schools and frequently indifferent to the values that we hold for our children.

The prerogative of a parent to exclude unwelcome educational influences is not easily exercised in the home today. At least one of these ubiquitous educators, the television set, has planted itself securely in the family living room, a permanent boarder, often loud-mouthed, garrulous, uncouth, and boring. Everyone fears that the Boarder is having a bad influence upon the children, but it is difficult to silence him and difficult to exclude him. He can be animated and given voice by any child over twelve months of age capable of turning a switch, and he can be silenced only by tirelessly vigilant parents. He could be excluded on grounds of corrupting the young, but sometimes he redeems himself after the children go to bed by a creditable performance of music or drama. "So you see," the parents say to each other, "if we got rid of the Boarder we would miss some Very Fine Programs."

### Violence in a Post-War World

The appetite for violence which so disturbs us in our children has been given strong nourishment and encouragement by mass media, but we cannot examine the influence of horror and crime programs without reference to the climate of our culture. It is not only through mass media that violence is transmitted in our culture. Violence is in the air and we are all affected by it.

After every war, the aggression that had been liberated for survival and had its legitimate target in the enemy, returns with the soldier to be subdued once again. But something remains, and without the sanctions of war and a target, it discharges itself in the cultural atmosphere—an aimless, free-floating aggression that roams the streets looking for something to do. The social institutions that normally reinforce the prohibitions against aggression have themselves been crippled by war. This means, of course, that an increase in acts of violence is a regular occurrence following war. And even when violence is not discharged through acts, it fills the imagination and makes itself felt in the culture. We should not forget that neither World War II nor the Korean War was concluded with a return to peace-time, and the threat of atomic warfare has never left us in fifteen years.

## Collective Daydreams

It is not easy to see the effects of omnipresent danger in our society. Certainly we behave as if the danger were not there. But if we want to know a society's state of mind, we should examine not only the external signs, but the myths and daydreams of that society. If a society faces the danger of extinction with a passive face, this tells us nothing in itself. But if that society is also addicted to collective daydreams of violence in which life is threatened by inhuman gangsters or monsters bent on world destruction, we must treat the daydream as the other side of the passive exterior. While it is true that fantasies of world destruction are as old as the race, when such fantasies take the form of a community daydream they tell us that the community is reacting inwardly to the great peril, that it recognizes the danger in fantasy while it ignores it in reality.

It would be folly to blame the vulgar crime shows of television for the disease that affects us and our children. We are united in these morbid daydreams of violence and horror, and their vulgarity should not hide from us the primitive fear that has made violence one of the forms of family entertainment.

For aggression must also be seen as a primitive defense against danger. It is regularly brought into service during wartime and doubtless has insured survival cf men in battle and of whole communities and nations in times past. Today, when the threat of extinction hangs over the whole human community, this preoccupation with violence may be seen as a reactivation of this archaic mode of defense.

Every child who has grown up during the past fifteen years has been confronted with a fact that no other child in the lifetime of the human family has had to face. He has known from early childhood that a weapon exists that can destroy him and his family and everyone and everything that constitutes his world, and there is no defense against this weapon and no possible flight from it; that it can be launched by an unseen enemy thousands of miles away or set off as a madman's caprice by a man at a control button. This is terrible knowledge for a child to own and there is something that is even more terrible in this for a child. Almost as soon as he acquires this knowledge, he will learn that his parents themselves are helpless against this danger, that they have no defense against the danger and no means of protecting him.

## A Primitive Defense

Now we know that in the ordinary course of child development, a child masters his fears in certain typical ways. First and foremost, he relies upon his parents to protect him at times of extreme danger and he endows them with magical properties in overcoming dangerous enemies or dealing with threats from the external world. Second, he relies upon his own reality testing to deal with many of these external dangers. A witch isn't real; monsters are only pretend. But now what happens to a child when reality confirms his most terrible fears, when the danger of total annihilation is uttered daily in the press, on the radio and television, and in the classroom?

When the worst fears of a child can be confirmed in reality, the child loses his own best means of dealing with external danger. And when he discovers simultaneously that his parents themselves are helpless against such a danger, he is left without defense and without an ally against extreme peril. None of us can imagine what it is like to be a child today, to be helpless against the most extreme dangers and to be confronted in his own living room, in his classroom, with the full knowledge of the real dangers that exist in our world.

The child who occupies himself with fantasies of destruction, his own fantasies or the packaged daydreams of the screen, is a child who is attempting to master danger by means of a primitive defense. The aggressive fantasies give the child the illusion of being active, of fighting against the very dangers that make him feel helpless.

## Aggression and the Social Goal

But now we come to the most complex part of the problem. We can understand to some measure the psychological forces at work here, but we are educators of children, and an educator cannot be content with an understanding of motive. He must ask, "How does all this affect a child's development, and how will this promote or retard our educational objectives for the child and the larger social goals that always determine child-rearing? If a child is reacting to the stress and dangers of these times by an increased pleasure in violence, will this serve his mental well-being, and will a child reared on this basis be equipped to deal with the problems of his society?"

We have learned through painful social experiments that a child's mental well-being depends in large measure on his control of aggressive urges and the employment of the energy of the aggressive drive for a vast range of mental activities that are far removed from the original mode and aims of the drives. We discovered through the period of licensed aggression of children from which our society has recently emerged, that children who were permitted free discharge of aggressive impulses were made as anxious in their own way as the severely inhibited child of another era. The child who was not required to control his aggression showed us that he was afraid of himself, afraid of his dangerous impulses and their consequences, and fearful of monstrous retaliation from the outside world. We learned that the child who freely discharged his aggression whenever the impulse seized him was a child who often suffered difficulties in learning, and showed little inclination toward intellectual and creative activities. There was, of course, no motive to employ aggressive energy in sublimated forms as long as it could be freely discharged in action. All of this has caused us to take a sober view of the management of aggression in the child.

We have also learned that in normal and healthy child development, aggressive fantasies have their place and may harmlessly fill a need while the child is learning to manage his drives. But when we find that fantasies of violence and destruction fill a large part of a child's imaginary world and crowd out or exclude other varieties of imagination, we are no longer dealing with healthy adaptive tendencies but deep anxieties which the ego attempts to master through repetition as in a terror dream. Whether the child is the inventor of the morbid fantasy or makes use of the morbid fantasies of comic books or screen stories, we know that the consuming appetite for such fantasies arises from deep and pervasive anxiety and that the morbid fantasy will not cure but may, perversely, create its own appetite for more and stronger doses.

## The Danger in the Defense

But now surely the question will be raised, "If we regard the increasing appetite for violence among children as a reaction to the tensions and real dangers which surround our children today, why shouldn't we speak of this behavior as 'adaptive' to a pathological world? If destruction threatens, isn't mobilization of aggression one of the ego's oldest measures to insure survival?"

It is true that aggression as a primitive defense against danger has served the human race for most of its history at times of great peril. And this unleashing of aggression was "adaptive," in that it worked for survival. But all this is past. For the first time in man's history, his survival depends solely upon his humanity. His intelligence, his morality, and his renunciation of destructive tendencies in his nature are the only measures he owns to meet the new future adaptively. The archaic defense of aggression and the unleashing of sadistic impulses will only bring him more rapidly to extinction.

## Learning to Modify Aggression

I do not think anyone who attempts to see a culture whole will accuse the mass media of responsibility for today's violence, but it is not difficult to show how mass media can affect children's attitudes toward violence and brutality, and to see the effect on children of the steady diet of murder and sadism provided by mass media today.

Mass media have not created the appetite for violence; they have only discovered an appetite and expend their talents on increasing the market for it. And they have discovered that one of their steadiest and most loyal consumer groups can be found among children. They are not motivated by a desire to corrupt the young; their only motive is to build a market for a breakfast food or a soft drink.

The manufacturer of breakfast foods is understandably outraged to hear the objections of educators. He does not consider himself an educator of children. But anyone who brings a child into contact with his ideas, anyone who purports to represent the adult world, and anyone who makes use of a child's imagination in any way becomes an educator of the child for all practical purposes. And if the average child spends only three hours a day before a television screen, we will have to admit that a substantial part of his education is in the hands of the manufacturer of breakfast foods, his script and ad writers.

What concerns us first of all is that certain of the educational aims of the mass media are directly opposed to the educational objectives our society holds for children. While all children manifest aggressive urges and all young children reveal pleasure in destruction and violence, we consider in our society—and in all civilized societies—that these aggressive and destructive urges must undergo a radical alteration in order for civilized values to survive. The aggressive drive and its original aims will be greatly modified in the course of a child's development so that its energy may serve useful social goals. In the civilized human being, we expect to see disgust and revulsion against sadism, the original infantile pleasure in destruction repressed and no longer discernible. This is one of the forms of repression that is absolutely necessary for the survival of human values, and today, one may add, it is absolutely necessary for the survival of the human race.

Now it is also true that even those of us who have acquired a civilized reaction of revulsion to sadism will discover that the repeated exposure to scenes of violence and sadism may partially wear away the feeling of revulsion. The flooding of our sensory organs with repeated, strong doses of horror, will eventually create an armoring of the personality against the onslaught; we raise the barriers against the overwhelming stimulus until we are no longer able to react appropriately. The danger for our children is self-evident. A child whose senses are flooded daily by the sight and sounds of brutality is in danger of losing the capacity to summon revulsion against brutality.

*Separating Sex from Brutality*

There is a second indictment to be brought against the education through mass media. Along with naked brutality is the admixture of sex and brutality found in movies, TV, and comic books.

Now, it may be argued that children themselves conceive of adult sexuality in sadistic terms, and this is true. But it is generally understood that it is the task of education to gradually achieve a separation of the sadistic elements from the sexual, and in fact, it is expected that a large measure of this sexually linked sadism undergoes repression in normal childhood. The child normally gives up his sadistic conception of sexuality through sex education and reality testing. For while he cannot, of course, make direct observation, he does make the observation that since the adults he knows do not behave like sadists in the daytime, it is highly unlikely that they should be sadists at night. It is worth mentioning now that children who are reared in homes where violence and cruelty erupt in their everyday family life will have great difficulty in giving up their sadistic-sexual fantasies because reality seems to support these fantasies. But now what happens to children today who do not experience brutality in their families but are witnesses of brutality on the TV screen, at the neighborhood movie house, or in horror comics? I would consider that insofar as their own parents present good models, the children may correct their sadistic-sexual fantasies, but I am certain that this education to reality is made infinitely more difficult for even the best of parents because of the education of the screen and comic books.

## Emphasis on Realism

Sooner or later, in all such discussion, the rebuttal of the fairy tale is brought in. What about the monsters of fairy tales and the cruelties of witches and ogres? Is there any difference between these monsters and the vampires and bat-men who entertain today's children? There are these differences. The fairy tale world is a frankly invented world, and the child who enters it makes a pact with a storyteller to willingly suspend belief. The fairy tale keeps its side of the bargain by never representing its people or its events as real and by presenting its story in such extravagantly fantastic terms that no child above the age of two with the word "pretend" in his vocabulary should have any trouble in naming this world as "pretend."

The child reader of the fairy tale supplies his own pictures, for the most part, and is not confronted by realistic representations of sadism and horror. The wolf who devours Little Red Riding Hood's grandmother does not emerge with bloody fangs panting for his next victim in a thirty-minute chase through the forest; he accomplishes this in one sentence in the standard version of the story: "The wolf ate up the grandmother." No sadistic lingering before the act and no lusting after the grandmother. No posturing as a human or a halfhuman; no pretense of being decanted in a madman's laboratory.

Apart from an over-enthusiastic approach to sadism and brutality, the movie and TV screen make a pact with their viewers which is very different from that which the fairy tale makes with its readers. If the fairy tale world is frankly unreal, the screen world attempts to make the unreal as realistic as possible, and employs all the techniques at its disposal to make the viewers feel that he is a witness, if not a participant, in the events which it represents. It is extraordinarily easy to do this with motion pictures. As soon as a picture is animated, it gives the illusion of reality. Even a screen presentation of a fairy tale will produce a very different effect from the story that is read. The witch in Snow White, who can be tolerated by most children in story form, may provoke terror in children who see the movie version. The animated picture makes the witch "real" to the child viewer.

To the child whose reality sense is not yet firmly established, the world of the screen is very close to the world of reality. If we question the young viewers, we will find that they believe that their TV heroes have a real existence some place, that when they leave the screen they pursue their vocations, eternally rounding up the bad guys, piloting ships through space, grilling arson suspects, and, of course, promoting the sponsor's product. And this means, too, that when the child views the screen stories of murder, brutality, and sadism, that the realistic presentation of these stories brings the child close to being an eye-witness or a participant.

I think it would not be far-fetched to propose that a large part of what a child views on the TV and movie screen is incorporated into his view of the world. We know that, throughout the early years of life, a child must construct the world of reality from his own observations. A story world and a world of the imagination can be put in their place by the young child by the time he enters school. But what does a child do with his screen world? To what extent are sadism, brutality, and sordid domestic affairs built into his view of the world?

## The Abstraction of Evil

Inevitably, too, the sponsors of these programs will rebut us with Huck Finn's alcoholic father, the vices of Mr. Fagin and his gang, Little Emily's fall from virtue, and a number of other seamy characters from the classics. "Why pick on us?" they say. "What's the difference as far as the kids are concerned?" The difference, we must make clear, is not to be found in comparative vice, but in the treatment of vice. Pap Finn had the good fortune to fall into the hands of Samuel Clemens, and while his vice is not a shade nicer than that of many a lout on a TV screen, I am in favor of introducing Pap and his delinquent son to any school-age child who cares to meet them. Huck's old man is a brute but he has psychological integrity as a character. He is, therefore, human. Unlike the brutes who emerge from the commercial arts, Pap is not an abstraction of a bad guy or a caricature of evil; he is thoroughly realized as a character and the problem of evil becomes a *human* problem in this work.

Evil is given a human connection by establishing it as a part of a character named Pap. Evil is human-centered throughout the complex development of the novel. Man's inhumanity to man is represented in the cruelty of a man to his son and again in the cruelty of the white man to the black man. When evil is represented as part of the human problem, we do not need to fear corruption of a child; it can only enlarge his humanity and give quality and depth to his moral judgments. It is the abstraction of evil in commercial fiction that corrupts.

## Only the Sound-Effects

Writers of movie and television scripts have neither the time nor the talent to invest their characters with a personality or a significant life. Neither their lives nor their brutal deaths can have meaning for the audience; for all practical purposes the victim is a corpse before he is murdered. A child who is exposed to the monotonous repetition of death and destruction in a mindless world cannot acquire a tragic view of death, he cannot experience grief, or sorrow or outrage or even simple human bewilderment before the fact of man's inhumanity. He only learns to brace himself for the sound-effects of death.

Among other reasons, we may object to the legion of crooks who invade the family television room because they have no reason to present themselves except to give a fast jolt to the psyche and fade out. An imagination that is treated to psychic jolts at frequent intervals may become restricted to a narrow range of emotion in which it requires strong excitement to produce pleasure. This accusation cannot be made against a literary work of merit, because if the work has merit at all, it has range and complexity. The brutality of Pap is not employed to slug the reader or to give him brief, sweet excitement; the brutality is part of the aesthetic scheme; it gives texture to a work that covers an extraordinary range of human emotion. A young reader does not know this, of course, but he experiences it as such. If he allows the novel to affect his imagination and if the work leads him into intimacy with its characters, he will know that Pap exists in the story in order to make the story and not for the purpose of titillating him.

## The Moral Issue

If we want to consider the issue strictly on moral grounds, I would like to argue that any work that deepens a child's imagination will strengthen his moral development. Morality, in the deepest sense, derives from the possibility in a human being of entering imaginatively into many lives and many egos. It is in this sense that literature may influence moral development.

We do not want a moral education for our children that derives from cheap "lessons." If, after an orgy of sadism, the television crook is rounded up and sentenced, the producer should not feel that he has paid his respects to civilized morality. The moral lessons of television crime fare teach that crime does not pay and the innocent will be avenged. But a stern morality needs to deal with the fact that crime often goes unpunished and virtue may go unrewarded, and the only conscience worthy of the name is one that can deal with these cruel facts and not yield an inch to the argument of gain. A stern conscience offers self-esteem as the only reward. And somewhere between the ages of three and sixteen, a child must learn to embrace this melancholy fact and find consolation in it.

We cannot single out commercial fiction in criticizing a culture that furnishes children with cheap codes of conduct. But there are few teachers as ubiquitous as that vulgar Boarder in the family room, and an instrument that has demonstrated its success in influencing markets cannot be lightly dismissed as an educator of opinion, of tastes, of manners and morals.

I do not mean, by this, that the vulgar fiction of television is capable of turning our children into delinquents. The influence of such fiction on children's attitudes and conduct is really more subtle. We need to remember that it is the parents who are the progenitors of conscience and that a child who has strong ties to his parents will not overthrow their teachings more easily than he could abandon his parents themselves. I do not think any of us here needs to fear this kind of corruption of our children. But the effectiveness of our moral education may be substantially reduced if a child's culture does not support the teachings of parents.

## The Gesture of Exclusion

How can we teach revulsion against sadism and the destruction of human life when the child's commercial fiction feeds the appetite for sadism and makes murder trivial? How shall we teach a child the difficult moral achievement of judging his own conduct and of becoming answerable to his own conscience when the crime story preaches its imbecile moral lessons for hours each day? The burden on the parent as moral educator becomes a very heavy one. A child who has strong ties of love will not repudiate his parents' teaching, but he will have great difficulty in summoning the emotional reactions that must accompany such attitudes when his culture makes a mockery of them. The result is not, then, a reversal of parental standards, but a blunting of moral sensibilities.

Then, too, we must reflect upon our position as moral educators when we teach our children to renounce sadism, and destructive tendencies within themselves, at the same time that we hold daily open house to the underworld of television, its gangsters, extortionists, and assorted ghouls in the family living room. It has always been the prerogative of parents to exclude unwelcome influences from the home, to declare their opposition to alien and hostile forces by not keeping company with them. This is not to say that one pretended they did not exist, which is an absurd position for a parent, but to make explicit the moral stand of the family through a gesture of inhospitality or exclusion. During the years that a child must learn his parents' stand on a variety of moral issues it is undoubtedly a help to him to know which ideas are given hospitality in his home and which are not. But how is he to make sense out of an ambiguous parental stand which deplores and abhors on the one hand and permits and entertains on the other?

## A Firm Parental Policy

Inevitably we are confronted with the ugly word censorship. As an adult I am opposed to any authority that attempts to judge what I may read or hear. But I do believe strongly that parents and our society have certain rights of censorship where children are concerned. I consider this part of the protective function of all adults on behalf of children. Children need the protection of adults against their own impulses and against overwhelming dangers on the outside. I do not mean by this a hovering and over-anxious protection on the part of adults, but a protection that grows out of adult wisdom and knowledge of child development.

No child can be asked to cope with a world that assaults his eyes and ears with the sounds of death and catastrophe for hours every day. In a world where a child's education still remained in his parents' hands, we cannot imagine a parent who would choose to entertain his children with stories of crime and horror for three hours a day or more; nor can we imagine parents introducing young children to stories of sordid bedroom intimacies, violent lovers' quarrels, underworld intrigue, and nightclub brawls. If parents, in their own education, choose to exclude certain types of experiences from the home, it is because they recognize that an immature ego cannot cope with massive excitement or omnipresent danger and needs the protective barriers provided by adults and by his home.

For these reasons I do not feel that parents need be faint-hearted about exercising their ancient prerogative of censorship on behalf of the children. We must all admit that such censorship is not easily exercised when unwelcome visitors can be admitted to the home by any child who can turn a switch, but a firm parental policy can go a long way in excluding the most objectionable programs and will go an equally long way in backing up the beliefs and standards of the home and in making the moral stand of parents explicit.

## 25

## The American Reading Problem

In 1955 a backward schoolboy called Johnny became the central figure in a national literacy scandal. Rudolf Flesch's *Why Johnny Can't Read* produced domestic ferment over such issues as phonics vs. "whole-word recognition," the controlled vocabulary, and reading texts. An exposé of primers turned up two vapid children named Dick and Jane whose ordinary discourse in fifty re-usable words would have unfitted them for the teaching of Yahoos. In the fever of reform a public-school system in Wisconsin restored the McGuffey readers in the early grades.

Anyone who has followed the Johnny story will know that Dr. Flesch's book was followed by a number of sequels. In Arthur S. Trace's *What Ivan Knows That Johnny Doesn't* (1961), we meet Johnny in a post-sputnik academic joust with a Russian boy in which, grade for grade, he again goes down to shabby defeat. In *Tomorrow's Illiterates*, a collection edited by Charles Walcutt (1961), Johnny is failed once more by consensus of a group of educators and a psychoanalyst. More recently Johnny made an appearance in the pages of *Partisan Review*: "Why Johnny Can't Write" (Gross, 1964). This was a review of Lynch and Evans's *High School English Textbooks* (1964) in which it was clear that the boy was getting deeper and deeper into academic peril. The reader who has followed Johnny in his downward path to wisdom must brace himself for the next volume in the series. If Johnny's instruction in phonics has removed the impediment to reading he may be a college freshman next year. The test is yet to come. He can sound out Raskolnikov. But will he dig big D.?

This decade of public commotion over reading methods and the teaching of literature has not yet produced major reforms. In *Innova-*

*tion in Education,* a collection of essays edited by Matthew B. Miles (1964), there are reports of sweeping curriculum changes in mathematics and the physical sciences. But nationwide research on the state of the curriculum in reading shows no significant changes in methods or in the curriculum itself during the past thirty years.

The curriculum that embraces reading in the early grades, and language and literature in the later years, is an edifice that has extraordinary resistance to time, climate, assault by enemies, or abrasion through use. The durable siblings, Dick and Jane, have survived their national scandal in robust health and are still in business in hundreds of schools throughout the country. As it turns out, there are also about a dozen more primer series in current use in which pairs exactly like Dick and Jane (Alice and Jerry, for example) exhort each other to run, jump, look, and see in a controlled vocabulary of fifty words. Teachers who have worked with these texts have expressed their opinions to me in language that is rich in gastrointestinal metaphor. The durability of these primers, then, cannot be attributed to the support of educators alone.

The same conservative tendency may be seen in the secondary-school curriculum. For thirty years *Julius Caesar, Silas Marner,* and *The Ancient Mariner* have been interred in the common tomb of the tenth-grade curriculum. By some remarkable consensus of a long dead committee, this ghostly company was assembled in the thirties and the order for release or amnesty never came through. They were there when I was in high school; they are still there twenty-five years later. I had always thought that they were brought together on the basis of a local or regional taste (not necessarily that of tenth-graders), but I have since learned that they constitute a kind of sacred fellowship in the tenth grade of schools throughout the country. No man can now say why Caesar has greater glory in the tenth grade than the ninth, or why Silas was elected for martyrdom when the rest of the George Eliot canon went scot-free.

This conservative tendency might speak for the enduring values of literature, except that the curriculum confers immortality with lavish impartiality. In one tenth-grade curriculum that I reviewed, I found *Julius Caesar, Silas Marner*—and *A Lantern in Her Hand* by Bess Streeter Aldrich (a best seller of the thirties). In the seventy-two high-school anthologies studied by Lynch and Evans, the drama selections include *Julius Caesar, The King and I, Life with Father,* and a substantial number of radio and television plays that might have been lost to literature if it were not for the intervention of the anthologists.

How a work gets into a curriculum is not so difficult to explain. The job is done by a curriculum committee that may fairly be compared to an ecumenical council. Modernizing the curriculum—which is sometimes done when a new chairman of the department is appointed—is so debilitating to a faculty, so costly in personal enmities and wounds, that I have never known it to happen twice in the tenure of one chairman. All this means that once Bess Streeter Aldrich gets locked up in the tenth grade, there is no academic machinery for bringing about her release. A curriculum committee is dissolved after its work is done, but there is no provision for a parole board or a board of review to investigate cases that have been committed on the basis of insufficient evidence.

All this sounds formidable in itself in considering change, but the problem expands as we study the other agencies that are engaged in the making and preservation of the curriculum. The manufacture of primers, textbooks, anthologies, "workbooks," and audio-visual materials is a major industry which exerts an influence in the setting of a curriculum that is comparable to that of any intramural agency within the school system. For while every school system does its own job of selection of texts from the materials offered by publishers, there is extraordinary uniformity among the texts available. This uniformity is not the result of conspiracy but of compliance on the part of the publishers with educational shibboleths such as the graded vocabulary and the "grade level" of literary works. And since the writers and editors of all these texts are chosen on the basis of conventional qualifications, the textbook industry inevitably supports the most conservative tendencies in the system itself. Innovation or novelty entails a heady financial risk.

But it is not inertia and conservatism alone that stall innovation in the schools. The introduction of a new curriculum is an undertaking of the same magnitude as that of retooling an industry. Within any local school system, the product of each third-grade classroom, for example, must be interchangeable with that of any other third-grade classroom on the same track. An innovation has to be system-wide. New textbooks must be introduced and other textbooks must be rewritten. Teachers must be retrained. Certification standards for teachers are usually involved. And with all this there must be agreement among the top brass regarding the need for, and extent of, curricular innovation. The seniority system practically guarantees that the top-echelon school people will not be innovators.

It is instructive to see how major curricular reforms have been achieved in fields other than English. The much publicized recent innovations in the teaching of physical science, for example, did not originate in the schools, but rather in the Physical Science Study Committee started in 1955 by Professor J. R. Zacharias of MIT. The striking feature about the project (and the one that was ultimately responsible for its success) was the fact that the physical scientists took upon themselves the job of developing new materials. They did not seek massive backing from school people but operated from the first on the assumption that "only physical scientists could define the structure of modern physical science." The new materials were devised, tested in practice (with the cooperation of a few institutions, mainly in the Boston area), and revised over a period of years. In time, scientists at five universities in the North and along both coasts began to use the Committee's materials to instruct high-school teachers in modern physical science at summer and in-service institutes. Estimates indicate that by 1962-63 about a fifth of all secondary-school physics students were using PSSC materials.

While this approach cost the Committee some support among professional educators, it is questionable in my view whether any educational innovation of such magnitude could have been achieved in such a short time if the innovators had chosen any other route. And in this case it was the classroom physics teachers who tested the materials and who played an active role in bringing curriculum changes into the system.

So far no Zacharias has appeared to lead the English curriculum out of the wilderness. If one does appear, he will most certainly get into a jurisdictional dispute that may tie up things for another decade. For while the professors of physics may define "the structure of physical science," and even a school bureaucrat cannot argue the point, there is no parallel for this authority in the hierarchy of English scholarship and teaching. A Zacharias-for-English who emerged from upper academia with a mission to define the aims and structure of a public-school education in reading, language, and literature would have his credentials challenged before he reached Morningside Heights. For whatever his qualifications might be in "defining the structure" of a college English program, he would have no credentials in the pedagogical science that underlies the public-school teaching of English. His academic views on the study of literature would be sternly challenged by another group of "definers," the curriculum-makers in the elementary and secondary schools. The public-school English curriculum is not seen by its makers as a formal course in the study of literature (even in high school it aims at little more than modest literacy on the student's part); they see it in terms of the acquisition of "reading skills," "the controlled vocabulary," "vocabulary building," the "grade level" of literary works, and the relationship of literature to the developmental needs of children. In all likelihood Zacharias-for-English would be deficient in these areas of pedagogical science.

To be sure, this emphasis on "reading skills" is not as arbitrary as it may seem. For it appears that much of the instruction in English during the first ten grades (and sometimes beyond) is still carrying the burden of teaching children and adolescents how to read—and by this I mean helping children achieve mechanical mastery of reading. The study of literature becomes incidental.

## II

The basic problem, then, is still reading, and thus the controversy over methods of reading instruction continues. Much of the primary teaching in reading still centers on "look-say" or "whole-word recognition." When the child shows initial mastery in the sight-reading of approximately three hundred words, which may occur in the second or third grade, he is introduced to phonics; by the sixth grade, he is presumably equipped to sound out any new word he finds in print.

Proponents of those reading methods that employ phonics from the very beginning of primary reading instruction claim that their students can read one thousand to three thousand words at the end of the first grade. While it may be argued that this in itself proves nothing, there are some crucial problems involved. First, the rate of building a reading vocabulary is progressive, and there is strong evidence that the "look-say" readers lag behind, grade for grade, the students who receive early phonics training. For example, a typical fourth-grade reading text geared to the whole-word recognition method will use a vocabulary of about fifteen hundred words. An instructional system that employs phonics from the start can work up to a ten-thousand word vocabulary in the fourth grade, as Trace shows in his analysis of Soviet readers. But the real significance of the reading-vocabulary ranges comes through in the reading materials themselves. Even in the second grade a child with a reading vocabulary of fifteen hundred words can be given selections that make no compromise with taste and engage his interest and imagination; and with a vocabulary of ten thousand words, a nine-year-old can tackle almost anything. But a vocabulary of one hundred and fifty words condemns a seven-year-old to Dick and Jane, and the slow accretion of vocabulary in the next two to four years reduces him to the relatives of Dick and Jane or, at best, a simple stripped-down story that provides reading exercise but no exercise of the imagination.

The so-called "controlled vocabulary" that is built into the look-say method and the graded reading texts that are employed in most public schools have their own rationale. The teaching of reading through whole-word recognition requires that students memorize each word by the way it looks on the page, much as a Chinese student must learn his ideographs. Since the word must be recognized by its shape alone, each word in the text has to undergo hundreds of repetitions, and new words can be introduced only slowly. Mastery of reading through a look-say method is a prodigious feat of memory for the child in the early grades. The problems of "reading disability" which have grown out of this method are the subject of a vast literature, but I can testify as a clinician that a very high proportion of such failures can in fact be attributed to the method. Very often the remedial measures used for these non-readers consist of nothing more than the teaching of a phonics method. But even the child who survives the look-say system is frequently a careless reader who produces bizarre misreadings and approximations and eccentric spellings.

Whether or not a child becomes an adequate or a good reader through the look-say method is closely linked to social class. The reasons are very complex, but one factor can be weighed heavily: a child who has a home that provides incentives to reading can become independent of the quality or method of school instruction, independent of the stifling primers and the tedious workbooks that destroy the appetite for reading in the early grades. The child who must depend entirely upon his school for instruction in reading and incentives will not fare so well. And while primary-school educators argue strongly that the underprivileged child does not have "reading readiness" and that cultural factors have depressed his I.Q. and his potential for learning, the question of reading method comes back into the picture again. Those systems which employ a phonics approach from the start have a very small percentage of reading failures *even among children with I.Q.s in the eighties and nineties;* nor does the social-class factor affect the ability to learn the mechanics of reading in those ways which are reported by the systems employing sight-reading methods. In *Tomorrow's Illiterates,* Walcutt claims that approximately one-third of young adults in America are "seriously retarded" in reading.

The question of whether today's children are reading better or worse than children of forty years ago cannot be fairly evaluated, since instruments of measurement and systematic collection of data are themselves not much older than the system of reading that is in dispute. I found one item, however, which is sobering: Walcutt reports that during the revision of the Stanford-Binet Intelligence Test in 1955 it was found that twelve-year-olds were reading on the average only as well as ten-year-olds had been reading twenty and forty years earlier, when the two previous editions of the same test had been issued.

The proponents of look-say have barricaded themselves behind a formidable wall of research findings which, they contend, support and justify the method. These findings, as well as the assumptions on which reading research has been based, have been given a rough going-over by a number of critics. Much of the early theorizing about whole-word recognition was derived from a Gestalt psychology that was badly mangled by the educational psychologists. In contemporary psychology, the theory collapses entirely. That which is seen as a single configuration, Donald Hebb (one of the leading figures in contemporary perceptual psychology) demonstrates, is actually achieved through an additive process in which the eye scans the figure but perceives it as a whole. The early proponents of look-say had correctly observed that good readers perceive words as wholes, then leaped from this observation to an untenable generalization—that is, if good readers read whole words, then good readers can be made through teaching whole-word recognition.

Pieties regarding research abound in the field of reading instruction today, but an independent analysis of this research by two social scientists (Barton and Wilder) shows that much of it is of low quality, conducted by poorly trained people, and is little influenced by findings in other disciplines. The elaborate teaching apparatus in the elementary-school reading program—the basal readers, the workbooks, the exercises, the building of "word attack skills"—is widely accepted by teachers as the sacred finding of research. But the reading researchers interviewed by Barton and Wilder seemed much less certain of their own product, and only a third agreed with the teachers on the scientific status of reading manuals.

A large part of the elementary-school student's time is devoted to the acquisition of "reading skills" through workbook exercises which are designed to develop mechanical mastery. They bore the young and add immeasurably to the revulsion against the subject, Reading. The scientific rationale of the workbook is dubious, but there is a consensus among teachers that they give wholesome occupation to two out of three reading groups during the time that the teacher is working with the third. The question may fairly be asked whether the same amount of time spent in reading books might not produce a reader with the same or better mechanical skills. There is the common sense argument that a story provides a bribe in reading that cannot be provided by an exercise book, that the child who simply reads books in quantity, following the lure of the story, can acquire "reading skills" effortlessly, quite unconsciously.

The effects of a reading program based upon a restricted vocabulary and simplified texts reach into all other parts of the curriculum in the elementary grades. The average child in the fourth grade with a reading vocabulary of fifteen hundred words must be provided with texts in history, geography, and physical science that do not tax his limited vocabulary and shaky mechanical skills. This means, of course, that the texts are severely restricted in content and that the diction is in a class with that of Dick and Jane. The poverty of these texts is tacitly acknowledged by the publishers who provide handsome color illustrations and attractive formats to lure the child into the bleak interior. The drab vocabulary and the mechanical rhythms of the prose have the effect of obliterating meaning and reducing all facts to the same order of importance. Thus there is a consistent downgrading in the teaching of all subjects to accommodate the limitations of the reading instruction program.

The effects of this downgrading are seen most clearly in the teaching of literature. As we have already noted, the problems of achieving simple mechanical skill in reading occupy a major part of the curriculum during the first six grades. The average child who has completed the typical fifth-grade reader has a reading vocabulary in the range of twenty-five hundred words. He has been cut off from the best of children's literature and provided with a kind of subliterary sludge that may permanently impair his digestion of printed material. In all this time, he may have encountered no work of literary merit—a fact which cannot be blamed so much on his teachers as on the failure of our better stylists to write in a vocabulary of fifty to twenty-five hundred words.

He may still be struggling with the mechanical problems of reading in the eighth or ninth grades, at which point the curriculum-makers introduce him to his literary heritage. In a typical eighth-grade anthology in a series called *Adventures in Literature*, the thirteen-year-old student will meet this extraordinary company: Longfellow ("Evangeline" and "Paul Revere's Ride"), Phyllis McGinley and Emily Dickinson, Charles Lindbergh, Robert Browning, William Shakespeare ("Under the Greenwood Tree"), Mary Roberts Rinehart, Dwight D. Eisenhower, and thirty-eight different writers of light verse, one-act radio plays, and sports stories whose names have not previously been linked with William Shakespeare. In this anthology Mark Twain is represented by a television play: "Tom Sawyer: The Glorious Whitewasher." Though Mark Twain thought he was writing a boys' book, his rating on the graded vocabulary list won't get him far with today's youth.

This brings us to the high-school years. In the seventy-two high-school English anthologies studied by Lynch and Evans, there are approximately seven hundred and fifty short stories of which only a fraction have any literary merit at all. The chief sources the anthologists draw upon are popular mass magazines, with the *Saturday Evening Post* and the late *Collier's* most favored, and *This Week, Woman's Day, Boy's Life, Seventeen, Ladies Home Journal,* and *Science Fiction* following just behind. Out of consideration for high-school students who are still struggling with reading, there are wholesale abridgements of stories in some anthologies in which the vocabulary, syntax, paragraphing, and even punctuation are simplified.[1]

The novel comes into these anthologies through excerpts (the first fourteen chapters of *David Copperfield*, the first 118 pages of *Great*

*Expectations,* a little over one-half of *Ivanhoe*) which have themselves been subjected to drastic abridgment. In one of the anthologies intended "for students of average or superior ability," the excerpt from *Great Expectations* has been edited in the interests of a simplified vocabulary, and the adapter has rewritten whole sentences. Lynch and Evans point out that "Dickens's own words, some of which rank as sixth-grade words on the Thorndike lists, are sometimes replaced by what Thorndike classed as third-grade words, although the volume is intended for the ninth grade." In order to "speed up the plot," such passages in *David Copperfield* as David's recounting of his birth and the history of the caul have been deleted. *Silas Marner* is also pruned of descriptive passages that might bore the young.

*Julius Caesar,* abridged and updated, is still enjoying a long run in the anthologies. And while Shakespeare has so far survived the axe of the Thorndike word list, the adapters have freely translated his lines whenever Elizabethan usage taxes the sixteen-year-old reader. "Good morrow, Caesar" becomes "Good morning, Caesar." "That plays thee music?" is given as "That plays the music?" "Thou," "doth," "prithee," " 'tis," "hath" are translated into modern English in many of the anthologies, notwithstanding dissonance or collapse of meter. The updating of the drama sections themselves results in the inclusion of works like Van Druten's *I Remember Mama,* Fletcher's *Sorry, Wrong Number,* Niggli's *This Bull Ate Nutmeg,* and Medcraft's *The First Dress Suit.* Only two of Shakespeare's tragedies (*Caesar* and *Macbeth*) are represented among the anthologies. *Hamlet* and *Lear* have both disappeared from the required reading list. Mindful of the treacheries of the curriculum committee, the thought occurred to me that *Hamlet* was traded for *The King and I,* and *Lear* for *Life with Father.*

The poetry sections of these anthologies show remarkable agreement in the selection of works. Lynch and Evans note that some of the editors borrow from each other, textual errors included. Where time has not yet sanctified poetic merit, the judgment of the anthologists is both prudent and catholic. Among contemporary poets Auden, Eliot, and Spender have sparse representation. Dylan Thomas does not appear at all (Booze? Marital infidelity?). Dorothy Parker, Ogden Nash, Phyllis McGinley, F. P. Adams, and Louis Untermeyer have made it. So has Eugene Field, whose "Little Boy Blue" is included in five eleventh-grade anthologies.

The editorial apparatus of these anthologies is illuminating. Here, for example, are topics in one anthology suggested for twelfth-graders in connection with their reading of *Macbeth*: (*a*) a character sketch of Macbeth or of Lady Macbeth, (*b*) a letter Lady Macbeth might have written in answer to her husband's, (*c*) the doctor's report on Lady Macbeth's illness, (*d*) a pastoral poem (reported by Lynch and Evans).

Classroom teaching follows the same pattern. I turned up these items from a teacher's manual in a major and top-ranking school system:

> "The Necklace." Suggested topics for essays: (*a*) "On Being Honest." (*b*) "Things I have Lost." . . . "The Raven." (*a*) "A Weird Experience." (*b*) "My Parakeet's Vocabulary." . . . (Eleventh Grade) "To a Waterfowl." "Thanatopsis." (*a*) "I agree (disagree) with Bryant's philosophy." . . . "The Pit and the Pendulum." (*a*) "If Poe were alive today, he would be (would not be) an outstanding writer of crime stories." . . . (Twelfth grade) *Macbeth*. (*a*) "compare or contrast Macbeth with a dictator of recent or current times." . . . "Locksley Hall." (*a*) "The World in 2060." "Take some single aspect of it. Consult your teacher." . . . "Song from Pippa Passes." (*a*) "I once felt just as Pippa does." (*b*) "I often feel as Pippa does."

One that I like best, and one that should give scope to the eighteen-year-old imagination, concerns "The Passionate Shepherd to His Love." Manual editor to teachers: "There are possibilities here for a composition based on very clever or very idealistic thinking, by having the student modernize the thought in the poem. For instance, if a young man today said to his girl, 'Come with me [sic] and be my love,' what would he offer her comparable to that offered by the shepherd?" This provocative question might easily lead to a twelfth-grade riot if it were not for the foresight of the anthologists who keep an eye on these things. The deletion of the word "live" and the twitching of the meter at the amputation site will go unnoticed.

This "how would you feel if" approach is almost certain death to the imagination and to the appreciation of literature. The student is left with the feeling that the ultimate values of literature are attained through a mystic union with ravens and waterfowl. He is diverted from the task of taking a story on its own terms, taking the characters as given, and examining the problem as it is worked out in these terms. He is under the impression that it is he who imparts value to the work by liking or not liking, consenting or not consenting, and by having common ground with the characters: "I once felt just as Pippa does."

## III

A fair percentage of the graduates of these programs in high-school English will go on to college. Here, in a last desperate attempt to consummate the marriage, the student and literature are brought together for a compulsory year or two. In all but a few institutions in the country (those that command the top secondary-school graduates) the first-year course in English is called Freshman Composition. Here a corps of young Ph.D.s or not-yet-Ph.D.s are assigned their first teaching labors. They must weed the freshman idiom of barbarisms and neologisms and clear out the underbrush in the wildly untended growth of entering student prose. This is energetic teaching which involves the instructor in reading and commenting on fifty to two hundred essays a week. Under the most favorable circumstances the student's exercises will produce a tidier exposition. But the faulty idiom persists like a tic, and after this year of rigorous study the habitual language patterns reassert themselves and cause consternation among the faculty in senior college and graduate school. In the faculty dining room the quality of student writing ranks next to the quality of institutional food as a topic that brings everyone warmly together. It is commonly believed that if the English Department were on the ball and drilled those kids in the elements of grammar and usage, these outrages would stop.

But formal drill in the language is not what these students need. As a matter of fact, the typical high-school curriculum in English includes killing doses of drill in grammar, usage, and mechanics. And since the medicine has no effect in the ninth grade, it is administered regularly in the tenth, eleventh, and twelfth grades in the desperate hope that some of it will stay down. Jacques Barzun, speaking of his highly selected graduate students at Columbia, says ". . . I find one in ten who needs coaching in the elements of literacy—spelling, punctuation, sentence structure and diction. And these students cannot write because they cannot read."

Barzun has not overstated the case. His estimate of one in ten gives

Columbia a high batting average among graduate schools. Among undergraduates, even in our best schools, the student who does not require coaching in the elements of literacy is in the minority. And the reason is, as Barzun has put it, that *they cannot read.* A good reader's ear and eye have undergone a training that cannot be duplicated by exercises, teaching machines, or any formal teaching measures.

The year of freshman composition will not supply the missing elements in the student's preparation for reading or writing. If the student is lucky he may pass the rest of his years in college without writing another essay outside of the English department. The short-answer quiz has replaced the essay exam and the term paper in all but a few departments of undergraduate education, and with careful planning and course selection a student can receive his diploma without further examination of the state of his literacy.

In most colleges, a sophomore course called Introduction to Literature actually completes the student's obligatory education in literature. Since only a fraction of the student body will return for further study in the English department, this course represents the all-out effort of the curriculum committee to bring the world's great works together before time runs out. It has all the aspects of a funeral feast.

## IV

The entire curriculum, from first-grade reading through high-school English, is a pretentious joke, of course. No one—not even the educationists—makes any serious claims for it. The only defense offered is that this is the best we can do in a program of mass education. European systems, our school people say, work with an academic elite, whereas ours must deal with a heterogeneous population, etc.; comparisons are therefore irrelevant.

Arthur Trace makes a grade-by-grade comparison of sample texts employed in our country in the teaching of reading and literature with those of the Soviet Union. Soviet students are taught to read according to a phonics system. Only a few weeks are devoted to the teaching of the Cyrillic alphabet and to practice in reading words and short sentences. The students then proceed to their first-grade reader, which has some 130 selections and a vocabulary of two thousand words. The second-grade reader has about 165 selections and a vocabulary of approximately four thousand words. This progression leads

up to the fourth-grade reader which has longer selections and a vocabulary of about ten thousand words. (A typical American fourth-
grade reader has a vocabulary of eighteen hundred to twenty-five
hundred words.)

These Soviet readers include pieces aimed purely at Communist
indoctrination and exemplary pieces (like those of our old McGuffey
readers) aimed at character building, but they also include literary
material of high quality from the first grade on. In the first-grade
reader (for seven-year-olds) Trace found Tolstoy represented by three
stories, two anecdotes, a fable, and a fairy tale; there were three poems
by Pushkin, one fable by Krylov, a poem by Nekrassov, and one by
Lermontov; there were many anonymous tales from the Russian
folklore tradition; there were several selections by well-known contemporary Soviet authors. Altogether, Trace estimated that about a
third of the selections in the first-grade *Rodnaya Rech* readers had
genuine literary merit, and some were written by Russia's greatest
authors.

In each of the successive readers the number of literary selections
increases. Of the 77 selections in the third-grade reader Trace examined, more than half were of established literary value (stories by Tolstoy, Pushkin, Gorky, Chekhov, Turgenev, fables by Krylov, poems by
Nekrassov and Pushkin).

In the fifth grade (age eleven) the Soviet student begins a formal
study of literature on an elementary level. He is introduced to literary
forms and the analysis of literary works. The organization of texts
from the fifth through the tenth grades encourages a historical study
of Russian and Soviet literature (not, however, in strict historical sequence) and a beginner's appreciation of the tendencies at work in the
different literary epochs.

All of this is not as formidable as it sounds. The selections in the
fifth through the seventh grade are often short—an excerpt from *War
and Peace*, a Nekrassov poem, stories by Chekhov and Gorky, biographical sketches of the significant literary figures—but the emphasis is on the work itself. This program, in the hands of a good teacher,
can provide the eleven-to thirteen-year-old student with an approach
to the reading of literature. His eyes and ears can be educated to the
elements of style, the qualities of language, and the repertory of literary values that give meaning to a work. The fifth-grade pupil in the
Soviet Union will probably not get more than a rudimentary sense of

these things, but he begins an education in reading that leads him into a full-scale exploration of major literary works in the eighth and ninth grades. The ninth-grade literature program, for example, includes Tolstoy's *War and Peace* in its entirety, Chekhov's *The Cherry Orchard*, Shakespeare's *Hamlet*, and Goethe's *Faust, Part I*. As an indication of the thoroughness with which such works are studied, Trace points out that teachers are instructed to spend fourteen class periods on Turgenev's *Fathers and Sons* and twenty-eight hours on Tolstoy's *War and Peace*.

This curriculum, for an unselected population of school children, resembles in all essentials the curriculum in most European school systems which our educators have dismissed as "elite." Now it is very possible that a fair number of Soviet school children are bored or find the curriculum too demanding. It is very likely that the Soviet school system has some teachers who cannot measure up to the demands of such a rigorous program. And even with good teachers and good students there is no guarantee that a good curriculum on paper will produce the desired result. Nevertheless, a curriculum designed with these objectives provides a framework in which under optimal circumstances the elements of appreciation can be taught. The American public-school curriculum that I have described cannot, in itself, produce anything better than a market for the *Reader's Digest*. It is sobering to remember, too, that a great many of our teachers today—elementary and high school both—are themselves the products of this shabby education in English, an education which ends for a high proportion of them at the close of the compulsory college course, Introduction to Literature.

## V

There are proposals for reform of the curriculum in English. And while they show zeal on the part of the agencies involved, they resemble in disconcerting ways a slum rehabilitation program. Since no one is willing to condemn the entire structure as unsound, the plans call for shoring up the sagging floors, patching the bad spots in the draughty upper stories, and surveillance to insure compliance with the minimum standards of the code. A proposal (by Lynch and Evans) to get rid of some of the undesirable tenants in the high-school anthologies has been criticized as unrealistic. Of course, if they were evicted there would be no place for them to go.

In a nationwide survey of teachers of English, the National Council of Teachers of English found that the average elementary teacher has devoted less than 8 percent of his college work to English. About half of all secondary-school teachers of English lack college majors in the subject. One half of the secondary-school teachers responding to this survey rate themselves as not confident in their ability to teach literature and language; two thirds do not feel prepared to teach composition.

In the face of these and other lamentable findings, the NCTE manages a brave face. Phrases like "massive frontal attack" and other warrior slogans appear in the concluding section of its report. But as the section goes on, the metaphors of battle recede and the plan itself is disclosed in the idiom of the teacher's college catalogue. Such terms as "language arts," "basic language skills," "reading skills," "trends in content and methodology" break out like an old rash, and it soon becomes clear that the "massive frontal attack" will employ the same old strategies on a larger scale. The recommendations envision "a massive program of carefully planned summer and year-round institutes on the content of English . . . to improve the basic competency in English of the majority of elementary and secondary teachers now assigned instructional responsibilities in the subject." Courses in rhetoric and practical methods of teaching English are given highest priority in the NCTE's recommendations. But this emphasis on training in "methods" is hard to take seriously after 166 pages of information and statistics which show that a majority of our English teachers do not have even a rudimentary education in the subject. There is even some question as to whether they have any serious interest or pleasure in the subject they are teaching. Only 35 percent of elementary-school and 44 percent of secondary-school teachers rated courses in literature as "of great interest and value" for their own continuing education—although 67 percent of the latter gave this rating to courses in "Practical Methods of Teaching English."

I will concede with the educators that "you have to begin somewhere" and that some form of large-scale in-service training of teachers is urgently needed. But such a training program needs to take a hard look at the facts. A teacher who does not regard his own study of literature as "of great interest and value" will not profit from a course in the methods of teaching literature. And if this absence of interest is reflected in his own reading, he will not profit from a course in rhetoric, or "language skills," or grammar and usage.

No one can argue against an effort to raise minimum standards, but I regret that the NCTE has not made equally strong recommendations for the raising of the maximum standards that now prevail. An investment of millions of dollars in the postgraduate education of several thousand *good* teachers of English with demonstrated capacity and qualifications might elevate the low ceiling of the curriculum and start some fresh currents moving. And here I do not envision "methods" and "language arts" courses taken in night school, but a rigorous, full-time, fully subsidized postgraduate program in English in which study of the language and study of literature are at the center. Also, it goes without saying that if we want to prevent the complete decay of instruction in English, the whole system of undergraduate training of teachers will have to undergo a revolution.

But teacher training alone does not hold the key to a revitalization of the English curriculum, and even a corps of topnotch teachers will not be able to work effectively within it as it stands today. There is no part of this curriculum that can be singled out for repair. It all hangs together, from the first grade through the twelfth, a dilapidated structure based upon bad reading, poor instruction, repellent texts, and a degraded literature. The entire structure must be rebuilt. Sending teachers to summer school, renovating textbooks and anthologies, reforming the program in rhetoric or grammar or literature will all prove futile if a substantial part of the school population is struggling with the mechanics of reading throughout most of the twelve years of compulsory education.

There are few signs that such a wholesale reform of the curriculum will be initiated by either the schools or the professional organizations of English teachers. While the spirit of reform is running high in English education today, the proposals that have come to my attention are mainly in the direction of technological innovation. The use of electronic devices, teaching machines, and language laboratories are widely endorsed "to supplement the efforts of the classroom teacher" in the instruction of reading, spelling, and certain aspects of grammar. We may expect to spend millions on such devices in the years to come. The very fact that they can be seriously offered as solutions to our national literacy scandal tells us how far removed we are from understanding the psychological base of language learning, in which I include learning to read.

Psychologically, the acquisition of speech and the process of learning to read are intimately related. Both derive from a human center. In the absence of human connections, the child will not acquire speech. By this I mean something more complicated than the self-evident fact that the child who does not hear human speech cannot learn to reproduce it. In the absence of human ties, of human partners, a child will have no incentives to learn to speak, even if he has the opportunity to hear others speak.

A child acquires speech not through simple imitation of sounds, but through a dialogue with human partners. The first words are expressions of need, articulations of wants, summonings of loved persons and objects through magical invocation of the name. Through words the child unites himself with his human partners. In the absence of human partners a child may learn to imitate sounds or parrot speech patterns, but he will not acquire a meaningful language. This has been clinically demonstrated in the tragic cases of infants and young children who have never known human ties. No amount of instruction in speech will teach these children—even at the age of four or five or older—to use words to communicate needs or designate objects. There is only one measure that has been found effective in bringing about the development of meaningful speech in these children—the provision of a substitute mother, or sometimes a psychotherapist, to whom the child can attach himself and with whom he can form a human partnership.

The second point that should be made about early speech development is that it is unsystematic and cannot be reduced to formal teaching procedures. The child acquires a vocabulary through discovery and repetitions in contexts; in other words, learning is associative and not logical. Here the clinical demonstration may be seen in dream language and other examples of the primary process of thinking. It is only later in the development of the child that language acquires some degree of independence from need and from dialogue and can be employed for the expression of abstract ideas and for the ordering of thought.

The learning process in reading affords some close parallels to this beginning phase of speech development. Once again we have the discovery of words through a human partner, in this case the teacher. Once again words are initially invested with meaning through need and through pleasure: the mastery of even a few words gives the beginning reader a sense of exaltation, as if he magically possessed the thing through naming it, just as he once magically summoned a loved person by naming her. And the lure that was provided in early speech development, the discovery of a world of objects and their associations, has its equivalent in early reading in the lure of the story and world of the imagination. The acquisition of new words in reading follows the genetic sequence of speech development. Meaning is acquired in context, and the vocabulary expands through associative paths, unself-consciously, without logical progression, independent of order in instruction. The eye is trained through the exercise of reading. No instructional device has matched the story and reading in quantity for incentive, pleasure, and painless mastery of the symbol system.

The failure of our present methods of reading and language instruction derives essentially from a failure in understanding the psychology of language. The teaching machines that loom in the future are only the absurd extensions of a pedagogy that has lost the connections between language and a human center and is urged on by a lunatic science to the last frontier. The child who learns to read words in a crowded classroom with an indifferent teacher and her mechanical aids has been deprived of the vital human connections that are indispensable for learning to read and pleasure in reading. Long before the teaching machines came into vogue we created mechanical readers through mechanical teaching.

The child who must spend six years or more under our present teaching methods in order to achieve a reading capacity of twenty-five hundred words will lose all pleasure in reading, and even the most arduous wooing may not bring him back to the state of readiness of a six-year-old. With more perseverance than an elementary-school student, I would not spend six years in studying a foreign language for this result. Mechanical mastery of reading must be achieved in ways that give increments of pleasure, and pleasure in mastery itself, or all motive will be destroyed. Those methods of reading instruction that give early mastery of mechanics and make way for the lure of the story at the earliest possible stage have the greatest potential for creating readers.

The "graded vocabulary" of our current texts is another affront to the learning of language. I was much entertained by the word lists compiled by Sylvia Ashton-Warner in her teaching of Maori children. These children, who correspond to a group that we call "the culturally deprived," could not be lured into the standard primers (from the description of the texts, a New Zealand or British version of *Dick and Jane*). It occured to Miss Ashton-Warner that the words of these texts were without value or meaning to the children and she began to experiment with a method in which the children provided their own word lists to the teacher. These words were written down on cards and given to the child to take home for study. The cards, greasy and mangled in the children's hands, became treasured possessions. And the children learned their words quickly.

One child's list included the following words: ghost, jet, jeep, skellington [skeleton], bike, aeroplane, sausage, porridge, egg, car, beer, jersey, kiss. Another child had these: peanut, cake, ghost, bed, kiss, socks. A third had: beer, pudding, bus, darling, kiss, ghost. Not at all, of course, like the words in a graded vocabulary. As a writer and a connoisseur of word values, Miss Ashton-Warner went unerringly to the source of the reading difficulty. She also had a natural understanding of word magic and translated this into a teaching method. Notice the repetition in the private lists of "ghost," for example, and "kiss"—the first a fear word and the second a love word. To be able to read "ghost" and write "ghost" is conjury for the child (and not only the Maori child). When you name the ghost you have him in your power. You can call him up and put him down through the magic act of reading. When you name "kiss" and read "kiss" you are united with a loved person, and you unlock a whole glossary of associated words, and with them experiences and states of feeling in which pleasure, comfort, and protection can be magically revived. The reading vocabulary of these Maori children expanded according to no laws of logic or "form perception"; each new word unlocked associated groups of words, which is in itself an interesting demonstration of the repetition of beginning speech patterns in early reading.

Miss Ashton-Warner apparently had good results in engaging her "unteachable" children in reading because she understood words and word magic in a profound psychological sense. And if the method still popularly employed in our schools has been a failure, it is because the method does violence to the natural evolution of language.

The long years spent by our children in mastery of the mechanics of reading rob them of pleasure and discoveries in literature, but also rob them of the possibility of addiction, which is one of the characteristics of the good reader. The addiction to reading is acquired at an early age—usually, I believe, under eight or nine. The addict reveals himself through an insatiable appetite, an almost compulsive need to take in printed matter (even the legend on a can label or soap wrapper rivets the eye and must register its message). The book addict suffers certain types of disturbance when the supply is low or when he is cut off from the source of it. This is not pathological: the addict may be a healthy adult or child in all respects.

The critical period for becoming addicted is early childhood, the time when urges are felt as irresistible and objects that gratify the urge are also experienced as irresistible. The educator who wishes to capitalize on the addictability of the child at this age must insure early and repeated gratifications from stories told and stories read. It goes without saying that the urge is indiscriminate and that repeated gratifications from television or comic books can also result in a durable love affair. But if the educator's aim is to create readers, he must understand addiction and the forms of literary gratification that insure it in early childhood. Instruction that gives imperfect mastery of mechanics even at the age of twelve and later, has not only missed the critical period but has built up an aversion to reading which will resist the wooing of the most ardent teacher.

The educator who understands the meaning of language learning will know that it is human-centered from the start and that when it is deprived of its human connections it loses its own vital substances. It refuses to be automatized. For all the early years of education it requires a human partner, as if its origins in a human partnership had imprinted this condition. In reading, in language study, the teacher must become the human partner. If there is any part of this curriculum in which a machine can do as well as a good teacher, it has not yet been demonstrated. If we have tolerated the idea at all, it must be that it sometimes happens that a mechanical teacher will not do much better than a mechanical device. But why settle for either?

If the early teaching of reading and language is human-centered, and if addiction has done its work, there will come a time in childhood when pleasure in reading and in language achieve a certain degree of independence from the human partners who had served as teachers. The dialogue that had originated between the child and his family and the child and his teachers is no longer the indispensable component in learning and in pleasure. The book itself has taken over as a partner and is invested with some of the qualities of a human relationship. In this way literature becomes an extended dialogue.

## Note

1. These statements apply to texts which have been designed for use in all three tracks in high school—college preparatory as well as vocational and general.

## References

Ashton-Warner, S. (1963). *Teacher.* New York: Simon and Schuster.

Flesch, R. (1955). *Why Johnny Can't Read.* New York: Harper.

Gross, M. W. (1964). Why Johnny Can't Write. *Partisan Review,* 4:627.

Lynch, J. J. and Evans, B. (1964). *High School English Textbooks.* Boston: Little, Brown and Co.

Miles, M. B., ed. (1964). *Innovation in Education.* New York: Bureau of Publications, Teachers College.

Trace, A. S. (1961). *What Ivan Knows That Johnny Doesn't.* New York: Random House.

Walcutt, C., ed. (1961). *Tomorrow's Illiterates.* Boston: Little, Brown and Co.

# 26

# The Science of Thought Control

The events of the past thirty years have created a kind of monstrous laboratory for the study of the enslavement of the human ego. The Moscow Trials confronted us with the spectacle of a man who had been brought into morbid alliance with his own persecutors, a man who confessed to crimes he had never committed, professed beliefs that negated his own history, and held "truths" that contradicted the evidence of his own senses. In an ecstasy of self-abomination many of these accused men demanded the extreme penalty from their judges. Later, we learned through Hitler's concentration camps that systematic terror and degradation can strip personality to its naked foundations, that hunger and extreme peril can enslave a man to his persecutors, and that when the work of enslavement is completed the rags of personality can be made over so that a man finally comes to resemble his own jailers.

It was the Chinese Communists who gave us the term "brainwashing" and demonstrated through the conversion of Western civilians and prisoners of war that their methods of thought reform were not to be conceived of as a kind of black magic practiced by totalitarian regimes upon passive and enslaved citizens. The reports of our own repatriated prisoners of war collapsed a whole body of popular theories. We were without any explanation for the fact that a man born to freedom and reared in a democratic creed should surrender a part of his mind to his enemy. Official and public reaction was, in itself, without precedent in history. There were no denunciations of the converts and the collaborators as traitors, or any public demonstrations against them. They were visited by psychiatric teams appointed by their government, and brought back as mentally afflicted men.

Once again, we have learned that freedom of thought is not alone a human right conferred upon a man by his government and guaranteed by its laws. The ultimate guarantees of freedom are invested in the human ego. As the pragmatic psychology of tyranny has known for centuries, there are conditions under which the ego will surrender its autonomy. The methods for enslaving the ego and even the methods of "thought reform" are not entirely new. But we are the first generation in history to acquire a scientific psychology of tyranny and mental enslavement. We can now begin to understand the process of mental enslavement, and the morbid attachment of a man for his persecutors. With this knowledge we shall not banish devils from the human scene; but for those who find cold comfort in scientific revelation, these investigations of contemporary psychology afford a considerable advance over the modern demonology that has invaded so much of our thinking about mental enslavement.

Among the most brilliant and illuminating contributions to our understanding of the psychology of mental enslavement are Bruno Bettelheim's studies of individual and mass behavior in the concentration camp society. Before being imprisoned in 1938–39 at Dachau and Buchenwald, Bettelheim had undergone a personal analysis and had already become interested in psychoanalytic research and applied psychoanalysis. Under the early impact of imprisonment in Dachau, Bettelheim began to experience changes in his own personality, and to protect himself against the danger of disintegration which he saw among his fellow inmates, he undertook to employ his psychological knowledge in a strict analysis of his own behavior and that of his fellow prisoners and the guards and SS men in the concentration camp community. By such means he was able to preserve his personality from destruction and achieve a kind of autonomy in an environment that had, as its calculated aim, the complete subjugation of the individual and the annihilation of the individual will.

Some years after his release and his immigration to the United States, Bettelheim gathered together his observations in a study called "Individual and Mass Behavior in Extreme Situations" (1943). This study with some modifications forms the center of a new work, *The Informed Heart* (1960), in which he addresses himself to the problem of autonomy and submission in contemporary society.

According to Bettelheim, the war against the human spirit within the camps was not a matter of a grand-scale unleashing of sadism, but a policy deliberately aimed at creating the docile and enslaved personality. Moreover, this destruction was carefully carried out in a series of stages.[1] The first stage Bettelheim refers to as "traumatization," a massive assault upon the personality and the body which, in psychological terms, paralyzes the ego and lays the groundwork for drastic personality changes. A kind of ritual initiation took place during the transport to camp, when the prisoners were exposed to almost constant physical and mental torture. Suffering may unite men through identification with each other, but the Gestapo made sure that this could not happen. No prisoner was allowed to care for his own or another's wounds. Prisoners were forced to hit one another, to accuse themselves and others of vile actions, to curse their religion, to denounce their wives as adulteresses and prostitutes. Any failure to obey the orders to hit and to vilify, or any help given a tortured prisoner, was swiftly punished by death.

This "initiation"—whose purpose, of course, was to break the prisoner's resistance to changing his external forms of behavior, as a preliminary stage in breaking his resistance to internal personality changes—usually lasted for about twelve hours, often longer. The real world was transformed into a nightmare, and the only possible way in which the ego could deal with this was to make the new reality "not real," to experience it as if it were happening to someone else. This "denial of reality," Bettelheim points out, was a first step in developing new psychological mechanisms for survival in the camp, a necessary adaptation to overwhelming experiences, but one that already signified a major personality change.

Upon entering the camp, the prisoner became a number, and not only in a metaphorical sense. Thereafter the camp officials addressed him by his number; and the prisoner was compelled to refer to himself by number and not by name. Thus the very symbol of personal identity, one's name, began to lose its connections with the personality, and with the body, and the stranger taking over from within acquired the absolute anonymity of the serial number.

The extent to which this had the effect of reducing the prisoner to the helplessness of childhood may be seen in one example among many that Bettelheim gives. Permission had to be sought from the guards to use the latrines: "Jewish prisoner number 34567 most obediently prays to be permitted to ———." To complete the degradation many guards withheld permission, or asked baiting questions to further humiliate the prisoner. If permission was granted, the prisoner was required to report back later (using the same formula). Here, it was as if the man were reduced to the state of earliest childhood, and the training for cleanliness repeated once again.

The constant threats of lashings from the guards served further to undermine a man's image of himself as a man; they were like the threats of punishment in childhood. Even the work assigned to prisoners was often nonsensical and childish: for example, a prisoner (especially if he was new) might be required to carry heavy rocks from one place to another and then pick them up and carry them back.

The impotent rage of the prisoner was another factor in his reduction to a condition of pure submissiveness. For there was nothing to do with this rage except turn it back upon the self or project it onto a suitable object. Fear of one's own internalized rage, fear of its destructive power, produced a feeling not unlike that of childhood, of being helpless before an internal danger, the danger of one's own impulses. Bettelheim shows how this internalized rage played an important role in the submission to the SS. The power of the objectively real danger represented by the SS man was augmented in the destructive fantasies of the prisoner, so that the SS man grew omnipotent in the eyes of the prisoner and the prisoner became more submissive out of the magnitude of the danger. A fair proportion of the internalized aggression built up in all prisoners was also discharged in endless, petty quarrels among themselves, like the quarreling of children. How could it be otherwise? Yet such petty warfare among the prisoners worked once again against any group cohesion or support for disintegrating personalities, and consequently only served the purposes of the Gestapo psychological program.

The prisoner soon learned that there was no possibility of asserting his individual will or influencing his environment through his own actions. As in a nightmare, there was unremitting horror—bleak timelessness and no hope of deliverance. No man was ever permitted to believe that he might some day be released. And as a monstrous symbol of death and the eternity of this hell, no clocks nor watches were permitted the prisoners. There remained one last freedom: the choice to live or die.

The problem, as Bettelheim puts it, was how to survive as a man, not a walking corpse," as a debased and degraded but still human being." To react emotionally to the torture or abuse or death of a comrade was suicidal. Yet, to preserve his humanity in the concentration camp a man had somehow to find a way of keeping alive his inner feelings even though he could not act upon them.

Those persons who blocked out neither heart nor reason—neither feelings nor perception, but kept informed of their inner attitudes even when they could hardly ever afford to act on them, those prisoners survived and came to understand the conditions they lived under. They also came to realize what they had not perceived before; that they still retained the last, if not the greatest, of the human freedoms: to choose their own attitude under any given circumstances.

Those who were unable to do this ended by becoming empty of human feeling, and shameless in their degradation. Finally, many of them came to resemble their jailers. Old prisoners, it could be observed, modeled themselves on the SS, taking over their methods of handling traitors within the group and outdoing the SS in cruelty and torture. They scavenged for old pieces of SS uniforms, or tried to sew and mend their prison garb to resemble the uniforms. They took pride in producing at roll-call the snappy SS salute, standing rigidly at attention. And there was a terrible irony in the taking over by the prisoners of a favorite SS game, the object of which was to determine who could stand being hit the longest without uttering a complaint.

The remaking of a man in the image of his enemy is a highly complex psychological process. Bettelheim makes it clear that we are to understand this pathological identification as a primitive type of defense, an attempt to protect the ego against a great and overwhelming danger. "Like the child who identifies with the parent, this identification helped prisoners to know intuitively what the SS expected of them." Such knowledge, and the behavior based on it, may often have saved a prisoner's life. But the price he paid was the altering of his own personality into the very type of person the SS was trying to produce.

## II

If we set aside our revulsion at the idea of a man who makes himself over into the image of his persecutor, there is much to be learned from such behavior. Let me, in the following remarks (which are strictly my own, and not in anyway Bettelheim's), attempt a brief sketch of the psychology of the process.

The fear of ego extinction, loss of the self, is one of the primordial fears of mankind. Whether the threat of dissolution comes from within (as in psychosis) or from without (as in the concentration camp), the ego characteristically falls back upon its earliest and most primitive defenses—the very ones, in fact, that were first employed in childhood development to guard the emerging ego against extinction. Among the most important of these is the mechanism of "identification." Before a self emerges in infancy there is an undifferentiated oneness with the mother, a state of relative freedom from tension as long as needs are satisifed. With the emergence of a self, however, comes tension, for separateness from the mother brings about in the child an acute awareness of the need for a person outside the self who is the giver of satisfactions, and a corresponding awareness of the danger of losing this person. In adapting to this new state of separateness the infant makes use of a mental mechanism that recreates in psychic terms the earlier oneness with the mother; he makes her part of himself, as he will do ever afterward with every loved person in his lifetime.

We have seen that certain measures employed by the Gestapo to break down prisoner resistance had the effect of reproducing the condition of biological helplessness in infancy. The prisoner was completely dependent upon his jailers for the satisfaction of the most elemental body needs. Hunger and danger enslaved him to his jailers who had absolute power over life. The ego, robbed of its capacity for defense against danger, was obliged to find survival techniques in an environment of unremitting peril, and one that was carefully contrived to sustain it in childlike dependency.

The ego, when it fears its own extinction, revives its oldest mechanisms in order to bind itself more closely to a world that is slipping away. It seeks to unite with a human object; and in repetition of its beginnings, the ego may find in body and survival needs the connection between it and the human objects that wield power over life. The ego protects itself against danger by identifying with the powerful persons and assuming their attributes. In this way, I suspect, the prisoner in the concentration camp found himself in grotesque alliance with his own persecutors. He borrowed the attributes of his jailers in order to prevent his own ego from dying. It appears, then, that the process by which a man can be made over in the image of his enemy is a perversion of the very process that gives birth to the human ego.

From analogy with the process of ego development we can see that, when this kind of identification between the prisoner and his jailer takes place, it is possible for the jailer to exert a strong educational influence upon his prisoner. If, in pursuit of its purposes, the state should see fit to indoctrinate or to bring about a conversion to its ideology, the very circumstances in which a prisoner through survival needs becomes attached to his jailer and has formed a primitive identification with him will provide the exact conditions for blotter-like receptivity, "taking in" and "swallowing whole," that is required in the school of demagoguery.

We have a clue, then, as to how when the human ego is forced into regressive modes of functioning, mental processes revert to archaic patterns; it is this ego regression that provides the favorable condition for a conversion experience. And this leads us to another part of the story.

## III

When the reports of the Moscow Trials of the 1930s first appeared, Western psychologists were as baffled as the layman. It was not difficult to guess how the false confessions were obtained. But there was nothing to explain how so many of the defendants had come to *believe* in the false confessions they were making. In the show trials, it would have been possible for any defendant to repudiate his false confession before the world press, since the death penalty was inevitable in any case. Yet one after another of the alleged conspirators accused himself of treachery, of sabotage, spying, counter-revolutionary actions, and assassination plots—and in language of fervent self-abasement. Nor could this be explained by the expectation of mercy, for in the final statement to the court the prisoner often ended with an impassioned plea for the most severe verdict, the deserved penalty of death.

Arthur Koestler in *Darkness at Noon* constructed a plausible picture of how the Moscow confessions were obtained. His Rubashov was broken down through an ideological inquisition to which, as a party official who had impeded political objectives through his own individual actions, he was vulnerable. But—as John Rogge has pointed out—this explanation does not help us in trying to understand the confessions of non-Communists to Communist inquisitors. How can we explain an Oatis, for example? Not only did Oatis confess to espionage and later testify against twelve alleged accomplices, but after his release he refused to repudiate his confession. When he was questioned about why he had made the confession in the first place, he firmly denied that he had been tortured. He could only say enigmatically that "psychology" had been used. Among others during the postwar period who confessed to Communist inquisitors were Vogeler, Cardinal Mindszenty, Archbishop Grosz, and scores of Catholic and Protestant clergymen in the satellite countries.

The inquisitional methods of the Chinese Communists were borrowed from the Soviet Union, but the Chinese gave larger scope to the inquisition by uniting it with a program of thought reform. The Chinese Communist prison became the center of a grueling and intensive re-education program in which confession served to "cleanse" the prisoner of ideological sins, and group study was then combined with certain extraordinary types of group pressures to build a new identity in the prisoner. The effectiveness of the program was seen in the degree to which even Western non-Communists came under its influence.

Robert Lifton, whose book *Thought Reform and the Psychology of Totalism* appeared last year, was one of the psychiatric investigators assigned in 1953 to examine repatriated prisoners of the Korean war. From the stories of the repatriates he was able to piece together a great deal of information about Chinese Communist confession and re-education techniques, but he soon saw that many of the profound questions raised by this inquiry could best be explored through a study of men and women who had been "reformed" within China itself. Returning to Hong Kong in 1954, he began to search out both Western civilians and Chinese who had experienced "thought reform," and for seventeen months he conducted psychiatric studies of a number of these people. In the summary that follows I have used material from both his 1956 essay in *Psychiatry* and his recent book.

The arrest typically took place at midnight. A squad arrived at the house, conducted a search, and led the prisoner, blindfolded, to a house of detention. This was followed by a stage that Lifton calls the "Emotional Assault." There were day and night interrogations under bright lights. The prisoner was told: "You are here because you have committed crimes against the people. Confess and your case will be quickly solved and you will soon be released." The prisoner was given no rest for consecutive days and nights. When he appeared near collapse he was taken to his cell, but wakened in an hour to be brought back for further interrogation. Continued denial of guilt put hand-cuffs and chains back on the prisoner.

Up until this point the Chinese inquisitional method closely re-sembles that of the Russians. But now we encounter an element that is uniquely Chinese, and part of the thought-reform program. It is called "Struggle," and at this stage in the procedure takes the form of a group inquisition conducted by the prisoner's cell mates. The pris-oner is always placed in a group of other prisoners who are more ad-vanced in their reform process, and whose task now is to help him make his confession. The foreign victim sits in the middle of the floor while his cell mates shout invectives at him and denounce him as an arch criminal. (The prisoner is interrogated at night and "struggled" by his cell mates during the day; thus he is virtually without a moment of freedom from accusations of guilt.)

All this is accompanied by the reduction of the prisoner to com-plete helplessness and dependency upon his cell mates. One of Lif-ton's informants, a Dr. J., describes how, with his hands chained be-hind his back, he had to eat like a dog using only his mouth and his teeth. When he needed to urinate his cell mates opened his trousers. After defecation a cell mate cleaned him. He was left unwashed for weeks, tormented by lice. The day and night torments and interroga-tions, sleeplessness, hunger, diarrhea, filth, rapidly bring the personal-ity toward a crisis. Every part of the process (which is strikingly sim-ilar to Bettelheim's description of the concentration camp methods) is designed to effect a destruction of the self-image and a weakening of the boundaries between the ego and reality. But at the point of crisis in the ego, when surrender is imminent, an abrupt change of tactics is introduced by the interrogators. They switch to softness and le-niency, expressions of concern for the prisoner's health, and apologies for their harsh treatment of him. They hold out promises that things will be more comfortable for the prisoner if he cooperates. At this point the prisoner experiences a tremendous gratitude toward his jailers, a feeling akin to love. He is now ready to make his confession.

The confession to crimes that were never committed begins with an acknowledgment by the prisoner that he is guilty "from the peo-ple's standpoint" of ideological crimes—his capitalist thinking, his service in behalf of capitalist groups are crimes against the people of China. Once the prisoner can even provisionally accept the "people's standpoint" he is able to see himself as an enemy of the revolution. And as he becomes more deeply involved in his confession and the scrupulous self-searching that is demanded by it, as he is "struggled" by his cell mates and his "judge" (instructor), who help him make his confession, he begins to accept, increasingly, the definition of crime "from the people's standpoint" and to regard himself as a criminal.

But the gap still has to be bridged between confession to ideological crimes and confession to criminal acts which the prisoner must invent, naming fellow conspirators, giving details of the "plot," and so on. This bridge is built by means of a fantasy which always has its basis in actual events. (There really was a man named X. The prisoner and X did see each other frequently.) The confession as composed and as written and rewritten over a period of months and even years is *the prisoner's own invention* and he improves on it as he goes along. Lifton says: "As the confession develops, the prisoner finds it looming before him as the basic reality of his immediate world. What he admits and what he writes become standard truths." Lifton observed that the degree of blurring of reality varied greatly among prisoners. Some prisoners came to believe in their inventions, but many were aware of the falsehood and distortion. During the writing of the confession, the prisoner is guided by his judge. The prisoner's failure to come up with satisfactory confessional material can result in renewed "struggle" in the cell.

There follows the period of re-education. The prisoner becomes part of a study group which is in session for ten to sixteen hours a day. One person reads selected material and each of the group is expected to give opinions and criticize the views of the others. Each must learn to express himself from the "correct"—that is, "people's"—viewpoint. Particular emphasis is put on "thought problems," on "wrong thoughts" or "bad thoughts," in an unending confessional—the self-denunciation, casting out of evil.

During this time there is also an individual approach to the prisoner and his re-education (which may go on for several years). His judge, or instructor, supervises the prisoner's education and his progress. The judge keeps a case file, receives reports, conducts interviews himself with the prisoner. The prisoner, Lifton observed, forms a complex and ambivalent relationship to his analyst. Eventually the prisoner is put to work on the final draft of his confession and gets ready for his trial. All prisoners, of course, plead guilty. The prisoner is sentenced, sometimes to as much as ten years; but in the case of Westerners there is a show of leniency, and in many instances the Westerner is expelled at this point.

In Lifton's analysis the elements of the process are "death and rebirth." "The 'reactionary spy' who entered the prison must perish; in his place must arise a 'new man' resurrected in the communist image." In fact the words "to die and be reborn" are often used by officials, Lifton points out, and the prisoner himself may use them in describing his experience.

In the context of "death and rebirth" Lifton shows how the process aims at annihilation of the prisoner's former identity and the building of a new identity. (The destruction of the old identity is accomplished, as we have seen, by techniques strikingly similar to those in the concentration camps described by Bettelheim.) The ego is brought rapidly to the last crisis before surrender. At this point, many prisoners reported, came severe depressions and suicidal thoughts. Many others experienced delusions and hallucinations. The alternatives appeared to be psychosis or death. In this extremity, relief is offered to the prisoner from the outside. The sudden leniency and affectionate concern for the prisoner's welfare come as a flood of relief. The dying ego is rescued, and there is the promise of rebirth through confession and reform.

The confession represents an expulsion of the old identity, metaphorically a vomiting forth of the bad, the repudiated, the poisonous attributes of the old self. In some of Lifton's reports we see a kind of orgy of self-abomination, a confessional outpouring that gathers momentum and seems to take possession of the personality; it goes on as if through a will of its own. (Analogies with some types of religious experience come to mind.) And as the confessional orgy gathers momentum, the penitent finds himself with an increasing sense of submission to his jailers. The confession is an ecstasy of surrender.

The compulsion to confess has its origins in underlying forces that are not yet well understood. Yet once this process is set in motion it releases deep and secret reservoirs of feelings, the "free-floating" guilt that exists in every personality and is always available to attach itself to images and ideas, symbols that it selects for one or another reason. The prisoner, by adopting the "people's standpoint," Liften shows, is able to channel these non-specific feelings of guilt into a paranoid, pseudo-logical system. The prisoner learns to regard his past actions as evil and destructive and can charge the most prosaic events of the past with the strong emotion that has broken through to the surface of consciousness.

In reading Lifton I was struck by the fact that the making of the confession, the invention of a fictional criminal past, bears certain resemblances to the making of a dream or a delusion. I do not attribute this idea to Lifton, I am simply following a train of thought of my own. A dream or a delusion always has its point of origin in a piece of reality. In the regressed state induced by sleep or certain mental disturbances, strong unconscious impulses and ideas are liberated and unite with certain emotionally charged events of present reality to produce the imagery of the dream or the delusion. The dream representation is, then, a condensation of actuality and the repressed past.

Something analogous happens in the making of the confession. In the long months of writing and rewriting the confession the prisoner searches for real events and persons in his past and elaborates his fiction of criminal activities from the tiny core of reality. Like the delusion, or the dream, or the "big lie," this small piece of truth at the center gives the illusion of veracity. And, again in analogy to delusional formation, the powerful charge of emotion from unconscious sources, the overwhelming feeling of guilt, is invested in the fictional self-representation of "criminal," "spy," "saboteur," in the confessional narrative. Perhaps in the same way that a powerful dream is experienced and even remembered uncertainly as "real," the fictional confession is made real by the strength of the real emotion. The genuineness of the feeling of guilt authenticates the fictional representation of guilt.

Lifton makes it absolutely clear that programs of thought reform are not "irresistible." There were men and women who successfully resisted and retained integrity of personality. Among those who experienced thought reform there was a wide range in the degree of conversion. And in follow-up studies, it is seen that even the successful converts altered belief in varying degrees after being released from prison and establishing contact with another environment. The inference is that successful thought reform can be maintained and integrated only when the environment continues to reinforce the ideology.

Who is most susceptible to thought reform? Among the Chinese intellectuals, Lifton found, not unexpectedly, that the young people, the late adolescents, constituted the group ready-made for ideological rebirth. This is because adolescence in itself constitutes an "identity crisis" (Erik Erikson's term); it is the time for psychological rebirth. Among other susceptible types, both Chinese and Western, Lifton found that a "totalism" in the basic structure of personality (i.e., an "all or nothing" principle, a value system committed to absolutes of good and evil and unable to tolerate, either within the personality or without, the existence of impurities or imperfections) united with the totalism of the Communist ideology in the process of conversion.

Who is least susceptible to thought reform? A prisoner who maintained his critical faculties during the thought reform procedure, who had a theory about what was going on and an awareness of being manipulated, was provided, as Lifton puts it, with "one of the rewards of knowledge: a sense of control." As in any other situation of extreme danger, knowledge about the forces that threaten will give back to the ego the feeling of being in control. Lifton further observed that the successful resister avoided emotional involvement with his teachers and fellow prisoners, and maintained as far as posible his independence from the communication system of thought reform. "Humane stoicism," Lifton noted, also served many resisters well. But the fourth and most important resistance technique Lifton calls "identity reinforcement." By this he means that the prisoner maintained contact with his own identity, with his own history, his personal values, his interests, his vocation. As one of the priests said, "To resist . . . you must affirm your personality whenever there is an opportunity. . . ."

One last point: Lifton saw no evidence that "an authoritarian personality" was more susceptible to thought reform than a "liberal." Among the converts he found both. What appeared to be crucial in the conversion experience was the degree to which personal identity could be undermined through the guilt-producing tactics of thought reform.

## IV

The brainwashing and concentration camp studies have together illuminated many obscure problems in the area of ego autonomy. Conversely, some of the researches in ego autonomy have provided startling insights into certain aspects of the brainwashing experience and the behavior generally of human beings under extreme conditions.

At McGill University, Woodburn Heron, W. H. Bexton, and a team of psychologists studied the effects of isolation on human subjects. Student volunteers were paid to lie twenty-four hours a day on a bed in a soundproof room. They wore goggles that admitted light but prevented patterned vision. They were asked to stay in isolation as long as they could (it was a rare subject who was able to remain longer than two or three days) and at intervals, during and after isolation, they were tested.

It was found that within this comparatively short isolation period, mental functioning altered measurably. There was a marked decline in reasoning and complex problem-solving ability. (All subsequent sensory-deprivation studies confirm these findings.) All but a few of the subjects experienced hallucinations,[2] and all reported confusion, inability to concentrate, and diffuse anxiety sometimes bordering on panic.

Of special interest is the "propaganda study" which was part of the experiment; it offers a fascinating insight into one of the psychological conditions that may produce "false belief" during the brainwashing procedure. The "propaganda" was a ninety-minute recorded talk which argued for believing in various types of psychic phenomena (telepathy, clairvoyance, ghosts, poltergeists). After the subject had been in isolation for approximately eighteen hours, he was told that he could listen to a series of records if he wished. Attitude tests were administered to the subjects before and after their exposure to this propaganda, and a control group was employed for comparison. As measured against the control group, the subjects in isolation showed a significant change in attitude regarding psychical phenomena following exposure to the propaganda material.

Two important points can be made here. Sensory deprivation produces regressive modes of thinking and perception, with a corresponding loss of autonomy in the ego. In a stimulus void (such as the isolation room) a hunger for sensory stimulation and for information develops. Against this background, the repetitive information droned out on the phonograph record produced such an impact upon the mind that many subjects experienced it as "truth."

The reports of prisoners who have undergone brainwashing bear striking similarities to the reports and observations of the subjects in sensory-deprivation studies. In brainwashing, regressive modes of thought appear; the ability to reason and to judge becomes progressively weaker; hallucinations are reported; and a panic that is greater than the fear of objective danger overcomes the prisoner: the fear of dissolution of the self and of personal identity, which probably corresponds to the panic states reported among the sensory-deprivation subjects.

As the psychologist David Rapaport suggests, the brainwashing techniques deliberately make use of physical isolation to break down the prisoner; but the prisoner has been isolated in a larger sense, from the external world and from all the sources of information that normally feed his personal ideology. The only information he gets in the immense psychic isolation of the prison is that which his jailers offer him: the relentless grinding out of accusations, exhortations, and lessons in the new ideology.

The problem of ego autonomy and surrender has also been approached through studies of hypnosis: Merton Gill and Margaret Brenman's *Hypnosis and Related States* (1959) furnish important data and theoretical formulations for the analysis of brainwashing. In hypnosis, the ego is induced temporarily to surrender certain of its vital functions, to give these functions and their control to another ego, that of the hypnotist. In order to bring this about, the hypnotist must employ methods that center all attention upon himself. He must interfere with and block certain ego functions that are vital for reality testing, the "I" sense and the sense of voluntariness, in order to take them over himself and achieve the necessary influence over the subject.

The hypnotist's patter and his instructions to concentrate on a single object are aimed at restricting the sensory intake, at excluding so far as possible the sensory data that normally preserve contact between the ego and the environment. As in the sensory-deprivation experiments I have described, the exclusion of normal stimuli has the effect of promoting regression. But at the same time the absence of any other stimulation permits the utterances of the hypnotist to achieve a great impact (analogous to the propaganda records in the isolation chamber). Gill and Brenman compare the brainwasher's unending barrage of talk about guilt and the new ideology to the hypnotist's patter; it commands the subject's attention and deprives him of free energy with which he might feed his sense of identity and his personal ideologies. The brainwasher—like the hypnotist (and unlike the phonograph record)—can make use of a human relationship and dependency to exalt his utterances and charge them with meaning beyond that of words themselves.

Under normal circumstances, if illness or incapacity immobilizes a person even temporarily, there may be anxiety, a sense of childlike helplessness, and an altered self-image. Those who take over the functions of the incapacitated body are endowed with highly magnified powers by the helpless person. When the hypnotist prevents his subject from engaging in motor activity he is taking an important step in acquiring control of his subject. The brainwasher, too, deprives his subject of freedom, even putting chains on him. The prisoner is not permitted to carry out bodily functions with any freedom; toilet, sex, and sleep behavior are rigidly controlled. Of course, the psychological influence and power of the brainwasher are greatly magnified (as compared with the hypnotist's) by the real power he holds over his subject, and by the fact that his subject, like the hypnotist's, is being coerced into surrendering autonomy.

Yet both the hypnotist and the brainwasher, when successful, bring about surrender of the ego because they are able to capture an archaic tendency in the core of the ego itself, a longing to abdicate, to lose itself, to merge with the outer world once again in primal oneness. It is as if there remained in the human personality a regressive longing for the union and complete fusion that preceded the first differentiation of *me*-ness and *other*-ness, the terrible solitude and tensions of separateness.

Both Bettelheim and Lifton make the strong point that there were men and women in the concentration camps and the prison camps of Communist China who did not surrender their minds to the enemy. And, in what I presume to be independent analyses of the data, both authors come to similar conclusions on this point: a man who is deprived of his name, of his intimate human ties, his vocation and all the external nutriments for his personal ideology, can only preserve his identity by feeding it from within. He tells himself who he is by keeping alive his past, his personal values, the memories of loved persons, his intellectual armament. To achieve this in a hostile environment, one's personal identity must have a relatively high degree of independence from the environment. It was not moral belief alone that sustained the ego in extremity, but the degree to which conscience was internalized in personality and the relative independence of conscience from the environment. In the extreme situations in which the ego and its moral organization is cut off from its external nutriments and may even find itself in an environment that opposes its values, the internalized conscience may take over the function of the absent environment, *so that it supports itself, in effect, and provides its own nutriments.*

So the vulnerable center is "I." But it would be just as true to say that the invulnerable center is "I." There is no black magic in the possession of alien powers that can enslave the human mind. The methods employed to create total submission and conversion are neither mysterious nor irresistible, in the last analysis. The limits of the human body are known, circumscribed and predictable, and this ancient knowledge can be employed to bring about confession and subjugation of the human will. But surrender of the mind and conversion to an enemy's ideology must engage the ego in a choice, not a rational choice (since it may be dictated by a genuine peril to the ego's survival) and yet a moral one, if we are to give any meaning to moral behavior. The ultimate danger to personal autonomy, then, comes from within; the ultimate guarantees of freedom are invested in the ego itself.

## Notes

1. We must remember that Bettelheim is describing the concentration camps of 1939 and 1940 which at that time were largely for the internment of political prisoners. The extermination camps did not come into existence until a later date.

2. These should not, however, be confused with the hallucinations of psychosis. The subjects—except in three cases—did not suppose that the images which presented themselves were real.

## References

Bettelheim, B. (1943). Individual and Mass Behavior in Extreme Situations. *Journal of Abnormal Psychology*, 38:417–452.

——. (1960). *The Informed Heart.* New York: Free Press.

Gill, M., and Brenman, M. (1959). *Hypnosis and Related States.* New York: International Universities Press.

Lifton, R. (1956). Thought Reform of Western Civilians in Chinese Communist Prisons. *Psychiatry*, 19:173–195.

——. (1961). *Thought Reform and the Psychology of Totalism.* New York: Norton.

# 27

## Morals and Psychoanalysis

A *review of* Freud: The Mind of the Moralist *by Philip Rieff (New York: Viking, 1961) and* Psychoanalysis and Moral Values *by Heinz Hartmann (New York: International Universities Press, 1960)*

Can one derive an ethic from a psychology and its psychotherapeutic method? Freud himself maintained the physician's and scientist's neutrality on problems of moral conduct, while conducting his private life according to his own strict moral code. There is no contradiction here, if we understand that moral neutrality is the necessary condition for scientific investigation and is not the condition for governing behavior or instinctual drives. Freud specifically disclaimed the use of psychoanalysis as a guide to the right conduct of life. And yet Philip Rieff is right when he claims that nonetheless there are intellectual and moral implications in the writings of Freud. Ideas that have played a crucial role in the moral revolution of our time, though neutral in the scientific sense, have lost moral neutrality upon challenging established beliefs and altering man's image of himself.

Ironically many of the cultural changes which psychoanalysis produced were not, strictly speaking, derived from psychoanalytic theory or therapy but were magnificent errors in interpretation, ideas that lost their identities while traveling. Repression, for example, first introduced by Freud in 1895 as a factor in neurosis, emerged later in the popular culture as a psychic evil, the deterrent to health, happiness, and successful art. Between 1900 and 1905 Freud began to see that the mechanism that he had isolated in hysteria was a normal and indispensable component of psychic functioning, that repression was not in itself pathological. From approximately 1905 until the present a correct statement of Freud's views on repression would include these two points: (1) repression is not, in itself, pathological; (2) it is not repression *qua* repression that creates neurosis but *unsuccessful* repression. When it breaks down and an intolerable wish threatens to break through into consciousness a conflict will arise that may initiate a neurosis. There is nothing, then, in this view (which pre-dates the popularization of psychoanalytic ideas) that recommends the theory to those who seek health through the casting off of moral restraints or to those who try to rear healthy children by avoiding "repressions." The error in transmission of the idea in popular culture certainly influenced conduct in many spheres. Changes in child-rearing methods and the sexual morality of adults are attributable, at least in part, to the popular belief that repression is a danger to psychic health. In such instances new standards for conduct claim the authority of psychoanalysis, though the influential idea is a distortion of the scientific concept.

It is not an easy job to establish the links between Freud's ideas and their product in social behavior, attitudes and the self-image of modern man. Philip Rieff is a sociologist who brings to this study a considerable erudition and a discerning eye for forms and patterns in behavior. He describes a new moral type that has emerged in the past half-century, the product of diverse historical and socio-economic tendencies, one that needed a psychological rationale for its introversion of interest and found it in Freudian psychology. The new moral type Rieff calls "psychological man." He emerges quite convincingly from Mr. Rieff's examination. But the connections between the modern type, and the influential psychoanalytic ideas that have formed him are not so convincing, and here Mr. Rieff encounters difficulties.

Psychological man is described by Rieff as the dominant moral type of our time, "specially adapted to endure his own period: the trained egoist, the private man, who turns away from the arenas of public failure to re-examine himself and his own emotions." Rieff identifies a new kind of conscience, a reasoned, scrupulous examination of self and motive, one that is guided by the scientific ideal of neutrality and the Freudian "ethic of honesty," a conscience that measures good by personal health-values and substitutes reasoned self-judgments for guilt. Because moral aspirations may endanger his health-values, psychological man does not aspire. Because social protest is for him only the externalization of an inner struggle with authority, psychological man looks inward for solutions. And if virtue is the civilized mask for base longings, the new morality is compelled to question the legitimacy of good.

The caricature obliges us to recognize a number of traits that are identifiable as modern and a considerable number of beliefs that claim the authority of psychoanalysis. Rieff himself, by examining the entire body of Freud's works, identifies him as the educator of psychological man. Psychological man appears as the personification of the ego, judiciously regulating the demands of the id and the demands of the superego. The moral neutrality of psychological man suggests the moral neutrality of the analyst and the analytic method, in which the patient is asked to suspend his critical attitude; and the reasoned morality of psychological man may be taken as the triumph of the therapeutic ideal in which the irrational dictates of the superego are overcome by rational thought processes. Above all, Freud discovered the tyranny of conscience and, in Rieff's view, made guilt a disease. "Freud," says Rieff, "can conceive of a person's feeling guilty not because he has been bad but because, as a result of his repressions, he is too moral. This is one source of his influence: his diagnosis that we are sick from our ideals and that the one practical remedy lies in an infusion from below."

A large part of Mr. Rieff's argument rests upon his erroneous conception of the superego. Rieff sees the superego as "imposed or superinduced on the real individual (ego)" which he understands to imply an alienation of "the social personality (superego) from the genuine self (ego)." Rieff appears to believe that the superego is almost entirely unconscious, which then leads him to say, "Implicitly Freud presumes that the decisions of conscience are invariably irrational; indeed conscience is defined as being—it is a powerful rhetorical affront—no less irrational than the instinctual id." Rieff speaks of "the ostensibly amoral knowledge of the ego." And later: "Against the rigid moralizing tyranny of conscience, Freud posed a flexible but highly limited administration by the rational ego. . . . Thus narrowly defined, reason makes a weak champion."

Now, of course, if conscience is irrational and the "amoral" ego is weak against its tyranny, the whole question of values, moral choice, and moral responsibility is thrown into confusion, and this is exactly what Rieff sees as the implications of Freudian psychology. And if guilt is the manifestation only of pathology, the place of guilt as a moral restraint can also be disputed.

In Freud's view the concept superego embraces both conscience and ideal self and is conceived as a permanent organization within the personality, an internalized moral system that may exert its influence without coercion from external forces. Part of the superego is unconscious. The superego is part of the ego; its values and standards of conduct are an integral part of the ego, and one can speak of the two institutions as merged for all practical purposes. It is only when conflict arises that a division between them can be observed. We cannot speak of the "amoral" knowledge of the ego, for the ego as properly defined is the possessor of moral knowledge and the executor of moral functions. The superego makes no decisions, "rational" or "irrational." Only the ego can make decisions, for it is the ego that judges, reasons and acts.

The sense of guilt, Freud says, is an expression of the tension between the demands of conscience and the actual attainments of the ego. In *The Ego and The Id, Civilization and Its Discontents*, and in other works, he makes it very clear that he regards guilt feelings as normal and indispensable for the functioning of personality. The signal of guilt becomes a warning and usually an effective deterrent to conduct that is incompatible with moral standards. The experience of guilt feelings and self-criticism for failure to measure up to the ego-ideal provides the motive for modification of the personality. Freud differentiates between a "normal, conscious sense of guilt" and the guilt feelings encountered in neuroses, which arise from unconscious forces and derive their energy and their malignant character from an internal conflict that grows on secrecy and engages the ego's defensive measures to keep it from entering consciousness. In this way a neurotic patient may be burdened with intolerable guilt without knowing the reason for it. In such instances we have a disease of conscience, and the sense of guilt which normally serves as a guardian of internal moral laws is now given over to the disease to persecute the personality for unknown crimes.

Psychoanalysis treats the diseases of the superego, but it does not abolish the superego. The superego is an indestructible part of the ego. If it were possible to abolish it the entire structure of personality would collapse. A successful psychoanalytic therapy strengthens the superego by partially freeing it from irrational forces. It restores guilt feelings to appropriate moral functions, making available a store of energy for constructive action bound in disease to magic acts of repentance, self-abasement and avoidance.

If there are any moral implications that can be derived from psychoanalytic therapy it might be said that a man who has achieved relative freedom from magic and the demands of the drives may have relative freedom to choose. But the question of moral choice cannot be dealt with apart from the question of moral imperatives, and here the relevance of psychoanalysis is important. Heinz Hartmann, probably the outstanding psychoanalytic theorist today, takes up the problem of psychoanalysis and moral values in his recent essay, written for a psychoanalytic audience. Psychoanalysis, he says, presents us with a psychology of moral behavior. Through Freud we have come to understand how moral imperatives are derived from the earliest love ties of child to parent and the means by which moral imperatives are internalized in personality. But a psychology of moral behavior cannot be taken as a guide to moral conduct. (In the same way, I would suggest, a psychology of art cannot give us standards by which to judge art. Rieff gets sidetracked here, too.) Moral imperatives, therefore, cannot be *derived* from psychoanalysis, or from psychoanalytic therapy or from any system of "health-values." The "thou shalt" and "thou shalt not" can only achieve their imperative quality through the unique conditions provided by the dependency of the child upon his moral teachers and are given permanence in character through his identification with them.

The analysis of moral imperatives in psychoanalytic therapy does not deprive them of their power to influence moral judgments. (As examples I would point out that the analysis of incestuous wishes toward the mother will not lead to incest; the analysis of destructive wishes toward the father will not lead to murder. Analysis deprives the unconscious incestuous and murderous wishes of their power to contaminate areas of normal functioning, to inhibit the sexual function, or work, or to create symptoms.) Psychoanalysis, therefore, can confirm the existence of moral motivations in human character that are permanent and irreversible.

Hartmann demonstrates very clearly that moral imperatives which are themselves the most stable class of values, constituting the earliest and most powerful voice of conscience, cannot be subjected to objective tests; their validity as a guide to moral behavior is beyond proof and beyond rationalization. A man who cannot bring himself to murder does not ask himself, like Raskolnikov, "After all, why not?" He cannot. The "thou shalt not" requires no verification.

Hartmann criticizes the tendency today to substitute health-values for moral values, sometimes formulated as "there are not moral or immoral people, there are only healthy and sick people." There are many neurotics, he points out, who are "highly moral" and often socially useful, while there are many "healthy" people who are neither. Since health valuations do not have the psychological character of moral imperatives, Hartmann argues, there is a psychological error in the implication that they can substitute for "genuine moral valuations"—and by "genuine" he means integrated into character.

Hartmann notes that people who have undergone analysis certainly do not have a uniform hierarchy of moral values or similar moral codes. (This is a strong argument against the belief that psychoanalysis indoctrinates or that a system of health values can be derived from the theory or therapy psychoanalysis.) This is not to say that psychoanalysis cannot have an influence on moral life, but that it does not provide standards of conduct based on health ethics. Hartmann quotes Freud: "Why should analyzed people be altogether better than others? Analysis makes for unity but not necessarily for goodness." Hartmann expands these remarks: "If moral inadequacy is due to neurotic causes, successful analysis can remedy it. The more successful integration psychoanalysis promotes may have an effect also on moral conduct. . . . The broadening of self-awareness, which is, of course, a regular result of analysis, can influence the degree of consistency of the 'moral system,' etc."

Has psychoanalysis contributed to the devaluation of moral values by the unmasking of moral pretense? One must realize, writes Hartmann," that in addition to moral pretenses there are moral motivations which have the full dynamic significance of independent forces in the mental economy. The discovery by psychoanalysis that highly valued moral behavior may have roots in instinctual tendencies or self-interest has led to the mistaken view that high valuation is an illusion." Hartmann speaks of this as "the genetic mistake." (To illustrate: if moral revulsion against sadism is a reaction-formation against the infantile pleasure in destruction, is moral revulsion devalued by its origins in an opposite tendency? The psychoanalytic view is that the later moral attitude has achieved independence from its instinctual origins, that it has autonomy in the sphere of mental operations and has validity for what it is, a stable and permanent moral attitude that guarantees against the return of the instinct.)

There is the common belief that psychoanalysis empties the contents of the id and brings the instinctual life and unconscious mental processes under the control of the ego and rationality. (Rieff, too, is inclined to see psychoanalytic therapy in this light.) Hartmann, who has much to say about rationality in the volume under discussion also touched on this problem in an essay published twenty years ago and recently reissued (*Ego Psychology and the Problem of Adaptation*). Hartmann suggests that a misconception has arisen out of Freud's statement, "Where id was, there shall ego be." "It does not mean," Hartmann comments, "that there has ever been, or could be, a man who is purely rational; it implies only a cultural historical tendency and a therapeutic goal" [expressed in relative terms]. "There is no danger that the id could ever be 'dried up' nor that all the ego functions could be reduced to intellectual functions." This "rational" man if he could be produced, would be a "man without qualities" says Hartmann, borrowing Musil's phrase.

It should be mentioned that Hartmann in his essay on moral values does not alter in any way Freud's own views on the psychology of moral behavior or the position he stated for psychoanalysis in regard to moral values. Rieff is under the impression that there is a "school" of ego psychology that has revised Freudian psychology and has "attacked" (Freud's) "weakling conception of the ego." Hartmann is in fact one of the leading scholars in the field of ego psychology but the theorists in this field (Rieff mentions Kris, for example) are not members of a deviant or revisionist wing of psychoanalysis. They are in the mainstream of Freudian psychoanalysis. It was Freud himself who in the 'twenties turned the attention of analytic scholars to the study of the ego and who laid the theoretical groundwork for an ego psychology.

Finally, something must be said about the most unsettling question that arises out of Freud's writings, the question of moral responsibility. If unconscious wishes can motivate behavior is a man fully responsible for his actions? Does he have moral responsibility for ideas of which he has no conscious knowledge? Does he have moral responsibility for his dreams? Rieff understands Freud to give moral absolution for unconscious thoughts. Rieff writes: "We cannot be held responsible, Freud argues, for the thoughts expressed in our dream life." He cites as authority Freud's essay, "Moral Responsibility for the Content of Dreams" and, unaccountably, he has exactly reversed Freud's statement! This is what Freud said:

> Obviously one must hold oneself reponsible for the evil impulses of one's dreams. In what other way can one deal with them? Unless the content of the dream (rightly understood) is inspired by alien spirits, it is part of my own being. If I seek to classify the impulses that are present in me according to social standards into good and bad, I must assume responsibility for both sorts; and if, in defense, I say that what is unknown, unconscious and repressed in me is not my "ego," then I shall not be basing my position upon psychoanalysis. . . .

Rieff's psychological man, the man of reasoned morality, prudently steering his course by self-interest and health-ethics, is worth the attention bestowed upon him by a social scientist. He remains unclaimed by psychoanalysis, and the authority of psychoanalysis which Rieff claims for him is not supported by the theory or the therapeutic method of psychoanalysis. Rieff could have made a stronger case for his new moral type if he could have separated the scientific idea from its later forms as it became absorbed into the culture. A scientific idea may retain its integrity as long as it retains its connection with science and its methods. When it passes over into popular usage it inevitably acquires new meanings and uses which are no longer subjected to definition or to scientific validation. The term "repression," for example, as it was absorbed into popular culture and usage has lost nearly all connections with Freud's concept of repression, except through the name itself. In contemporary thought and morality the concept of repression has probably had little influence outside of psychoanalysis, psychiatry, psychology, and related fields. But the popular term "repression" with its uncertain antecedents in the concept has probably been one of the most influential words in the twentieth century. If this concept goes astray in Greenwich Village shall we hold Freud accountable for the wayward idea in the same way that a father is responsible for his delinquent minor? And whose concept of repression are we talking about? Freud's or Mabel Dodge Luhan's?

The example of "repression" above is my own, but I wish to illustrate in this way the hazards of tracing influential ideas. Mr. Rieff's new moral type reflects with startling accuracy a psychological attitude and system of beliefs that might be called "the popular Freud," Freudian ideas that were made over in popular usage and lost their connections with the original concepts. Strictly speaking, these are no longer "Freudian ideas." Freud's "influence" on contemporary ideas and morality cannot be traced from his writings to the social product without accounting for the reshaping of these ideas by popular usage and by other historical and cultural tendencies of the times. It might even be said that the popular Freud has had vastly greater influence upon contemporary ideas and morals than the scientist Freud.

# 28

# Kafka and the Dream

For most of his life, it appears, Kafka lived on terms of dangerous intimacy with the world of the dream. He possessed a kind of sensory knowledge of the dream and the dimensions of consciousness which could only be achieved by a man who had an extraordinary relationship to his own inner life. This knowledge did not come from a clinical study of his own states of consciousness, and I feel certain that it did not come from psychoanalytic texts. Kafka was not an academic student of the mind. He was, however, a meticulous observer of his own mental activity.

There is evidence that he experienced mental states in which dream-like images and fantasies emerged, then were caught and held in consciousness, naked specimens of unconscious productions. Often he preserved these things in his notebooks, recorded along with the texts of nocturnal dreams, obsessional thoughts, fragments of memories, and hundreds of other bits and pieces of the disordered contents of his inner world. Here and there in the Kafka stories a piece from this attic debris makes its ghostly reappearance. In many instances a dream, a fantasy, or a piece of imagery recorded in the notebooks becomes the starting point for a sketch or a story. There is evidence, then, that he not only made exhaustive investigations of his own mental processes but also made use of his discoveries in his writing.

Introspection for Kafka was not a reflective process but a disease, the compulsion of his morbid guilt, which drew him deeper and deeper into psychic depths in hopeless pursuit of the crime and the judgment. It was an obsessional occupation which became a torment for him and slowly widened the gap between himself and the real world. In 1922 this estrangement reached a critical point and Kafka viewed his mental state with alarm. On January 16 he writes: "This past week I suffered something very like a breakdown . . . " " . . . impossible to sleep, impossible to endure life, or, more exactly, the course of life. The clocks are not in unison; the inner one runs crazily on at a devilish or demoniac or in any case inhuman pace, the outer one limps along at its usual speed. What else can happen but that the two worlds split apart, and they do split apart, or at least clash in a fearful manner. There are doubtless several reasons for the wild tempo of the inner process; the most obvious one is introspection, which will suffer no idea to sink tranquilly to rest but must pursue each one into consciousness, only itself to become an idea, in turn to be pursued by renewed introspection." And later in the same entry: "The solitude that for the most part has been forced on me, in part voluntarily sought by me—but what was this if not compulsion too?—is now losing all its ambiguity and approaches its dénouement. Where is it leading? The strongest likelihood is, that it may lead to madness. . . ." Later that month the panic gives way to melancholy resignition. On January 28 he writes: " . . . for I am now a citizen of this other world, whose relationship to the ordinary one is the relationship of the wilderness to cultivated land. . . ." And on the following day he writes: " . . . it is only that the attraction of the human world is so immense, in an instant it can make one forget everything. Yet the attraction of my world too is strong. . . ."

The mental crisis did not end as he feared in madness, but in disease. This was the year of the onset of Kafka's tuberculosis. He understood his illness and wrote to Brod, "My head has made an appointment with my lungs behind my back."

Of the two worlds, Kafka's and "the human world," it was the first that he knew best. Kafka wrote about himself, his inner experience, and the struggle with nameless tyrants, the lustful couples who copulate within the sight of the law, the endless tribunal, the comic-tragic bureaucrats and corrupt officials—all of these were not conceived as allegories for his time but were events of inner life. (His own comments and interpretations of his works repeatedly bear this out.) If his writings achieve the effect of satire and broad social caricature, it is because the dream is in itself a caricature of life; the dream is in one sense an allegory. Moreover Kafka knew this and understood it very well. In a conversation Janouch says to Kafka: "The *Metamorphosis* is a terrible dream, a terrible conception." Kafka replies: "The dream reveals the reality, which conception lags behind. That is the horror of life—the terror of art. . . ."

I think it is also a mistake to look upon his writings, as Charles Neider proposes, as "freudian allegories" or to speak of Kafka's deliberate use of "freudian symbols." If Kafka was acquainted with psychoanalytic ideas (and there is some evidence for this), he did not pluck his symbols from clinical texts like an amateur with a drugstore dream book. The use of the term "freudian symbols" is, in itself, an embarrassment in considering this view, for Freud was not the inventor of dream symbols but their investigator, and he repeatedly acknowledged his debt to the creative writers who were the discovers of symbolism, including that of the dream.

No formula for dream interpretation exists in psychoanalysis. A dream, a symbol, can be properly interpreted only through the personal associations of the dreamer. While Freud brought attention to a number of "universal" symbols, he repeatedly stressed the multideterminants in symbol choice, and hence the futility of assigning a single meaning to a symbol. Neider's extrapolation of symbols, his mechanical interpretations, and codification of the symbol types result in a piece of analysis which is psychoanalytically unsound and which debases the work studied. It is worth mentioning, too, that many of the symbols which he has dealt with are interpreted arbitrarily by him and without the authority of clinical investigation. So far as I know no clinical investigator has found that a court stands for "the unconscious" or a boarding house for "the preconscious," and I think it very unlikely that this will ever be demonstrated.

Moreover, we must admit that even those symbols which are properly speaking "universal" are not in themselves the material for creative work. Symbols are sterile things in themselves; it is only when the symbol is animated through personal experience, when it acquires dimensions of meaning and ambiguity, that it can evoke emotional reactions.

Kafka may have profited from the psychoanalytic investigation of dreams and dream symbolism, but he wrote out of inner experience. An investigation of Kafka symbolism will demonstrate repeatedly how little he was influenced by the arbitrary dream symbol. It seems to me to be as unprofitable to try to understand Kafka and his writing in terms of "freudian symbols" as it is to understand a dream apart from the dreamer's own associations.

If Kafka knew the world of the dream better than the rest of us, he was not indebted to Freud but to his personal suffering. He called himself, at last, "a citizen of this other world." He was not like the rest of us, the nocturnal visitors, who are favored on return with a merciful amnesia or dim recall. He had taken up his ghostly residence there, and habituation had given his eyes a special kind of night vision so that the forms and events of the dream which ordinary dreamers call uncertain and indistinct were tangible and real, capable of description in fine detail. Even the texts of his own dreams, recorded in his notebooks, are remarkable for the recall of detail and the visual preciseness.

The danger in such intimacy with the dream world is that the connections to the other world may be lost, and this danger was real and known to Kafka. His writing was the bridge, the connection betweeen the two worlds; it was the strongest of the bonds which united him with the real world. And the writings themselves told the same story of the danger, or the failure, or the impossibility of human connections.

He wrote his biography in his symbolism of lost connections—the intercepted letters, the interrupted coitus, the telephones with the connections to nowhere. There is the indescribable loneliness and sadness of the little train in "The Railroad of Kalda" which makes its way into the frozen interior of Russia and regularly comes to its end in the middle of the wilderness, never to reach its destination. It is a train without mission, bearing a tiny freight and a few passengers in the course of the year, running its course between nowhere and nowhere. At the train stop the company's agent dwells in solitude in an abandoned wooden shed, in despair of life and afraid of death. The Kalda story, too, is unfinished. No man can write the end of his autobiography.

These symbols of lost connections, like all powerful symbols (and unlike those symbols which are plucked cheaply from dream books), are highly stratified and rich in latent meaning. They speak of the failures in human connections and communication which are recurrent motifs in Kafka's writing and his life. The wretched railroad of Kalda, once conceived by its owners in a surge of capitalist daring and hope, has come to nothing, a toy train chugging its way through vast space to its absurd and melancholy end in the wastes. This is the parable of Kafka's failure in the eyes of his father. And the ridiculous railroad, this mockery of men's extravagant hopes and ambitions, is Kafka's symbol for the failure of his own ambitions, and for the failure of his lifelong struggle with an unconquerable opponent, here represented as the vastness of a wilderness which cannot be spanned by the tiny train, in real life by the figure of a giant, the father, before whom Kafka remained an insignificant dwarf as boy and grown man. It is the symbol for the unfinished work, the uncompleted writings. It is the comment on Kafka's religious views, the failure to reach anything "beyond." And it is the symbol of biological failure. The little train which is never to reach its destination speaks eloquently and touchingly of Kafka's sexual impotence. The little train comes to its end in the middle of the wilderness, a full day's journey from Kalda, discharges its few passengers, its small freight, and returns. And the ground of this tiny settlement was frozen solid, we are told. "I was too weak to conquer the soil," said the company's agent. "A stubborn soil that was frozen solid until spring and that even resisted the sharp edge of my new axe. Whatever seed one sowed in it was lost."

It is a striking fact that Kafka, the "citizen of this other world," should have established his human fellowship in his writings through the fraternity of the dream. He had only the frailest connections with what he called "the human world," and his life was a tragedy of lost and broken communications with that world. Yet his literary genius was most pronounced in his ability to communicate elemental emotion and primal experience. It is a communication which is direct and powerful and owes its effect to a profound insight; it is the creation through the device of the private dream of a world of collective memory where each man can know his fellow.

## II

It is probable that when the current enthusiasm for Kafka has run its course Kafka will emerge with less stature as a writer but with undiminished prestige as an innovator in the technique of the psychological novel. For Kafka has brought a thoroughly original and revolutionary approach to the problem of the representation of psychic dimensions in literature.

We must consider that the discoveries of psychoanalysis have made demands upon the writer which are entirely unlike those of other systems of ideas. A theory of biology, of society, of politics, or of history can be given suitable expression within the framework of a narrative without straining the conventional means of communication. But a scientific theory of psychic dimensions and the primary processes of thought and imagery make unique demands upon the writer's equipment and his technique when he attempts to represent these ideas in his work.

Language, itself, as an instrument of the reasoning ego, seems opposed to working for unreason in the service of the unconscious. The higher order of thinking which is implicit in language is incompatible with the archaic mental system which governs the primary thought processes. The dream, for example, doesn't "speak" a language. It can only represent words and ideas through pictures. The spoken word or phrase, if it comes into the dream at all, is torn from the context of waking life and played back like a dusty record. Similarly, the writer's conventional devices of narration oppose the representation of unconscious thought processes. The story teller gives order to his materials; the dreamer gives disorder to his. The story reveals, makes explicit, intends to communicate its meaning; the manifest dream conceals, disguises, has no intention of communicating.

It is understandable, then, that the writers who have attempted to bring this dimension of mind into the scope of their work have usually found it necessary to experiment upon the language itself and the techniques of narration. In one way or another these writers tried to recreate the world of the unconscious by borrowing the method of unconscious thought processes, the so-called "primary process." The dream's method of plastic representation, ellipsis, condensation, and symbol formation, provided models for a new writing. The writer's problem of narration of unconscious mental processes also found solutions in the model of the dream. The dream dispenses with logical connections. Its contents are brought together only because of their associative links and without regard for order or coherence. Its meaning can only be established through translation. The transposition of unconscious thought processes in writing led to various types of "stream of consciousness" writing which, like the dream, could be understood only through interpretation.

Kafka did not trouble himself at all with the mechanical problems of entering the dream world. He found an easy solution to the problem of the language barrier. He simply walked through it. His prose style which Mann described as "a conscientious, curiously explicit, objective, clean, and correct style" undergoes no distortions, employs no language tricks, and is perfectly consistent and reasonable in the reporting of events, real or delusional.

No one has succeeded with this device as Kafka has. No one else can evoke the world of the dream with such chilling authenticity. Kafka's so-called "dream technique" springs from a conception of the dream as a work of art. Kafka explored the aesthetic properties of the dream. He understood the primary relationship between unconscious mental processes and the form and composition of the dream. By taking the dream as his model in his own compositions, he achieved the perfect formal conditions for the representation of unconscious experience. Now this, in itself, is not an innovation; experimental writers of this century have turned to this method of composition repeatedly in the attempt to evoke the qualities of the dream. But when Kafka unites the structural aspects of the dream with his narrative technique, his compositions achieve the most extraordinary effects of the dream itself. This is all the more impressive when we regard the seeming artlessness, the unambitious character of his narrative technique. It is simply the narration of a dream by a dreamer.

> One evening I returned home to my room from the office somewhat later than usual—an acquaintance had detained me below at the house entrance for a long time—opened the door (my thoughts were still engrossed by our conversation, which had consisted chiefly of gossip about people's social standing), hung my overcoat on the hook and was about to cross over to the washstand when I heard a strange, spasmodic breathing. I looked up and, on top of the stove that stood deep in the gloom of the corner, saw something alive. Yellowish glittering eyes stared at me; large round woman's breasts rested on the shelf of the stove, on either side beneath the unrecognizable face; the creature seemed to consist entirely of a mass of soft white flesh; a thick yellowish tail hung down beside the stove, its tip ceaselessly passing back and forth over the cracks of the tiles.
>
> The first thing I did was to cross over with long strides and sunken head—nonsense! nonsense! I kept repeating like a prayer. . . .

The effect of this passage, the immediate sense of the nightmare, is achieved not by its contents alone, not by the stove monster, but by the prose treatment. It is the conventional narration, the factual, ordinary rendering of this event which produces the effect of the uncanny. This is entirely in accord with the psychological mechanism in the experience of the uncanny by which unreal events are perceived as real, the inanimate is animated, and the delusion or dream obtains conviction. Kafka demonstrates by this technique that the quality of uncanniness which we attribute to the dream and the delusion is not a property of the dream itself or of unconscious experience; it belongs to the ego, the representative of consciousness and reality, and is produced when a repressed idea is given illusory confirmation by an event in consciousness with the effect of momentarily breaking off the ego's contact with reality.

Now since the uncanny is not a quality of the dream itself, but derives from an impairment of an ego faculty, that of reality testing, a narrative which attempts to simulate the experience of dreaming or to evoke the "uncanniness" of the dream must deceive the critical and judging faculties of the ego through a prose which apparently sustains logic and belief at the same time that it affirms the delusion. The ideal prose for this treatment is everyday speech, a factual narration in simple declarative sentences. The narration of events and visions from a night world in the ordinary, accustomed prose of waking life produces exactly that sense of dissolving reason which makes reality a dream and the dream a reality, in essence the quality of uncanniness.

Let us consider whether the same effect could be achieved through an experiment upon the language itself and the mode of narration. Now a prose which attempts to evoke the experience of dreaming by borrowing the method of the dream work must break up the structure of speech in order to bring it into a primitive system of thought. Syntax has no place in primary mental processes, and such a narrative needs to free itself from the order and restriction of language, yet cannot abandon it completely for functional reasons. Meaning will suffer through this treatment, of course, but this is a dimension of mind which is cut off from the higher mental faculties, has no reason of its own, no order or coherence, and for many purposes of the writer the obscurity and ambiguity of this liberated prose will strengthen the analogy to dreaming. Similarly, by abandoning the patterns of everyday speech, the writer can introduce phrasing and rhythms which recall the fluidity and merging forms of unconscious thought processes. Such a radical departure from the spoken language can include words themselves. The dream can be taken as a model for bold invention and license in language. For although it "speaks no language," it represents the word in visual forms and symbols which both mask and unmask the language of waking life and reveal the infinitely ramified structure of meaning. The writer who takes this license of the dream for himself can achieve dimensions of meaning and a richness of allusion unparalleled in everyday speech. It is unnecessary to add that these experiments upon the language demand such powerful gifts of imagination in a writer that they have only rarely produced important results.

This writing which bends the language, changes its order, its accustomed phrasing and usage, can achieve many effects of its own in the representation of unconscious mental processes, but it cannot achieve the effect of the uncanny or cause the reader to experience the dreamlike narrative as a dream. We stand outside of the dream in reacting to this writing; certain sensory effects of the dream are induced in us, but we are not deluded. Our knowledge that this is unreal or that this is a dream is not even momentarily destroyed. This is because the distortions of language have already stamped the experience as unreal. It is analogous to a situation described by Freud in his essay on "The Uncanny." He demonstrates that the feeling which we describe as uncanny is always dependent in fiction or in life upon the appearance of unreal events as real, but when, as in fairy tales, the setting and the frankly animistic character of the events depart from the world of reality from the start, the feeling of uncanniness cannot be obtained. In the fairy tale or any fictional form that by its setting or form of presentation states its unreal character, the reader *willingly* participates in the delusion. In producing the experience of the uncanny in fiction, the writer must take care to exclude his reader's judgment and criticism and cause him to participate in the fictional delusion without a moment's reflection or the exercise of consciousness.[1]

The authentic dream quality, which Kafka achieves, owes a large part of its effect to narrative devices which temporarily dissolve the reader's sensory contact with reality and cause him to fall back upon archaic forms of thinking. Kafka erases the boundaries between reality and the dream; his transition from one world to another is as imperceptible as the moment between waking and sleeping. In much of Kafka's writing there is this ghostly treading between two worlds, made all the more sinister by the insubstantial and muted forms of reality and the electrifying clarity of the delusion and the dream. The passage from the ordinary event of coming home from the office and hanging up a coat to the extraordinary vision of a monster occurs without an interval. In analogy with the dream the interval does not exist; it is not remarked upon for the same reason that no man knows the moment he falls asleep, loses this self for the other self in the dream, or leaves his bed to flee through hollow corridors. In recreating through the narrative the psychic transition from waking to dreaming, Kafka brings the reader directly into the dream. He causes the reader to suspend reason and criticism, to submit to the delusion, through the simple device of juxtaposing reality and the dream in agreement with the psychic experience of the emerging dream.

The effect is strengthened when the narrative, as in the stove-monster sequence, proceeds to treat fantastic events as real in the same way that events of the dream are experienced as real by the dreamer. The narrator did not imagine that he saw a monster; he *saw* it; and the description of the monster in fine detail supports the delusional effect in much the same way that the eye-witnesses of flying saucers support their delusions through minute descriptions of the little men, their clothing, and the size and appearance of the craft.

Kafka's use of metaphor must also be considered in a study of his "dream technique." In the dream a metaphor is represented in its literal aspect. In the metaphor, for example, it is "as if" Kafka were a species of vermin; in the story, "Metamorphosis," as in a dream representation, he *is* a noxious bug. In many places in Kafka's diaries we can trace the evolution of a story or details of a story from a metaphor. In the "Letter to My Father," for example, Kafka has the father answer his reproaches in an imaginary speech in which the father says, "And there is the fight of the vermin, which not only bite, but at the same time suck the blood on which they live. . . ." In the diaries he speaks of the broken engagement with F. B. as "the tribunal in the hotel," and employs other metaphors to represent his engagement as "an arrest," himself as "a criminal." Later, in *The Trial*, we see the concrete representation of these metaphors (though I do not wish to imply that the meaning of the work is contained in these metaphors alone). Similarly we can find the genesis for the story, "The Burrow," in these remarks in his diary, October 6, 1915: "Various types of nervousness. I think noises can no longer disturb me, though to be sure I am not doing any work now. Of course, the deeper one digs one's pit, the quieter it becomes, the less fearful one becomes, the quieter it becomes." In "The Burrow" he represents his illness, his fear of life, in a literal treatment of the metaphorical allusion. The small, frightened animal has dug deep into the ground, and with cunning and ingenuity he has created a labyrinth in which he is snug and safe and which assures him escape in case of danger. "But the most beautiful thing about my burrow is the stillness."

## III

In any circumstances, the relationship between art and the dream is difficult to analyze. The psychoanalytic investigator needs to bear in mind Trilling's insistence that the dream-art analogy must be corrected to allow for the artist's conscious command of his fantasy. He quotes Lamb: "The . . . poet dreams being awake. He is not possessed by his subject but he has dominion over it."

Kafka provides a special case for the study of the relationship between the dream and creative work. He has given us evidence that he employed his dreams and the productions of dream-like states in his writing. In his diaries Kafka records a large number of his own dreams. Many of these are terror dreams, dreams of torture, mutilation, flight from attackers, of lepers and whores and disease, filth, excrement, and monotonously, regularly, dreams of the father, the formidable opponent who cannot be conquered and who cannot be escaped. A number of these dreams become the starting point for a story or a sketch in the diaries, so that we can if we wish examine the relationship between the two.

Like all victims of recurrent terror dreams, Kafka suffered from insomnia. He feared sleep; he feared his dreams, and the struggle against sleep and the yearning for sleep were in themselves a repetition of a lifelong struggle, as if sleep had become the formidable opponent who could not be conquered and to whom it was dangerous to submit. In a conversation with Janouch he says, "Perhaps my insomnia only conceals a great fear of death. Perhaps I am afraid that the soul—which in sleep leaves me—will never return. Perhaps insomnia is only an all too vivid sense of sin, which is afraid of the possibility of a sudden judgment. Perhaps insomnia is itself a sin. Perhaps it is a rejection of the natural."

He wrote at night: "Wenn es nicht diese grauenvollen, schlaflosen Nächte gäbe, so würde ich überhaupt nicht schreiben. So wird mir aber immer meine dunkle Einzelhaft bewusst."* But the apparitions of the dream which he fended off through sleeplessness forced their way into the fantasies and obsessive thoughts which occupied him at these times. These fantasies were themselves very close to dream productions and were the sources of a number of stories and sketches. On one occasion Janouch attempts to pin down Kafka on the meaning of *The Verdict*. Kafka, after some embarrassment, says, "*The Verdict* is the spectre of a night." "What do you mean?" "It is a spectre." "And yet you wrote it," Janouch says. And Kafka replies, "That is merely the verification, and so the complete exorcism of the spectre." So that writing for Kafka was also the rite and the magic act for the subduing of his disturbing visions. In another conversation with Janouch he allies writing and conjuration: "Das Schreiben ist eben eine Art von Geisterbeschwörung."**

Kafka has left us an extraordinary record for the study of the relationships between his dreams and dream-like fantasies and his writings. I am particularly interested in the dream-story sequences in his diaries which show us how he worked with the materials of his own dreams. In each of these we see how the problem of the dream is taken up in the waking state, and how the elements of the dream are recomposed in the story.

In the example which follows, I employ a method of analysis which requires some justification to begin with. I am committed, of course, to the psychoanalytic principle that a dream or an imaginative work cannot be fully analyzed without the associations of the dreamer or the artist. In these studies of the dream-story sequences, it can be demonstrated that the elements of the story which are related to the dream can be regarded as associations to the dream, that is, that the story takes up the dream thoughts, the latent content of the dream, and develops these thoughts in a new composition. (This does not mean of course that the latent *meaning* of the dream is made conscious to the writer, or that the story is an explication of the dream by the writer.) In analyzing the dream-story sequences, I also make use of any other source materials, circumstantial or historical, which have a

---

\* "If it were not for these sleepless nights I would probably not write at all. But then I would never be aware of my dark isolation."—Ed. trans.

\*\* "Writing is always a kind of exorcism."—Ed. trans.

demonstrable relationship to the content of the dream or the story. When Kafka tells us the circumstances under which the dream is dreamed or the story is written, we can assume a relationship between these circumstances and the production of a dream or a story that can be safely employed in an analytic investigation. We are justified in making the same use of a biographical fact (like the relationship of Kafka to his father) when this information is required for analytic study. Similarly, when Kafka shows preference for a certain type of imagery, we can regard this imagery as over-determined in the psychoanalytic sense and can draw inferences from its use in other writings which we are permitted to employ in the present investigation. So far as possible I have avoided any arbitrary interpretations of symbols.

### The Dream of the Letter and the Merchant Messner Sketch

In the diary entry for November 24, 1913 (also during the period of struggle against marriage with F. B.), Kafka records a dream which is followed by a story in which certain elements of the dream are employed. *The dream:*

> I am sitting in the garden of a sanatorium at a long table, at the very head, and in the dream I actually see my back. It is a gloomy day, I must have gone on a trip and am in an automobile that arrived a short time ago, driving up in a curve to the front of the platform. They are just about to bring in the food when I see one of the waitresses, a young delicate girl wearing a dress the color of autumn leaves, approaching with a very light or unsteady step through the pillared hall that served as the porch of the sanatorium, and going down into the garden. I don't yet know what she wants but nevertheless point questioningly at myself to learn whether she wants me. And in fact she brings me a letter. But I open it and a great number of thin sheets covered with writing come out, all of them in the strange handwriting. I think, this can't be the letter I'm expecting, it is a very thin letter and a strange, thin, unsure handwriting. I begin to read, leaf through the pages and recognize that it must be a very important letter and apparently from F.'s youngest sister. I eagerly begin to read, then my neighbor on the right, I don't know whether man or woman, probably a child, looks down over my arm at the letter. I scream, "No!" The round table of nervous people begins to tremble. I have probably caused a disaster. I attempt to apologize with a few hasty words in order to go on with the reading. I bend

over my letter again, only to wake up without resistance, as if awakened by my own scream. With complete awareness I force myself to fall asleep again, the scene reappears, in fact I quickly read two or three more misty lines of the letter, nothing of which I remember, and lose the dream in further sleep.

*The story:* In the story which follows the dream entry in the diary, the dream details of "a message" and "an interruption" are brought together again. Following is a summary of the sketch:

The old merchant Messner, laboriously ascending the stairs to his room, is confronted by a young man who has stationed himself in a dark corner. The merchant "still groaning from the exertion of his climb" demands to know who this is and what he wants. The young man introduces himself as a student named Kette. He has come to deliver a message to the merchant. The student wishes to discuss the message in Messner's room. Messner obstinately refuses. "I do not receive guests at night." If the student wishes to give him the message, he can give it now, in the hall. The student protests. The merchant dismisses him curtly. He is not interested in the message. "Every message that I am spared is a gain. I am not curious." He enters his room, locks the door upon the protesting Kette. A moment later there is a persistent knocking on the door. "The knocking came the way children at play scatter their knocks over the whole door, now down low, dull against the wood, now up high, clear against the glass." The merchant approaches the door a stick in hand. "Is anyone still out there?" "Yes. Please open the door for me." Messner opens the door and advances toward the student with his stick. "Don't hit me," the student warns him. "Then go!" The merchant points his finger at the stair. "But I can't," said the student and ran up to Messner so surprisingly. . . .

The story breaks off here, just as the dream breaks off at the point, "I have probably caused a disaster" and with the dreamer's hasty apology.

Certain elements of the dream reappear in the story. In the dream someone, "probably a child," interrupts the reading of the important message, invades the privacy of the dreamer through spying upon the letter. In the story a young student interrupts the old man, creates a disturbance late at night, disturbs the privacy of the merchant. The connection between the child in the dream and the student is further suggested by the knocking on the door in the story which is likened to the knocking of children at play. The antagonists in the dream, the dreamer and a child, become the merchant Messner and the student Kette. The "merchant" is a familiar character in Kafka's writings. He is Kafka's merchant father. *Kette*, chain, might signify the bond which tied Kafka to his father. (See also Kafka's own analysis of the name Georg Bendeman in *The Verdict* in which he identifies *Bende* with bonds, the bonds between father and son. *Diaries*, I, p. 278.) The symbolism becomes clear. The chain, the bonds which tie father and son cannot be severed. Here the link to F. B. in the dream is seen, for Kafka himself understood and explicitly stated in his diaries and his own analysis of *The Verdict* that it was the tie between himself and his father which made marriage with F. B. impossible.

The message in the dream is contained in the letter, but it is a message which is not received, so to speak, because of the interruption. When the dreamer returns to it after waking, he can read a few more "misty lines," none of which he remembers, then loses the dream in further sleep. In the story, too, the message is never delivered. The merchant does not want to hear it. (In both instances the nature of the message is not known.) The letter, the message, seem to belong to the group of "lost communication" symbols in Kafka's writing which were mentioned earlier and are analogous, particularly, to the telephones in *The Castle*. They are failures in human connections, of course, here represented in the dream by the symbol of a letter from a woman and in the story by the message for the man. His life conflict is delineated in these terms. He cannot receive a woman's love (he cannot read the letter in the dream), and he cannot give his love to a man (the thwarted message for Messner in the story).

In examining the connections between the dream and the story, we should give our attention to those details which are most highly charged with feeling. In the dream it is the interruption, the invasion of privacy, and the "no" which create anxiety in the dreamer. These details must be highly over-determined in the dream with threads leading to the dream day and current experience and other threads leading back to infantile experience. It is possible that those details represent (among many other things) the conflict over marriage which was uppermost in Kafka's thoughts during this period. For Kafka saw marriage as an invasion of his privacy, "then I'll never be alone again," and an interference with his writing, "But then would it not be at the expense of my writing? Not that, not that!" (Both quotations are from his "Summary of all the arguments for and against my marriage," July 21, 1913.) But also he desired this marriage and in his list of arguments there is one in favor of marriage, "Inability to bear life alone." I think, then, that these thoughts made their way into the dream details. He is "eager" to read the letter which has a connection with F., but "someone" interferes, invades his privacy, and his cry of "no!" is the vehement protest against marriage, the invasion of his privacy, the interference with his work.

But these interpretations would account only for those motives in the dream that are provided by a current conflict. These details must also have threads which lead back into infantile experience. In an early draft of this paper, I attempted to reconstruct a childhood memory from these details which I could not support on any basis except clinical experience in dream interpretation. While such tentative constructions are allowable in psychoanalytic investigation, the test of validation is provided by the live patient or subject of the investigation, i.e., the patient will confirm or not confirm the analyst's construction. In this case, it seemed, the subject of my investigation could never offer the necessary confirmation. His diaries and recollections provided me with nothing more specific for my purposes, and while I thought I found evidence in certain of his writings, the use of imaginative works for "evidence" could bring forth the same criticism as the use of dream details for "evidence." We still don't know if it really happened. So, in this earlier draft I wrote in a tentative construction based on these dream details which read as follows: "The details in the dream suggest a crisis in childhood, an interruption by a child, an invasion of privacy, and a severe prohibition represented by the 'no!,' an early disaster which caused a small child to tremble in fear. (In the dream reversal 'the round table of nervous people began to tremble.')" I could not pursue this further and I was also bothered by the fact that the connecting links between the dream details, my reconstruction, and the Messner-Kette story could not be clearly established.

Last year the text of Kafka's "Letter to My Father" was published in full for the first time. In a long outpouring of old griefs and reproaches, there is one memory to which Kafka himself attached the greatest importance and which provided unexpected confirmation of my construction and the connecting links between the dream and the Messner-Kette story.

There is only one episode in the early years of which I have a direct memory. You may remember it, too. Once in the night I kept on whimpering for water, not, I am certain, because I was thirsty, but probably partly to be annoying, partly to amuse myself. After several vigorous threats had failed to have any effect, you took me out of bed, carried me out onto the *pavlatche* (a balcony) and left me there alone for a while in my nightshirt, outside the shut door. I am not going to say this was wrong—perhaps at the time there was really no other way of getting peace and quiet that night—but I mention it as typical of your methods of bringing up a child and their effect on me. I dare say I was quite obedient afterwards at that period, but it did me inner harm. What was for me a matter of course, that senseless asking for water, and the extraordinary terror of being carried outside were two things that I, my nature being what it was, could never properly connect with each other. Even years afterwards I suffered from the tormenting fancy that the huge man, my father, the ultimate authority, would come almost for no reason at all and take me out of bed in the night and carry me out onto the *pavlatche*, and that therefore I was such a mere nothing for him.

This memory has made its way into the dream and the story. I would like to propose from the evidence of Kafka's recorded dreams and his stories that this experience was not the only one in which he disturbed his father at night with disastrous consequences, for the theme of sexual observation occurs repeatedly in Kafka's dreams and his writings. But he is probably truthful in saying that this episode is the only one of his early years of which he has a direct memory, for such infantile sexual scenes as I have inferred from the material ordinarily undergo repression. It is even probable that Kafka's memory of the disturbance at night which he describes obtained its dreadful proportions in his child's eyes from an earlier interruption the memory of which was repressed. We would then regard the memory which was retained in consciousness as a screen memory, that is certain qualities of the repressed experience are displaced onto the later, more innocent interruption at night, the one that survives in memory.

But for our purposes here we can work best with the memory which Kafka has given us, the crisis at night which led to the forceful eviction of a small boy and the punishment of being locked out on a balcony. For it is clear that Kafka has written into the Messner-Kette story the scene of this childhood calamity, the disturbance at night which provoked his father's anger. The details are there: the interruption at night, the student's plea to be heard, to deliver the message, the merchant's angry refusal, the locking out of the intruder, the persistent demands of the student, the menacing reappearance of the merchant, with the command to leave, and the student's last protest. With very few changes, the story of the childhood crisis is retold. The conflict between a small boy and his father becomes a conflict between two strangers, an older man and a student, aptly named Messner and Kette. It is a compact statement of the idea that the conflict between father and son persists unchanged in the adult years of the son. The story is unfinished. It breaks off when the merchant commands the student to leave. " 'But I can't,' said the student and ran up to Messner so surprisingly. . . ." We are reminded of the dream now which ends abruptly at the point, "I have probably caused a disaster," and with the dreamer's hasty apology.

Now I think we can understand the relationship between the dream of the letter and the story. It is as if the dreamer takes up the problem of the dream in the waking state, searches for its meaning, and comes up with a memory, an association to one of the dream elements. It is probable that the dream details of the interruption by the child, the cry "No!" and the observation "I have probably caused a disaster," those details which are highly charged with feeling, lead the dreamer's waking associations back to the event in childhood. The story then makes use of the memory, recasts and resets it as the encounter between the merchant Messner and the student Kette.

But then we need to ask, "What is the motive in *writing* the story, or, more exactly, in putting this memory into the form of a story?" By doing this Kafka attempts to get rid of the painful effects of this memory through repetition, through experiencing it once again in order to overcome it. He gives the childhood event a second existence in the story. The original conflict led to disaster because the antagonists were a small boy and his powerful father. In the new edition he tries out the event once again with the antagonists a young man and an old and wheezing merchant, as if this time there might be hope for a different outcome. But the young man is defeated by the old man once again as if the problem can find no solution in the imagination either.

We have seen the connection between details in the dream, a memory, and a story, but in reading the story of Messner-Kette we feel that in the process of re-working these details into a story something got lost. There is an emptiness in this story which we cannot immediately account for when we consider its source in a dream and a memory which were highly charged with emotion. Now the effect of this story is certainly intended by Kafka; it is satirical, absurd, and its author is saying, "Here is a spectacle for you! A young man and an aging man are like a small boy and his father, but the old man still has his power and the young man is still a weakling, a child who whimpers at night outside his father's room." But even the irony is weakened in this story by the absence of any emotional quality.

It seems that in the process of utilizing a dream detail and a memory in a story the ideational content was preserved but the emotional content was lost. We have already mentioned as one of the advantages of a conscious fantasy over a dream that the conscious ego can control the quantities of affect and can admit into consciousness only those quantities which can be tolerated. It is even possible for the ego to permit a fantasy or a memory to emerge into consciousness while its accompanying affects are held back by the repressive mechanisms. In this way once painful memories appear in consciousness as empty or disembodied images, ghosts of themselves which hold no real terror because they are not alive, are not animated by the original full charge of energy. Similarly, the grossest, the most naked sensual fantasies can be admitted to conscious expression if they are deprived of their accompanying affects. The quality of the mental production is then altered accordingly so that the fantasy seems dead, unreal.

Now this is a quality which appears very strongly in Kafka's writings. Think of the torture in "In the Penal Colony," the scene, "The Whippers," in *The Trial*. The detachment which accompanies these descriptions is the mental quality of the writer who admitted these awful visions into consciousness by making them silent, by anesthetizing the vital parts. Only in this way could he confront his spectres without dread. Kafka's people, the people of his stories, are the product of this emotional isolation. They do not live; they imitate the living. They are human abstractions and abstractions of human qualities exactly as dream people are. We could never believe in Kafka's people if we did not take them as dream people and accept Kafka's world as a dream world.

From these ideas on the defenses against affect which Kafka employed in his writing, I think I can also deduce the reasons why so many of his stories are unfinished. Frequently Kafka's stories and sketches break off at the critical moment as a dream breaks off when a signal of danger occurs. It seems probable to me that at those points in Kafka's stories where a strong emotion threatens to break through the defenses, the story breaks off. We never find out what it was that the student Kette was about to do or say at the critical point in the Messner-Kette story. The story breaks off just as the dream breaks off and this may be for the same reasons.

## IV

In this example we see how the story takes up the problem of the dream, how the latent dream thoughts are transformed in the waking state and worked into a new composition. The story stands in the same relationship to the dream as a dreamer's waking associations to his dream and its elements can be regarded as associations to the dream. There is this difference, of course: ordinarily when a man pursues his thoughts in relationship to a dream, these thoughts, if they are free associations, will emerge in a formless, chaotic stream. Now Kafka does bind these disordered elements together in a narrative, but the narrative is as indifferent to the conventions of story telling as is the manifest dream. The comparison between these two should be closely examined. The latent dream thoughts are themselves disordered fragments and what we call the manifest dream, the "story" of the dream, is the attempt on the part of the dream work to give a semblance of order and coherence to materials which have no logical connections and are governed by primitive thought processes. Freud called this aspect of the dream work "secondary elaboration." The resulting "story" in the dream when considered as a composition is loosely and often indifferently strung together in a narrative which combines its elements without regard for compatibility, temporal sequence, or the boundaries of space. (While many dreams do present an intelligible facade, when we say "like a dream" we usually mean the disordered dream, the absurd dream.)

Kafka's stories, as in the example studied, are associations to the dream and are also composed like the dream. The so-called "dream technique" is like the dream's own method of composition, the process of secondary elaboration. There is no doubt that Kafka deliberately employed this device of the dream for reproducing the effect of the dream in his stories. But I think it is also true, as I mentioned earlier, that his gift in recreating the dream world in his stories derived from illness. I want to emphasize that I do not think Kafka was psychotic, but the danger of psychosis was very real, probably as real as he feared. He never actually lost touch with reality, never lost his citizenship in the real world even when he pronounced himself "a citizen of this other world." His writing must be considered as his strongest bond to the real world and may even be responsible for maintaining his contact with reality.

I think I can support this last statement from certain remarks of Kafka regarding the conditions under which he wrote. If it were not for the sleepless nights he would not write at all, he says. (This should not be taken literally, of course, but it is a fact that most of his writing was the work of these sleepless nights, and we have seen the close connection between these nocturnal fantasies and the anxiety dreams which he warded off through insomnia.) He himself connects his fear of sleep and his fear of death. "Perhaps I am afraid that the soul—which in sleep leaves me—will never return." In psychological terms, he is afraid of sleep because in sleep he loses the self, or awareness of self, and there is the danger that he may not recover it. This is a common fear in severe neuroses, where the danger of losing the self and the ties to reality is real. This extreme peril to the ego gives rise in many serious neuroses (and psychoses as well) to creative spells in which the ego attempts to counteract the loosening of its bonds to reality by energetically recreating aspects of the objective world. (Ernst Kris develops this psychoanalytic idea in a group of brilliant essays dealing with the phenomenon of restitution in art.) But the restitutive function of art is not confined to morbid states, and I feel that I am doing this psychoanalytic theory an injustice by introducing it in this context. In Kafka's case, however, we need the clinical observations on restitution in order to explain the function of writing in his neurosis. Only one who is in great danger of losing the self and the real world will fear sleep as Kafka did. This explains why Kafka wrote only of himself. He needed to affirm and reaffirm his uncertain existence in the real world through creating images of himself, through giving himself an existence on paper. In this way his writing preserved his ties to reality.

The problem of art and neurosis is often brought in irrelevantly to the study of a work. In Kafka's writing the problem not only is relevant but intrudes itself into the study of his works. We cannot understand his writing without understanding him, and this must be counted as a failure in the work. The ambiguity of his writing has given rise to a Kafka criticism in which the works have stimulated impressions and fantasies like the ink blots on the Rorschach test. With the publication in recent years of the Kafka notebooks, letters, conversations and miscellaneous pieces, Kafka as Mystic, Kafka as Cabalist, Kafka as Prophet, Kafka as Social Critic, and a large number of other Kafkas have receded, and we are left to read Kafka as Joseph K. and as Gregor Samsa, a man who has less to say about the world he lived in than about the world that lived in him.

Kafka offers himself and his disease as a symbol which exercises an extraordinary attraction in our time. For mental illness is the romantic disease of this age just as tuberculosis was in the past century. His writing is expiation, atonement, an extreme mortification before his human judges, and the bond he creates between himself and his reader is in part the bond of guilt, of unconscious sin. But this does not account for his vogue during the past twenty years. The awe and mysticism which surround the figure of Kafka and his writings bring to mind those feelings which are aroused in us by a premonitory dream. When the events of the dream or of inner life are reproduced in the world of reality, we are inclined to endow both the dream and the dreamer with magical and divine qualities. The events of our recent history have appeared to us like the full-scale performance of Kafka's tormented dreams. The peril to our reason has given a significance to Kafka's writings which, we must grant, was not altogether his intention.

Kafka appears, finally, as a crippled writer, a man in whom the disease and the art were united in a kind of morbid love so that neither could set the other free. "Die Kunst ist für den Künstler ein Leid, durch das er sich für ein neues Leid befreit," he said.* His writing represented, among other things, an attempt to free himself from neurotic suffering, to repeat and to relive it in order to conquer it. But behind each door with Kafka there was another door, as in the imagery of the legend "Before the Law." An unending chain of events led backward into earliest times, and the conquest of danger and of suffering was a succession of battles in which a new enemy grew in the spot of the last

* "Art is a sorrow for the artist through which he frees himself for a new sorrow."— Ed. trans.

*Applications*

one vanquished, and the new enemy was only a replica of the one who came before.

The disease which produced extraordinary dreams exerted its morbid influence on the creative process as well. The striving for synthesis, for integration and harmony which are the marks of a healthy ego and a healthy art are lacking in Kafka's life and in his writings. The conflict is weak in Kafka's stories because the ego is submissive; the unequal forces within the Kafka psyche create no tension within the reader, only a fraternal sadness, an identification between a writer and reader which takes place in the most solitary regions of the ego.

*Note*

1. For another treatment of the "uncanny" in Kafka's writing, see M. B. Hecht, "Uncanniness, Yearning, and Franz Kafka's Works," *Imago* (April 1952).

# 29

# Two Modern Incest Heroes

Freud has shown that the theme of incest in its manifold disguises is ubiquitous in the literature and art of all ages and all times. The variations upon this theme are produced by the culture and the forms and symbols which it lends to disguise, by the degree of repression which the culture dictates and by the personality of the artist who employs these materials in his work.

But until this century no writer had to contend with the idea that the universal dread of incest had its origins in a repressed wish. Freud's discovery, the unmasking of one of the great tragic themes of literature, has the effect of releasing a profound and melancholy joke from the depths of the myth. The comedy turns on the point that the object of moral dread is the object of desire, an irony that does not easily lend itself to literary treatment of incest and one that gives little scope to incest as a tragic theme. This is not to say that incest is no longer a tragic theme—it will probably endure as long as the human race—but a writer who makes use of the psychoanalytic insight in a contemporary treatment of the incest theme will find that the insight robs the work of tragic import. An Oedipus, not-knowing, who is drawn to his mother by irresistible external forces, is a tragic figure, but an Oedipus in a contemporary version who reveals the motive of unconscious seeking of the mother has cheated us out of the vital secret, and in giving himself away his tragedy is diminished.

In this respect and others it can be argued that psychoanalysis has inhibited the modern writer to a far greater extent than it has liberated him. The insights of psychoanalysis cannot be ignored by a novelist writing today—but what is to be done with them? A clinical

insight does not stir old ghosts in the psyche and bring forth unremembered feelings. On the contrary it behaves like a conjurer's trick
to put down the ghosts and quiet the turbulence below. (In crude
analogy with the therapeutic effects of interpretation.) If a writer
wishes to produce the emotional effects of an incestuous conflict he
will do much better with the conjuring tricks of his trade than those
of the psychoanalyst. If he can conceal and disguise the conflict and
smuggle it past the cold clinical eye of the modern reader the story
may get through and surprise the unguarded regions of emotion. But if
he writes a psychoanalytic version of an incestuous conflict he runs
the risk of creating a clinical document.

In the case of the classic incest drama, the tension is sustained
through the device of "not knowing," that is innocence of motive. And
if *Oedipus Rex* has lost none of its power over a modern audience,
even one that "knows" the internal motive, it is because we have entered the dramatist's conspiracy not to know, that we accept for this
moment the conventions of both the drama and another time and
suspend beliefs that might interfere with enjoyment.

But a psychoanalytic version of Oedipus leaves the writer with no
place to hide the motive. The play can't be written without the play-
within-the-play and when the motive of unconscious seeking enters
the story it has the effect of dissolving the tension. If dread, horror,
and shame are the emotional concomitants of incest they are best
sustained in a narrative in which the internal motive is concealed. For
emotion is reinforced and heightened by the contributions of energy
from unconscious sources. It is the unknown danger that raises the
intensity of feeling. In the case of incest the unknown danger is the
wish, and if a modern writer lays bare the unconscious motive in his
narrative he will reduce the intensity of feeling. In this way the identification of motive has the same effect upon the narrative as the interpretation of a dream, that is, when the motive is brought into consciousness the accompanying affects are diminished.

Even D. H. Lawrence could not extricate himself from this dilemma. All the fine prose and the marvelously wrought flower imagery in *Sons and Lovers* cannot overcome the clinical drabness of the
mother-son love. And while Paul's later sufferings and failures in love
are given complexity and texture by the device of the interlocking
theme of mother-son love, once mother-love is given a strong statement in the story Lawrence cannot surprise the emotions, and the

tragedy of Paul seems a little commonplace to the modern reader who has ripened on the psychological novel.

All of which brings up another problem in the use of psychoanalytic insight in a literary work. Is the Oedipus complex, the clinical syndrome, material for a tragedy? If we remove ourselves for a moment from our time and our infatuation with mental disease, isn't there something absurd about a hero in a novel who is defeated by his infantile neurosis? I am not making a clinical judgment here, for such personal tragedies are real and are commonplace in the analyst's consulting room, but literature makes a different claim upon our sympathies than tragedy in life. A man in a novel who is defeated in his childhood and condemned by unconscious forces within him to tiredly repeat his earliest failure in love, only makes us a little weary of man; his tragedy seems unworthy and trivial.

Now we can argue that the irresistible fate of Oedipus Rex was nothing more than the irresistible unconscious longings of Oedipus projected outward, but this externalization of unconscious conflict makes all the difference between a story and a clinical case history. We can also argue that the three brothers Karamazov and Smerdyakov were the external representatives of an internal conflict within one man, Dostoevsky, a conflict having to do with father-murder and the wish to possess the father's woman. But a novel in which one man Karamazov explored the divisions within his personality would scarcely merit publication in the *Psychoanalytic Quarterly*.

It is a mistake to look upon the Oedipus of Oedipus Complex as a literary descendant of Oedipus Rex. Whatever the psychological truth in the Oedipus myth, an Oedipus who is drawn to his fate by irresistible external forces can carry the symbol of humanity and its archaic crime, and the incest that is unknowing renews the mystery of the eternal dream of childhood and absorbs us in the secret. But a modern Oedipus who is doomed because he cannot oppose his own childhood is only pathetic, and for renouncing the mystery in favor of psychological truth he gives up the claim on our sympathies.

I am suggesting that a case history approach to the Oedipus complex is a blind alley for a storyteller. The best gifts of the novelist will be wasted on the reader who is insulated against any surprises the novelist may have in store for him. Incest is still a durable theme, but if it wants to get written about it will have to find ways to surprise the emotions, and there is no better way to do this than that of concealment and symbolic representation. And the best way to conceal and disguise the elements of an incest story is not to set out to write an incest story. Which brings to mind another Lawrence story and some interesting comparisons in the treatment of the Oedipal theme.

"The Rocking Horse Winner" is also a story about a boy's love for his mother. If I now risk some comparisons with *Sons and Lovers* let it be clear that I am not comparing the two works or judging their merits; I am only singling out differences in treatment of a theme and the resultant effects. "The Rocking Horse Winner" is a fantasy with extraordinary power to disturb the reader—but we do not know why. It is the story of the hopeless love of a little boy for his cold and vain mother. There are ghostly scenes in which the little boy on his rocking horse rocks madly toward the climax that will magically give him the name of the winning horse. The child grows rich on his winnings and conspires with his uncle to make secret gifts of his money to his mother. The story ends in the child's illness and delirium brought on by the feverish compulsion to ride his horse to win for his mother. The child dies with his mourning mother at his bedside.

I had read the story many times without asking myself why it affected me or caring why it did. But on one occasion when I encountered a similar fantasy in a little boy who was my patient I began to understand the uncanny effects of this story. It was, of course, a little boy's fantasy of winning his mother to himself, and replacing the father who could not give her the things she wanted—a classical oedipal fantasy if you like—but if it were only this the story would be banal. Why does the story affect us? How does the rocking exert its uncanny effect upon the reader? The rocking is actually felt in the story, a terrible and ominous rhythm that prophesies the tragedy. The rocking, I realized, is the single element in the story that carries the erotic message, the unspoken and unconscious undercurrent that would mar the innocence of a child's fantasy and disturb the effects of the work if it were made explicit. The rocking has the ambiguous function of keeping the erotic undercurrent silent and making it present; it conceals and yet is suggestive; a perfect symbol. And if we understand the rocking as an erotic symbol we can also see how well it serves as the symbol of impending tragedy. For this love of the boy for his mother is a hopeless and forbidden love, doomed by its nature.

We are also struck by the fact that this story of a boy's love for his mother does not offend, while the incestuous love of the man, Paul Morel, sometimes repels. It's easy to see why. This love belongs to childhood; we accord it its place there, and in Lawrence's treatment we are given the innocent fantasy of a child, in fact, the form in which oedipal love is expressed in childhood. And when the child dies in Lawrence's story in a delirium that is somehow brought on by his mania to win and to make his mother rich, the manifest absurdity of such a disease and such a death does not enter into our thoughts at all. We have so completely entered the child's fantasy that his illness and his death are the plausible and the necessary conclusion.

I am sure that none of the effects of this story were consciously employed by Lawrence to describe an oedipal fantasy in childhood. It is most probable that Freud and the Oedipus complex never entered his head in the writing of this story. He was simply writing a story that wanted to be told, and in the writing a childhood fantasy of his own emerged. He would not have cared why it emerged, he only wanted to capture a memory to play with it again in his imagination and somehow to fix and hold in the story the disturbing emotions that accompanied the fantasy.

In our own time we have seen that the novelist's debt to psychoanalysis has increased but that the novel itself has not profited much from this marriage. Ortega's hope that modern psychology might yet bring forth a last flowering of the novel has only been partially fulfilled. The young writer seems intimidated by psychological knowledge; he has lost confidence in his own eyes and in the validity of his own psychological insights. He borrows the insights of psychology to improve his impaired vision but cannot bring to his work the distinctive vision that should be a novelist's own. He has been seduced by the marvels of the unconscious and has lost interest in studying the surfaces of character. If many of the characters in contemporary novels appear to be the bloodless relations of characters in a case history it is because the novelist is often forgetful today that those things that we call character manifest themselves in surface behavior, that the ego is still the executive agency of personality, and that all we know of personality must be discerned through the ego. The novelist who has been badly baptized in psychoanalysis often gives us the impression that since all men must have an Oedipus complex all men must have the same faces.

## II

I have argued that Oedipus of the Oedipus complex has a doubtful future as a tragic figure in literature. But a writer who has a taste for irony and who sees incest in all its modern dimensions can let his imagination work on the disturbing joke in the incest myth, the joke that strikes right at the center of man's humanness. Moral dread is seen as the other face of desire, and here psychoanalysis delivers to the writer a magnificent irony and a moral problem of great complexity.

There is probably some significance in the fact that two of the best incest stories I have encountered in recent years are burlesques of the incest myth. The ancient types are reassembled in gloom and foreboding to be irresistibly drawn to their destinies, but the myth fails before the modern truth; the oracle speaks false and the dream speaks true. In both the farmer's tale in Ralph Ellison's *Invisible Man* and in Thomas Mann's *The Holy Sinner*, the incest hero rises above the myth by accepting the wish as motive; the heroic act is the casting off of pretense.

Thomas Mann wrote *The Holy Sinner* in 1951. It was conceived as a leave-taking, a kind of melancholy gathering-in of the myths of the West, "bevor die Nacht sinkt, eine lange Nacht vielleicht und ein tiefes Vergessen."* He chose a medieval legend of incest, Gregorius vom Stein, and freely borrowed and parodied other myths of the West, mixing themes, language, peoples, and times in a master myth in which the old forms continually renew themselves, as in his previous treatment of Joseph.

But *The Holy Sinner* is not simply a retelling of old stories for an old man's entertainment. Mann understood better than most men the incest comedy at the center of the myth and the psychological truth in which dread is shown as the other face of longing was for him just the kind of deep and complicated joke he liked to tell. And when he retold the legend of Gregorius he interpolated a modern version in which the medieval players speak contemporary thoughts in archaic language; while they move through the pageantry of the ancient incest myth and cover themselves through not-knowing, they reveal the unconscious motive in seeking each other and in the last scene

---

* ". . . before night falls, a long night perhaps and a deep forgetting."—Ed. trans.

make an extraordinary confession of guilt in the twentieth-century manner.

Grigorss is the child of an incestuous union between a royal brother and sister, the twins Sibylla and Wiligis. He is born in secrecy after the death of his father and cast adrift soon after birth. The infant is discovered by a fisherman who brings him home to rear him. An ivory tablet in the infant's cask recounts the story of his sinful origins and is preserved for the child by the monks of a monastery in the fishing village. Grigorss, at seventeen, learns his story and goes forth as a knight to uncover his origins. His sailing vessel is guided by fate to the shores of his own country at a time when Sibylla's domain is overrun by the armies of one of her rejected suitors. Grigorss overcomes the suitor in battle, delivers the city from its oppressors and marries Sibylla who had fallen in love with the beautiful knight the moment she saw him.

Sibylla is pregnant with their second child when she finds the ivory tablet concealed by her husband, and the identities of mother and son are revealed. Grigorss goes off to do penance on a rock for seventeen years. At the end of this period two pious Christians in Rome receive the revelation which leads them to seek the next Pope on the rock. Grigorss comes to Rome and becomes a great and beloved Pope. In the last pages of the book Sibylla comes to Rome to seek an audience with the great Pope and to give her confession. Mother and son recognize each other and, in Mann's version of this legend, make a remarkable confession of guilt to each other, the confession of unconscious motive and unconscious knowledge of their true identities from the time they had first set eyes on each other.

Mann allows his story to be told with heavy piety and solemnity by a monk who is at great pains throughout to see that the reader draws the correct moral lesson from this tale. The monk is a windy old bore who deplores and shudders but recounts this history of abominations with an unhurried detailing of events. And all the while he is telling his pious monk's story Mann has teased him into telling a scandalous modern version. For the innocents in this medieval incest tale are our contemporaries in the same way that we are theirs, and as the myth knows many forms and no time, these sinners give the wink to their formal pageantry and, without shifting for a moment the Gothic mask, play Freud's version behind the monk's story, the play within the play.

Sibylla has a dream before giving birth to her son. "She dreamed that she gaved birth to a dragon who cruelly tore her womb. Then he flew away, which caused her great mental anguish, but came back again and gave her even greater pain by squeezing back into the torn womb." In the first encounter between Sibylla and the knight Grigorss who has come to deliver her, the mother is stunned by the resemblance of the boy and her brother with whom she sinned. She is also disturbed by the fact that the material of the garment which Grigorss wears is identical with that in which she wrapped her infant son in preparation for his voyage in the tiny cask. With all this—and her old dream of the dragon, too, Sibylla in the monk's tale is unable to draw any conclusions regarding the possible identity of the young knight and finds easy rationalizations for her disturbing thoughts. She is already in love. The monk reflects briefly on this womanish nearsightedness but can make nothing of it.

Behind this ornate and florid monk's tale Mann carries on his burlesque. He allows his incest hero and his mother to know and not know, to carry on the most preposterous self-deceptions and to enjoy their incest to the utmost while subduing their secret knowledge. This is the kind of exquisite joke that Mann is particularly fond of telling, one that he brought to perfection in the lyric wedding night of Jacob and his false bride. The comedy turns on the indifference of Nature to the means by which she attains her end, her disregard for the images of love which she serves, and the conspiracy through which she smuggles her claims at night while men protest that it was dark, they were ignorant, and they had been deceived.

In *The Holy Sinner* the ardor of the sinful pair is unspoilt for two years. When a gossipy maid leads Sibylla to the ivory tablet in Grigorss' room, the whole story comes out in the open and the lovers discover their incestuous relationship. The scene of discovery is played in operatic style with shrieks, swoons, and ritual breast-beating. When the noise subsides the incest hero is found racked by bourgeois torments. Now should Sibylla be called "mother" or "aunt"; is their child his wife's grand-daughter, and what is his relationship to his own child? What is he? Grigorss goes off to his rock to do penance and Sibylla humbles herself by caring for lepers.

In Mann's last chapter Sibylla makes a pilgrimage to Rome to confess her sins to the great Pope Gregorius whose fame has spread throughout the world. In the Pope's chambers the old incest comedy is renewed and mother and son resume the pretense of not knowing each other.

Sibylla makes her confession of incest which ends with the most extraordinary confession of all:

> . . . How by the finding of the tablet, she sobbed, the identity of child and spouse had been frightfully revealed and her soul for horror had swounded, but only in play-acting-wise, for on top the soul pretends and makes to-do the diabolical deception practiced on it, but underneath, where truth abides in quietness, the identity had been known at the first glance, and conscious-unconscious she had taken her own child for husband, because again he had been the only one equal in birth. . . .

And the Pope replies:

> Great and extreme, woman, is your sin, and to the very bottom have you confessed it to the Pope. This thoroughness to the uttermost is greater penance than when according to your sin-husband's arrangement you washed the feet of beggars. . . .

The Pope reminds her that however grave the sin, true repentance will bring salvation. And then He makes his confession:

> The measure of the sinfulness . . . is controvertible before God, the more so that thy child in that place where the soul makes no pretense, likewise very well knew that it was his mother whom he loved.

He brushes aside Sibylla's protests.

> . . . A youth who sets out to find his mother and wins by conquest a wife, who, however beautiful, could be his mother, must reckon with it that she might be his mother whom he marries. So much for his understanding. But to his blood the identity of wife and mother was familiar long before he learned the truth and play-acted about it.

The story ends when the Pope and Sibylla drop the last pretense of not knowing and acknowledge that each had recognized the other at first sight in the Pope's chambers and that the time had come to end the play-acting between Pope and penitent—son and mother, to unblind themselves in spite of shame.

The story ends with this extraordinary confession, the confession that Freud forced from this reluctant century. This most durable myth of sin can no longer shelter man from knowledge of his own sinfulness. In Mann's story the Christian ideas of sin and salvation are given a new and imponderable dimension in the last act. Mann's pious monk wants us to believe that it was penance, the most extreme humiliation before God which freed the sinners from their terrible crime. But the Pope speaks clearly for Mann: it is this confession from the depths, the casting off of pretense, that earns them God's mercy.

The monk tells us, too, that "it is wise to divine in the sinner the chosen one, and wise that is too for the sinner himself. For the divining of his chosen state may make him worthy and his sinfulness fruitful so that it bears him up for high flights." This is one of the points in Mann's story where the monk and the modern man traveling in opposite directions pass each other with a flash of recognition, for in modern psychology it is recognized that the aspect of man that is instinctual and may give rise to evil and criminal impulses will also give rise to the highest ideals and social attainments.

Ralph Ellison brings together a Negro Sharecropper and a white philanthropist for the impossible meeting, the meeting which has been postponed until the white man's Judgment Day. It is the meeting that reveals the motive in the white man's abhorrence of the Negro, the black sin which is cast out in dread and loathing and rediscovered in a black brother with dread and loathing. The sin is, of course, incest, and the impossible meeting is the confrontation of the white man with his sinful motive. The meeting is envisioned by Ellison with supererb wit.

Mr. Norton, the white philanthropist, appears in the early part of the novel as the distinguished visitor to the campus of a southern Negro college. The narrator, then a student, is appointed chauffeur to Mr. Norton during his visit and unwittingly steers him to the fateful meeting with the farmer, Trueblood. Mr. Norton has dedicated his life to the improvement of the Negro. His work is a monument to his dead daughter, and he speaks lyrically of her beauty, her purity and her goodness. His love for his daughter and his good works for the Negro are the two sustaining forces of his life. We do not understand yet how they are connected.

Mr. Norton has an extraordinary introduction to Mr. Trueblood, the Negro sharecropper of local fame, who has impregnated both his daughter and his wife. In fascinated horror Mr. Norton confronts the sharecropper.

"Is it true . . . I mean did you?"

"Suh?" Trueblood asked . . .

. . . "You have survived," he blurted. "But is it true . . . ?"

"*Suh?*" the farmer said, his brow wrinkling with bewilderment. . . .

. . . "You did and you are unharmed!" he shouted, his blue eyes blazing into the black face with something like envy and indignation. . . .

"You have looked upon chaos and are not destroyed!"

"No suh! I feels all right."

"You do? You feel no inner turmoil, no need to cast out the offending eye?"

"*Suh?*"

"Answer me!"

"I'm all right, suh," Trueblood said uneasily. "My eyes is all right too. And when I feels po'ly in my gut I takes a little soda and it goes away."

Trueblood is urged to tell his tale.

One night in the crowded family bed of the sharecropper's cabin Trueblood lay next to his grown daughter and found himself in a dream. It was a distorted dream of intercourse in which the dreamer finds himself in a white man's house in the bedroom of a white lady. There follows a nightmare sequence in which the dreamer tries to escape from the embrace of the white woman and flees through the door of a grandfather clock, running with pounding heart through a hot, dark tunnel.

When the dreamer wakens he finds himself on top of his daughter in a sexual embrace. It is the moment before the climax. And here is the farmer's dilemma: If he moves to withdraw he will sin. If he stays he will sin. He cannot act without moving and he cannot move without sinning. Trueblood (urged on by his daughter) stays to sin.

Now the farmer's wife, Kate, is aroused and goes mad with horror and revulsion. Kate, posing as God's wrathful instrument, grabs an axe and brings it down upon her husband who lies hypnotized before this terrible judgment. But at the last minute he cannot bring himself to submit to the axe and turns his head to one side. The axe strikes the side of his face. Kate, ready to strike again, poises the axe and then Trueblood sees it stop, "like somebody done reached down through the roof and caught it." The axe falls behind her at this time, and Kate stumbles out the back door and vomits.

Trueblood leaves his home and, following the myth, becomes a wanderer shunned by all men. In exile he ponders his guilt. Did he sin or didn't he sin? Is a man responsible for his dreams? Trueblood does not appeal to God for a judgment, and God remains silent during Trueblood's exile. A man of a more philosophical turn of mind might have spent the rest of his life wandering in the wilderness pondering his guilt. But Trueblood is a practical man. When he finds that he cannot know his crime or his guilt, he accepts the impossibility of knowing and sees the absurdity of his exile for an unjudged crime. He decides to return to his family.

At this point Trueblood breaks with the myth. And from that moment the myth collapses, all the actors in the ancient pageant lose their lines, and the myth goes off on a lunatic rampage reversing its prophecy. Trueblood returns to his family and his sin brings him undreamed of prosperity.

Trueblood becomes an embarrassed hero, a contemporary marvel for his white neighbors, the man who committed the blackest sin and lived to tell the tale. The white folks come to visit him and hear his story, the plain white folks who are his neighbors and educated white folks from the university who write articles about him. They pay him well for his story and take good care of him and his family. Trueblood and his pregnant daughter and his pregnant wife are perversely rewarded for sin.

The argument is subtle, here. Mr. Ellison does not consider incest a laughing matter, of course. But he understands that the inmost core of the incest myth contains a grotesque comedy, the comedy of knowing-not knowing. He has expertly brought off the bitter joke that Mr. Trueblood's dream-sin is the white man's dream-sin and that Trueblood is rewarded for offering himself as a symbol and taking the white man's sin on himself.

Ellison's tale is marvelously contrived to state the dilemma of the man of our times who can no longer hide behind the myth. He has written a kind of incest comedy in which moral dread is exposed as the other face of desire, but in this treatment he reveals an irony of such magnitude that the ancient myth acquires a new dimension as tragedy. As in the classical model the tragedy proceeds through its inevitable phases by means of the device of "not knowing," but "not knowing" in this modern incest tale is a species of self-deception, the denial of the sinful motive in the unconscious.

There are two incest heroes in Ellison's story—or one, if you like— for Mr. Trueblood is Mr. Norton's brother of the dream, his black self.

Mr. Norton who listens to Mr. Trueblood's dream with dread and fascination is the witness to his own dream. Mr. Norton's dream-sin of incest is concealed from him and from the world. He atones by creating monuments to the sacred memory of his daughter, and his good works for the Negro are the symbols of his guilty partnership with the Negro: the Negro sins for Mr. Norton and Mr. Norton atones. Mr. Trueblood who sinned in a dream and wakened to find himself embracing his daughter is stripped of pretense and the protection of the myth. He is confronted with his naked self and the testimony of his dream and the act. He can still take refuge in the myth by submitting to the classical fate; for an instant he offered himself to the axe and then refused; for a short time he exiled himself but chose to come back. He became a hero because he refused to hide behind the cowardly deceptions that cloak sin; he faced the truth within himself. In this way Trueblood rose above the myth and escaped the tragic consequences. He reverses the classic fate of the incest hero. Instead of an Oedipus blinded we are given an Oedipus newly sighted.

Norton is Oedipus blinded in this story, for when he is confronted with Trueblood's dream-sin, which is his own, he refuses to see and is carried from the scene unconscious. In one of the funniest and saddest chapters of the story, the unconscious Mr. Norton is carried off to a whorehouse frequented by the Negro inmates of a local insane asylum and lies serenely unconscious in the midst of brawling and whoring while the lunatics speak unquieting truths about the white man's sickness and the black man's sickness. They are not heard, and when Norton is revived by a lucid madman (once a prominent Negro psychiatrist) everyone works quickly to put Mr. Norton together again, to shore up the fictions and pretenses, to tell him what he wants to hear and show him what he wants to see. The young Negro student who had unwittingly led Mr. Norton to the sharecropper's cabin is hastily expelled by his college for his part in bringing about the impossible meeting.

Did Mr. Trueblood sin? Mr. Ellison puts the moral problem with great delicacy and sees it in all its complexity. Is a man morally responsible for his dream? This is undoubtedly one of the most bothersome questions to emerge with Freudian psychology. Freud himself addressed himself to the problem in a little known and rarely remembered essay called "Moral Responsibility in Dreaming." Freud says "yes," and such is the confusion generated by psychoanalysis that nobody remembers that Freud himself gave cold comfort to the dream-sinners, that conscious-unconscious a man cannot escape moral responsibility; he alone is the inventor of his dream.

Trueblood, the modern incest hero, is obliged to judge his own case and cannot find the verdict. He is guilty-not-guilty in the uncertain class of modern criminals still waiting judgment with Joseph K. But he is not afflicted with their disease; he does not torment himself with unanswerable questions, and he cannot bring himself to atone for a crime that cannot be judged. There are no heroes in Joseph K.'s court-room. K. submitted to the knife and others are consumed by their disease. But Trueblood became a hero because he refused the refuge of mind-sickness, and his manhood refused the axe. He did not bargain with God in the wilderness, but fairly judged his own worthiness to live and manfully returned to his living.

Now of course Ellison is not writing a case for incest. Mr. Trueblood's prosperity is a bitter joke, and to understand the joke in all its complexity we need to study the conduct of God, Himself, during this case. For it strikes us that God showed a considerable disregard for the conventions of the incest tale. His judgment appears to be far more lenient than that of Trueblood's human judges. He stayed the hand of Kate Trueblood when she brought the axe down the second time and was satisfied that the sinner should bear his judgment in the unhealing sore, the mark of the axe's first blow. When Kate, posing as God's wrathful instrument, demanded the sacrifice of Trueblood's manhood, God gave no sign when the axe descended for its first blow and seemed to wait for the sign from Trueblood. Trueblood's instinctive turning aside was the affirmation of his manhood, and God, approving, stayed the hand of Kate when she was about to bring the axe down for the second blow.

When Trueblood goes forth into the wilderness we are given no sign as to God's intentions. The myth supports the interpretation that God looks favorably upon wandering in the wilderness for crimes of various classes, but when Trueblood decides to go home and face his crime and assume his masculine prerogatives, God approves and rewards him by causing him to prosper. This suggests to me that God is sick of naked and sightless fools wandering in the wilderness and that any man who wants to go home and face up to things may get His blessings.

Both Mann and Ellison have created in their incest tales a heroic image of man that is entirely modern—"Freudian," if you like—a man who rises above the myth by acknowledging the unconscious motive. Both Grigorss and Trueblood refuse the refuge of the myth, the refuge of "not knowing," and by undeceiving themselves they reverse the prophecy. We are left to conclude that it is the myth that destroys and that the heroic act for modern man is the casting off of pretense.

There is even the strong suggestion in *The Holy Sinner* that the unmasking of sinful motives by psychoanalysis may initiate a new progress in the moral evolution of mankind in which the "know thyself" of psychoanalysis will bring moral wisdom in place of moral tyranny.

When Grigorss was found by the searchers after seventeen years of penance on the rock, he had lost his human form and had shrunk to the size of a small animal. The animal had protected itself against hunger and the assaults of weather by periods of long hibernation. After receiving the messengers Grigorss assumed his human form, and with his new birth came new wisdom. The new-born man, the Pope, was the man who had learned that he had carried his sin within himself in the form of a wish, that he had deceived himself in order to satisfy his longing. And it was this "confession from the depths" that freed him and restored him to human stature.

# Chronological Bibliography of the
# Selected Writings of Selma Fraiberg

1945 The Spontaneous Drama as a Technic in Group Therapy. *Nervous Child*, 4:252–273.

1947 A Casework Program in a Summer Camp. Ann Arbor: Univ. of Michigan. Mimeograph.

Studies in Group Symptom Formation. *Amer. J. Orthopsychiat.*, 17:278–289.

1950 (with L. Fraiberg) Hallowe'en: Ritual and Myth in a Children's Holiday. *Amer. Imago*, 7:289–328.

On the Sleep Disturbances of Early Childhood. *Psychoanal. Study Child*, 5:285–309.

1951 Applications of Psychoanalytic Principles in Casework Practice with Children, Parts 1 and 2. *Quart. J. Child Behav.*, 3:175–197, 250–275.

Clinical Notes on the Nature of Transference in Child Analysis. *Psychoanal. Study Child*, 6:286–306.

Enlightenment and Confusion. *Psychoanal. Study Child*, 6:325–335.

1952 A Critical Neurosis in a Two-and-a-Half-Year-Old Girl. *Psychoanal. Study Child*, 7:173–215.

Some Aspects of Casework with Children: Part 1, Understanding the Child Client; Part 2, Helping with Critical Situations. *Social Casewk.*, 33:374–381, 429–435.

1954 Counseling for the Parents of the Very Young Child. *Social Casewk.*, 35:47–57.

Helping Children Develop Controls. *Child Study*, 32:12–19.

Tales of the Discovery of the Secret Treasure. *Psychoanal. Study Child*, 9:218–241.

1955 Psychoanalytic Principles in Casework with Children. New York: Family Service Association of America. Pamphlet.

Some Considerations in the Introduction to Therapy in Puberty. *Psychoanal. Study Child*, 10:264–286.

Teaching Psychoanalytic Theory to Social Work Students. *Social Casewk.*, 36:243–252.

1956  Kafka and the Dream. *Partisan Rev.*, 23:47–69.
      On Therapy. *Child Welfare.*, 35:11–12.
      Some Aspects of Residential Casework with Children. *Social Casewk.*,
          36:159–167.
1957  Professional Responsibility in Casework Treatment of Children. In
          *Direct Casework with Children*, ed. J. Regensburg & S. Fraiberg,
          pp. 15–39. New York: Family Service Association of America.
          Pamphlet.
1959  An Appraisal of Group Methods in Casework Agencies. In *Group
          Methods in the Practice of Casework*. New Orleans: Tulane
          Univ. School of Social Work.
      *The Magic Years: Understanding and Handling the Problems of Early
          Childhood*. New York: Scribner's.
1960  The Mass Media: New Schoolhouse for our Children. *Child Study*,
          37:3–18.
1961  Homosexual Conflicts. In *Adolescents: Psychoanalytic Approach to
          Problems and Therapy*, ed. S. Lorand & H. I. Schneer, pp.
          78–112. New York: Hoeber.
      Morals and Psychoanalysis. *Partisan Rev.*, 28:109–117.
      Psychoanalysis and the Education of Case Workers. *Smith Coll. Stud.
          Soc. Work*, 31:196–221.
      Two Modern Incest Heroes. *Partisan Rev.*, 28:646–661.
1962  The Science of Thought Control. *Commentary*, 33:420–429.
      Technical Aspects of the Analysis of a Child with a Severe Behavior
          Disorder. *J. Amer. Psychoanal. Assn.*, 10:338–367.
      A Therapeutic Approach to Reactive Ego Disturbances in Children in
          Placement. *Amer. J. Orthopsychiat.*, 32:18–31.
1963  Contributions of Psychoanalysis to Medical Practice with Adoles-
          cents. *Clin. Proc. Child. Hosp.*, 19:45–51.
1964  (with D. Freedman) Studies in the Ego Development of the Congeni-
          tally Blind Child. *Psychoanal. Study Child*, 19:113–169.
1965  The American Reading Problem. *Commentary*, 39:56–65.
      A Comparison of the Analytic Method in Two Stages of a Child Anal-
          ysis. *J. Amer. Acad. Child Psychiat.*, 4:387–400.
      Management of Disturbed Children in Foster Care. *Feelings*, 7,
          Nov.-Dec.
1966  Further Considerations of the Role of Transference in Latency. *Psy-
          choanal. Study Child*, 21:213–236.
      (with B. L. Siegel & R. Gibson) The Role of Sound in the Search Behav-
          ior of a Blind Infant. *Psychoanal. Study Child*, 21: 327–357.
1967  The Analysis of an Eight-Year-Old Girl with Epilepsy. In *The Child
          Analyst at Work*, ed. E. R. Geleerd, pp. 229–287. New York:
          International Universities Press.
      The Origins of Human Bonds. *Commentary*, 44:47–57.
1968  The Origins of Identity. *Smith Coll. Stud. Soc. Work*, 38:79–101.
      Parallel and Divergent Patterns in Blind and Sighted Infants. *Psy-
          choanal. Study Child*, 23:264–300.

(with J. F. McDermott & S. I. Harrison) Residential Treatment of Children: The Utilization of Transference Behavior. *J. Amer. Acad. Child Psychiat.*, 7:169–192.

1969  (with M. Smith & E. Adelson) An Educational Program for Blind Infants. *J. Spec. Educ.*, 3:121–139.

Libidinal Object Constancy and Mental Representation. *Psychoanal. Study Child*, 24:9–47.

1970  The Muse in the Kitchen: A Case Study in Clinical Research. *Smith Coll. Stud. Soc. Work*, 40:101–134.

1971  Intervention in Infancy: A Program for Blind Infants. *J. Amer. Acad. Child Psychiat.*, 10:381–405.

Separation Crisis in Two Blind Children. *Psychoanal. Study Child*, 26:355–371.

Smiling and Stranger Reaction in Blind Infants. In *Exceptional Infant*, vol. 2, ed. J. Hellmuth, pp. 110–127. New York: Brunner/Mazel.

1972  (with E. Adelson) Mouth and Hand in the Early Development of Blind Infants. In *Third Symposium on Oral Sensation and Perception*, ed. J. Bosma, pp. 420–430. Springfield, Ill.: Thomas.

Some Characteristics of Genital Arousal and Discharge in Latency Girls. *Psychoanal. Study Child*, 27:439–475.

1973  (with E. Adelson) Self-Representation in Language and Play: Observations of Blind Children. *Psychoanal. Quart.*, 42:539–562.

1974  Billy: Psychological Intervention for a Failure-to-Thrive Infant. In *Maternal Attachment and Mothering Disorders: A Round Table, Sponsored by Johnson and Johnson Baby Products Co.*, ed. M. Klaus, T. Leger & M. Trause, pp. 13–19. Sausalito, Calif.

Blind Infants and Their Mothers: An Examination of the Sign System. In *The Effect of the Infant on Its Caregiver*, ed. M. Lewis & L. A. Rosenblum, pp. 215–232. New York: Wiley.

The Clinical Dimension of Baby Games. *J. Amer. Acad. Child Psychiat.*, 13:202–220.

(with E. Adelson) Gross Motor Development in Infants Blind from Birth. *Child Dev.*, 45:114–126.

Legacies and Prophecies. *Smith College School for Social Work*, 1:1–8.

1975  The Development of Human Attachments in Infants Blind from Birth. *Merrill-Palmer Quart.*, 21:315–334.

(with E. Adelson & V. Shapiro) Ghosts in the Nursery: A Psychoanalytic Approach to the Problems of Impaired Infant-Mother Relationships. *J. Amer. Acad. Child Psychiat.*, 14:387–421.

1976  (with V. Shapiro & E. Adelson) Infant-Parent Psychotherapy on Behalf of a Child in a Critical Nutritional State. *Psychoanal. Study Child*, 31:461–491.

(with E. Adelson) Self-Representation in Blind Children. In *The Effects of Blindness and Other Impairments on Early Development*, ed. Z. S. Jastrzembska, pp. 136–159. New York: American Foundation for the Blind.

(with E. Adelson) Sensory Deficit and Motor Development in Infants

Blind from Birth. In *The Effects of Blindness and Other Impairments on Early Development*, ed. Z. S. Jastrzembska, pp. 1–28. New York: American Foundation for the Blind.

1977 (with E. Adelson) An Abandoned Mother, An Abandoned Baby. *Bull. Menning. Clin.*, 41:162–180.

Congenital Sensory and Motor Deficits and Ego Formation. *Annual Psychoanal.*, 5:169–194.

*Every Child's Birthright: In Defense of Mothering.* New York: Basic Books.

(with L. Fraiberg) *Insights from the Blind: Comparative Studies of Blind and Sighted Infants.* New York: Basic Books.

1978 (with C. Aradine & V. Shapiro) Collaborating to Foster Family Attachment. *Amer. J. Matern. Child Nurs.*, 3:92–98.

Future Care of Mothering Disorders. *Birth and Fam. J.*, 5:239–241.

(with J. Bennett) Intervention and Failure to Thrive: A Psychiatric Outpatient Treatment Program. *Birth and Fam. J.*, 5:227–230.

The Invisible Children. In *The Child in His Family: Vulnerable Children*, vol. 4, ed. E. J. Anthony, C. Koupernik & C. Chiland, pp. 287–302. New York: Wiley.

Notes on Infant and Pre-School Programs in Jerusalem. Mimeograph.

Psychoanalysis and Social Work: A Reexamination of the Issues. *Smith Coll. Stud. Soc. Work*, 48:87–106.

1979 Psychiatry and Infant Mental Health. Unpublished manuscript. Univ. of Michigan.

1980 (Editor, with L. Fraiberg) *Clinical Studies in Infant Mental Health: The First Year of Life.* New York: Basic Books.

1981 (with A. Lieberman, J. Pekarsky & J. Pawl) Treatment and Outcome in an Infant Psychiatry Program: Parts 1 and 2. *J. Preventive Psychiat.*, 1:89–111, 143–165.

1982 The Adolescent Mother and Her Infant. In *Adolescent Psychiatry: Developmental and Clinical Studies*, ed. S. C. Feinstein, J. G. Looney, A. Z. Schwartzberg & A. D. Sorosky, pp. 7–23. Vol. 10. Annals of the American Society for Adolescent Psychiatry. Chicago: Univ. of Chicago Press.

Pathological Defenses in Infancy. *Psychoanal. Quart.*, 51:612–635.

# Index